Documentary Voice & Vision

Learn the creative and technical essentials of documentary filmmaking with *Documentary Voice & Vision*. This comprehensive work combines clear, up-to-date technical information, production techniques, and gear descriptions with an understanding of how technical choices can create meaning and serve a director's creative vision. Drawing on the authors' years of experience as documentary filmmakers, and on interviews with a range of working professionals in the field, the book offers concrete and thoughtful guidance through all stages of production, from finding and researching ideas to production, editing, and distribution. *Documentary Voice & Vision* will help students and aspiring filmmakers think through research and story structure, ethics, legal issues, and aesthetics, as well as techniques from camera handling to lighting, sound recording, and editing. The book explores a full range of production styles, from expository to impressionistic to observational, and provides an overview of contemporary distribution options.

Documentary Voice & Vision is a companion text to Mick Hurbis-Cherrier's *Voice & Vision: A Creative Approach to Narrative Film and DV Production*, and employs a similar style and approach to that classic text. This book is written from the perspective of documentary filmmakers, and includes myriad examples from the world of non-fiction filmmaking. A robust companion website featuring additional resources and interactive figures accompanies the book.

Kelly Anderson's documentaries include *My Brooklyn* (2012) and *Every Mother's Son* (2004, with Tami Gold). Her work has been screened on the PBS series *POV* and on HBO, and she was nominated for a national Emmy Award. She is a Professor in the Department of Film and Media Studies at Hunter College, City University of New York.

Martin Lucas is a documentary filmmaker and educator with over 30 years of experience making and speaking about documentary worldwide. His most recent film, *Hiroshima Bound* (2015), is a personal exploration of coming to terms with the Atomic Bomb. He teaches in the Department of Film and Media Studies at Hunter College, City University of New York.

Mick Hurbis-Cherrier teaches film production and screenwriting at Hunter College, City University of New York. Professionally, he has worked as a screenwriter, director, cinematographer, and editor. He is the author of *Voice & Vision: A Creative Approach to Narrative Film and DV Production*, 2nd ed. (Focal Press) and the coauthor of *Directing: Film Techniques and Aesthetics*, 5th ed. (Focal Press) (with Michael Rabiger).

"An impressive book! The authors have expertly drawn upon their filmmaking skills and integrated it with decades of teaching experience to incorporate theory with practice. *Documentary Voice & Vision* is both an essential reference for students and an informed update for skilled professionals."
—**Arthur Dong, Distinguished Professor in Film, Loyola Marymount University, Director, *Coming Out Under Fire, Licensed to Kill, Hollywood Chinese, The Killing Fields of Dr. Haing S. Ngor***

"This is a very comprehensive guide to contemporary documentary filmmaking. Embedded in the history of the form but also using a wealth of current examples, it is rich in aesthetic, practical and technical knowledge."
—**Tony Dowmunt, Professor, Department of Media and Communications, Goldsmith's College, University of London**

"*Documentary Voice & Vision* is a comprehensive resource for documentary film production, balancing practical, technical information, and historical insight into documentary practice and methods. This textbook provides a valuable line of inquiry into the ethical, storytelling, and aesthetic issues documentary production students face. The text features real world examples from contemporary documentary filmmakers and serves as a wonderful tool for any documentary production class."
—**Jamie Meltzer, Associate Professor, Documentary Film and Video, Stanford University**

"*Documentary Voice & Vision* offers an expansive soup-to-nuts approach to advanced non-fiction filmmaking and is remarkably comprehensive in scope. The book guides the filmmaker through the myriad hurdles of documentary production, deftly interweaving detailed practical information and relevant case studies."
—**Jan Krawitz, Professor, MFA Program in Documentary Film and Video, Stanford University**

"*Documentary Voice & Vision* is amazingly comprehensive. No more need to cobble together different materials on storytelling, styles, history, theory, production techniques and the latest technical aspects of documentary filmmaking—it's all here in a single book! Anderson and Lucas have combined their years of documentary experience in the field and the classroom with the insights of dozens of filmmaker colleagues working in all aspects of the genre. The emphasis on effective observational filmmaking techniques and the breadth of coverage on sound is particularly impressive. Whether for undergraduates wanting to explore non-fiction, graduate students working on a documentary thesis project, or experienced professionals looking for an updated understanding of the field, *Documentary Voice & Vision* is an essential tool."
—**Johnny Symons, Assistant Professor and Documentary Program Coordinator, School of Cinema, San Francisco State University**

"Anderson, Lucas, and Hurbis-Cherrier have done an extraordinary job providing an in-depth understanding of how documentaries are made from both an aesthetic and technical perspective. Superb book."
—**Sam Pollard, Producer/Editor, *4 Little Girls, Eyes on the Prize, Sinatra: All or Nothing at All, When the Levees Broke: A Requiem in Four Acts***

Documentary Voice & Vision

A CREATIVE APPROACH to Non-Fiction Media Production

KELLY ANDERSON & MARTIN LUCAS

With Mick Hurbis-Cherrier
Illustrations by Amy Saidens

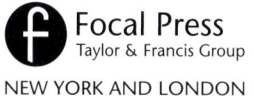

Focal Press
Taylor & Francis Group
NEW YORK AND LONDON

First published 2016
by Focal Press
711 Third Avenue, New York, NY 10017

and by Focal Press
2 Park Square, Milton Park, Abingdon, Oxon OX14 4RN

Focal Press is an imprint of the Taylor & Francis Group, an informa business

© 2016 Taylor & Francis

The right of Kelly Anderson and Martin Lucas to be identified as authors of this work has been asserted by them in accordance with sections 77 and 78 of the Copyright, Designs and Patents Act 1988.

All rights reserved. No part of this book may be reprinted or reproduced or utilised in any form or by any electronic, mechanical, or other means, now known or hereafter invented, including photocopying and recording, or in any information storage or retrieval system, without permission in writing from the publishers.

Trademark notice: Product or corporate names may be trademarks or registered trademarks, and are used only for identification and explanation without intent to infringe.

Library of Congress Cataloging in Publication Data
Anderson, Kelly.
Documentary voice & vision : a creative approach to non-fiction media production/Kelly Anderson & Martin Lucas, with Mick Hurbis-Cherrier; illustrations by Amy Saidens.
pages cm
Documentary voice and vision
Includes bibliographical references and index.
Includes filmography.
1. Documentary films—Production and direction.
2. Cinematography. I. Lucas, Martin (Director) II. Hurbis-Cherrier, Mick. III. Saidens, Amy, illustrator. IV. Title. V. Title: Documentary voice and vision.
PN1995.9.D6A53 2016
070.1′8—dc23
2015031297

ISBN: 978-1-138-18804-4 (hbk)
ISBN: 978-1-138-79543-3 (pbk)
ISBN: 978-1-315-75842-8 (ebk)

Typeset in Helvetica
by Florence Production Ltd, Stoodleigh, Devon, UK

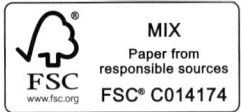

Printed and bound in the United States of America by Sheridan

For Tami Gold, George Stoney, and Brian Winston,
whose passion and commitment inspired us to make,
teach, think, and write about documentary film.

Contents

ACKNOWLEDGMENTS xix
INTRODUCTION xxi

Part 1 ■ DEVELOPING YOUR DOCUMENTARY

CHAPTER 1: FINDING AND DEVELOPING IDEAS
- **What is a Documentary?** 3
- **Where Do Documentary Ideas Come From?** 3
- **Your Artistic Identity** 7
- **Research** 8
- **The Importance of a Hypothesis** 10
- **"Casting" Your Documentary** 11
  - Active vs Passive Characters 12
  - Juggling Multiple Characters 13
- **The Value of the Documenting Process** 14
- **Feasibility** 14
- **The Specific and the Universal** 14

CHAPTER 2: DOCUMENTARY STYLES
- **A Brief and Selective History of the Documentary** 18
  - Impressionistic Filmmaking 20
  - Dziga Vertov and Reflexivity 21
  - The British Film Movement and the Expository Film 22
    - *TV Documentary as a Subgenre of the Expository Style* ... 23
  - Observational Filmmaking 23
  - From the Observational to a Reemergence of the Reflexive 26
  - Reenactment in Documentary 27
- **Conclusion** 28

CHAPTER 3: STRUCTURING THE DOCUMENTARY
- **Basic Approaches to Documentary Storytelling** 29
  - Drama: Goals, Conflict, and Stakes 29
  - Dramatic Structure 30
    - *Opening* 30
    - *Introducing the Conflict* 32
    - *Rising Action* 32
    - *Climax* 33
    - *Results and Ending* 33
  - Imposing a Structure on Real Life? 34
  - Rhetorical Structure 34
  - Mixed Approaches 36
- **Alternative Structures** 36
- **The Short Documentary** 37

Issue-Based Films 37
Profile of a Person 38
Portrait of a Place 38
Single Event Story 39
Process Film 39
Conclusion 40

CHAPTER 4: THE DOCUMENTARY PROPOSAL
Proposal Elements 41
Introduction or Synopsis 42
Background 42
Rationale 43
Project Description 43
    Main Characters 44
    Events You Will Film 44
    Structure and Style 44
    Themes 45
    Treatment 45
Distribution Plan 46
    Target Audiences 46
        Film Festivals 46
        Television 46
        Theatrical 46
        Educational Institutions 47
        The Internet 47
        Community-Based Screenings 47
    Community Partners 47
    Goals 47
Personnel 47
Budget 47
Funding Sources 48
    Foundations 48
    Government Funding 48
        State Arts Councils and Humanities Councils 48
        National Endowment for the Arts 48
        National Endowment for the Humanities 48
        Corporation for Public Broadcasting 48
    Cable TV 49
    Crowd-Sourced Fundraising 49
Fiscal Sponsorship 49
Project Timeline and Status 49
Trailers and Sample Reels 49
Conclusion 49

CHAPTER 5: DOCUMENTARY ETHICS AND LEGAL ISSUES
Responsibility to your Subjects: Subject Relations and Release Forms 51
Who Gets to Represent Whom? 54
The Impact of Money 56
Handling Delicate Situations 56
Responsibility to Your Audience: Objectivity and Fairness 57
Responsibility to Other Creators: Intellectual Property Rights 58
Fair Use 59
Conclusion 59

Part 2 ■ PRODUCTION

CHAPTER 6: PLANNING THE SHOOT

- **Crew Size** 63
- **Crew Responsibilities** 65
- **Locations** 65
  - Permits and Location Agreements 66
  - Location Aesthetics and Meaning 68
- **Equipment** 69
  - Lighting Considerations 69
  - Sound Recording Preparation 69
- **Insurance** 70
- **Crew and Communication** 70
  - The Call Sheet 71
- **Scheduling** 73
- **Budgeting** 73
  - The Budget Topsheet 74
  - The Detail Budget 79
  - Budgeting for a Low-Budget Documentary 79
  - Cost Reports: Knowing Where You Are 79
- **Conclusion** 82

CHAPTER 7: ORGANIZING CINEMATIC TIME AND SPACE

- **The Visual Language of Documentary** 83
- **Shots, Sequences, and Scenes** 83
- **The Frame and Composition** 85
  - Dimensions of the Frame 85
  - Shot Composition and the Graphic Qualities of the Frame 85
  - Closed and Open Frames 86
  - Deep Frames and Flat Frames 86
    - *Receding Planes, Overlapping Objects, and Diminishing Perspective* 86
    - *Horizontal and Diagonal Lines* 86
    - *Deep and Shallow Focus* 87
    - *Shadows* 88
  - Balanced and Unbalanced Frames 88
  - Rule of Thirds, Looking Room, and Lead Room 88
  - Shot Size 90
  - Shot Size and Character Identification 90
  - Camera Angles 91
    - *High and Low Angles* 91
    - *Front to Back Angles* 92
    - *The Horizon Line* 92
- **Camera Moves** 93
  - Pivot Moves 93
  - Zooming In and Out 94
  - Dynamic Moves 94
  - The Moving Frame and Perspective 95
  - Motivation and the Moving Camera 97
  - Adjusting Your Shot 97
- **Shooting with Editing in Mind** 98
- **Collecting Visual Evidence** 99
- **Covering Observational Scenes** 99
  - Filming Group Interactions 102
  - Walking and Talking, Showing and Telling 103
  - Entering and Exiting the Frame 104
  - The Long Take 104

CONTENTS

- Stylized Expressive Sequences 105
- Infographics and Animation 105
- Conclusion 106

CHAPTER 8: THE DIGITAL VIDEO SYSTEM
- **Film: A Mechanical and Chemical Medium** 107
- **Video: An Electronic Medium** 108
  - Analog vs Digital Video 110
  - The Video Image Today 110
    - *Recording Formats* 110
    - *Media Formats* 110
    - *Display Formats* 110
    - *Audio/Video Codecs* 111
  - Broadcast Standards 111
  - Resolution 112
  - Aspect Ratio 113
  - Scanning Type 113
    - *Interlaced Scanning* 113
    - *Progressive Scanning* 114
  - Frame Rate 114
- **Time Code** 116
- **Types of Digital Video Cameras** 116
  - Hybrid Large Sensor Cameras 118
  - Mirrorless Shutter Cameras 118
  - Minicams 118
  - The Ultra High End: 4K and More 119
  - The Basic Video Camcorder: Exterior 120
    - *The Body* 120
    - *Viewfinders and LCD Viewscreens* 121
    - *The Lens* 121
    - *Servo Zoom Control* 122
    - *Media Bay* 122
    - *DC Power* 123
    - *Camera Function Menus and Switches* 123
    - *Audio and Video Connectors, Inputs and Outputs* 125
    - *External Microphone Inputs* 125
    - *Other Connectors* 125
  - The Basic Video Camcorder: Interior 126
    - *The Image Sensor* 126
    - *Three-Chip vs One-Chip Cameras* 127
    - *White Balance* 127
    - *Gain* 128
    - *Shutter Speed* 129
    - *ND Filters* 129
    - *The Analog-to-Digital Converter* 129
    - *The Digital Signal Processor* 129
    - *Signal Compression and Codecs* 130
    - *Color Encoding and Subsampling* 131
- **Data Rate** 132
- **Monitoring and Display** 132
- **Broadcast Standards Worldwide** 135
- **Conclusion** 136

CHAPTER 9: THE LENS
- **The Optics of the Lens** 137
- **Focus** 138

   Adjusting Focus during a Take 140
    Selective Focus 141
 Focal Length 141
  Focal Length and Sensor Size: Crop Factor 144
  Prime and Zoom Lenses 145
  Focal Length and Lens Perspective 146
 Aperture 148
  Lens Speed 149
 Depth of Field 150
  Other Factors Impacting Depth of Field 151
  The 1/3–2/3 Rule 152
 Conclusion 152

CHAPTER 10: CAMERA SUPPORT

 The Handheld Camera 153
 Shoulder Mounts 154
 The Tripod 155
  Tripod Head 157
   Pan and Tilt Locks 157
   Pan and Tilt Dampers 157
   Pan Handle 157
   Camera Mounting Plate 158
   Head Mount 158
 The Monopod 159
 The Dolly 160
  Sliders 162
 Jib Arms and Crane Shots 162
 Stabilizing Arm Systems 162
 Drones 163
 Underwater Photography 164
 Conclusion 164

CHAPTER 11: BASIC LIGHTING FOR DOCUMENTARY

 Why Light? 165
  Lighting as Respect 166
 Elements of Exposure 167
  Monitoring Exposure 168
 The Fundamental Sources of Light 168
 Three Essential Properties of Light 169
  Intensity 169
  Quality 170
  Color Temperature 171
 Controlling Light 171
 Basic Lighting Equipment, Filters, and Gels 172
  Lighting Units 172
   Open-Faced Lights 172
   Fresnels 173
   Soft Lights 173
   Fluorescent Lights 174
   LED Lights 174
   HMI Lights 175
   Reflectors 175
  Camera Filters and Lighting Gels 175
   Altering Light with Filters 175
    Neutral Density Filters 176
    Diffusion Filters 177

   Polarizing Filters 177
   Graduated Filters 178
  Altering Light with Gels 178
   Color Conversion Gels 178
   Color Conversion Gels and Mixed-Lighting Situations 179
   Neutral Density Gels 179
   Diffusion Media 180
  Basic Grip Gear 181
   Stands 181
   Gear for Light Control 181
   Clamps 182
   Miscellaneous Grip Gear 182
   The Ditty Bag 183

CHAPTER 12: LIGHTING AND EXPOSURE—BEYOND THE BASICS

Lighting Interviews 186
 Three-Point Lighting 186
  Key Light 187
  Fill Light 187
  Backlight 188
Lighting Styles 188
 Lighting Ratios 189
Exposure Control and Metering Light 190
 Manual Exposure Control 190
  The Incident Light Meter 191
 The Gray Scale 191
Lighting Observational Scenes 192
Set Lights, Specials, and Practicals 194
Stylized Lighting 194
Exterior Lighting 196
 Location Scouting and Time of Day 196
 Check the Weather 196
 Subject and Camera Positions 196
 Sun plus Bounced Light 197
 Shade plus Bounced Light 197
 Dusk-for-Night 197
 Shooting at Night 197
 Camera-Mounted Lighting 198
Exposure: Beyond the Basics 198
 Contrast Range 198
 Dynamic Range 199
  Shooting with Dynamic Range in Mind 200
  Characteristic Curves and Gamma 200
   Black Stretch, Knee, and Log Gamma 201
   Color Settings 203
Conclusion 203

CHAPTER 13: SOUND BASICS AND EQUIPMENT

The Importance of Sound 205
Sound Recording Today 205
Understanding Sound 206
 Frequency (Pitch) 207
 Amplitude (Loudness) 207
  Inverse Square Lawv 208
 Quality (Timbre) 208

Velocity 208
Production Sound 208
Sync Sound 209
Wild Sound 212
Room Acoustics 212
Digital Sound Recording 213
The Basic Signal Path 213
Balanced vs Unbalanced Audio Signals 214
Digital Audio Quality: Sampling Rates and Bit Depth 214
Production Sound Tools 216
Sound Recording on Video Camcorders 216
The Digital Sound Recorder 216
   Microphone Inputs 217
   Level Controls and Meters 217
   Playback, Controls, and Outputs 218
   Digital Recording Media 218
      Flash Memory Recorders 218
      Hard Drive Recorders 219
Portable Field Mixers 219
Microphones 220
   Dynamic, Condenser, and Electret Condenser 220
   Microphone Frequency Response 222
   Microphone Directionality 222
      Omnidirectional 222
      Cardioid 223
      Hypercardioid and Shotguns 223
   Microphone Usage Types 223
      Handheld 223
      Shotgun 224
      Lavalier 224
      Wireless Microphones 224
      Pressure Zone Microphones (PZMs) 225
      Onboard Microphones 225
Microphone Support 225
The Importance of Headphones! 225
Conclusion 226

CHAPTER 14: LOCATION SOUND TECHNIQUES

The Sound Recordist's Job 227
Sound and the Documentary Crew 227
Before the Shoot: Prepping and Scouting 228
On Location: The Shoot 229
Evaluate the Location 231
Devising a Sound Recording Strategy 231
Setting Up Your Equipment 233
   Setting Levels 234
      Setting Levels on a Peak Meter 234
      Setting Levels on a VU Meter 236
      Setting Tone 236
Recording Your Audio 237
Riding the Gain during Recording 237
   Limiters, Microphone Attenuation, and Frequency Filters 237
Headphone Monitoring 238
Microphone Technique 239
   Booming: Clean Sound, Consistency, and Being On-Axis 239
   Boom Technique 240

　　　　　Recording Room Tone 241
　　　　　Wind Noise 241
　　　　　Doing a Sound Report 241
　　　Conclusion 242

CHAPTER 15: INTERVIEWING AND WORKING WITH SUBJECTS
　　Building and Maintaining Relationships 243
　　On-Camera Interactions with Subjects 244
　　　Interviewing 244
　　　　　Preparing for the Interview 244
　　　　　Interview Location 245
　　　　　Setting up the Interview: Visual Considerations 248
　　　　　　　Eyeline and Subject Placement 248
　　　　　　　Framing Considerations 250
　　　　　Conducting the Interview 250
　　　Directing Participants in Cinéma Vérité Scenes 252
　　Conclusion 253

CHAPTER 16: PRODUCTION PROCEDURES, ETIQUETTE, AND SAFETY
　　On the Documentary Set 255
　　Set Etiquette: Human and Material Resources 255
　　　Respect and Protect the Location 257
　　　Respect Your Equipment 257
　　　Food and Breaks 258
　　Production Safety and Security 258
　　　Prepare for Safety 259
　　　Production Insurance 260
　　　Employment Rules and Workman's Compensation 260
　　　International Travel 260
　　　Common Sense 261
　　　Rest and Health 261
　　　Weather 262
　　　Risky Locations 262
　　　　　Water 262
　　　　　Air 262
　　　Security 262
　　　Electricity and Safety 263
　　　　　How Much Electricity? 263
　　　　　Electrical Loads and Time 264
　　　　　Splitting the Load 265
　　　Lighting Safety Tips 265

Part 3 ■ POSTPRODUCTION

CHAPTER 17: POSTPRODUCTION WORKFLOW AND THE PROCESS OF DIGITAL EDITING
　　Postproduction Overview 269
　　　Postproduction Workflow 270
　　The Process of Digital Editing 272
　　　The Basic NLE System 273
　　　　　The Hardware Setup 273
　　　Setting Up Your NLE Project 274
　　　Ingesting Your Video 274

Working Natively vs Transcoding	275
Frame Rate Considerations	275
Working with Proxies ("Off-Line" and "Online" Editing)	276
Ingesting Audio	277
Syncing Picture and Sound	277
The NLE Software Interface	278
The Project Window (Avid) or Project Panel (Premiere Pro)	278
The Preview Monitor (Avid) or Source Panel (Premiere Pro)	278
The Timeline Window	278
The Sequence Monitor (Avid) or Program Panel (Premiere Pro)	282
Menu, Icon, or Keyboard: Take Your Pick	282
Making Simple Edits	283
Split Edits	288
Editing Stages	289
Reviewing Raw Footage	289
Paper Edit	289
Rough Cuts	290
Rough Cut Screenings	291
Building Your Soundtracks	291
The Fine Cut and Picture Lock	292
Finishing	292
High-End Finishing Workflows	292
Mastering	293
Overview of Editing Stages	293

CHAPTER 18: WRITING AND STRUCTURING THE DOCUMENTARY

Where to Begin?	295
Story Elements: Character, Exposition, and Plot	296
Structural Elements: Observational Scenes, Interviews, and Visual Evidence	298
Observational Scenes	299
Interviews	300
Visual Evidence	300
Chronology: How to Handle Time	301
Writing Narration	302
Third-Person Narration	302
First-Person Narration	302
Writing Narration	303
Styles of Narration	303
Writing the Essay Film	304
Conclusion	306

CHAPTER 19: THE ART OF DOCUMENTARY EDITING

Editing Expository Films	307
Editing Impressionistic Films	310
Associative Editing	311
Observational Documentaries and the Continuity System	313
Continuity of Mise-en-Scène (Shared Shot Content)	313
Continuity of Performance, Actions, and Placement	314
Continuity of Spatial Orientation	315
Avoiding "Too Similar" Shots	316
Cutaways	317
Timing, Rhythm, and Pacing	318
Timing	319
Rhythm	319

Pacing 319
Editing Patterns 321
Image Transitions 322
The Cut 322
The Dissolve 323
The Fade 323
Conclusion 323

CHAPTER 20: ARCHIVAL STORYTELLING

Archival Research 325
Talk to Somebody! 327
Ways of Using Archival Material 327
Metaphorical Imagery 330
Organizing Your Material 330
Using Metadata 331
Who Owns an Image? Copyright and Fair Use 331
Public Domain Materials 333
Clearing Rights 333
The Ethics of Using Archival Material 335
Technical Issues 335
Documents 336
Conclusion 337

CHAPTER 21: SOUND DESIGN AND FINISHING

Types of Sounds: Speech, Sound Effects, and Music 340
Speech 340
Sound Effects 343
Ambient Sounds 344
Music: Source and Score 346
Common Music Pitfalls 347
Sound Perspective 348
Sound Design Strategies 349
Sound Editing 351
Building Your Audio Tracks 351
Refining Your Sound Design 351
Splitting Tracks and Checkerboarding Your Audio 352
Finessing Your Audio 352
The Sound Mix 353
Step 1: Audio Sweetening 353
Audio Filters 354
Filters for Frequency Equalization and Noise Reduction 354
Filters for Reverb and Echo 355
Filters for Amplitude Compression or Expansion 355
Filters for Sibilance Suppression or "P" Popping 356
Step 2: Creating Audio Transitions 356
Step 3: Audio Level Balancing 357
The Reference Track and Establishing Average Level Range 357
Adjusting the Other Tracks 357
NLE Systems and Audio Levels 357
Step 4: The Mix Down 358
Sound Mixing Tips 359
The Mix Environment 359
Audio Monitor Reference 359
Advanced Sound Editing and Mixing Programs 359
Why Go Pro? 360

CHAPTER 22: FINISHING PICTURE AND MASTERING

- **Color Correction vs Color Grading** 363
- **Color Correction in Your NLE System** 363
  - Adjusting Brightness and Contrast 364
  - Adjusting Hue and Saturation 364
- **Titles and Credits** 368
  - Lower Thirds 370
- **Mastering Your Project** 372
  - Output Formats 373
  - Digital Cinema Package (DCP) 373
  - Exhibiting on Disc 375
    - *Pressed or Burned?* 375

CHAPTER 23: DISTRIBUTING YOUR DOCUMENTARY

- **Film Festivals** 378
- **Theatrical** 380
- **Semi-Theatrical** 382
- **Broadcast and Cable** 382
- **Educational** 382
- **Home Video (DVD)** 383
- **Streaming/Video on Demand** 383
- **Impact: Engagement Campaigns** 383
- **Conclusion** 388

NOTES 389
GLOSSARY 397
FILMOGRAPHY 435
PHOTOGRAPH AND ILLUSTRATION CREDITS 443
INDEX 445

Color plates can be found between p. 226 and p. 227

Acknowledgments

Documentary filmmaking is a collaborative art, so it stands to reason that a book about the topic, especially one with the scope of the current volume, could not have been made without the support and insights of many people.

First and foremost, we are deeply indebted to Mick Hurbis-Cherrier, the author of *Voice & Vision: A Creative Approach to Narrative Film and DV Production*. This book is a companion to that excellent resource, and we thank Mick for his generosity in coming up with the idea of a companion documentary book, his trust that we had the breadth of vision and expertise to do it, and for his guiding hand and wise feedback throughout. We also owe a special thanks to Gustavo Mercado, who did all the illustrations in the original book. His deep technical knowledge and pedagogical ability are evident in everything he does, and many of his images were inspirations for the illustrations in this book.

We also wish to thank our colleagues in the Department of Film and Media Studies at Hunter College, City University of New York, for their ongoing support and creative inspiration. In particular, we are grateful for the support we receive from James Roman, Peter Jackson, Renato Tonelli, Andrew Lund, Tami Gold, Stuart Ewen, Shanti Thakur, Michael Gitlin, and Ricardo Miranda.

This book would not be what it is without our students at Hunter College, at the undergraduate level and in the MFA program in Integrated Media Arts, over the past several decades. Their astute questions and observations about documentary have informed our teaching in myriad ways, and that is reflected in this book. Several Hunter students and alumni helped out in the production of this book specifically, including Shaun Persaud, Roberto Mendez, and Christine Chee. The unsung heroine of this book is Julia Main, who stuck with us throughout the process, and without whose organizational skills this book could not have survived past its infancy.

We also want to thank those filmmakers whose support you will find evidence of in our pages. We are indebted to them for providing much of the "meat" on the bones of the book, in the form of interviews we conducted with them. They include Pamela Yates and Paco de Onís, Nathan Fitch, Edin Velez, Jay Rosenstein, Tami Gold, Lynne Sachs, Annie Goldson, Julie Gustafson, Keith Wilson, S. Leo Chiang, David Alvarado, Andrew Lund, Ann Bennett, Iva Radivojevic, JT Takagi, Annukka Lilja, Brian Boyd, and Brian Lerch.

In addition, there were many times we reached out to expand our own knowledge of specific areas. We are more than grateful to Robert Bahar for allowing us to adapt his excellent article on documentary budgeting, first published on the International Documentary Association's website. Others to whom we owe thanks for sharing their expertise are Gary Griffin, Keith Shapiro at Frame:Runner, Gisburg Smialek at Harvestworks, Jon Miller of Icarus Films, and Basil Tsiokos. Veronique Bernard shared invaluable insight about development, Sabine Hoffman contributed thoughts about editing, and Deirdre Fishel shared her editor's valuable time and her AVID project. Thank you to Daniel Brooks and Fiona Boneham, and their son Lochlan who plays the trumpet.

We are also appreciative of all the people whose likenesses appear in these pages because they are part of illustrations we use as examples. These include Mariaelena Gonzalez, Harley Spiller, and Justin Hill, as well as countless others who appear in the films represented but remain unacknowledged.

We are grateful to President Jennifer Raab, Provost Vita Rabinowitz, and Dean Andrew Polsky at Hunter College, who supported us with grants for research and editing. We also wish to thank the creative team at Focal Press, particularly Emily McCloskey, Elliana Arons and Tamsyn Hopkins for their patience and quick responses throughout this process.

No acknowledgment would be complete without mentioning Jay Rosenstein, whose thoughtful comments made this book a much better one than it would otherwise have been.

To our families, especially Prudence Hill and Sofia Velez, we offer love and appreciation for their patience as we worked on a book that seemed to have no end.

Introduction

Documentary filmmaking is a practice that encompasses many different objectives, ways of working, and philosophies about media-making and even about reality itself. It is a bit of an octopus, with one foot in television, another in art practice, and another in journalism, not to mention social sciences such as anthropology. It certainly has a lot in common with its cousin, fiction filmmaking—the border that separates them is sometimes fiercely defended, while at other times it seems to disappear completely.

The debate about what constitutes documentary is as old as the form itself. We believe that it is often a useful debate, and have devoted some time in this text to the history and evolution of the form. A key concept is that documentary films are stories, but they draw their material from an encounter with reality. The desire to explore the real world, attend to real events, draw on history in the form of images old and new, sit with people and ask them questions about their lives, use tools like graphics, maps, and sound, all in the interest of telling a story about the world—all of this and more goes into any definition of documentary. As varied as their relationships to the real world are, documentary films—whether a call to action, a look at a way of life that deserves recognition, an account of an event, or a portrait of a community—can get to the heart of an issue and an audience in a way that is both passionate and cogent. Documentaries engage the heart and the intellect in a way that perhaps no other form can.

We believe the book you are holding is as thorough an introduction to the making of documentaries as you will find. In its pages, you will find discussions of everything from a CMOS sensor to tools for creating a social justice outreach plan for your film, from suggestions for ways to interact with your subjects to ideas about postproduction workflows. While this is an eminently practical book, it is not a technical manual. It is, rather, a book that believes creativity can reach its highest potential when informed by a thorough understanding of media-making techniques. It is also based on the idea that any new technology is only as significant as the new storytelling approaches it has to offer.

Speaking of technology, we have chosen to use the word "film" to refer to a documentary produced in any type of media, whether electronic, chemical, or digital. In this text, we have decided not to include film as an acquisition medium. We are aware that some documentarians are working with film because of its aesthetic possibilities, but it seems that for documentary, digital video in one form or another is the primary production medium.

Documentary Voice & Vision is based on our own pedagogical philosophy, developed over decades of teaching—often together—at Hunter College in New York City. It also draws on decades of documentary filmmaking experience, in contexts ranging from the most mainstream to the highly alternative. Our belief is that the best documentary filmmaker is one who is informed by a broad range of theoretical approaches drawn from critical theory, documentary studies, and the study of visual culture, as well as by a thorough knowledge of the history and practice of the form. Our impetus for the book was our desire to see the kind of book we would like to teach with ourselves, one we didn't find elsewhere. We have, however, found inspiration for various parts of this book in other very insightful sources, and we have referenced them so you can consult them yourselves.

For people who are passionate about documentary film, as we are, these are heady times. When we started to write this book, we realized quickly that we were not simply putting what we knew, the content of our lectures, down on paper. Instead we were at times on a breakneck journey through a rapidly changing terrain. On the one hand, tools for making documentary films are becoming more available by the day, and new technologies are making it possible to capture images and sounds in ways that were unimaginable even five years ago. On the other hand, there is a flourishing of interest in the documentary form, as evidenced by the explosion of documentary film festivals, collectives, online communities, and more. A key reason for this explosion, we believe, is the rise of a new digital citizenship in the age of the Internet and a healthy belief in questioning the authority of traditional sources of information. More than ever, people are finding in documentary filmmaking a tool for a rich range of social expressions whether artistic, entertaining, informative, personally expressive, activist, or investigative. It is precisely in this proliferation of methods, approaches, platforms, and audiences that complex choices, as well as opportunities, lie.

The book tracks the production process closely, offering chapters on each step of making a documentary. We have devoted the first five chapters of the book to various aspects of preproduction: how to find and develop ideas in Chapter 1, and how to think about the advantages and drawbacks of different stylistic approaches in Chapter 2. Then we move on to thinking about how to structure a documentary story in Chapter 3, and how to present your ideas to others in Chapter 4. As we note, documentary practice is an engagement with real people in ways that have very real consequences, so in Chapter 5 we take a look at the ethical and legal considerations involved.

The next group of chapters looks at the production phase, from planning in Chapter 6 to the visual language of the cinema, and documentary coverage specifically, in Chapter 7. In Chapters 8 and 9, we cover the nuts and bolts of cameras and digital imaging, as well as lens optics, and the expressive capabilities of these technologies. Audio equipment and recording practices are addressed in Chapters 13 and 14. We follow with an overview of postproduction in the digital era in Chapters 17 through 22, looking at workflow, editing techniques, ways of working with archival material, and sound and picture finishing. We end with a chapter on distribution that we believe is unique in its emphasis on social impact as well as financial return.

We don't believe there is one kind of successful documentary. Some films seek a broad audience, others a specific one. Some aim to interrogate the language of documentary, or its relation to the real; others use the immediacy of the form to expose situations around the world that need calling attention to. Still others are lyrical expressions of individual experience. But in all cases there are practices and principles makers try to adhere to. There is equipment, and ways of using it, and the people you encounter, and ways of working with them.

Documentary filmmaking is a practice with a shared culture. For the making of this book, we've reached out to many people. Some are friends and colleagues, others experts in the field previously unknown to us. The result is, we believe, a very up-to-date account of how documentaries are made, and of how you can make the best use of the tools available to express your creative vision.

We're strongly aware that documentary filmmaking is a collaborative art form. We hope this book will be useful not just to people who aspire to direct films, but to those who hope to become cinematographers, sound recordists, editors, colorists, distributors, or educators. For others, making a documentary may be something they are hoping to teach themselves outside of school or the workplace. We hope this book will be a useful companion for them as well.

As of its publication date, this book is up-to-date in terms of technology and practices. However, as we note throughout the text, the methods of making documentaries, the forms that they take, the platforms they appear on, and the ways they will engage their audiences are all changing rapidly. Our companion website (www.routledge.com/cw/Anderson) will contain the book's appendices, including examples and interactive features, and will be updated regularly.

Despite recent developments, however, we believe that many of the issues that makers engage with today are inherent to the form. With that in mind, we've chosen to examine a cross section of documentaries, some historically significant films that represented major paradigm shifts in the way documentaries were made and received, others because they illustrate specific points, and others simply because we like them. We've also used examples from our own work, not to blow our own horns but because we know why we've made the choices we've made, and can illustrate subtle ideas fairly readily. At the end of the book, you will find a listing of all the documentaries referenced, with links that will help you find them either for individual viewing or institutional purchase.

One significant area that we have not addressed is the explosion of Internet-based documentary forms. Under the banners of "expanded documentary," "interactive documentary," "cyberdocs," "docmedia," and more, the Internet and the computer have offered a range of tools that are creating rich and exciting new forms. While we firmly believe that the utopian possibilities offered by this new cyber-terrain are worth exploring, we have decided that an investigation of techniques and approaches in this area is beyond the scope of our book, except in a modest way in the area of distribution.

Documentary is a universal language, and this is something we've tried to keep in mind. We both live and teach in the United States, so in many ways the book is based on that experience. On the other hand, documentary making is a global practice, with exciting work and valuable traditions on every continent. From the shores of Hudson Bay to Patagonia, from the Cape of Good Hope to Lapland, documentary stories are conceived, filmed, edited, and shown. No one group or region has a monopoly on documentary filmmaking. While making and showing documentary films can present challenges everywhere, the nature of those challenges varies widely from region to region and country to country. In some places, the biggest problem is standing out from the crowd; in other areas, the problems are with offering points of view that challenge reigning authority or wisdom, while in other areas, the basic infrastructure of digital distribution and screening is lacking. But these are all obstacles worth overcoming and goals worth fighting for. The rewards of this work can be great. They include the possibility of presenting a picture of the world, or at least part of it, to an audience that wants not just to be entertained but to be informed. They also include an engagement with people about things you feel are critically important. We hope you will join us on a journey into the vibrant, challenging, and rewarding arena of documentary filmmaking.

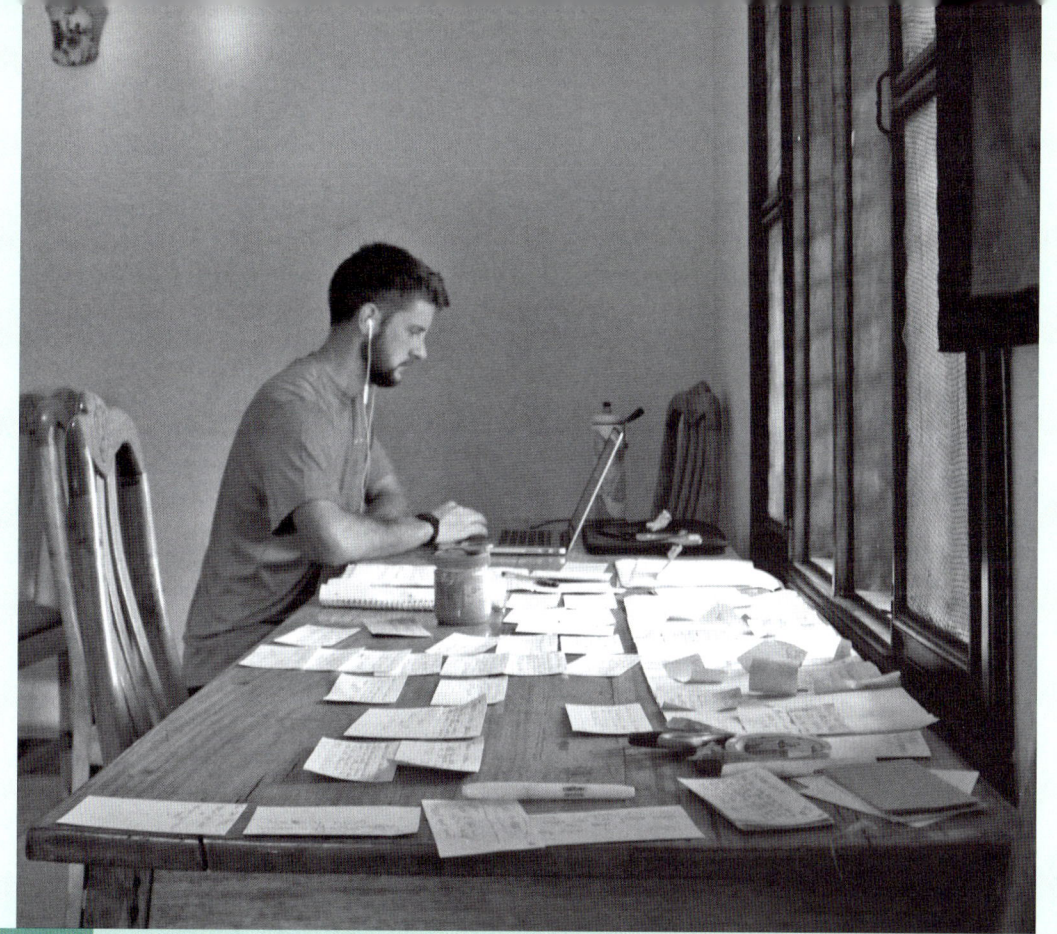

PART 1 DEVELOPING YOUR DOCUMENTARY

CHAPTER 1

Finding and Developing Ideas

WHAT IS A DOCUMENTARY?

Documentary as a form has many points of origin. Some people look to Robert Flaherty's footage of Inuit life in Northern Canada in *Nanook of the North* (1922), others to works by Dziga Vertov and his innovative portrait of urban life in the new Soviet Union in *Man with a Movie Camera* (1929). For many others, the edifying documentaries of the 1930s British documentary movement, described by founder John Grierson as a "creative treatment of actuality,"[1] still serve as defining models for today's documentarians. Wherever we locate its origins, at its most basic, documentary film offers us some kind of vision of how the real world looks and operates. Documentary filmmaking is a fascinating pursuit because it allows us to comment on our society, offers us a glimpse of other ones, and may even exhort our audiences to change the world we live in. As we will explore in this chapter, documentary makers use a wide variety of elements including interviews, records made while historical events unfold, archives of sound and image, and even actors to offer viewers something that is both non-fiction and a story.

As we will see in the coming chapters, "documentary" describes a whole field of film-making, from educational films to activist ones, from hard-hitting video journalism to lyrical poetic expressions. But every documentary starts with an idea not just about the real world, but about the process of representing reality as well.

WHERE DO DOCUMENTARY IDEAS COME FROM?

All documentaries start with a moment of insight, with somebody (usually the producer or director) realizing that a particular person, subject, or event would make a great non-fiction film. That "aha!" moment is the beginning of months, or often years, of work. Sometimes it's a question that won't let go of you until you explore it more deeply.

For one of our students, Nathan Fitch, that moment came a few months into his time in the Peace Corps. He was working on the tiny Pacific island of Kosrae, part of the Micronesian archipelago. He recounts:

> *I visited a remote village with several of my fellow volunteers. As I trudged through the hot sand, I saw a man seated in the shade of a coconut palm. He was wearing camouflage fatigues. Eager to test out my burgeoning language skills, I accosted him in the local language, "Len wo. Kom fuhka?" (Good day. How are you?). He squinted up at me, then replied in English flavored with a Southern drawl. "Hey man, I'm doing good. How are y'all making out?" I was shocked, for few of the young people I had met were confident speaking English—especially to a stranger.*
>
> *I asked the man, "Have you lived in the US?" "Yes sir," the man replied, "I've been in Fort Benning and Fort Carson. Just got back from Iraq a few days ago for some R&R." "Iraq?" I confirmed. The man nodded. "Yep, stationed right outside of Baghdad. I'm heading back there next week."*
>
> *There were many things I might have asked this soldier had I lingered longer, a cascade of questions that would have highlighted my ignorance of the geopolitics of*

the region that I now called home. Questions like, "Why are you fighting for the US in Iraq, when I, a US citizen, am not?" "What is it like to leave such a peaceful place for the turmoil of war?" "What is it like to return?" It was these questions, and the somewhat guilty understanding that he was serving in my place so that I could be in the Peace Corps, that were the impetus for my documentary Island Soldier *(Figure 1.3).*[3]

Every documentary filmmaker has their own process for finding the seeds of a good film. And like most people involved in creative endeavors, many experience self-doubt and some anxiety about their ability to come up with a good topic and stick with it. It can be reassuring to remember, as choreographer Twyla Tharp puts it, that "there are no creative geniuses . . . in order to be creative, you have to know how to prepare to be creative."[4] Many people report that breakthrough ideas came while they were cleaning the house, taking a shower, or out for a walk. But these moments of creative breakthrough can only come when combined with everyday practices that pave the way. For documentary filmmakers, this often means keeping track of the people, social patterns, trends, and events that are occurring in our communities, country, or world. Many have rituals that include things like keeping a journal, clipping (or, increasingly "bookmarking") articles from newspapers, magazines, or blogs they read every day. As Graeme Sullivan suggests, "art practice can be seen as a form of intellectual and imaginative inquiry, and as a place where research can be carried out that is robust enough to yield reliable insights that are well grounded and culturally relevant."[5] Other rituals keep filmmakers in touch with their creative potential. Filmmaker Luis Buñuel, for example, committed to having coffee with one particular producer every day, and to

ARE DOCUMENTARY FILMMAKERS ARTISTS?

In a 2014 essay "Reflections on Getting Real: Debunking Five Myths That Divide Us," documentary filmmakers Pamela Yates and Paco de Onís write about the common misperception that filmmakers who tackle human rights abuses, or illuminate social issues, are not artists:

We give equal weight to being artists as well as human rights defenders. We know that as we get better and better as artists, we create wider audiences with far greater impact. Because we aren't just developing a narrative story arc, we are developing ideas across the length and breadth of the documentary film. It's the interplay of the two that creates dramatic tension. The power and beauty of cinema are our artistic and political tools. Our canvas is global; our palette, the human condition.[2]

One only has to look at a documentary like Rithy Panh's *The Missing Picture* (2013), about the Cambodian genocide, or Ari Folman's *Waltz with Bashir* (2008), about the Israeli invasion of Lebanon in 1982, to see the incredible range of creative practices that documentary filmmakers are using to tell stories about real-life events (Figures 1.1 and 1.2). While documentaries like these redefine the genre through their nontraditional use of animation, even more traditional approaches have extensive creative dimensions that overlap with those of fiction film, theater, photography, painting, and even music.

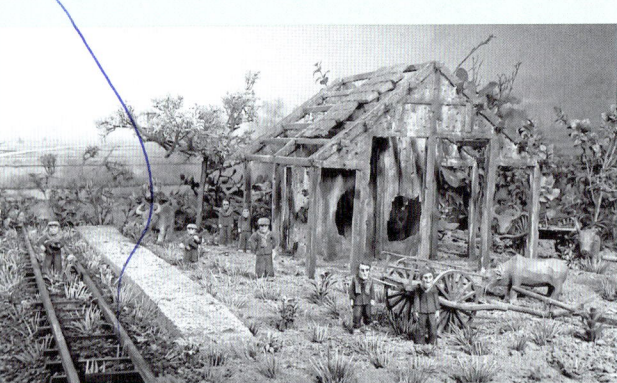

■ **Figure 1.1** Rithy Panh uses clay figures, archival footage, and his narration to recreate the atrocities Cambodia's Khmer Rouge committed between 1975 and 1979 in *The Missing Picture*.

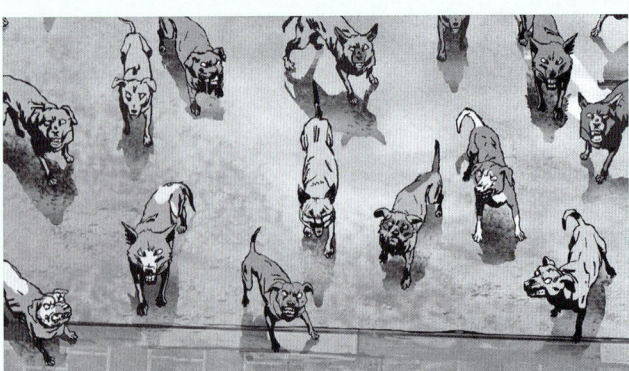

■ **Figure 1.2** Animation provides compelling visuals for *Waltz with Bashir* while recreating the traumatic psychological experiences of veterans of the 1982 Israeli invasion of Lebanon.

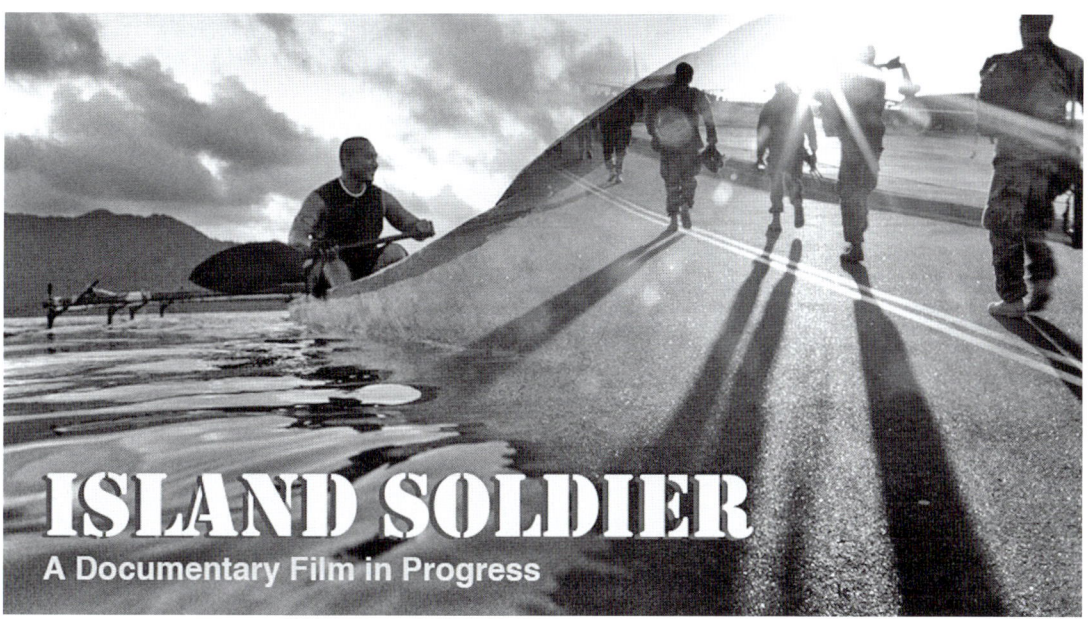

Figure 1.3 Nathan Fitch's film *Island Soldier* (2016) started from a chance encounter on a small Micronesian Island.

telling him a story. While not every story was worthwhile, the practice of coming up with a story a day to tell his producer created enough good ideas that Buñuel was able to make at least a movie a year for most of his working life.[6] The important thing is that you create a routine that works for you, and that you follow it consistently.

In addition to being curious, documentary filmmakers tend to be passionate and interested in communicating their ideas and experiences to others. Jay Rosenstein, the director of *In Whose Honor?* (1997), about the controversy around the use of Native American mascots in sports, recounts the moment he realized he needed to make a documentary about the topic (Figure 1.4):

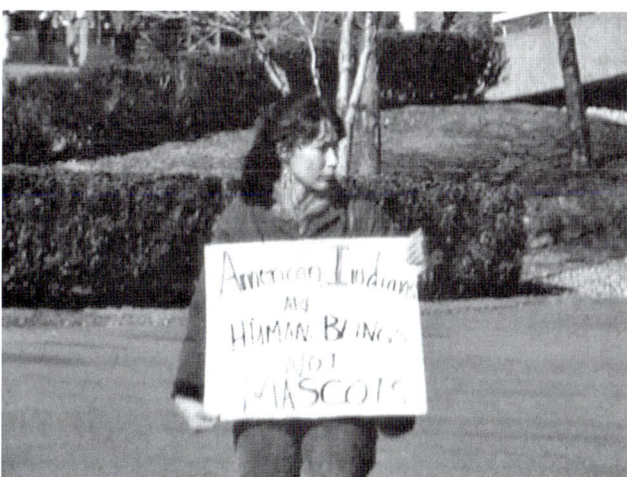

Figure 1.4 Charlene Teters, a Spokane Indian woman whose activism sparked Jay Rosenstein's interest in the use of Native American mascots in sports. Her story became the centerpiece of *In Whose Honor?*

I heard this woman, Charlene Teters, speak. She is a Spokane Indian, and she was talking about the University of Illinois mascot Chief Illiniwek (Chief Illiniwek is a pretend Indian that dances at football and basketball games). I had never heard an Indian person talk about the mascot. I was kind of stunned, and very moved, and I thought "Everybody needs to hear this." And so the film became a way for me to try to get Charlene's voice and her message out to people who couldn't or wouldn't otherwise hear it. So sometimes you just learn information that isn't known, that you think should be known, and you become passionate about spreading those ideas.[8]

Other filmmakers use the process of making documentaries to better understand their world. When he began the film that would eventually become *The Thin Blue Line* (1988), director Errol Morris was making a documentary about Dr. James Grigson, a Dallas psychiatrist who had testified for the prosecution in many

PART 1
Developing Your Documentary

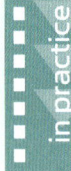

■ PAVING THE WAY FOR CREATIVITY

On a trip through Europe, video artist Edin Velez came up with a ritual that ultimately helped him conceive of an idea that would define his work for decades to come. He decided to create a collage journal as a way of testing out different ways of layering images in a single frame (Figure 1.5).

For me, creating small works, not necessarily in your primary medium, is one of the best ways to tap into creativity. It's always nice to set up a certain number of rules, because if it's too open people tend to flounder. So I decided that each page had to be finished before I left the location I was in, and I could only use photographs I took or other things I found in that location. It was very freeing to make the journal, because unlike making a video, where you're concerned about showing it to people, this was a very personal book and I didn't expect to show it to anybody. The beauty of allowing yourself moments to explore is that out of all this you will have ideas that will be cheesy, and ideas that make you cringe, but then you will have great ideas you never expected to have. You are focusing on the simple task of cutting and gluing images, but what you are really doing is placing your mind in that creative zone. It puts the mind in a place where it allows concepts and ideas to flow from unconscious to conscious.[7]

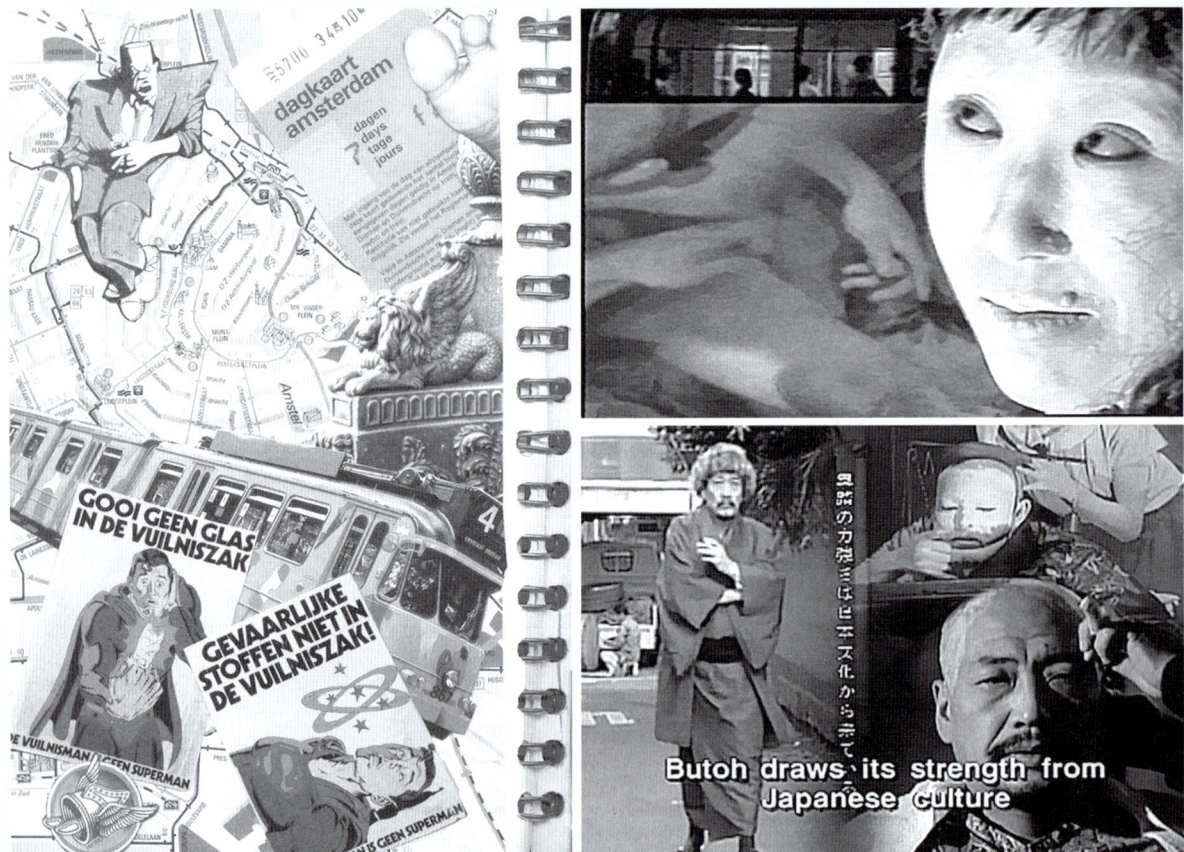

■ **Figure 1.5** Using small exercises to stimulate creativity. Filmmaker Edin Velez's collages (left) helped him develop the ideas about image layering that were later incorporated into his video work. The still frame on the top right is from his highly layered film about the traditional and the contemporary in Japanese culture, *The Meaning of the Interval* (1987). At bottom right is a frame from *Dance of Darkness* (1989).

death penalty cases. Along the way, Morris interviewed Randall Adams, one of the "cold-blooded killers" (Grigson's words) that Grigson had helped put on death row, and his film took a completely different turn. He explains:

> *As I read about Adams' story I slowly but surely became convinced that there had been a terrible miscarriage of justice. And then the movie changed. It was no longer a movie of Dr. Grigson. It was a movie about Randall Adams. That was the beginning of close to two years of tracking people down, interviewing them, of doing research. The Thin Blue Line isn't telling the story of a murder case, it's not about an investigation. It is an investigation! The investigation was done, in part, with a camera—culminating with David Harris' confession to me. It was on tape—following the malfunctioning of my camera in my interview with him—the tape on which he essentially confesses to the murder!*[9]

YOUR ARTISTIC IDENTITY

Whatever topic you choose, your film will be different than somebody else's documentary on the same topic. This is because we each have a particular set of experiences and worldviews that shape our **artistic identity**.

How do you discover your own artistic identity? This is a lifelong process, and your own artistic identity will evolve through every creative endeavor you take on, starting with the very first films you make as a student. It can be helped along by forcing yourself to think through your own ideas and opinions about your subjects, investigating where and how you have developed your particular point of view, and grounding your film in your own unique **stylistic approach** (Chapter 2). In *Directing the Documentary*, Michael Rabiger creates a "self-inventory" that helps readers understand the marks their life experiences have left on them, and translate that into a worldview that is reflected in their films.[10] What are your "hot" issues, the ones that will prompt you to engage, question, and communicate with an audience? Discovering these is critical to your development as an artist.

Many documentary filmmakers report that while their topics change from film to film, there are consistent deeper themes that permeate them all. Whether your films will be built around the complex dynamics of family relationships, the quest for identity, struggles for equality, or some other theme is something you will have to discover for yourself.

One of the biggest obstacles to finding your artistic identity as a documentary maker lies in the prevalent notion that documentaries should be "objective" and refrain from having a point of view. If you start with a point of view, it is thought, you risk losing objectivity and risk distorting the truth. Documentary is often misunderstood as a form of news reporting, which is constrained by television network practices of representing "both sides" of an issue, and where editorializing or personalizing is discouraged. Since most situations in life involve more than two sides, and presenting life in its complexity is part of good documentary filmmaking, it's helpful to jettison this idea of objectivity and replace it with a sense of fairness—to your audience, to the subjects of your film, and to yourself. Reaching a real understanding of the world around us, and the relations of cause and effect in it, can only be seen as a dynamic and ongoing effort. Documentaries have the potential to explore the personal and human dimensions of issues, incorporating layers of information that are broader than the facts journalists traditionally work with. If documentary filmmaking is indeed "the creative treatment of actuality," that creativity is fueled by your individual passion and perspective.

The best documentaries are usually made by people who have strong ideas and opinions, but aren't afraid of changing or revising those ideas when presented with new information.

Documentaries are not the last word on a topic; they are better understood as supporting and enhancing the discussions that society needs to have. For example, Davis Guggenheim's *An Inconvenient Truth* (2006), featuring former Vice President Al Gore, reframed the issue of global warming in such a compelling way that it became a policy debate. Precisely because it took a strong point of view, it opened doors for a broad public discussion that was heard as far as Washington DC.

RESEARCH

Once you have a strong story idea, you need to start your research process. You will need to become, at least for the time you're making the film, an expert in the area you are exploring. You may begin by looking for articles, books, and other sources on the Internet and in the library. If you have access to licensed databases like Lexis-Nexis or JSTOR (often available through universities or libraries), your research will be much more thorough than if you rely on a browser-based search engine (like Google).

Before getting too far into your research, it's important to find out what other films have been made on your topic. Watching any other films that deal with similar issues will help you find an angle that hasn't been explored yet. While there is no guarantee that no one else is making a film on a similar subject at the same time as you, your goal is to make something that feels fresh in terms of topic, approach, or perspective.

It is also important to find out, in the research phase, what **archival footage** and **stock footage**, photographs, and sound recordings exist that you might want to use. This search can be time consuming, but the payoffs can be large. For coauthor Kelly Anderson and Allison Lirish Dean's film *My Brooklyn* (2012), about the redevelopment of a popular African-American and Caribbean shopping district in Downtown Brooklyn, finding the photographs that Jamel Shabazz took in Brooklyn during the 1980s (and securing his permission to use them) was essential to setting the mood and tone of the entire film (Figure 1.6).

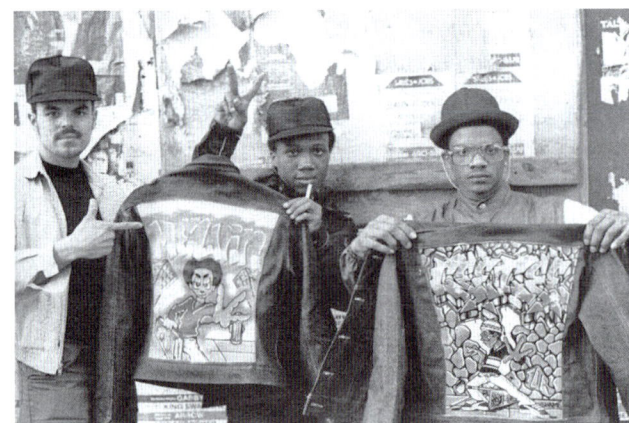

■ **Figure 1.6** Photographs by Jamel Shabazz are essential to the storytelling in *My Brooklyn*.

Soon, though, you will need to get out of the comfort of your home and start to engage with people in person. Whether they are going to be on-screen, provide you with background information, or simply connect you to other people and resources, a documentary needs people in order to be successful. Sometimes an email approach is the best way to make initial contact, but soon afterwards you should pick up the phone or go visit in person.

It can be intimidating to go into unfamiliar situations, but as long as you take precautions to stay physically safe, in-person visits will usually yield the best results. On the positive side, there are few things more thrilling than walking into a new environment, seeing things you have never seen before, meeting people and sharing ideas, and building trust. Making a documentary gives you license to talk to people you wouldn't otherwise approach, and ask questions that might otherwise seem intrusive. Finding people who see the world in ways that help you understand things from new perspectives is one of the joys of documentary work, and anybody who sticks with documentary filmmaking will tell you that for

■ RESEARCH: WHERE TO BEGIN

Print: Periodic literature (newspapers, journals, magazines)
    Online databases
    Books on your topic
    Primary source documents
    Still photographs

Films on your topic:
    Good for background information and ideas
    Make sure you aren't reinventing the wheel!
    Can provide leads for archival and stock footage (Chapter 20)

Internet: Organizational websites (may have reports, research, white papers)
    General Internet searches (and Google alerts)

People: Academics, activists, or other official or unofficial experts

all the difficulty and fear of the unknown that you have to confront, as long as you approach people with humility and respect, the process can be extremely rewarding.

For example, when coauthor Martin Lucas was making the film *No Room to Move!* (1993) for the United Nations Population Report, he decided to focus on rural-to-urban migration in Mexico. He found himself knocking on the door of a family home in a quiet country town during Holy Week, solely because there was a bright green Mexico City taxicab some 250 miles from home, parked in front. He introduced himself and his crew to the complete strangers who were living there. He says,

> *I would have never knocked on that door if I wasn't making a film. But the pressure of knowing I needed an interview subject made me do it, and the cabbie ended up being a great subject for our film. When he heard we were making a film sponsored by the United Nations, and that we thought of him as an expert, he was happy to help out. As it turned out, this man ended up serving another purpose: he knew everybody in the area and became the crew's "ambassador" as they searched for others to talk with.*[11]

Organizations or professional researchers with an interest in your subject area can be invaluable. For *Every Mother's Son* (2004), their film about excessive use of force by police officers, coauthor Kelly Anderson and Tami Gold relied on the attorneys representing their main subjects for information and primary documents such as recordings of 911 calls, crime scene photos, and transcripts of court proceedings. While this material could likely have been obtained by filing requests with the NYPD or the courts, it saved the filmmakers a lot of time and energy to go through the lawyers. And since in this case the lawyers also had an interest in publicizing their cases, the collaboration worked for everybody involved.

For *My Brooklyn*, Anderson and Dean gained a tremendous amount of information from community-based organizations with an interest in their film's topic. Several labor-intensive surveys and reports had been published by groups like Families United for Racial and Economic Equality (FUREE) and Good Jobs New York. While it was important for Anderson and Dean to understand that these organizations had their own agendas and perspectives on the topics of development and gentrification, the research found in these documents was invaluable.

Organizations that have spent years working on an issue can also be helpful in identifying possible subjects for your film, and help you gain access to those people. When approaching organizations, the goal is to be transparent about what you are doing and why, and to establish a relationship of mutual trust. This does not mean, however, that you agree to collaborate with them on the vision for your film, or that you will allow them to review the film before it's made. We will address these issues in more depth in Chapter 5.

Keep in mind that organizations may be understaffed and not have the resources to cooperate with your requests. Sometimes, spending time building relationships can pay off in the long run. Offering to shoot an event for a group (even if it's something you don't want to use in your film), or to edit something for their website, or just participating in one of their events or campaigns, can be a nice way to make a relationship more reciprocal.

The situation is different when you are approaching people or organizations who have reason to think your film might portray them in a less than positive light. For public officials, corporate executives, or others in positions of power, it is sometimes best to wait to approach them, since you may only get one chance to get them on camera. People who are used to dealing with the media will need to be approached after your research is done and you have a clear sense of what you want from them, or they can "run away" with the interview, leaving you with little you can use.

Whoever you are approaching, prepare a few (short!) sentences describing what your film is about, why you are making it, and what you hope it will accomplish. Be prepared to answer the question "Why me?" And remember, your job is to listen to them, not convince them you are the expert.

THE IMPORTANCE OF A HYPOTHESIS

Once you have an idea for a documentary, and maybe some characters in mind, it's time to develop a **hypothesis**. Your hypothesis is a basic *claim* about your subject, and it acts as a map, giving you a way to move forward with your research. Even though your hypothesis may change over time, it's essential to have because without it, your film will be in danger of losing its focus at any time.

Let's imagine you decide to make a film about "university tuition increases." Congratulations! You have found a documentary topic. A topic is an area of interest, but it takes research to turn it into a story you can actually film.

The first thing to figure out is what you are trying to say about tuition increases. Your research will help you develop a point of view on your subject, and also help you narrow down a broad topic to something less abstract. Your sample hypothesis at this point might be:

Rising tuition costs are affecting students.

At this point the hypothesis is based on your gut instinct, but you can't rely exclusively on instinct. Don't be paralyzed, however, by the possibility that your hypothesis might not turn out to be true. The point of a hypothesis is to take a stance that you can begin to test.

Let's say you actually interview some students and they tell you that they are struggling to make ends meet and stay in school. This allows you to restate your hypothesis with more urgency:

Cutbacks and increases in fees are jeopardizing student dreams of a college education.

Now you are convinced there is a problem, but you don't know how widespread it is. How much has tuition gone up? Are there cases of students dropping out of college that can be attributed to these increased fees?

You find data to suggest that fees have increased substantially and that graduation rates have stalled. You can now move past your previous hypothesis to state:

Cutbacks in financial aid and increases in tuition are actually making the possibility of completing college difficult for a substantial number of students.

Let's say, as you start shooting, you interview an economics professor who not only studies these trends but has witnessed them in her school over the years. She tells you there is a clear link between public college education and the ability of a society to be viable in an era of economic globalization. You also might spend more time filming with individual students and their families. All this might lead you to a more urgent and dramatic thesis:

> *Cutbacks and increases in tuition are resulting in the first generation of Americans at risk of being less well educated than their parents, jeopardizing the nation's ability to be competitive globally.*

Now you have a really interesting and compelling point of view, and a point that you think your film will make. While this process of stating and refining what your film is about starts during preliminary research, you must see it as ongoing. As you talk to more people and learn more during your production process, your views will continue to develop and change.

Your hypothesis needs to be something you care about, and your personal stake in it should be clear to you. In the case of tuition increases, you might feel that every society owes its young an equal opportunity, and that this opportunity is under threat. On a more personal level, you might have had to struggle for your own education. Or it might be the opposite: your parents' sacrifices might have made it easier for you to go to college and you feel like others deserve a similar chance. No one reason is better than another. What is important is that you are aware of your own motivations and values, and that you have a strong sense of where you are heading while continuing to stay open to new perspectives on your topic.

Should you talk to people who will contradict your thesis? The answer goes back to the idea of a documentary as part of a larger conversation in society. Films thrive on conflict, and you will do well to have a variety of perspectives represented. Let's imagine your college administrators believe that tuition is not a key factor influencing student retention. Including their perspective will likely make your film more interesting and complex, and strengthen your credibility.

"CASTING" YOUR DOCUMENTARY

The next step is to find real people who can embody the issues in a way that puts flesh on the bare bones of your hypothesis. Documentary filmmakers have varying criteria about what makes a person a good choice to feature in a film. Here are some things to consider:[12]

- Does the person present well on screen? Many directors do a test shoot to see if the person's personality, passion, or conflicts translate on camera. Some refer to people "popping" on screen, or just being "cinematic" or "charismatic." The criteria for this will differ from director to director, but there's no doubt you will come across people who seem like great possibilities for your film when you meet them, only to find they can't hold an audience's attention on screen. Being able to recognize this early on will save you (and your subject) time and stress.
- Do they have a goal, and are they willing to let you follow them to try to reach it? It is sometimes said that "action is character." People who aren't trying to achieve things, and encountering obstacles along the way, can make for boring films.
- Be careful about quirkiness as a major draw, especially for its own sake. "Colorful" characters can be appropriate for short films, especially if their quirks express something deeper that touches on a more universal theme. For longer films, there needs to be more at stake or it will risk becoming "one-note"—repetitive, and therefore boring.
- Many documentary filmmakers report that they are drawn as they have a personality that is not too guarded, nor too smooth, people whose "performances" of themselves contain cracks that allow us to see their internal as well as their external struggles. This kind of underlying conflict, especially when married to an external goal the audience can relate to, can be perceived by audiences and be deeply compelling.

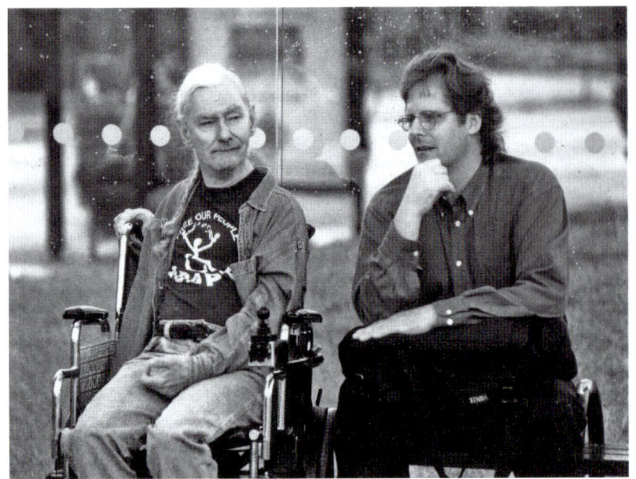

■ **Figure 1.7** Walter Brock (left) with Arthur Campbell Jr., the main character of his documentary *If I Can't Do It*. Photo by Noel Saltzman.

People who are highly articulate can be useful for your film, especially if they are going to fill the role of experts who will be explicating complicated history or information. Don't eliminate people just because they aren't traditionally articulate, however. If we never choose people who aren't "good talkers" to be on camera, we will unintentionally end up excluding whole groups of people from the media landscape. An example of a different approach is seen in Walter Brock's *If I Can't Do It* (1998), about Arthur Campbell Jr., a disabled man who is pushing for independence and equal opportunity (Figure 1.7). Instead of having Campbell's sister speak for him as an interpreter, Brock allows Campbell to speak for himself, even though it is difficult to decipher his language. Brock explains:

> *Nothing in my life prepared me for my first sight of Arthur. There he sat in his wheelchair, drooling, arms flailing, making loud noises that I could not imagine made sense . . . I want viewers to experience the discomfort that I felt, to process and examine it, and come out on the other side of that discomfort with a greater sense of acceptance and tolerance.*[13]

Active vs Passive Characters

Many documentaries begin with a character trying to achieve something that matters to them. The protagonist of *In Whose Honor?*, Charlene Teters, wants the University of Illinois (and all sports teams) to stop using their Indian mascots. In *The Wolfpack* (2015), Crystal Moselle's fascinating documentary about a group of brothers whose father keeps them locked away in an apartment on the Lower East Side of Manhattan, the protagonists share the goal of breaking free so they can experience the world outside. Over the course of most documentaries, the characters try to accomplish things, find obstacles in their way, and either succeed or fail in their attempt to surmount the obstacles. To maximize the possibility that your film will be dramatic, look for people who are trying to do something about their circumstances, not people who are passive victims of circumstances beyond their control. Another way to think of this is that you want characters who are closely involved in the issue you are exploring. While there is a role for secondary characters, there is no substitute for subjects who have something deeply significant to them at stake.

Sometimes, people who are more passive than active can function in a dramatic way. *Nobody's Business* (1996), an experimental documentary by Alan Berliner, would seem to be about Oscar Berliner, the filmmaker's father. Oscar is a tragic character, seemingly victimized by age, lack of friends, and life circumstances. If he were the film's only subject, this would likely present problems. But the other main character in the film is the filmmaker, Alan. In this interview, he explains how his father's passivity was actually what motivated him:

> *The kinds of messages I was getting from my father were becoming very difficult for me to accept: That the misfortunes of his life had overtaken him. That he had somehow become a victim of circumstances . . . Oscar Berliner cannot live for 79 years and tell me his life is nothing, was nothing. I'm much too alive as a human being to accept that attitude from him. So the more he articulated his own ordinariness, the more motivated I became to prove him wrong.*[14]

The filmmakers' need to challenge his father about precisely his passivity becomes the conflict that drives this highly dynamic and entertaining film (Figure 1.8).

Not all documentaries follow characters over time. Documentaries can take many forms, and conflict can also be metaphorical, a conflict of ideas or theories about how the world works. An example of a more conceptual conflict would be Charles Ferguson's *Inside Job* (2010), about the 2008 financial crisis, which we will discuss further in Chapter 3. The important thing is that there be something at stake for you, for your characters, and for your audience.

Juggling Multiple Characters

Often filmmakers cast a wide net, filming multiple characters and narrowing the list down over time. Sometimes a subject ends up "on the cutting room floor" because the actual course of their story hasn't produced enough interesting conflict. Remember, we are dealing with reality here, and nobody can predict for certain what will happen in the course of filming. At other times, you reframe your topic as you get more information, and a character who seemed essential in the beginning ends up being less important.

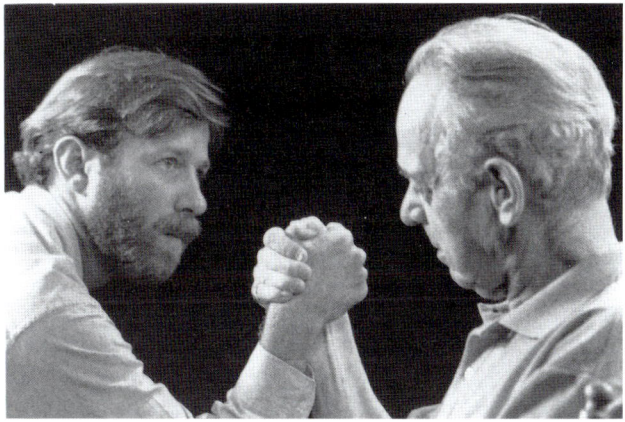

■ **Figure 1.8** Alan Berliner's active efforts to pull out the story of his extremely reticent father provide the central conflict that is the engine of *Nobody's Business*.

It can be taxing for audiences to follow multiple characters, so casting sometimes involves making sure each character is distinct from the others and carries a specific part of the story you are trying to tell. For *Every Mother's Son*, Anderson and Gold followed four mothers for several years before deciding their film could only accommodate three main characters. "People were confusing two of the characters' storylines," says Gold. "We ultimately decided that each of the women needed to be very different—physically and in terms of the details of their story—in order for people to not get confused."[15] They also decided that, even though in reality there was a lot of commonality between the women's stories, each mother's story *as presented in the film* needed to illuminate one aspect of the issue of police brutality, without a lot of overlap. Gold says,

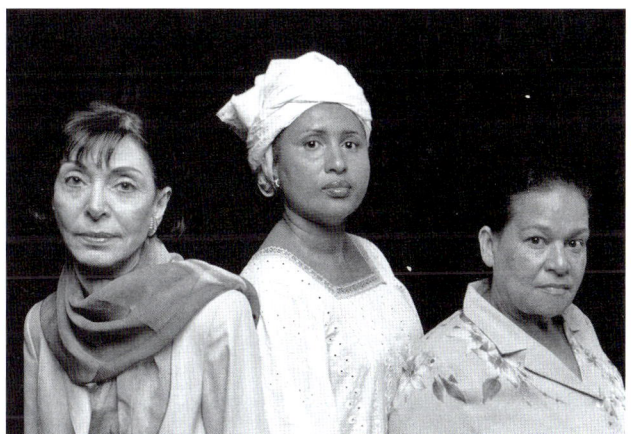

■ **Figure 1.9** *Every Mother's Son* follows three mothers (from left, Doris Busch-Boskey, Kadiatou Diallo, and Iris Baez). Each character represents an aspect of the problem the film illuminates. Photo by Anna Curtis.

> Iris Baez's story became about how difficult it is to have abusive officers removed from the force, Kadiatou Diallo's story became about racial profiling and the ways that aggressive stop-and-frisk tactics can lead to disaster. And Doris Busch-Boskey's story illuminates the ways incidents of police abuse are covered up, and victims of police abuse are demonized. Together, the three cases allowed us to address a very complicated situation in an accessible way, and telling it through the mothers' points of view made it emotionally compelling for audiences" (Figure 1.9).[16]

THE VALUE OF THE DOCUMENTING PROCESS

While **interviews** are a common staple in documentary, real events and processes that can unfold in front of the camera will be uniquely compelling to audiences. Using the tuition example, imagine you discover that students are planning to interrupt a meeting where university trustees are expected to approve a tuition increase. This situation would seem an important dramatic addition to your story. Or you could take another approach, starting your tuition story with a shot of a student moonlighting at a fast food outlet, throwing out the trash in front of the store at 2 AM, and then studying at a table. A scene like this would give your viewers an idea of the difficulties of student life. It could also be used to support the testimony of students, parents, college officials, and others you might interview.

One key point is that the image of the student who is working nights puts a face on the larger issue. Documentary stories are best when about people, not "issues" or "problems." A specific person shown in their daily environment, or a concrete situation, can illuminate the larger issue in a way that resonates. It is the specific details and the nuance that make the story worth watching for others.

FEASIBILITY

It's important to be realistic about what you can accomplish with the time and resources you have available to you. There is no point in embarking on a history of the origins of the Vietnam War if you have three months and no budget for clearing archival photos. If family commitments, job obligations, or finances limit your ability to travel, it makes sense to choose a subject close to home. Following a documentary story often means you need to drop everything and run to shoot an event that is unfolding, and taking geography into consideration is wise.

Similarly, you need to make clear to possible film subjects that there will be some real time commitment when they agree to be part of your film. Filming with someone who is impatient to see you gone is likely to produce unusable material.

Finally, institutions can make life tricky for filmmaking. Schools, hospitals, and other government agencies can be suspicious of press and concerned about negative publicity, not to mention genuinely concerned about the privacy of students, patients, or clients. You need to make sure that before investing a lot of time in a story that relies on access to such institutions, you have permission (in writing) to film.

It is also important to make sure that you have explicit permission to film with your subjects, and the traditional and still the best way to do this is with a written **release form** (Chapter 5). You don't want someone to decide two months into filming that they no longer want to participate. You should be particularly careful with minors, where you will need to get parental permission and expect constant supervision.

THE SPECIFIC AND THE UNIVERSAL

It is important to remember that making a documentary film means creating a story that draws on the realities in front of your camera, for an audience that doesn't know the specifics, or what is at stake, or even why they should care. You may not be able to predict how your film will reach its audience, but you can make a story that has the potential to speak to universal themes. Every good story should have the potential to resonate on multiple levels, and part of your skill as a storyteller involves maintaining an awareness of the links between the specific reality in your film and the universal issues that you understand as being at stake.

An example is Paco de Onís and Pamela Yates' *State of Fear* (2005) (Figure 1.10), about the Peruvian government's war on the Shining Path guerrilla group. The film documents how a legitimate fear of terrorism was used to undermine democracy, making Peru a virtual dictatorship where official corruption replaced the rule of law. Although the film was made entirely in Peru, and didn't address the international context at all, people in other countries found it resonated strongly for them as well. De Onís explains:

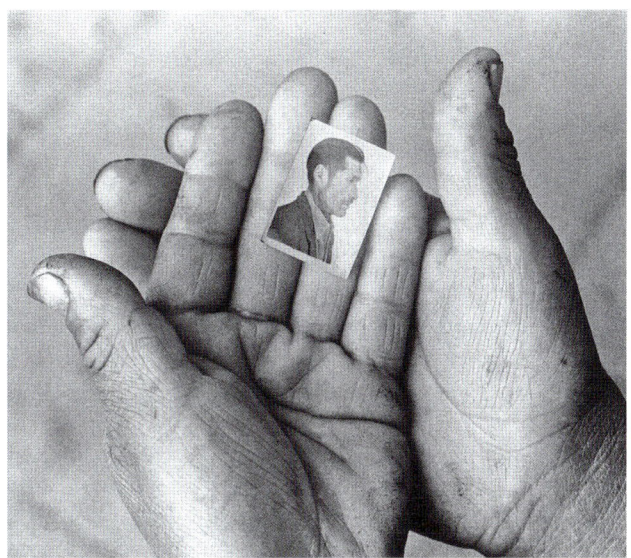

We got an email from a guy in Nepal who said he had read about State of Fear, *and it sounded a lot like the story of Nepal. Because they had this king, King Gyanendra, and he said he reminded him a lot of Fujimori (in Peru). He said he'd like to screen the film in Nepal, so we sent it. And he said at the screening, you could hear a pin drop. Everybody was looking at Peru but thinking "this is Nepal." So then he asked if they could make a Nepalese version of the film, doing a voiceover, and we said "sure." They used it in organizing meetings for months, as a way of talking about what was going on in Nepal. He was part of a pro-democracy group, and they eventually prevailed.*

■ **Figure 1.10** State of Fear was about Peru from resonated in Nepal because of its universal themes. Photo by Vera Lenz / http://skylight.is.

State of Fear was about Peru. We never mentioned other countries, or US influence or anything like that. It was about their own war on terror, as they themselves describe it. Their truth commission was looking back on 20 years of the war of terror, and we were just entering the global war on terror. The film got translated into 48 languages. It went to 154 countries, because every country in the world was grappling with this "security vs. civil liberties" thing. It just resonated everywhere.[17]

Not all documentaries translate across cultures and countries this dramatically, but you should always be asking yourself what the larger themes are in your work, and how they will translate to people beyond you and your team.

■ RESEARCH CHECKLIST

1. Come up with possible topic:
   - Is there a reason to make this documentary? What will it contribute to the public's understanding of the subject? If other films exist on the subject, can you show it from a new angle?
   - Is there conflict, a clear struggle over something that matters? What is at stake at a local level, and in terms of the big picture?
   - Is there an unfolding story that you can capture as it's happening? It's much easier and more powerful to capture in the present than have people telling what happened in the past (though often you end up with a lot of this anyway).
   - If you are telling a story that happened in the past, are there people who can tell what happened from their personal experience? Others (historians, for example) who can talk about it? Can you find visual documentation (archival footage, stills) that you can use to help tell the story?
   - What is the main point you want to make with the film (your "hypothesis")? Keep revising this as you research and even as you shoot.
   - Is there one or more organizations you can work with? How can you build trust and a relationship with them? Can they connect you with people and help with research?
   - Is it feasible? Can you get access to the places and people you need to make it? Do you have the written permissions you need to actually film with the people and in the locations you need?

- Do you have the financial resources to back up your project? Have you looked for hidden costs like archival rights, or travel expenses, or equipment rentals that may present obstacles later?

2. Research
    - Using the Internet, publications, phone calls, and meetings with people, find out as much as you can about your topic.
    - Meet with potential organizations and people who can help you. Be sensitive about taking up their time. Do not promise them the world. Be clear that you are not working for them, but that you are interested in their input on your idea. Ask them if they are willing to share resources (information, research, contacts) with you. Identify a contact person at the organization that can be your liaison.
    - Identify possible events to shoot. Get permission to shoot them.
    - Identify key players on the issue who you can touch base with periodically to find out what's happening in the world of your subjects.
    - Identify people to interview. (You do not have to do pre-interviews on video, but you should meet them or talk to them on the phone.)
    - Build relationships with anybody and everybody you need cooperation and trust from.
    - Find archival footage sources for material you might need, newspaper articles, still photos, etc.
    - Keep refining your perspective on the issues and revisiting your hypothesis.

CHAPTER 2

Documentary Styles

Once you have an idea and have completed basic research, it's time to think about the **stylistic approach** you would like to take with your documentary. While it might seem at first glance that all documentaries use similar techniques, there is in fact a wide range of creative approaches documentary filmmakers use to represent the world around them. The elements of each documentary style—whether narration, interviews, archival footage, reenactments, or an on-screen filmmaker—are picked up or rejected by filmmakers for a variety of reasons. Some filmmakers use the same approach their entire careers, while others adapt their approach to fit the subject matter of each film.

Whichever style (or combination of styles) you choose, it is important to realize that the *way* you represent the world is as meaningful as the subject matter you choose. Your message to an audience is a combination of **content** and **form.** Being intentional about the choices you make when you film people, places, and events and edit them together is a critical part of being a documentary filmmaker.

It is impossible to understand documentary styles without a sense of the history of the documentary **genre**. Over the course of more than a century of documentary practice, people have adapted various moving image technologies (film, video, and digital media) to capture images of the real world and present them to audiences. At critical junctures, specific technological developments opened up new possibilities, changing the course of the documentary form. Equally important were the social contexts in which the films were made; as social trends brought new issues into focus, documentary filmmakers took up those issues. As governments, citizens, corporations, educators, and others realized the particular power of the documentary, they also contributed to the development of this body of work.

When you set out to make a documentary film, you are stepping into a tradition that spans from approximately 1895 to the present. It is important to know this history because you do not have to reinvent the wheel each time you make a film. Past filmmakers have struggled with issues of content, form, and ethics, and have created a legacy of stylistic approaches we can borrow from, adapt, and even oppose.

Because documentary films represent real people and situations, questions around their **veracity**, or truthfulness, have been part of their development since the beginning, and have actually contributed to the form itself. Here is a sampling of the questions that recur:
- Are documentaries "true"? How representative are they of the world they depict?
- What is included or excluded, and what are the implications of those choices?
- Did the presence of the camera impact what we see unfolding on the screen?
- Who is making the film? Funding it? What is their relationship to the issues or the world represented in the film?
- Who is speaking in the film, and for whom?

Some filmmakers see their work as an opportunity to converse with their peers about these questions, and about documentary itself. As filmmaker Lynne Sachs says:

> *I like it when the community I'm making the films about is interested in watching the film. I want it to be compelling and accessible to them, and for them to feel good about the way that their lives are represented on the screen. But I also want people who are really interested in cinema (and might not care about the issue at all) to look at my films and think that I'm doing something for the field that we're in, that I'm taking this medium to a place it hasn't been before.*[1]

Whether or not you are interested in a conversation with other filmmakers about documentary form, understanding the possibilities and constraints of any given style will help you make critical choices about crew, equipment, and a host of other production decisions you will have to make before you even start shooting. A firm grasp of what is involved in each approach will also prove invaluable in editing, when you start to see the real possibilities of your footage, and to reconcile your ideas about what you were *trying* to make with what you actually *have*.

The following brief and very selective historical survey will give you a sense of the evolution of the documentary, and prompt you to think about questions of form, audience, and ethics as you begin to find your own place in the documentary tradition.

A BRIEF AND SELECTIVE HISTORY OF THE DOCUMENTARY

Many individuals contributed to the development of film technology in the late nineteenth century. Some, like Etienne-Jules Marey and Eadward Muybridge, were trying to slow down nature in order to observe it and better understand phenomena like animal motion (Figure 2.1). The development of the actual motion picture camera is attributed to Thomas Edison, working in New Jersey, and the brothers Louis and Auguste Lumière in France. Edison's camera required electricity, and thus confined his **mise-en-scène** to a stage where he filmed circus performers, athletes, and staged productions. The Lumière camera, by contrast, was hand-cranked and portable, freeing a small army of operators to travel and document daily life in cities across the globe (Figure 2.2). In each location, the Lumière operators would film during the day, develop their film, and present it that same night for local audiences. Because of the Lumière camera's mobility, and these operators' interest in filming the world outside the studio, we locate the beginning of the documentary tradition in these 50-second films, which were called "actualities" at the time.

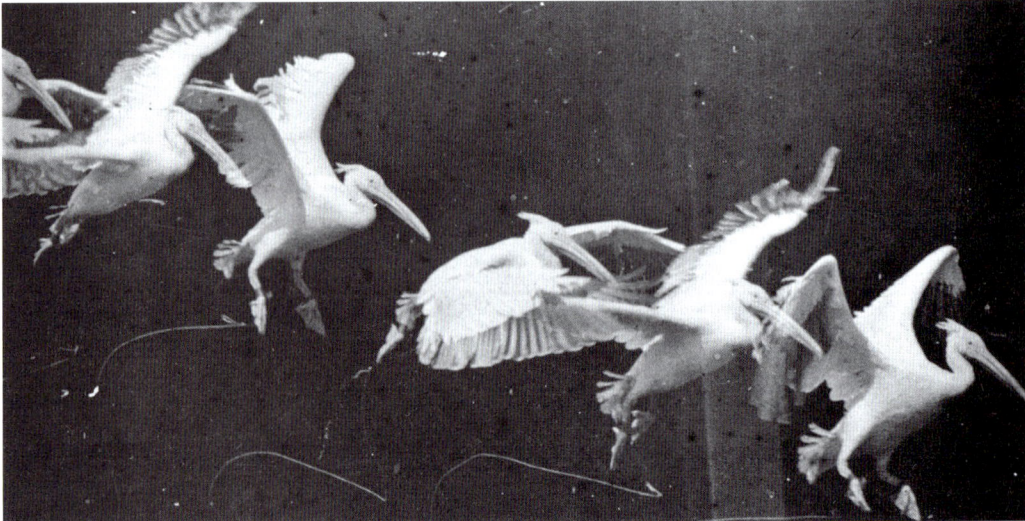

■ **Figure 2.1** In 1888, doctor and physiologist Etienne-Jules Marey invented a method of producing a series of successive images of a moving body on one piece of film in order to be able to study its exact position in space through time, which he called "chronophotographie."

Filmed with a stationary camera, on black-and-white film in one continuous take, the Lumière films are simple by today's standards. But in a time when travel was out of most people's reach, these films provided a glimpse of life in other countries and on other continents, and they satisfied a public curiosity about lives, customs, and cities not their own. Many contemporary documentary filmmakers pick up a camera and travel to other places, following the same impulse that pushed the Lumière camera operators across the globe to bring images home to audiences in Europe. While the issues involved in representing people of other races, classes, and cultures have been rigorously debated in the intervening century, the role of the documentary in sharing information and experiences across cultures remains an important part of its social role, and a common practice.

If turning a camera on other societies and foreign lands has been a constant in documentary, so has using the documentary camera to explore our own society. In the early Lumière film *Workers Leaving the Factory* (1895), we see a very early representation of "regular" people who are workers, not nobility or people with high social standing (Figure 2.3). To this day, those people or groups neglected by mainstream media, and marginalized more generally, are important documentary subject matter. The Lumière brothers were likely less interested in this than the generations that followed in their footsteps, but "giving voice to the voiceless" has been a justification for the documentary since its inception.

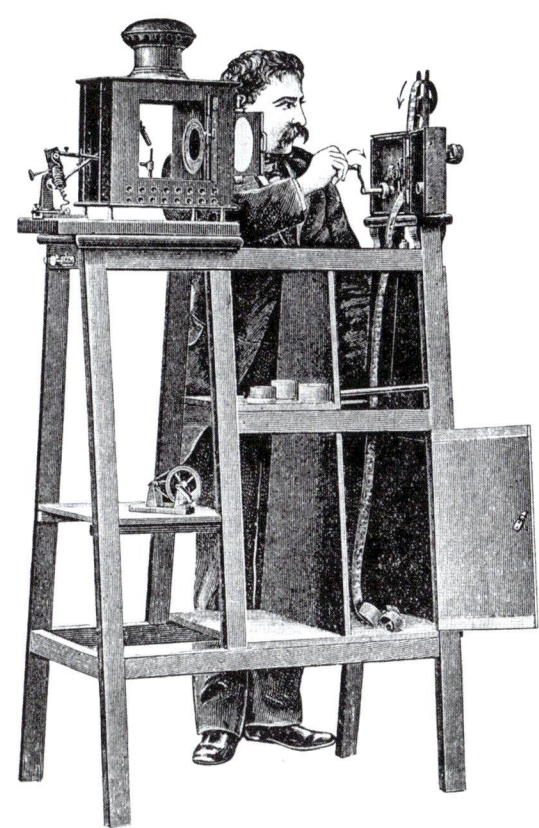

■ **Figure 2.2** The Lumière cinématographe was a relatively portable hand-cranked camera. Its portability allowed operators to travel all over the world and document daily life. For this reason, the Lumière Brothers are considered by many to be the first documentary filmmakers.

The Lumière films also invite us to explore the question of documentary from the audience's point of view. Why do people watch non-fiction films? What is the appeal? If we are going to make films for an audience, these are important things to consider. Georges Sadoul, in *Histoire Générale du Cinéma*, writes that audiences were less interested in the main action in scenes of people playing cards or feeding a baby (two early Lumière films) than in the details of leaves rustling in the background of the shot, or the dust from a brick wall being demolished.[2] As editor and film theorist Dai Vaughn writes, "People were startled not so much by the phenomenon of the moving photograph, which its inventors had struggled long to achieve, as by the ability of this to portray spontaneities of which the theatre was not capable."[3]

In his 1945 book *The Theory of Film*, Béla Balázs wrote about the particular power of documentary images (in this case footage of military battles):

> *This presentation of reality by means of motion pictures differs essentially from all other modes of presentation in that the reality being presented is not yet complete; it is itself still in the making while the presentation is being prepared . . . The cameraman is himself in the dangerous situation we see in this shot and it is by no means certain that he will survive the birth of his picture. It is this tangible being-present that gives the documentary the peculiar tension no other art can produce.*[4]

This quality of "being-present" is not just a feature of war documentaries. It is a central aspect of the power of all documentaries. There is a spontaneity to events that unfold while you are filming that can serve your film well. Contemporary examples include Laura

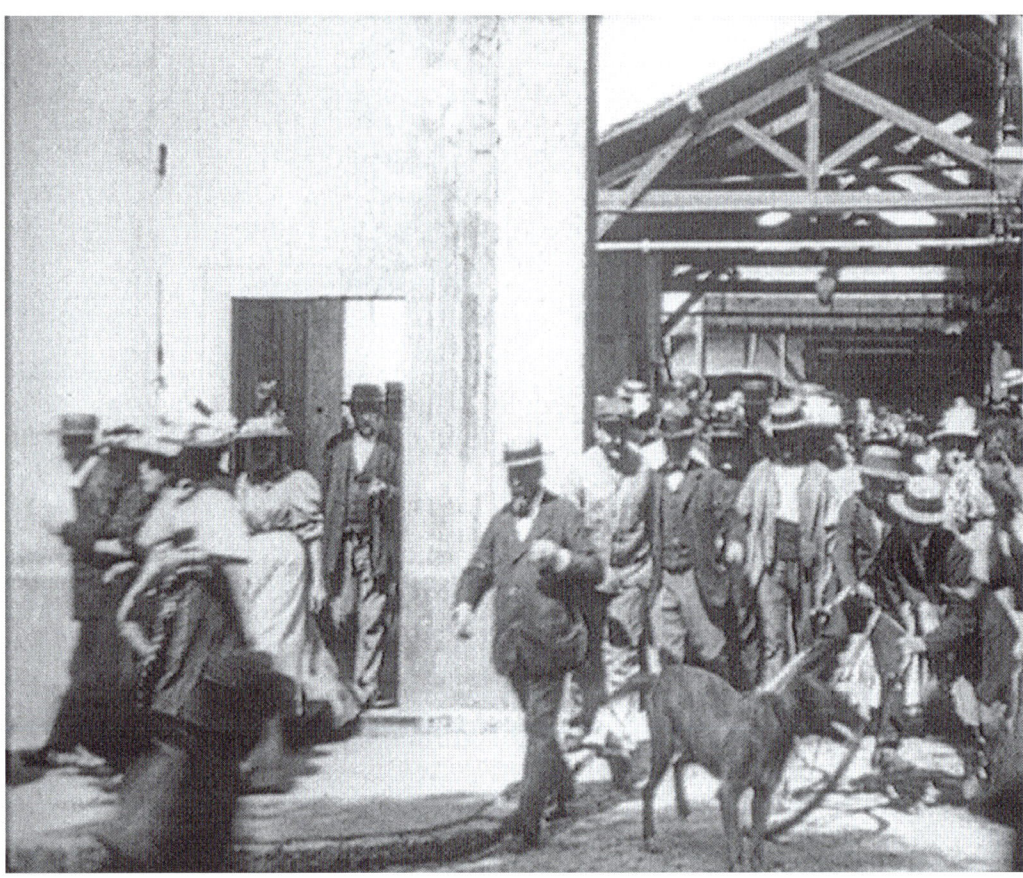

■ **Figure 2.3** A still from *Workers Leaving the Factory* (1895).

Poitras' interview with whistleblower Edward Snowden in the Academy Award®-winning documentary *CitizenFour* (2014), where the presence of the camera itself in a Hong Kong hotel room is part of the drama because we know this man (and perhaps even Poitras) may be arrested for sharing confidential state department information.

Impressionistic Filmmaking

Much as viewers of the first Lumière films were awed by the details of nature like leaves rustling, early documentary filmmakers were captivated by the ability of the camera to capture the poetry of everyday experience. Dutch filmmaker Joris Ivens, in his film *Regen* (*Rain*, 1929), shows us what seems to be a passing shower in Amsterdam (Figure 2.4). The filming took four months, however, and the attention paid to each frame is clear in the film's precision and beauty. Ivens' filmmaking is referred to by historian Erik Barnouw as "painterly,"[5] and by others as **impressionistic**. Whatever this style of filmmaking is called, it is characterized by an attention to the composition of the frame, including textures, movement, light, and shadows. This approach relies on metaphor, inference, and lyricism more than direct argumentation or human dramas.

In poetic documentaries, we can find breathtaking moments. A more lyrical approach can also strengthen the more literal points a film is making by inferring more than can be said in words, and conveying emotions as well as rational arguments. Filmmaker Fred Barney Taylor's portrait of science fiction writer Samuel Delany, *The Polymath* (2008), uses a series of long elegant takes that emphasize patterns of light and the texture to evoke an imagined meeting between Delany's grandfather and poet Hart Crane on the Brooklyn Bridge (Figure 2.5). The recreation of this poetic, timeless space for the viewer reinforces the film's overall story by giving us a sense of Delany's inspiration and imaginative abilities.

Handsworth Songs (1986), by John Akomfrah and the Black Audio Collective, uses the impressionistic style combined with more expository elements to create a nuanced and layered exploration of the uprisings in the Birmingham district of Handsworth in 1985. The film uses footage of protests and news coverage of the events of the sort used by many historical documentaries. It also, however, presents hidden narratives about racism and the black immigrant experience by layering fiction and poetry over archival images of West Indians arriving in England in the 1950s. *Handsworth Songs* was both celebrated for trying to create a new filmic language and attacked for failing to speak clearly enough to audiences, a tension that will always be a risk for those working in a more impressionistic mode.

Dziga Vertov and Reflexivity

Dziga Vertov, a Soviet filmmaker and founder of the Kino-Pravda ("film truth") movement in the 1920s, was another pioneer of the documentary genre. Among many achievements, Vertov included the process of making the film within his films, a practice that later became known as **reflexivity**. In *Man with a Movie Camera* (1929), Vertov includes many shots of his cameraman, Mikhail Kaufman, climbing smokestacks and riding in moving cars with his camera, to demystify the filmmaking process by showing that films are made by actual people. At one point in the film, Vertov cuts from a shot of children to the same shot on actual film, in the editor's hands. We then see Elizaveta Svilova, the editor, cutting the film with scissors and joining the shots together, and we watch the edited sequence. This **sequence** literally shows the audience how the film is constructed, frame by frame. Reflexivity was important to Vertov because the audiences for his films included a wide range of Russian citizens, many of them illiterate peasants who had likely never seen a film in their lives. Vertov was attempting to help audiences understand that what they were seeing is *not reality, but a representation of it*. This marked the beginning of a long tradition in documentary of demystifying the process behind the product, and encouraging audiences to retain a critical perspective as they watch.

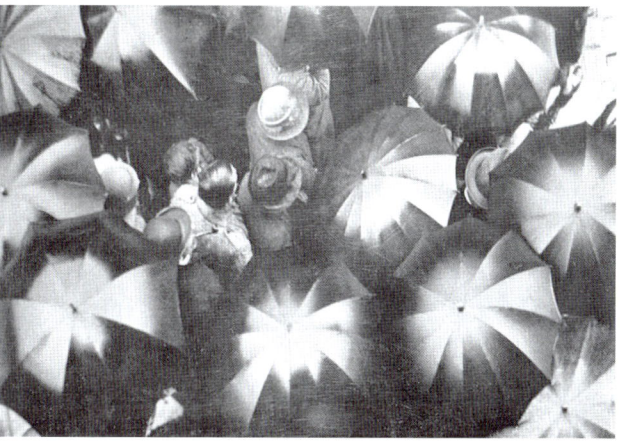

■ **Figure 2.4** *Regen* (*Rain*) takes an impressionistic approach to representing a passing rain shower in Amsterdam. Note the attention to the composition of the frame, and the pattern created by the light on the umbrellas.

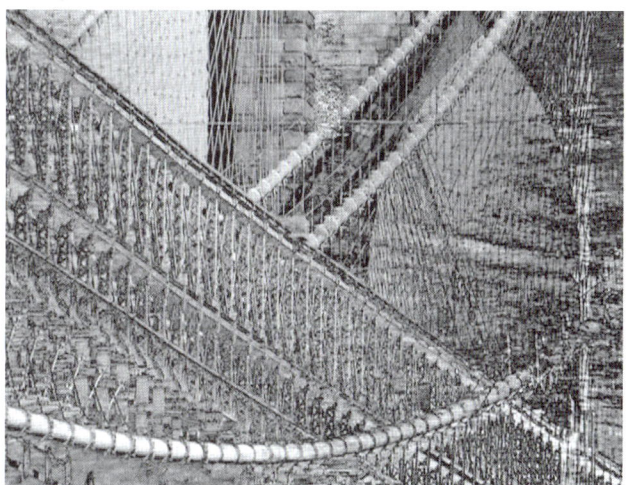

■ **Figure 2.5** *The Polymath*, a portrait of writer Samuel Delany, uses impressionistic visuals of New York City to give us a sense of Delany's imaginative abilities.

Reflexive films take many forms and are among the most intellectually engaging in the documentary genre. This style reemerged with force in the 1960s, 70s, and 80s, when a critique of authority and the rise of people's movements established the importance of letting audiences know not just that the film is constructed, but who is constructing it, from what perspective, and to what end. A notable example is Rea Tajiri's *History and Memory: For Akiko and Takashige* (1991), about the internment of Japanese–Americans during the Second World War. The film uses clips from Hollywood movies and US government propaganda films to show how a nationalistic official perspective on the internment was constructed—even literally—by showing the film **slate** and call for "action" as internees are posed before the camera.

Tajiri uses a first-person **narration**, which lays bare her own subjectivity, as a driving force in the film. This is another common characteristic of reflexive films. She also uses interviews with relatives to excavate a suppressed history. In her narration, she says:

> *I began searching for a history, my own history, because I had known all along that the stories I had heard were not true, and parts had been left out. I remember having this feeling growing up that I was haunted by something, that I was living within a family full of ghosts. There was this place that they knew about. I had never been there, yet I had a memory for it.*
>
> **History and Memory: For Ashiko and Takashige. Dir. Rea Tajiri. Women Make Movies, 1991. DVD**

Her investigation reminds us that nothing can be taken at face value—that histories, like memories, are subjective and incomplete. The same is true of the documentary film.

The British Film Movement and the Expository Film

In the 1930s, documentary took a new turn, based on the need for some kind of forum for addressing social problems of the era, from global economic depression to the rise of fascism. Often when people think of a documentary, it is the **expository** documentary developed at this time they have in mind. In fact, the very term "documentary" was originally coined at this time by famed British filmmaker, theorist, and producer John Grierson. Grierson saw the huge potential for film to help create discussion of social issues on a national level. Inspired by the revolutionary films of Soviet makers including Vertov and Sergei Eisenstein, Grierson sought to infuse the documentary with the poetry of everyday life, a more **realist** approach that would elevate the form above the standard non-fiction fare of travelogues and newsreels:

> *[A] sense of social responsibility makes our realist documentary, a troubled and difficult art, and particularly in a time like ours... Realist documentary with its streets and cities and slums and markets and exchanges and factories, has given itself the job of making poetry where no poet has gone before it, and where no ends, sufficient for the purposes of art, are easily observed.*[6]

One of the most well-known films of this era is *Housing Problems* (1935), directed by Arthur Elton and E.H. Anstey, who worked for Grierson at Great Britain's Empire Marketing Board. While the film has drawn criticism for posing the poor as victims of circumstance who can be rescued by enlightened public policy, its innovative use of **sync sound** allowed slum dwellers to speak for themselves about their housing conditions on film for the first time (Figure 2.6). Sync sound also allowed the filmmakers to feature officials and experts, making it an early example of expository documentary. This style has persisted to the present day. In these films, you will find a belief in the value of a well-written voiceover, a mix of witness and expert testimony, footage shot in common locations of people engaged in everyday activities, and a willingness to use teaching tools such as maps and diagrams, all devoted to giving a viewer the tools for discussing and exploring important social issues.

Jay Rosenstein, a more contemporary practitioner of expository documentary, says:

> *With* In Whose Honor? *(1997) I knew much of the information in the film would be controversial to a fair number of people, and the first time they would be hearing it. I decided to couch it in a style of storytelling—the expository style—that maybe people would be more comfortable and familiar with. If the film had been more experimental, it wouldn't have been as effective as political advocacy, which is really what it was.*[7]

One of the key social values of documentary film is its ability to explore and convey complex problems facing society in an accessible way. In a world where the causes of social problems are complex, documentaries excel at revealing links and drawing connections that might not be readily visible to people. They also link the lives of regular people to the larger picture. The expository style is often chosen by documentary filmmakers who want their films to have broad social impact.

The expository style is also often used because it is efficient, and offers the possibility of delivering information in narration or text where it may not emerge organically from your footage. Rosenstein says:

> I'm trying to impart a certain amount of factual information in my films. And you can usually explain something in narration much more efficiently and concisely than a character can. Also a lot of what is in the film happened before I started shooting, and I couldn't see a way of making that film effectively in any other way.[8]

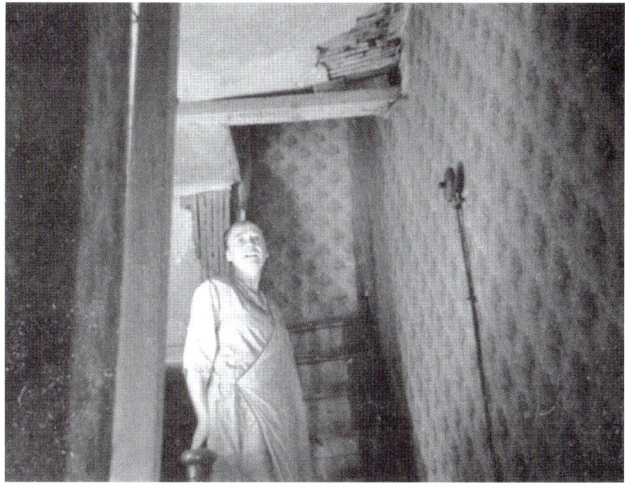

■ **Figure 2.6** *Housing Problems* pioneered the use of interviews and expert testimony, hallmarks of the expository style.

While the expository mode continues to be one of the most popular approaches, it does have dangers. Perhaps the strongest is the tendency for expository films to become illustrated lectures and therefore dryly didactic. One way to avoid this trap is to make use of strong **visual evidence,** images that convey the story you are trying to tell with little or no explanation (Chapter 7).

In *In Whose Honor?*, Rosenstein develops a sequence that shows bumper stickers and signage of the Chief Illiniwek mascot on cars, homes, and stores (Figure 2.7). Even though nobody in the film speaks explicitly to this issue, the shots provide visual evidence that the power of the mascot extends far beyond the sports field, and that it won't be easy to get people to let go of their allegiance to it. This visual evidence moves the discussion to less abstract, more emotional turf where human emotions and loyalties are central.

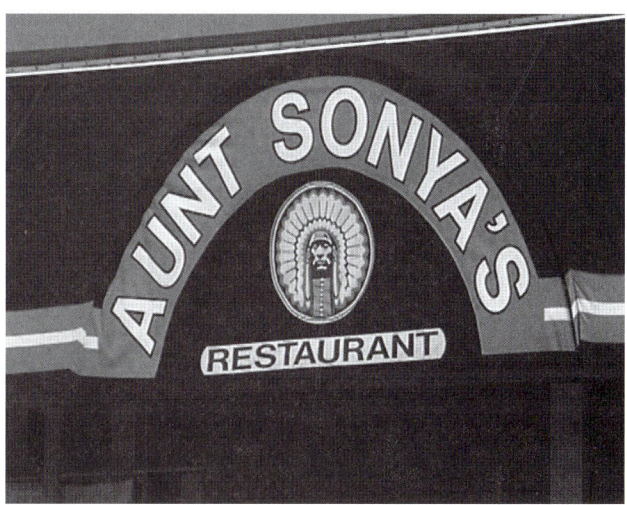

■ **Figure 2.7** *In Whose Honor?* uses visual evidence to show you how prevalent images of Chief Illiniwek are in Champaign, Illinois.

TV Documentary as a Subgenre of the Expository Style

Television is such a major platform for non-fiction material that the type of documentary seen on TV has come to define the form in the popular imagination. While most TV documentaries fall into the expository category, it would be limiting to conflate the two. One way of understanding the difference is to think of the "news documentary" as a subgenre of the expository form. The news documentary, which has ancestors in both radio and television, tends toward an on-air host or reporter. At its worst, this kind of filmmaking takes a news radio-style script and illustrates it with highly literal visuals, rarely pausing for breath. At its best, it is more akin to investigative journalism. Examples of the latter type include the BBC's *Panorama* or PBS's *Frontline*, which are heavily researched and often break important stories that have not appeared in other media. They depend on multiple teams to cover events in different regions of the globe and build an authoritative case using strong, verifiable evidence. In addition, these programs often find characters whose personal involvement and concern can help humanize the issue at stake and avoid overtly didactic or "preachy" filmmaking.

Observational Filmmaking

One of the most influential developments in documentary style was the advent of **cinéma vérité** and **direct cinema** in the 1960s. These styles sprang from a desire by filmmakers in the early 1960s to get closer to reality with new portable technologies including lightweight 16mm cameras, zoom lenses, and portable tape recorders capable of capturing sync sound. While two major schools of **observational filmmaking** emerged, both are characterized by the use of small crews with lightweight handheld equipment, filming unscripted action with a highly observational "fly-on-the-wall" approach. The advantage of this method is that life as it unfolds can be very engaging, and filming it observationally puts viewers in the action in a way that no interview or voice-over commentary can do. Unlike the Lumière films, which were observational from a distance and used a static camera, these filmmakers put themselves and their cameras in the center of the action, filming from multiple perspectives and using **continuity style editing** to create a sense of a seamless reality (Chapter 19). Looking at a story that seems to "tell itself," viewers can make up their own minds how to understand an issue or whether to believe a character. Albert Maysles, who with his brother David and others in the United States developed a style that came to be known as "direct cinema," says:

> *On television they'd rather take a shortcut and have somebody tell you what happened. We had this revolutionary idea about how to make a documentary with no staging, no narration, no host, no music. Just let it happen, and be at the right place at the right time, and you'll have a film.*[9]

It is not surprising that this approach appeared at a moment when people were starting to question authority and where having someone tell you about the world had become less convincing than seeing it for yourself.

One drawback of a direct cinema approach is that you have to spend significant amounts of time in a situation to capture moments and images that are, in fact, revealing. These filmmakers spend days, weeks, or months on location filming. That closeness means a real chance to learn about the ins and outs of a situation, and to observe people changing as they confront the obstacles and challenges facing them. But it can also require extensive resources.

A critique of direct cinema is that it is overly naive about the possibility of capturing "the truth." No camera is a "fly on the wall", unseen to subjects. The presence of the camera and the fact that people know they are being recorded necessarily alter the course of the events being captured. People may ignore the camera, but how much their behavior changes because of its presence is open to debate. A classic example is *An American Family* (1972), a 12-hour PBS series produced by Craig Gilbert that was built around the daily drama of one American family, the Louds. This particular drama ended in a divorce, raising the question of whether the stresses of being on camera, and seen by millions, may have altered the reality being filmed. There is no way of knowing, but as a documentary filmmaker, you should always keep in mind that your presence is a factor in the situation you are documenting.

The influence of the filmmaking process asserts itself during the postproduction process as well. Fred Wiseman, the maker of films such as *Titicut Follies* (1967) (Figure 2.8) and *High School* (1968), says:

> *Say you're at a place for four hundred hours and you shoot forty hours and you use nine hours. All that is selection, all that is choice. Sure. But really all I'm saying is that I try to make the selection based on my view of the experience as filtered through what I was before the film and what happens while I'm there. This means not only for the period of time that I was at the institution, but also sitting in front of the movieola trying to think through . . . what the experience meant to me.*[10]

The cinéma vérité movement in France emerged when makers like Jean Rouch challenged the idea that the camera could capture reality, or life as it would have occurred if the camera wasn't there. Rouch believed in the power of the filmmaker to *catalyze* events, and this school of a more **participatory** observational filmmaking came to be known as cinéma vérité. Erik Barnouw writes, "The direct cinema documentarist took his camera to a situation of tension and waited hopefully for a crisis; the Rouch version of cinéma vérité tried to precipitate one."[11]

In Rouch films such as *Chronique d'un Eté* (*Chronicle of a Summer*, 1960) (Figure 2.9), made with Edgar Morin, we also find a reflexivity that has its roots in Vertov. We see the film's participants discussing the shooting process with Rouch and Morin, and at the end of the film we see them watching themselves on the screen, and discussing how they feel about their representation. The film ends with Rouch and Morin discussing whether their film "experiment" has been a success.

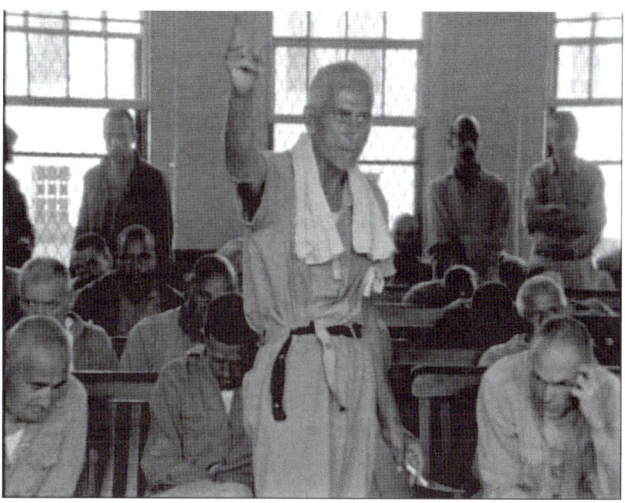

■ **Figure 2.8** Direct cinema films like *Titicut Follies*, about a Massachusetts psychiatric hospital, strive to capture life "on the fly," as though the camera isn't there.

While the debates between the practitioners of direct cinema and cinéma vérité might seem theoretical, there are practical applications to the arguments. When should you interfere in an observational situation, and when should you sit back and let it unfold? Julie Gustafson describes how, while filming *Casting the First Stone* (1991), a film about women on both sides of the abortion debate, not intervening was the right choice:

> *There is an incredible scene where Joan and her husband are having dinner, and she says, "You know, he didn't want me to get arrested." They had just served us lunch, and I had put the camera down, and very quietly got up and picked it up again. The soundman didn't realize what I was doing, but I knew the wireless microphone was on her, and didn't want to interrupt the conversation, because by then already the husband and wife were arguing, and I knew it was an incredible scene. And that's where the documentary turns to drama. You don't interrupt, you do whatever you can to get the scene.*[12]

On another occasion, Gustafson decided to provoke a response, albeit subtly:

> *In the case of* The Pursuit of Happiness *(1983), which was about whether Americans do or do not pursue happiness, I was filming the main character doing the dishes. And after a while I asked her, from behind the camera, "What do you think happiness is?" She answered, but kept doing the dishes, and it became an interview but also turned back into a vérité scene. I have found this to be a very effective, very informal strategy.*[13]

Another cautionary note for an observational filmmaker is that placing an audience inside a situation with limited contextualization can mean leaving out significant portions of the big picture. As documentary scholar Brian Winston suggests, it is easy to confuse access to an

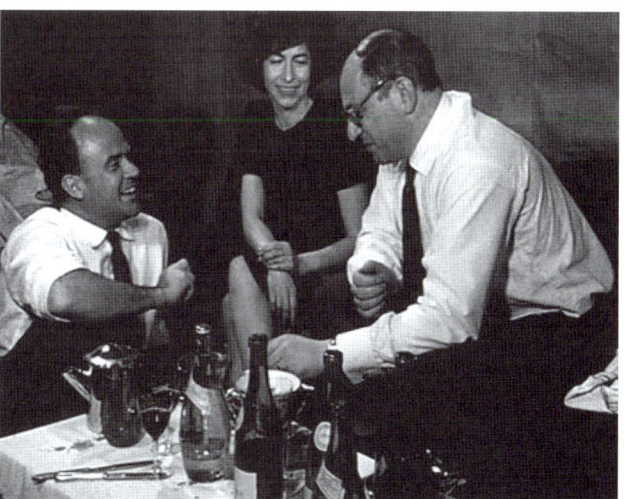

■ **Figure 2.9** *Chronique d'un Eté* (*Chronicle of a Summer*) is an example of Cinéma Vérité. In this scene, the filmmakers include a discussion about the filmmaking process with one of their main subjects.

interesting situation for a film idea, skipping the need for background research to shape your hypothesis. This can result in a close-up view without much context.[14]

Restrepo (2010), the Oscar®-nominated 2010 documentary about the war in Afghanistan, took filmmakers Tim Hetherington and Sebastian Junger on 10 trips to the Korengal Valley with troops of the 173rd Airborne Brigade. While the film was highly and deservedly praised by critics, others have pointed out that a significant facet of the experience was essentially left out. There were no interviews with the Afghanis that the Americans, whose valiant efforts are so closely portrayed, were there to protect. Nor did the filmmakers include experts who might have offered an analysis instead of an easy identification with the US military. As journalist Nick Turse suggests, the result is a film that provides a limited point of view on the war, and offers the experience of combat as the whole of the geopolitics of war.[15]

From the Observational to a Reemergence of the Reflexive

The 1960s political movements—antiwar, Women's Liberation, Black Power, and others—shook Americans' belief in the official version of events presented, in expository form, by television news journalists. The development of portable 16mm film equipment that could record sync sound and the creation of a consumer video camera by Sony in 1967 introduced the possibility that communities could represent themselves. "People taking charge over their own lives was one of the battle cries of the late Sixties," noted public access television pioneer George Stoney.[16] Media representation was no exception. Documentaries had long focused on the plight of the less advantaged in society, and advocated for change, but now those communities wanted to take control over how they would be represented.

In the 1970s and 80s, this tendency toward self-representation was also fueled by identity politics, political movements based on the common experience and concerns of groups identified on the basis of gender, race, ethnicity, sexual orientation, or HIV status. The practices of these groups included consciousness-raising, celebrating the pride and integrity of marginalized groups, excavating ignored or suppressed histories, and focusing on personal experience. Many of these practices involved employing documentary film as a way to document process and influence majority opinions. More and more, individuals were making documentaries that spoke from an intensely personal, subjective position. Many of these films used narration, but they eschewed the "voice of god" omniscient narration of the expository film, and spoke in the first person instead.

A notable example of this kind of work is Marlon Riggs' *Tongues Untied* (1989), about the experiences of black gay men. The film is intensely personal as well as reflexive. Unlike Vertov's form of reflexivity, which deconstructed the filmmaking process, *Tongues Untied* goes further to take apart the idea that there is a fixed position from which we can speak. Riggs appears in the film, speaking to the camera. He tells us how he identifies with other gay men, but when he is subjected to racism within the gay community, he identifies as a black man. The film presents us with the idea that people's identities are flexible and can coexist. Riggs' film reminds us of the power of telling personal histories, and about how individual voices can be powerful representations of a collective (Figure 2.10).

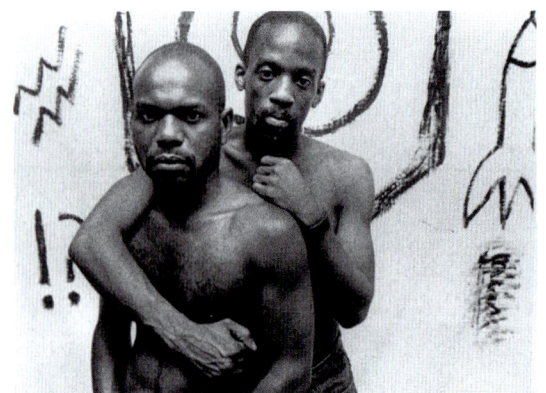

■ **Figure 2.10** *Tongues Untied* takes a highly subjective, personal approach to present audiences with a look at gay, black male identity.

Not all identity subgroups are based on ethnicity, sexual orientation, or gender. They can also be geographic. In *Stranger with a Camera* (2000), Elizabeth Barret uses an **essay documentary style** to investigate the circumstances surrounding the 1967 death of Hugh O'Connor in Eastern Kentucky. O'Connor, a filmmaker from the National Film Board of Canada, was killed by a local man, Hobart Ison, after filming images of one of Ison's tenants, a coal miner. Barret uses a narration written in the first person, foregrounding her identity as a filmmaker from the Appalachian region. In the film, she says:

> *These are the mountains I come from in Eastern Kentucky. The killing that happened here had a lasting effect on the lives of everyone who lived through it, and now that includes me. Over the years I learned what had happened, but I wanted to go beneath the surface, to find out why it happened. What brought these two men—Hobart Ison with his gun, and Hugh O'Connor with his camera—face to face in September of 1967? As someone who lives in the community that I document, what can I learn from this story, now that I have stood on both sides of the camera?*
>
> **Stranger with a Camera. Dir. Elizabeth Barret. Appalshop, 2000. DVD**

What follows is an unusually nuanced and deep exploration of the ethics of documentary representation. As someone with a foot in both the filmmaking world and the world of those represented in the many documentaries about Appalachia, Barret's first person position gives her **authority** with the audience. The conflicted nature of her position—she is critical of the O'Connor murder, but also understands the historical pain this community has felt over its representation as an impoverished backwater—is the dramatic engine driving this film.

Reenactment in Documentary

Finally, there is the tricky ground of **reenactment** in documentary. For an art form that depends by definition on its close relationship with the real, reenactment can be a touchy subject. For many viewers, reenactment suggests actors pretending to be Roman Legionaries at Hadrian's Wall, or patriotic Continental soldiers in Concord, Massachusetts. Historically, stilted action and overly literal interpretations gave reenactment a mediocre reputation. It does, however, seem to be having a bit of a heyday as filmmakers explore the porous boundary between documentary and fiction forms.

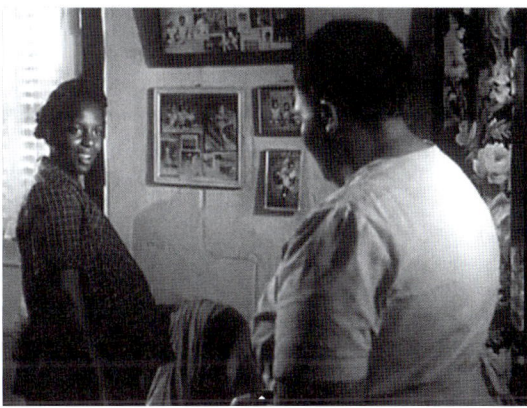

■ **Figure 2.11** In this scene from *All My Babies*, "Miss Mary" Coley and one of her clients reminisce. While the scene is staged for the camera, the participants are not actors, but the real subjects of the documentary.

One important area of reenactment in documentary, is that of people performing their own lives. This tradition goes back to the 1930s. A classic example is George Stoney's *All My Babies: A Midwife's Own Story* (1952). This portrait of Georgia midwife "Miss Mary" Coley is built around staged scenes where Coley, with some of the mothers whose children she helped deliver, recounts the story of her own career (Figure 2.11). This approach empowers people to be experts on the story of their own lives, and is likely to remain a useful tool for documentary.

The postmodern era has brought different approaches to reenactment. One of the most notable examples is Errol Morris's *The Thin Blue Line* (1988). The film is an investigation of the murder of a police officer, and the subsequent trial and conviction of suspect Randall Adams. There is one key witness, the partner of the murdered officer. But this officer's testimony, even about her own location at the moment when her partner had approached a stopped vehicle on a dark Dallas highway, is in doubt. A key detail is a milkshake that has landed in a position that makes it unlikely that Officer Teresa Turko was where she said she was at the time of the shooting (Figure 2.12).

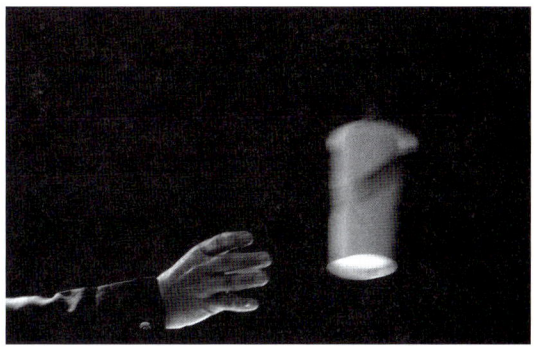

■ **Figure 2.12** The flying milkshake becomes a key detail in the reenactment of the killing of a police officer in *The Thin Blue Line*.

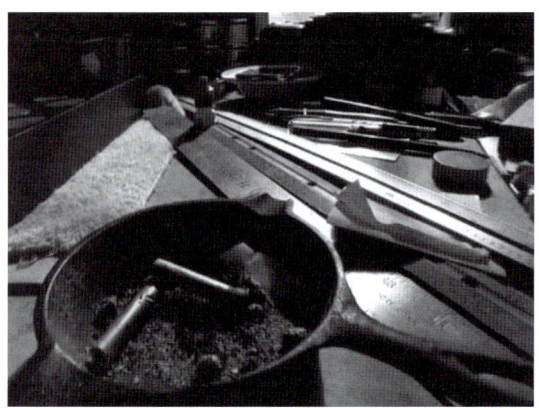

Figure 2.13 Direct sun is used as a hard backlight and also bounced back onto the talent to provide a soft key (left). When subjects are in the shade (right), a reflector can bounce sunlight back onto the subject to get a better exposure and contrast range.

As director Morris notes:

Where was Turko when the shooting occurred? In the car? Out of the car? How many people were in the suspect vehicle? Two people? One person? What did the driver look like? Did he have bushy hair? Sandy-blonde hair? All of this is critical information in deciding who did it, who killed the cop.

How do you represent this in a movie? How do you evaluate the nature of competing and conflicting evidence? It is through reconstructing the past with reenactments.[17]

Here, the reenactments do not offer us reality, but differing versions of the facts from different witnesses, versions that change substantially during the course of the film. As Morris notes, his reenactments invite not the suspension of disbelief, but the opposite: the suspension of belief in the truth of the image.

Another approach to reenactment is offered by films like Bianca Giaever and Rachel Antonoff's short documentary *Crush* (2014). The film's soundtrack is a straightforward account by Antonoff's parents, of how they first met. The images offer a contemporary reenactment of a college romance in 1972 that develops as the account proceeds. In a cheerful comedic sendup of young love, the actors lip-synch the narrative while going from a dorm room to a pumpkin patch to a laundromat.

A more subtle approach is offered by filmmakers who seek to evoke the past through recreated situations, where the "enactment" is more one of memory. Sasha Wortzel, a graduate of Hunter College's Integrated Media Arts MFA Program, made a short documentary *Paint It Again* (2011) that explored the home shared by a woman and her late partner of over 40 years. Now the home of only one surviving partner, the house is full of artifacts that hold memories and hint at a life shared in this space—a life that is now gone. A mix of quiet spaces and period music creates a sense of what is lost when a loved one dies.

CONCLUSION

With all these styles available—impressionistic, reflexive, expository, observational—it can be difficult to find your way. All of these approaches have advantages and drawbacks. Most filmmakers end up borrowing, mixing, and adapting strategies from multiple traditions. Also remember that the content of your film will, to a great extent, determine your documentary's style.

Think about the story you are trying to explore. Can you follow it in real time and watch it unfold? If you can, then an observational approach could be appropriate. Are you involved in an area where policy discussions are central? Then interviews and a more expository approach may work for you. If you are taking on a story that is about your own history, or that you are connected to in a personal way, some reflexivity may be in order.

Finally, there is no way to grow as a documentary filmmaker without watching films. Think about the documentaries you admire and why they touch or speak to you. Look at how other makers structure their storytelling. Take advantage of what is available on the Internet, in libraries and universities, and screening in theaters, at festivals, and in community spaces near you. Seeing how others approach subjects and solve problems will enrich your own sense of what is possible.

CHAPTER 3

Structuring the Documentary

> *We can tell people abstract rules of thumb which we have derived from prior experiences, but it is very difficult for other people to learn from these... We can more easily remember a good story. Stories give life to past experience. Stories make the events in memory memorable to others and to ourselves. This is one of the reasons why people like to tell stories.*
>
> Roger C. Schank, from *Tell Me A Story*[1]

■ BASIC APPROACHES TO DOCUMENTARY STORYTELLING

Documentaries are a form of storytelling. They originate from someone trying to communicate an experience, information about an issue, or an idea about the world we inhabit. And they speak to an audience in an organized fashion. As we saw in the last chapter, documentaries take many forms. Some are more literal and communicate more directly, while others employ more **observational** or **impressionistic** methods. But whatever their stylistic approach, documentaries take us on a journey over time, often using storytelling techniques that have emerged over thousands of years and that humans—even across many cultures—recognize.

Broadly speaking, documentaries draw on two of the oldest traditions in Western culture: **drama** and **rhetoric**. In drama lies the origins of stories of human life—the myths that explain human fate, our gods, our hearts. The origins of rhetoric lie in the political speeches, debates, and discussions that were at the heart of ancient Greek and Roman democracy. These are two distinct approaches. Some documentaries will favor one or the other approach, while many use a combination. Also, being a creative form, documentaries usually don't fit entirely into neat categories and very often use and blend methods beyond the scope of these two traditions.

Drama: Goals, Conflict, and Stakes

What makes any story compelling is, on some level, conflict. In **character-based** films, the conflict could be between two characters (see *Nobody's Business*, pp. 12–13), a person's internal conflict with themself (see *Fog of War*, p. 318), or a person's conflict with a social institution or barrier. At other times, it could be the conflict a community faces when it finds itself up against larger outside forces like a corporation or a political structure (see *A Village Called Versailles*, pp. 42–45). In this type of film, characters want things and have **goals**. They want to save the family farm, understand their parents better, fight discrimination, or simply find self-determination in one form or another. They act and struggle to get what they want or need, while facing opposition and **obstacles** that they either overcome or fail to overcome. In character-driven documentaries, the relationship of conflict to story is similar to the way things work in narrative fiction storytelling (see Dramatic Structure, p. 30).

Some documentaries, however, are based more on information and argument than characters in conflict (though they may include characters as part of a strategy to humanize the issues). In these cases, conflict is present too, but in a slightly different form. Here, we find that conflict is closely related to the idea of stakes. **Stakes** refer to the investment the characters in a film, or the audience, have in the outcome of the story or argument. Why does it matter if a character achieves their goal? What will happen if they don't? Why do we, as an audience, care about whether charter schools are better than public ones, or vice versa, to use the example of Davis Guggenheim's Waiting for Superman (2010)? What's at stake, in the case of Waiting for Superman, could be the future of quality education as a right all people share equally. In order for the audience to be connected to your film, you need to make sure they understand the stakes as you see them.

Often filmmakers will start to screen an early cut of a documentary, only to find that it fails to engage a viewer. Asking "Why does this film matter?" or "Why do you care about this?" can often reveal the underlying investment that they (and often their characters) have in the outcome of the situation documented in the film. Identifying the stakes in a film is critical because without stakes, there is no drama. In another way, the question of stakes involves us as audience members. It is a particular characteristic of documentary that its audience is, by definition, part of the world of the film. In a well-crafted documentary, we care about the issues at hand, or about what happens to the people in the film, because their issues are our issues. We might be literally facing the same problem they are, but even if we aren't, our shared reality bonds us with them and creates an ethical framework within which we are asked to care about what happens.

Dramatic Structure

A film must move. A documentary must start somewhere and take us to a different place. What moves it forward is its **dramatic structure**. Many documentaries, especially those that are character-based, make use of the three-act structure first defined by the Greek philosopher Aristotle. Aristotle posited that a story must have "a beginning, a middle and an end." While this might seem obvious—what film doesn't have a beginning, a middle, and an end?—it becomes more useful when we realize the difficulty of keeping an audience engaged over time. Some films, especially in their early forms (before editing is finished), seem to stall, repeat themselves, or lose the narrative thread that keeps the audience fully engaged. Often, this is because the **dramatic structure** has not been fully or thoughtfully worked out.

Documentary makers do not just deliver information; they shape it into a compelling story by creating provocative questions in the mind of the audience that need to be answered. What's going to happen next? Will she find justice? How can this go on? What does the other guy think? Why did he do that? And so on.

One major way of moving things forward is through the introduction and resolution of conflict in individual scenes, and in the story as a whole. Here, a traditional narrative **dramatic arc** (Figure 3.1) can be extremely helpful in thinking about your documentary's structure.

Here are some brief definitions of the various parts of the dramatic arc.

Opening

The **opening** of your film is one of the most important, and most difficult, parts to conceptualize and create. It must, at a minimum:
- draw the audience into your story
- give them a basic sense of what the topic is
- introduce your audience to at least one of the main characters
- establish the style of your film, including major elements
- give your viewer a sense of the scope of the discussion (is this about one person, or a community, or an issue as it impacts people in many places?)

CHAPTER 3
Structuring the Documentary

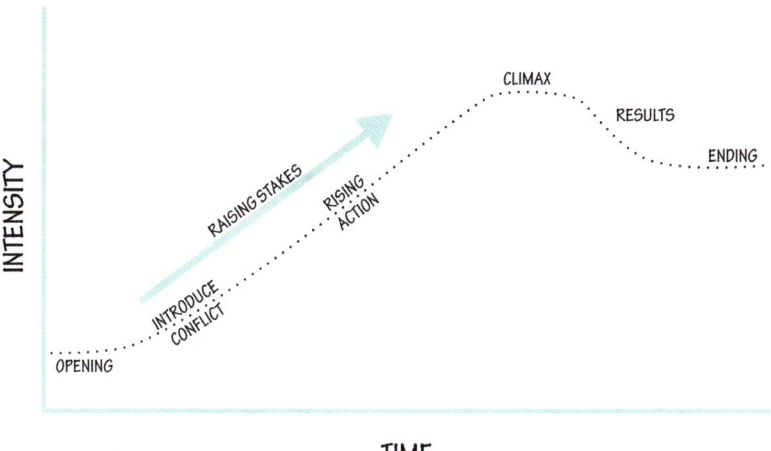

■ **Figure 3.1** The stages of the basic documentary dramatic arc.

Finally, your opening should include a **narrative promise**. This is hard to define exactly, but it means that you give your audience a taste of what is to come and a sense of what they will get from watching your film. For coauthor Kelly Anderson and Tami Gold's documentary *Every Mother's Son* (2004), about abuse of force by New York City police officers, the promise suggests,

> *If you stick around for the next hour, you will learn something about issues of police use of deadly force. While this film foregrounds the experience of family members of people killed, it will also include the perspective of law enforcement.*

The stakes are clearly very high and stark in this film—life and death, safety and loss—but defining the stakes, no matter how dramatic or subtle, is equally important for all films.

Openings often include **exposition**, information the viewer needs to know in order to understand what's happening on the screen. Exposition can take the form of narration, text on screen, interviews with subjects or experts, dialogue between characters, or a visual that gives us information about where we are, who is involved, or what is happening. While it can, and should, occur at multiple points in your film, it is particularly necessary in the opening moments of your documentary.

Sheila Curran Bernard, in her book *Documentary Storytelling: Creative Nonfiction on Screen*, defines exposition as "the information that grounds you in a story: who, what, where, when and why. It gives audience members the tools they need to follow the story . . . and, more importantly, it allows them inside the story."[2]

In *Every Mother's Son*, the exposition includes two text cards that place the story in the context of a wider national debate about policing:

> *In the 1990s, under Mayor Giuliani's administration, policing in New York City became more aggressive—a pattern that could be seen in many cities across the United States.*
> *This film tells the story of three women—Iris Baez, Kadiatou Diallo and Doris Busch-Boskey—who turn the tragedy of having a son killed by police into an opportunity for change.*
>
> *Every Mother's Son.* **Dir. Tami Gold and Kelly Anderson. New Day Films, 2004. DVD**

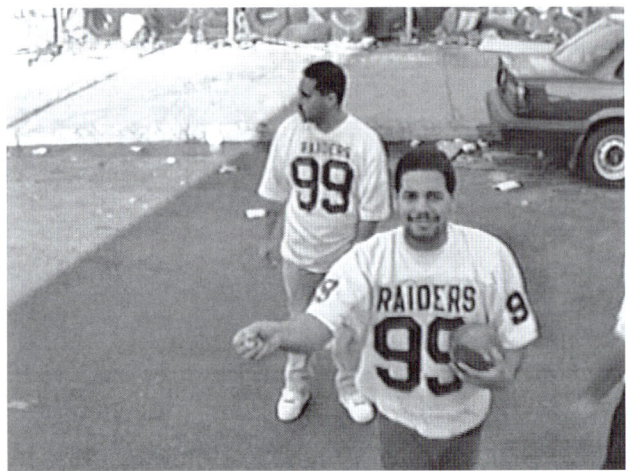

Figure 3.2 In *Every Mother's Son*, the conflict is introduced when a wayward football hits an NYPD patrol car and police officer Francis Livoti puts Anthony Baez in a chokehold.

These two cards give the audience a very basic outline of what is to come, but leave out enough information about the specifics of the stories for the audience to remain engaged. Finding the balance between giving viewers enough information, while keeping them curious enough to keep watching, is one of the challenges of any kind of storytelling.

Following *Every Mother's Son*'s introductory text cards and opening titles, we see images of Iris Baez, one of the film's three main characters, walking in her Bronx neighborhood. We hear her talking about raising children—six adopted and five biological. "We have two kitchens—this is for the early eaters, and upstairs is for the night eaters," she explains with a smile from a seat in the "downstairs kitchen." The images here include children running around the house, and playing outside in the yard. This sequence is part of the exposition of the film. It gives us information about who Iris is, the kind of close-knit family she heads up, and the deep identification she has with being a mother. We also receive visual information (graffiti-covered walls in the neighborhood, the elevated subway rumbling overhead) that tells us this family isn't wealthy, and that they live in a part of town that is far from the luxury skyscrapers and power brokers of Manhattan.

Introducing the Conflict

Soon into any film, you must introduce the central conflict that sets the film in motion, often called the "inciting incident." In a character-driven film, it may be the point where an event happens that changes the course of the main character's life. In *Every Mother's Son*, this moment occurs when several of the Baez boys are playing football in the street and the ball hits a police car, resulting in a confrontation with Officer Francis Livoti (Figure 3.2). Within minutes, Anthony Baez is dead, and questions abound: What happened? Did Anthony die of an asthma attack, as the NYPD claimed, or did Livoti choke him to death? How will the Baez family deal with this tragedy, and will the city take any responsibility? It's important to remember that as a documentary filmmaker you not only deliver information; you also must raise provocative questions that need answers. This lies at the center of involving the audience in your story.

Rising Action

The **rising action** is the bulk of the film. Here we develop the voices, the events, and the nuances that contextualize the basic conflict to create a larger and more complex picture. As scenes play out, we see the stakes escalate for the characters and for the audience. In *Every Mother's Son*, we eventually meet three mothers whose sons were killed by NYPD officers under circumstances that seem unjust. The rising action of the film is each mother's attempt to understand what happened to her son, the realization that something profoundly wrong has occurred, and an effort to get some form of justice. At each turn, obstacles present themselves: a "blue wall of silence" in the police department that makes it difficult to find information, district attorneys who fail to make indictments despite ample evidence that a murder has occurred, a political structure that is complicit with the police department. There are also obstacles that are internal to the characters, including debilitating depression and loss of hope that make it difficult to persevere. Each of these obstacles adds information, adds dimension, and raises the stakes as the mothers and we, as viewers, realize that the desire for justice isn't just an individual matter. Each obstacle is a learning moment for the audience, as we come to understand that without policy reforms, these mothers' sons will, in fact, have died in vain.

When you are embarking on a character-based documentary, make sure that your subjects have goals that you can articulate, and that there are likely to be obstacles along the path they take to achieve those goals that you can highlight. This will ensure that your film has enough conflict to keep the narrative moving forward and the audience engaged as you layer on factual information for context.

Climax

The **climax** of a film is the moment of highest emotional impact, where the conflicts that have been put into motion come to a head. This is where the efforts of the characters lead them to go toe-to-toe with whatever is opposing them, whether that opposing force is a person, an institution, or something more abstract like ignorance or apathy. In *Every Mother's Son*, this is the moment where the three mothers connect with one another, and take their individual stories to a more collective level, joining forces to fight for policy changes. The climax always occurs near the end of the film.

Results and Ending

After the climax, you generally give the audience some time and information that allows them to process what has happened, and to think about what it means. Obviously, in a documentary, we cannot manufacture resolutions or happy endings. The actual conflict may be too pernicious to be resolved, but you need to tell us where we have come as a result of all of this information, and effort. Are we enlightened? Has our awareness of our world been expanded? And, of course, you must tell us where we are leaving the characters. If there is no resolution for them, is there hope? Have their voices been heard? For *Every Mother's Son*, the resolution lies in the mothers' commitment to continuing to work to change policing policy, so that their sons' deaths will not be in vain. We also receive information, via text cards, about where each mother's legal case stands in 2004, when the film ends.

If you analyze the structure of documentaries, you will see many variations on the traditional dramatic arc. *Every Mother's Son*, for example, had three separate stories integrated into one film. Its dramatic arc looks something like this (Figure 3.3).

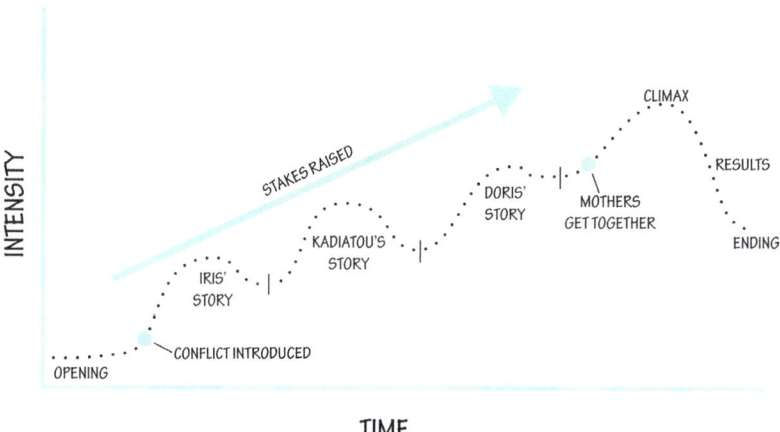

■ Figure 3.3 Story arc for *Every Mother's Son*.

There are three individual stories, and each plays out in full before we move to the next. The first is Iris' story, and it contains its own opening, conflict, goals, obstacles, and rising stakes. At the height of its dramatic arc, we leave this story and pick up Kadiatou's. Hers has its own arc, and then we leave it and begin Doris' story. With multiple stories like this, there is always a danger of them feeling too similar. In *Every Mother's Son*, this is avoided by having each story introduce a new set of issues related to police brutality. This developing revelation of the complexity of the issue keeps the audience on their toes as they develop a more complete understanding. The final climax of the film, when the mothers come together to fight for justice, is the highest emotional point because it offers a potential real-world resolution to a devastating problem.

Some films with multiple characters intercut the stories more often, which would result in another dramatic arc involving parallel action across multiple stories. So you could start with character A, go to character B, then character C, and then repeat several more times over the course of the film. The result would be a different type of dramatic arc. Trying to map out your own film's arc can be a very useful exercise.

Imposing a Structure on Real Life?

Structure and story should be part of your concern from the beginning of your research process, and should periodically be rethought, along with your hypothesis, throughout production. This might seem counterintuitive. Unlike fiction films, documentaries are based on "real life." How then can we impose a story structure on them? The answer to that question brings us to one of the most unique, challenging, and thrilling aspects of documentary: the tension between what exists in the world and your representation of it on screen. Questions of story will determine which parts of a real situation you will capture, how you will film them, and how you will assemble what you've shot in the edit room. If you are sensitive to your story as it unfolds, the people, their goals, and the events will suggest an appropriate structure. You must be willing to allow for new chemistry and new possibilities as production unfolds. Keep in mind all the time how an audience, unfamiliar with the world you are exploring, can be brought into this world of people, events, and issues, and how they are to truly understand it. You will never be able to represent everything that happened; your film will necessarily only show some aspects of what actually occurred, and from certain perspectives. Shaping your representation so that it is true to your understanding of events, and also has compelling narrative structure, can be challenging.

Rhetorical Structure

Often documentarians find themselves wanting to explore an issue in a way that gives audiences more information or analysis than can be delivered by simply following individual stories. This is where more overtly rhetorical approaches to documentary come in, and where we tap into the goals of educating an audience that have always characterized many documentary films (Chapter 2).

Let's say you wanted to make a film about the 2008 financial crisis. One approach might be to follow an individual who is losing their home because of a badly structured mortgage. This would be emotionally moving, but might not lead to a serious analysis of the root causes of the crisis. Another approach might be the one that director Charles Ferguson takes in *Inside Job* (2010). This film presents a carefully structured argument, using a narration read by actor Matt Damon and interviews with a variety of influential figures to provide the core points. There is much at stake, as the film states that the global recession "cost the world tens of trillions of dollars, rendered 30 million people unemployed and doubled the national debt of the United States."

This film, which is expository in style, employs a rhetorical approach. Rhetoric is concerned with the impact of a message on an audience. Examples of rhetoric include political speeches, lectures, and legal arguments. Many documentaries borrow from these traditions as they explore real-life situations and conflict, crafting arguments through the presentation of events, evidence, information, and analysis.

In *Inside Job*, Ferguson lays out an assertion: an out-of-control and unregulated financial sector caused the 2008 global financial crisis. Much like a courtroom argument, *Inside Job* presents evidence in the form of documents, testimony at hearings, and interviews with people actually involved in the events. It also uses expert testimony, including interviews with former New York Attorney General Eliot Spitzer, several business professors at prestigious universities, politicians such as Representative Barney Frank, and journalists. Finally, employing some excellent on-camera interviewing, *Inside Job* uses a strategy akin to legal cross-examination, as in the following exchange about whether the government under President George W. Bush had neglected to heed warnings about the looming financial crisis. David McCormick, Under Secretary of the Treasury for International Affairs from 2007 to 2009, is being interviewed (Figure 3.4):

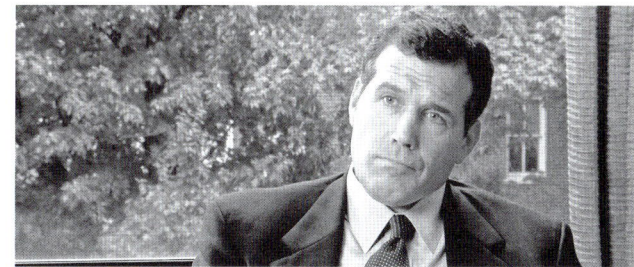

■ **Figure 3.4** Charles Ferguson's interview with David McCormick, Under Secretary of the Treasury for International Affairs, in *Inside Job* feels very much like a courtroom cross-examination.

> McCormick: Secretary (of the Treasury) Paulson spoke throughout the Fall, and all the potential root causes of this, and there are plenty, he called them. So I'm not sure . . .
>
> Andrew Ferguson (Director, off-camera): You're not being serious about that, are you?
>
> McCormick: I am being serious. What would you have expected? What were you looking for that you didn't see?
>
> Ferguson: He was the senior advocate for prohibiting the regulation of credit-default swaps, and also lifting the leverage limits on the investment banks. He mentioned those things? I never heard him mention those things.
>
> McCormick (to the camera operator): Could we turn this off for a second?

The exchange is damning evidence of the cover-up and spin used by government officials and others to deny their responsibility for the crisis. Ferguson also keeps viewers engaged by introducing us to different categories of players. First we meet the bankers, then the government officials who are supposed to be regulating them, and finally the academics who are generally thought to be more impartial, only to find they are also part of the

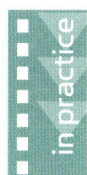

■ HEARING BOTH SIDES OF THE ARGUMENT

Jay Rosenstein's *In Whose Honor?* (1997), about the use of Native American mascots in sports, takes a strongly critical position on the Chief Illiniwek mascot used by the University of Illinois sports teams. In his film, he allows administration officials who support the mascot to speak at length, however. He explains why:

> I made sure to include characters who would vocalize the other side, including trustees from the university, the head of the alumni association, the Chief Illiniwek at that time, and a state representative who proposed a state law that would make Chief Illiniwek the official mascot by state law. I also did a bunch of "man on the street" interviews, going out to the tailgate parties before the games and asking various people how they felt about the mascot.
>
> In allowing these people to speak, I was presenting arguments that were contrary to the point of view of my film. If you are going to make an argument, and you ignore the other side, ultimately you undercut what you are trying to achieve and you make your own argument weaker. I've always felt that by acknowledging the other side, and at the very least trying to counter some of their arguments, not only do you strengthen the film, but you enhance its credibility too.
>
> Audiences are inherently skeptical, and nobody wants to be given a one-sided argument about an issue. Addressing their doubts about your film's messaging head-on is a powerful way to strengthen your claims. And a good conflict between perspectives also builds dramatic tension.
>
> If you are sort of afraid that the counter-argument will overtake your argument, then maybe that should be a sign that you don't have such a strong argument to begin with![3]

problem. In this film, the stakes are so high, and the argument is so well-crafted, that even in the absence of strong character development the film has a gripping narrative arc.

One rhetorical strategy used in *Inside Job*, and in expository documentaries in general, is the **refutative argument**. This involves presenting the opinions of people who counteract the essential claim of the documentary. To continue the court analogy, this is similar to a courtroom defense and prosecution presenting evidence as vigorously as possible, and refuting the veracity of their opponents' arguments. With documentary, the theory is that the truth will be revealed in the end.

Mixed Approaches

In most contemporary documentary films, dramatic and rhetorical storylines coexist and run parallel throughout the film. If you are making a documentary that deals with big policy issues, it's very common to personalize the argument with dramatic human stories. If you are a filmmaker with an amazing human drama, you may want to broaden out the issues the characters are dealing with so that the stories resonate on a more societal or universal level.

Another way to think of a mixed approach is that there is always a tension between a subject in your film being who they are, a real person with a real life, and the role they play in your film as a representative of an issue. It's up to you to contain that tension in a creative way so that viewers see the way larger issues impact people's lives, without turning your subjects into illustrations, or losing the bigger picture that gives their story broad appeal.

ALTERNATIVE STRUCTURES

Some films resist conventional structures altogether, whether rhetorical or dramatic. There are many reasons for an alternative approach. Some makers want to create a more nuanced approach to documentary "truth," even to question the idea that anything is really knowable. Others seek a language that is more aesthetic and associative, and less linear. *Watermark* (2013) is a documentary film by Jennifer Baichwal, in collaboration with photographer Edward Burtynsky, about human interaction with water (Figure 3.5). Baichwal says:

> *I would say the film is more philosophically based than narratively based. It's not a story with a beginning, middle and end. It's like beads on a string that are tied together by this theme of human interaction with water. And there are these little existential moments where you as a viewer get to be in the rice paddies for a moment, or the construction site of the Xiluodu Dam or at the Kumbh Mela with 30 million other people making a sacred vow. The rhythm of it was intended to flow a bit like water.*[4]

It's important, however, to take a pause before deciding to abandon a dramatic or rhetorical structure for your film. One of the reasons *Watermark* is able to hold viewers' attention for 92 minutes, despite a lack of traditional dramatic structure, is the breathtaking cinematography by Nick de Pencier, and the acute directorial eyes of Baichwal and Burtynsky. As de Pencier explains, "(Ed Burtynsky) doesn't choose subjects that don't resonate with layers of meaning and information underneath." The film, which is based on Burtynsky's photographs, works without a lot of exposition because the image itself is dense with meaning.[5] In this way, the film is similar to the impressionistic films described in Chapter 2.

Also remember that just because your film eschews traditional structure, it does not mean that it has no structure. Every filmmaker, no matter what their approach, needs to be clear about the particular organizing principle of their story. Every film must have a conscious and thoughtfully constructed organization of material to create a compelling experience that can communicate to a viewer. As Baichwal explains, in her films there is no shortage of advance planning and thinking about questions of structure and theme: "We always have an outline and a vision and a philosophical idea of what we're trying to do, and then we go into the field."[6]

THE SHORT DOCUMENTARY

Many documentaries are much shorter than the feature-length examples we have discussed above. Many run 2 to 3 minutes, others 10 to 15, and they are typically structured differently from longer works. If you are just starting out making documentaries, it is a great idea to make short projects to hone your technical and storytelling skills. Creating short documentaries will allow you to explore a variety of themes, styles, and structures within a short period of time. In addition, you will be able to spend much more of your time actually making the film, rather than trying to find the resources required for a feature.

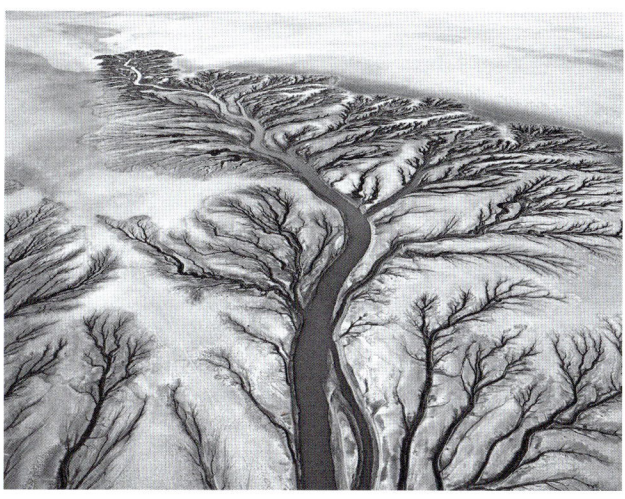

■ **Figure 3.5** *Watermark* builds its case about humans' interaction with water through a structure based on thematic imagery rather than a traditional dramatic or rhetorical structure.

The short form isn't always a "stepping stone" to feature documentary production, however. Many filmmakers prefer the short form and make short documentaries their entire lives. Keith Wilson, whose short film *The Shrimp* (2009) is analyzed below, says:

> *Early in my career I subscribed to the widely held belief that the ultimate filmmaking goal was feature length fare. But my interests are wide-ranging, my attention span is short, and my financial resources are limited. So I gravitate towards short films that are conceptually contained and formally focused, because they make my life as a creative person sustainable.*[7]

Short documentaries don't have much time for character development, or for conflict to develop organically, and most don't follow the traditional dramatic arc. Instead they tend to fall into one of these categories:
- Issue-Based Films
- Profile of a Person
- Portrait of a Place
- Single Event Story
- Process Film

Issue-Based Films

Issue-based short documentaries present us with a quick glimpse of a social problem. They often begin with a presentation of the problem, then delve into possible causes, and end by providing us with some potential solutions. They have little time for character development, but people often function as experts or eyewitnesses. An example is Meerkat Media's *Every Third Bite* (2008), a 9-minute documentary about the phenomenon of "bee colony collapse." We meet one scientist, and several beekeepers in Nantucket (MA), Chicago, Long Island (NY), and New York City. Through interviews, mostly with beekeepers as they work, we learn that millions of bees have abandoned their hives, about the connection between bees and agriculture ("every third bite of food we eat is pollinated by a honeybee"), and that large-scale industrial honey production is a likely cause of the problem. We are also presented with a solution in the example of small-scale farmers, even some who are farming on rooftops in the city, as a way of creating employment as well as saving bees.

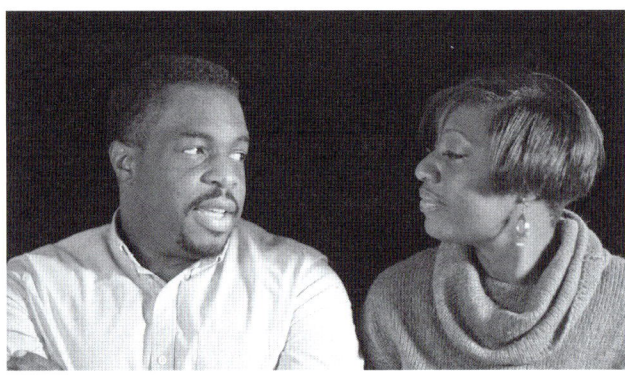

Figure 3.6 *A Conversation with My Black Son* is an example of an issue-based short documentary on the New York Times Op-Docs Video Channel.

The New York Times Op-Docs Video Channel (www.nytimes.com/video/op-docs/), which premiered on the newspaper's website in 2012, is a good place to view and analyze issue-based short documentaries. An example is Geeta Gandbhir and Blair Foster's formally sparse but powerful 5-minute film *A Conversation with My Black Son* (2015). This short documentary consists entirely of parents, sitting before a black backdrop, talking about why and how they talk to their black sons about interactions with police. The comments at first address why they feel the need to have this conversation, and how they feel about it, then what they tell their children specifically. The intimacy and honesty of their accounts is disarming, and invites all parents to share a common love for their children and come to terms with a world that treats them differently based on race. The piece ends with several of the parents talking directly to camera, as if to their sons, telling them how much they love them and why. Over the end credits, the parents hold up pictures of their sons. It is the first time we see them, and seeing such small children after hearing the burden society places on them is heartbreaking (Figure 3.6).

Profile of a Person

Many short documentaries take the form of a personal profile. With the right choice of subject, this is a highly economical form because the filming is generally contained to interviews with one person and some observational footage of them doing what they do. The key is to find a person whose life will resonate beyond their specific story, touching on broad themes that have universal appeal. An example is *Marie's Dictionary* (2014), a 9-minute and 30-second documentary by Emmanuel Vaughan-Lee about Marie Wilcox, the last fluent speaker of the Native American Wukchumni language (Figure 3.7). The film is based on interviews with Marie, her daughter, and her grandson. We see many beautiful shots of Marie working on her dictionary as she discusses her 7-year effort to create it. We then see how her grandson has begun recording her dictionary so that there will be an audio as well as a written record of the language. Observational moments showing interactions between these three characters enrich the documentary by giving us a deeper sense of who these people are, and their relationships to one another. In one scene, we see that Marie is frustrated with her daughter, who has trouble pronouncing the Wukchumni words. Later, though, we see Marie conversing with her grandson, who seems much more fluent in the language. This gives us hope that this nearly extinct language may survive after all. The film works because of the strength of its characters, but also because it speaks to important themes of cultural preservation and identity. Like most successful portrait documentaries, it touches on an issue as it presents us with a person.

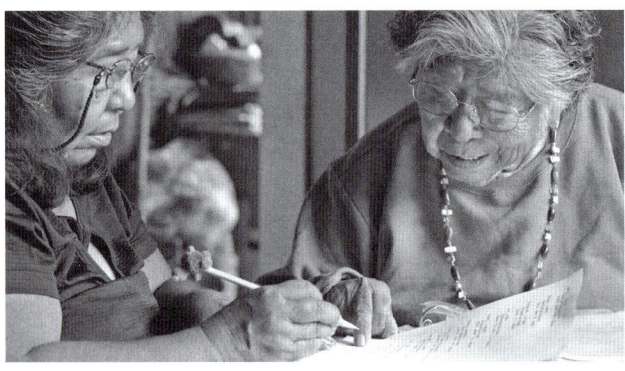

Figure 3.7 Marie Wilcox (right) and her daughter work on the Wukchumni dictionary in *Marie's Dictionary*.

Portrait of a Place

Another strategy for making a story feasible for a short documentary is to confine shooting to one place. Elizabeth Lo's 8-minute film *Hotel 22* (2015), shows us one night on the #22 bus, a 24-hour route that has attracted many homeless people displaced by the tech boom in California's Silicon Valley (Figure 3.8). Shot in a purely observational style, with no interviews at all, the film is a slice of life that conveys a sense of what it's like to be homeless and have to sleep on a bus. We witness "regular" passengers berating the homeless for being there, and the homeless riders asking the bus driver to turn up the heat so they won't be cold. The structure follows one night, beginning with people waiting for the bus and ending with police waking everyone up and making them leave the bus so morning commuters can board.

Single Event Story

Just as it sounds, these short documentaries are built around a single event or occurrence. They often contain a mini dramatic arc, building to a climactic moment. An example is *Last Minutes with ODEN* (2009), a 6-minute documentary by Eliot Rausch (Figure 3.9). During the first minute of the film, we are introduced to Jason Wood. While seeing images of Jason carrying and riding his bike, with an emphasis on his tattooed arms, we learn that he is a former drug addict who was incarcerated for 10 years, and that he has a dog—ODEN—who has been a constant companion to Jason and his friends through many hard times. "My dog would get right next to them, and he wouldn't leave, he was so loyal, he was so down for the guys I loved," Wood says. "He showed me, through his example, how to love, and I loved him." At this point, there is the introduction of the conflict: we see ODEN, and he has only three legs. The story builds as we see observational footage of Jason on the phone crying, picking his dog up from a friend's house, and bringing him to various people to say goodbye. Through this footage, we realize that the dog is sick and will be put to sleep. The climax of the film is ODEN's death as he is euthanized by a veterinarian. The result and ending are the aftermath, as we see Jason Wood and others crying, and then Jason biking as we hear him reflect on how ODEN's unconditional love transformed him by teaching him to let down his guard and love people.

Process Film

Some short films focus on a process. Keith Wilson's 15-minute *The Shrimp* (2009) is about shrimping on the Gulf Coast, and draws its structure from the life cycle of one shrimp (Figure 3.10). Except for a brief bit of context in the form of text cards at the beginning, which lets us know that "shrimp are an important source of food, income and culture for communities along the American South's Atlantic Seaboard and Gulf Coast" and that "the viability of commercial shrimping is threatened by pollution, oil spills and cheaper foreign imports," we are told very little and left to draw our own conclusions. Part of the film's appeal, in fact, is our recognition that the story is structured to show us every phase of the food chain from catching shrimp, to cleaning, cooking, and eating it. Finally, in a humorous twist, the camera tracks across a row of houses and we hear water (and probably more) running through pipes. At a sewage treatment plant we see water being treated, and eventually returning to the spawning grounds where future shrimp will

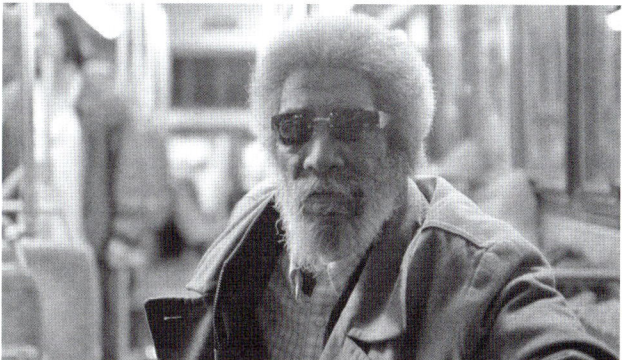

Figure 3.8 A city bus in California's Silicon Valley has become an unofficial homeless shelter in the short documentary *Hotel 22*.

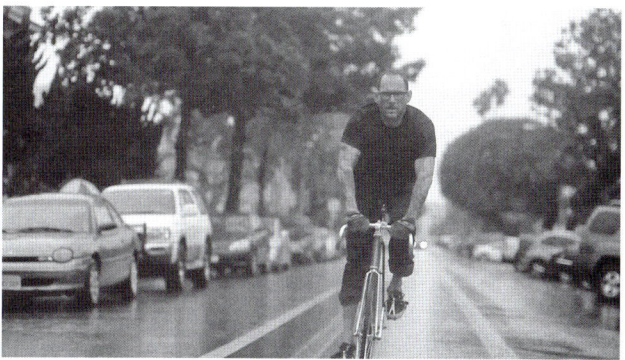

Figure 3.9 Jason Wood in *Last Minutes with ODEN*.

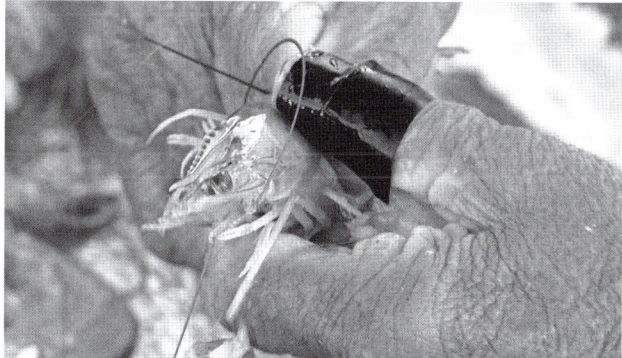

Figure 3.10 *The Shrimp* uses the life cycle of a shrimp to tell us about an important Gulf Coast industry threatened by pollution.

be born and the cycle will recur. Wilson's film reminds us that attention to story structure in the preproduction phase will bear fruit all the way down the line.

CONCLUSION

In this chapter, we have tried to provide some guidance about how documentaries are commonly structured. While these ideas will likely be helpful, structure is something that emerges organically as you work. It is a dynamic process, not a static one. No quantity of organizational charts or structural containers will ever be a perfect fit for your material. This is why documentary filmmaking is exciting and challenging: you are creating the language to describe the world in a new way as you go.

CHAPTER 4

The Documentary Proposal

A documentary **proposal** is usually developed as you seek funds, or other support, for your film. Competition for documentary funds is intense. Whether you are approaching a foundation or a television network, or launching a crowd-sourced funding campaign, you need to be able to communicate your vision for your film clearly and powerfully if you expect to be successful in your fundraising efforts.

The proposal serves a second function as well. It can help you move from an *idea* for a film to a solid *plan* for production. The proposal serves as a repository for your evolving ideas about your film, and it is often rewritten several times while you are in preproduction (and even in the production and postproduction phases). A proposal is an opportunity to see your film without scheduling a single interview or lifting any equipment. It is a way of visualizing how your story will unfold, who the characters will be, what elements you will use, and what the structure will be. During this phase, the larger social implications of your topic start to come into focus. Often the proposal is developed in collaboration with other people you will be working with, such as a producer or associate producer. Creating the proposal can be a fruitful exercise that helps everybody "get on the same page" before you actually go into production, when there is less time for working out differences of opinion or vision. For this reason a proposal is essential, even for short films that might not involve a formal fundraising proposal.

Once production begins, it can be easy to lose your sense of why you began making your film and what you think it is about. After all, there is a big difference between a documentary idea and the messy reality you are likely to be confronted with when you begin actual filming. Your proposal can be a kind of "home base" that allows you to check in on your original ideas about your film. While you are always free to change your concept, and documentaries always evolve, the proposal can be a helpful way to remember your intentions and make sure you don't get pulled in unproductive directions. So even if you are not planning on raising outside funds for your documentary, do not skip this essential part of the process! As you write your proposal, you will be consolidating your research, thinking through stylistic approaches, lining up the elements necessary to tell your story, choosing which characters you will follow, and deciding what events you will shoot. Perhaps most importantly, you will discover for yourself what you hope your film will communicate, and why it should be made.

PROPOSAL ELEMENTS

Each funding entity has slightly different requirements for what a proposal must include. If you are using your proposal to raise money, you will inevitably end up with several different versions of the same basic proposal. Most filmmakers have a longer proposal (5 to 10 pages) as well as a shorter version that can be consolidated into a two-page **letter of inquiry** required by many funders as a first step through the door. Most of your proposals will include some of these elements.

Introduction or Synopsis

The **introduction** or **synopsis** is a concise, one-paragraph description of your project. It includes what the film is about, how long it will be, and what the general significance of the story is. This part of the proposal orients the reader, giving them a basic sense of the topic and scope of your project. The proposal for S. Leo Chiang's film *A Village Called Versailles* (2009) (Figure 4.1), which received funding from the Independent Television Service (ITVS) and aired on PBS' documentary series *Independent Lens*, opened with this synopsis:

> *A Village Called Versailles is an hour-long documentary about Versailles, an isolated community in eastern New Orleans originally settled by Vietnamese "boat people." In the aftermath of Hurricane Katrina, Versailles residents have impressively risen to the challenges by returning and rebuilding before any other neighborhood in New Orleans, only to have their homes threatened by a new government-imposed toxic landfill just two miles away. A Village Called Versailles will recount the empowering story of how this group of people, who have already suffered so much, turn a devastating disaster into a catalyst for change and a chance for a better future.*[1]

This synopsis tells us, in a nutshell, who the film is about and where it unfolds. It also gives us a sense of the story, including the conflict and what is at stake for the community represented. Finally, this synopsis hints at the ways this specific story will resonate more universally by tapping into a theme that many communities can learn from: "turning disaster into a catalyst for change and a chance for a better future."

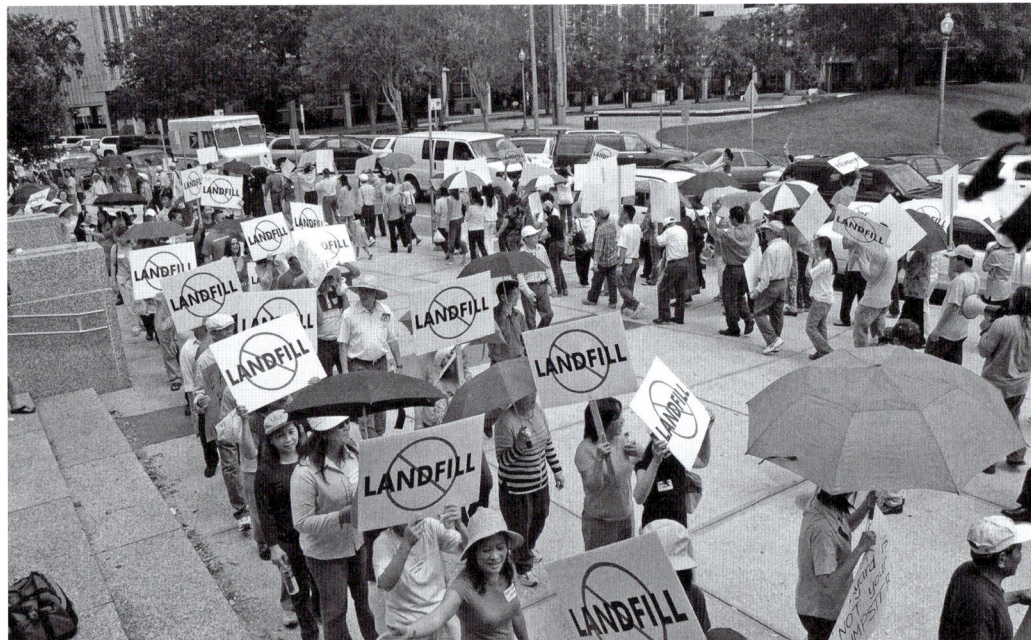

■ **Figure 4.1** *A Village Called Versailles* documents the impact of Hurricane Katrina and its aftermath on the Vietnamese community in New Orleans.

Background

In this section of the proposal, you provide the basic information your reader needs to understand the issue your film is dealing with. Background information is contextual—it may or may not presented in your final film. For *A Village Called Versailles*, background might include how Vietnamese refugees came to settle in New Orleans and the obstacles they faced, what Versailles was like before Hurricane Katrina, how hard it was hit and the damage it sustained, and a sense of how the Vietnamese community was absent from the national media coverage of the disaster.

Here are some excerpts from Chiang's proposal that would be considered background:

The name "Versailles" refers to "Versailles Arms," the New Orleans East public housing project where a group of Vietnamese refugees was first resettled in 1975. This unusually tight-knit group, most of whom are devout Catholics with roots in the same three rural North Vietnamese villages, had been forced to flee their homes twice already in their life time—first from North to South Vietnam to escape communist persecution in 1957, and then from the Vietnam War to New Orleans in 1975 through a Catholic refugee-resettlement program. Surrounded by lush wetlands and humid climate reminiscent of the Mekong Delta, the Versailles clan was grateful to find peace on the easternmost edge of New Orleans. Some took jobs in factories. Some worked in construction. Those who were fishermen back in Vietnam joined the shrimping industry along the Gulf Coast, and those who were business owners began opening small grocery stores all around New Orleans. The community grew steadily through the '80s and the '90s.

Thirty years after their arrival, however, Versailles is at a crossroads. The elders look at their American-born, hip-hop-loving grandkids with suspicion, questioning the cultural allegiance of the youth and fearful of them moving away and leaving the community behind. The youth, on the other hand, dismiss the elders as out-of-touch and yet are frustrated by the lack of trust from the Viet-speaking older generations. Legally citizens of the US, but uncomfortable being American, Versailles residents are perpetual outsiders in the city of New Orleans, largely ignored by the government. All of this, of course, is about to change.[2]

Rationale

A **rationale** will tell the readers why your film *needs to be made*. While documentaries can be entertaining and should definitely be engaging, this part of the proposal is an opportunity to explain why your film is important, and what impact it can have. Here is an excerpt from Chiang's rationale for *A Village Called Versailles*:

For a public television audience bombarded with mostly negative images and stories from New Orleans through other media outlets, A Village Called Versailles will take a different, positive point of view on the Katrina disaster. The mainstream media has largely left out the struggles of the 30,000-plus Gulf Coast Vietnamese in covering Hurricane Katrina. The film will serve the Asian-American audience by telling the Katrina story from the Vietnamese-American point of view, which has not been done thus far. Also, at a time when being religious is often equated with divisive, bigoted fundamentalism at home and abroad, A Village Called Versailles will serve the communities of faith by showing how a church and its leaders can unify a group and bring about positive social change during times of crisis. The film will also appeal to immigrant groups in general, who can all relate to the Versailles community overcoming obstacles to integrate their traditional roots with their American surroundings.[3]

A rationale can also include an overview of what other films exist on your topic and how your documentary differs from what is already out there. It can also explain why you are the best person to make this film because you have a personal connection to the issue, or some particular knowledge or experience.

Project Description

This is your chance to explain in detail all the **elements** that will comprise your film, and how each functions in the telling of the story. These might include **interviews** and

observational footage, as well as **archival** materials like old film footage or still photographs (for a more complete list of possible documentary elements, see Chapter 7). It is understood that once you start production, the reality you encounter might differ from what you describe in your project description. This is your chance to pull together all the research you have done and take your best shot at imagining what your film might actually look like when it is completed.

In the project description, you should include:

Main Characters

Who will be in your film and what role will they play? Is this a portrait of one individual, or do you have several characters who represent various points of view on the events in your film? In David Alvarado and Jason Sussberg's film *The Immortalists* (2014), about the science of life extension, each character is given a metaphorical role in the proposal. Dr. Aubrey de Grey, a scientist with "a two-foot-long red beard and bottomless appetite for beer and thorny scientific problems," according to Alvarado, is given the title "The Crusader."[4] Dr. Leonard Hayflick, a professor of medicine at the University of California who has studied the cell biology of aging his entire professional career, is given the title "The Forefather."[5] This is a clever way to help readers understand the basic role each character plays in the film as they read the proposal.

Events You Will Film

What will be unfolding that you can film in the present? Which characters are involved? How will these scenes contribute to the story of your film? In *The Immortalists*, a potentially dry scientific topic is brought to life by the filmmakers' efforts to film their characters in visually engaging pursuits and situations: a super-marathon in the Himalayas, a naked picnic one of the scientists has with his wife, and a debate between one of the main characters and the old guard at Oxford University.

Structure and Style

Will your film be mostly observational, or will it be told through archival footage and interviews? Will there be any **narration**? If yes, is it third-person or in a first-person, more **reflexive** style (Chapter 2)? Will your film follow a narrative **dramatic arc**, or use a more **rhetorical** strategy (Chapter 3)? Try and imagine how your story will unfold, what you are building towards, and what viewers might take away from your film.

Here is a paragraph from S. Leo Chiang's proposal for *A Village Called Versailles* that addresses both structure and style:

A Village Called Versailles utilizes a traditional linear documentary structure. The chronological unfolding of events so compellingly propels the story forward that attempting to play with the timeline will only weaken the narrative. News clips of New Orleans Mayor Ray Nagin's various announcements will provide the context of what is happening in New Orleans at large during the storm, the flood, and the aftermath.

We plan to incorporate a sizable amount of third-party media, including news footage (from both mainstream and Vietnamese-language news outlets), home videos, video footage from other filmmakers, photos and newspaper headlines. We plan to build a visual language so that certain characteristics of each specific type of material become an advantage instead of a liability. For instance, the shaky low-resolution home video footage of the storm and the landfill protest are jump-cut to add energy, grit, and a sense of authenticity. The visual formality of local and network news clips will give authority when the story needs it. Finally, beautiful twilight shots of Versailles shot on a tripod will emphasize serenity.[6]

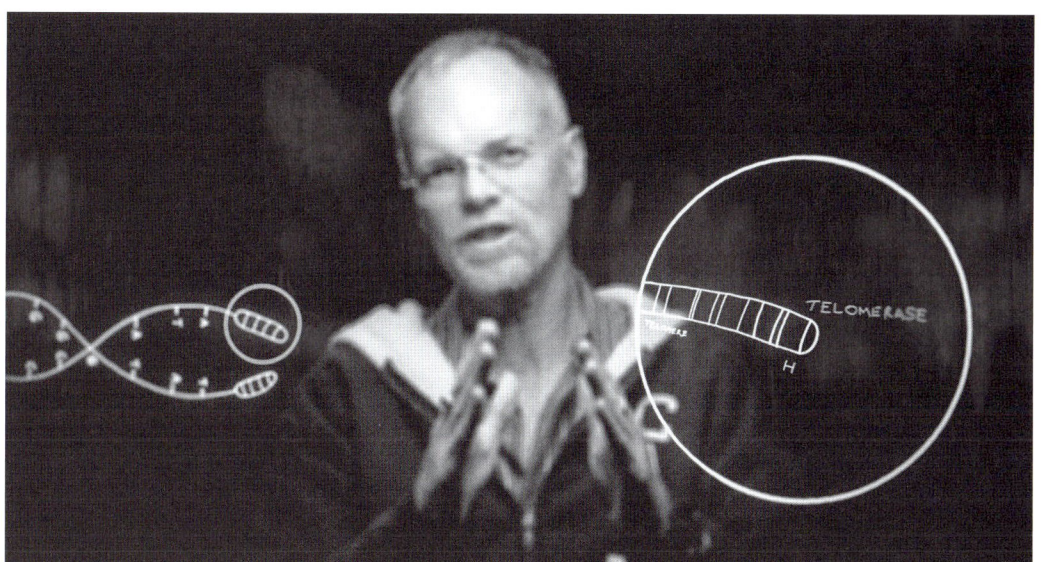

Figure 4.2
The Immortalists uses animation to illustrate scientific concepts.

The Structure and Style section is also where you should indicate your intention to use elements like graphics or animation. In *The Immortalists*, the main interviews are set in front of a black background, which is then used as a space for animation that illustrates some of the more complex scientific concepts in the film (Figure 4.2).

Themes

Themes are the deep central ideas that may not be referenced directly but are at the core of your film. In *A Village Called Versailles*, themes include resilience in the face of adversity, immigrant struggles to retain cultural values while also trying to adapt to a new environment, the possibility of turning disaster into a better future, and the importance of community involvement in post-disaster reconstruction. For *The Immortalists*, themes include the human desire to live forever, conflicts between different generations of scientists, and the challenges of human relationships.

Treatment

Not all funders require a **treatment**, but some do and in either case it can be extremely useful to try and write one for your film. Unlike a project description, which allows you to explain why you are using certain elements or approaching things a certain way, the treatment includes *only what the viewer will see and hear as they watch the film*. It is a present-tense prose description of your film, without technical terms (like camera angles or shot sizes). Of all the elements of a proposal, this is perhaps the most important, as it communicates most directly what the film will actually be. Here is an excerpt from the treatment for *A Village Called Versailles*:

The film opens with a montage of familiar yet still violent images of the Katrina devastations, followed by unfamiliar images of Vietnamese elderly in traditional clothing and conical straw hats, thrusting their fists skyward and chanting "We are united, and we are powerful!" We meet FATHER VIEN NGUYEN, the pastor of the Mary Queen of Vietnam Catholic Church. "We never considered not returning," he says emphatically. "It was a matter of fact that when we could return we WOULD return." Sunset. Terraced vegetable gardens line the Maxent Canal. An old man shuffles through a parking lot full of Vietnamese business signs. Teenage boys play hoops in the FEMA trailer park. "We Vietnamese are an agricultural people," Father Vien continues. "We have a saying—the place where we bury our placenta, that is home. So we're connected to the earth where we live. We are tied to that land."[7]

A treatment can run anywhere from two to four pages for a feature-length documentary, or a page for a short film. As with the project description, it is understood that what you write in a proposal during the preproduction stage is not set in stone. This is your best attempt to visualize what your film will be, based on your research to date.

Distribution Plan

Most funders give money to documentary projects because they believe the film can have an *impact*. Your distribution plan is your opportunity to explain how your film will reach people and help create some kind of education, enlightenment, or social change. In developing your distribution plan, it is a good idea to list the various **target audiences** you have in mind, as well as the **platforms, strategies,** and **venues** you will use to reach them. Many films start out with a very specific target audience and end up "spilling over" into a larger community of viewers. Here are some things to think through as you develop your distribution plan:

Target Audiences

Who are you making your film for? There is always a tension between speaking to a specific audience and wanting your film to appeal more broadly. But as S. Leo Chiang says, "Knowing who you are telling your stories to will make you a better storyteller. Keep thinking about the audience for the film you want to make—who they are, where they are, what they are interested in, and why."[8]

A target audience can be specific, like the Vietnamese community in New Orleans, or as general as Americans who watch public television. Strange as it may seem, speaking to a specific community will not necessarily lessen your film's appeal to a more general audience. At the same time, however, if you are aiming for a general audience (like a theatrical release or broadcast) it's important to remember that there may be certain facts and background information they will need to follow your story.

Once you have defined your target audiences, you need to think about how, and where, they are likely to encounter your film. **Venues** include actual screening locations like film festivals, theaters, or community centers such as churches or schools. **Platforms** include distribution mechanisms like broadcast or cable television, video-on-demand websites like Netflix, Amazon, or iTunes, and mobile applications for streaming media. Most films use a variety of these routes to reach their audiences. See Chapter 23 for a more detailed discussion of distribution. For now, though, here are a few examples to consider including in your proposal:

Film Festivals

Don't just write about your desire to get into Sundance or a list of other top-tier festivals, even if you hope your film will make it there. Are there festivals that have a track record of showing films like the one you hope to make? Niche festivals are often a good target if your film fits their mandate (examples of these include a robust circuit of Jewish film festivals, environmental film festivals, and human rights film festivals). For students, taking advantage of student film festivals (and the student categories of larger festivals) can be a good strategy for lessening what is likely to be intense competition.

Television

Many filmmakers hope for a broad general audience for their films, and television is still one way to get millions of people to see your film. There are several excellent series on public television (*POV* and *Independent Lens*, among others) but the competition for limited slots is intense. Cable television is another option for television distribution.

Theatrical

A theatrical release is generally defined as a week or more in one theater, with multiple screenings per day. While some notable documentaries have turned a healthy profit in theaters, relatively few documentaries get real theatrical releases. Some filmmakers will arrange their own short runs (called "four-walling") to qualify for Academy Awards® or secure a review in a major newspaper.

Educational Institutions

High schools, colleges, and universities are rich opportunities for engaging faculty and students with your work. If this is a target audience for you, your proposal should include a sense of which disciplines or departments you hope to reach, how you might reach them (possible examples are professional conferences, or direct mail), and any resources like study guides you will provide to help educators include your film in their lesson plans.

The Internet

Increasingly, the Internet is the place where people watch films, including documentaries. Here you can explain what your plans are for allowing online streaming and/or downloading of your film and, most importantly, how you will drive people to your film. Just because it's online doesn't mean people will find it and watch it!

Community-Based Screenings

From a social change perspective, one of the best ways for people to encounter your film is in a group setting. Your distribution plans should include a list of organizations that might sponsor or help publicize screenings of your film. Often community screenings are followed by a discussion with guest speakers or a facilitator that guides a discussion.

Community Partners

It can strengthen a proposal to have a commitment from specific organizations to work with you in the distribution phase. A letter from the local PBS station, or other broadcaster, can also be persuasive.

Your partners might agree to sponsor a series of screenings or house parties, or publicize a broadcast or internet streaming campaign. Whatever their participation, reaching out and having a real conversation (and obtaining a letter of commitment) is critical. Anybody can include a list of organizations in their proposal. Demonstrating that you have actually begun speaking with people working on your issue will bolster your credibility with funders.

Goals

Finally, whether they are as specific as having people participate in a campaign or as general as "raising awareness" about an issue, the goals of your distribution strategy should be as clear as possible. While you can never know for sure where your film will end up and what impact it might have, preparing the way for its life in distribution is essential, even at the proposal stage.

Personnel

This section is where you include short biographies of the key people working on your film, including yourself. Try to include information that makes the case that the film will get made, and be of high quality. If you are lacking in experience, it can be helpful to bring on more seasoned people in roles like "Executive Producer" or even "Producer." Minimally, your personnel section should include the Producer, Director, Director of Photography, and Editor.

Other titles, like Executive Producer, Associate Producer, Archival Footage Researcher, and Sound Recordist, can also be included but are not essential. There is more information about developing a documentary crew in Chapter 6.

Budget

Budgeting for a documentary is a complicated and nuanced business, and we will address it further in Chapter 6. For now, it is important to give your funders a sense of how much money you think you will need to complete your film, and to create a budget that seems realistic and professional. Many filmmakers budget for what they need in an ideal world, and end up making the film for less.

An important distinction is made in budgeting between **in-kind** and cash support. In-kind support is donated and can include the producers' and directors' time, as well as items like office rent and equipment rental. Most budgets will have separate columns for cash items and in-kind items. It's important to indicate in-kind support, and translate it into currency worth, because funders like to see that there are others who believe in the project and are supporting it.

Budgets generally include an "expense" and an "income" section. In the latter, list projected sources of income even if they haven't been committed to yet. Your projected income should equal your expenses.

Funding Sources

Documentary films vary widely in the amount of support they will need, but no film is made without some. Most cobble together funding from a variety of sources, and continue fundraising throughout production and even postproduction. Here are some examples of where you can find funding for documentaries.

Foundations

Nonprofit foundations often represent at least a portion of the funding sources for a documentary. Some, like the Ford Foundation and the MacArthur Foundation, have funding specifically targeted at documentary production. Smaller foundations specializing in documentary include Cinereach and The Fledgling Fund. Other foundations without a history of media funding may nevertheless be interested in your documentary because they care about the issue you are addressing.

Government Funding

There are various ways to access public funding for the arts, including documentary filmmaking. Some of these in the United States include the following:

State Arts Councils and Humanities Councils

Many states have arts funding available to residents of that state that can be used for documentary filmmaking. A quick Internet search should let you know whether your particular state has such a council and whether you are eligible.

National Endowment for the Arts

The National Endowment for the Arts (NEA) does not support individual artists, but does support organizations that work with media artists.

National Endowment for the Humanities

The National Endowment for the Humanities supports film projects with significant humanities content.

Corporation for Public Broadcasting

There are a variety of ways to access public broadcasting money in the United States. The most common is through ITVS (Independent Television Service), which funds independent work for public television broadcast. Eligible projects also receive funding through the Minority Consortia, including the Center for Asian American Media, the National Black Programming Consortium, Native American Public Telecommunications, Native Public Media, Pacific Islanders in Communications, and Latino Public Broadcasting.

Cable TV

Many cable stations commission or acquire documentary programming. Some of those most friendly to independent producers include HBO, National Geographic, the Independent Film Channel, the Sundance Channel, and Al Jazeera US.

Crowd-Sourced Fundraising

Increasingly, filmmakers are turning to platforms like Kickstarter.com or Indiegogo.com to raise funds in small increments from friends, family, and other supporters. These campaigns are labor-intensive but provide a good opportunity for bypassing traditional gatekeepers, and allow you to reach out and begin to build an audience before your film is finished.

In other countries, the landscape will look slightly different, but you are still likely to find a mix of public and private financing for films, as well as commissioning entities like television stations. Big funders in Europe include BritDoc Foundation (Channel 4), the BBC, Arte (French/German TV), and many others. In Canada, the Canada Council for the Arts and the National Film Board of Canada are noteworthy.

Fiscal Sponsorship

For tax reasons, many funders only give money to nonprofit organizations (in the United States, this means those with an official 501(c)(3) IRS status). Since most filmmakers aren't themselves nonprofit organizations, many nonprofit organizations have developed **fiscal sponsorship** programs that allow individual filmmakers to receive funding from foundations.

Project Timeline and Status

When will you begin and finish shooting? When will editing begin and for how long? Most importantly, when will you be finished? How much work has already been completed? Anybody putting money into your project will want realistic answers to these questions, and a clear picture of your timeline.

TRAILERS AND SAMPLE REELS

Many funders will require that you provide a **trailer**, **sizzle reel**, or **work sample**, either on a DVD or via an online link. If you are in the preproduction stage, you might be asked to provide a sample of previous work to show that you are capable of completing a high-quality project. For students and other emerging filmmakers, a lack of previous work can be a real obstacle and is best overcome by providing a work-in-progress sample.

Work-in-progress samples are longer than trailers or sizzle reels, which typically run for less than 2 minutes and are paced very quickly. A sample reel is a collection of your best material, and it should give viewers a sense of the style of your documentary and the range of material you have shot. While you obviously want to avoid giving potential funders long selections of unedited video, your sample reel should be paced slowly enough so that viewers can understand what they are watching. Sometimes a text card can be used to set up the material so that viewers can easily see where it fits into your overall plan.

CONCLUSION

Developing a solid proposal requires that you understand the topic as well as the underlying themes of your documentary. It also requires that you think carefully about your stylistic approach, what elements will be necessary to achieve your goals, and the resources necessary to acquire them. For all these reasons, the proposal is not just a bureaucratic chore. It is a critical part of the creative process, and one that should be revisited often throughout production and postproduction.

Documentary Ethics and Legal Issues

CHAPTER 5

A documentary film production involves an intense and often intimate interaction with the real world. It is an encounter with other human beings, many times in complex and difficult circumstances. And it is an attempt to represent aspects of that world to a larger audience. In addition, documentaries often incorporate the creative works of others, which forces you to confront issues of ownership and authorship. All of these circumstances offer particular ethical and legal challenges.

Why do we need "ethics"? In the largest sense, ethics suggests some kind of common code of conduct for morally correct behavior. Documentary filmmaking involves real people who can be misrepresented, exploited, or otherwise harmed by your actions. When we are representing others, we are taking responsibility for how they are seen in the larger public sphere, often by millions of people. In addition, we are showing audiences a picture of the world that we claim is valid. How do we understand our responsibility to an audience that is depending on us to raise issues in a useful and truthful way?

An ethics of documentary would fall under the category of "applied ethics," akin to legal, medical, and journalistic ethics where philosophical and moral principles are applied to real-world situations. But documentary makers don't have boards, licenses, or one organization that we all belong to, like the American Medical Association (AMA) for doctors. Nor do we take any professional oath. Is there a specific need for a set of standards like other professions maintain? Because documentary filmmaking is so varied in practice, it would seem impossible to create such a specific code. However, the issues that face documentary filmmakers are as morally complex as those of any other profession, and the implications can be just as serious.

RESPONSIBILITY TO YOUR SUBJECTS: SUBJECT RELATIONS AND RELEASE FORMS

In documentary filmmaking, the relationship between you (the representer) and your subject (the represented) is by definition unequal. As the filmmaker, you hold most of the power. This relationship is formalized in the **release form** you ask people to sign when you begin filming with them. A release form is a legally binding contract between the filmmaker and the subject being filmed, stipulating that the subject consents to being filmed and included in the final work. Releases are generally worded very broadly, so that filmmakers can use the footage for promotion, or reassign rights to third parties. Many beginning filmmakers find asking someone to sign a release form daunting, but it is critical that you get releases. Networks and distributors will not enter into an agreement to show or distribute your film without a full set of release forms. Contrary to popular mythology, asking someone on camera to say they grant you permission to use their interview will not be considered sufficient by most broadcasters and distributors. In addition, having a signed release protects you from legal challenges over privacy and libel. For sample release forms, see our companion website (www.routledge.com/cw/Anderson). While specifics vary from country to country, the standard release forms are similar in the United States, the United Kingdom, and other Commonwealth countries.

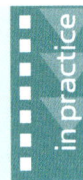

■ WHEN DO YOU NEED TO GET A RELEASE?

While some networks might insist that every person whose face you see in a documentary must be covered by a signed release, most typical practice suggests that you need a release in a situation where someone actually speaks with you. A variety of courts in the United States have made decisions that someone whose picture is taken while on a public street cannot sue an artist for the use of their image.[1] In many situations where documentary filmmakers work, however, the space is not public. A football stadium, a nightclub, a hospital—all these will present specific issues. One common answer for events or crowded spaces is to post a sign indicating that there will be filming, and that entering the locale indicates consent. Often this will be combined with a suggestion to stand in a certain area where the camera will not be pointed if you don't want your image to be taken. Schools also raise specific issues, because children are minors. Filming children in a classroom will require getting a consent form signed by the guardian of each child in the class. Other schools take the precaution of getting blanket consents from parents at the beginning of the term. Hospitals raise other issues, as patients have specific legal privacy rights.

In addition to obtaining releases from people, it is usually important to obtain a **location permit** when shooting on private property or any kind of institutional or restricted locale. There is more on location permits and agreements in Chapter 6.

Veteran documentarian Tami Gold suggests that getting a release is not so much an unpleasant chore as it is a key step in building a productive relationship of mutual trust:

> *The big challenge for documentary filmmakers is building relationships. One of the reasons I love release forms is that asking for the release stops the process and allows the person to think. It establishes a contract. It basically acknowledges that they have rights, and they might not feel comfortable signing them away, but some of it can be negotiated. I'm not saying it's easy. Sometimes it's hard to go to people and ask them for permission to use their image or their interview. On the other hand, it is our responsibility to take their rights seriously, and be clear about the terms of the relationship.*[2]

Gold's dynamic understanding of the maker's relationship to their subjects underlies good filmmaking and richer storytelling. Why? Because a documentary film is only as good as the filmmaker's relationships with their subjects. The more people trust you, the more willing they will be to invite you into their lives in difficult moments and to share their deeper feelings with you on camera.

The introduction of the release form is also your chance to discuss the long-term relationship between you and your subjects. For many filmmakers, this is the point where you can negotiate other questions involving editorial control and how much involvement you are willing to offer. Are certain topics off-limits? Will you show subjects a cut before exhibiting the film? Will you offer them some level of control? Despite a shared perspective you may have, and your efforts to treat people fairly, your goals as a filmmaker are never identical with those of your subjects. Often the process of filmmaking is a strong bonding experience, and it is important to establish boundaries early on so that subjects don't later expect something you can't or won't deliver.

It is not uncommon for a subject to have second thoughts about being in a film, especially if their situation changes or tension develops with the filmmakers. Without a signed release, a subject can legally and legitimately insist on being removed from the project, leaving you in one of the worst binds filmmakers can find themselves in.

CHAPTER 5
Documentary Ethics and Legal Issues

Even when you have consent, participants can feel misled. French documentarian Nicolas Philibert selected Georges Lopez and the students in his one-room rural school from over a thousand possible schools to be the focus of a film, and then spent seven months filming with him and his pupils to make the hit documentary *Etre et Avoir* (2002) (Figure 5.1). The film was a big success, and brought in some 2 million euros for its producers.

In a lawsuit waged by Lopez against the film's producers, Lopez claimed he was not given a clear picture of the scope of the project, and demanded 250,000 euros on the grounds that the film was partially his creation and that his teaching methods were his intellectual property. Philibert in return asserted that "one of the founding principles of documentary filmmaking is to not install relationships of subordination. If you start paying people in documentaries, they become your employees." The French court ruled against Lopez, noting that he was basically doing what he would normally do: teaching kids. Lopez didn't pick shots, or define the film's approach. He did spend time answering questions, but again, that is typically what interviewees do in documentaries, and he had given his consent for that.[3,4]

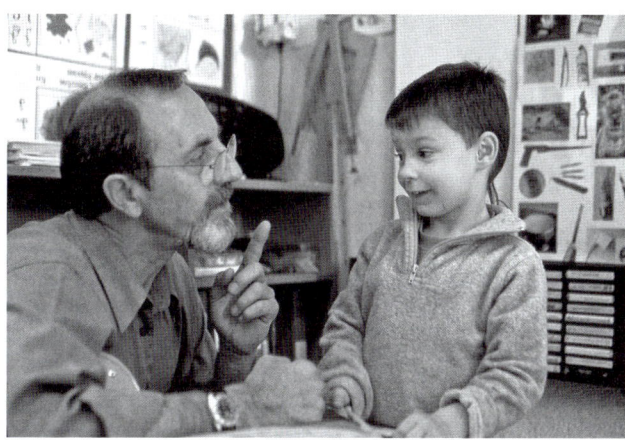

■ **Figure 5.1** Georges Lopez, a teacher in a French village school, is the main character of documentary *Etre et Avoir* (2002). The film's success led him to sue the filmmaker.

The film's producers did offer Lopez some money by way of settlement, but he turned it down. They had also done something rather atypical initially: they had contributed support to the school itself. While it is difficult to draw general conclusions from one case, it is worth remembering that as a filmmaker, you should try to present a realistic sense of what the outcomes might be for participation in your film project.

One important way of thinking about this comes from social science research; it is the idea of **informed consent**. This principle suggests that you make it clear to your subjects what your film is about and what their role will be, and what the possible consequences of participation might be. The practical realities of merging these ethical standards with normal production practice are difficult but worth contemplating. In addition to making ethical sense, informed consent is prudent for the filmmaker. Contracts are only binding if both parties understand what they are signing. If a subject who appears in your film shows up in court and says, "They just told me I had to sign this and never explained what it was," they may have a case.[5]

Producer and attorney Andrew Lund makes the point that in order for your subject to grant informed consent, you need to understand the release form yourself. Pulling a release form off the Internet and handing it to your subject is not responsible or reasonable. Take time to understand exactly what the release says before presenting it to anybody. Finally, make sure the release asks only for what you really need. Lund says:

> *Some release forms are much broader than you need, and asking subjects to sign them can be damaging to your relationship. Many releases give the filmmaker the right to reassign the rights to use the footage to any third party, regardless of who they are and what they are using it for. A subject should be able to agree to be in your film, and grant you any rights necessary to distribute your film, without giving you the right to license the footage for use in a beer commercial! It's not hard to craft an agreement that allows you the rights you need to make and distribute your film, without making your subject unnecessarily vulnerable.*[6]

Who Gets to Represent Whom?

Questions of voice, authority, and authorship became a serious concern among anthropologists in the 1950s, and the concerns flowed through to documentary filmmaking. Who can represent someone else, and with what intention? These questions are even more acute when we consider that documentary filmmakers often come from more privileged environments than those they are representing, and that simply having the means, training, and outlets to represent others creates an inherently unequal power dynamic.

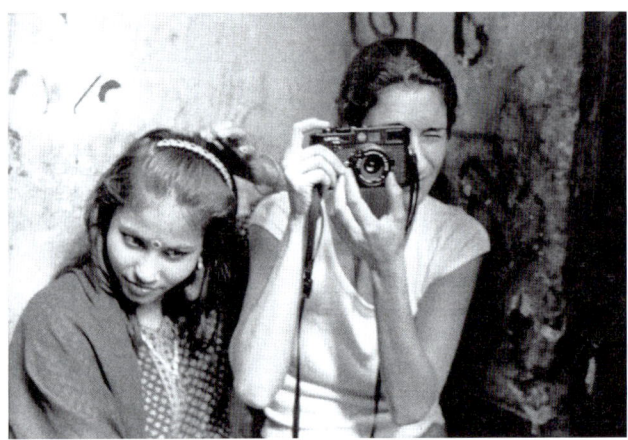

■ **Figure 5.2** Zana Briski, the director of *Born Into Brothels*, with one of the Indian children who were her subjects. Photo by Tumpa.

Zana Briski, the director of *Born into Brothels* (2004), started by teaching photography to the children of Indian sex workers in Kolkata (Figure 5.2). In the course of her work, she became deeply involved in the lives of the children who were the subjects of her Academy Award®-winning film. She ended up not only using the images taken by the children to describe their reality, but transforming their lives extensively, even taking them on trips abroad and getting them into boarding schools. Although money generated by her project provided real opportunities for at least some of the children, the film triggered a storm of criticism in India.

> *In their advocacy of Sonagachi's children ... the directors have turned the tables on their mothers (and fathers). We see them at their worst: drugged, screaming at the children, shooing them away when clients arrive, fighting with one another, obstructing Briski's efforts to give her students a future. If the children of Sonagachi enjoy moments of intimacy or comfort with their parents, we are not privy to them. It may just be possible that this is, in fact, the reality of the lives of the children Briski documents. No effort, however, is made to lead the audience into the shoes of the sex workers:* Born into Brothels *reduces them to props.*[7]

Others felt her approach was paternalistic, a criticism that resonates particularly strongly, given the history of colonial domination in India. A review in the Indian national magazine *Frontline* summarized this criticism: "If *Born into Brothels* were remade as an adventure-thriller in the tradition of *Indiana Jones and the Last Crusade*, its posters might read: 'New York filmmaker Zana Briski sallies forth among the natives to save souls.'"[8]

While for some Indians Briski's film had a paternalistic flavor, it can also be said that as an outsider, she was offering a voice to children who would otherwise live their lives in the shadows of a society that offered them no voice and no future. Before making the film, she spent three years working with the children on photography projects, and she continued to work with them, even setting up a foundation to help support their life goals. For her, the involvement and the effort to empower specific children highlighted a terrible inequality. And the specific act of giving the children cameras and encouraging them to see and document the world around them was empowering as well as very moving for audiences, as the film's many awards attest.

One solution to the problem of relating to subjects is to have the community represent itself. In the late 1960s, new portable video equipment first made filming by nonexperts possible, and documentary makers such as George Stoney, working with Challenge for Change and the National Film Board of Canada (NFB), developed a documentary approach that put the camera in the hands of the communities being represented. Films like *You Are on Indian Land* (1969) and *VTR St. Jacques* (1968) allowed people to represent their own situations and represented a notable breakthrough in the understanding of local issues and marginalized communities.

While self-representation is an important development in documentary history, it does not necessarily guarantee a good film. Often people will represent themselves the way they want to be seen, rather than in the most insightful way. Many of the best documentaries create a picture of a situation from multiple, often conflicting, points of view. For this and other reasons, most documentary filmmakers still end up in the more ethically challenging situation of representing others. This is not necessarily negative. An outsider can often see patterns and relationships that the people involved cannot see clearly. This is particularly true in our modern era of globalization where even the most local issues can be affected by outside players and forces.

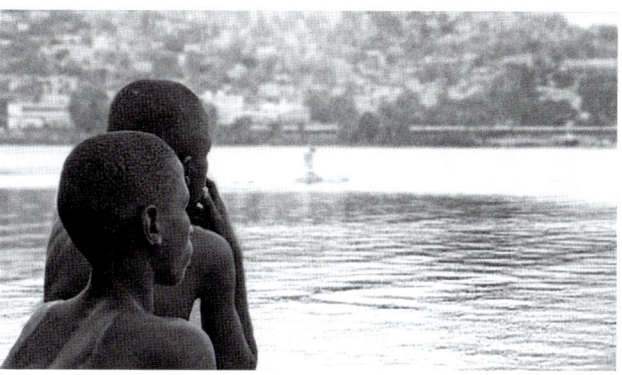

Figure 5.3 In *Darwin's Nightmare*, director Hubert Sauper draws on a range of local knowledge and knits it into a dense tapestry based on his outsider perspective on the situation in Tanzania.

Some films, although made by outsiders, can be very helpful in creating an understanding of the predicament a community is facing. In Hubert Sauper's *Darwin's Nightmare* (2004), the residents of a fishing town on the shores of Tanzania's Lake Victoria live harrowing lives, exporting giant fish, surviving on the edge of starvation, devastated by AIDS and poverty, while the wealth they produce flows to European arms manufacturers supplying endless African wars (Figure 5.3). Sauper makes a point of building his investigation with local knowledge from interviews with people others would overlook: security guards, street kids, prostitutes, as well as foreign pilots and factory owners. By bringing all of these players together with an eye towards the larger picture, the filmmaker helps us see that this is not a local problem, but a perverse system in which globalization as well as the demands of normal European and American consumers are the core problem.

At other times, outsiders can tell a story that would be unsafe for locals to expose. An example is *Burma VJ: Reporting from a Closed Country* (2008), a film by Danish director Anders Ostergaard about undercover video journalists in Burma. The film could not have been made by filmmakers within that country because of the repressive nature of the government. It was nominated for a Puma Creative Impact Award for "putting the issue of Burma firmly on the international agenda," "helping to bring about the release of [opposition leader] Aung San Suu Kyi," and "inspiring a new generation of VJs and independent journalists within Burma."[9]

There are simply no hard and fast rules about who gets to represent whom, and under what circumstances. Probably the best advice is to think seriously about the privileges you have and consider the impact of your filming on those you are representing. Ask yourself why you want to do the story you are doing. In *Directing the Documentary*, Michael Rabiger suggests you check your "embedded values," and ask yourself key questions about your assumptions about class, race, appearance, speech, and background. Also, try to consider how you are representing the environment, family or social dynamics, and who has or gets authority in your work.[10]

Of course, many times, power relations will be reversed and filmmakers will find themselves speaking with subjects who represent power and authority, whether social or political. How do our obligations to them differ? Legal opinion in the United States suggests that public officials can be held to different standards based on the public's "right to know" in a democratic society, including a higher burden of proof for libel, which means that you may be on safer ground exposing information about them than about a private citizen.

But what about people who are not political figures? Very often, documentary filmmakers find themselves in the position of making the lives of the rich, powerful, and privileged uncomfortable. Here, the rights of individuals might be trumped, at least for the filmmaker, by the greater good. In *Inside Job* (2010) for example, filmmaker Charles Ferguson feels free to put his interview subjects, who are some of America's key financial players, on the spot, to the point where some of them walk off the set to escape his grilling. His logic is that these are the extremely powerful members of the financial community, the government, and academia whose collusion allowed the 2008 financial crisis to take place, so why ask only softball questions that allow them to use his film as another opportunity for a PR spin?

In real life, of course, people fall on a spectrum in terms of how much power and responsibility they have, and documentary filmmakers are no exception. This means that you as a filmmaker will always have to make difficult decisions. These decisions will resonate out in the world, so make sure that you can live with them.

The Impact of Money

Paying subjects is a deeply thorny issue in documentary circles. It is anathema in journalism, because it is considered to compromise the integrity of the source. But in documentary, you are sometimes asking people to be involved with your project for weeks, months, or even years. While most documentary filmmakers do not pay their subjects directly, they may seek to compensate them in some way for their time. Whether this happens before production or after the film is completed varies. We do know anecdotally that some filmmakers feel an ethical responsibility to the people whose stories make their films possible, and that sometimes this translates into a financial giveback. A very public example would be Zana Briski, who as mentioned above actually set up a foundation to fund the educations of the children who are featured in *Born into Brothels* (www.kids-with-cameras.org). One big problem with paying people up front is that it may make them feel obligated to spin a story to meet your expectations. A workaround is to pay subjects for **exclusivity**, compensating them for not offering their story to another media maker for a specific period of time.

Another key principle derived from journalistic ethics is that you should not accept support from sources who have an interest in how things are represented in your film. The Radio-Television News Directors Association cautions against "accepting gifts, favors, or compensation from those who might seek to influence coverage."[11] This is a tricky area for documentary filmmaking, where funding is hard to come by and where it is common for an organization interested in a specific topic to support media production about that area. It is up to you to be clear with funders that you plan to stay independent and represent things as you see them. Be aware that if there is any possibility of exhibiting on US public television, you will be dealing with strict guidelines for funding from interested parties. According to PBS, these guidelines are intended to ensure that:

> *editorial control of programming remains in the hands of the producer, that funding arrangements will not create the perception that editorial control was exercised by someone other than the producer, or that the program was inappropriately influenced by its funding sources.*[12]

Handling Delicate Situations

Because many documentaries deal with subject matter that is controversial or that exists at the margins of society and legality, you will undoubtedly need to confront situations where it's unclear whether you should film or not. These include:
- Situations where people are doing something illegal
- Situations where violence is occurring in front of the camera
- Surreptitiously gathered images

- Illegally obtained footage
- Situations where your footage may put the subject at risk

All of these situations present moral dilemmas. Filming people injecting illegal narcotics, for example, can be seen as damaging to their reputations, putting them at legal risk, and gratuitous (meaning you are showing the act for sensational reasons that are not integral to the story). But the same material might also be significant as a way of representing a social reality that many would rather ignore. It depends on the context you establish, and the relationship of the scene to the overall thesis of your film. Only you can make the decision, and decide that you are including potentially sensational material for the right reasons.

Obtaining material illegally seems like an unwise thing to do, and it can be. But what if you are a journalist who gets inside information about malfeasance in high places? You may feel that there is a "right to know" that overrides the government's information restrictions. For example, laws promoted by agricultural interests in Utah and Iowa have made the recording of undercover videos showing animal cruelty in farming practices illegal. You might decide that breaking this law to expose inhumane farming practices is a risk you are willing to take in the interest of public education and debate on the issue. Clearly we can't advocate breaking the law. You should assess the risks of any potentially illegal action for yourself.

The same is true for images that are gathered surreptitiously. In the case of Ying Chang, Peter Kwong, and Jon Alpert's *Snakeheads* (1994), the filmmakers were trying to explore illegal trafficking in indentured labor and posed as labor contractors. They arranged a meeting with traffickers in a restaurant in China, and filmed the meeting with a hidden camera (Figure 5.4). They used the material in the film to show how brazen the trade in human beings is. We see them bargaining over price, quantity, and delivery dates, creating incontrovertible evidence for the existence of the trafficking problem they are highlighting.

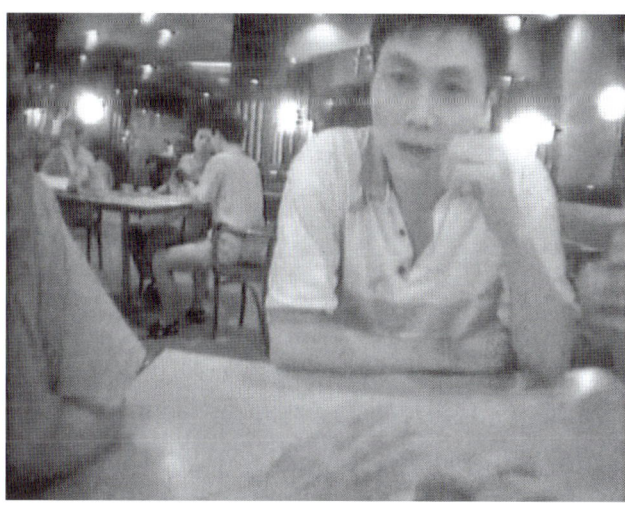

■ **Figure 5.4** This meeting with labor traffickers in a restaurant in China was filmed with a hidden camera for a documentary exposé of the trade in human beings, in *Snakeheads*.

Putting your subjects at risk by, say, outing them as lesbian or gay, is something else you need to discuss with them before it happens. Similarly, there are times when subjects may be put at risk because of repressive governments or other social factors, and speaking publicly may lead to retaliation later. While you can never be sure of the consequences your film will have, it is crucial that you think these possible outcomes through and be as responsible as you can.

■ RESPONSIBILITY TO YOUR AUDIENCE: OBJECTIVITY AND FAIRNESS

Ethics also involves your responsibility to a viewing public. Here is where terms like **bias**, **balance**, and **objectivity** are commonly discussed. There are important overlaps between documentary practices and journalistic ones, and important differences.

In decades of teaching documentary, the authors have found that students cling to the idea that documentaries should be "balanced" and "objective," meaning that they should not take sides or claim a strong position, especially one far outside of the mainstream. This problematic expectation emerges from the history of American television news. As Barry Hampe states:

> *The very notion of objectivity in documentary is a fairly recent development in the history of the genre. It is an outgrowth of the peculiar rules governing American network television, and a basic misunderstanding of both the requirements of journalistic objectivity and of the nature of scientific objectivity. Certainly the pioneers of documentary made no pretense of using a journalistic approach in their films, and would have found any discussion of journalistic "objectivity" totally irrelevant. They unashamedly used the documentary to make as powerful a statement as they could manage about something they considered important.[13]*

The early Soviet documentaries, as well the British documentaries described in Chapter 2, would seem to support this claim. The way journalists tend to approach balance is by giving a counterpoint to every point. The problem with this is that a false balance can actually obscure reality. For example, even though 99 percent of scientists believe that global warming is caused by human activities, a study of articles in The New York Times, The Wall Street Journal, The Los Angeles Times, and The Washington Post between 1988 and 2002 showed that 53 percent of stories gave equal attention to scientists who claimed global warming was a natural phenomenon.[14] This fulfilled the need for balance, but created a false impression of controversy in the scientific community, where actually there is strong consensus.

For contemporary documentary filmmakers, ideas of objectivity and balance have largely been replaced by one of "fairness." We can still borrow certain principles from journalism, such as the idea that facts should be verifiable. You should resist omitting or obscuring evidence or information that contradicts your central claims. Anderson and Gold's *Every Mother's Son (2004)*, for example, was built around the idea that the young men killed were innocent. If the filmmakers had discovered, in the process of making the film, that one of them had actually been carrying a gun, or was involved in a crime at the time they were killed, it would have been inappropriate and misleading to eliminate those facts from the film's representation of the events.

The line between what is acceptable and what isn't can be blurry. Michael Moore ignited a huge controversy when he manipulated the chronology of events in his film *Roger and Me* (1989). He claimed that a cash register was stolen during Ronald Reagan's visit to an Italian restaurant, but it had been stolen a few days earlier. Moore portrayed the construction of the Auto World theme park and a Hyatt Regency hotel as happening after the mass layoffs of General Motors workers in Flint, Michigan, in 1986, when in fact they were built before. Moore dismissed the criticism as a nonissue, arguing he was making a "movie" rather than a news documentary.[15] Some critics called Moore to task for these lapses, while others defended them as necessary for exposing the "larger truth" of corporate America's indifference to its workers. Where you draw the line on these types of issues will be your own decision, but be aware that sloppiness can open the door to criticism.

RESPONSIBILITY TO OTHER CREATORS: INTELLECTUAL PROPERTY RIGHTS

The digital age and the advent of the Internet have made literally billions of images, sounds, and moving image clips available at the push of a button. Documentary filmmakers, who are often talking about historical events or faraway places, often find themselves wanting to use material produced by others. The ethical aspect of this is clear. If you use someone else's footage, music, or imagery, you need to get their agreement or compensate them in some way. This is a standard aspect of filmmaking. Typically, when you buy the right to use a still image, a piece of music, a sound effect, or a film clip in your work, you will have to sign a **licensing agreement** that spells out the specific ownership rights you are obtaining and what you are paying in return for those rights.

Copyright laws, which started in England in the 1700s, acknowledge the rights of the creator in any work. These laws vary from country to country. Currently in the United States, they protect a work for up to 75 years after the death of the author. The goal of copyright is to protect work long enough for the maker to profit from it. While the rights of the maker are acknowledged, they have to be seen in relation to other rights, broadly speaking the right to speak of and from a common culture.

Culture is a shared field, a common heritage that artists can draw on. Digital media and the Internet have contributed to the spread of **remix culture,** where creators can easily borrow and adapt images and sounds created by others. In addition, since the advent of the electronic age, big players in the entertainment industry have been working to protect their own interests by extending the reach of copyright law. This has brought the broader discussion of cultural production underlying intellectual property into new prominence. Documentary filmmakers can find themselves on conflicting sides of these debates. On the one hand, we rely on sales of our work to make back money spent on production and to support ourselves. On the other, we find ourselves increasingly burdened by expensive licensing fees for film clips, songs, and photographs. One alternative to clearing images is to use materials with Creative Commons licenses, which are more flexible and vary their permissions with the use to encourage sharing (Chapter 20).

Fair Use

There is some flexibility in copyright law that can be of specific benefit to documentary filmmakers. **Fair use** is a doctrine written into law in some countries, including the United States, which allows creators to use copyrighted material in certain specific contexts (see Chapter 20 for a more complete discussion of fair use). One of the most important aspects of fair use is the idea that you can use copyrighted material if you are offering a social or political critique of the material. An example would be Robert Greenwald's documentary *Outfoxed: Rupert Murdoch's War on Journalism* (2004). In order to support his claim that a pervasive right-wing bias and a lack of journalistic standards pervades Fox Network despite its claims to offer "fair and balanced" journalism, Greenwald made extensive use of Fox's own broadcasts. He intercut the footage with interviews with former Fox News reporters, analysis of specific coverage, and a look at Fox's position in the larger media sphere. In this case, the use of Fox's broadcast material was firmly situated within a critique and was thus covered by fair use (Figure 5.5).

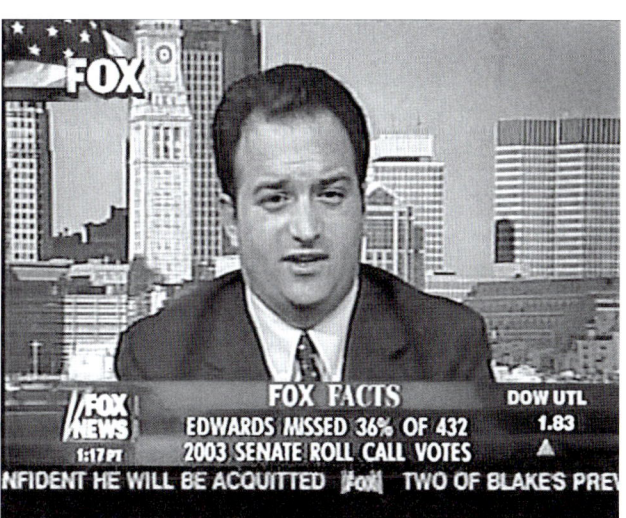

■ **Figure 5.5** *Outfoxed: Rupert Murdoch's War on Journalism* uses images from Fox News, under "fair use" doctrine, to critique that network's news handling practices.

Finally, there are no copyright issues when using material that is in the **public domain**. The public domain is the term for material that has aged out of copyright, was produced before copyright existed, or was produced for the public (typically material made by government agencies). For more information on where to find public domain images, see Chapter 20.

CONCLUSION

This chapter has offered a variety of very important concerns for filmmakers. Remember it is a guide, not a roadblock! In our experience, students may become overwhelmed or even paralyzed by the kind of questions we are raising in this chapter. The point of ethics is not to prevent you from doing things, but rather to help guide you toward a practice that is thoughtful, rich, and responsible to both your subjects and your audience.

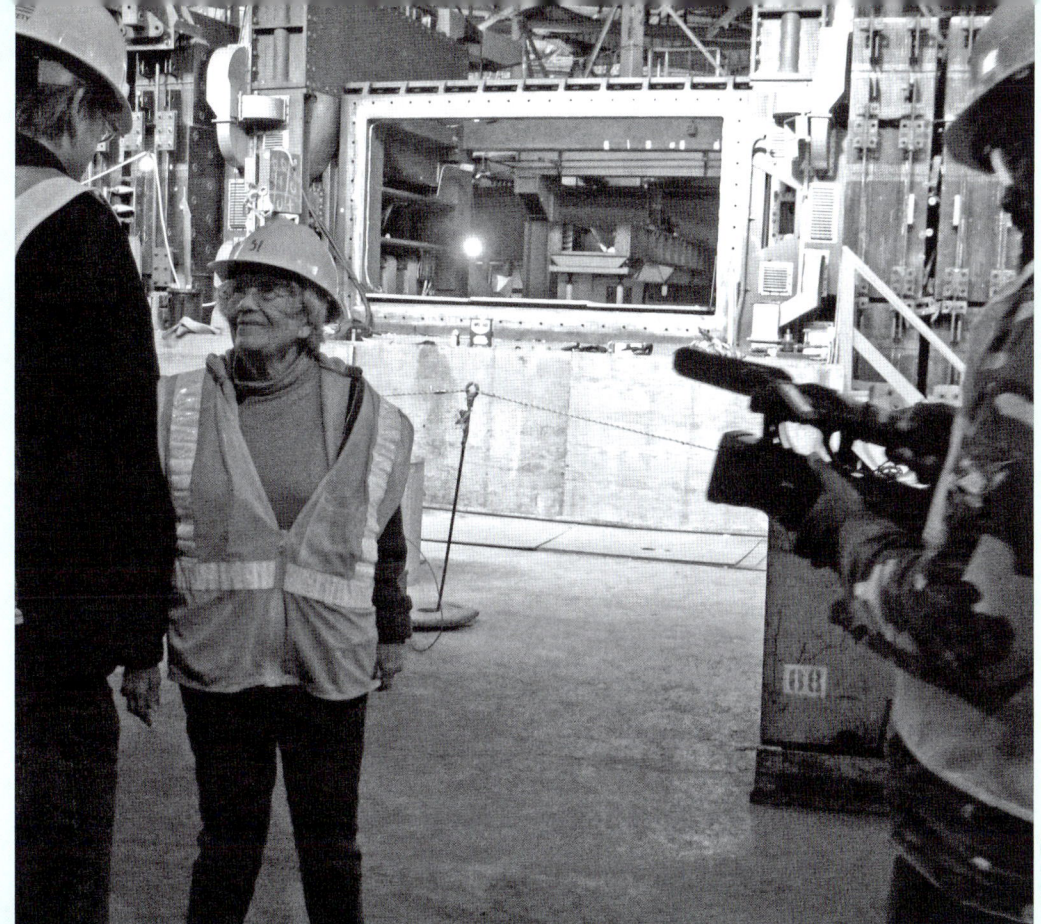

PART 2 PRODUCTION

CHAPTER 6

Planning the Shoot

Making a documentary, on any scale or in any format, is a multipronged effort. On the one hand there is the creative dimension, which involves conceptualizing a project (sometimes called **ideation**), writing the proposal and treatment, developing your style, finding subjects to follow and people to interview, visualizing the shots and sequences, and so on. Then there is the practical dimension of documentary film production, which involves the organizing of time and personnel, coordinating travel and locations, dealing with equipment and workflow, and working with budgets.

These **production management** aspects of a film have a big impact on what audiences see on screen. All filmmakers have had the unpleasant experience of losing a day of shooting because someone forgot to pack a critical piece of equipment, or to confirm with an interviewee. Often these mistakes can cost dearly—when you are dealing with real-life events, there is sometimes no "rain date." Many events happen only once, and if you arrive late, or without batteries, or if you weren't even aware that a critical event was taking place, you risk losing the moment forever.

The creative side of filmmaking and the practical side need to remain in close dialogue with one another for the duration of every film project, big or small. Balanced and proper attention, as well as a healthy collaboration between crew members, assure a successful process and a satisfying project. Every film shoot, from the smallest to the largest, involves unforeseen challenges, extenuating circumstances, and unanticipated difficulties. To deal with these adequately, you must make sure that all of those production elements that you can control, plan, and prepare for are taken care of.

CREW SIZE

The smallest documentary crew is the "one-man band," where one person directs, films, and handles sound (Figure 6.1). There are advantages to a small crew; it keeps the budget down and heightens the intimacy of a shooting situation. Some experienced filmmakers create wonderful work flying solo, but having one person do everything is not an advisable choice for the beginning filmmaker. Even seasoned professionals usually prefer to hand off some responsibilities to others.

For example, remaining conscious of sound while handling the technical and creative aspects of camerawork is challenging for even experienced filmmakers. A separate sound person is a great investment. They can get a microphone closer to your subject, and more specifically positioned, resulting in noticeably better sound. A sound recordist can also adjust sound levels as you film, avoiding overmodulation and guaranteeing a healthy sound level throughout (Chapters 13 and 14).

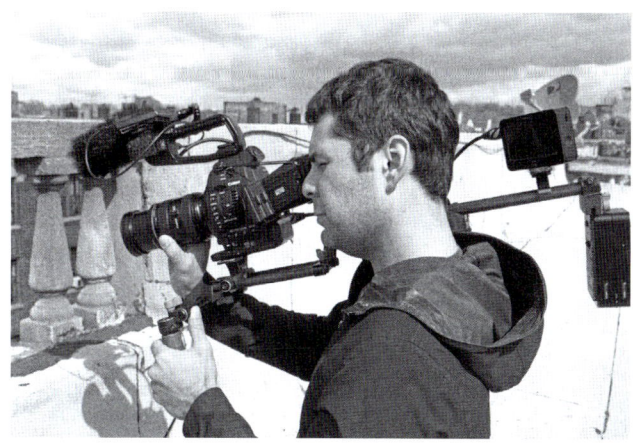

■ Figure 6.1 "One-man band" filmmaking. Here cinematographer David Alvarado works with a Canon C100 camera and two camera-mounted microphones: a short shotgun and a wireless microphone receiver (with the transmitter on the subject).

David Alvarado, who directed (with Jason Sussberg) and did the camerawork for *The Immortalists* (2014), explains that crew size depends on the situation you are shooting in.

For some really intimate stuff I'd rather just shoot it and do the audio myself. In my thesis film I shot a love scene between a person with a traumatic brain injury and his girlfriend. I didn't want somebody with a microphone up in their business. If you think about the standard car interview, you put a lavalier on the person, put a microphone on top of the camera, and you can't get better audio than that. But if it's a vérité event, where one person is going to be going around talking to different people—people who aren't miked—there's no way around having a separate sound recordist. Because if you can't hear somebody saying something, the scene is really kind of lost.[1]

Many directors prefer to bring in a separate cameraperson. This leaves the director free to focus on directing, conducting interviews, and connecting with their subjects. This is another wise choice. Most interviewing conventions require that your interviewee avoid looking directly into the camera lens, and often this is achieved by having the interviewer sit next to the lens while they are asking questions and listening to the person being interviewed. This setup makes it almost impossible to shoot and interview at the same time.

Throughout documentary history, there have been many two-person directing teams where one person shoots and the other interviews and does sound. A veteran example is the team of David and Albert Maysles (Figure 6.2). But very often a director will prefer not to handle any of the technical aspects so they can focus on other things, which would result in a three-person team (Figure 6.3). You can also find **production coordinators**, **associate producers**, and/or **production assistants** on many documentary shoots.

Nowadays, with most documentaries shooting onto card media, the crew will likely include either a **digital loader** or a **digital imaging technician**. These jobs are similar in that they involve downloading media from the cards into a computer or onto hard drives, but the digital imaging technician will also be involved in media management, preparing media for editing, transcoding, syncing picture, and sound, and other advanced tasks.

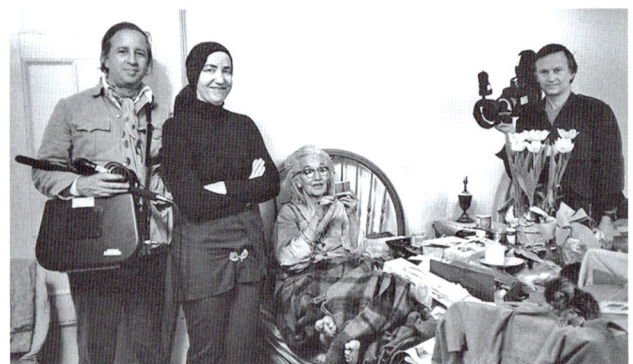

■ **Figure 6.2** Albert (right) and David Maysles make up a two-person crew for this scene with "Big Edie" and "Little Edie" Bouvier for their film *Grey Gardens* (1973).

A large documentary crew may include a **gaffer** and **grips**. A gaffer helps with lighting, while grips handle any complicated camera support (dollies and cranes, for example) and deal with any electrical needs that go beyond the basics. Larger crews may also include a separate sound mixer to accompany the boom operator, an assistant camera person, a driver, several production assistants, and even hair and makeup. In the end, you will find the style that works best for you. Just remember that filmmaking is hard work, and much is gained by bringing together the talents and energies of more than one person.

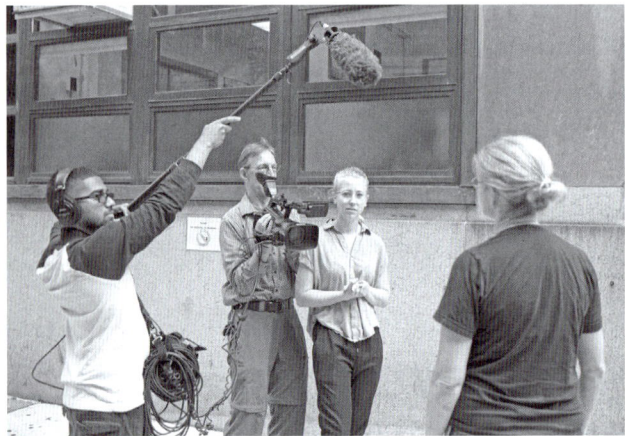

■ **Figure 6.3** This typical three-person documentary crew has a director working with a sound recordist and cinematographer.

CREW RESPONSIBILITIES

The **documentary director**'s role is to be responsible for the vision of the film, making sure that all the things you will film and all the other elements you gather have the potential to add up to a coherent story (no small task!), and communicating this vision to the crew. Before production, the director should meet with the **cinematographer** to discuss the look and shooting style of the film. They also decide which events, people, and environments to shoot, and are responsible for developing fruitful working relationships with the subjects of the film. The director's preparation for a shoot can include coming up with interview questions, developing shot lists, and, in the case of a highly constructed film, even storyboarding. While shooting more observational scenes, preparation involves having a strong sense of the dramatic core of your story so that you can recognize and capture important moments that unfold spontaneously.

The **documentary producer**'s job varies from project to project, but it always includes raising the funds for the film, budgeting, and making sure the film is delivered on budget. Producing may also involve hiring crew, finding film subjects and locations, and helping develop the vision for the project. Quite often, the director and the producer on a documentary are the same person. A **line producer** is a producer who focuses specifically on the daily logistics of the shoot.

The **cinematographer** is responsible for shooting the film, including lighting interviews and scenes, capturing the image, framing the compositions, choosing the length of the shots and deciding which elements within the frame to emphasize—often in a series of split-second decisions. Since it's impossible to storyboard observational documentary scenes because you don't know how the action will unfold, the cinematographer needs to communicate with the director before shooting to develop a clear understanding of the story, including who the central characters are, and what action is important. Together they devise a shooting strategy for every event they shoot. See Chapter 7 for more on coverage for documentary scenes.

A **sound recordist**'s primary function is to make sound recordings of outstanding quality, free from interference and all unwanted noise. They also work to ensure that the location is as quiet as possible. The sound recordist decides on a sound recording strategy for a given scene, and places microphones. On a documentary, the sound recordist often operates a boom mic and carries a recorder and/or mixer in a shoulder-mounted bag. In addition to synchronized production sound, they may also record sound effects, ambience, and other nonsynchronous sound elements to be used in editing (Chapters 13 and 14).

An **associate producer** or **production coordinator** handles a variety of tasks including confirming locations and meeting times, coordinating transportation, helping things stay on schedule, making sure release forms are signed, and generally providing backup for the director and other crew.

Production assistants lend extra help to a production, whether that means running to the next location with extra equipment, grabbing lunch or parking the car. In foreign locations, the production assistant will be replaced by a **fixer**, someone who knows the lay of the land, speaks the local language, or has other specialized knowledge that will help ease your way.

LOCATIONS

Documentaries are rarely shot on a stage or set. You will most likely be filming where the action is unfolding, whether in someone's home, in an office, driving in a car, or outdoors. The unpredictable nature of capturing reality makes planning difficult, but there are things you can do to maximize the possibility of success. While a **location scout** is a defined job in fiction filmmaking, in documentary it is typically someone on the production crew—the director, producer, cinematographer, or a combination—who will be involved in location choices. For instance, if you want to interview someone, they may offer you a choice of their office or their home. You may actually decide you would prefer them walking around their neighborhood to add a bit of dynamism to the interview. Each of these three options offers advantages and disadvantages.

When possible, it is a good idea to do a **location survey** ahead of time. This may occur a few days, or a few hours, before the shoot. Note that location surveys are not the same thing as "location scouting." Scouting means trying to find a location to film in, while the survey helps you plan a shoot in a location you've already picked. The location survey allows you to develop a sense of how your action might unfold, and where you can place the camera to capture things from the most advantageous points of view. If you are going to use lights, a survey will allow you to develop a plan for what lights to bring. It's a good idea to scout for AC outlets. Figure out where you can park your vehicle, and whether there is a separate entrance for freight (bulky equipment will often be considered freight and banned from passenger elevators). Once you are at your location, try and find a secure place where you can store equipment, and where you can **stage** from if you need to be portable and run somewhere with your subjects. Bring a notebook and sketch the dimensions and layout of your locations. This will help you remember, and to communicate later with crew members who haven't seen the location.

Surveying locations is also important for sound. Often people will describe their environment as "quiet," but when you arrive to film you find there is a loud air vent, or a barking dog next door, or that the location is right below a flight path. Any of these could necessitate finding a new location, but if you don't realize the problem exists until an hour before the interview, there is likely not going to be much you can do. The specifics of the **sound scout** are covered in Chapter 14.

Permits and Location Agreements

One other key aspect of any location survey is getting location permits (for public spaces) and location agreements (for private property). Different municipalities handle permits differently. The organization Film London notes, "Whatever location you are using, no matter how public it seems, it is likely you'll need to notify or get permission from somebody."[2] Permits issued by New York City's government are designed for feature film crews and will generally not be needed for a documentary crew. However, it is worth noting that it was only in 2006 that New York stopped demanding a permit for any filming with a tripod on city streets. Some public locations, such as parks, universities, or monuments, will require permission for any "professional" use of their space, which usually means filming with an obvious crew, a lot of equipment, and/or a tripod. While not every camera set up on a street will bring down the arm of the law, in this security-conscious age, certain locations—bridges and tunnels, for example—are subject to special restrictions. Transportation systems are another complex area. If you want to film on a bus or train, you are well advised to seek official permission. In some countries, "panorama rights," or the right to take a picture of a building or monument, may be subject to restrictions as well.

Keep in mind that some locations may seem to be public even though they are actually private. When you are filming in a private location you don't need a permit, but you should have a signed **location agreement** that indicates the owner's permission for your filming (Figure 6.4). This will be something your insurance agents will need to have in the case of any claim.

Rules vary from place to place. It's also important to remember that these rules are often contested, and interpreted differently by law enforcement. Talking with other journalists or filmmakers in a particular place, and even consulting with legal entities such as an

LOCATION CONTRACT

Date _____

Permission is hereby granted to _____

_____

(hereinafter referred to as "Producer"), to use the property and adjacent area, located at

_____

_____

for the purpose of photographing and recording scenes (interior and/or exterior) for motion pictures with the right to exhibit and license others to exhibit all or any part of said scenes in motion pictures throughout the world; said permission shall include the right to bring personnel and equipment (including props and temporary sets) onto said property, and to remove the same therefrom after completion of work.

The above permission is granted for a period of _____

from _____

at the agreed upon rental price of _____.

Producer hereby agrees to hold the undersigned harmless of and from any and all liability and loss which the undersigned may suffer, or incur by reason of any accidents or other damages to the said premises, caused by any of their employees or equipment, on or about the above-mentioned premises, ordinary wear and tear of the premises in accordance with this agreement excepted.

The undersigned does hereby warrant and represent that the undersigned has full right and authority to enter into this agreement concerning the above-described premises, and that the consent or permission of no other person, firm, or corporation is necessary in order to enable Producer to enjoy full rights to the use of said premises, hereinabove mentioned, and that the undersigned does hereby indemnify and agree to hold Producer free and harmless from and against any and all loss, costs, liability, damages or claims of any nature, including but not limited to attorney's fees, arising from, growing out of, or concerning breach of the above warrant.

_____   _____
Signed   Company

_____   _____
Title   Signed

                                 _____
                                 Address

■ **Figure 6.4** Here is a sample location agreement (also called a "location contract").
Courtesy of Renato Tonelli, Dept. of Film and Media Studies, Hunter College.

attorney or the American Civil Liberties Union, can be helpful if you think you are being stopped from doing something you have a right to do.

Location Aesthetics and Meaning

The right location can add value and meaning to your film. Remember, viewers notice everything in the frame, and where people are interviewed can communicate information as strongly as what they say. In S. Leo Chiang's film *Mr. Cao Goes to Washington* (2012), the first Vietnamese-American US congressman is supported by Louisiana Republicans who see an opportunity to elect a Republican for the first time in decades. Cao's campaign chairpersons are filmed in their home, and Chiang chose his frame very carefully. The resulting image suggests that the people running Cao's campaign are wealthy and likely conservative, but it is all visual information that the viewer can interpret on their own (Figure 6.5).

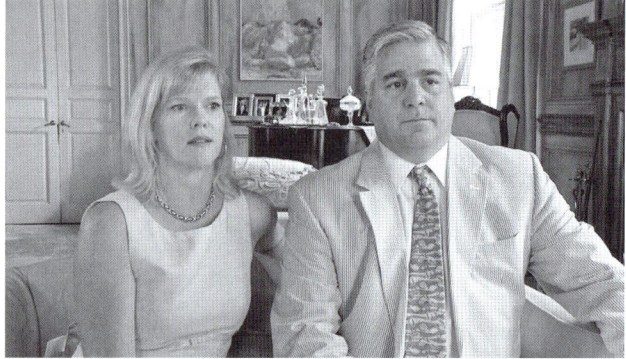

Figure 6.5 The choice of this location in *Mr. Cao Goes to Washington* helps define the characters and adds to the overall meaning of the shot.

When you are setting up an interview or scene, some directors opt to "dress the set" by rearranging objects, decorations, or furniture. Most try not to create a false sense of what the place usually looks like. Always be careful with people's belongings to avoid breakage or damage. When possible, take photographs of a location before you alter it so that you know exactly how to return it to its original state when the shoot is over.

It is quite common for people to clean up their home or office before a camera crew arrives. Sometimes this can create problems, for nothing speaks more eloquently about the busy life of a person than the natural chaos of their workspace. In order to avoid having the natural character and color drained from your location, you can ask people to avoid tidying up for you (while understanding that people have to right to some control over how they are represented). An example of a location that would have been ruined by over-cleaning is the office of Ron "Disaster Master" Alford, a clutter intervention specialist profiled in coauthor Kelly Anderson's documentary *Never Enough* (2010), about people's relationship with their material possessions. Alford's office is so cluttered that it contributes a sense of irony to the scene (Figure 6.6).

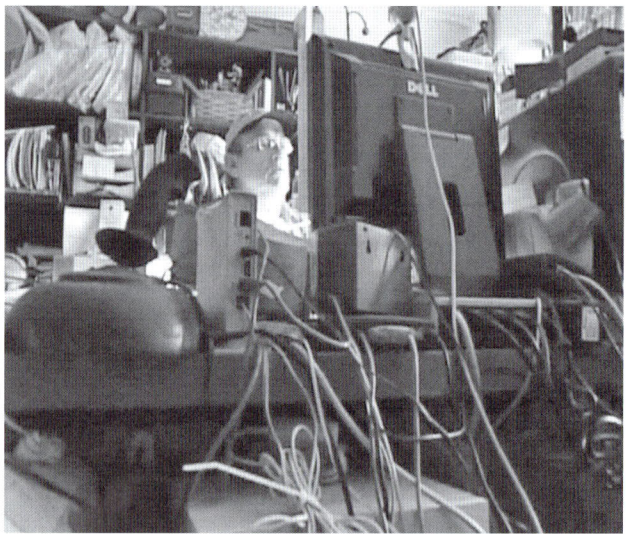

Figure 6.6 Ron Alford's cluttered office in *Never Enough* reveals character and provides an ironic twist given Alford's work as a de-cluttering consultant.

While in documentary, you can't always control the location of an event, there are times when you can persuade an interviewee to allow you to film them in the better of several options. Most corporate offices, for example, are visually boring, generic, or characterless, not to mention too cramped to allow for varied camera positions. They also tend to have sound problems. Often an interview at home or in some other location will work just as well and lend something important to your film. In *The Immortalists*, for example, one of the main characters, scientist Aubrey de Grey, has a punting boat hobby. Alvarado and Sussberg interviewed him boating on a canal, and the results reveal the beauty

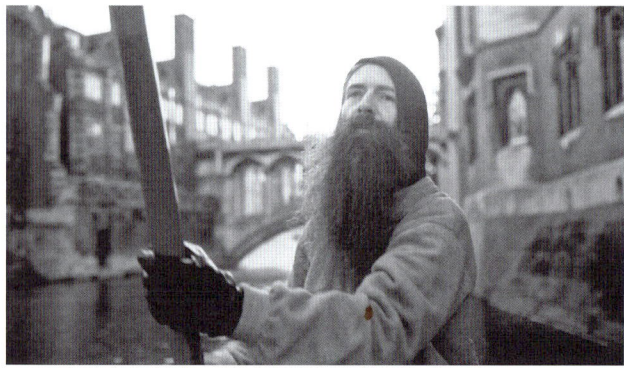

Figure 6.7 In *The Immortalists*, Aubrey de Grey is interviewed while on a punting boat. The location reinforces his solitary nature and unique personality.

of the medieval Cambridge locale and communicate something about the unique personality of de Grey, a loner who marches to the beat of his own drummer (Figure 6.7).

EQUIPMENT

There are important decisions to be made about equipment before you shoot for even a day. What kind of look do you want your film to have? Which camera and supporting equipment will allow you to achieve your goals? Is there anything in the shooting environment that makes for special equipment demands? What does your budget allow? Do you need to be highly portable, or will you use heavier equipment to get more constructed shots? Will you shoot handheld, or will you need a tripod? What are the sound recording requirements and challenges? Is there any specialized equipment (shoulder mounts, sliders, lights, microphones, field monitor) you will need? Location surveys and conversations with your key crew members will help you decide the answers to these questions.

It is also a good idea to develop a backup plan, so if you have equipment failure, you have some way of obtaining equipment on short notice. Equipment breaks down often, especially in humid or dusty conditions, so plan accordingly. The chapters on cameras and lenses (Chapters 8 and 9), camera support (Chapter 10), and sound recording (Chapters 13 and 14) will help you understand what equipment is suited to various circumstances.

THINGS TO CONSIDER WHEN SCOUTING A LOCATION:

1. **Shot opportunities.** Does the location offer the space and visual qualities needed for your film?
2. **Light considerations.** Does the location have natural light? What kind of lighting will you need to bring in?
3. **Power.** What kind of electrical supply is available? How is it fused? Where are the outlets? (Chapter 16)
4. **Sound considerations.** What kind of acoustics does the location have? Where can you detect potential problems? (Chapters 13 and 14)
5. **Storage and staging area.** Identify where equipment can be left, where you can lay out your lighting equipment, etc.
6. **Safety and security.** Is this a secure area? Will you need to leave someone to watch equipment? Where are the exits? Sprinkler systems and alarms?
7. **Logistics.** Where can you park? Where are the bathrooms? Where and what will you eat?

Lighting Considerations

Will you be using artificial lighting or working exclusively with natural light? Many of today's cameras can perform well in low light, but in some situations adding light will produce a better image and give you more flexibility in achieving your aesthetic goals. If you are bringing lights, make sure you have enough extension cords and adapters for getting grounded power cables into ungrounded sockets (Chapter 16). Many lights used for video draw a lot of electricity, so be sure you know where the fuse or breaker box is, and that you can access it during production. Colored gels (blue and orange) can be useful in situations where you are mixing artificial and natural light. Even if you aren't bringing lights, are there reflectors or other lighting tools you can bring with you to shape, diffuse, and/or block the available light? And finally, lights are bulky and weighty. You'll need someone to carry them, and help setting them up. You may need to consider getting a **gaffer**.

If you are shooting outdoors, it's a good idea to consider what time of day it will be. Direct overhead sunlight can be harsh, and a reflector or diffusion, or a plan to shoot where there is shadow, can be helpful.

Sound Recording Preparation

One of the first determinations you need to make when approaching sound is whether you will be shooting **single-** or **double-system sound**. This will depend largely on what camera you are using. Digital single-lens reflex (DSLR) cameras, because of the low quality of their sound, typically require that sound be recorded separately on a **digital audio recorder**. Professional camcorders will allow sound and image to be recorded together on the same medium. More attention will be given to sound recording setups in Chapters

13 and 14. For now, the important point is that you need to think carefully about sound and develop a strategy for your particular shoot before you arrive on set. Understanding how you plan to work with sound will determine what equipment you'll need to secure before the shoot.

Documentaries usually use some combination of wireless microphones, a boom pole and a directional microphone, a portable mixer, and headphones. Make sure that you have a hardwired backup for wireless mics, as interference can occur with even the best wireless microphones. The dynamics of your shoot will determine what specific equipment you will need. Will you be following one person, or covering a group? If you are following a main character and are planning to put a wireless microphone on them, is there a chance they will be interacting with other people whose sound you will want to pick up? Do mics need to be hidden? Are you going to be outside or indoors? If the location you are going to record sound in is very "live," you should plan to bring sound blankets and cover some of the hard surfaces to reduce echo. Again, all of these contingencies are covered in Chapters 13 and 14.

If you are shooting to digital media, you will also need to think about the computer and/or hard drives that you will need in the field to back up your media. And, make sure you have enough audio cables and batteries to power your mics and mixers. Finally, make sure you can carry your entire setup comfortably, without compromising your portability.

INSURANCE

Production insurance is required by many funders and broadcasters, as well as by many municipalities or private entities that grant location permits. While it is tempting to go without insurance on low-budget productions, it is not a good idea. Packages are available for specific periods of time, or yearly. A film production insurance package will cover liability (necessary if anybody injures themselves on your shoot or claims you harmed their property). It will also cover loss or damage to production equipment, whether rented or owned.

Workers' compensation is also a necessity for hired crew; you need to get it to comply with the law. Your insurance broker can arrange this for you, or if you are using a **payroll service** they can take care of it.

Errors and omissions insurance protects you from claims involving violation of certain personal rights such as invasion of privacy, libel, or slander. This is especially important for documentary makers, but you don't need to secure this policy until you have completed editing. The important thing at this stage is to make sure you have personal release forms from all participants in your documentary, and sources for any controversial claims you will be making.

If you are a student, your school should have information about where and how to acquire production insurance. If you are an independent filmmaker, there are several insurance companies that cater to low-budget films. In the United States, the Independent Film Project (www.ifp.org) and Fractured Atlas (www.fracturedatlas.org) are good places to start. For the United Kingdom, try the BBC's site.[3]

CREW AND COMMUNICATION

Regular and precise communication with your crew is paramount and is at the heart of successful directing. Good communication begins when someone agrees to work with you, whether for a day or for a longer term. You should work out specifics *before* you are actually on location, including:

- How many days will they work, and what are those days?
- How much will you pay them?
- Will they be treated as independent contractors, or employees? (Chapter 16)
- Are they expected to bring their own equipment? If so, are you compensating them for that?
- How will they get to the location and home again? Are you covering transportation costs?
- How long is a day's work? Will you pay them overtime for a longer day than anticipated?
- If you are going out of town, will you pay them for travel days? At what rate?
- What can they expect in terms of hotels and/or meals?
- What kind of support will they have, in terms of other crew?

Often these terms are solidified in a **deal memo** signed by the producer and the crew member. Having everybody on the same page from the beginning of production will ensure that things go smoothly.

You should have meetings with at least your key crew members prior to shooting to discuss your goals for the project, what you will be shooting, aesthetics, your opinions on your subject, and anything else that seems relevant. Listen to their ideas and contributions. As the director, you will ultimately call the shots, but the success of your film depends on everybody sharing your vision and feeling invested. Also, people will bring ideas to the table that you can use.

It is critical that you take the time to show appreciation for your crew's work. Whether people are paid or working for free, letting them know you value their contribution to your documentary will go a long way. Make sure you credit everybody who works on, or contributes to, your film. Keeping a list throughout production is a good idea since it's always hard at the end to remember every shoot in detail.

If you are using free production assistants or interns, it's nice if you can figure out a way that they can gain valuable experience on your film set. Interns expect to have to do a certain amount of running around for coffee, or feeding the parking meter, but facilitating a relationship with professional crew members who can help them learn skills is priceless and likely the reason they are working for free. Be generous with your time and contacts.

The Call Sheet

A **call sheet** is a one- to two-page document that is circulated before a shoot to everyone involved in a production (Figure 6.8). It is a vital tool that will help ensure everybody knows the following:
- Where they need to be, and at what time
- How they get to and from the location
- What they need to bring (clothing, equipment)
- Contact information for everybody on the production
- The schedule for the day
- Health and safety information

There is a sample documentary call sheet in Figure 6.8, and on our companion website (www.routledge.com/cw/Anderson).

Call Sheet #1 – Monday 6th July 2015

Film Title		
Unit Call Time: 08:00	Weather: Temp: Sunrise: Sunset: Humidity	Cloud / Sun / Chance of rain Highs of 85 degrees 05:06 20:57 60-70%

Main Production Contact		Name & Number	
Director: Line Producer: Camera: Production Assistant: Client Contact: Location Contact:	Name Name Name Name Name Name	Number Number Number Number Number Number	Email Email Email Email Email Email

Preliminary Schedule - Subject to change

Time	Action	
08:00 09:00 12:00 18:00 19:00	Unit Call & Setup Roll Camera Lunch Wrap Crew leave	Unit Wrap Time: 18:00

Location

30 Main St.
Anyplace, USA

Tel:

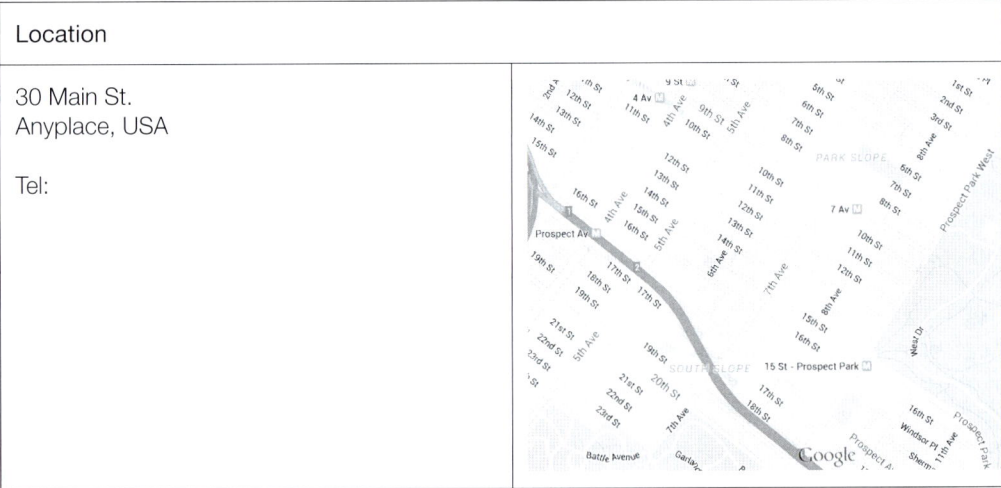

Health & Safety

- All crew to wear protective footwear (No flip flops, sandals or open toe shoes)
- All crew to wear sensible clothing (No shorts. Only jeans or long trousers permitted)

Production Requirements

Media: To be downloaded and backed up on set.
Parking: On site
Toilets: On set
Medical: List nearest hospital.

■ **Figure 6.8**
Sample call sheet.

SCHEDULING

Be realistic about how long it will take to pick up the equipment and travel to the location, set up, shoot, and pack up in each location. Remember, all this takes time! People should be at the location *at least* an hour before you plan to start filming. It is rarely advisable to film in more than two or maybe three locations in a single day (depending on how long you will be in each place).

While documentaries are by nature unpredictable, it is important to develop and maintain a schedule for the full production. This schedule should include how many production days remain, travel required for each one, what equipment is needed, how many crew members will be needed, and so on. This schedule is essential for budgeting.

BUDGETING

A good budget requires research, planning, and a vision for what you would like your documentary to be. As such, it is more than a requirement you need to produce for funding proposals. It is an essential part of your preproduction process and, in combination with cost reports, your budget is a flexible tool you will use throughout the filmmaking process to align your vision with your resources and make the most of the support you have available to you.

"Don't Fudge on Your Budget: Toeing the Line Items" is an excellent article on budgeting for documentaries that was written for the International Documentary Association's website (http://documentary.org/docbudget) by Robert Bahar.[4] We are grateful to Mr. Bahar for allowing us to adapt that article and his extensive insights for much of this section and the section below it on cost reports.

Bahar lays out a series of questions you must answer before you begin budgeting. They include:
1. What is the story you're trying to tell and what will it require? Possibilities include:
    a. Interviews (how many?)
    b. Observational shooting (how many days?)
    c. Archival materials or stock footage (how much?)
    d. Graphics and/or animation
    e. Narration
    f. Music
    g. Reenactments
2. How long will you need for each stage of production? Stages of production include preproduction, production, and postproduction. Are there any special constraints on the schedule (like a tight shooting window or a hard delivery deadline)?
3. How long will the film be? What equipment will you need for shooting and editing? How many people will be on your crew? What will your shooting ratio be? How much travel will be required? What acquisition format will you use? What will you need to "deliver" (if you have been commissioned) or have in hand for your own distribution?

One question that will inevitably come up as you start this process is, "How can I make a budget if I don't know how much money I'll be able to raise?" Bahar addresses this:

> *While some filmmakers are lucky and persistent enough to raise the necessary funds before they begin, a vast number begin shooting and even editing while still fundraising. In these cases, you'll probably need two budgets. The first budget should include "professional" rates and will be the budget that you'll submit to potential funders. The second should be the "bare bones" budget that you'll keep hidden in your desk drawer. This will be the absolute minimum amount of money needed to complete the project in a way that is acceptable to you.[5]*

In order to delve into budgeting more deeply, Mr. Bahar presents a sample documentary budget, which we have adapted for use here (Figure 6.9). Please note that this budget is for a professional feature-length documentary. *The total of $452,544 is much higher than most filmmakers, especially students or emerging filmmakers, spend!* The vast majority of independent documentaries are made for much less than $450,000, and students' documentaries can be made for a few hundred dollars. In this example, though, we are including all of the relevant expenses, at realistic rates, so that you will know what things cost in the real world, and can make your own decisions about what to cut. Do you want to bring down your number of shoot days? Pay yourself or your crew members less? Edit for fewer weeks? Use your own apartment or house as your production office? These are all choices that you are free to make, and should do based on your own circumstances. The sample budgets in this chapter are available in Excel format on our companion website (www.routledge.com/cw/Anderson).

The Budget Topsheet

The **topsheet** is a one-page summary of the budget. It generally includes some basic facts about the project, based on your production schedule. Our sample budget includes the following **constants**:

> Format: HD
> Research Phase: 6 weeks
> Prep for Shooting: 3 weeks
> Days of Shooting: 25 days (20 with sound recordist) over 8 weeks
> Wrap Shooting and Prep for Editing: 1 week
> Editing: 20 weeks
> Sound and Picture Finishing: 3 weeks
> Locations: Based in Los Angeles, includes 2 trips to New York City and 1 trip to Houston, TX

The topsheet then summarizes the budget by its major categories:

Topsheet: Sample Documentary Budget

Account	Description	Amount
1000	Project Development	$30,854
2000	Producing Staff	$70,000
3000	Rights, Music, Talent	$26,350
4000	Crew and Personnel	$150,680
5000	Production Expenses	$23,674
6000	Travel	$6,636
7000	Postproduction	$54,320
8000	Insurance	$10,300
9000	Office and Administration	$24,955
10000	Publicity	$1,300
SUBTOTAL		**$399,069**
CONTINGENCY (8%)		$31,925
FISCAL SPONSOR FEE (5%)		$21,550
GRAND TOTAL		**$452,544**

CHAPTER 6
Planning the Shoot

Program: **SAMPLE DOCUMENTARY BUDGET**
Format: HD

Producer/Director: Great filmmaker

Locations: Los Angeles, New York, Houston

Budget date: 6/1/2015

Research:	6	weeks
Prep:	3	weeks
Shoot:	25	days (over 8 wks)
Wrap:	1	weeks
Edit:	20	weeks
Total Post:	23	weeks
TOTAL:	41	weeks

	PROJECT DEVELOPMENT	#	UNIT	X	PRICE	TOTAL $ COST
1000	PRODUCING & PRODUCTION STAFF - RESEARCH/DEVELOPMENT PHASE					25,954
1010	Director/Producer/Writer	1	flat		5000	5,000
1020	Producer	1	flat		3000	3,000
1030	AP/Researcher	1	flat		2000	2,000
1040	DP	5	days		750	3,750
1050	Sound	5	days		700	3,500
1060	Editor	2	weeks		2500	5,000
1070	Production Assistants	5	days		150	750
1089	Union and Guild Fees		%			0
1099	Personnel Taxes (FICA, Medicare, payroll)	15,000	payroll		7.65%	1,148
1099	Personnel Taxes (Fixed due to wage limit - FUI, NY SUI, NY Re-Empl)	5	employees		361.30	1,807
1100	RESEARCH					1,500
1110	Books	1	allow		300	300
1120	Videos, screenings	1	allow		150	150
1130	Research meetings with potential advisors, allies, etc.	1	allow		400	400
1140	Research travel	1	allow		500	500
1190	Misc research	1	allow		150	150
1200	PRODUCTION & POST PRODUCTION OF FUNDRAISING SAMPLE					3,400
1210	Rights, Music and Talent	0	allow		0	0
1220	Production Expenses					
1221	Camera/Lighting/Grip Equip Rental	5	days		200	1,000
1222	Sound Equip Rental	5	days		150	750
1230	Travel (none)	0	days		0	0
1240	Post production (none, edited and finished on edit system)	0	allow		0	0
1250	Insurance	1	allow		1,000	1,000
1260	Office & Admin	1	allow		500	500
1270	Promotion & Publicity	0	allow		0	0
1290	Miscellaneous	1	allow		150	150
	TOTAL					30,854

	PRODUCING STAFF	#	UNIT	X	PRICE	TOTAL $ COST
2000	DIRECTORS, PRODUCERS, WRITERS					70,000
2010	Director/Producer/Writer	1	flat		50,000	50,000
2020	Producer	1	flat		20,000	20,000
2030	Executive Producer		flat		0	0
2035	Associate Producer		flat		0	0
2040	Writer		flat		0	0
2089	Union and Guild Fees		%			0
2099	Personnel Taxes (FICA, Medicare, payroll)	0	payroll		7.65%	0
2099	Personnel Taxes (Fixed due to wage limit - FUI, NY SUI, NY Re-Empl)	0	employees		361.30	0
	TOTAL					70,000

	RIGHTS, MUSIC & TALENT	#	UNIT	X	PRICE	TOTAL $ COST
3000	STORY & OTHER RIGHTS					500
3010	Story Rights		flat		0	0
3020	Title Report	1	flat		500	500
3090	Miscellaneous		allow		150	0
3100	ARCHIVAL PHOTOGRAPHS & STILLS					4,000
3110	Researcher (contractor)	1	weeks		1,400	1,400
3120	Preview fees	1	allow		150	150
3130	Shipping/messenger	1	allow		100	100
3140	Stills licensing	10	stills		200	2,000
3150	Stills duplication costs	1	allow		200	200
3190	Miscellaneous	1	allow		150	150
3200	STOCK FOOTAGE & FILM CLIPS					6,850
3210	Researcher (contractor)	1	weeks		1,400	1,400
3220	Preview tape fees	1	allow		150	150
3230	Shipping/messenger	1	allow		100	100
3240	Stock footage licensing	60	seconds		80	4,800
3250	Stock footage transfer costs	1	allow		250	250
3260	Feature Film clip licensing		seconds		0	0
3280	Feature Film clip transfer costs		seconds		0	0
3290	Miscellaneous	1	allow		150	150
3300	TALENT					0
3310	Union & Guild Performers		allow		0	0

Figure 6.9 A detail budget for our sample project. Courtesy of Robert Bahar.

PART 2
Production

		#	UNIT	X	PRICE	TOTAL $ COST
3320	Union Narrator		allow		0	0
3398	Union & Guild Fees		allow		0	0
3399	Personnel Taxes (FICA, Medicare, payroll)	0	payroll		7.65%	0
3399	Personnel Taxes (Fixed due to wage limit - FUI, NY SUI, NY Re-Empl)	0	employees		361.30	0
3400	**MUSIC/COMPOSER**					**15,000**
3410	Composer *(all-in package includes musicians, score, and recording session)*	1	flat		15,000	15,000
3420	Music Supervisor (songs, etc.)		flat		0	0
3430	Add'l Music Rights (songs, etc.)		allow		0	0
3489	Union and Guild Fees		%		0	0
	TOTAL					**26,350**

	CREW & PERSONNEL	#	UNIT	X	PRICE	TOTAL $ COST
4000	**PRODUCTION STAFF**					**82,317**
4010	Line Producer		weeks		1,600	0
4012	Unit Production Manager		weeks		1,200	0
4015	Production Coordinator	41	weeks		800	32,800
4020	Director's Assistant		weeks		600	0
4030	Director of Photography	25	days		750	18,750
4035	"B" Camera Director of Photography		days		700	0
4040	Assistant Camera		days		400	0
4060	Sound Recordist	20	days		600	12,000
4065	Add'l Boom Operator		days		400	0
4050	Gaffer		days		700	0
4070	Hair/Makeup/Wardrobe Stylist w/kit		days		500	0
4080	Production Assistant #1 (Prod Ofc during prep + shoot period)	12	weeks		600	7,200
4081	Production Assistant #2 (On-Set, Manages media & drives)	25	days		175	4,375
4098	Union & Guild Fees		allow		0	0
4099	Personnel Taxes (FICA, Medicare, payroll)	75125	salary		7.65%	5,747
4099	Personnel Taxes (Fixed due to wage limit - FUI, NY SUI, NY Re-Empl)	4	employees		361.30	1,445
4100	**EDITORIAL STAFF**					**68,363**
4110	Editor *(independent contractor)*					
	Prep/consult during shoot	0	week		2,500	0
	Edit period	20	weeks		2,500	50,000
	Post sound, online, color correction	1	weeks		2,500	2,500
4120	Assistant Editor					
	Setup edit room & system	1	weeks		1200	1,200
	Log/capture/ingest all footage	5	weeks		1200	6,000
	On-call - rest of edit period	15	days		240	3,600
	Post sound, online, color correction	3	weeks		1200	3,600
4198	Union & Guild Fees	0	allow		0	0
4099	Personnel Taxes (FICA, Medicare, payroll)	14400	salary		7.65%	1,102
4099	Personnel Taxes (Fixed due to wage limit - FUI, NY SUI, NY Re-Empl)	1	employees		361.30	361
	TOTAL					**150,680**

	PRODUCTION EXPENSES	#	UNIT	X	PRICE	TOTAL $ COST
5000	**CAMERA**					**7,074**
5010	Canon C100 Mark II package with 3 lenses	1	allow	0.50	9999	5,000
5011	64 GB SDXC cards	4	cards	0.50	64	128
5012	Canon BP-975 Battery	3	batteries	0.50	214	321
5013	Field laptop w/built-in SD card reader	1	allow	0.50	1200	600
5020	Carrying Case	1	allow	0.50	250	125
5021	Tripod	1	allow	0.50	1500	750
	Note that the camera package is budgeted at 50% of the purchase because either (1) it will be rented from a crew member under a funder's policy that rentals cannot exceed 50% of the purchase price or (2) the entire kit will be purchased at the beginning of project, and will then be sold at the end of the project for 50% of the original purchase price. Also note that on-set drives are listed under 5600.					
5030	"B" Camera pkg rentals	0	days		500	0
5031	"B" Camera accessories	0	days		150	0
5090	Miscellaneous	1	allow		150	150
5100	**SOUND**					**3,450**
5110	Sound equipment rentals	20	days		150	3,000
5120	Sound equipment purchases	0	allow		0	0
5130	Batteries & Expendables	20	days		15	300
5190	Miscellaneous	1	allow		150	150
5200	**LIGHTING & GRIP**					**2,850**
5210	Lighting & grip package rental	25	days		100	2,500
5220	Lighting & grip purchases	0	allow		0	0
5230	Expendables	1	allow		200	200
5290	Miscellaneous	1	allow		150	150
5300	**STUDIO FACILITIES**					**0**
5310	Studio facility rental		days		0	0
5320	Electricity & facility charges		allow		0	0
5390	Miscellaneous		allow		0	0
5400	**SET DRESSING**					**0**
5410	Set dressing for studio interviews		allow		0	0
5490	Miscellaneous		allow		0	0
5500	**WARDROBE**					**0**
5510	Wardrobe rentals for studio interviews		allow		0	0
5520	Wardrobe purchases for studio interviews		allow		0	0
5590	Miscellaneous		allow		0	0

■ **Figure 6.9** A detail budget for our sample project—*continued*

CHAPTER 6
Planning the Shoot

		#	UNIT	X	PRICE	TOTAL $ COST
5600	**PRODUCTION FILM & LAB**					**1,150**
5610	Field Drives - LaCie Rugged Drives	4	2 TB Drives		250	1,000
	(Assume max 4 hrs/~64 GB per day, 140 hrs total, need 2.5 TB total, x2 for mirror)					
5620	Tape Stock	0	tapes		0	0
5690	Miscellaneous	1	allow		150	150
5700	**LOGGING + TRANSCRIPTIONS**					**4,200**
5710	Transcriptions	35	hours		120	4,200
	(Assume 35% footage are interviews to be transcribed)					
5720	Logging verite footage (PA1 in-house)	0	allow		0	0
5800	**LOCAL EXPENSES**					**4,950**
5810	Gas/Mileage (based on current IRS mileage rate)	2000	miles		0.575	1,150
5820	Parking lots & fees	1	allow		400	400
5830	Meals (Dir/Prod, DP, Sound, PA)	75	meals		18	1,350
5840	Snacks/Craft Service	25	days		20	500
5850	Location Fees, Permits, Gratuities	1	allow		400	400
5880	Loss, Damage & Repair	1	allow		1000	1,000
5890	Miscellaneous	1	allow		150	150
	TOTAL					**23,674**

	TRAVEL	#	UNIT	X	PRICE	TOTAL $ COST
6000	**TRAVEL EXPENSES - NEW YORK**					**3,518**
6010	Airfare					
	Dir/Prod, DP from LAX to NYC	2	roundtrip		500	1,000
6020	Add'l baggage fees for equipment	2	fees		150	300
6030	Hotel					
	Dir/Prod, DP in NYC	4	hotel nights		300	1,200
6040	Incidentals & gratuities	2	days		60	120
6050	Local Transportation/Car Rental	2	days		200	400
6060	Per Diem (includes travel days) check current IRS rates					
	Dir/Prod	3	days		58	174
	DP	3	days		58	174
6090	Miscellaneous	1	allow		150	150
6000	**TRAVEL EXPENSES - HOUSTON**					**3,118**
6010	Airfare					
	Dir/Prod, DP from LAX to Houston	2	roundtrip		400	800
6020	Add'l baggage fees for equipment	2	fees		150	300
6030	Hotel					
	Dir/Prod, DP in Houston	4	hotel nights		250	1,000
6040	Incidentals & gratuities	2	days		60	120
6050	Local Transportation/Car Rental	2	days		200	400
6060	Per Diem (includes travel days) check current IRS rates					
	Dir/Prod	3	days		58	174
	DP	3	days		58	174
6090	Miscellaneous	1	allow		150	150
	TOTAL					**6,636**

	POST PRODUCTION	#	UNIT	X	PRICE	TOTAL $ COST
7000	**EDITORIAL EQUIPMENT & FACILITY**					**11,575**
7010	AVID or Premiere System, Monitors & Software	1	allow	0.50	4500	2,250
7020	Audio interface and monitor speakers	1	allow	0.50	1000	500
	Note that the edit system is budgeted at 50% of the purchase because either (1) it will be rented from a crew member under a funder's policy that rentals cannot exceed 50% of the purchase price or (2) the entire kit will be purchased at at the beginning of project, and will then be sold at the end of the project for 50% of the original purchase price.					
7030	Hard Drives/RAID 5 System	1	allow		2500	2,500
7050	Equipment Repair	1	allow		500	500
7060	Technical Support	1	allow		500	500
7070	Edit room rental	5.75	months		750	4,313
7071	Edit parking spaces (x2)	5.75	months	2	75	863
7090	Miscellaneous	1	allow		150	150
7100	**EDITORIAL SUPPLIES**					**1,020**
7110	Edit office supplies	5.75	months		95	546
7120	Edit meals & snacks	5.75	months		95	546
7130	Edit gas & mileage	250	miles		0.51	128
7140	Blank DVD media for screeners, etc.	1	allow		250	250
7190	Miscellaneous	1	allow		150	150
7200	**FORMAT CONVERSIONS**					**850**
7210	Upconversions SD to HD (incl. stock) Convert Archival to File for NLE	1	allow		700	700
7220	Downconversions HD to SD (incl. stock)		allow		0	0
7230	PAL-NTSC transfers (incl. stock)		allow		525	0
7290	Misc format conversions	1	allow		150	150
7200	**GRAPHICS & MOTION CONTROL**					**5,000**
7210	Graphics & Titles Designer	1	flat		5,000	5,000
7220	Motion Control (still photographs)	0	hours		250	0
7300	**ONLINE EDIT**					**0**
7310	Online Suite		hours		400	0
7390	Miscellaneous		allow		150	0

■ **Figure 6.9** A detail budget for our sample project—*continued*

PART 2
Production

		#	UNIT	X	PRICE	TOTAL $ COST
7400	**COLOR CORRECTION**					12,000
7410	Color Correction	30	hours		400	12,000
7500	**POST SOUND**					12,000
7510	Sound design, edit, mix, layback (combined pkg)	1	flat		12,000	12,000
7520	Voiceover Recording		hours		0	0
7590	Miscellaneous		allow		0	0
7600	**OUTPUT**					2,050
7610	Online Suite		hours		400	0
7620	Output texted, color corrected HDCAM SR Master	1	allow		950	950
7630	Output textless, color corrected HDCAM SR Master	1	allow		950	950
7640	Audio Layback		hrs		250	0
7650	QC		hrs		150	0
7690	Miscellaneous	1	allow		150	150
7700	**TRANSFERS & DUPLICATION (DELIVERABLES)**					3,850
7710	HDCAM SR Clones (Txtd & Txtlss)	2	tapes		700	1,400
7720	Downconversion to DBC (Txtd & Txtlss)	2	conversions		800	1,600
7730	Digibeta (DBC) Clones (Txtd & Txtlss)	2	tapes		200	400
7740	Beta SP copies NTSC	0	tapes		70	0
7750	DVD Copies	100	dubs		3	300
7790	Misc transfers	1	allow		150	150
7800	**SUBTITLING**					0
7810	Translation & Subtitling		minute		14	0
7820	QC		minute			0
7800	**SUBTITLING & CLOSED CAPTIONING**					2,000
7810	Translation & Subtitling	0	minute		12	0
7820	QC of Subtitles	0	minute		5	0
7830	Closed Captioning	1	allow		2,000	2,000
7900	**ADDITIONAL REQUIRED ITEMS**					3,375
7910	Transcription for "as-broadcast" cut	1	allow		350	350
7910	Transcription for Rough Cut #1, RC #2, and Fine Cut for Funder review	3	cuts		300	900
7920	Clones of all master media (approx. 20 TB across 5 x 4TB drives)	5	drives		425	2,125
	TOTAL					**54,320**

	INSURANCE	#	UNIT	X	PRICE	TOTAL $ COST
8000	**INSURANCE**					10,300
8010	General Liability insurance package	1	year		2,300	2,300
8020	Errors & Omissions Insurance	1	allow		4,500	4,500
8030	Equipment Insurance	1	year		1,000	1,000
8040	Business Auto Liability	1	year		1,500	1,500
8050	Worker's Compensation	1	year		1,000	1,000
	TOTAL					**10,300**

	OFFICE & ADMINISTRATION	#	UNIT	X	PRICE	TOTAL $ COST
9000	**OFFICE/ADMIN**					13,850
9020	Office Supplies	10	months		100	1,000
9030	Photocopy & Fax	10	months		50	500
9040	Postage	10	months		100	1,000
9050	Telephone	10	months		75	750
9060	Office Meals	10	months		120	1,200
9070	Production Office Rental	10	months		750	7,500
9071	Production Ofc Parking Spaces (x3)	10	months	3	75	750
9089	Loss, Damage & Repair	1	allow		1000	1,000
9090	Miscellaneous	1	allow		150	150
9300	**PROFESSIONAL SERVICES**					11,105
9310	Legal	1	allow		5,000	5,000
9320	Accounting & Bookkeeping Services	10	months		500	5,000
9330	Taxes	1	allow		800	800
9340	Copyright Registration	1	allow		55	55
9350	International Currency Exchange Gain/Loss		allow		0	0
9360	Bank Charges	1	allow		250	250
	TOTAL					**24,955**

	PUBLICITY, PROMOTION, WEBSITE	#	UNIT	X	PRICE	TOTAL $ COST
10000	**PUBLICITY STILLS**					1300
10010	Photographer	1	flat		1000	1,000
10020	Film, Processing, Prints	1	allow		300	300
	TOTAL					**1,300**

	SUBTOTAL					399,069
	CONTINGENCY		8.0%		399069	31,925
	FISCAL SPONSOR FEES		5.0%		430994	21,550
	GRAND TOTAL					**452,544**

■ Figure 6.9 A detail budget for our sample project—*continued*

The Detail Budget

Creating a **detail budget** (Figure 6.9) requires a lot of research. You will need to call potential crew members, vendors, postproduction facilities, hotels, and airlines for estimates (and to start negotiating rates).

You will note that our sample budget includes a number of line items where no money is being spent. Normally, these "empty" or "zero amount accounts" would not be shown, but they are included here to make the sample budget more useful as a template, so that you don't forget anything when you begin making your own budget.

Budgeting for a Low-Budget Documentary

As we discussed, $450,000 is a lot more than most documentary filmmakers will ever have to spend on a production, but the same principles can be applied to a lower-budget documentary. A budget of just under $20,000 might look more like the one in Figure 6.10.

Constants:

Format:	HD
Research Phase:	3 weeks
Prep for Shooting:	1 weeks
Days of Shooting:	10 days (10 with sound recordist) over 3 weeks
Editing:	6 weeks
Sound and Picture Finishing:	1 week
Locations:	All local, no travel

In this budget, there are some important things to note. First, there is no money allocated for the creation of a fundraising sample. You (the producer/director) are working without pay, and doing the editing yourself, without an assistant. The cinematographer and sound recordist are budgeted at a very low daily rate. There is $1,000 budgeted for some assistance with sound and picture finishing in your Nonlinear Editing System (Chapters 21 and 22). There is a small budget for licensing still photos, but not for archival or stock footage. You will do your own transcriptions. There is a small (5 percent) contingency, but no fee for a fiscal sponsor.

Every part of a budget reflects your priorities, your ability and desire to work for free, and your ability to negotiate rates with service and equipment providers. It's always a balancing act between what you need and what you can afford.

Cost Reports: Knowing Where You Are

A budget is not something to be written and left in a file cabinet. It is a living document, and if you keep careful track of your expenses and compare them to your budget periodically, you'll have a powerful tool for managing your production. For example, suppose you're early in the edit process and your editor asks whether the production can afford to keep the assistant editor on for two additional weeks. You have money in the bank today but if you spend it now, you worry that you will not be able to cover costs later. How do you make a good decision?

The answer is to look at your cost report. A cost report shows where you are in comparison to your budget at a given time, and is usually created on a periodic basis. The faster you're spending money, the more often you should create cost reports. Many funders will require cost reports at certain regular intervals.

PART 2
Production

Program: **SAMPLE SHORT DOCUMENTARY BUDGET**
Format: HD

Producer/Director: Great filmmaker

Locations: New York

Budget date: 6/1/2015

Research:	3 weeks
Prep:	1 weeks
Shoot:	10 days (over 3 wks)
Wrap:	0 weeks
Edit:	6 weeks
Total Post:	7 weeks
TOTAL:	14 weeks

	PROJECT DEVELOPMENT	#	UNIT	X	PRICE	TOTAL $ COST
1100	RESEARCH					200
1130	Research meetings with potential advisors, allies, etc.	1	allow		100	100
1190	Misc research	1	allow		100	100
	TOTAL					200

	RIGHTS, MUSIC & TALENT	#	UNIT	X	PRICE	TOTAL $ COST
3100	ARCHIVAL PHOTOGRAPHS & STILLS					500
3140	Stills licensing	5	stills		100	500
3400	MUSIC/COMPOSER					500
3410	Composer (all-in package includes musicians, score, and recording session)	1	flat		15,000	500
	TOTAL					1,000

	CREW & PERSONNEL	#	UNIT	X	PRICE	TOTAL $ COST
4000	PRODUCTION STAFF					5,000
4015	Production Coordinator	3	weeks		500	1,500
4030	Director of Photography	10	days		200	2,000
4060	Sound Recordist	10	days		150	1,500
4100	EDITORIAL STAFF					1,000
	Post sound, online, color correction	1	weeks		1,000	1,000
4120	Assistant Editor					
	TOTAL					6,000

	PRODUCTION EXPENSES	#	UNIT	X	PRICE	TOTAL $ COST
5000	CAMERA					2,050
5010	Canon C100 Mark II package with 3 lenses	10	days	1.00	200	2,000
5011	64 GB SDXC cards	2	cards	0.50	50	50
5100	SOUND					1,250
5110	Sound equipment rentals	10	days		100	1,000
5120	Sound equipment purchases	0	allow		0	0
5130	Batteries & Expendables	10	days		15	150
5190	Miscellaneous	1	allow		100	100
5200	LIGHTING & GRIP					600
5210	Lighting & grip package rental	5	days		100	500
5230	Expendables	1	allow		100	100
5600	PRODUCTION FILM & LAB					220
5610	Field Drives - LaCie Rugged Drives	2	1 TB Drives		110	220
	(Assume max 4 hrs/~64 GB per day, 140 hrs total, need 2.5 TB total, x2 for mirror)					
5800	LOCAL EXPENSES					1,240
5820	Parking lots & fees	1	allow		200	200
5830	Meals (Dir/Prod, DP, Sound, PA)	30	meals		18	540
5840	Snacks/Craft Service		allow		200	200
5880	Loss, Damage & Repair	1	allow		300	300
	TOTAL					5,360

■ **Figure 6.10** Medium-sized sample budget for a short documentary.

	TRAVEL	#	UNIT	x	PRICE	TOTAL $ COST
6000	TRAVEL EXPENSES - NEW YORK					500
6050	Local Transportation/Car Rental	10	days		50	500
	TOTAL					500

	POST PRODUCTION	#	UNIT	x	PRICE	TOTAL $ COST
7000	EDITORIAL EQUIPMENT & FACILITY					2,600
7010	AVID or Premiere System, Monitors & Software	5	weeks	1.00	500	2,500
7090	Miscellaneous	1	allow		100	100
7200	GRAPHICS & MOTION CONTROL					300
7210	Graphics & Titles Designer	1	flat		300	300
7700	TRANSFERS & DUPLICATION (DELIVERABLES)					30
7750	DVD Copies	10	dubs		3	30
	TOTAL					2,930

	INSURANCE	#	UNIT	x	PRICE	TOTAL $ COST
8000	INSURANCE					2,500
8010	General Liability insurance package	2	months		1,250	2,500
	TOTAL					2,500

	PUBLICITY, PROMOTION, WEBSITE	#	UNIT	x	PRICE	TOTAL $ COST
10000	PUBLICITY STILLS					200
10010	Photographer	1	flat		200	200
	TOTAL					200

	SUBTOTAL					18,690
	CONTINGENCY (5%)					935
	GRAND TOTAL					19,625

■ **Figure 6.10** Medium-sized sample budget for a short documentary—*continued*.

EXCERPT FROM A COST REPORT

ACCT	DESCRIPTION	UNIT	x	RATE	BUDGET	PREVIOUS COSTS a/o 12/31/2004	COSTS January 2005	ACTUAL COST TO DATE	COMMITTED COSTS	ESTIMATE TO COMPLETE	ESTIMATED TOTAL	VARIANCE UNDER / (OVER)
5000	CAMERA				7,600	3,650	730	4,380	730	3,220	8,330	(730)
5010	DP Camera Operator	10 Days	1	400	4,000	2,000	400	2,400	400	1,600	4,400	(400)
5020	"B" DP Camera Operator	0 Days	1	0	0	0	0	0	0	0	0	0
5040	Camera Package Rental	10 Days	1	$250	2,500	$1,250	$250	1,500	250	1,000	2,750	(250)
5050	Add'l "B" Camera Rental	0 days	1	$0	0	$0	0	0	0	0	0	0
5900	Misc / add'l camera equip	1 Allow	1	$300	300	$0	0	0		300	300	0
5999	Personnel Taxes (FICA,	4000 %	1	20.00%	800	400	80	480	80	320	880	(80)
6000	SOUND				6,100	3,000	630	3,630	630	2,420	6,680	(580)
6010	Sound Operator	10 Day	1	400	4,000	2,000	400	2,400	400	1,600	4,400	(400)
6011	Sound Op - Prep Days	Days	1	400	0	0	0	0	0	0	0	0
6020	"B" Sound Operator	Days	1		0	0	0	0	0	0	0	0
6040	Sound Package Rental	10 Days	1	$100	1,000	500	100	600	100	400	1,100	(100)
6050	Add'l "B" Sound Rental	Days	1	$0	0	0	0	0	0	0	0	0
6080	Batteries & Accessories	1 Allow	1	$300	300	100	50	150	50	100	300	0
6999	Personnel Taxes (FICA,	4000 %	1	20.00%	800	400	80	480	80	320	880	(80)

(1,310)

5 shoot days 1 shoot day   1 shoot day 4 shoot days

■ **Figure 6.11** Excerpt from a sample cost report. Courtesy of Robert Bahar.

By examining the report, you'll quickly be able to see if you're under budget in some areas and can allocate extra money to keep the assistant editor on, or if you're over budget in most areas and simply can't afford the additional expense.

A short excerpt from a cost report is shown here (Figure 6.11). In the left section you see the project budget. The center section shows "actual costs" that have already occurred. The right section shows "committed costs" (things you have agreed to pay in the future) and the "estimate to complete" for each line item. This "estimate to complete" column is the most subjective and perhaps the most important. It is where a producer must decide how much more money to spend in a given area. By making good decisions, you can keep the overall project from going over budget. For example, in the excerpt shown here, the camera department is running over budget by $530. This cannot be avoided, so the producer has reduced the amount that will be spent in the sound department by $530 to compensate. The two variances balance each other out and the project remains on budget. Without a cost report, the producer wouldn't have known that the camera department was over budget. And without creating cost reports frequently enough, there wouldn't have been time to make an adjustment in another department to balance things out.

A good cost report also lets you predict future problems. For example, if early in production you see that you're spending more on production than you had planned (because you are shooting more each day), you can predict that the amount of time and money needed to log, transcribe, and digitize the footage is likely to increase as well. As in the previous example, it may not be desirable to reduce the amount that's being shot, but perhaps everyone can agree to conserve money in another area to keep the project on budget.

CONCLUSION

While these production management tools might seem to be adding extra labor to your project, they will in fact save you time, energy, and money by allowing you to think through your project on paper before you get out into the field. Call sheets, budgets, and cost reports are also a great way of keeping all the members of your crew on the same page. In addition, when you have wrapped and your funders want to know how their money was spent, it's much easier to just print out an updated budget than to have to assemble one after the fact. These are a few reasons why production planning is important. They are also excellent skills if you want to be employable on other people's films.

Organizing Cinematic Time and Space

CHAPTER 7

> *Film is a medium. A medium is based on an agreement, a contract that has developed over a long period during which the speaker and the listener, the picture maker and the viewer, performer and audience, have established a system of meanings: a vocabulary, syntax and grammar of the language being used. For this reason, language emerges slowly, and will continue to evolve for as long as audiences and authors develop new ways of expressing themselves.*
>
> **Alexander Mackendrick, *On Film-Making*[1]**

THE VISUAL LANGUAGE OF DOCUMENTARY

Cinema is an art that offers a rich visual language that has developed over a 100-year history and is still growing. In documentary, this visual language references reality, but it is definitely not the same thing. Rather, it is a *story* about the real, and many of the conventions and expectations that make up the visual language of fiction filmmaking apply in documentary as well. In this chapter, we will look at how choices in framing, angle, movement, camera placement, and editing drawn from different strands of filmmaking offer documentary filmmakers a variety of tools to say what they want to say.

Remember that cinema is a living language with an ever-expanding vocabulary and ever-evolving syntax. The fundamentals in this chapter are just the beginning of how we speak in film. Just as in writing, the cinematic language can be bland or expressive, prosaic or poetic, utilitarian or profound. You can certainly customize cinematic language to your own expressive purposes, but it's essential to have a firm grasp of the basic conventions first.

SHOTS, SEQUENCES, AND SCENES

Film scholars and practitioners alike have long referred to the cinema as a language, which means that it is a shared system of terms, symbols, and syntax used to communicate thoughts, feelings, and experiences. In written language, we use letters, words, sentences, and paragraphs. In the visual language of cinema, we have three basic building blocks: the **shot**, the **sequence**, and the **scene**.

The **shot** is the smallest unit of the film language. A shot is a continuous moving image, unbroken by an edit. Technically speaking, a shot is the footage generated from the moment you turn on the camera to the moment you turn it off—also called a **camera take.** However, these shots are often divided into smaller pieces, which are used independently in the editing stage, and each one of these pieces is also called a shot. Shots can be as short as a few frames or as long as your camera will allow before you run out of tape or data storage space.

Each shot in a film builds on the others, so that by arranging shots in a particular order you can create meaning. For example, if Shot A is an exterior shot of the United Nations (UN) building in New York City, and shot B is of a woman giving a speech, we understand that this woman is addressing an audience inside the UN building. If Shot A were cut next

THE RAW MATERIALS OF YOUR DOCUMENTARY: THE ELEMENTS

Before you can start building your documentary, you need to decide what the filmic "ingredients" will be. You know from Chapter 2 that there are many stylistic approaches, but all of them use some combination of the following **elements**:

Video (sometimes with accompanying audio)
- Interviews: formal ("sit-down") or more casual (mobile, handheld)
- Observational footage of events as they are unfolding
- Visuals that aren't part of an observational scene: landscapes, establishing shots, **visual evidence** (sometimes called **B-roll**)
- **Archival footage**: generally historical material (Chapter 19)
- **Stock footage**: generally suggests contemporary footage shot by someone else
- Still photographs: can be historical or contemporary
- Documents: newspapers, letters, official reports, or other primary source documents
- Titles: opening titles, end credits, IDs (**lower thirds**), text cards
- Graphics and animation: illustrations or computer-generated elements, often used to present complex information (**infographics**) or to suggest personal memory or experience
- Reenactments (Chapter 2)

Audio Only
- Narration
- Music
- Wild or ambient sound
- Sound effects

From a directing point of view, you need to figure out which elements you will need in order to establish and maintain the style of your film, and express what you want to convey about your subject.

to a shot of the Empire State building, and then the Chrysler building, a viewer would start to understand that this might be a film about New York City, or the architecture of skyscrapers. In other words, a shot alone has meaning, but much of a single shot's meaning depends on its context. A juxtaposition of shots often adds up to more than the sum of its parts.

Because images and editing function in tandem, they must both be considered as you devise your visual strategy. In documentary, you usually can't plan out your film, shot by shot, before you go into production as can be done with fiction filmmaking. You can, though, consider what you will film and how the shots you gather might fit together. This is what is referred to as "shooting for the edit." As filmmaker S. Leo Chiang notes:

> *I really think if you are going to be a shooter or a director for documentaries, you really should learn how to edit. Because then you will have the experience of wishing you had a particular shot. And then, when you go back into the field to shoot you will think, "Yes, I can shoot this speaker all I want, but if I don't have any reaction shots of people listening, this scene is not going to work."*[2]

A **scene** is a dramatic unit in which action ostensibly happens over a continuous time and within a single location. A scene is usually composed of multiple shots, taken from different vantage points and with various shot sizes. An editor will cut these together using the conventions of continuity editing (Chapter 17) to create a sense that the scene is unfolding continuously. Scenes are clearly delineated by any break in time or place—as soon as you cut from a scene in a bedroom to the street, for example, audiences understand that you have ended one scene and begun another.

A **sequence** is a part of a film, usually longer than a shot or a scene, that is unified by a theme or a larger idea. It could include more than one scene, a montage (Chapter 19), and/or a series of interview bites combined with visual evidence. The idea is that a sequence has a major role to play in your story, and should have its own dramatic arc. You should be able to articulate where your sequences begin and end, and what specific ideas and meaning they bring to your documentary.

THE FRAME AND COMPOSITION

Dimensions of the Frame

Aesthetic considerations concerning the graphic and compositional aspects of your shots begin with the frame. The **frame** has two definitions. The *physical frame* is each individual still image captured on film or on video, which, when projected as a series, creates the illusion of motion (Chapter 8). The **compositional frame** (Figure 7.1) is a two-dimensional space defined by its horizontal (**x-axis**) and vertical (**y-axis**) dimensions. Within this space, we can perceive a third dimension, depth (**z-axis**), which is created through graphic illusion.

The frame is your canvas, the rectangular space in which you determine the parameters of the viewer's perspective. The frame essentially crops the real-world environment and determines what the audience sees and what they don't see. Images and action outside the boundaries of the frame are referred to as **off-screen**. Framing your shot, deciding what to show and what *not* to show, is a highly significant creative decision.

The relationship between the width and the height of the frame is called the **aspect ratio** and is derived by dividing the width of the frame by the height. There are several different aspect ratios used in film and video. The aspect ratio of broadcast **standard-definition (SD)** video (Chapter 8) is 1.33:1, generally expressed as 4 × 3 when referring to video. Nowadays, most film and video cameras have a wider aspect ratio, which elongates the horizontal dimension. The American theatrical release aspect ratio is 1.85:1, the European theatrical release aspect ratio is 1.66:1, and the **high-definition (HD) broadcast** aspect ratio is 16 × 9 (or 1.78:1). This last aspect ratio has become the most common for contemporary documentary filmmaking and the current established standard for broadcasting. Aspect ratio has significant impact on the compositional possibilities of the frame (Figures 7.2 and 7.3).

Shot Composition and the Graphic Qualities of the Frame

Working within the parameters of a given aspect ratio, a filmmaker has a broad palette of aesthetic choices when designing the composition of a shot. There are no absolute rules concerning visual style except that the choices you make should emerge from the dramatic needs of your documentary story and should reflect your own creative ideas. Even as the reality around you is changing, you need to be thinking about how to frame your shot with authority—whether that means moving yourself or your subjects, or communicating precisely with your crew.

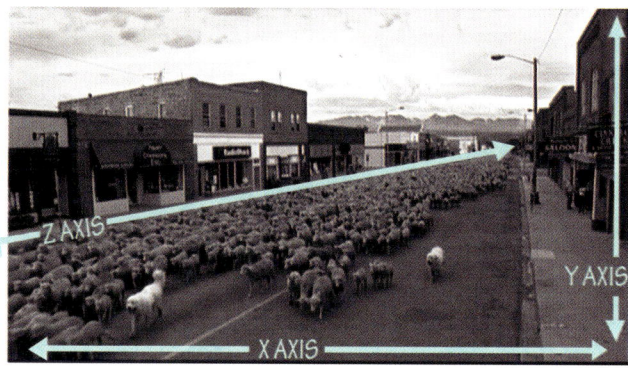

■ **Figure 7.1** The Compositional Frame. Although we work with only two dimensions (the x- and y-axes), we can imply depth by emphasizing the z-axis. This still is from Ilisa Barbash and Lucien Castaing-Taylor's *Sweetgrass* (2009).

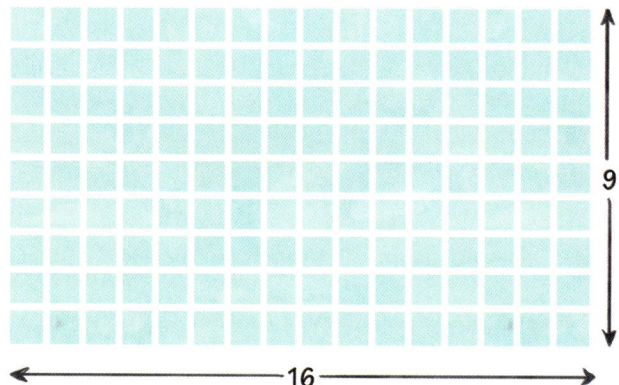

■ **Figure 7.2** Aspect ratio is determined by dividing the width of the image by its height. Since this is a ratio, it can be expressed in full numbers or decimals. The HD video frame is 16 units across and 9 units high, so it can be said to have an aspect ratio of either 16 × 9 ("sixteen by nine") or 1.78:1.

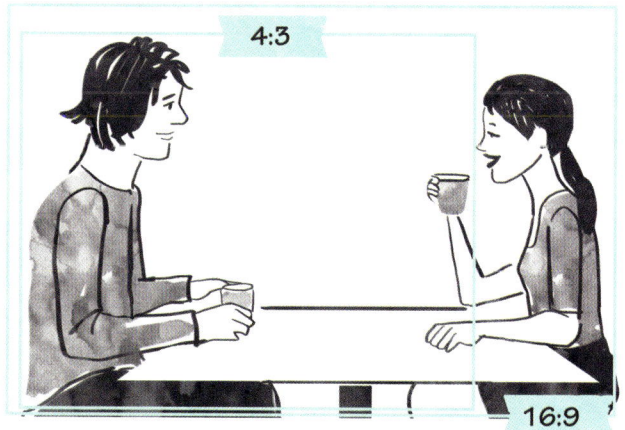

■ **Figure 7.3** In this illustration, you can see the compositional possibilities of two common aspect ratios, 4:3 and 16:9. In the 16:9 frame, you can include both subjects, but with the 4:3 frame you would either have to frame the shot more widely or pan from one subject to the other to see them both.

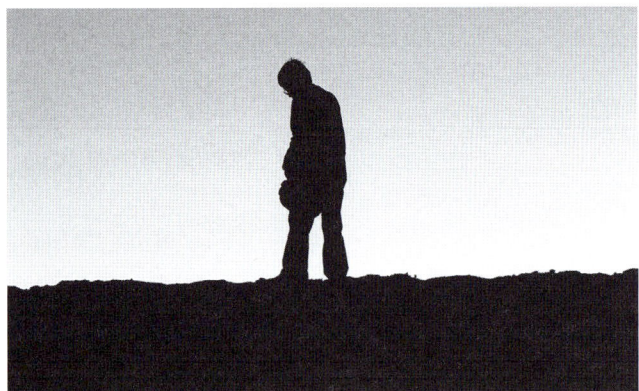

Figure 7.4 This closed frame from Patricio Guzman's *Nostalgia for the Light* (2010), of a mother who searches for her murdered son's remains in the desert, emphasizes her isolation.

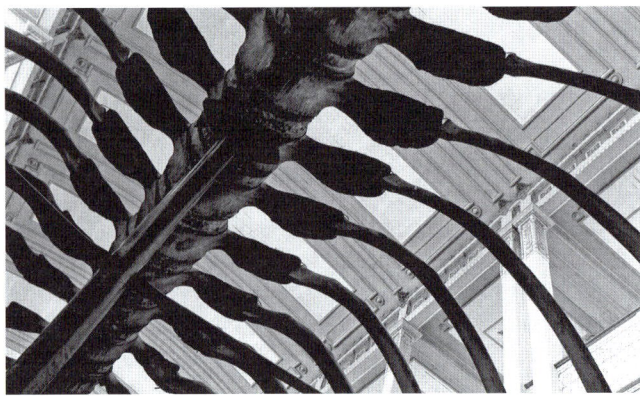

Figure 7.5 In this open frame shot, also from *Nostalgia for the Light*, we are forced to decipher an image (a whale skeleton) by imagining the off-screen space of this natural history museum.

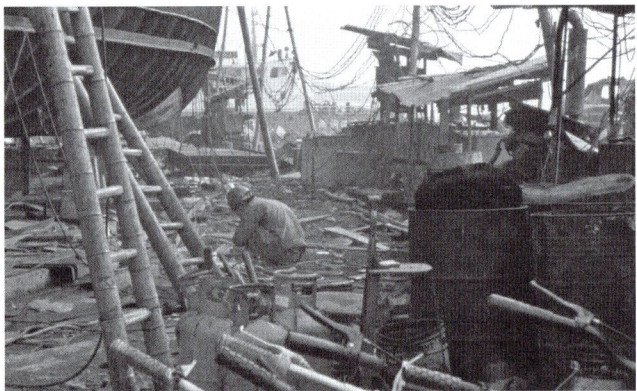

Figure 7.6 This deep frame from Jennifer Baichwal's *Manufactured Landscapes* (2006)—which includes bicycle handlebars and ladders in the foreground, the looming ship hull on the left, and another boat passing in the background—emphasizes the complexity of economic forces in China today.

Closed and Open Frames

A **closed frame** means that all of the essential information in the shot is neatly contained within the parameters of the frame (Figure 7.4). An **open frame** leads the audience to consider the area beyond the edges of the visible shot (Figure 7.5). This is not necessarily an either/or choice. A shot can begin as a closed frame and then an unexpected intrusion from beyond the edge of the frame can suddenly disclose the larger off-screen environment. Also, sound or dialogue coming from off-screen can serve to open a frame, because it asks the audience to imagine the space beyond the edges of what is visible.

Deep Frames and Flat Frames

We refer to a frame that accentuates the compositional element of depth (z-axis) as a **deep frame** (Figure 7.6), and one that emphasizes the two-dimensionality of the image as a **flat frame** (Figure 7.7). The graphic factors that are used to create the illusion of depth are the same ones that are minimized to create a flat frame.

There are several ways of establishing depth in a frame:

1. Receding Planes, Overlapping Objects, and Diminishing Perspective

People share a perceptual understanding that smaller objects appear to be farther away, while larger objects appear to be closer. This means you can achieve a feeling of deep, receding space by placing objects along the z-axis to define foreground, midground, and background planes. Related to this is the idea of **object overlapping**, which means that when we see one object overlapping another, we understand that the object that is partially concealed is further away. Conversely, by reducing the z-axis space to two or even a single plane by putting an interviewee against a wall, we flatten the perspective and the space appears shallow (Figure 7.7). Also related to the notion of receding planes is **foreshortening** or **diminishing perspective** (Figure 7.8).

2. Horizontal and Diagonal Lines

Shot head-on, lines or objects in a horizontal arrangement will obviously look, well, horizontal. But shot from an angle, a horizontal line appears to recede into the distance on a diagonal. For example, if you shoot a tombstone head-on, the composition will appear flat. But if you move the camera 45 degrees (or more) to the side, so that the line of

CHAPTER 7
Organizing Cinematic Time and Space

87

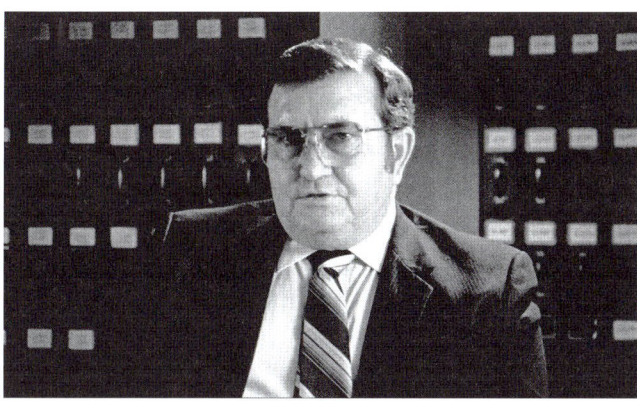

Figure 7.7 In *The Thin Blue Line* (1988), director Errol Morris uses a flat frame to create an "unreal" feeling. This strategy also gives us a feeling of being trapped in a tight space with the interviewee.

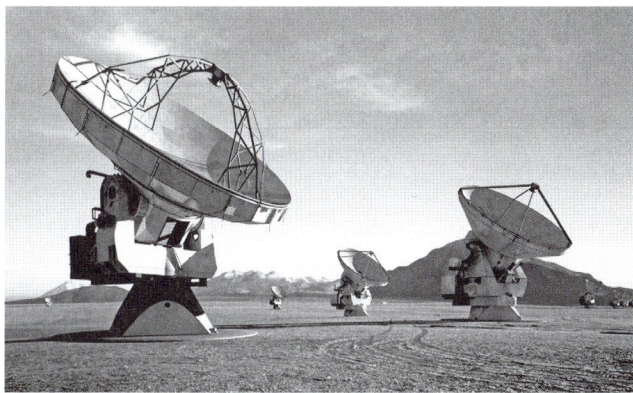

Figure 7.8 This long shot from *Nostalgia for the Light* uses receding planes and diminishing perspective to show the vast size of this radio telescope array in Chile's Atacama Desert.

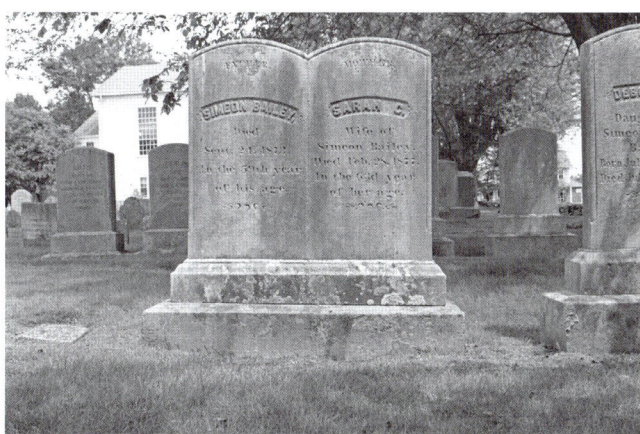

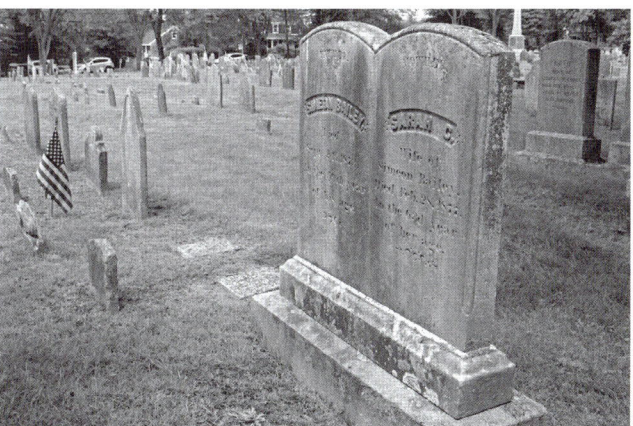

Figure 7.9 In the figure on the left, putting the camera directly facing the tombstone creates a certain formal feeling, emphasizing perhaps the way memorials have stood through time. The image on the right, taken at a 45 degree angle, creates depth in the frame and gives a more elegiac feeling, emphasizing the numbers who have found rest in this graveyard.

gravestones recedes diagonally along the z-axis, then you've created depth in the frame (Figure 7.9).

3. Deep and Shallow Focus

The **depth of field** of a shot is the range of distance along the z-axis where objects appear to be in sharp focus. Manipulating depth of field can encourage or discourage attention to background and foreground information. With a **deep depth of field** we can see objects along the z-axis, from foreground to background, in crisp detail (Figure 7.10). With a **shallow depth of field**, only a single vertical plane is sharply defined and objects in front of or behind that plane are blurry (see Chapter 9 for more about depth of field). Shallow depth of field is becoming more common in documentary because of the prevalence of large-sensor cameras. For more on the relationship between sensor size and depth of field, see p. 151. For an example of an image with a shallow depth of field, see Figure 8.12 (top).

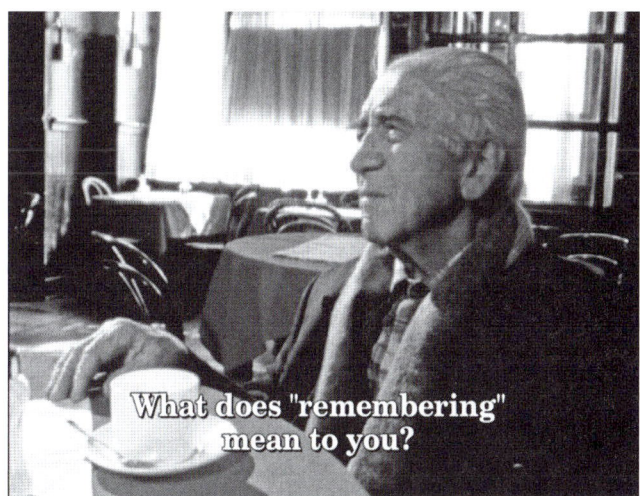

Figure 7.10 This interview subject in Patricio Guzman's *Chile, Obstinate Memory* (1997) is framed poignantly in a cafe where the empty seats are made clearly visible by framing and the deep depth of field. The shot emphasizes the fact that this is a man who is telling a story that is rarely heard.

4. Shadows

Shadows add depth to just about any image because they accentuate the dimensionality of your subject and their environment (Figure 7.11). Eliminating shadows, therefore, conceals depth and leads to a flatter image. Adding shadows through lighting or shooting at a time of day like morning or late afternoon, when there are more shadows, are common ways of using light and shadow to create more depth in the frame. See Chapters 11 and 12 for information about controlling light and shadow.

■ **Figure 7.11**
Shadows create depth (left). Eliminating shadows creates a flatter image (right).

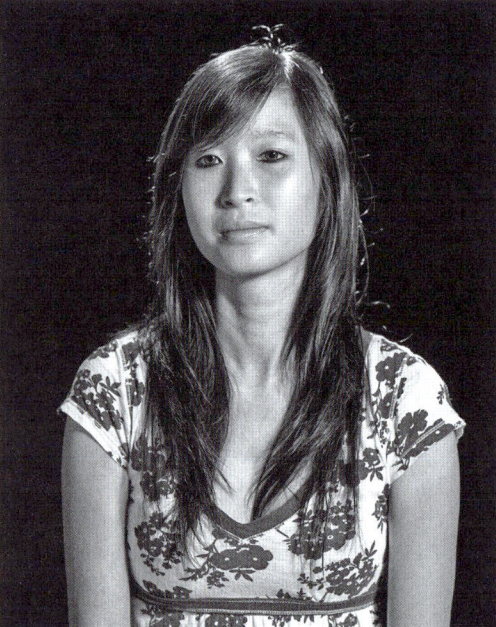
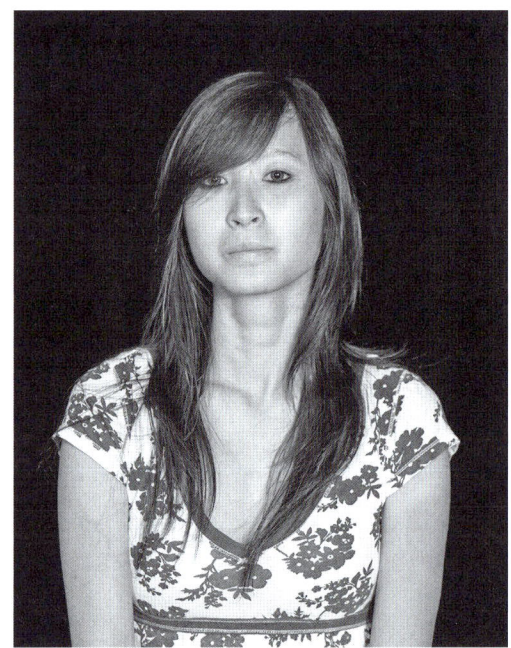

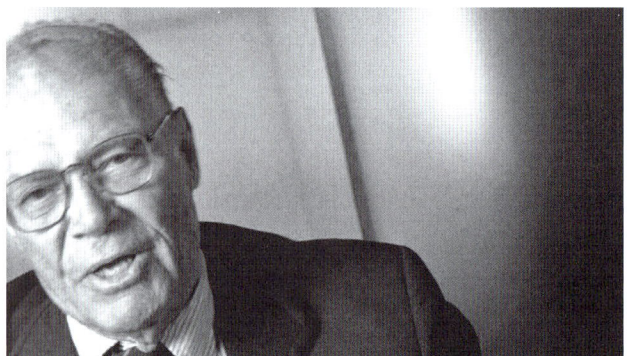

■ **Figure 7.12** Errol Morris's *Fog of War* (2003) is built around a series of interviews with Robert McNamara, all shot on the same set. Here, the unbalanced framing gives as much space to the gray "fog" of the background as to the main character, creating a sense of unease.

Balanced and Unbalanced Frames

The principle of compositional balance begins with the understanding that objects in your frame carry a certain visual weight. Size, shape, brightness, and placement can all affect the relative weight of an object in the frame. How you distribute this visual weight within the frame—equally or unevenly, symmetrically or asymmetrically—gives your composition a sense of stability or instability (Figure 7.12). There is no value judgment attached to balanced and unbalanced frames; neither is better than the other. Like all of the other aesthetic principles in this section, the right choice is the one that is appropriate for the mood you are creating and the story you are telling.

Rule of Thirds, Looking Room, and Lead Room

Cinematic composition, like any other art form, has certain classic principles that have developed over time. Film and video, being two-dimensional representational art forms that developed after painting and photography, have been influenced by many earlier ideas about composition. One such idea is the **rule of thirds**, which is often used as a guide for framing human subjects and for composition in general.

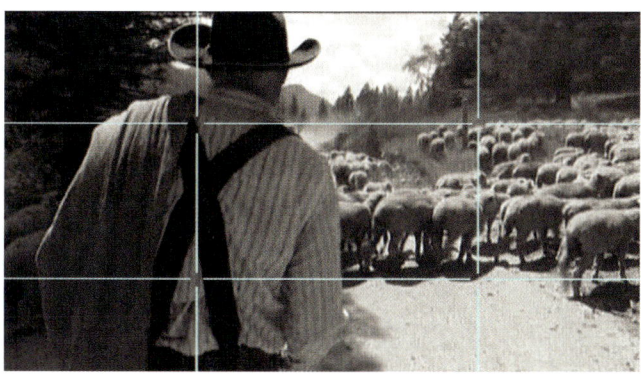

■ **Figure 7.13** This frame from *Sweetgrass* suggests how, according to the rule of thirds, compositional "sweet spots" occur at the intersection of the lines. Notice that the sheep herder is placed on the left vertical line, and the sheep are assembled between the two horizontal lines.

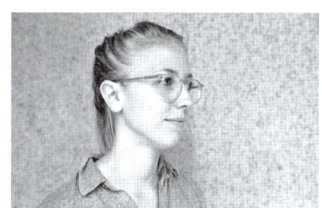 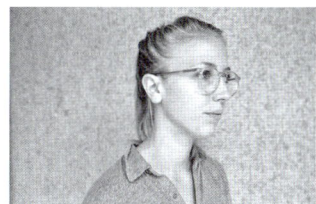

■ **Figure 7.14** Looking room. A subject should be placed along the vertical third line opposite the direction they are looking (left) as opposed to in the center of the frame (right).

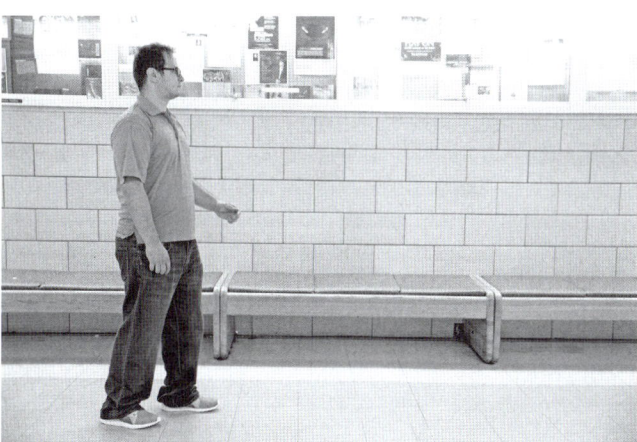 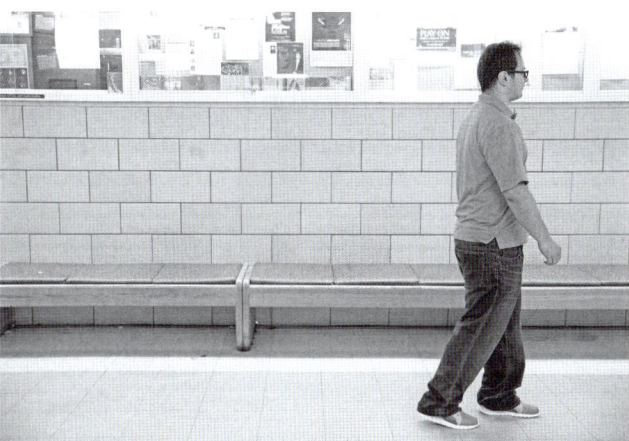

■ **Figure 7.15** Lead room. Give a walking subject ample room in front of them (left) to avoid an awkward frame (right).

First, divide the frame into thirds with imaginary lines along the horizontal and vertical axes. Then, place significant objects, focus points, and elements of interest along these lines. The intersections of the lines are known as "sweet spots," and placing objects at those sweet spots draws the eye to them and creates a pleasing frame (Figure 7.13). For the human face, for example, this might mean placing the eyes along the top third horizontal line. For a figure, it could mean placing the person to one side or the other, along the left or right vertical line. Bear in mind that the rule of thirds is just a guide, a convention, and not really a rule at all. While it is often employed and can be a useful starting point, it is by no means a requirement for a well-composed shot.

If your subject is looking or moving toward one side of the screen, traditional composition dictates that you should place them along the left or right vertical third line *opposite* the direction in which they are looking or moving. This extra vertical space, to one side or the other, is called **looking room** (Figure 7.14) or, for a moving figure, **lead room** (Figure 7.15). The extra space provides a sense of balance because the direction of the gaze, or movement, itself carries a sort of compositional weight. It also keeps the viewer from feeling like the subject is pushing, or about to go beyond, the edge of the frame.

Shot Size

Shot size refers to the size of your subject relative to the frame. This is determined by two factors: (1) the proximity of subject to camera (the closer the subject is to the camera, the larger they will appear) and (2) the degree of lens magnification (the more your lens magnifies the subject, the larger they will appear). Dramatically speaking, you select a shot size based on the narrative emphasis, visual information, and emotional impact you need at a particular moment. As the following figures show, there are a wide variety of shot sizes to choose from (Figure 7.16).

The frame of reference for any discussion of shot size is traditionally the human form, but the following shot designations work for nonhuman subjects as well:

- An **extreme long shot** (**ELS**) or **wide shot** is a shot that shows a large view of the location, setting, or landscape. Even if there are people in the shot, the emphasis is on their surroundings or their relationship to their surroundings.
- A **long shot** (**LS**) is generally a shot that contains the whole human figure. It's a good choice when you need to show larger physical movements and activity.
- A **medium shot** (**MS**) frames your subject from approximately the waist up. This shot can show smaller physical actions and facial expressions while maintaining some connection with the setting. The location is no longer the emphasis of the shot, however, as the viewer is now drawn closer to the subject.
- A **medium close-up** (**MCU**) is generally from the chest or shoulders up. The emphasis of this shot is now facial expression, but some connection to the body more generally is maintained.
- A **close-up** (**CU**) places the primary emphasis on the face or another part of the body. Small details in features, movements, and expressions are emphasized in this very intimate shot.
- An **extreme close-up** (**ECU**) is a stylistically potent shot that isolates a very small detail or feature.
- **Two shots, three shots,** and **group shots:** As these labels imply, the two shot includes two subjects, the three shot includes three subjects, and shots that include more than three people are referred to as group shots.

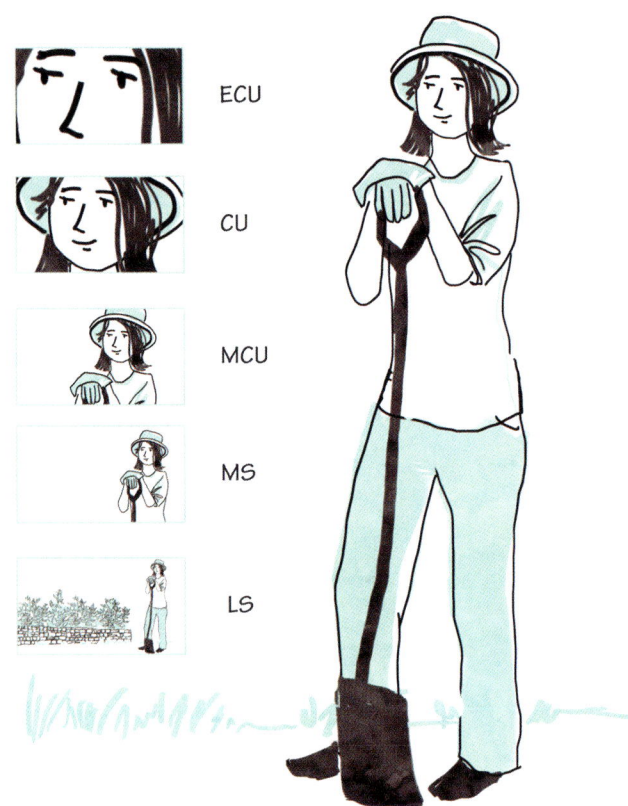

Figure 7.16 This illustration gives a sense of various shot sizes as they relate to the human subject.

Often the names of shot types refer to their function in editing. An **establishing shot**, for example, refers to anything that will give the viewer a sense of the location where a scene will unfold. Similarly, a **cutaway** shot is filmed with the acknowledgment that it will likely be used to help "smooth out" discontinuity in the main action or interview (Chapter 19).

Shot Size and Character Identification

In observational films, the framing will vary within a scene. Sometimes a shot will offer information about the environment, while at other times the subject's emotional state or focus of interest might be dominant. In general, the long shot gives us information about place, but does not give us intimacy, while the close-up shot gives us very little information about the larger situation, but tells us a lot about the individual featured. Understanding this, a filmmaker is able to precisely modulate the emotional involvement as well as the understanding the audience has at any given moment (Figure 7.17).

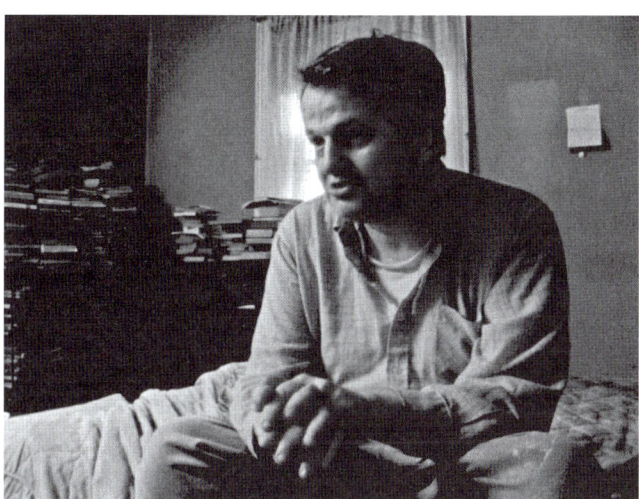 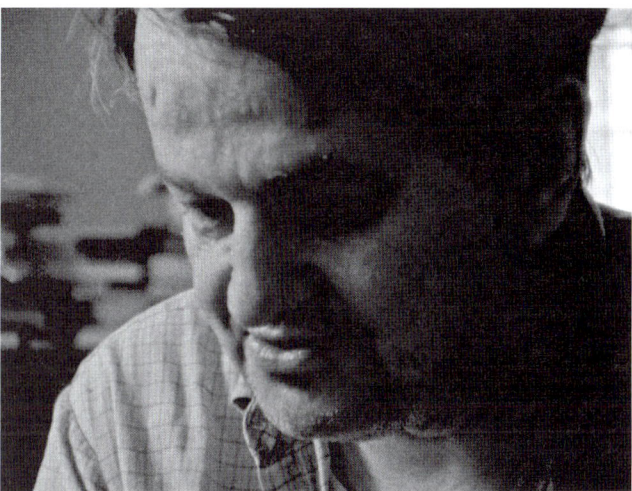

■ **Figure 7.17** This interview with Charles Crumb, the brother of the cartoonist who is the subject of Terry Zwigoff's *Crumb* (1994), was filmed by Maryse Alberti. The interview starts with a relaxed medium shot, and moves to a close-up as Charles speaks of the depression that has haunted him throughout his life.

In documentary interviews, filmmakers generally choose shot sizes in the range of medium shot, medium close-up, and close-up. This allows the audience to identify with the interview subject yet, with the wider shots, allows for the environment to provide some context. Another common strategy is to use the close-up or extreme close-up when the discussion becomes more personal or intimate.

Camera Angles

The horizontal and vertical angles you are shooting from have a dramatic effect on your image no matter what size the subject is in the frame. Simply moving the horizontal or vertical position of the camera, relative to your subject, can be a powerfully expressive technique that establishes the viewer's relationship to your subject.

1. High and Low Angles

Using the human form for our reference, the **eye-level** shot is one in which the lens of the camera is positioned at eye level with your subject, regardless of whether they are sitting, standing, or lying down. Raising the camera above eye level yields a **high-angle** shot, and below eye level gives us a **low-angle** shot (Figure 7.18). An eye-level shot can encourage a connection with a subject, while extreme high or low angles tend to be more emotionally remote but very dynamic.

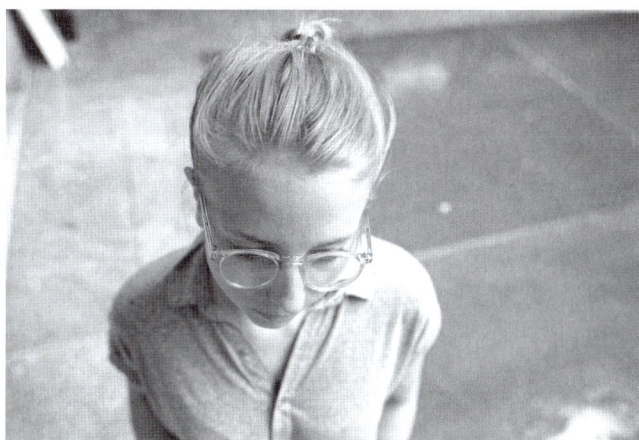 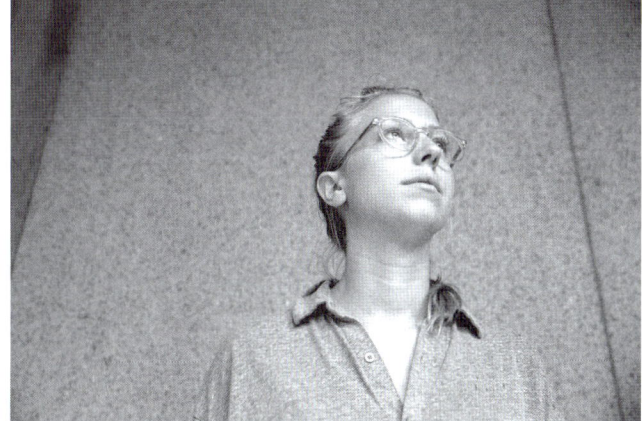

■ **Figure 7.18** High-angle (left) and low-angle (right) shots.

2. Front to Back Angles

The camera can be anywhere from directly in front of your subject to directly behind them. In a **frontal shot**, the camera is positioned directly in front of your subject. This is a common angle for interviews, though not the only option. Moving the camera along a horizontal arc to the side, we progressively move through **three-quarter frontal**, **profile shot**, **three-quarter back**, and finally to **shooting from behind** (Figure 7.19). As we move the camera angle from the front to the back of the subject, we drastically change the relationship of the viewer to the subject. Looking directly at a subject's face is an intimate perspective and can elicit strong engagement, a profile shot is a somewhat neutral point of view, and hiding the face by shooting from behind or from a three-quarter back position can encourage the audience to identify with a character by aligning their visual point of view with that of the subject.

■ **Figure 7.19**
Front to back camera angles: frontal (A), three-quarter frontal (B), profile (C), three-quarter back (D), and shooting from behind (E).

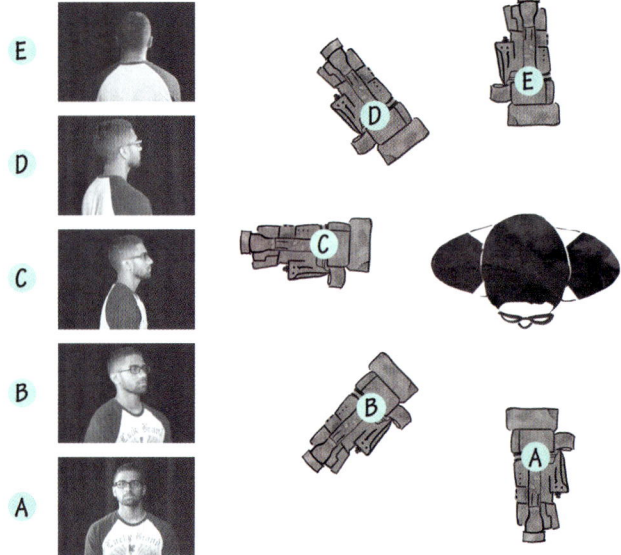

3. The Horizon Line

In documentary, we usually put effort into keeping the frame parallel with the horizon, but sometimes there is a reason to tilt the camera to the side. Tilting the camera laterally so that the horizon of your composition is oblique is called a **canted angle** (or **Dutch angle**) (Figure 7.20). A canted shot can infuse a scene with tension, imbalance, or disorientation.

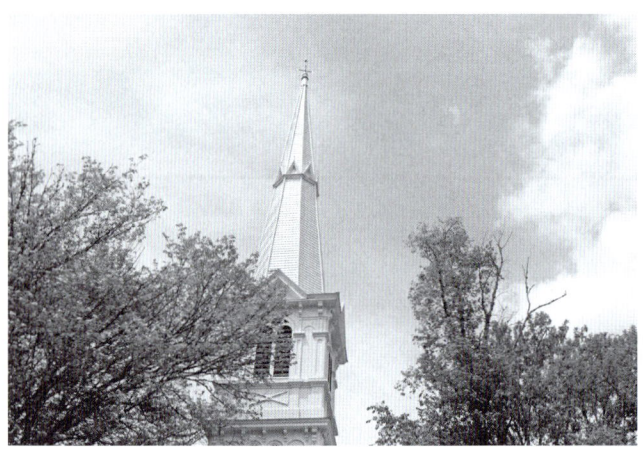
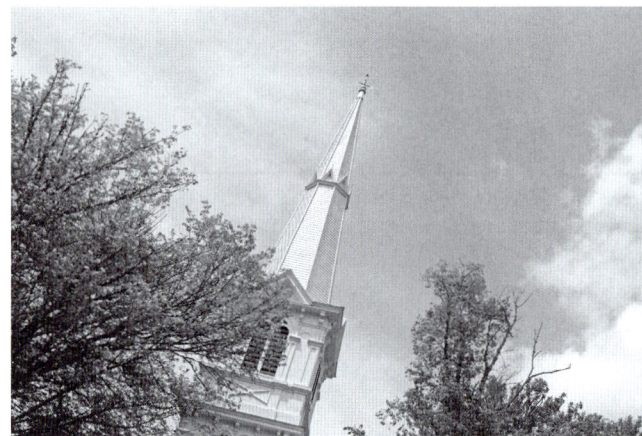

■ **Figure 7.20** Two shots of the same church steeple. The standard angle on the left gives a sense of the prosaic, while the canted angle on the right adds a feeling of disorientation.

FRAMING AND CAMERA ANGLES IN MANUFACTURED LANDSCAPES

Jennifer Baichwal's *Manufactured Landscapes* (2007) follows photographer Edward Burtynsky as he documents the monumental transformation of Planet Earth by modern industry. From the floor of a Chinese factory a kilometer long to the world's largest dam, and from recycling centers the size of mountains to the graveyards of the world's largest ships, the film asks complex and troubling questions about the irreversible impact of globalized manufacturing on life itself.

Baichwal uses all of the weight of framing, angle, and camera movement to emphasize the idea of human beings surrounded by a landscape that they have created but that threatens to overwhelm them.

Consider the various shots of a Chinese electronics factory in Figure 7.21. A long shot establishes the location and gives us a sense of its tremendous size. The medium shot provides a sense of the people in this context, and what they do. A close-up of a worker encourages us to identify with her and empathize with how it might feel to work on such a repetitive task 12 hours a day. Finally, an extreme close-up shows how small the parts they must work with are, and allows us to see that what they are assembling is a product we use every day: a steam iron. By simply changing the framing, the director allows us to view the same situation from multiple vantage points, each one giving a slightly different understanding of this reality.

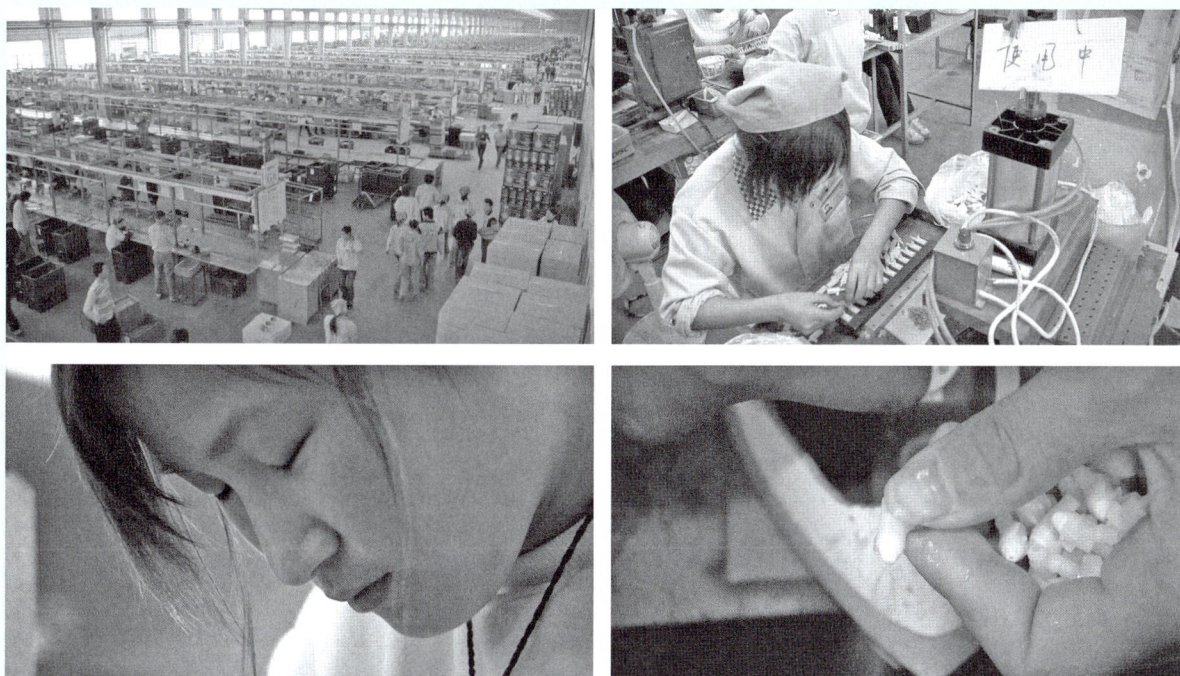

■ **Figure 7.21** Various shot sizes help tell the story in *Manufactured Landscapes* including a long shot (top left), a medium high angle shot (upper right), a close-up (bottom left) and an extreme close-up (bottom right).

CAMERA MOVES

Up until now, most of the discussion has been about static camera framing, but many shots involve camera movement that changes the frame over time. Sometimes we need to move to follow a subject, while at other times we decide to change the frame to reveal new information.

Pivot Moves

Pivot camera moves involve pivoting the camera, horizontally or vertically, from a stationary spot. This can be done on a tripod or with a handheld camera as long as the location of the camera doesn't change, just its horizontal or vertical angle.

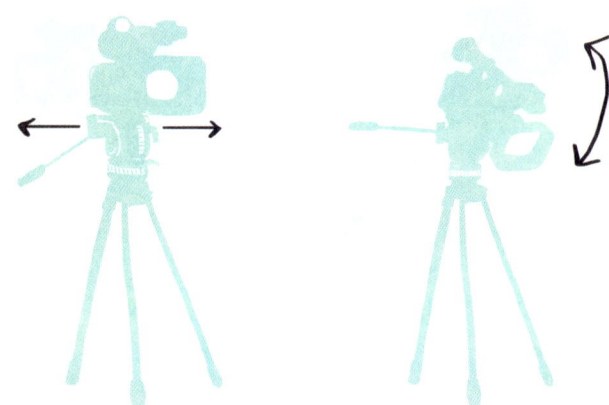

■ **Figure 7.22** Pivot moves. In a pan (left), the camera moves left or right on the tripod's axis. A tilt (right) shifts the camera's perspective vertically on the tripod's axis.

A **pan** scans space horizontally by pivoting the camera left or right (*pan left* and *pan right*). A **tilt** shifts the camera perspective vertically, with the lens facing up or facing down (*tilt up* and *tilt down*) (Figure 7.22). A pan or a tilt that moves from one subject to another is called **panning from/to** and **tilting from/to**. For example, you pan *from* the man at his desk *to* the window across the room. A pan or a tilt that follows a subject as they move is called a **pan with** or **tilt with** (this move is also called a **follow pan** or **follow tilt**). For examples of what these moves look like, see our companion website (www.routledge.com/cw/Anderson).

Zooming In and Out

Zooming in or **zooming out** refers to changing the image size by manipulating the focal length of the lens (Chapter 9). It is common in documentary to zoom out from a detail to reveal its context, or vice versa. During an interview, a slow zoom in can be used to emphasize an emotional high point.

Dynamic Moves

Dynamic camera moves involve a mobile camera, which means literally moving the entire camera in space, horizontally (left or right), closer or farther (forward or backward), or even vertically (up and down). These moves can be accomplished handheld, or with special camera mounting equipment.

A **tracking shot** is a term used when you move the camera in order to *follow* or *track with* a subject. You can *track* left, right, forward, or backward to follow the movement of your subject. In Robert Drew's classic cinéma vérité documentary *Primary* (1960), Ricky Leacock's handheld camera follows presidential candidate John F. Kennedy as he struggles to move from the street through a cheering crowd to the stage. The high angle and continuous tracking shot gives weight to the mass emotion raised by Kennedy (Figure 7.23).

Dolly shots are moving shots in which the camera moves closer to, or farther away from, the subject. To **dolly-in** or **dolly-out** means to move the camera closer to or farther away from the subject, respectively. In *Night and Fog* (1959), Alain Resnais employs slow, deliberate dolly-in shots with a 35mm camera on tracks to link postwar Auschwitz and the history of the Holocaust (Figure 7.24). The slow movement through the sunny countryside gives the film an elegiac quality, emphasizing our distance from the past while echoing the movement of the trains that brought victims to their deaths in the camps. In effect, it creates a degree of identification and empathy by putting us on the same path as the victims of the holocaust.

The term "dolly" originally referred to a wheeled platform with a mounted camera; however, in modern documentary the dolly may be a tripod in the back of a pickup truck, or even a small lateral **slider** mounted to a **tripod** (Figure 10.14).

Lifting the camera up and down is called **booming** ("boom up" or "boom down"). This can be done with a handheld camera or mechanically with a boom or jib arm (Figure 7.25). A **crane shot** is one in which the camera is raised very high in the air, certainly above a human subject's head. This requires a special, and expensive, piece of equipment called a crane or, for smaller cameras, a **jib**. The specific equipment and techniques used for dynamic camera moves are discussed in more detail in Chapter 10.

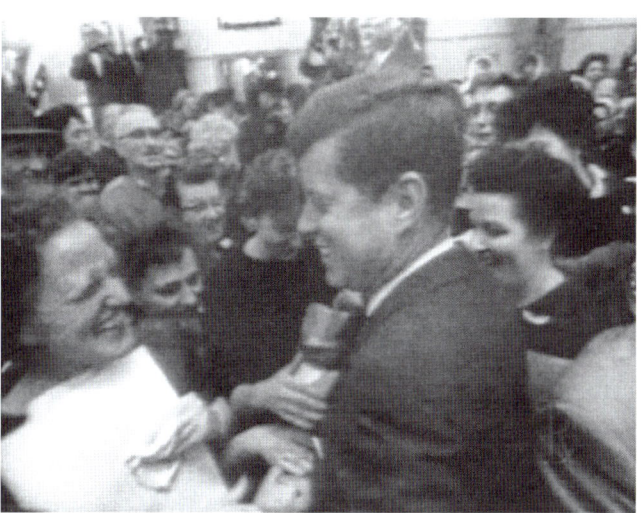

■ **Figure 7.23** In *Primary*, Ricky Leacock's camera uses a tracking motion to follow a young John F. Kennedy through a throng.

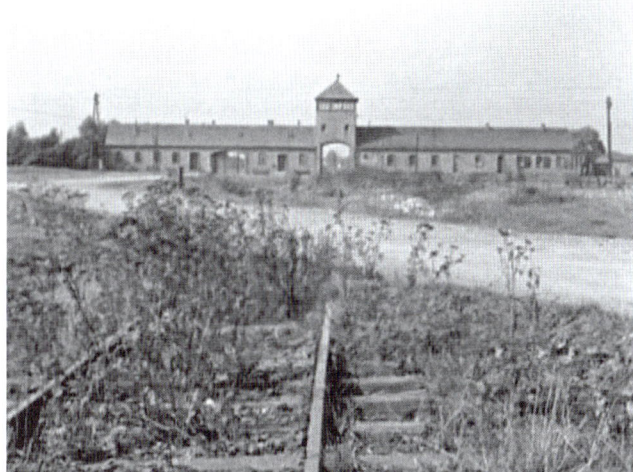

■ **Figure 7.24** In *Night and Fog*, cinematographer Sascha Vierney uses a dolly shot to encourage us to occupy the perspective of Holocaust victims being brought to Auschwitz.

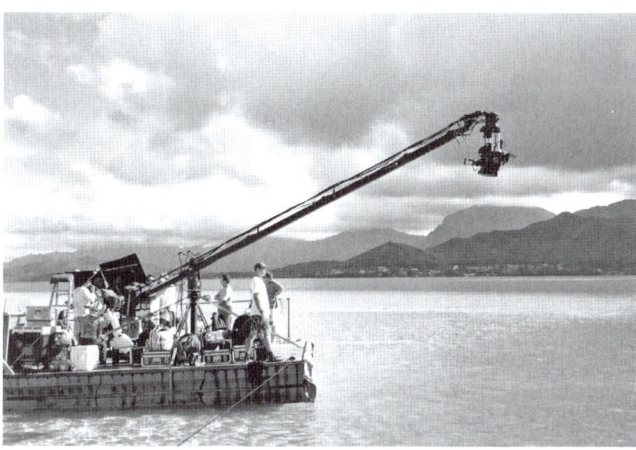

■ **Figure 7.25** A camera on a jib. Photo by Jai Mansson.

All of these moves—pans, tilts, dollies, tracking, booming, and zooming—can be combined. For example, following the trajectory of a helium balloon just as a child lets go of it would require panning and tilting simultaneously, and one might even want to zoom in.

The Moving Frame and Perspective

Although the general directions of the frame shifts are similar (i.e., left to right or up and down), there is a big difference between pivot camera moves (pans and tilts) and dynamic camera moves (dolly, track, and boom). Think of the camera as essentially the seat from which an audience member views the world of your film. With pivot camera moves, this perspective point of reference remains fixed. Panning or tilting the camera is the equivalent of having them turn their head left and right or up and down. With a dynamic camera, you are essentially moving the viewer through the space of the film.

Here's an example of the difference. Let's say we are filming a runner, jogging down a street. First, let's shoot the run with a follow pan, placing the camera at the halfway mark along his path (Figure 7.26). The beginning of the shot is quite frontal, looking into the runner's face. When he hits the midpoint mark, directly in front of the camera, he will be seen in profile and, continuing, when he reaches the end of his path, we will be looking at his back. It's the perspective of a stationary spectator—as if we were sitting on a bench watching him run past us.

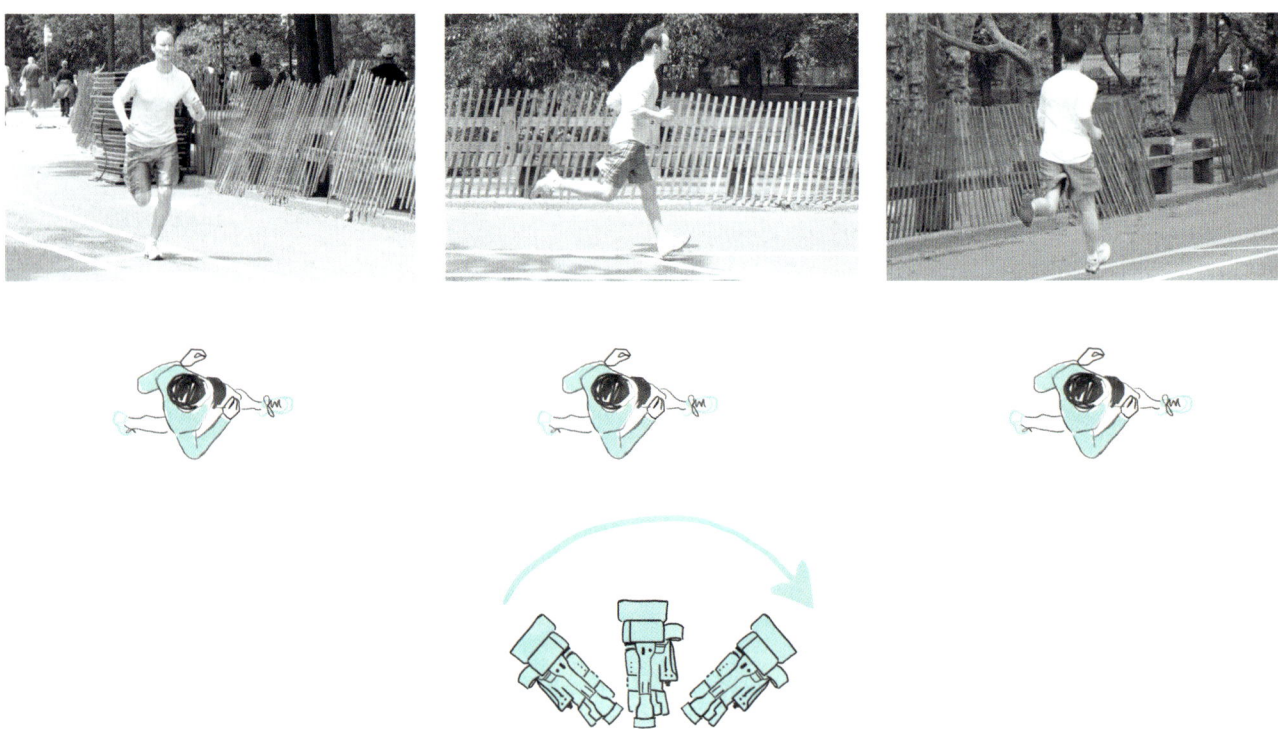

■ **Figure 7.26** In a pan, a subject is viewed from one stationary point as the shot progresses. In this example, the runner is facing the camera at the beginning of the shot and is seen from behind at the end of it.

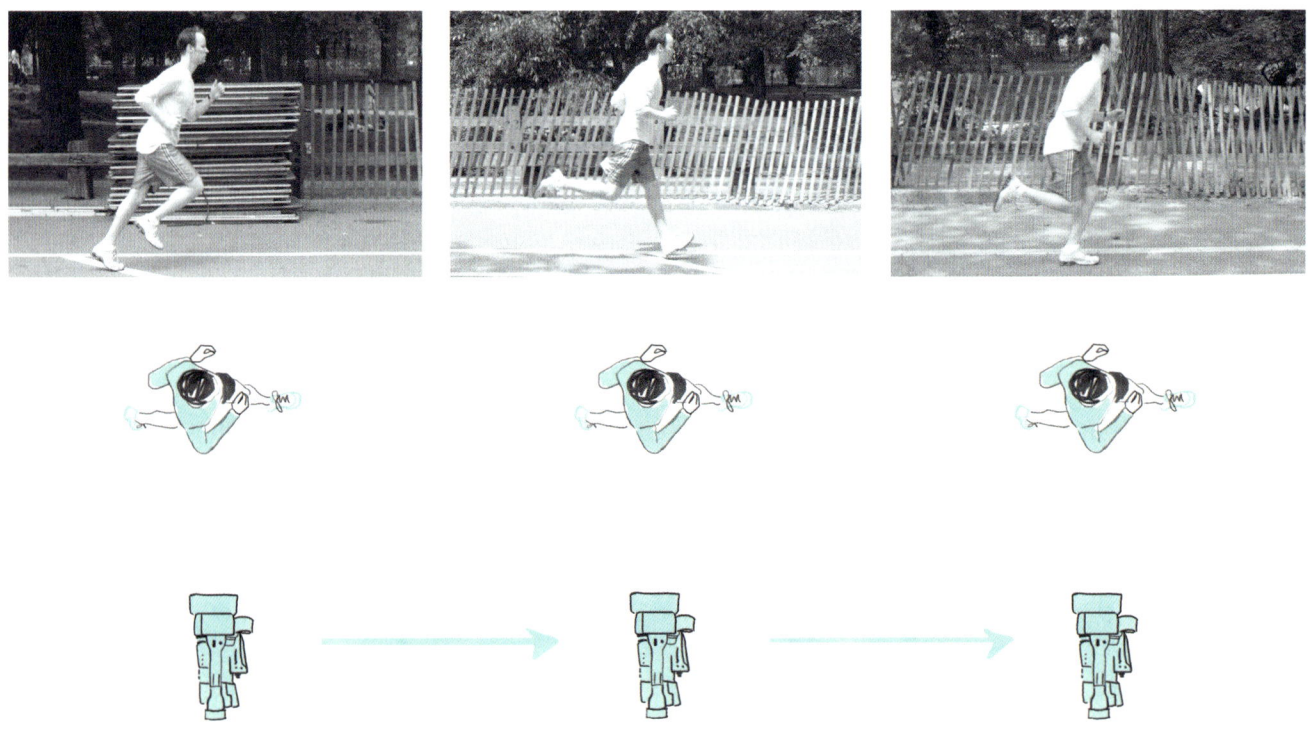

■ **Figure 7.27** Here the camera tracks with the runner, maintaining a consistent profile angle.

Now, let's go back to the beginning of the runner's path and shoot his run with a tracking shot (Figure 7.27). We begin alongside the runner, in profile, and as he moves, our camera tracks along with him. As he reaches the midway point and then the end of the path, the runner remains in profile because we have been moving parallel to him. In this shot, the viewer, like the camera, is a runner too, a participant moving through space just like the runner. For video examples of pivot and dynamic camera moves, go to our companion website (www.routledge.com/cw/Anderson).

Motivation and the Moving Camera

A camera move, whether it's a pan, track, or zoom, is a promise. It promises viewers that they are going to receive a new piece of information, a new perspective, or a new understanding by the end of the camera's journey. Let's say you are shooting a long shot of a mountain range and you pan right. The pan promises the viewer that they will see something in addition to those mountains. Maybe the move reveals a forest fire raging on the south slopes, or perhaps a cowboy comes into view in the foreground. Or maybe the pan of the mountains goes on and on, and the move reveals that our character is surrounded by mountains on all sides. One name for a shot like this, and it speaks to its storytelling function, is a **reveal**. A reveal uses a camera move to give new, and sometimes startling or significant, information within a single shot. What, how, and when you reveal—or conceal—details are very important factors to consider when you devise camera moves of any sort. A move that accomplishes nothing more than a static shot would break its promise of showing something else and it is considered an "unmotivated move."

In documentary, where situations are fluid and changing all the time, you will find yourself reframing constantly to accommodate changes in the unfolding action. Deciding when to use a camera move such as a pan or a zoom requires quick thinking as well as an eye for what is happening outside the frame. Say you are shooting a scene with two people in conversation, and you are filming one person talking in a medium shot. While making sure you are in focus and have a well-composed shot, a good cinematographer will also be keeping an eye on the person who is listening. If their reaction is interesting or significant, this might mean that you should make the decision to pan to show the reaction.

It is important to know in advance where your move will begin and precisely where it will end. A common problem with inexperienced cinematographers is that they begin a camera move without knowing exactly where they are going, and wind up fishing around for a place to land, making the move look sloppy. The alternative is to know how to think on your feet, and begin and end your camera moves in places that make sense. In some situations, you will be able to practice the move before you actually execute it. At other times, you will be making decisions on the fly, as Maryse Alberti does in this scene from *Crumb* shown in Figure 7.28

Adjusting Your Shot

Whether you're executing a pan, tilt, dolly, or tracking shot, a camera move is a clear and substantial alteration of the subject or composition. A **camera adjustment**, on the other hand, is a slight shifting of the frame to maintain your composition on a person or object that is moving only a little. For example, if you are filming someone in a medium close-up while they speak to someone else off-screen, they may shift from one foot to the other or take a step forward or back, or even just shift their gaze from screen right to screen left. Each one of these changes requires a minor adjustment of the frame to maintain a balanced composition. The person operating the camera needs to anticipate these small movements and adjust accordingly. For this type of small adjustment, we sometimes say that the camera is "breathing with the subject." A common error in a documentary interview, for example, is to "lock off" the tripod and presume that the subject will stay in exactly the same place. As a rule of thumb, always keep controls on the tripod loose and be ready to adjust when someone sits back, leans forward, or turns to the side. Even if your subject

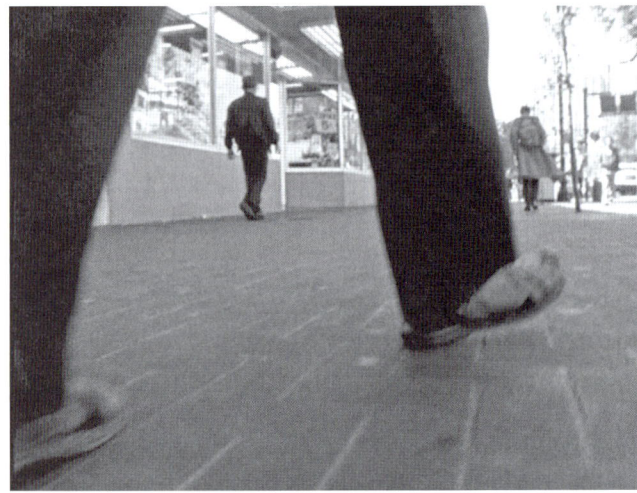 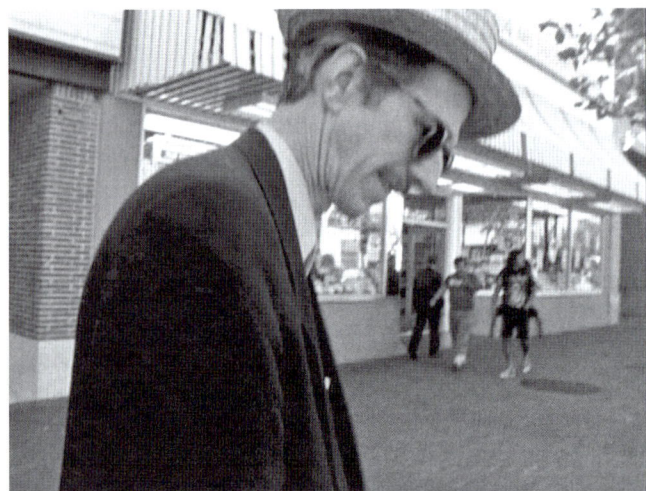
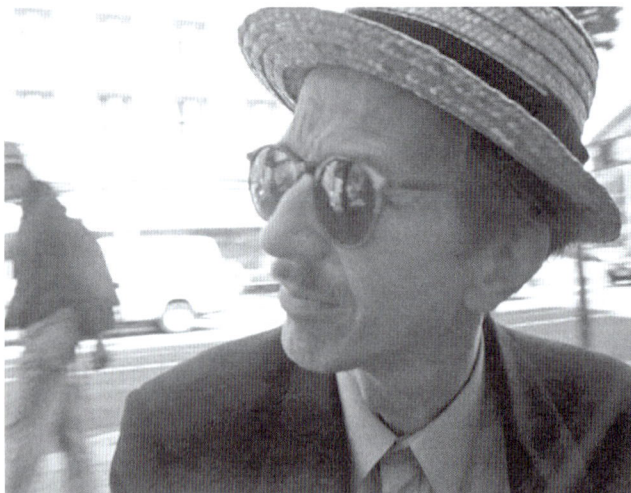 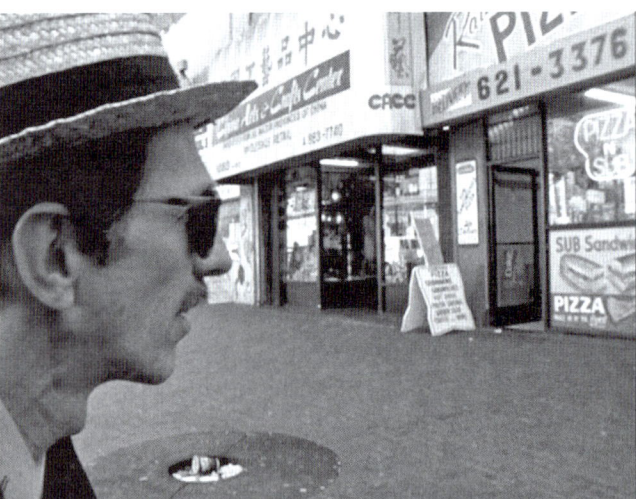

■ **Figure 7.28** This single shot in *Crumb* is the last of a series that follow cartoonist Robert Crumb down the street. At the beginning of the shot, the camera is very low, following his legs as he walks (top left). The camera then booms up as Crumb pauses and looks at a bench (top right). It comes back down as Crumb sits (bottom left), and then tracks around him to get a profile (bottom right).

doesn't move much, the looser camera will give your interview a more dynamic and responsive feel.

SHOOTING WITH EDITING IN MIND

The way events are presented to us in a documentary film may be very different from the order in which they actually occurred. In addition, documentary films often have a high **shooting ratio,** meaning that the amount of material recorded is much greater than what actually ends up being used in the final film. All this means that the filmic reality of the documentary is to a great extent created in the edit room, after much or all of the film has already been shot. This means that as you go into a situation to film, you should have a sense of how the event you are filming might translate into a scene that will work for your film. While you can never predict exactly what will happen while you are filming, having an idea of what might occur will allow you to think through a strategy for shooting and to be flexible if and when things change. Otherwise you risk being left without the elements you need to construct your scenes. An example would be to make sure you collect establishing shots of your location, as well as enough cutaways of significant details in the environment, before you wrap up filming for the day.

This sense of your approach and storytelling strategy will dictate how you **cover** everything you shoot. **Coverage** refers to your strategy for filming the **pro-filmic reality**: what you will shoot, where you will position your camera, and how you will select and arrange your frame. This can apply to both observational and more expository modes of documentary. For an observational film that depends on the creation of a continuous time and space experience, you will need to approach your coverage with the rules of **continuity editing** in mind (Chapter 19). If you are doing a project that is based more on an expository or rhetorical approach, your coverage might include both interviews and various types of **visual evidence**.

COLLECTING VISUAL EVIDENCE

Whether you are shooting an observational film or a more expository one, you will need to collect imagery. Strong visuals are more than "something to look at" while you are listening to an interview or narration. They should, in and of themselves, contribute important additional information and meaning to the film. As Barry Hampe says, in his book *Making Documentary Films and Videos*:

> *Evidence shows the audience something both real and true which they can understand to be a portion of the documentary argument. A strong visual demonstration will almost always be the best evidence you can use. The minute you find yourself thinking about visuals or B-roll footage, an alarm should go off in your head to tell you that you lack the visual evidence you need and are relying on words to tell your story. Show us what happened, instead.*[3]

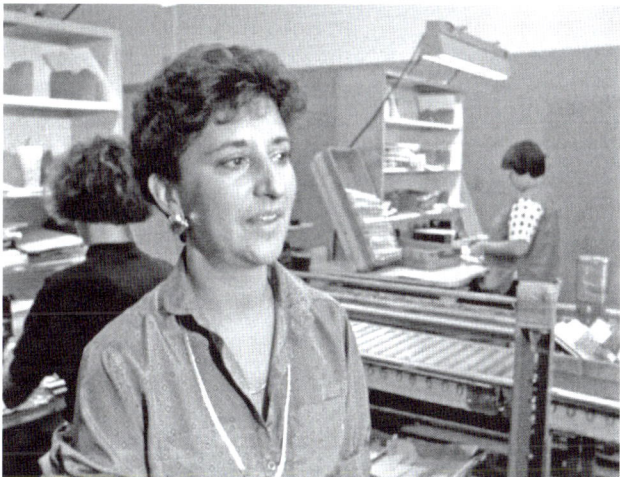

■ **Figure 7.29** In *Roger and Me*, Michael Moore offers strong visual evidence for the depopulation of Flint, Michigan, in this scene at the Flint post office, where three women are needed to handle the growing number of change of address forms.

Students often refer to documentary visuals as **B-Roll**. This term, used in broadcast journalism to refer to images that will accompany a voice-over narration, limits the possibilities for visual material because it implies that visuals are just illustrations to back up **voice-over** or **narration**. Visuals, on the contrary, are at the heart of documentary filmmaking. Sometimes they will simply illustrate what is being said, but at other times they can function independently as powerful evidence backing up a claim, or refuting one.

A great example of a documentary that offers strong visual evidence for its points is Michael Moore's *Roger and Me* (1989). One line in Moore's voice-over refers to the fact that the city of Flint, Michigan, is depopulating because General Motors is closing its operations there. To underline this idea, Moore cuts to a scene at the local post office, where there are three women who are working full-time just processing "change of address" forms (Figure 7.29). They talk about how this part of the job keeps them all busy as we watch them work, and they mention that a new computer will help them. This evidence is anecdotal (they give us no firm numbers), but the visuals create an indelible impression of the size of the exodus from Flint.

COVERING OBSERVATIONAL SCENES

Unlike live television and studio programs, which are shot using multiple cameras, documentaries are generally filmed using a single camera and then edited together in postproduction. It is increasingly common to shoot with two cameras so their angles can be intercut, but multiple camera setups remain relatively rare in documentary. Building observational scenes, which as we have mentioned rely on an illusion of continuous time and space, require much skill on the part of a director and cinematographer. In fiction filmmaking, continuity of performance and actions is achieved by having the actors run through the scene many times, and changing the camera angle or lens between takes. As long as the actors do and say the same thing each time they do the scene, and the cinematographer follows the rules of continuity (explained below), the various takes will cut together in editing. In documentary, however, the editor must comb through hours of footage, looking for shots that can be cut together seamlessly to convey the action of the scene.

Depending on your philosophy, it may be acceptable during production to ask a subject to repeat an action. It is quite common, for example, to ask someone to "go back inside and come out through the door again, without looking at the camera." Documentary will never resemble the highly controlled world of fiction filmmaking, but seasoned camera operators and directors will be keeping track of what they have shot and what might be needed in editing to make a scene work.

In order for your scene to cut together in a way that appears seamless, you will need to shoot with the rules of **continuity editing** in mind. This is covered in more detail in Chapter 19, but for now we will stress that you will need a *variety of shots* that have *different framings*, shot from the same side of the room or location. What this means is careful thinking on your feet so that you give the editor a useful selection of shots to work with.

One of the main rules of continuity is the 180° principle, which ensures that the viewer understands the physical space of the scene and the relationships between characters and objects in that space. Practically speaking, this means that when you begin to shoot an observational scene, you should draw an imaginary line called the **180° line** or **line of action**. This usually follows the direction a character is looking, called their **sightline**, or the direction the character travels in the frame, called their **screen direction**. The 180° principle tells us that, to maintain consistent spatial orientation, all shots used in a sequence must be filmed from one side of the line, giving us a 180° arc where we can place our camera. Crossing the 180° line with the camera reverses both the looking and moving directions of our subject and breaks spatial continuity.

Here is an example of a common way of approaching a two-person interaction that involves following the 180° principle: the **shot/reverse shot** technique. Consider a scene from Zachary Heinzerling's *Cutie and the Boxer* (2013), a documentary about the chaotic 40-year marriage of the painter Ushio Shinohara and his wife Noriko. The scene shown in Figure 7.30 involves a conversation between Ushio and Noriko about money Ushio has just received for some artwork. The first shot is a wide-angle of Ushio and Noriko sitting at the table. It acts as a **master shot**, establishing the space and where the characters are relative to one another and their environment.

As the conversation progresses, there are medium shots and close-ups of each person. Importantly, while Heinzerling moves the camera closer to Noriko to shoot the shots of Ushio alone, and closer to Ushio to shoot Noriko, he never moves the camera to the other

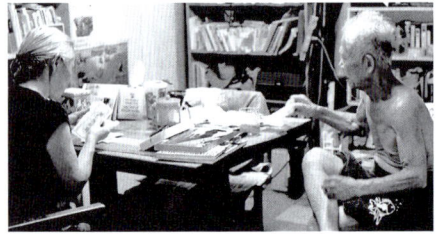
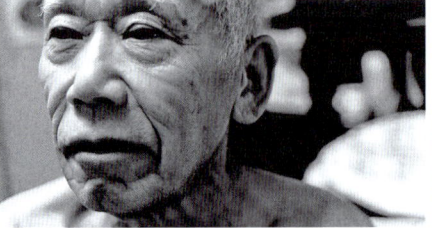
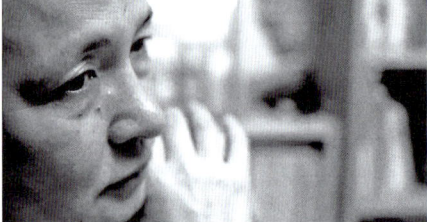

■ **Figure 7.30** Shot/reverse shot coverage in *Cutie and the Boxer*. The left shot is a master shot with both subjects. The middle and right shots are close-ups, which alternate as the discussion unfolds (see Figure 7.31 for an overhead diagram of subject and camera placement).

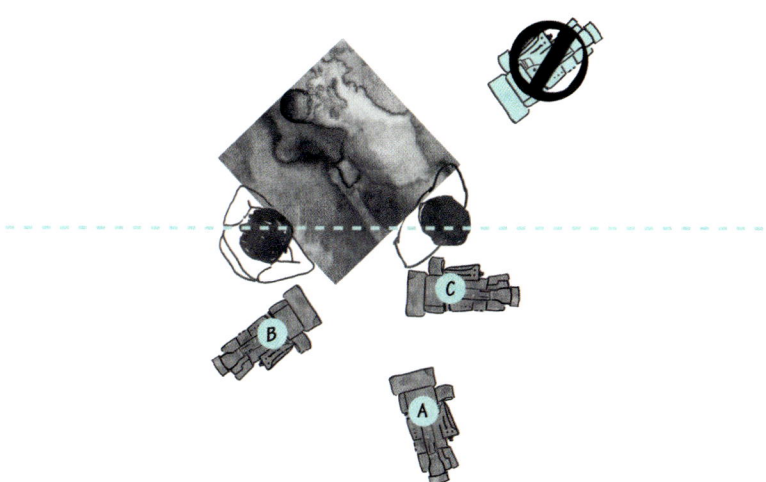

■ Figure 7.31
Overhead blocking diagram of the scene in Figure 7.30. Note the 180° line, which the camera cannot cross without disrupting spatial continuity.

side of the table. Positioning the camera on the other side, by the bookshelves, would have jumped the line of action and disrupted the spatial continuity of the scene (Figure 7.31).

How do we organize space for a more complex scene in which one of our characters moves around, disrupting the original line of action? What happens if a third person comes into the scene, causing our characters to shift their sightlines? The truth is, we are not stuck with only one 180° line in every single scene. It's very common for there to be shifts within a single scene. And in documentary, audiences tend to be forgiving of small disruptions in continuity.

Shooting a scene like the one described above presents challenges for even seasoned documentary cinematographers. A variety of shots must be filmed, from many angles, if the editor is to have enough material to work with. Deciding on your angles, and when to change your position, takes experience and an ability to keep your eye on what is going on outside the frame, as well as staying attuned to the emotional tenor of the interactions between the people you are filming.

When shooting a conversation between two people like the one between Ushio and Noriko in *Cutie and the Boxer*, when is it best to stay in the wide, establishing shot? When should you move to capture a shot of just one person talking? When is a good time to capture **reaction shots** of the person listening (like the shot of Noriko in Figure 7.30, right)?

About shooting another, very similar scene between Ushio and Noriko in *Cutie and the Boxer*, Heinzerling says:

> In shooting, what you are really paying attention to are reactions and body language. If you have a good sound recording you are going to be able to use the conversation, even if you don't film the person on camera. So I always think it's better to stick with one person for a long period of time, where you are getting a variety of reactions and getting into the rhythm of the scene, as opposed to worrying, "What is that person saying?" and "I need to make sure that I get that exact point where he says that great line." Forget all of that. You'll find those moments in body language and in their faces, I think. You have an outline of what you are supposed to get, but rarely does the scene equal what you thought it would be. It's so much more important to make sure that you have coverage.[4]

Another key question in deciding how you will cover a scene is **point of view**. Since your camera becomes the eyes of the audience, camera placement is a powerful storytelling tool. S. Leo Chiang's film *Mr. Cao Goes to Washington* (2012) follows Joseph Cao, the first Vietnamese-American US Congressperson, as he navigates the difficulties of being a rookie Republican congressman representing a largely African-American, Democratic district in Louisiana. Chiang explains how knowing your story helps you figure out your coverage:

> *I knew this was going to be a "fish out of water" story, a story about an outsider who is kind of on the margins of everything that he's a part of. He's a Republican in a majority Democratic district. He's a Vietnamese American in a majority African American district. His party doesn't really want him, and the Democrats don't really like him. How does somebody like that survive?*[5]

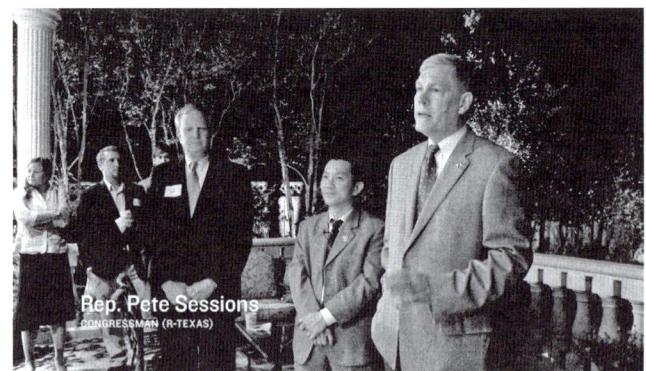
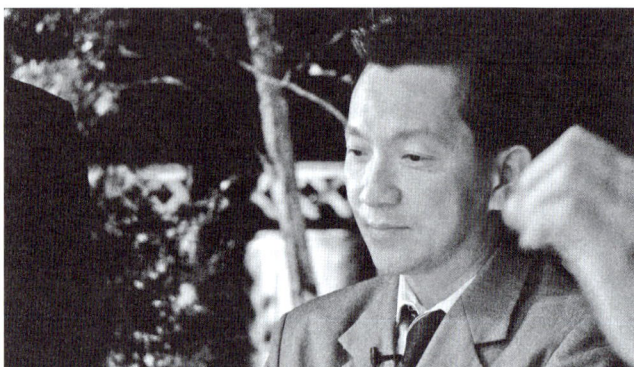

■ **Figure 7.32** In *Mr. Cao Goes to Washington*, we see more of Joseph Cao's reactions than of Rep. Sessions' speech.

In one very telling scene, Cao is at a Republican Congressional Campaign fundraiser and conservative Texas Congressman Pete Sessions is speaking about how Obama is destroying America by "putting us on a path to Central Europe." Chiang keeps the camera on Cao almost the entire time, even though Cao doesn't say a word (Figure 7.32). Chiang explains:

> *I always ask myself, "Whose scene is it?" I don't really care about Pete Sessions. I can hear what he's saying, but if I'm on him I don't necessarily get any additional information. I'm curious what Cao's thinking when he's hearing all these things that he disagrees with. And that happened a lot. I think he disagreed a lot with what the Republican Party—especially the more conservative faction of the Republican Party—had to say. So it was always interesting to watch his face and see how he was reacting.*[6]

Filming Group Interactions

Many documentary scenes involve more than two subjects. There are many different approaches to shooting groups of people, but the 180° rule applies to these as well. Choose your camera position and stay on one side of the line. Sometimes it's simplest if you can divide your group into two smaller groups (a single speaker vs a group listening, or placing yourself so that half the people are on one side of you, and the rest on the other). Then you can conceptualize the camera placement for the scene exactly like a two-person interaction.

For example, in *Mr. Cao Goes to Washington*, Joseph Cao gives a talk to a group of Young Republicans. Chiang draws the imaginary line using Cao's sightline to the audience, and keeps the camera on one side of the line while capturing a variety of shots (Figure 7.33).

There will be more complex scenes where you need to cross the line to cover the action you need. One way to do this is to move the camera, while it is running, as you cross the line. Then, include that shot in your sequence. This will reestablish the 180° degree line and your audience will not be disoriented. Another way is to use a neutral shot, like a cutaway, that doesn't include the subjects in the previous shot.

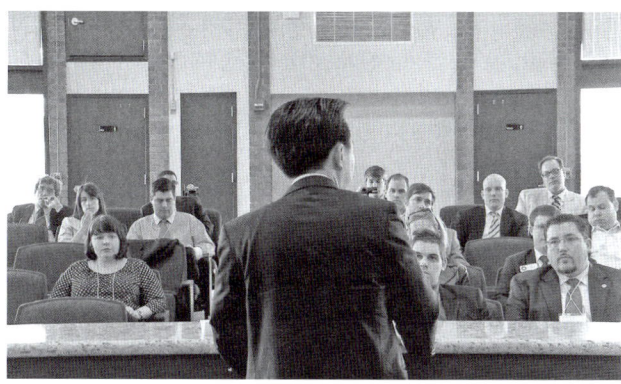
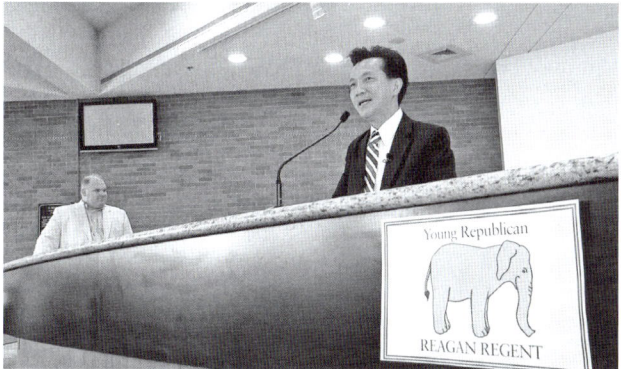
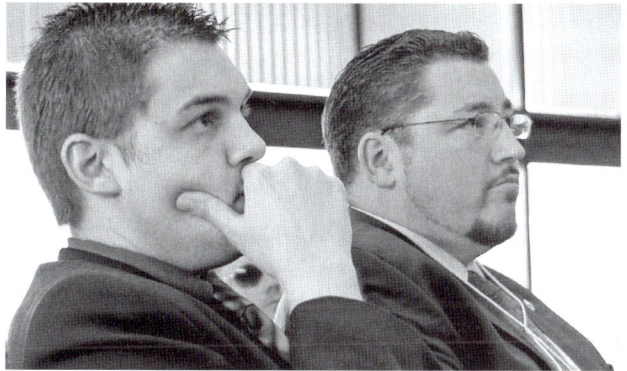

■ **Figure 7.33** Coverage of a simple group scene in *Mr. Cao Goes to Washington*. Director Chiang keeps the camera on one side of the 180° line.

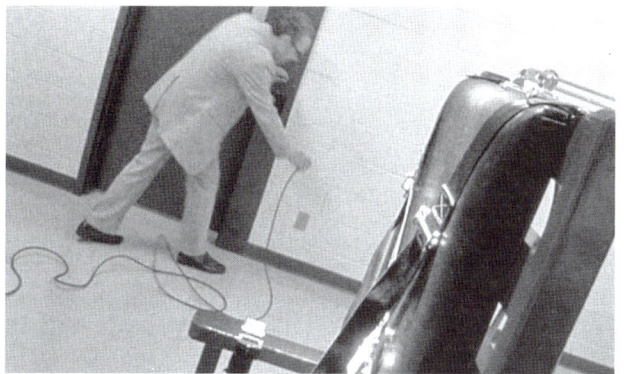
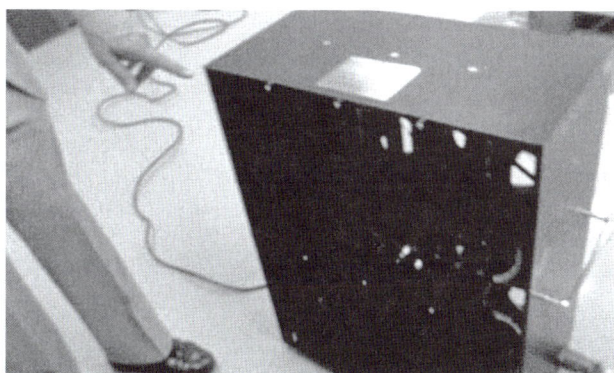
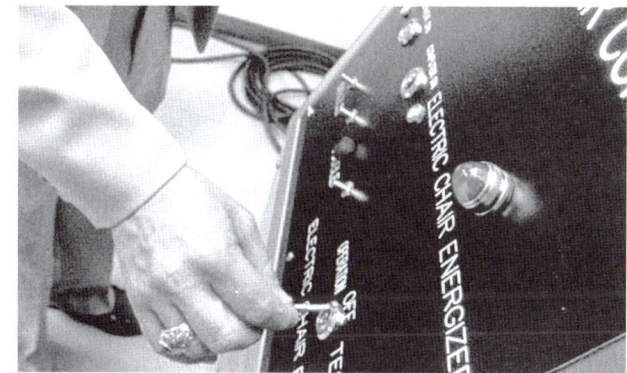

■ **Figure 7.34** A variety of still images from a "show and tell" sequence in *Mr. Death: The Rise and Fall of Fred A. Leuchter, Jr.*

Walking and Talking, Showing and Telling

Because formal **sit-down interviews** can get tedious for an audience, many filmmakers prefer to shoot their subjects in another, more dynamic, environment. The **walk and talk sequence** is one strategy for this. It involves walking with the subject, tracking backwards or alongside them as they talk. This is a good choice for films where the environment is part of the story. An example would be having a subject walk around their childhood neighborhood as they reminisce about the past.

Another version of this approach is the **show and tell sequence**, where the subject explains something to an off-screen director. The cinematographer will usually work handheld (Chapter 10), following the subject and filming a variety of camera angles and cutaways to allow the sequence to be edited together seamlessly using continuity conventions. An example is a sequence in *Mr. Death: The Rise and Fall of Fred A. Leuchter, Jr.* (2009), Errol Morris' film about an execution technician who becomes an infamous Holocaust denier. In the sequence, Leuchter shows Morris an electrocution system he

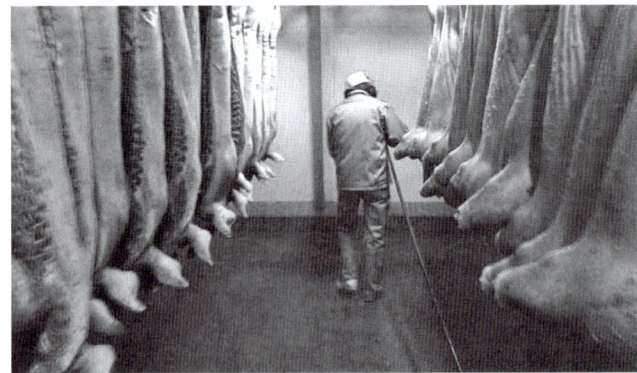

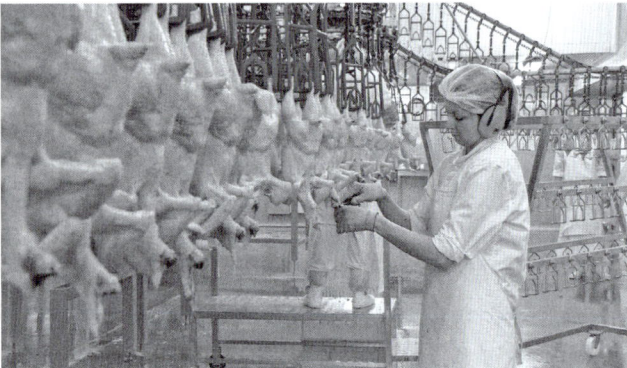

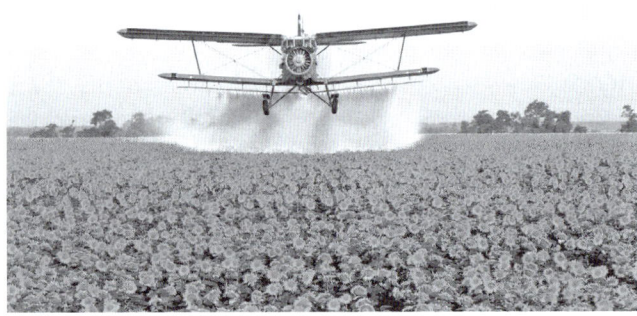

■ **Figure 7.35** Long takes in *Our Daily Bread*.

developed for a prison in Tennessee (Figure 7.34). Cinematographer Peter Donahue covers the scene with shots of Leuchter talking, as well as with a variety of shots that help tell the story and make editing smooth.

When filming any scene where a subject moves through space, it is important to think about one final principle of continuity: **screen direction**. Basically this principle dictates that the movement of a character (or a car, or animal) through the frame establishes their screen direction and the axis of action. For us to maintain a strict sense of continuity and progress toward a destination, we must maintain this screen direction from shot to shot by staying on the same side of the 180° line. This means that if a subject enters frame left and exits frame right from one shot, the following shot should also involve them traveling from left to right. Otherwise, they will appear to have switched directions and be traveling back to their original departure point.

Maintaining only one screen direction over the course of a long traveling sequence can get monotonous for a viewer, however. It is possible to change screen direction and still maintain the feel of a character's progress toward their destination. One strategy involves showing the character changing direction within the shot. Another is to film the subject from a neutral angle, like heading right towards the camera. After this shot, you can move your camera to the other side of the subject's path and it won't appear that they are reversing direction.

Entering and Exiting the Frame

Allowing moving subjects to enter and exit the frame in each shot is especially useful when it's time to edit a moving-through-space sequence. Cutting from the moment a subject exits the frame to the moment they enter the frame is a very smooth edit, although it is not necessarily the one you need make. By allowing a moving character to enter and exit the frame, you give the editor a range of possible places in which to cut into the action.

The Long Take

Some directors, instead of relying on cutting to tell their story, prefer to shoot in long takes. This approach allows the actions and relationships of an entire scene to develop within a single shot, in real time. These shots can be as long as several minutes. Consider that the average shot length in a conventional documentary runs around two to six seconds, and you'll have a sense of what a radical aesthetic departure the long take is. Because one essentially never cuts into a master shot, there is no question during production about spatial orientation, or matching shot content or actions. By the same token, the long take makes it impossible to cut out extraneous actions, terrain, or time. This real-time unfolding of events gives the viewer a long time to ponder the image, and that is the power of this shot. Viewers are asked to look, think, and then consider again what it is they are seeing, as the film flows on in the real time of everyday life. They are also given the opportunity to choose for themselves what part of the scene to pay attention to, rather than have the editor dictate what they should see and when. In the appropriate story, this immersion into a single perspective for a long unbroken period can communicate the feeling of truly being "in the moment" instead of witnessing an abbreviated construction of it, and this can be profound.

An example of the long take can be found in *Our Daily Bread* (2005), Nikolaus Geyrhalter's documentary about modern industrial food production. The film opts to depict each scene, whether it is showing us meat processing or a chicken farm, in long uninterrupted takes (Figure 7.35).

The opening shot, of a worker hosing down the floor of a slaughterhouse, lasts more than a full minute. On both sides, we see pig carcasses. The absence of cutting creates a powerful emotional effect as we are forced to experience the uniform size and shape of each animal, and the scale of this operation. In subsequent shots, the long duration forces us to be present with what is happening, and to question our complicity with this system of food production that reduces all life—plant, animal, and even the human workers—to a uniform commodity.

STYLIZED EXPRESSIVE SEQUENCES

Errol Morris is a documentary filmmaker who creates resonant, stylized visual sequences that work in many ways to complement, and sometimes contradict, what is being said in his interview footage. In *Mr. Death: The Rise and Fall of Fred A. Leuchter, Jr.*, there is a montage (Chapter 19) that accompanies Leuchter's account of how he met his wife (Figure 7.36).

The images feel exquisitely planned, as if they came from a big-budget commercial rather than a documentary. This is not surprising, since Morris also directs TV commercials, and cinematographer Peter Donahue had worked mostly on commercials prior to this film. The **sound design** (Chapter 21) also contributes to the feeling of heightened reality. Morris has recruited his subject (Leuchter) as an actor in these scenes, blurring the boundary between fiction and documentary. Finally, our curiosity about how these images relate to the subject of the film draws us further into the film's world as we wait for their significance to be revealed. Eventually we are told that Leuchter met his wife, a waitress, in the coffee shop where he has breakfast.

INFOGRAPHICS AND ANIMATION

Many documentaries rely on graphics and/or animation to convey complex information. **Infographics** can be a powerful way to help your audience absorb critical information that is dense. These can be as simple as text cards over moving images, or a slow zoom into on a map, as S. Leo Chiang does in several of his films (Figure 7.37).

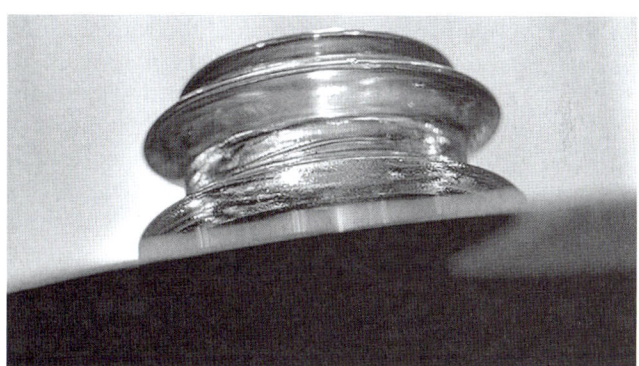
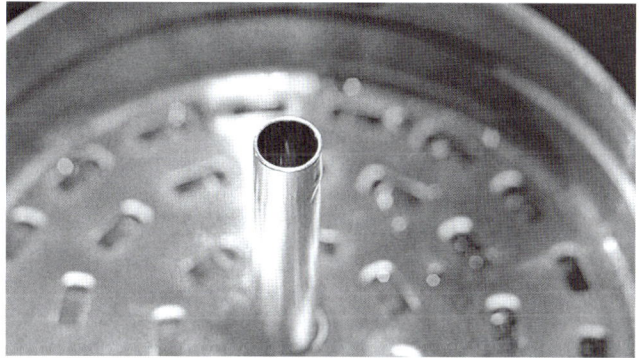
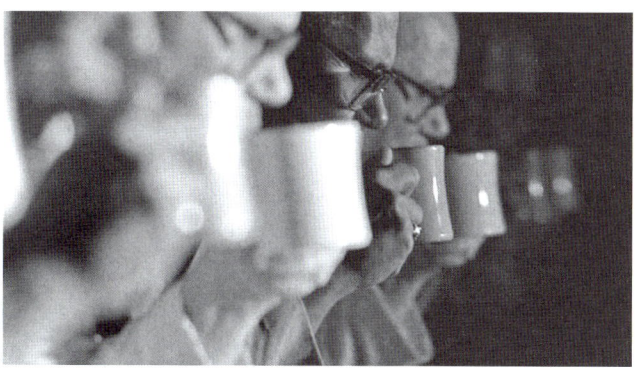

■ **Figure 7.36** Images from the "coffee montage" in *Mr. Death: The Rise and Fall of Fred A. Leuchter, Jr.*

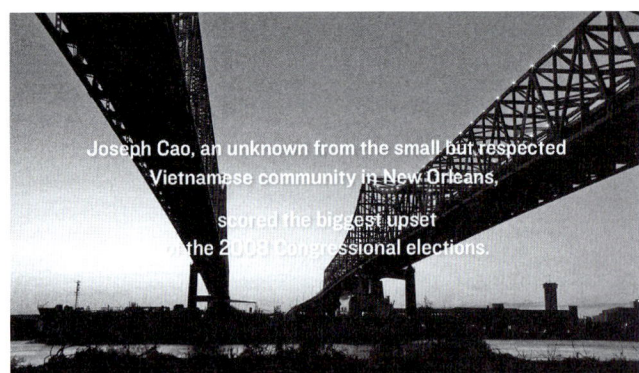 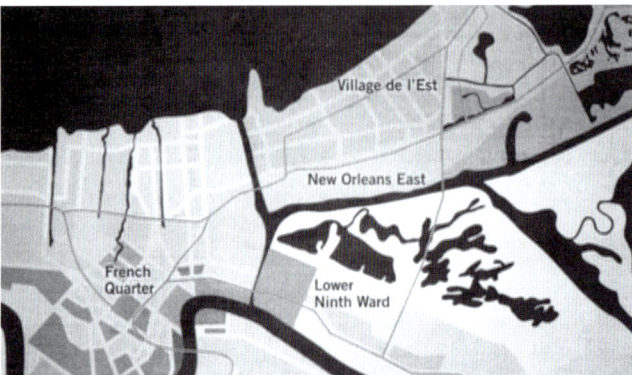

■ **Figure 7.37** Text cards give us critical establishing information in *Mr. Cao Goes to Washington* (left). An animated map shows us where New Orleans' Vietnamese community is located in Chiang's *A Village Called Versailles* (2009).

■ CONCLUSION

It is essential that anyone hoping to tell stories with moving images develops a deep working knowledge of the concepts of framing, composition, and coverage. It is with these building blocks that you will build your documentary, weaving together story, information, meaning, and emotion. Being aware of the expressive power of camera angles and moves allows one to conceive of shots, sequences, and scenes that are narratively and emotionally eloquent. When it comes to the aesthetics of the still or moving frame, we have only laid the groundwork in this chapter. There are many factors that contribute to the graphic qualities of your images: choice of imaging format, lens selection, camera support, lighting design, exposure, and frame rate, just to name a few. In the next chapters, we look at the impact of camera and format choice, and lens optics, on your documentary.

CHAPTER 8

The Digital Video System

When you pick up a camera—whether it is your smartphone or a sophisticated high-resolution video camera—you are in fact inserting yourself into a history that spans almost 150 years. Today's cameras, even **high-definition** (HD) video cameras, rely on the same basic principles that drove the earliest motion picture systems. As a professional media maker who seeks to be in control of the aesthetic possibilities of the medium you are working in, you will need to understand a complex array of specifications: frame rates, aspect ratios, resolutions, sampling, and data rates. Each of these has much to do with technological innovations that occurred at various points in the history of the film, and then the video, moving image. Understanding those principles is critical if you are going to make the best use of the technology available to you today, and tomorrow.

FILM: A MECHANICAL AND CHEMICAL MEDIUM

As early as the 1880s, people, especially scientists, were trying to find ways of reproducing motion so they could analyze natural phenomena around them. Forms of photography had existed since the 1830s, but the glass or metal plates, and the long time necessary to fix the image in silver halide crystals, made it unfeasible to capture subjects in motion. It was only in the 1890s that the Lumière brothers in France and Thomas Edison in the United States pioneered the first systems for capturing motion and playing it back for audiences.

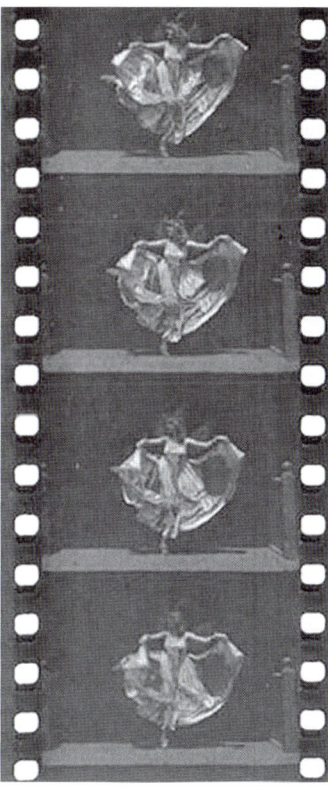

Film is a mechanical and photochemical motion picture system. It creates the illusion of motion through the rapid presentation of a series of sequential photographic images fixed to a flexible and transparent strip of cellulose or acetate. A film camera gathers light from the outside world through its lens, and focuses that image onto the film to create exposures. A film projector pushes light from within the apparatus, through the images and through a lens, to focus and project that image onto a screen.

The early films were recorded and played back at a **frame rate** of about 16 frames per second (fps), resulting in the **flicker effect** we associate with early motion pictures. Eventually a frame rate of 24 fps became standard. Each frame is projected onto a screen and held stationary long enough for the viewer to register the image before it is quickly replaced with the subsequent still image, which is again held for a fraction of a second, and so on. The viewer perceives this rapid presentation of still images as motion through the perceptual phenomenon known as **short-range apparent motion**.[1] Simply put, when shown a rapidly changing series of sequential still images in which there is only a slight difference from image to image, humans process this visual stimulus with the same perceptual mechanism used in the visual processing of real motion. This mechanism transforms the series of still images into motion through the psychological and physiological interpolation of information between the still frames. This "magic" is what creates the possibility of recording and playing back motion in film and video (Figure 8.1).

■ **Figure 8.1** A 35mm filmstrip of the Edison production *Butterfly Dance* (ca. 1894–95).

From the film medium's earliest days, directors used it to create non-fiction stories. As discussed in Chapter 2, the Lumière brothers used film to record early scenes of real life, called "actualities." Robert Flaherty's *Nanook of the North* (1922), about the life of an Inuit family in Northern Canada, is often considered the first "documentary". Others, including John Grierson's team at the Empire Marketing Board in the United Kingdom, used film to create monumental works about British workers and industry, including *Drifters* (1929), about herring fishermen, and *Song of Ceylon* (1935), about the colonial tea trade. These films relied heavily on visual storytelling and narration, as the technology for portable **sync sound** did not yet exist. During the late 1950s, Robert Drew and Ricky Leacock pioneered the use of a crystal-sync motor that would allow sound and picture recorded separately to be synchronized in postproduction. This was a major development for documentary, as filmmakers were free to shoot in places that had not been documented before, and could record people talking in the field on truly portable equipment. As Erik Barnouw wrote in his seminal history of documentary, "Field footage began to talk."[2] An early example of these new **direct cinema** films was Drew's *Primary* (1960), which caught the drama of a political campaign featuring candidate John F. Kennedy with an immediacy audiences had not seen before. Over the entire history of film, including documentary, technological advances were driven by filmmakers trying to do things that had never been done before. As new equipment opened up new possibilities, the form itself changed.

VIDEO: AN ELECTRONIC MEDIUM

While film cameras and cinematography emerged from the world of still photography, the ancestor of modern video technology is radio. As early as the 1920s, scientists were working on the developments that would lead to television and modern video. The biggest issue facing them was how to take a two-dimensional electronic image and turn it into a continuous signal so that it could be transmitted or broadcast. The answer developed by scientists, such as John Baird in Scotland and Vladimir Zworikin in the United States, was to "scan" the image, breaking it down into a series of lines of picture information that could be fed over a wire to a transmitter as a continuous electronic signal. The first scanners were mechanical, but scientists quickly realized that they could control a beam of negatively charged electrons using a ring of magnets to "paint" a picture on the end of a cathode ray tube (Figure 8.2). This scanning process is still at the heart of video image capture and reproduction today.

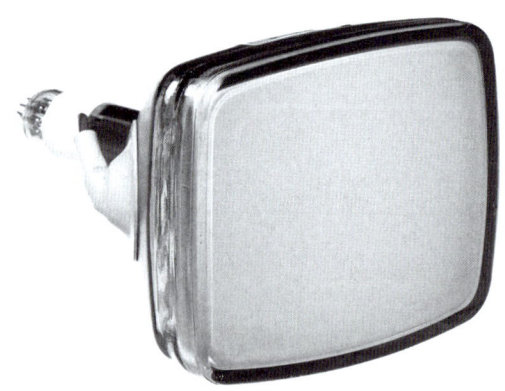

■ **Figure 8.2** The cathode ray tube emits a beam of high energy electrons, which hit the end of the tube painted with phosphors, causing it to glow momentarily.

By the late 1930s, the United Kingdom, Germany, and the United States had video transmission systems that could capture picture and sound in one location and send it almost instantaneously over fairly long distances. During the early years of television, electronic recording devices did not exist. The only way to record those images was to film them from a television screen. TV remained basically a "live" medium until the development of a viable recorder and videotape by the Ampex Corporation in 1956. The early recorders were expensive and bulky, making them appropriate only for network television use.

The late 1960s were a watershed moment for documentary. In 1967, the Sony Corporation developed inexpensive portable video recording equipment that offered, finally, a real alternative to film (Figure 8.3, top left). One of the biggest attractions was the possibility of shooting for extended periods of time on a very inexpensive medium, magnetic tape. A black-and-white camera and a microphone were connected by cables to a battery-operated open reel video tape recorder. At first the output was not considered broadcast

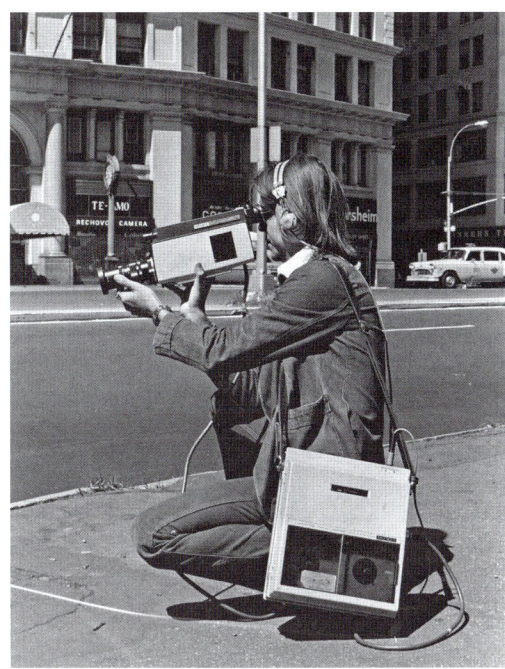
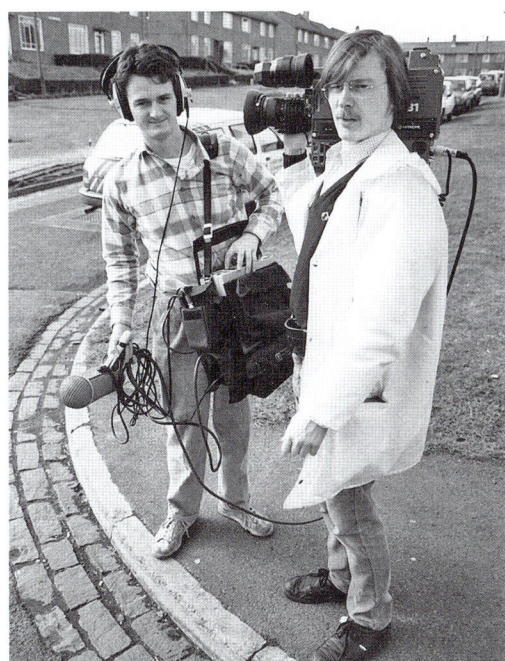
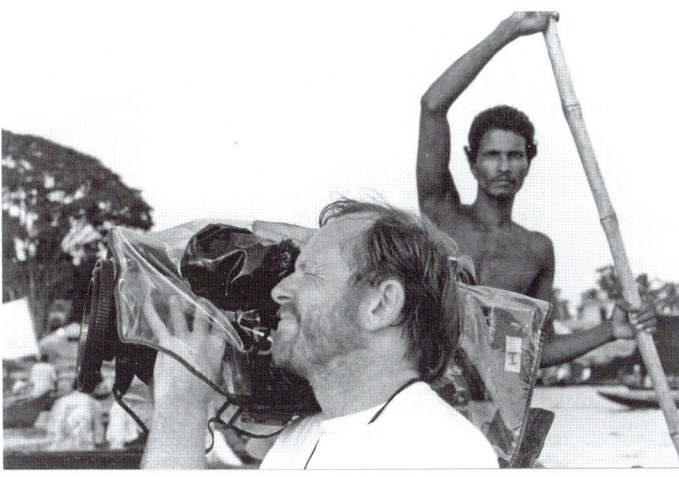

■ **Figure 8.3** Edin Velez, an early video "pioneer," with a Sony Portapak (top left). On the top right are Philip Johnston and Ian Bodie with a typical 1980s video equipment package: a U-matic camera and separate recording deck. The development of the CCD sensor allowed for the consolidation of camera and recorder in the form of the camcorder in the 1980s (bottom), pictured is cinematographer Gary Griffin shooting Prudence Hill's *Three Women* (1995) in Bangladesh.

quality, but the airing of Susan and Alan Raymond's Emmy-award winning *The Police Tapes* on ABC in 1977 meant that portable video was here to stay (Figure 8.4). In addition, the video equipment was simple to operate in difficult circumstances and much more light-sensitive than film, allowing for night shooting with only street lighting as illumination, giving viewers access to a world that had never before been shown on screen.

In the early 1970s, Sony developed a color video cassette recorder for more professional use. It used a 3/4" tape format, called U-matic, and the deck still had to be connected to the camera with a cable and carried separately, often by the sound recordist (Figure 8.3, top right).

In the 1980s, the camera and the video tape recorder were married into one unit, and the modern camcorder was born (Figure 8.3, bottom). This development was very important

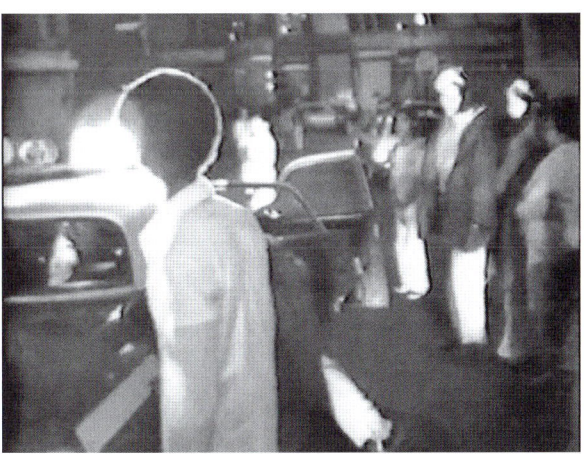

■ **Figure 8.4** *The Police Tapes*, for which Susan and Alan Raymond spent three months filming police in the South Bronx, opened new ground for documentary by using simple black-and-white portable equipment designed for amateur use.

for documentary as it allowed a single individual to record both sound and image. Over the years, development of smaller and smaller tape formats such as Hi-8 and MiniDV consolidated this trend, making unobtrusive cameras and a truly personal approach to documentary possible.

Analog vs Digital Video

For most of its history, video was an **analog** medium. This meant that the light and color of the image corresponded to the strength and frequency of its analogous electronic signal. At the turn of the twenty-first century, the "digital revolution" transformed media production. Digital media involves creating, recording, and disseminating video and audio by transforming light and sound values into **binary code**, or a series of ones and zeros. There are numerous advantages to digital media, including superior resolution, greater flexibility for creative manipulation, and the ability to make copies with no generational loss. Importantly, the advent of digital media meant not only better quality imagery, but material that could be edited on a computer, transforming the workflow for documentary filmmakers. More recently, the advent of digital video precipitated another revolution by delivering HD video formats in addition to the **standard-definition** (SD) formats that were previously available. In this book, the term "digital video" encompasses both SD and HD formats. We will explain what these different formats mean in detail later in this chapter.

The Video Image Today

While the film system has remained virtually unchanged in well over 100 years, video technology seems to be in a perpetual state of rapid evolution. New video cameras and **formats** are introduced almost yearly, and swift technological obsolescence is the rule rather than the exception. Unfortunately, the world of video engineers, corporations, and government committees have not managed to coordinate their efforts to establish a single national video standard, let alone a worldwide standard. With enormous profits on the line, corporate rivals and nations continually race to develop their own superior systems in the hope that theirs will become the new standard. Current count reveals dozens of major digital video formats, making the world of video production seem like a technological tar pit for emerging filmmakers and veterans alike. Most filmmakers deal with these issues when confronted with having to make choices among the bewildering variety of cameras available. Before we launch into a discussion of camera choices, though, it is important to consider the complex world of digital video formats. In video, format can mean a number of things, and these fall into four broad categories.

Recording Formats

Recording Formats (also called **acquisition formats**) determine the way a particular system, like a camera, encodes and records video. Current examples include AVCHD, XAVC, HDV, and MXF. Older tape-based examples include DVC-Pro, DVCam, and miniDV. Recording formats have unique technical specifications including **resolution**, **aspect ratio**, **data rate**, and **encoding system**.

Media Formats

The physical medium on which video data is recorded is often referred to as its **media format**. Historically most video formats were tape-based, but these have largely been replaced by file-based media formats that record on various forms of solid-state memory. Examples of popular media formats today include P2, SDHC/SDXL, CF, and SxS cards (pp. 122–124). Most of these media are capable of handling many different recording formats.

Display Formats

Display formats are a set of specifications for how video is broadcast, received, and displayed. In the United States, they are codified in a set of nationally mandated digital television broadcast standards devised by the **Advanced Television Systems Committee**

(ATSC). Examples include 1080i and 720p (both HD formats) and 640 x 480 (an older, SD format). In addition, there are a variety of formats used for Internet streaming on services like Vimeo and YouTube, which are not subject to regulation. **Digital Cinema** has separate sets of format specifications, established by film studios under the **Digital Cinema Initiative (DCI)**, which specifically address digital theatrical projection.

Audio/Video Codecs

A **codec** (short for "compression/decompression") is a way of reducing digital file size to make the large amounts of information generated by digital media production easier to store and transmit. These are not technically formats, but they are so integral to the process of working with, within, and across formats (in recording, editing, and distribution) that a filmmaker must be able to identify them and understand their function. The most commonly used codecs are those approved by the Motion Picture Experts Group including MPEG-2, MPEG-4, and H.264. Related to codec is **data rate**, which is explained in detail below.

In the United States and globally, there are a wide variety of acquisition, media, and display formats, as well as dozens of audio and video codecs. They are constantly evolving, and it would be folly to try to cover them all in detail. But in the world of digital video, knowing some technical information is imperative in order to make informed creative choices and to develop a smooth creative and technical process from preproduction to distribution. It is worth noting that while there are a huge variety of options in terms of format, all of these must fall into a set of specific categories that define image size, frame rate, and other key aspects of the video signal so that we can record material that viewers can watch, whether on a television, a computer, or a digital theater projector.

Broadcast Standards

In the United States, **video standards** are defined by the ATSC and are summarized in Figure 8.5. The ATSC, like the **National Television System Committee (NTSC)** before them, is a consortium of engineers, telecommunications companies, and government policy makers who are responsible for setting video standards. These standards ensure compatibility between digital image recording and display systems across all nations that adopt the standard (these include the United States, Mexico, Canada, and other countries in Central America, the Caribbean, and the Asia Pacific region). The analogous standards consortium in Europe is the **European Broadcast Union (EBU)**. The **International Telecommunications Union (ITU)**, a specialized agency of the United Nations responsible for issues that concern information and communication technologies, is also involved in

ATSC Digital Television Standard Video Formats				
	Resolution		Aspect Ratio	Frame Rate
	Vertical	Horizontal		Progressive • Interlaced
HD	1080	1920	16:9	24/23.976 30 (60i)
				30/29.97 29.97(59.94i)
HD	720	1280	16:9	24/23.976
				30/29.97
				60/59.97
SD	480	704	16:9, 4:3	24/23.976 30 (60i)
				30/29.97 29.97(59.94i)
				60/59.97
	480	640	4:3	24/23.976 30 (60i)
				30/29.97 29.97(59.94i)
				60/59.97
ITC Ultra High Definition 4K Standard Video Formats*				
UHD	3840	2160	16:9	24/23.976p
				30/29.97p
				60/59.97p
*The ATSC is developing ATSC 3.0 standards that will include 4K for 2016.				

■ **Figure 8.5** The ATSC standards for recording and exhibiting video were last revised in 2006. The new standards, including for Ultra High Definition (4K), are due out in 2016. The International Telecommunication Commission's standards for 4K broadcast are included here as they are currently available on many 4K cameras.

defining standards globally. There are a variety of features that these standards define, including **image resolution**, **scanning type**, and **frame rate**.

Figure 8.5 lists the 17 digital video format standards supported by the ATSC broadcast system. Seven of these are HD formats and the rest are SD. Remember, the standards are not just for broadcast display, but for the capturing of images as well, and are reflected in the options available on your video camera.

Resolution

Whenever there is an evaluation of video image quality, you will hear the term **resolution**. Resolution generally refers to the ability to reproduce visual detail: sharpness of line, subtlety and degrees of luminance, as well as the accuracy of color. Video resolution is affected by a bewildering and complex array of factors. These include the format scanning system (**progressive** or **interlaced**), lens quality, the quality of the camera's electronics, the number of pixels in the sensor, sampling **bit rates**, **chroma subsampling**, and data **compression** (all explained later). To a great extent, though, resolution is a function of the number of pixels that make up the image (Figure 8.6). We can determine the pixel resolution of a given format by multiplying the vertical lines by the horizontal pixels. Standard-definition digital video (704 × 480, for example) contains a little more than 338,000 pixels with which to define the image. High-definition video, with a resolution 1920 × 1080, provides for 2,073,600 pixels per frame. With this greater resolution capacity offering more detailed visual information to the eye, it is no surprise that HD looks crisper and more vivid.

Occasionally, you will see or hear reference to 720p HD. This is an older HD format that you will find as an option on many cameras. One might wonder why anyone would use 720p HD, which has only half the pixel count of regular HD. This is where scanning frame rates enter into the resolution question. 1080i has twice as many total pixels, but the fact that it is an interlaced signal (p. 113) means that it creates a frame by making two fields, each lasting for a 1/60th second. Each field contains only half those lines (540). So in the final calculation, 720p, with its progressively scanned full image in each frame, delivers somewhere around 56 million pixels per second, while 1080i utilizes around 62 million pixels per second. This means that 720p only offers slightly less resolution in the image than 1080i.

It is important to understand that HD is a complete system of image creation and exhibition. To realize the improved resolution of HD, you not only need to shoot on HD

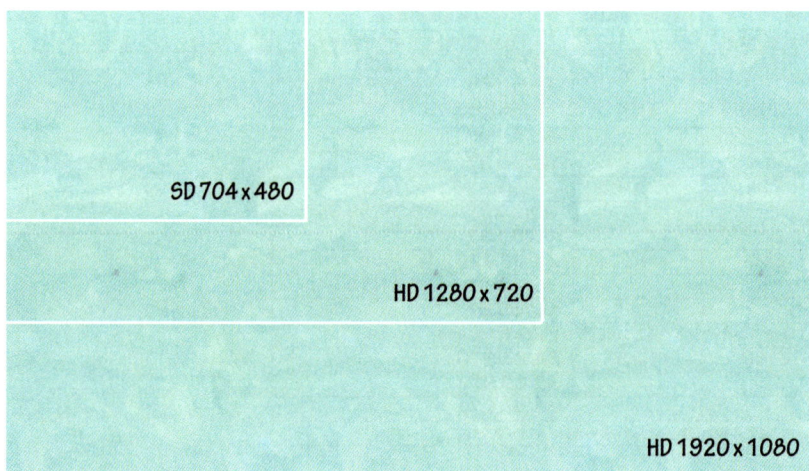

■ **Figure 8.6** The resolution of video formats can be roughly determined by multiplying the horizontal by the vertical pixels. This illustration shows the relative resolution capabilities based on pixel count.

but you also must master your final project on an HD format and display that image on an HD-capable monitor or projector. Shooting HD, but displaying the footage on an SD monitor, will reduce the quality of your original image to—you guessed it—480 lines of vertical resolution. Conversely, if your footage originated in an SD format, displaying it on an HD monitor will not increase the resolution quality.

Aspect Ratio

SD and HD have different **aspect ratios**. SD video has an aspect ratio of 4:3, of 1.33:1, while HD has an aspect ratio of 16 x 9 (or 1.78:1), making it closer to the widescreen film aspect ratio (1.85:1) familiar to theater-going audiences. See Chapter 7 for more on aspect ratios.

Scanning Type

As we discussed, digital video records and plays back images using an electronic process known as **scanning,** which analyzes the image line by line and outputs it for recording. As you can see in Figure 8.5, starting in the days of SD analog video, the video frame was split into a series of horizontal lines allowing it to be processed as a continuous stream of signal information. In the United States, there were 525 lines of picture, in Europe 625, and there were variations in other countries. Digital video offers two different methods for scanning a full frame of video: interlaced (i) and progressive (p) as well as different frame rates.

Interlaced Scanning

In the case of **interlaced scanning**, the camera's imaging device first outputs the odd-numbered horizontal pixel lines (1, 3, 5, 7, etc.), one at a time, from the top to the bottom, creating a half-resolution image that is called a **field** of video. Then, the imaging device returns to the top of the frame to output the even-numbered rows (2, 4, 6, etc.), from the top to the bottom, to fill in the rest of the information with a second field. These two fields of video are interlaced to make up one full frame (Figure 8.7). All this electronic information is then converted into digital data for storage on the recording media. During playback, the monitor or receiver duplicates the exact same interlaced process, line for line, field for field, and frame for frame, in perfect synchronization with the scanning used to record the image. The digital information is converted back into electrical voltage, which is then translated into light values (an image) as the electrical voltage causes the horizontal rows of pixels in a monitor to glow. In a **plasma display**, these pixels are colored fluorescent

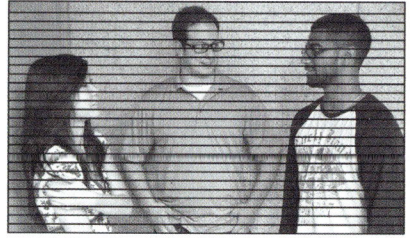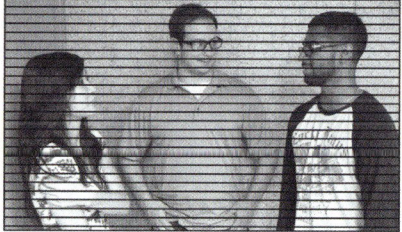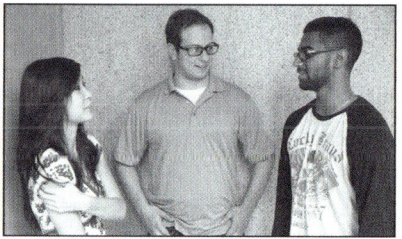

■ **Figure 8.7** Interlaced video. First, the odd lines are scanned, from top to bottom, then the even lines are scanned, creating the second field. The result is a full image.

cells, in an **LCD monitor** they are tiny LCD crystals, and in an **LED monitor** they are tiny LED lights. Interlaced scanning was developed as the standard scanning method for the original analog video systems because it refreshes the image more frequently to reduce flicker in the image.

When you see the scanning rate of 60i ("i" for interlaced) in the ATSC table in Figure 8.5, it means 60 fields of video information interlaced per second, for a **frame rate** of 30 fps. In other words, each field contains half the picture information, and lasts half as long as the full frame. Interlaced scanning has remained in the ATSC standards to ensure backward compatibility and as a way to deliver high-quality content at reduced signal **bandwidth**.

Progressive Scanning

Progressive scanning differs from interlaced scanning in that one frame is not made up of two interlaced fields (odd lines first, then even lines). Instead, with progressive scanning both the sensor and display are synchronized to scan a full frame of video (lines 1, 2, 3, 4, etc.) from top to bottom in a continuous line, like a farmer ploughing a field. There are no fields, just complete frames (Figure 8.8). Progressive scanning frame rates are written as 24p, 30p, and 60p ("p" for progressive). Although progressive scanning requires more processing power and bandwidth than interlaced video at the same frame rate, many cinematographers prefer its "filmic" look (see "In Practice: 24p or 60i?" on the next page).

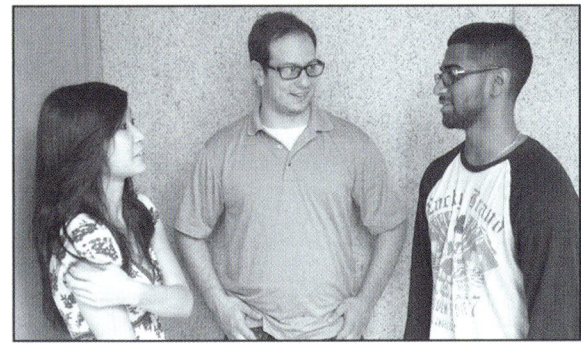

One serious problem occurs when you try to view an interlaced image on a progressive scan display (including computer monitors). The process of the progressive scanning pattern will present the two interlaced fields as slightly offset, which is especially noticeable with objects in motion (or during camera movements). The resulting image will have a **combing** artifact along edges in the image (Figure 8.9). To avoid this, the interlaced scanned video should undergo a process known as "de-interlacing" before it is displayed on progressive scan monitors.

Frame Rate

Frame rate refers to the number of still frames that are captured by a camera, or played back on a viewing system, over a specific period of time (usually 1 second). Digital video systems in North America run at a frame rate of 30 fps. In many parts of the world, including Europe, 25 fps is the standard. In the ATSC Video Format Standards table (Figure 8.5), you'll notice that there are whole number frame rates supported, like 30, 60, and 24. However, there are also frame rates listed that are ever so slightly slower than their whole number counterparts, namely 59.94, 29.97, and 23.976. These slowed-down frame rates (0.1 percent slower) are legacies of the old NTSC system, which remain with us in order for new equipment to stay compatible with SD format standards (which were derived from the NTSC system).

■ **Figure 8.8** Progressive scanning draws a full frame of video, from top to bottom, without skipping any lines.

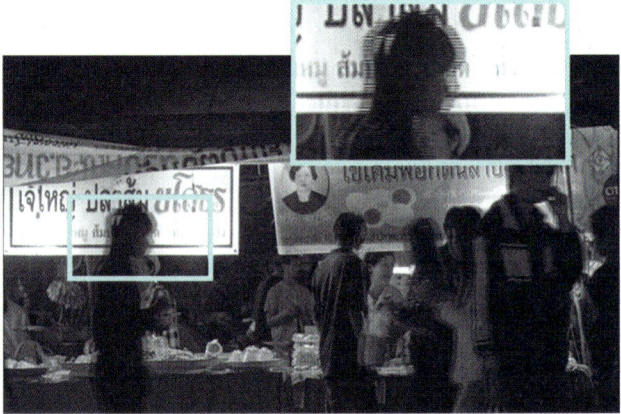

■ **Figure 8.9** When interlaced video is shown on progressive displays, a "combing" artifact occurs at the edges of moving objects caused by the displaced scan lines (notice that the stationary objects do not show any combing).

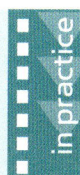

24P OR 60I?

Deciding whether to use a progressive or interlaced scanning mode is a complex question. While interlaced (60i) might seem like the obvious choice for anything headed for broadcast, some filmmakers find there is an aesthetic advantage to shooting 24p. (In many parts of the world, the choice is between 50i and 25p.) While it is hard to quantify the difference, the consensus suggests the way that 24p handles motion is more "filmlike" even for a project that will be shown in a broadcast context. On the other hand, if you want to capture the details of motion, as with sports, you may prefer the 60i rendition. Remember that many other factors, such as the size of the image sensor and the type of lens, are also part of the "look." Here are some documentary cinematographers on this topic:

S. Leo Chiang: *I mostly shoot on 24p. I just like the look of it. Most of the people I know shoot on 24p for their indie projects, although most freelance gigs with broadcasters I've done have been 60i. 60i feels more cold and traditionally "video like." 24p feels more "film like," more cinematic.*[3]

David Alvarado: *I shoot exclusively on 24p, but just for the look of it. If you want something to look cinematic and fluid, shoot 24p on 48 shutter speed. If you want it to look like television video, go for 60i or 30p. I think it's just a preference, so there's no right and wrong. Do a side by side comparison for yourself and see what you like most.*[4]

Vincent Laforet: *Film is just as much about what you DON'T show the audience as with what you DO. Motion blur, lack of sharpness, and movement all help to create movie magic. If images are too sharp and you see too much detail . . . that's not always a good thing.*[5]

Todd Grossman: *The creative choice between 24p and 60i can be a very subjective one. Whereas most high-end HD filmmakers will shoot 24p for the purpose of getting that film look, a lot of documentary and action-sports cameramen prefer 60i for the exact reason that others dislike it: the sharpness, clarity, and deep-focus ability are great for capturing the action.*[6]

Before the advent of color TV, the original NTSC black-and-white video signal was a nice and neat 30 fps. In the early 1950s, the NTSC developed the standards for color television and in an effort to make color television compatible with all preexisting monochrome receivers, the NTSC superimposed the color component on top of the existing black-and-white signal along a **subcarrier frequency** (3.58 MHz) rather than create a whole new, fully integrated signal. This ensured that even though a program was broadcast in color, viewers who owned black-and-white TV sets could still see it. However, this created interference between the two signals, and required that the frame rate be altered. The 30 fps signal (60 fields per second) became 29.97 fps (59.94 fields per second). Therefore, when we are talking about video production, the rate 60i (perhaps the most widely used) is actually 59.94 fields per second (29.97 fps). The 24p frame rate is actually 23.976. Most video cameras in fact shoot in these slowed-down frame rates, even if the frame rate options menu lists the rounded numbers.

While there are other options, filmmakers today will likely choose between shooting at a frame rate of 60i or 24p. The 24p frame (24 fps, progressive) was developed specifically to be compatible with, and to duplicate, the look of motion picture film, which runs at a frame rate of 24 fps. 24p video replicates some of the motion artifacts of film, giving it a so-called "film look" even when played back on 60i video monitors. Some people really like the 24p look, while others are not as convinced (see **"In Practice: 24p or 60i?"** above). If you are shooting 24p and planning to distribute on DVD or go to broadcast, you will need to convert to 30 fps through a **pulldown** process, so it's important to think through all stages of your project from production to distribution. This very common transfer process from a 24 fps system to a 30 fps system is explained in detail in Chapter 17.

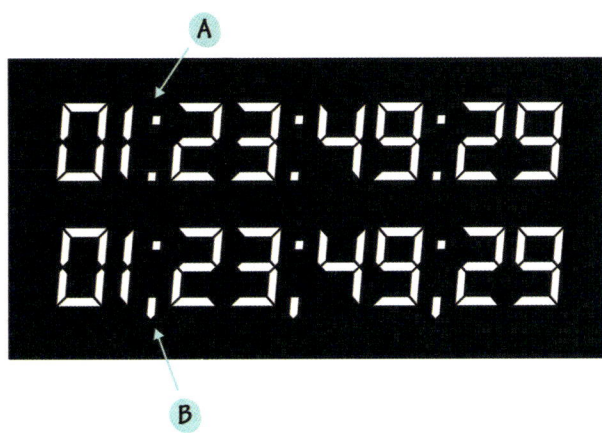

■ **Figure 8.10** Time code assigns a specific number to every video frame according to a format that indicates hours, minutes, seconds, and frames. Broadcast video uses only "drop frame" time code, easily identified by its use of semicolons (B), because it is time accurate. Some applications still provide the option to use "non-drop-frame" time code, which uses colons as separators (A).

TIME CODE

Regardless of the frame rate, every frame of a video recording is assigned a specific and unique number called **time code** (**TC**). Recorded right along with the video data for each and every frame is an electronic number with four sets of digits: hours, minutes, seconds, and frames. This numbering system is vital to the workflow of every video project. We use TC to quickly log, reference, or locate specific frames, to calculate the length of shots, scenes, and entire projects, to maintain audio and video synchronization, and to ensure frame-accurate edits. In short, TC, along with clip names, is the way we keep track of the frame-by-frame timing of every element, at every stage of a project. Virtually all video cameras have TC, although not all cameras allow you to set it to a number you want. Many offer a choice of two different flavors: **drop-frame time code (DF TC)** and **non-drop-frame time code (NDF TC)** (Figure 8.10). Why do we have two ways to count frames? Remember that in the early days of color television, it was found that the 30 fps signal produced interference between the sound and the color parts of the signal. The answer was to slow down the frame rate slightly (0.1 percent) from 30 fps to 29.97 fps.

Non-Drop-Frame Time Code (NDF TC) simply counts frames according to the original black-and-white video frame rate, assigning a new number to each video frame at a consistent rate of 30 fps. This seems simple, but it doesn't match real time and is rarely used. What looks like an hour of video in NDF TC is actually 1 hour and 3.6 seconds. That may not seem like such a big deal, but in broadcast television, where programs and commercials must conform to frame-accurate timing, it is crucial to have precise measurements.

Drop-Frame Time Code (DF TC) does not actually drop any video frames, but it does skip over some TC numbers from time to time in order to adjust the frame count to accurately reflect the true 29.97 fps of NTSC video. To be precise, the DF TC system skips over the :00 and :01 frame numbers once every minute, except for the 10th minute. Here is how the TC numbers change at each minute of footage (except for every 10th minute): 00;09;26;28, 00;09;26;29, 00;09;27;02, 00;09;27;03. After an hour of DF TC counting, we will arrive at TC 01;00;00;00 for exactly 1 hour of video footage. Most cameras will default to DF TC as this gives you a more accurate idea of your timing, and is what broadcasters require.

TYPES OF DIGITAL VIDEO CAMERAS

Historically, video cameras fell into fairly neat categories. Professional cameras were big, expensive, well made, and produced high-quality video. Consumer cameras were small, inexpensive, had an inferior image, but were easy to use. Today, small affordable cameras are delivering extremely high-quality images, so much so that professionals use them extensively. While consumer-level equipment tends to be fully automatic, many mid-level cameras offer control over basic and even more advanced functions that filmmakers can use to achieve sophisticated effects. For example the Canon XF300, at US $4,000, offers manual control over focus, aperture, frame rate, white balance, and data rate as well as professional audio inputs. These high-quality yet affordable video cameras may be too complex for the average consumer, but they are excellent when a polished and controlled look is important and a high-end, professional rig would be too big or expensive. In this book, we will focus on this mid-level range, and on some other cameras that are commonly used by independent filmmakers and students. There will always be trade-offs between cost and quality, but much of your decision about what camera to use will also be based on the particulars of your shooting situation and desired style.

One of the most important developments in documentary cinematography over the last decade has been the emergence of the **digital single-lens reflex (DSLR) camera** as a filmmaking tool. While the ability to shoot moving images with what was formerly a still camera was a feature intended for the consumer market, filmmakers seized on DSLRs and used them to create a new look in both documentary and narrative filmmaking. High-end DSLR cameras (like Canon's EOS series or Nikon's D series; see Figure 8.11) are designed with a large **complementary metal oxide semiconductor (CMOS)** sensor (see pp. 126–127), which takes high-resolution images, notably superior to those from previous generations of video cameras. In "movie-mode," the single CMOS sensor can capture and record 1920 × 1080 images at 24, 25, and 30 fps.

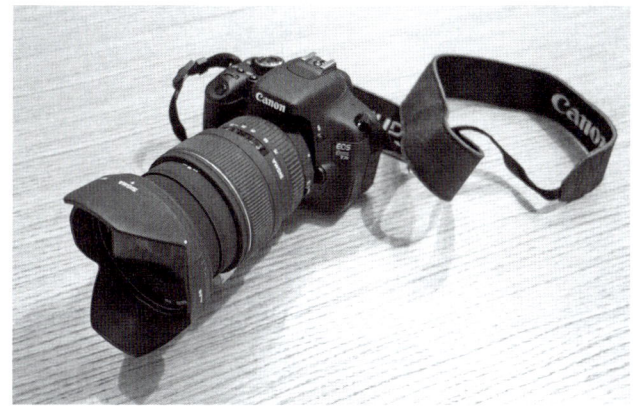

■ **Figure 8.11** DSLR cameras, such as this Canon T3i, are often used for documentary shooting.

A number of factors have made DSLR cinematography a very popular video production format: (1) an increase in SD and CF card storage capacity, and a drop in their price; (2) the fact that you can use an entire range of high-quality interchangeable lenses; (3) the large sensor and "big glass" make these cameras highly light sensitive, increasing control over depth of field (Chapter 9); (4) a substantially lower cost; and (5) the lightweight and compact body size, which can be helpful in situations where a large camera might impede intimacy (Figure 8.12).

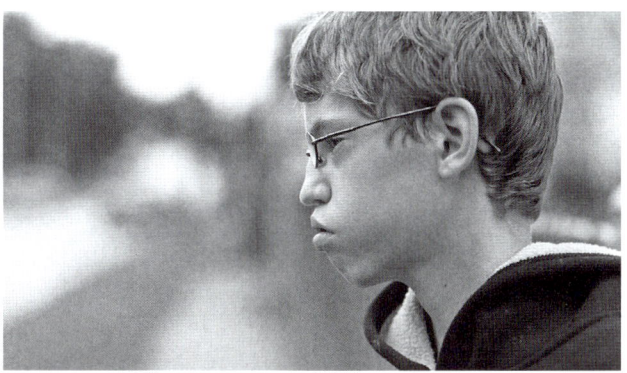

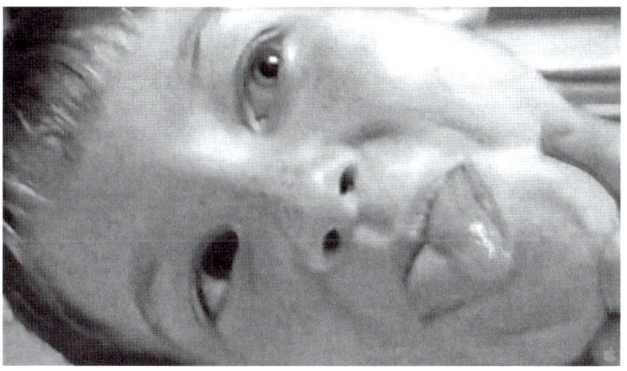

■ **Figure 8.12** *Bully* (2011), a documentary directed and shot by Lee Hirsch, takes advantage of the shallow depth of field (top) and intimacy (bottom) afforded by DSLR cameras.

There are downsides to DSLR video shooting. The shape and size of a DSLR camera, while perfect for still photography, is awkward for creating smooth camera moves and adjusting focal length and focus while shooting handheld, so most users will find that some sort of stabilizing rig is useful when shooting without a tripod (Chapter 10). Often these rigs can be more expensive than the camera itself. Another very important drawback for small crews is the fact that these cameras are poorly set up for audio recording, as they lack the XLR inputs that make single system shooting workable (Chapter 13). This means that in the field the filmmaker is dependent either on working **double-system**, with a separate sound recordist, or working with a rig that includes a microphone mount and bringing the audio in through a miniplug, which is an unstable connection and prone to interference. Another problem with single system sound is that in DSLRs, sound controls are often menu-based and therefore cumbersome to access, especially while shooting. Even with a shoulder mount (Chapter 10), the DSLR presents specific problems for observational shooting. Zoom lenses on DSLRs have less range (3:1 vs the 10:1 or 20:1 on a video camera) and the zoom has to be controlled manually instead of being motorized as on a video camera. In addition, the shallow depth of field gives a filmic look, but means that maintaining focus on a moving subject will be difficult. The autofocus capability of these cameras, while improving, is still not typically on par with that of camcorders. Finally, these cameras are designed for still photography, so shooting hours of moving footage can trigger overheating problems, which may result in camera shutdown. Despite these limitations, though, documentary filmmakers are making great use of DSLRs.

If you are planning to use this highly affordable camera type, you should be aware that there are two main groups of formats, based on sensor size. One, called **APS-C**, is loosely based on an older film format and measures 22mm x 15mm. The second is called **full 35mm** and is about 35mm x 24mm. Although they will both offer excellent results in terms of image detail and the ability to create shallow depth of field, the larger sensor generally offers superior image resolution and light handling capabilities.

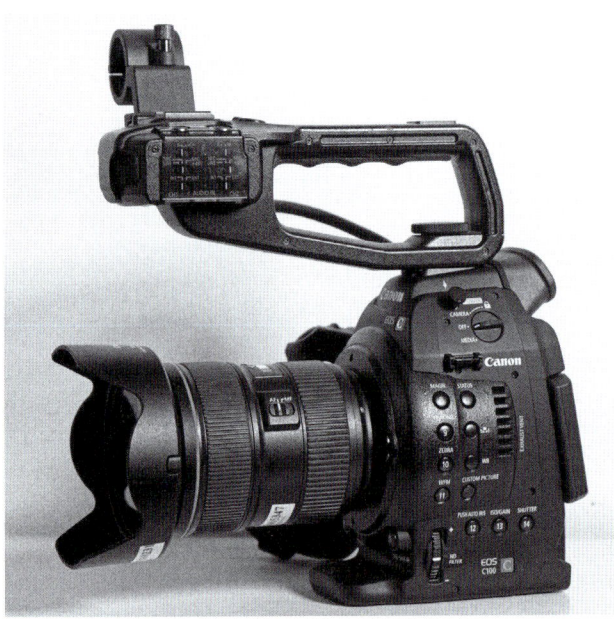

■ **Figure 8.13** The Canon EOS C100 is a good example of a hybrid camera that combines the large sensor and interchangeable lenses of the DSLR with some of the advantages of a video camera body.

Hybrid Large Sensor Cameras

One solution to the problems of the DSLR has been the **hybrid large sensor camera**, which attempts to bridge the gap between the ease of use of video cameras and the large sensors and interchangeable lenses of DSLRs. Like most compromises, these vary greatly in quality. One manufacturer, Canon, has attracted many users in the documentary field with its relatively inexpensive EOS C100 camera (Figure 8.13). This unit can be handheld and manually controlled, uses the popular Canon EOS lenses, and features XLR audio inputs for professional audio.

In the POV 2013 Documentary Filmmaking Equipment Survey,[7] the single-most used camera by documentary filmmakers was the Canon C300, indicating that this type of hybrid camera has already secured a primary place in the market. The C100, a less expensive version of the same camera, was close behind. While the survey hasn't been updated, anecdotal evidence suggests that this type of camera has only gained popularity among documentary filmmakers.

Mirrorless Shutter Cameras

DSLRs have a drop-down mirror that allows for through-the-lens viewing when shooting stills, something that is unnecessary for filmmaking. Another group of cameras that has found popularity is the **mirrorless shutter camera**. These are cameras that have a small body reminiscent of amateur point-and-shoot still cameras, and they have no optical viewfinder. Lacking the drop-down mirror that DSLRs use for viewing, they can be notably smaller and lighter. If you want a lot of resolution in a very small package, this may be the way to go. For an example, see the Lumix GH4 in Figure 8.15.

Minicams

One type of camera that has proved particularly useful for documentary shooting is a group of very small cameras with tiny sensors, fixed wide-angle lenses, and no viewfinder. These extremely small lightweight cameras are inexpensive, record to miniSD cards, and can be mounted anywhere, from skateboards to small aerial drones.

One recent documentary that made use of minicams to create a new visual aesthetic was *Leviathan* (2012), by Lucien Castaing-Taylor and Véréna Paravel (Figure 8.14). Their film uses tiny GoPro cameras to explore the sensation of being a fisherman (and a fish!) at sea. Paravel says:

Maybe because we attached those cameras to the fishermen themselves the result is an embodiment of this very cephalic point of view. It's not only the body that's moving, you're literally in their head, you're with them, you're a part of their actions, but your spatial and temporal orientation disappears and this is how you feel on a fishing vessel. So, we wanted to privilege this unique perspective, but we didn't want to limit it to the fishermen. Unlike in most documentaries where it's only the human subjects' perspective, we wanted to give the same ontological weight to the fishermen and their catch and it spread to the elements as well.[8]

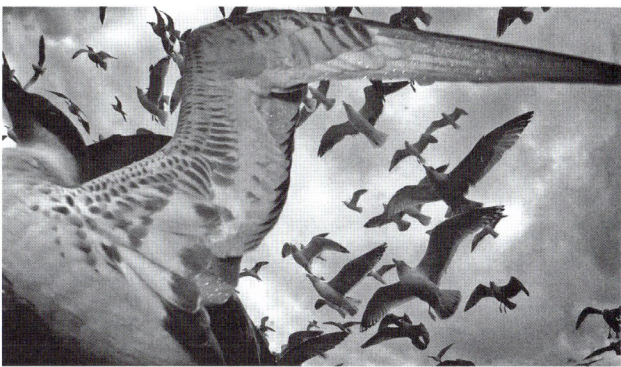

■ **Figure 8.14** *Leviathan* was shot mainly with small GoPro cameras whose wide-angle lens and ability to function under adverse conditions help give this film a look that critics have called "hallucinatory."

The Ultra High End: 4K and More

As mentioned above, a **4K image format** (exactly four times the size of an HD image) is available and cameras are being developed to take advantage of it. The format was originally developed for digital cinema cameras designed to shoot feature films, but several levels of camera are now available. A small camera offering 4K is the Lumix GH4, which can be held in the palm of a hand and is compatible with a documentary workflow (Figure 8.15, right). At the high end for documentary production is the SONY XDCAM PXW-FS7 (Figure 8.15, left), which offers good ergonomics for location observational shooting (including a servo zoom control and the ability to be mounted on the operator's shoulder), a lens mount that allows many types of lenses (using adaptors), and **Ultra High Definition (UHD) recording**.

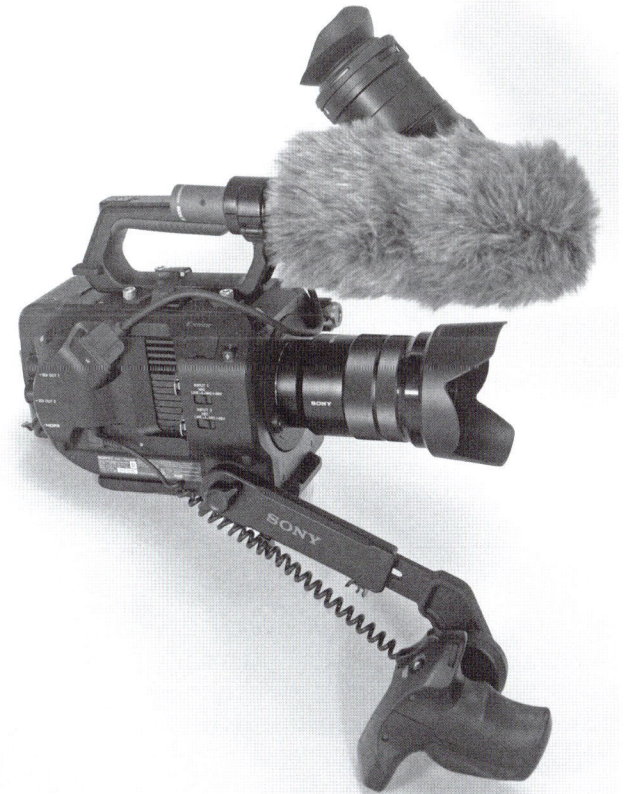
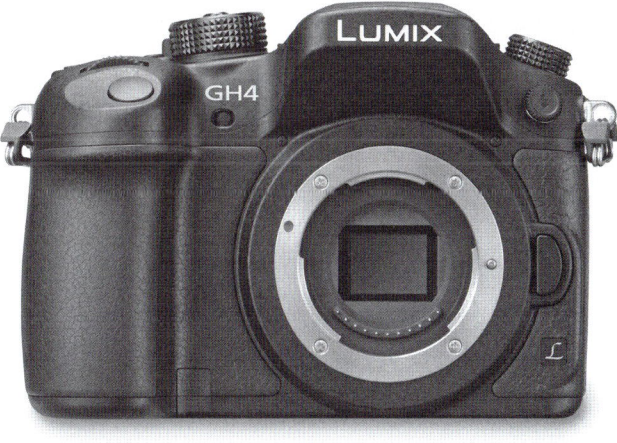

■ **Figure 8.15** The Sony PSW FS-7 (left) and the Lumix GH4 (right) offer a 4K image in two different handheld formats.

Figure 8.16
Comparison of the relative resolution capabilities between 720 HD, 1080 HD, 2K, and 4K formats based on pixel count.

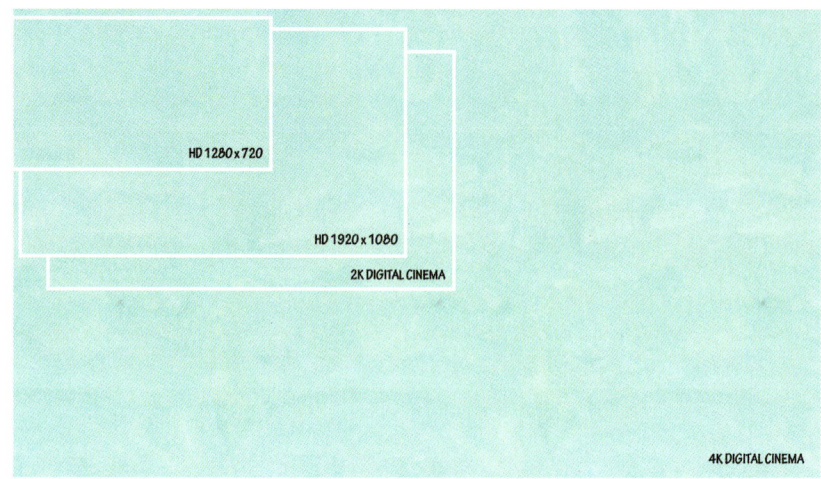

As with HD, there are several 4K format options including UHD (3840 x 2160) and DCI (4096 x 2160). Other available formats are 2K (2048 x 1080) and 2.5K (2560 x 1600 or 2560 x 1440) (Figure 8.16).

Another key area for makers interested in a higher quality image is the **bit depth** of the recorded signal (for more on bit depth, see pp. 129–130). Some professional video cameras record at various bit depths, typically 8-bit or 10-bit. Others, like the Sony PSW-FS7 (Figure 8.15, left), can record 8- or 10-bit internally or in 12-bit **RAW** uncompressed if you use an external, rear-mounted recorder. Other cameras allow you to bypass their image compression by sending the uncompressed signal out via the **SDI/HD-SDI** or **HDMI** output to a high-capacity hard drive.

So what's all that resolution for? These ultra-large resolutions do not conform to the ATSC standards because they're not intended for HDTV broadcast; they were developed for large screen theatrical projection. Broadcasters, led by NHK in Japan, are currently developing broadcast channels for the UHD format. Currently documentarians shoot 4K because it allows for cropping your image, as well as very high-end color correction, and you can "future proof" your work by creating a piece in a format that is likely to become standard in the near future.

The Basic Video Camcorder: Exterior

The standard camera design for documentary is the **camcorder**. While the name "camcorder" was originally given to video cameras that recorded image and sound together, the term is more commonly used now to differentiate video cameras from DSLRs. Most camcorders contain the same basic components and essential functions (Figure 8.17). As might be expected, the hybrid large-sensor cameras lack some of these functions, notably a motorized zoom lens, but share most other characteristics. We are devoting some time exploring the camcorder because despite the rising popularity of the DSLR and other camera designs, the camcorder remains a solid choice for observational documentary shooting on location.

The Body

The camcorder records single-system, which means that the body contains all of the electronic circuitry to gather and record both audio and video. Generally there are two types of camcorder bodies: shoulder-mounted cameras and smaller camcorders designed to be held in the operator's hands. Shoulder-mounted camcorders tend to be found on the high-end professional range, where cameras are heavier and larger. A shoulder-mounted camera allows for very stable handheld shots, while smaller cameras are more difficult to keep steady without a tripod or stabilizing rig (Chapter 10). Many filmmakers

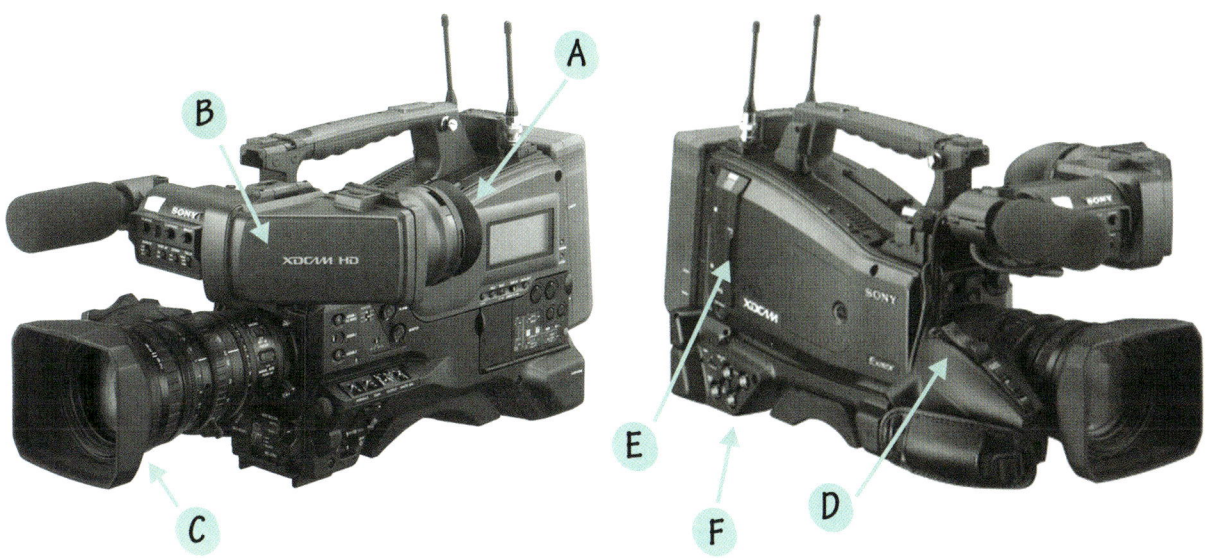

■ **Figure 8.17** Prosumer and professional video cameras have the following features: a viewfinder (A), an LCD viewscreen (B), a lens (C), a servo zoom control (D), a record media bay (E), external microphone inputs (not visible), and audio/video inputs and outputs (F). Pictured is the professional (and expensive) Sony PMW-400K.

find that the unobtrusiveness and mobility of a smaller camcorder allow for a greater sense of intimacy and spontaneity. One type of camcorder body is not inherently better than the other, but the difference in size and weight does have an impact on what you are able to do with the camera and so should be considered in tandem with your visual approach.

Viewfinders and LCD Viewscreens

Video camcorders have electronic **viewfinders** that allow you a glare-free look at the video image through an eyepiece that fits tightly against the camera operator's eye. This is extremely helpful for shooting in bright situations, when an LCD viewscreen (see below) is hard to see. The eyepiece contains a **diopter viewer**, or magnifying lens, that can be set for the camera operator's eye. This means an operator who normally uses glasses may be able to shoot without them.

Most camcorders also have an **LCD viewscreen** that flips or slides out to monitor your video. These screens are not as accurate as the viewfinder because changes in the viewing angle seriously alter the color and brightness of the image, as does the amount of glare the LCD screen catches from the ambient light. When shooting outdoors, an LCD **monitor hood** is essential for keeping sun glare from washing out the screen (Figure 8.18). Viewscreens are invaluable as a composition aid when you want to shoot from angles or create camera moves that make using the viewfinder difficult.

The Lens

The function of the lens is to gather the light reflecting off your scene and focus it onto the image sensor. Everything visual goes through the lens, so quality is important. A poor-quality lens will give you a poor-quality image. Lens quality is a major factor that separates consumer camcorders from those intended for professional use. Luckily for us, the dramatic improvement of video imaging devices has been paralleled by an evolution in the optical quality of lenses.

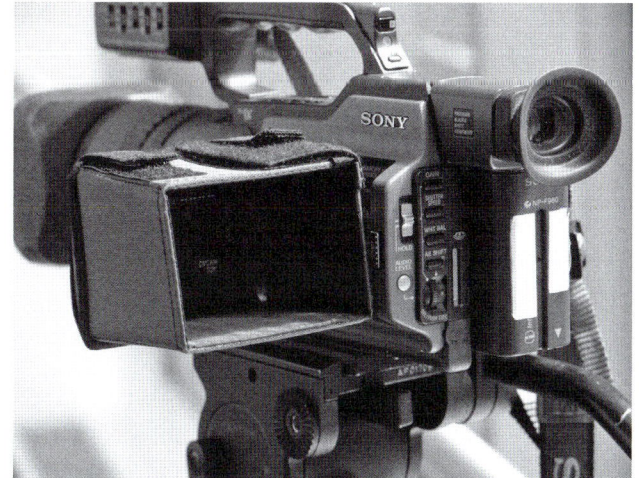

■ **Figure 8.18** An LCD monitor hood keeps sunlight from washing out the LCD screen when shooting in sunny locations.

The majority of mid-level and professional camcorders come with a **zoom lens**, which means that the lens has a range of **focal lengths** (Chapter 9). The zoom range of any specific lens is expressed in its magnification ability. With a 10 × 1 (or 10:1 or "ten to one") zoom lens, the degree of magnification increases 10 times over its full range. A 20x (or 20:1) zoom lens increases magnification by 20 times. The larger the magnification ratio, the greater the magnification power of the lens. Many cameras offer interchangeable lenses, so they can take advantage of a wide range of zoom and prime lenses. Cameras with fixed zoom lenses offer adaptors to extend the wide-angle or telephoto range of the lens. Consumer cameras under $1,000 generally come with a lens that is made of plastic or extremely low-quality glass elements. Plastic lenses are lighter and cheaper, but they are less sharp and often result in an image of lower resolution than the format is capable of producing.

The basic optical functions and compositional attributes of a lens are so important to the creative dimension of filmmaking that we have devoted an entire chapter specifically to this topic (Chapter 9).

Servo Zoom Control

Accompanying the zoom lens on most video cameras is the **servo zoom mechanism**, which enables you to glide through the zoom range, from wide-angle to telephoto and back, with the touch of a button (Figure 8.19). The servo zoom mechanism consists of a small motor operated by a **rocker switch**. Not all rocker switches are created equal, and this is another area that separates professional cameras from cheaper alternatives. A good-quality servo zoom is pressure sensitive. The harder you depress the mechanism, the faster the zoom, and the lighter you touch the button, the slower the zoom. This enables a camera operator to control not only the rate of a zoom, but also to taper it at the beginning and end of a shot. Most mid-level and professional cameras have a second zoom control on top of the body. In many cases, one or both switches can be set to respond more or less quickly to your touch.

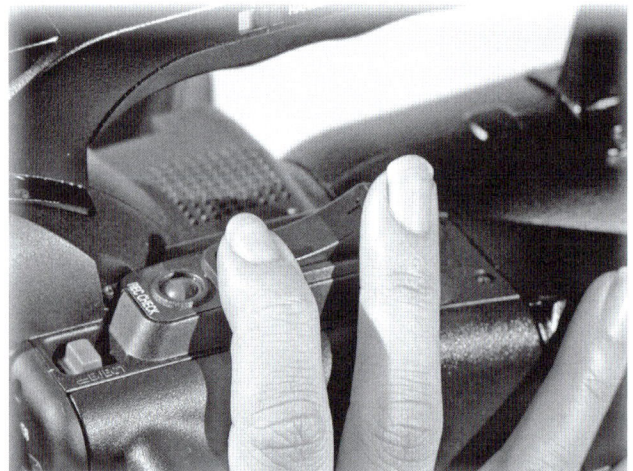

■ **Figure 8.19** The servo zoom rocker-switch allows the camera operator to glide through the entire range of focal lengths available on the lens. High-end cameras provide speed adjustments for this switch, allowing even greater control.

It's important to note that there are two types of zooms: optical zooms and digital zooms. They are not even remotely similar. An **optical zoom** adjusts the central lens element to magnify or demagnify the image. Although the composition and perspective of the image changes, the *resolution* of the video image remains the same. The optical zoom on most video cameras falls between the 10x magnification range and 20x magnification range. A **digital zoom**, on the other hand, is essentially an in-camera digital special effect in which the circuitry in the camera magnifies the captured video signal by selecting the central pixels and blowing them up. The loss of resolution quality is rapid and significant with digital zooms, and they should be avoided.

Media Bay

The **media bay** is where the video signal is recorded. Historically speaking, the signal was recorded on magnetic tape. However, as a shooting medium, the videotape cassette is now obsolete and **solid-state memory** cards are incorporated into every newly released camera. (Videotape remains a useful medium for project mastering and archiving.) Some common memory cards are the **Secure Digital (SD)** card (SDHC: up to 32 GB and SDXC: over 32 GB) and the **Compact Flash (CF)** card. While these are nonproprietary, others (like Panasonic's **P2** card and Sony's **SxS** card) are favored by specific manufacturers (Figure 8.20). HD video requires large amounts of storage space, so memory cards are compared (and priced) by their storage capacity, which depends on the size of the card as well as the video data rate of the shooting format (p. 132). In addition, some cameras come with solid state hard drives that offer substantially more storage.

Solid-state memory cards are referred to as **file-based media**, because each **camera take** is saved as a discrete digital file. In the field, you can see thumbnail images of every scene you've recorded. Footage recorded on any of these formats is immediately available for editing. Memory cards can also be off-loaded to portable hard drives in the field, allowing you to reuse them again and again. Many cameras offer two card slots in their media bay, allowing you to shoot continuously without interruption.

DC Power

Video cameras run on DC power provided by batteries or via an adaptor that transforms the AC power coming from the wall outlet into DC. Despite the unlimited power supply from an AC adaptor, most shooters only use batteries, preferring the freedom of not being tethered by a cord to the wall (Figure 8.21). Batteries need to be charged to work, and it takes time to charge them. Many student shoots are aborted early because no one remembered to charge the batteries. Modern batteries are typically lithium-ion, and they are rated in amp/hours. It is a very good idea to have a clear sense of how long the camera you are using can run on a particular battery, and to have plenty of backup power. Many crews will set up a charging station on location as part of their production workflow. It is worth mentioning that batteries don't hold their charge as long in extremes of heat and cold.

Camera Function Menus and Switches

Many cameras have their various functions and options embedded in a menu that can be accessed through buttons and viewed on the LCD viewscreen (Figure 8.22, left). On more professional cameras, some regularly used functions are located as switches, buttons, or wheels on the outside of the camera body (Figure 8.22, right), making them more easily accessible. You must consult your camera's manual to find out how to navigate all the camera's menus and control the functions you require for your shooting, and you should do this long before you are on location. With shooting options rapidly multiplying, camera function menus are getting longer and more labyrinthine with each generation.

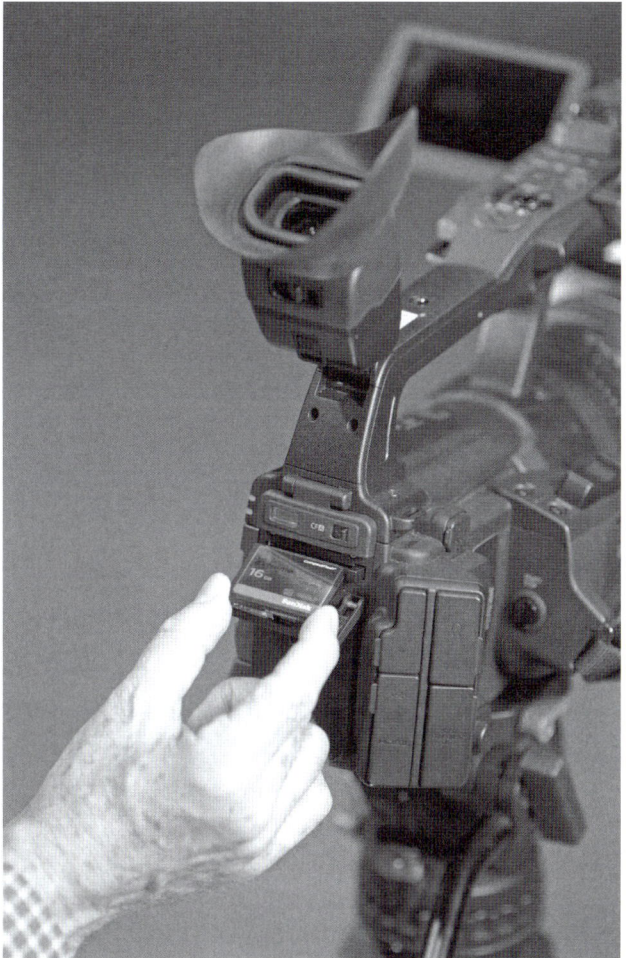

■ **Figure 8.20** File-based recording on solid-state memory cards, like the SD card pictured above, offers many advantages over tape and is now the standard. The camera pictured, the Canon XF300, has two slots to allow for longer, continuous recording.

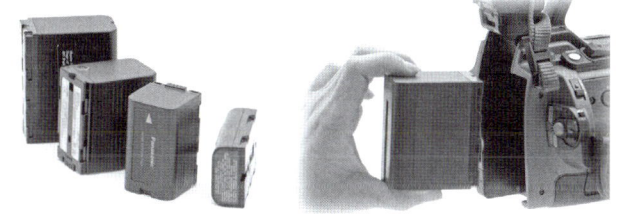

■ **Figure 8.21** Video cameras run on batteries available in a variety of sizes and power capacities.

One very important measure of a camera's capability as an expressive tool is the capacity for manual control of certain critical functions, namely **focus, exposure, white balance**, and **audio record levels**. Video cameras are designed by engineers and business people, not filmmakers, and the **auto functions** on a video camera are designed to give the user easily obtained, generally acceptable results. Point-and-shoot simplicity is what most home video shooters are looking for, and some of these functions can also be useful in a fast and unpredictable documentary situation. But if you are making a film you will want to show to an audience in order to move people and to communicate ideas and emotions,

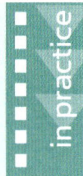

WHAT STORAGE MEDIA TO CHOOSE?

While your choice of camera will typically dictate which memory cards you use, within each memory card format are a variety of storage capacities. CF cards currently come in sizes from 2 GB to 256 GB, for example. Less obviously, memory cards come with a variety of read/write speed ratings, which dictate how quickly they can write the video files being stored on them. Manufacturers have periodically upgraded the specifications for their cards to keep up with the needs of video makers, so you aren't likely to have big problems. It is wise, though, to check the speed rating of any cards you purchase and compare it to the data rate settings of the camera. In other words, if your camera is set for a data rate of 50 Mbps (megabits/sec.), then make sure your card can write at least at that speed. Data rates are indicated by a "class" system on the card. The other big factor to think of is, of course, price. The best way to think of this is in "price per gigabyte." If you purchase a 16 GB card for $20, you are paying $1.25/GB. If you buy a 128 GB card for $300, you have voluminous storage, but you are paying closer to $2.35/GB, in which case the price may outweigh the convenience of the larger card. As bitrate options on cameras get higher, creating larger files, many people find themselves moving toward capturing video on external **solid state drives (SSDs)**. While not every camera can accommodate this, the external drive can store much more information than a memory card can. External drives can also record at compression rates that are higher than what cards can handle (like Apple's Pro-Res 422 format, for example).

Once you have picked the combination of image quality and storage method best suited to your project, it is wise to develop some kind of seat-of-the-pants idea of how many minutes of shooting equals how many GB of stored information. If you are filming at one GB per minute, you will go through memory cards fairly quickly, and you may want to invest in larger cards or an external drive despite the price.

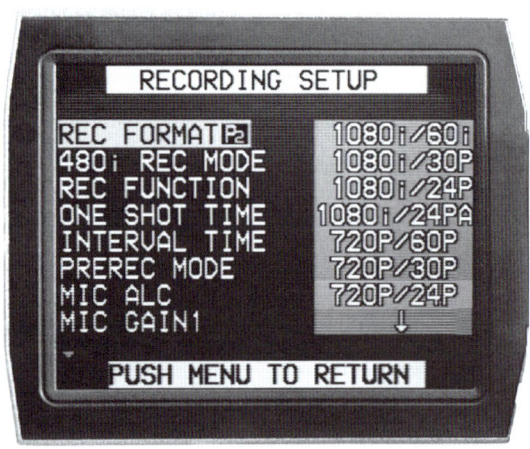
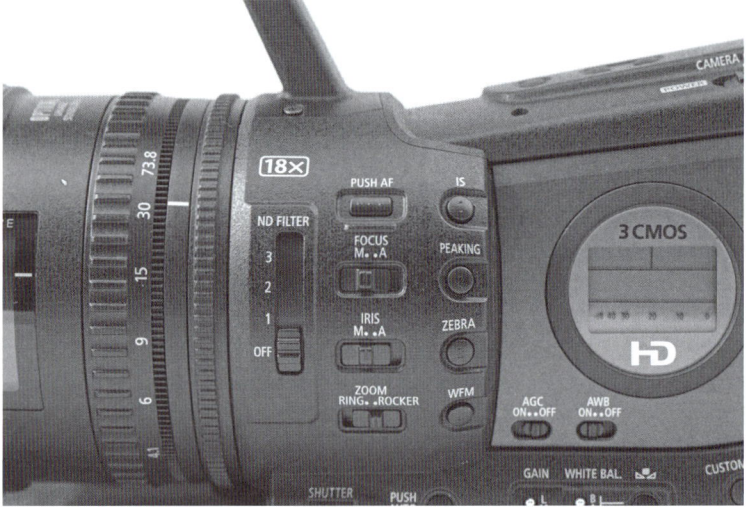

■ **Figure 8.22** Some video camera functions are embedded inside menus accessible on the LCD screen (left), while other more commonly used features (like the manual overrides for focus and iris) are sometimes found on the camera's body (right).

you need to be able to control all the elements that are part of your expressive and aesthetic palette. To leave these creative decisions up to a machine is to give away your voice. Cameras that do not allow you to set your own focus, sound levels, exposure, or white balance (usually the cheapest consumer cameras) severely limit your craft and are therefore less useful. All professional and most mid-level camcorders give you the option of **auto functions** or **manual override**, and you should immediately learn how to take control of your camera's image-making by turning off the auto functions in favor of manual control. We will look closer at how to use these functions in other chapters including Chapter 9 (The Lens), Chapters 11 and 12 (Lighting and Exposure), and Chapters 13 and 14 (Sound Recording Strategies and Techniques).

Audio and Video Connectors, Inputs and Outputs

Connectors are the way we get video, audio, and TC signals into and out of equipment. **Output connectors** are used for monitoring sound or picture, and transferring files. The main set of **input connectors** to consider when choosing a camera is the external microphone inputs.

External Microphone Inputs

External microphone inputs are especially important for documentary film production. The microphone input connection is another line demarcating professional and mid-level equipment from consumer cameras. The **onboard microphones** that come with many camcorders are insufficient for most filmmaking applications, where you need to acquire optimum-quality audio through careful microphone placement. All professional microphones use the locking three-pronged **XLR connector**. The advantages of this connector are a secure connection and **balanced audio**, which is much less susceptible to audio noise and interference. Many consumer cameras, including DSLRs, come with an 1/8" **miniplug connector** for an external microphone input. The primary shortcoming of this connector is its flimsiness. The miniplug can easily break or pop loose under the rigors of field production. The other shortcoming of the 1/8" **minijack** is that it is an unbalanced audio connection and is highly susceptible to interference (Figure 8.23).

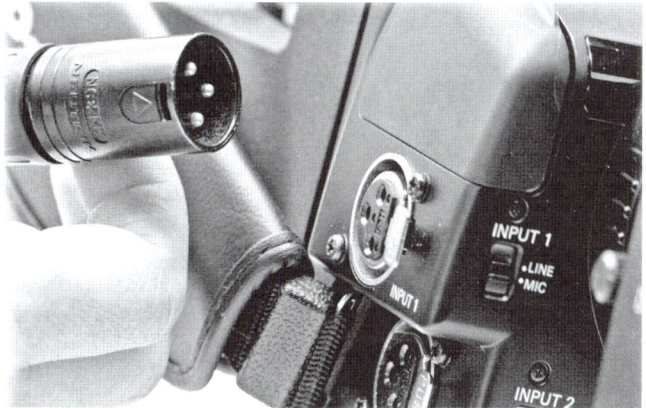
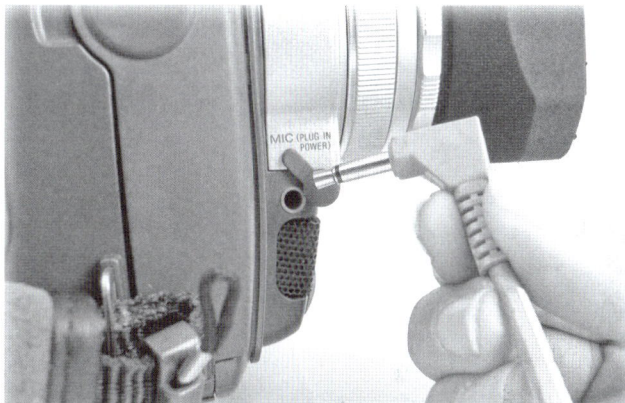

■ **Figure 8.23** While higher-end camcorders come with XLR inputs for professional microphones (left), consumer cameras often only have 1/8" connectors (right), which are prone to interference and are much less reliable.

Other Connectors

■ COMMON AUDIO AND VIDEO CONNECTORS

a. 1/8" miniplug (line audio and microphone audio)

b. XLR (line audio and microphone audio)

c. BNC (video and TC)

d. RCA (line audio and video)

e. HDMI type A (audio, video, and auxiliary data)

f. HDMI type D (audio, video, and auxiliary data)

g. Mini B USB (video and audio files to computer)

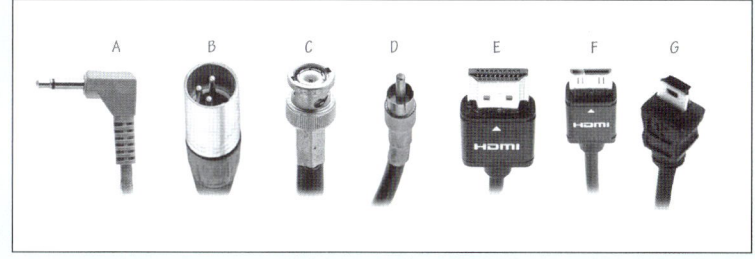

■ **Figure 8.24** Common connectors for video and audio production, and the types of signal they carry.

There are four common **in and out (I/O) connectors** on camcorders for outputting digital video and audio (Figure 8.24). On professional and mid-level camcorders, you'll find the **High-Definition Multimedia Interface (HDMI)** connector, and the **USB** (**2.0** and **3.0**). Older cameras may also feature a **FireWire** connector (also called **IEEE 1394**). These cables send digital data from the camera to a field monitor for viewing, or to your editing system. Professional cameras also come equipped with **SDI/HD-SDI** output (**Serial Digital Interface**), which uses the locking **BNC connector** (Figure 8.24). This interface can output uncompressed video (SD or HD) to a high-capacity hard drive (HHD) or an SSD for recording footage as you shoot. On consumer- and mid-level cameras, you may find an **RCA plug** providing a **composite video** output for an NTSC monitor. Every camcorder has its own audio and video I/O configuration; always check your camcorder's specific hardware. Also worth mentioning are TC I/O connectors, which allow you to synchronize cameras for multicamera shoots.

The Basic Video Camcorder: Interior

Video camcorders essentially turn light into data. The best way to understand the interior workings of a basic camcorder is to follow the progress of an image, which begins as light entering the lens and emerges as a stream of data recorded onto a memory card, hard drive, or tape (Figure 8.25).

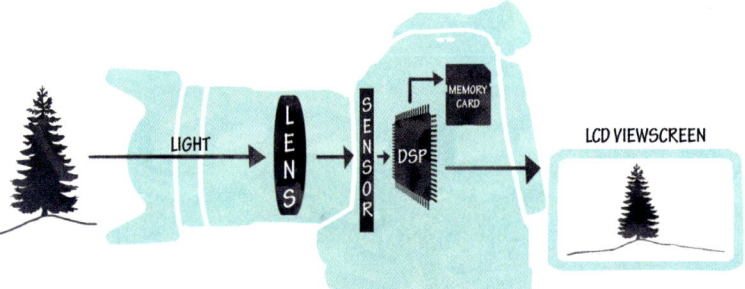

■ **Figure 8.25** This diagram shows the path of light through a Canon C100 camera as it travels through the lens, is registered by the sensor, is processed by the Digital Signal Processor (DSP), and finally sent to the recording media and the image display.

The Image Sensor

The recording of the image begins with the lens gathering light from the scene and focusing it on the **image plane**. In video, this image plane is the surface of the **sensor** – either a **charged coupled device (CCD)** or **CMOS sensor**. CCD chips, once standard in camcorders, are quickly being replaced by CMOS sensors in all new cameras (Figure 8.26). Each sensor is composed of hundreds of thousands to millions of light-sensitive photodiodes, called **pixels** (short for "picture elements"). When these pixels are struck by the incoming light, they register an electronic charge that corresponds to the light intensity hitting that particular spot on the sensor. At this point, the way CMOS and CCD chips handle the light signal differs. The CCD employs a **global shutter**, meaning all the pixels are exposed to light at the same moment and register a complete image. This image is then outputted line by line, amplified, and sent to the **analog-to-digital converter (ADC)**, where this analog signal is converted into digital data. The CCD then registers another complete frame and repeats the process. A CMOS imager, on the other hand, contains transistors with all the circuitry necessary for converting

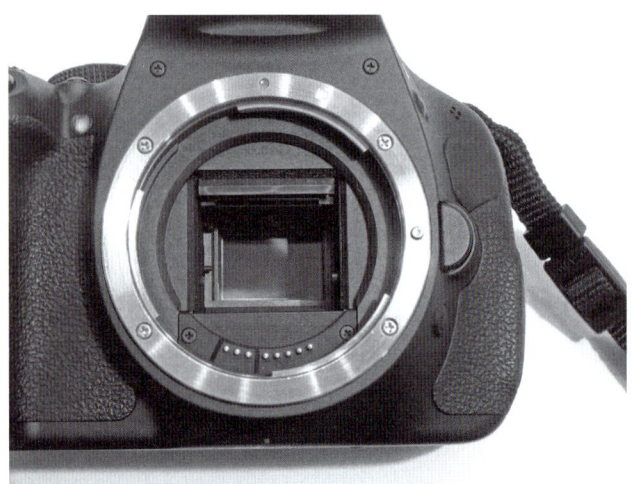

■ **Figure 8.26** A CMOS chip.

light values into voltage and then into digital data, all right behind each pixel on the sensor (Figure 8.27). Each pixel processes its own electronic charge and directly outputs a digital signal. However, rather than expose and then "read out" a complete frame, CMOS sensors have a **rolling shutter**, which exposes and reads out one line of pixels at a time. In other words, a CCD registers a complete frame and then outputs that frame line by line, whereas a CMOS sensor exposes and outputs one line at a time, eventually creating the complete frame. The rolling shutter is responsible for several characteristic artifacts, most infamously the **jello artifact** (also called "skew"), which occurs when there is horizontal movement in the frame, especially as a result of quick panning. With horizontal movement, it is possible for the top part of an object to be registered in one area of the frame, the middle scanned slightly later, and the bottom part registered even further along. The result is that vertical lines can appear slanted during the pan, and complex movement produces a wobbly, jello-like undulation in objects that should be stationary. With technological improvements, most of these artifacts are rarely seen with higher end cameras, but may still be seen with DSLRs.

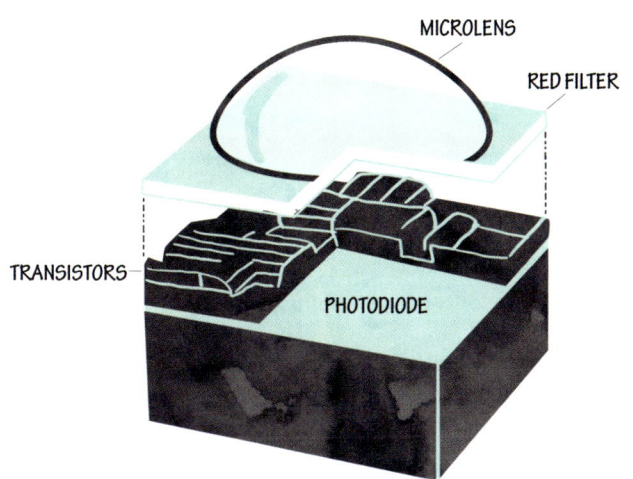

■ **Figure 8.27** One CMOS pixel. The light enters through the microlens, passes through a filter (in this case a red filter), and is converted to an electrical signal by transistors on the photodiode.

Three-Chip vs One-Chip Cameras

Cameras can have either three sensors, or one. In a three-chip camera, the light gathered from the lens first passes through a **prism block**. This splits the image into the three primary colors of light: red, green, and blue (**RGB**). These three images, identical except for their color, are reflected onto the **faceplates** of three chips, which register the relative light intensities and translate the information into a digital signal for each color. Traditionally, three-chip cameras produced a better image than a one-chip alternative, but recently very high-quality single-chip cameras have been developed. Examples of high-end one-chip camcorders include the Black Magic camera and the Canon C100 (Figure 8.13). One reason for their high quality despite the single chip is that the sensor is very large, with a correspondingly large number of pixels. These sensors include a **Bayer Pattern Filter**, which divides the pixels into three groups sensitive to three different colors of light creating Red, Green, and Blue signals on the one sensor (Figure 8.28).

White Balance

As we will see in Chapter 11, light from various sources has different color values. The sun is very blue, while a Tungsten light bulb is more orange (Figure 11.9). While the human eye compensates for these variations, your camera's ability to do this is limited. For your camera to reproduce colors accurately, you must take care to **white balance** each time you change location or lighting conditions. White balancing means adjusting the imager's color circuitry to compensate for the color temperature

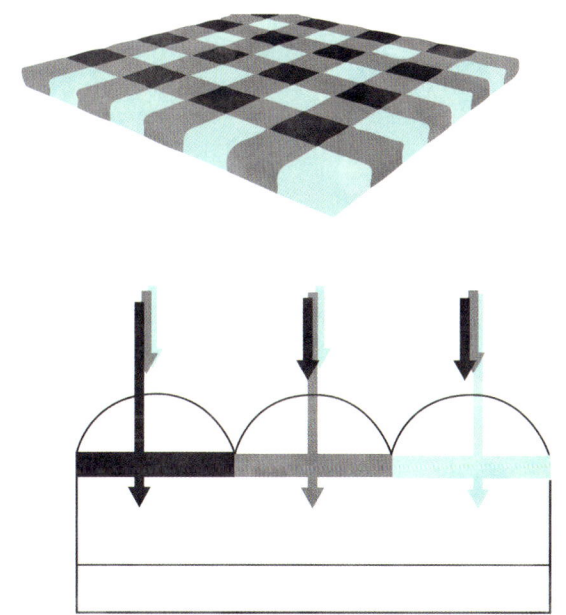

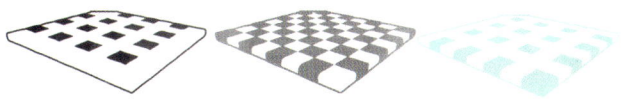

■ **Figure 8.28** A Bayer Pattern Filter separates light into three different colors in a mosaic pattern. The red pixels are on the right, the green (which predominate) are in the center, and the blue are on the left. (See plate section for color.)

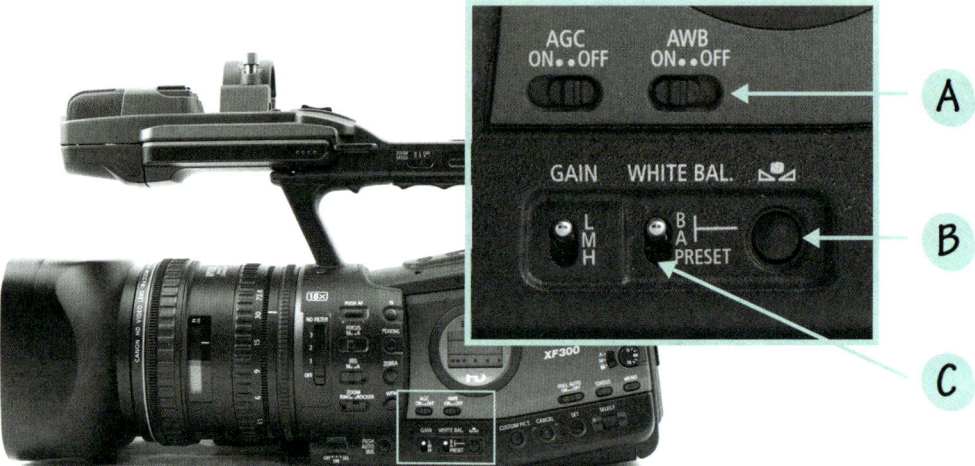

■ **Figure 8.29** White balancing. All video cameras have a way to balance the image sensors to a variety of color temperatures. On this Canon XF300, to do manual white balancing you must first switch off the auto white balance function (A). A user can then manually set color temperature balance for each scene (B) or recall daylight and tungsten presets (C). Also note the Gain Switch.

of different light sources. On nearly every video camera, there are two easily accessible color temperature presets, one for daylight (5,600K) and one for tungsten light (3,200K). In addition, many cameras provide a way to manually set white balance, which is more accurate than a factory preset. Setting white balance is accomplished by filling your frame with something white and matte (like a white card or sheet of paper) that is lit with representative light, and then pressing the manual white balance button (Figure 8.29). Whether the white card is reflecting the bluish tint of daylight, the amber tint of tungsten bulbs or the greenish hue of fluorescent lights, the camera adjusts the R, G, and B sensitivity levels until that card is rendered as "white." On many cameras, you can also assign these manually determined white balance settings to user preset buttons (Figure 8.29). Remember that white balancing must be done every time your light source changes! It may seem like a chore to reset white balance constantly, but it will soon become second nature, especially after a couple of shoots where all of your exteriors are blue or your interiors bright orange. Many documentary interiors offer a mix of different light color temperatures. You need to figure out what is important in the image, typically skin tones, and set your white balance for the light values hitting that subject.

It is worth noting that many DSLRs do not have a quick and easy way to white balance. You will likely have to enter the camera function menu system to access a manual white balance control. The same is true of smaller camcorders as well.

Gain

Gain is a measure of the electronic amplification of the video signal coming from the image sensor. Gain is important, as increasing it will increase the light sensitivity of the camera. This would seem to be an advantage. The problem is that increasing gain also increases the electronic noise that is visible in the image. Gain is considered an exposure adjustment (Chapters 9 and 11) of last resort, to be employed when you absolutely need to get the shot but there simply isn't enough light for a decent exposure. When you increase the gain, the image suddenly appears much brighter. Gain, however, seriously compromises image resolution and contrast and increases **video noise**, unwanted electronic aberrations and artifacts. Most cameras offer three preset gain settings: 0 dB for low gain, 9 dB for medium gain, and 18 db for high gain (Figure 8.29). These can sometimes be reset manually to offer less drastic boosts in light sensitivity. Most cameras also have an **automatic gain control (AGC)**, which, like most auto functions, should immediately be turned off in favor of the manual settings. On DSLRs, the gain is reflected in the ISO or "film speed" settings.

Here again, the camera will cheerfully boost the ISO to 1600 or even 3200 or more, but the result will be a very noisy image. As a rule, stick with an ISO of 800 or lower to avoid problems.

Shutter Speed

Shutter speed is an important variable. The standard exposure will be half that of the frame rate of the camera: for NTSC, it is 1/60th of a second for 60i and 1/48th of a second for 24p. For PAL, it is 1/50th of a second for 50i and 25p (Figure 8.5). Unless you have a good reason for changing your shutter speed, you are well advised to set this manually and leave it alone. Many cameras (especially DSLRs) will compensate for added light by changing the shutter speed to shorter amounts of time like 1/100th or even 1/1000th of a second. The problem with this is that the camera will appear to "stop" motion, giving moving objects and people a jerky look as they cross the screen. While this may be useful in certain applications, such as sports photography, in general it is undesirable, as the blur of moving objects filmed at 1/60th or 1/50th of a second appears much more natural to the human eye. Some cameras offer lower shutter speeds (achieved digitally), which can occasionally be helpful in low light situations.

ND Filters

Another option for controlling exposure is the **neutral density (ND) filter**. This is simply a gray filter that cuts the amount of light entering the lens. The advantage of using an ND filter is that it allows you to alter exposure without changing your f-stop, something you might want to do to maintain a narrow depth of field, for example (Chapter 9). ND filters are a common option in video cameras. They are mounted internally and adjusted through an external switch (Figure 8.30). If you are using a DSLR, you will need to mount an external filter. For more on ND filters, see Chapter 11.

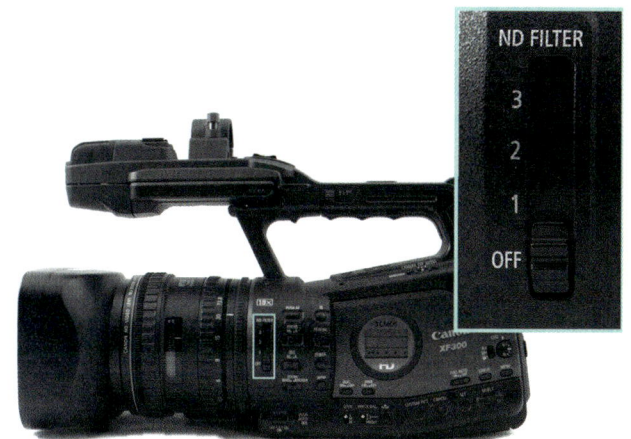

■ **Figure 8.30** Neutral Density switches activate filters that cut down on the amount of light entering the lens.

The Analog-to-Digital Converter

In cameras that use CCDs, each chip converts the light values that strike it into voltage, and sends this analog electronic signal to an **ADC**. There, the signal is transformed into digital data, meaning binary code (a series of 1s and 0s). Cameras with CMOS sensors don't have to do this, as the imager itself has circuitry that converts analog picture information to a digital signal. In all cameras, the audio input signals are converted from an analog electronic signal into digital data using an ADC.

The process of transforming analog information into digital data is called **quantizing**. It requires the camera to **sample** the constantly flowing stream of voltage information from each pixel and then ascribe to it discrete digital values. **Sample rates** are about 50 million samples per second and don't really vary for picture (although they can for sound). The amount of color information in each sample is expressed in terms of **bit depth**. The more bits, the larger the sample size (in bits/sample), and the better the color and image detail will be. Currently the standard for video is 8-bit per channel, which gives you 256 choices for each color. These choices combine (256 red values x 256 green values x 256 blue values) to offer a total of 16.7 million colors, also known as "millions of colors" (Figure 8.31).

The Digital Signal Processor

The digital video from the sensor(s) and the audio data from the audio ADC are sent to the **digital signal processor** (**DSP**) to create the final, digital signal. The DSP is the most complex part of the entire digital video system and works with algorithms specific to the camera's format (such as AVCHD, XMF, and XDCAM). Basically, the DSP combines the three sets of color information from the sensor(s) or determines the brightness and color

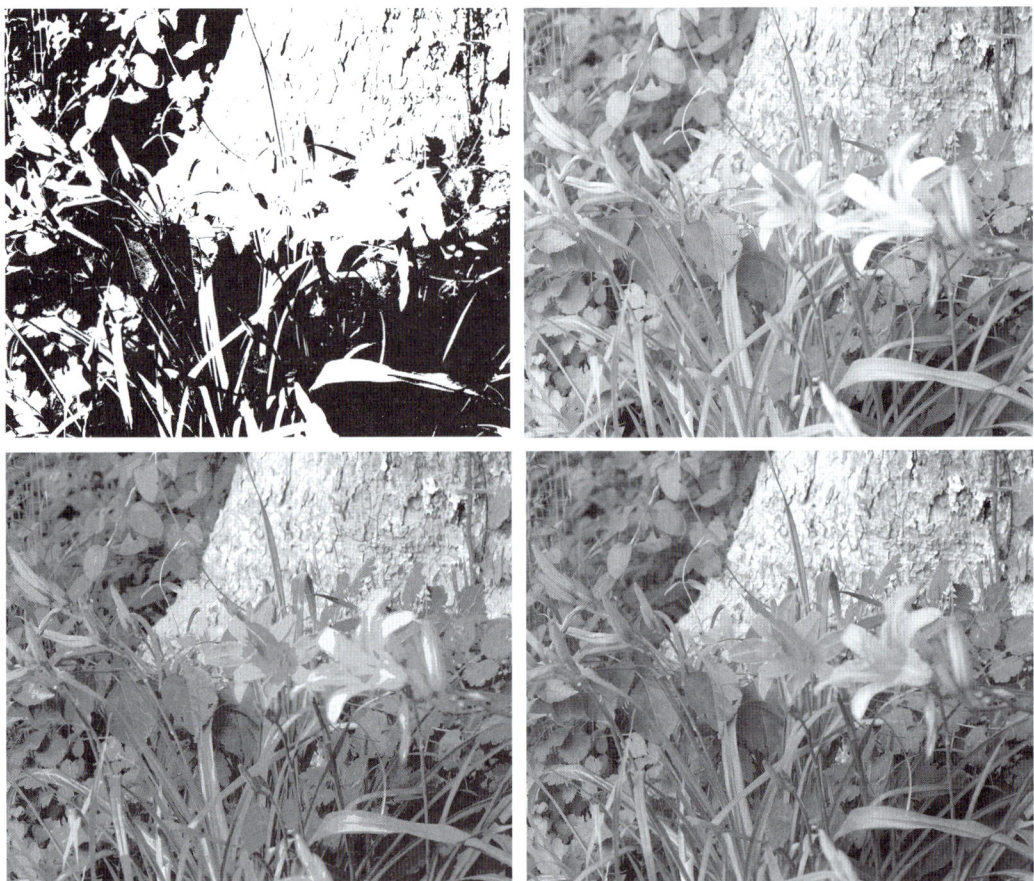

■ Figure 8.31
Bit Depth is an important aspect of the digital image. Shown here (clockwise starting with the upper left image) are 2-bit (black and white), 4-bit (16 shades of gray), 8-bit color (256 colors), and 24-bit color (16.7 million colors).
(See plate section for color.)

value of every pixel in every frame of video to create the full-color image, along with the audio signal. However, at this point, these uncompressed images contain an enormous amount of data. HD video generates around 150 MB/sec of data. At that rate, you would fill up a 64 GB memory card in about 6 minutes. This is simply way too much data to record easily on card media. So when processing raw video information, the DSP is forced to reduce the amount of data it sends to the recording media. To avoid losing too much resolution quality, the DSP uses two main processes to accomplish this reduction: **compression** and **color subsampling.**

Signal Compression and Codecs

The critical juggling act of all video formats is how to reduce the amount of image data while maintaining as much quality as possible. If you compress too much, the image quality suffers; if you don't compress enough, the files are too big and too slow to work with. **Compression** is the method used to reduce the amount of data by discarding visual detail that is either imperceptible to the human eye or redundant. The data compression algorithms are essentially software programs that perform a series of operations on the digital image. The programs that perform this compression are called **codecs** (for "compression/decompression"). There are multiple standard codecs in the world of digital video (MPEG-2, MPEG-4, and H.264, for example), with new ones being introduced regularly. However, when we are talking about video camera encoding, each manufacturer puts a proprietary codec as an envelope or **file wrapper** around the compressed file. For example, Panasonic's format utilizes the AVC-Intra codec, which is based on the H.264/MPEG-4 AVC standard (the codec used in Blu-ray). Sony uses the XDCam codec as a wrapper for MPEG-2 files. As you can imagine, there is constant negotiation with the most popular editing systems (AVID, Final Cut Pro, and Adobe Premiere Pro) to support these compression schemes, which, thankfully, they usually do (Figure 8.32). Recording formats and their proprietary codecs are numerous and constantly changing, so rather than look at them specifically, we will look at the essential principles of compression, especially as they pertain to image quality. Understanding some basics about compression is important because it has a bearing on choosing a shooting format, your anticipated workflow, and what viewers see on the screen.

Compression schemes use several approaches to shrinking file size. The amount of data kept can be surprisingly small. For HD video, the uncompressed file can be as much as 20 times bigger than the compressed file. In other words, the picture information is reduced to just 5 percent of its original amount, yet the image still looks surprisingly good. How does the codec achieve this? One strategy for compression is to remove redundant information. Redundant information is the data from visual details that are repeated, from pixel to pixel and frame to frame. For example, say you have a shot of a red ball rolling across a green lawn. The pixels along the path of the ball change from green to red as the ball travels, but the rest of the frame remains exactly the same green, frame after frame. It would take a great deal of space to re-record all of the common and repeated **luminance** (light) and **chrominance** (color) values for every pixel in every frame. For 1080i HD, we would need to re-record the same repeated "green" values 2,073,600 times for every frame (minus the red pixels that make up the ball). The codec reduces all of this common information to a smaller file size by recording the numeric value for "green" once and then indicating that every other pixel in each subsequent frame (except for the red ball pixels) is "just like that first one." The rest of the information is then tossed out. Later, when we play back that image, the codec decompresses that information by reconstructing the data through duplication of that one saved numeric value for the "green" areas of the frame. Video codecs can work so well that the compressed image is hard to tell from the uncompressed source image.

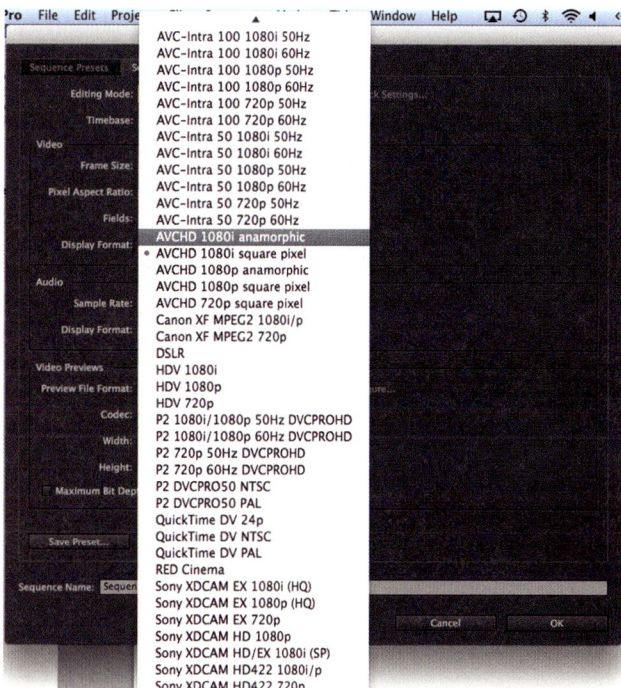

Figure 8.32 This setup menu in Premiere Pro reveals just how many format and codec variations exist these days.

Another key distinction among compression types is VBR vs CBR. Many compression types, including MPEG-2, are **variable bit rate (VBR)**. VBR codecs compress less when there is more movement or color shifting from frame to frame than when the image is more static. Others, like Apple ProRes 422, are **constant bit rate (CBR)**, meaning that they compress the image the same amount regardless of the content. VBR works very well for shooting and display, but it creates problems for editing systems because they prefer CBR data. Some edit systems can handle variable bit rate data better than others, but don't be surprised if you end up needing to transcode your VBR footage to a format more suitable for editing.

Color Encoding and Subsampling

The other main method codecs use to reduce file size is the elimination of color information. The video image has two components: the element of the video image that determines brightness (shades of black and white) is called the **luminance** signal, and the color component of the video signal is called the **chrominance** (or **chroma**). Chrominance is made up of **hue**, which determines the tint of a particular color, and **saturation**, which determines the intensity of the colors. An accurate color blend is created by mixing the chrominance and luminance information for the three primary colors (R, G, B) with the brightness information.

Color sampling refers to the number of times brightness (luminance) and color (chroma) information are measured and translated into data by the DSP. Color sampling is expressed as a ratio of luminance samples to blue samples to red samples (note that this is different from signal sampling and its relative, bit depth, which occur earlier in the analog to digital conversion). The information for green is not sampled because it can be interpolated given the data for luminance, blue, and red. Color sampling involves throwing away relatively large amounts of color information. Because the human eye is capable of perceiving very subtle variations in brightness but relatively fewer shifts in color tonalities, all video formats keep 100 percent of the luminance information, but much less blue and red information. A full sample is represented with the integer 4, so a color sampling ratio of 4:4:4 would mean that all luminance data, blue, and red colors are sampled equally and fully. A ratio of 4:1:1 would mean for each four luminance pixels, only one each of the blue and red pixels are saved.

Chroma subsampling is one way compression algorithms eliminate color data that may not even be perceptible in order to save space. Many HD cameras offer multiple color subsampling rates, including 4:2:2 and 4:1:1. Some cameras have 4:4:4 uncompressed (or **raw media**) available for external display or recording via a cable or external attachment. For an illustration of color subsampling, see our companion website (www.routledge.com/cw/Anderson).

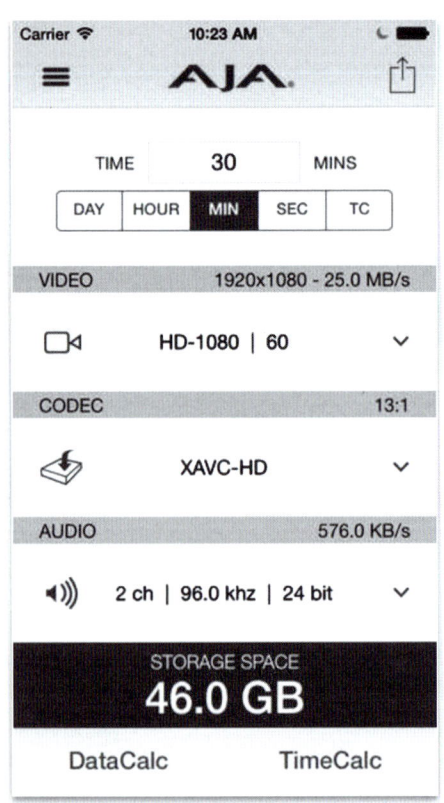

■ **Figure 8.33** Media data rate calculators, like this free one for iPhone from AJA Systems, are a handy tool for calculating data storage needs.

DATA RATE

Throughout your workflow, you'll need to be aware of the **data rate** for your particular format. The data rate is expressed as a **bit rate** in Megabits per second (Mbps). This determines, among other things, the amount of storage space you'll need for your project. Format data rates are determined by a number of factors, including whether you're shooting SD, HD, or 4K; the frame rate (60i, 24p); and the specific quantizing and compression factors of the record format (DVCPRO-HD, XDCAM-HD, AVCHD). Some cameras will let you choose the bit rate (35 Mbps or 50 Mbps, for example). Some broadcasters use bit rate to define minimum acceptable quality for broadcast. The BBC minimum standard for commissioned work, for example, is 50 Mbps. A media data rate calculator will give you a good idea of how big the files you accumulate will be at different data rates, so that you can make the best choice for your budget and workflow. There are many calculators you can download (as software or as smartphone apps) that include virtually every shooting format and codec available (Figure 8.33). Many cameras now list data rate options.

MONITORING AND DISPLAY

In addition to a viewfinder and an LCD viewscreen, most video cameras offer the possibility of sending a signal through connectors to an external monitor. These connectors are of several types, based on different analog and digital signal formats. In the field, you will typically use an external monitor either because the viewing options on your camera are poor, as can be the case with many DSLRs (Figure 8.34, left), or because there is some need for more critical viewing. A director and cinematographer might need to share input on the look of an image, for example, or there might be a particularly complex setup involving multiple light sources with different color temperatures. **Field monitors** are typically flat screen LCD displays, and come in a variety of sizes. Quality can vary widely, as can price. Typically those of smaller size, like 6 inches or less, will mount on the camera or the shoulder mount of a DSLR, while larger monitors can stand alone. Often they will come with a hood to isolate the screen from ambient light (Figure 8.34, right).

CHAPTER 8
The Digital Video System

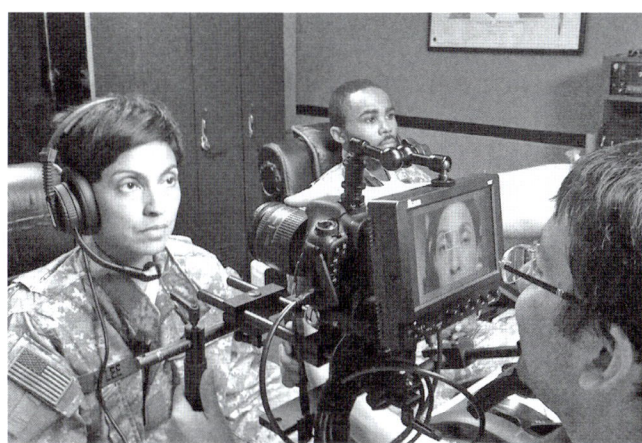
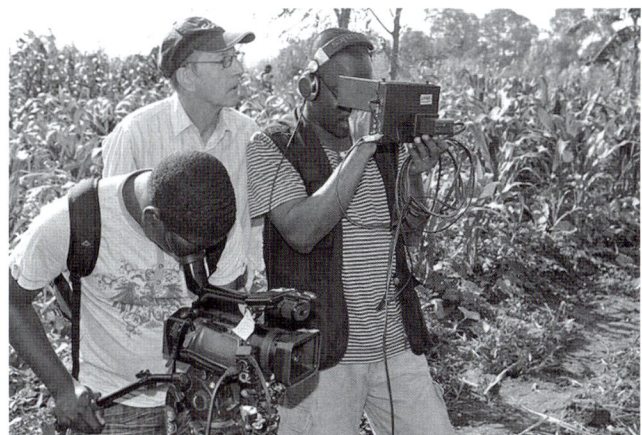

■ **Figure 8.34**
Shooting with a Canon 7D and a Marshall monitor mounted on the camera (left). A larger field monitor with a hood is useful for outdoor shooting (right).

If you use an external monitor, you will need to calibrate it. To do this, you should set your camera to generate **color bars**, usually a menu option. These bars allow you to set the color signal to match that of your camera's viewing system (particularly important for NTSC). Monitors vary widely in their ability to accurately render color and picture information, so use the information you get from them judiciously.

■ CALIBRATING A MONITOR

Calibrating a modern digital monitor means setting the white balance, the brightness, the contrast, and the chroma saturation. What follows is partially adapted from an excellent article by digital imaging technician Bennett Cain.[9]

The first question to ask yourself is "What standard am I setting the monitor to?" The standard for HD video, and the default for most digital cameras, is called ITU Rec 709. It comes from the International Telecommunications Union (p. 111), and Recommendation 709, which includes **color space**, among other things, and came out in 1990.

In the Rec 709 standard, the white should be set at a color temperature of 6500K or D65 (Chapter 11). On a Mac computer, there is a calibrating tool that can be used to make the color match this setting (Figure 8.35). If you have a choice for gamma, as you do on the Mac, you should set it at 2.2.

To set up an external monitor, you will use **color bars**. In the field, your camera can typically generate these. In the edit room, your nonlinear editing (NLE) system can generate color bars.

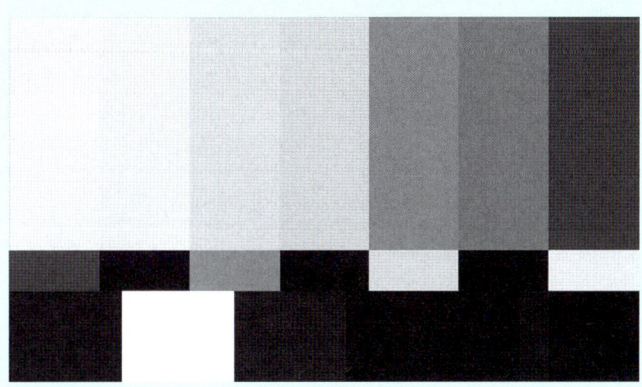

■ **Figure 8.35** In this window, you can see a representation of the Rec. 709 color space, with the small x marking the spot where a neutral white can be found. (See plate section for color.)

■ **Figure 8.36** This image shows a color bar display properly set for white, black, and chroma levels. (See plate section for color.)

Color bars vary depending on the hardware and software you're using. Standard HD bars will include the full color spectrum, plus black and white sections. First, take a look at what correctly set bars look like (Figure 8.36). The white setting, your luminance level, is subjective in the sense that you are setting it by eye. Typically, you will want to adjust the contrast until the white (second from the left on the bottom group, Figure 8.36) reaches a maximum, then back it off a little. Then you will want to set the black level using the three small black bars on the lower right (Figure 8.37). Basically, you want to set monitor brightness and contrast so that the difference between the center and the right bar just disappears. The settings for each variable might be adjusted through a knob or a menu item.

Higher end monitors will have a "blue gun" that provides a way of seeing only the blue signal. If you can do this, your calibration of color values will be easy (Figure 8.38).

If you don't have a blue gun option, you will have to adjust the chroma by eye. Everyone uses different clues, but a common one is the gray of the first bar on the top left, which should contrast notably from the white on the lower set of bars (Figure 8.36).

Again, every monitor is different, and there are many options for setting them. A high-quality monitor, whether for field or studio use, is quite expensive. The best advice is to do what you can in the field, record bars, and work with those to tweak your material when you get to the edit room. This will be especially useful if you've shot with more than one camera.

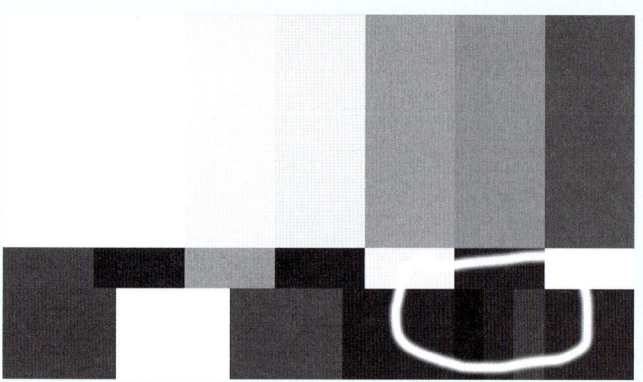 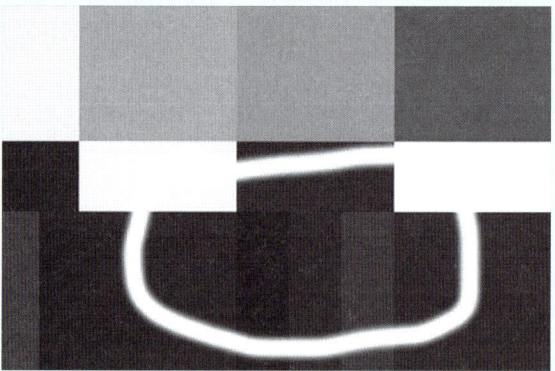

■ **Figure 8.37** In this typical color bar display, the brightness of the three small bars on the lower right (called the pluge, from "picture line-up generation equipment") can be used to set brightness level. In the close-up section of the bar display (right), the setting has been adjusted so that the difference between the two bars on the left of the pluge almost disappears. See color insert.

 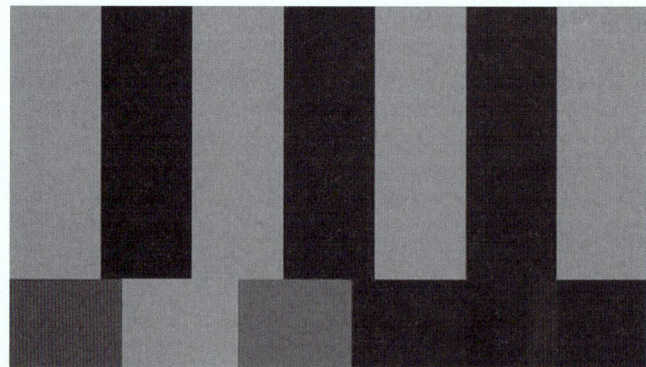

Figure 8.38 Setting up a monitor with a blue gun. Adjust the chroma level on the display until you're looking at solid, alternating bars of equal value. The image on the left shows an incorrectly adjusted chroma because the third and fifth bars show small stubs at the bottom. On the right, the chroma has been set properly. See color insert.

DOCUMENTARY IN 3D

The release of Werner Herzog's 3D documentary *Cave of Forgotten Dreams* (2010), about the prehistoric Chauvet cave paintings, and of Wim Wenders' *Pina* (2011), an Oscar®-nominated 3D profile of the famous choreographer Pina Bausch, opened a new chapter in the history of documentary. Although these projects were produced with large budgets by documentary standards, the availability of consumer-level 3D camcorders suggests that there is a real future for documentary in 3D (Figure 8.39). 3D cinematography was first introduced in the 1950s as one of several efforts to recapture viewers lost to television, and it has been regularly reintroduced (and improved) with each subsequent decade. There is a lot of debate as to what we are witnessing now, after the first decade of the twenty-first century. Some say that 3D digital video represents a "revolution" that will change filmmaking as we know it and make two-dimensional cinematography obsolete. Others claim this is a nostalgic craze, just another movie-making gimmick. Our opinion is that 3D is here to stay, and likely to improve rapidly. In fact, we are starting to see devices that make it possible to have a 3D experience in a home context. 3D probably won't displace 2D movies, but it will settle into its own market niche and share screens with traditionally made films.

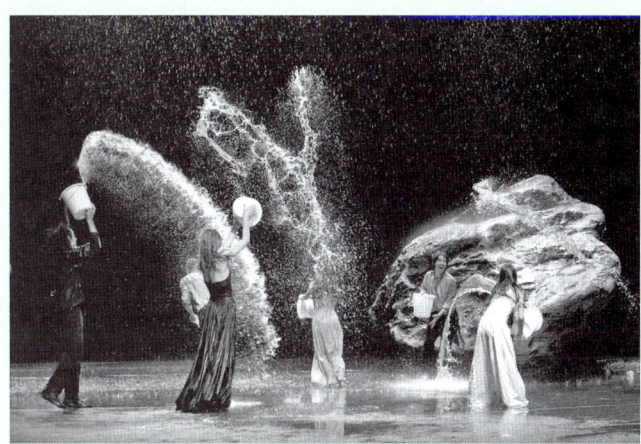

■ **Figure 8.39** *Pina*, the story of the life and work of modern dance choreographer Pina Bausch, was the first 3D film to be nominated for Best Documentary Feature at the Academy Awards®.

As with all new technologies, the availability of 3D is not a reason to use it. 3D was an appropriate technology for *Pina* because it served the story, putting viewers in the midst of the dancers to give a vivid sense of the physicality of the dance movements created by this leading choreographer.

BROADCAST STANDARDS WORLDWIDE

Once your documentary is finished, you will confront the sometimes daunting fact that broadcast standards vary from country to country. You will soon find that there are two main groups of television standards based on the historical standards of **NTSC** and Phase Alternate Line **(PAL)**. These standards ensure compatibility between image recording and display processes across all nations that adopt the standard.

In the United States, Canada, Mexico, South Korea, and some other countries in Latin America and Asia, the broadcast standard is defined by the **ATSC**, and is developed from the older NTSC system. Other digital television standards around the world are Digital Video Broadcasting-Terrestrial (**DVB-T**), which is used throughout Western and Eastern Europe, Russia, Australia, and many nations throughout Asia and Africa; Integrated Services Digital Broadcasting-Terrestrial (**ISDB-T**), used in Japan, Brazil, and most of South America; and Digital Terrestrial Multimedia Broadcast (**DTMB**), used by China and Hong Kong. As of the writing of this edition, global digital television standards were still in the process of being adopted by many nations. The target date for the complete global transition from analog to some form of digital broadcast is 2020. Just as the ATSC standards are based on the need for backward compatibility with the old NTSC standards, DVB-T is based on the widespread former European analog standards **PAL** and **SECAM** (Séquential Couleur Avec Mémoire). Many professional cameras have the capacity to switch formats based on these standards.

CONCLUSION

If you've read this chapter up to this point, you probably understand that the truest thing one can say about digital video is that it's constantly evolving, improving, and changing. Do not expect things to ever settle down to some sort of manageable stasis. Given the variety of options and the speed of technological change, you should try to think through your workflow carefully, and plan as far ahead as you can, thinking about postproduction as well as shooting. In addition, you need to consider that all of these new technologies come with advantages and trade-offs. One example might be 4K. The image is great, but if it comes in a camera that you can't actually handle easily, it might not be the best choice for an observational documentary. In addition, the workflow for 4K can add a big burden in terms of both budget and labor. Just remember that the quality of the image is important, but the story and your relationship with your subjects should be the main driving force behind any decisions you make about equipment.

CHAPTER 9

The Lens

It is often said that "the lens is the eye of the camera." This is true, in that light enters through and is controlled by the lens, and ultimately this light registers as an image. However, there are many things that human eyes and human psychology of perception do automatically which, on a lens, must be accomplished manually. **Focusing**, **exposure**, and **framing** are activities we rarely consciously think about, but on a lens we have to deliberately set each of these functions. These choices are, in fact, part of the creative potential of any lens and part of the aesthetic palette of a documentary filmmaker. Often there is no absolute "right" setting. Rather, you must find the appropriate setting for what you want to express. You must determine which parts of the frame you want to make soft or sharp, bright or dark. For every shot, you must also decide the size of the subject in the frame, as well as the visual perspective. Knowing how lenses work will help you capture your subject in a way that expresses exactly what you want to communicate to your audience. It is helpful to remember that the lens is much more than just the eye of the camera—it becomes the eyes of your audience.

THE OPTICS OF THE LENS

Regardless of whether you are using a smartphone, a digital single-lens reflex camera (DSLR), or a camcorder, the basic construction and function of camera lenses are the same. Broadly speaking, lenses are a series of polished glass sections called **lens elements.** These elements are held parallel to each other in a light-tight housing called the **barrel**, or **lens housing**. The function of these glass elements is to gather the light reflecting off a scene and bend the light through a process called **optical refraction**, forming a flat image on the camera's **focal plane**. The focal plane (also called the **recording surface**) of a video camera is the **faceplate** of the CCD or CMOS chip (Figure 9.1). Many cameras have an external marking that indicates precisely where the focal plane is located. The marking looks like this: ϕ. The image registered on the focal plane is both reversed and flipped. This flipping of the image occurs at the exact **optical center** of the lens and is later reversed on viewing. The distance between the optical center of the lens and the recording surface is called the **focal length** of the lens (pp. 141–148).

There are many lenses to choose from, and many variables on each, so understanding lenses in general will help you pick the right one to create the image you want. There are three critical aspects of every lens that you must learn to give you control of the image: **focus, focal length**, and **aperture**.

Video cameras offer different ways of controlling and monitoring these lens functions. Some use lenses with focus, aperture, and focal length settings etched into their barrels, and you can directly manipulate the lens yourself

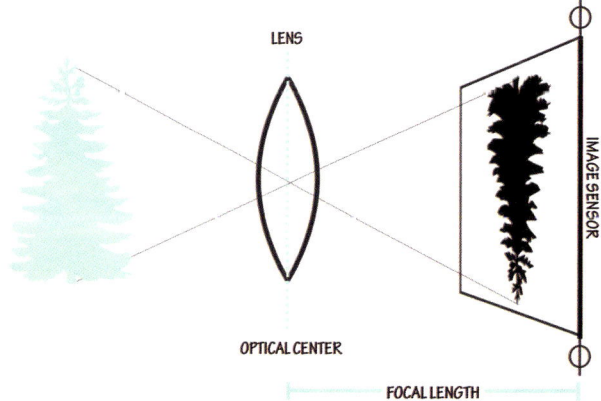

Figure 9.1 The function of a lens is to gather the light reflected off a scene and bend it so that it registers on the image plane (sensor). The distance between the optical center of the lens and the image plane is called the focal length of the lens.

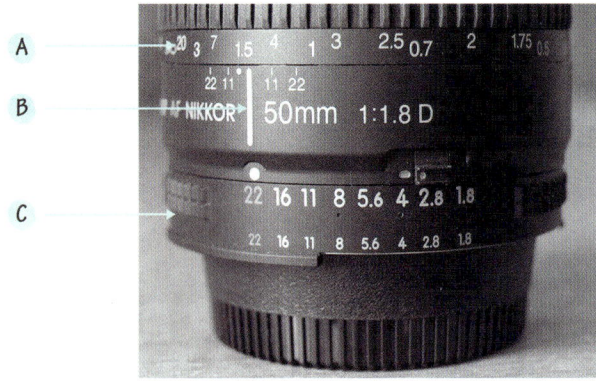
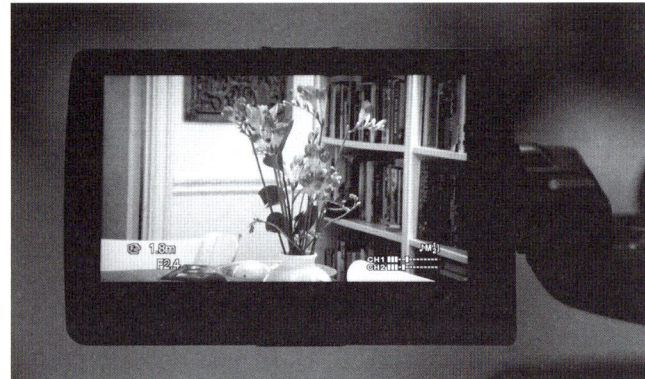

■ **Figure 9.2** Lens functions marked on a lens barrel: focal point in feet and meters (A), focal length indicator, or witness mark, with depth of field indications (B), aperture ring marked in f-stops (C).

■ **Figure 9.3** Lens functions indicated on a viewscreen.

(Figure 9.2). Many cameras, however, place some or all of that information in menus (Figure 9.3). It is important for you to familiarize yourself with these functions and figure out how to control your camera's lens manually before you shoot.

■ FOCUS

We all have some intuitive sense of what **focus** is. Images that appear fuzzy and indistinct are "out of focus" and images that are sharply defined and clear are "in focus." But to be more precise about it, focus can be defined as when a point on the subject is registered as a similarly sharp point on the focal plane (or sensor). The **focus ring** on a lens brings a subject into focus by very precisely moving the front element of the lens forward and backward in relation to the focal plane.

In documentary cinematography, the main task in a new situation is to identify the most important thing happening and make sure it is in focus and stays sharp. This can be challenging as people move around and events unfold.

When you focus the lens, you are adjusting what is called the **focus point**, or **plane of critical focus**. The plane of critical focus is the precise region in front of the camera that will be in sharp focus. If you set the focus ring for 10 feet, objects 10 feet from the camera's focal plane will be rendered sharply. If you set the focus ring to 30 feet, objects 30 feet from the focal plane will be in focus. Turning the focus ring moves the plane of critical focus along the z-axis, toward or away from the camera. The range of distances that you find on the focus ring scale will be from the closest to the farthest an object can be from the focal plane and still be in sharp focus. This range is usually **infinity** (represented on the focus ring scale with the symbol ∞) on the far end, and a few feet on the close end. While some lenses (called **macro lenses**) allow a much closer subject to be in focus, with most lenses a subject can't be closer than about 3 feet from the camera and be in focus. Focus is often indicated in both meters and feet, so be careful not to mix up these scales.

Setting the focus is done by turning the focus ring until the distance you want is lined up against a **witness mark**, which is a line etched into a non-movable part of the lens barrel (Figure 9.2). In documentary, you are rarely able to actually measure the distance between the subject and the camera, as you are probably capturing the action on the fly. In these cases, you can use other techniques to focus.

When shooting video, we can see the actual image that is being registered on the sensor, either through the viewfinder, an LCD viewscreen, or a larger field monitor, so focusing is usually done by eye. Some video camcorders offer a **focus assist** function, which enlarges a portion of the image to help you find critical focus (Figure 9.4).

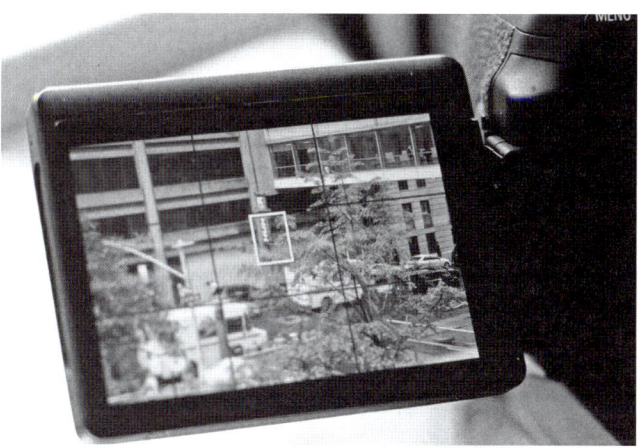 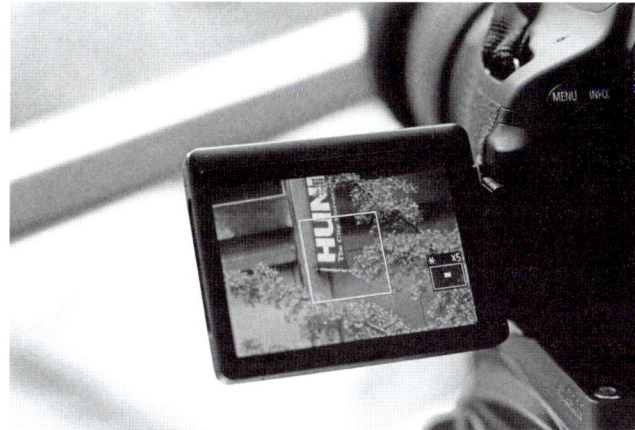

■ **Figure 9.4** The focus assist function. On the left is a shot as framed. On the right, the focus assist has been used to blow up the image to five times its original size to allow the operator to put the banner into sharp focus.

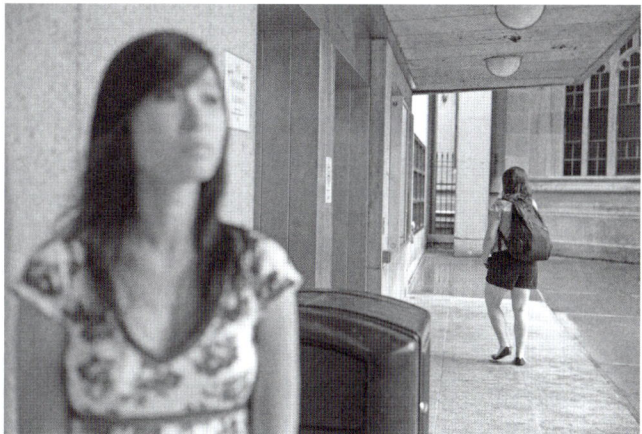 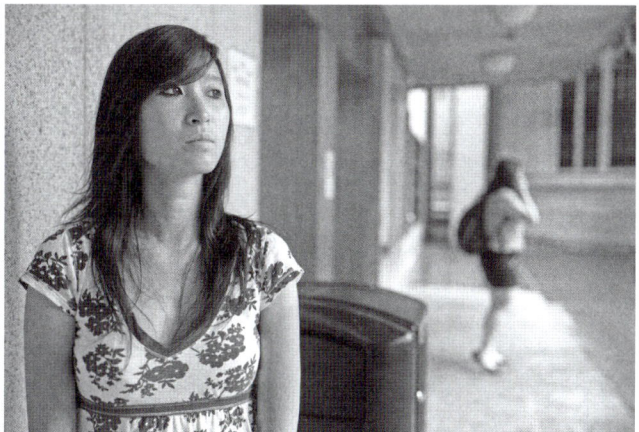

■ **Figure 9.5** The problem with autofocus. In the shot on the left, the camera's autofocus function has set the focus using the center of the frame, putting the main subject out of focus. In the shot on the right, the focus has been set manually to stay on the main subject in the left foreground.

If you are using a zoom lens (pp. 145–146), another common procedure for setting video focus is to zoom all the way in on a detail of what you want to have in focus (for example, the eyes of an interviewee), adjust your focus until the image is sharp, and then zoom out and find your frame. The subject will remain in focus even if you zoom in or out to get a closer or wider frame. This is called **presetting focus**.

Given the challenges involved in finding and maintaining sharp focus, you might be tempted to use **autofocus**. This strategy can create serious problems, however. One significant problem with autofocus is that it favors objects in the center of the frame, which might not be appropriate for the composition you want. Let's say you have a composition in which your subject is tucked over to the left of the frame, with a building behind her. It's likely that the camera will choose to set focus automatically for what is in the middle (a bystander in the background), leaving the main subject out of focus (Figure 9.5).

Autofocus also tends to shift focus in the middle of a take, especially when anything moves across the foreground of the frame. For example, if you are filming a wide shot of a house, and a person walks in between

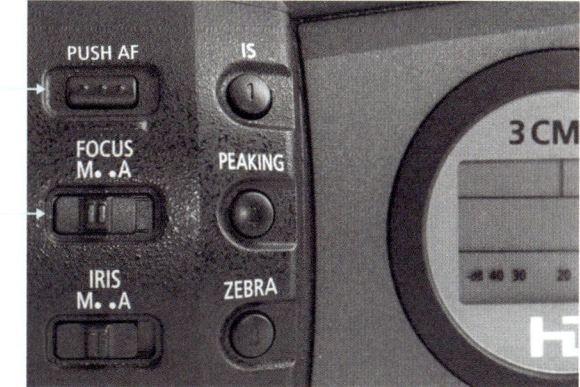

■ **Figure 9.6** The manual/automatic focus switch on a camera (A), and the push auto focus function (B).

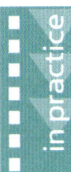

MAINTAINING FOCUS IN THE FIELD

As we have learned, focus is dependent on the distance between the subject and the camera. What that means in practice is that as long as the subject you want to have in sharp focus is kept at the same distance from the camera—even if in motion—you can avoid having them go "soft," or out of focus. A common shot in documentary is to have a subject walking towards the camera, with the camera operator walking backward, maintaining a consistent distance (Figure 9.7). This requires practice (and hopefully a production assistant to make sure you don't injure yourself as you are walking backwards or sideways).

When covering multiple subjects (for instance, around a table), this aspect of focus also means that you can pan from one subject to another and maintain focus as long as they are the same distance from the camera (Figure 9.8).

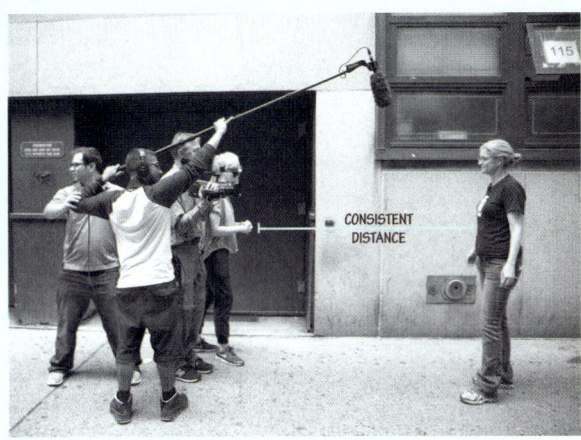

■ **Figure 9.7** When filming a subject walking towards the camera, the cinematographer can back up and stay in focus by maintaining a consistent distance between the camera and the subject.

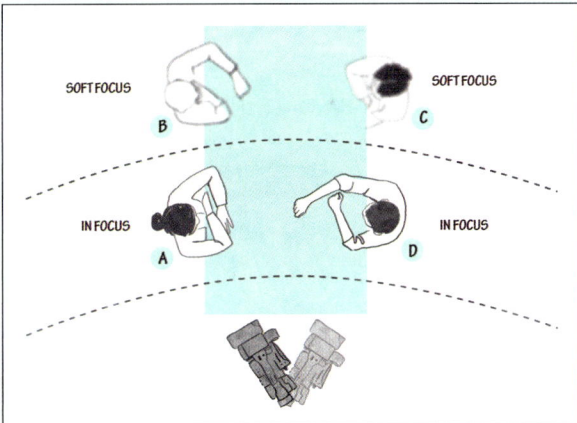

■ **Figure 9.8** In this situation with four people seated at a table, if subject (A) is in focus, the camera operator can pan with confidence to subject (D) knowing that, because they are the same distance from the camera, they will also be in focus. Subjects (B) and (C), however, will be out of focus because they are further away from the camera.

the camera and the house, the autofocus mechanism can start shifting arbitrarily from the house to the person and back to the house, "hunting" for focus but never quite settling. There is a popular technique that uses autofocus but avoids these pitfalls. You can start with autofocus enabled, make sure your subject is in the middle of the frame, and allow the autofocus to choose its setting. Then flip into **manual mode** and return to your original framing. When you readjust your frame with the subject to one side, the camera will hold your focus point. Some cameras have a "push auto" feature that temporarily engages the autofocus so that you don't have go to the trouble of switching back and forth between the auto and manual modes (Figure 9.6).

Adjusting Focus During a Take

There are times when you may need to change the plane of critical focus during a take, while the camera is running. Say an interview subject starts to lean in toward the camera. You can't afford to zoom in to preset focus again, so you make a slight adjustment by turning your focus ring a small amount in the right direction (something you learn by doing). When a larger adjustment is required or a change in focal point is used as part of a conscious strategy to shift the audience's attention, it is called **pulling focus**.

One type of pulling focus is **follow focus**. Follow focus is used when your subject is moving along the z-axis either closer to or farther away from the camera. Let's say you have a shot in which a subject begins 30 feet away from the camera, then moves to 20 feet away,

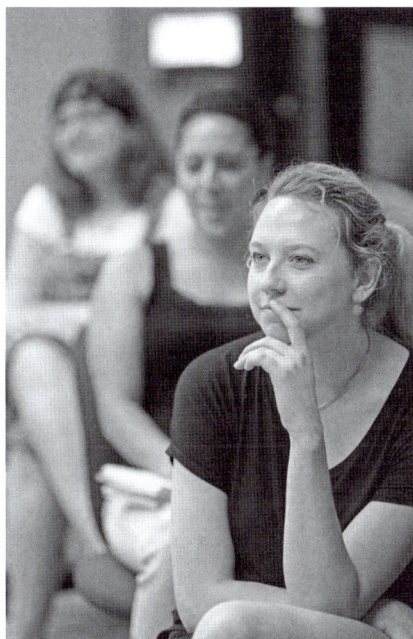 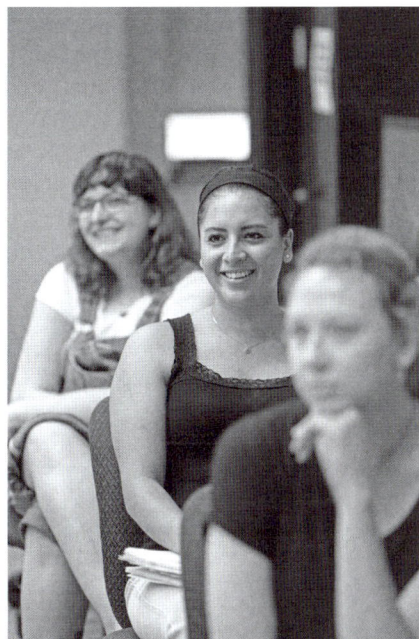 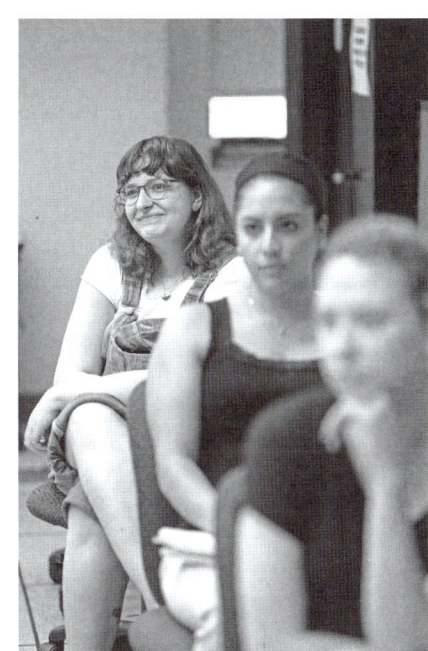

■ **Figure 9.9** Selective focus is used here to draw the viewer's attention to three different parts of the image.

and finally comes to rest 10 feet from the camera. You must adjust the plane of critical focus to follow your subject's progress, preferably in smooth, controlled movements.

In dramatic filmmaking, a camera assistant would adjust the focus ring as the subject hits predetermined marks, but in documentary this is usually done "on the fly," monitoring the results with your eye. Experienced documentary camera operators develop a keen ability to follow a moving subject and keep them in focus through large or small focus adjustments, as well as by maintaining an awareness of the camera-to-subject distance. Like any other specialized skill, the ability to focus quickly and accurately must be practiced so that it becomes as instinctive as a pianist who does not need to look at her fingers to see what keys she's supposed to play.

Selective Focus

As we have discussed, a primary task of the documentary cinematographer is keeping the main action in focus, even as people and objects move around. However, there are also creative decisions to be made about what constitutes the "main action" in a scene. Let's say you are filming a conversation happening at a dinner table, where the parents are discussing money issues in the family. Their son is in the background, and out of focus. You notice out of the corner of your eye that he looks upset. Adjusting your lens so that the child comes into sharp focus, even as the parents continue to speak, could make a strong impact and even change the whole point of the scene. You would be using the power of **selective focus** to direct your viewer's eye to an important aspect of a scene (Figure 9.9). Making these decisions is an important creative skill, and being able to execute them in rapidly evolving real-life situations involves much practice.

FOCAL LENGTH

We all have an intuitive knowledge of what **focal length** is, even if we don't know the term. The idea of "zooming in and out" is something even children are familiar with. What is actually happening when we "zoom" a lens is that we are changing the **focal length**. The **focal length** of a lens determines the degree of magnification or demagnification of the subject being filmed (whether it looks "big" or "small" in the frame).

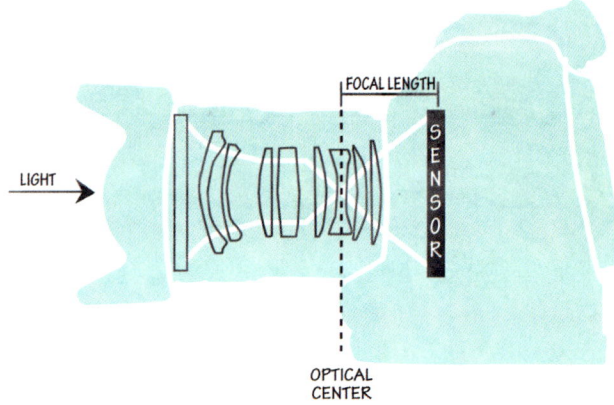

■ **Figure 9.10** Focal length and the optical center of a lens with multiple elements (a compound lens).

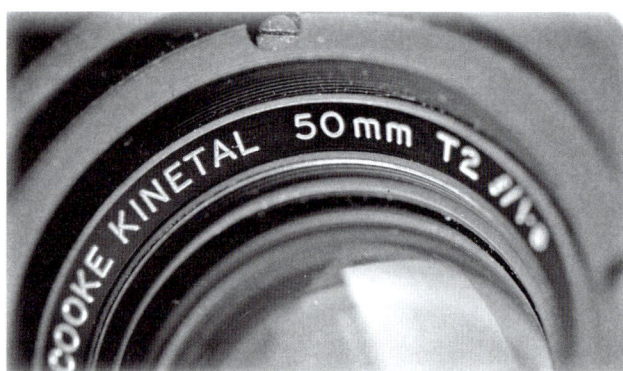

■ **Figure 9.11** Focal length marking on a lens.

As shown in Figure 9.1, focal length is determined by the distance between the **optical center** of the lens (the point at which the image flips) and the focal plane (the image sensor). This distance is usually measured in millimeters (25 mm, 75 mm, 150 mm, etc.). Most lenses are **compound lenses** (made up of multiple glass elements) and in these cases the optical center is calculated by the manufacturer and is difficult to locate physically by eye (Figure 9.10).

The focal length of a lens defines the **angle of view**, which in turn determines the image size within the frame. The exact focal length of a lens can be found etched into the front of the lens (Figure 9.11).

There are three broad focal length classifications for lenses: **wide-angle** (short lenses), **normal** (medium lenses), and **telephoto** (long lenses). The longer the focal length, the more the subject is magnified. The shorter the focal length, the smaller the subject appears, and the farther away objects appear (Figure 9.12).

A **normal lens** approximates the same perspective and image size that the human eye would see if one were to stand in the same spot as the camera. Although this sounds like a nonscientific description, human visual perspective is indeed the intended reference point.

Wide-angle lenses are those with focal lengths shorter than normal lenses, which is why they are commonly referred to as **short lenses**. Wide-angle lenses broaden the angle of view, reducing the size of any given subject in the frame and allowing us to see more of a situation. For example, if you are filming a three-person conversation, the wide lens allows the viewer to see all the participants and gauge their reactions. Wide-angle lenses are often used to shoot observational footage for documentary, because they make small camera movements less obvious.

An extreme wide-angle lens, with an angle of view greater than 180°, is also called a **fisheye lens**. These lenses can provide an interesting perspective on events, but be careful as they can distort people's faces (Figure 9.13). In some cases, the distortion is desirable. Dan Geva's *Description of a Memory* (2006) is a reexamination of a 1960 documentary by filmmaker Chris Marker. Geva's film questions all images, particularly of his homeland Israel. He uses the fisheye lens extensively throughout the film. Its distorted images push the viewer to question which is the correct angle to view a memory from, and what is at stake in our encounter with images of a country and a people.

Telephoto lenses have a longer focal length than normal, which is why they are commonly referred to as **long lenses**. These enlarge the size of the subject in the frame and narrow the angle of view. This narrow angle of view also has the effect of flattening out the image, actually altering the perspective to make objects and faces look less round (the opposite of the fisheye). While we normally think of the telephoto as offering us a close-up look at something far away, it is also common to use a telephoto for an interview as the flatter image can be flattering to the human face. In fact, a medium telephoto lens on a still camera is often referred to as a "portrait lens."

CHAPTER 9 | 143
The Lens

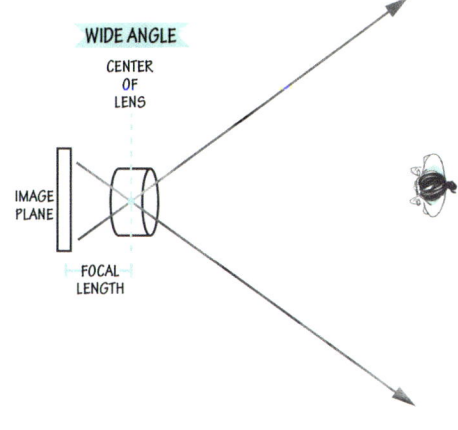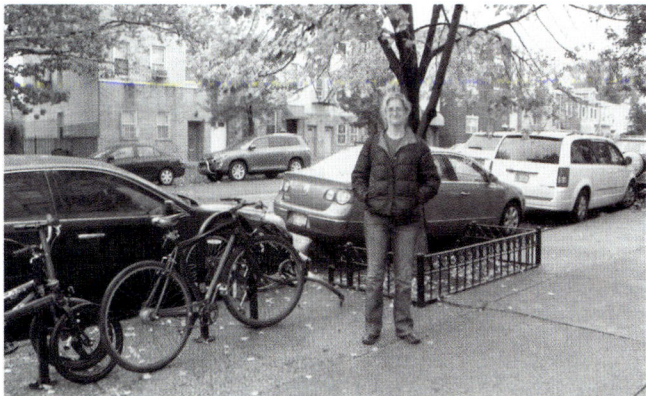

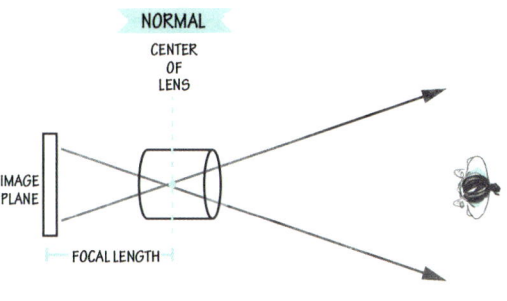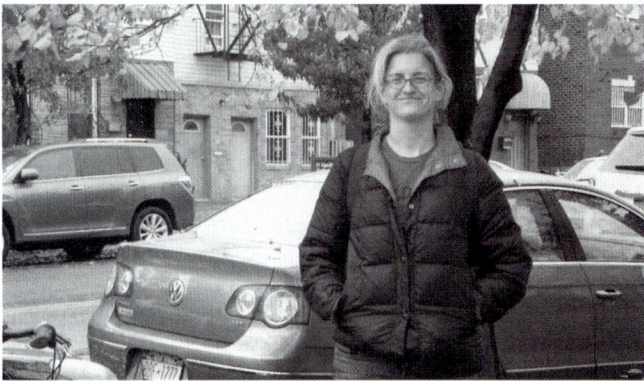

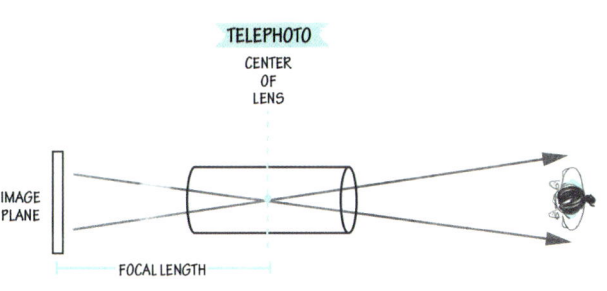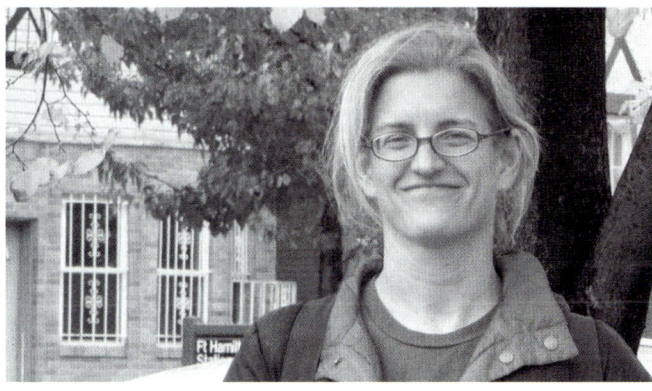

■ **Figure 9.12** Focal length affects angle of view.

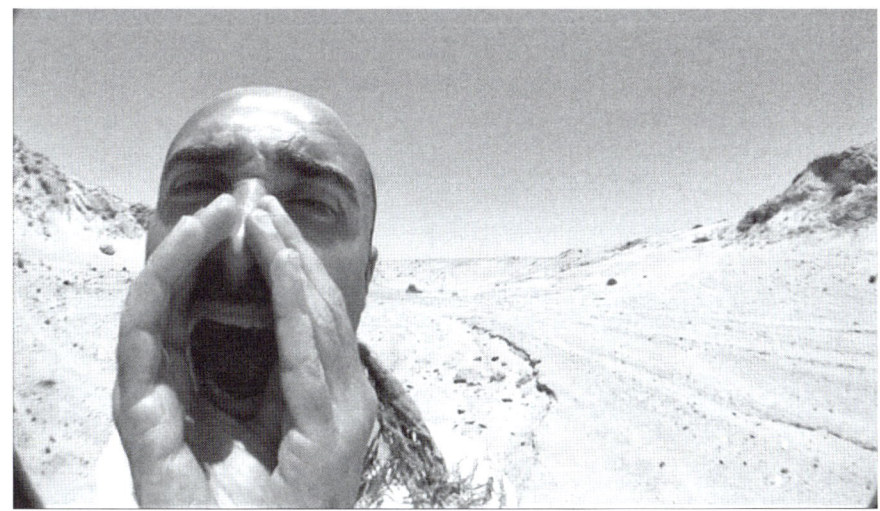

■ **Figure 9.13**
A fisheye lens creates a distorted close-up image of a man's face while emphasizing the vast loneliness of the desert in Dan Geva's *Description of a Memory*.

Focal Length and Sensor Size: Crop Factor

Focal length measurements are not absolute indicators of image size. There is a relationship between focal length and format size, so that a wide-angle lens always has a shorter focal length than a long lens, *for a particular camera*. However, the actual focal length in millimeters varies in relation to the size of the camera's sensor.

Consider this frame, a medium shot, filmed with two cameras with very different sensor sizes (Figure 9.14):

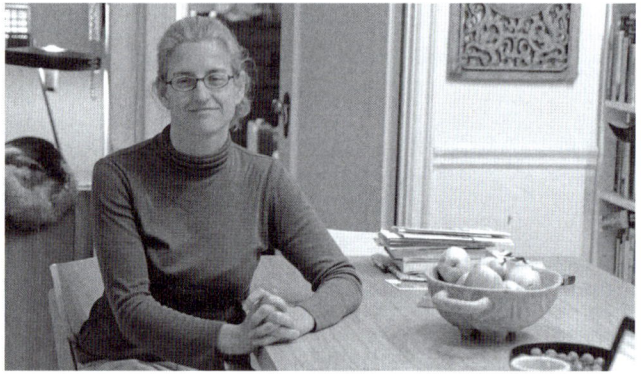 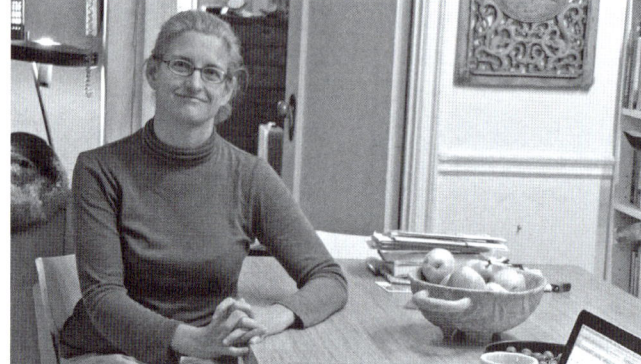

■ **Figure 9.14** Focal length varies according to sensor size. The image on the left was shot with a larger sensor (and longer focal length), while the image on the right was shot with a smaller sensor and shorter focal length. Interestingly, they look relatively the same, as the field of view is equivalent.

On the left, the image was filmed using a Canon T3i DSLR camera, which has an APS-C sensor measuring 22.2 x 14.8mm. The image on the right was filmed using a Sony HXR-NX5U, with a considerably smaller sensor size of 1/3 inch (4.6 x 3.7mm). Even though the shots look more or less "normal" in terms of magnification and angle of view, the shot filmed with the Canon T3i was made with a lens with a focal length of 60mm, while the same shot on the HXR-NX5U had a focal length of 12mm (about 5x smaller).

Because of their ubiquity in both still and moving image photography, the focal lengths of 35mm cameras have come to be used to define lens capability for other sensors. This is known as the **crop factor**. On a 35mm camera, for example, a normal lens has a 50 mm focal length. If you use a camera such as a DSLR with an APC chip, which is closer to 22mm wide, you will have a crop factor of about 1.6. This means that the same 50 mm lens will behave like an 80 mm lens would on the full frame 35mm camera. In other words, your 50 mm lens is now a telephoto. On the 1/3 inch chip camera, the crop factor is about 7. So a 50 mm lens would be the equivalent of a 350 mm lens. When you look at the specifications for a video camera, you will notice that the focal length is often expressed in terms of its 35mm equivalent.

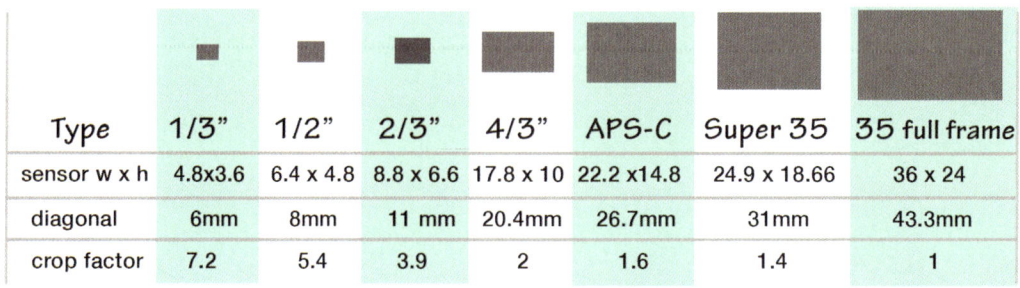

Type	1/3"	1/2"	2/3"	4/3"	APS-C	Super 35	35 full frame
sensor w x h	4.8x3.6	6.4 x 4.8	8.8 x 6.6	17.8 x 10	22.2 x14.8	24.9 x 18.66	36 x 24
diagonal	6mm	8mm	11 mm	20.4mm	26.7mm	31mm	43.3mm
crop factor	7.2	5.4	3.9	2	1.6	1.4	1

■ **Figure 9.15** This chart shows the size of the sensor for a variety of digital cameras and the corresponding crop factors in relation to the full 35mm frame.

All this means that it is very important to know what sensor size your camera has, and what the crop factor will be, before making assumptions about what field of view a particular focal length will deliver (Figure 9.15). One useful tool is a crop factor calculator, such as Abel Cine's (www.abelcine.com).

Prime and Zoom Lenses

Lenses that have one fixed focal length are called **prime** lenses. These lenses are very common in narrative film production, and more recently in DSLR documentary shooting. However, most documentary filmmakers prefer to use **zoom** (or **variable focal length**) **lenses**, which offer a continuous range of focal lengths, because of their flexibility in situations where stopping and changing a lens might mean missing the action.

Zoom lenses are constructed with a mix of stable and movable lens elements. The moveable elements can shift forward or backward to physically shift the optical center of the lens, and therefore change the focal length (Figure 9.16).

Zooming in increases the magnifying power of the lens by adjusting the optical center *away* from the focal plane. This makes the focal length longer, creating a **telephoto** effect. **Zooming out** moves the optical center *back* toward the focal plane, shortening the focal length and causing the image to become more wide-angle. Zooming is accomplished with an adjustable **zoom ring** that allows the filmmaker to manually set the desired focal length, or with a **servo zoom motor**, which allows you to move from one focal length to another smoothly during a shot (Figure 9.16).

Different zoom lenses offer different ranges of focal lengths, and this range is often stated as a ratio. A 21:1 zoom lens (also stated 21x) is one that increases the focal length 21 times over its full range, going, for example, from 5.7 mm to 120 mm (Figure 9.17).

Using the actual zoom movement as part of a shot is common in documentary filmmaking. As documentary cinematographer S. Leo Chiang explains:

> *Having worked with camcorders for so many years, I learned to incorporate the servo zoom into my shooting style. I often do a zoom-pan combination (start with an extreme close-up of a subject's fidgeting hands, for example, and zoom out while panning up to her worried face). In editing, these short and smooth moves add a nice energy that static shots do not have.*[1]

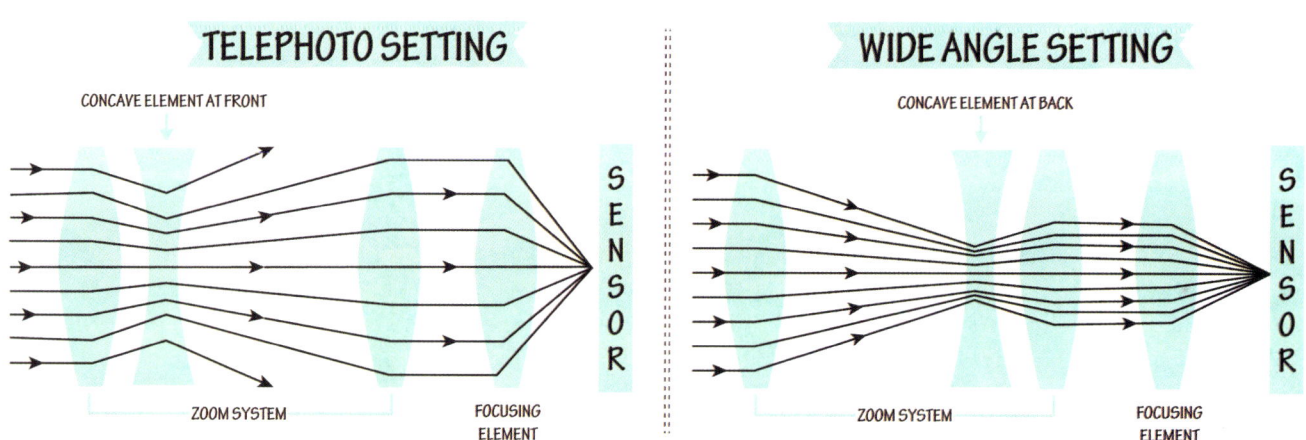

■ **Figure 9.16** Changing focal length on a zoom lens involves moving a group of lenses in relation to a focusing lens element.

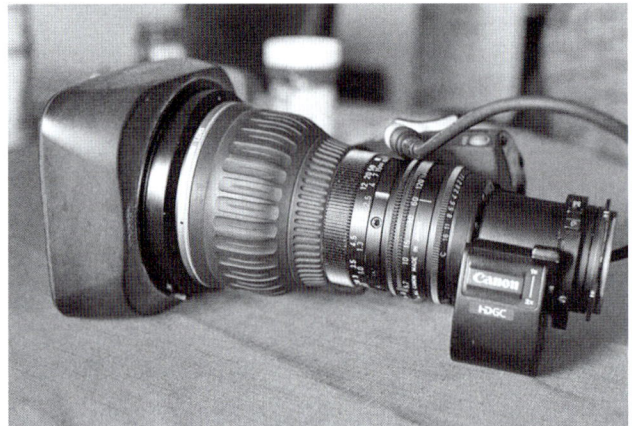

Figure 9.17
This Canon 21x zoom lens has a wide setting of 5.7mm and a long setting of 120mm, giving it very broad range of focal lengths. Photo by Kitmondo Marketplace.

Zoom lenses are very convenient, as they offer a wide range of focal lengths in one lens. For documentary, which calls for flexibility and spontaneity, they are indispensable. There can be trade-offs, including light loss and optical aberrations, but most documentary cinematographers are willing to pay that price.

Focal Length and Lens Perspective

Imagine you want to show a subject in a close-up shot. One approach would be to keep your distance and zoom in. Another would be to use a wide focal length and get close to the subject. These two approaches will give you very different shots with a different sense of space. This difference is called **perspective**. Consider the difference between these two images (Figure 9.18):

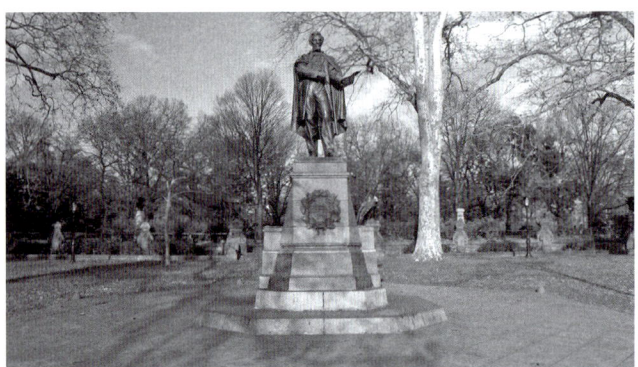
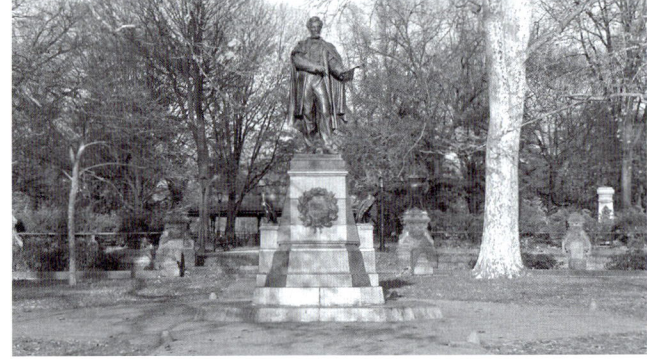

Figure 9.18 Focal length and perspective.

In the image on the right, which was taken from far away using a long (telephoto) lens, the trees behind the statue much closer than in the second image, where the camera has been moved closer to the statue feel and a wide-angle lens was used. Notice that the size of the subject (the statue) has not changed, but everything around it has.

Perspective has to do with how far apart or close together objects appear to the viewer, as well as how much information appears in the frame. This can be separated into horizontal and vertical effects, along the x and y axes, and depth effects along the z-axis (the depth dimension). Compare the two examples in Figure 9.19. Both are long shots where the subjects are nearly identical in size, and the horizontal center of both frames is the same (no left-to-right angle adjustment); however, the shot taken with the wide-angle lens and camera moved closer (A) includes the Gothic windows behind the farthest subject, as well as some bulletin boards on the wall to the left (to the left of the frame). Shot B, of the same subjects taken using a longer focal length and moving the camera back, has narrowed the field of view to exclude these details.

CHAPTER 9
The Lens

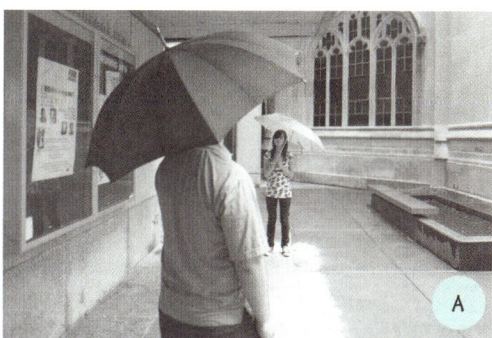
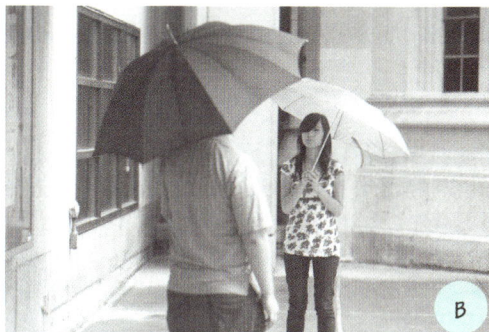
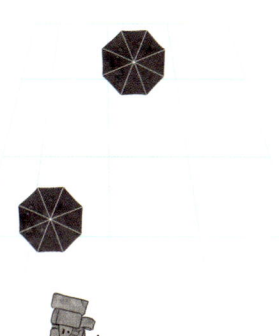
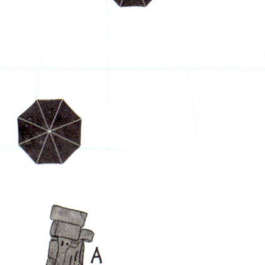
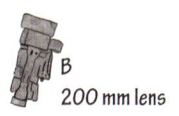
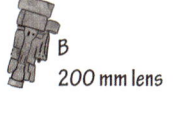

■ Figure 9.19
Focal length and perspective.

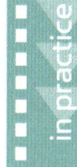

■ USING A TELEPHOTO LENS TO CONDENSE SPACE

In *Lessons of Darkness* (1993), about the oil fires that raged in Kuwait after the 1991 Gulf War, Director Werner Herzog used extremely long lenses to compress space along the z-axis, creating an other-worldly landscape that brought the fires extremely close to the firefighters battling them (Figure 9.20). This spatial compression also suffused the image with the shimmering thermal waves associated with extreme heat. The emotional impact is one of being in hell. Herzog explained that he wanted to depict "a crime against Creation itself."[2]

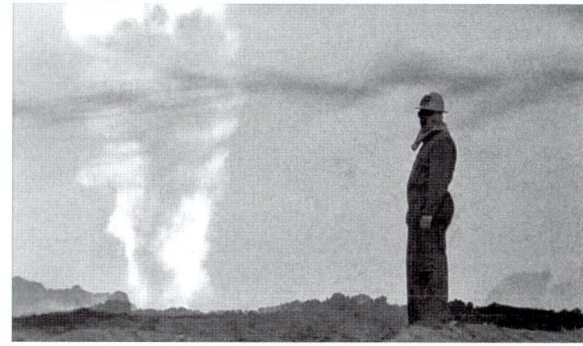

■ Figure 9.20 Long lenses compress space in *Lessons of Darkness*. Cinematography by Simon Werry, Paul Berriff, and Rainer Klausmann.

Changing the focal length also significantly alters the perception of depth in the frame. A normal lens replicates the same perception of depth that our eyes see. For example, if we use a normal lens to frame a subject in a medium shot with another object 5 feet behind, that object will indeed seem like it is 5 feet behind the subject. Wide-angle lenses tend to exaggerate depth along the z-axis, making objects look farther apart. Long lenses tend to compress space, making objects look closer together. For example, in Figure 9.19, the subjects have not physically moved between shots A and B, but they look much closer together in shot B, taken with a 200 mm lens, than in shot A, taken with a 50 mm lens. In documentary, this lens functionality is sometimes used to make spaces look more crowded (by using a long lens) or sparsely populated (by using a wide-angle lens).

You may be tempted to use the telephoto capability of a lens to "get closer" to your subject because it is easy, but keep in mind that the flat perspective can have a subtle surveillance effect. Moving physically closer to your subject with the camera may create more interaction with your subject, offering your audience a feeling of being there in the space of the subject rather than being outside peering in.

APERTURE

Another adjustable ring found on all professional lenses is the **aperture ring** (or **f-stop ring**). The aperture ring controls the **iris**, a diaphragm inside the camera made up of flat, metal blades. These blades overlap in such a way that they create an opening that is nearly circular. This opening is called the **aperture** and all light gathered by the lens must pass through the aperture before it is registered on the sensor. By adjusting the aperture ring, the iris either opens to allow more light in, or closes to allow less light to reach the sensor. The most important purpose of the iris is to control the amount of light striking the sensor. Allow too much light through the lens and you will have a washed out, **overexposed** image. Block too much light and you will have a dark, **underexposed** image.

The size of the aperture opening is calibrated to a scale called the **f-stop scale**, which is either etched into the aperture ring or displayed in the viewfinder. The f-stop scale typically includes the settings f/1.4, f/2, f/2.8, f/4, f/5.6, f/8, f/11, f/16, and f/22. Partial f-stops, in between these primary ones, are marked on some lenses. At first, f-stops can be confusing because the smaller the f-stop number, the larger the aperture opening. Conversely, the larger the f-stop number, the smaller the aperture opening. So a setting of f/2 lets in a lot of light, while at f/16 the aperture is only the size of a pinhole (Figure 9.21).

Each number on the scale is called a **stop**. There is one stop between f/4 and f/5.6, and two stops between f/4 and f/2. Going down or up one stop on the scale exactly doubles or halves the amount of light allowed to pass. Expanding the aperture (smaller f-stop number) is called "opening up" the lens. Reducing the size of the aperture (larger f-stop number) is called "closing down" or "stopping down." Opening up to f/4 from f/5.6 allows in twice as much light, while closing the aperture to f/2.8 from f/2 cuts the light in half.

As you can imagine, this range of f-stops gives you a huge amount of control over the actual amount of light hitting the camera's sensor. In the case of Figure 9.22, which shows a lens with a range from f/2.8 to f/22, there is a range in light levels of some 256 times higher or lower. How do you access the iris control? This varies hugely. If you have a DSLR with an older manual lens, you turn a ring that is marked on the lens, as in Figure 9.2. However, most modern cameras offer some other route to controlling aperture. A typical mid-level camera will have an iris control on a ring, but no numbers. You will only see the exact f-stop setting in the viewfinder. Other cameras, usually smaller and less expensive ones, will have only a menu option.

As with focus, there is not one single "correct" exposure for any video frame. There is a range of possible exposures you choose from in order to achieve the mood, style, and

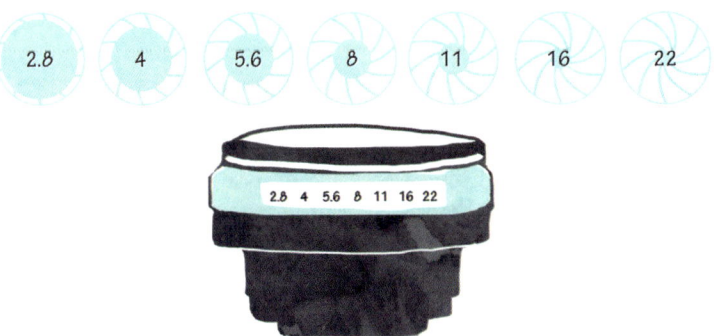

■ **Figure 9.21** The f-stop scale.

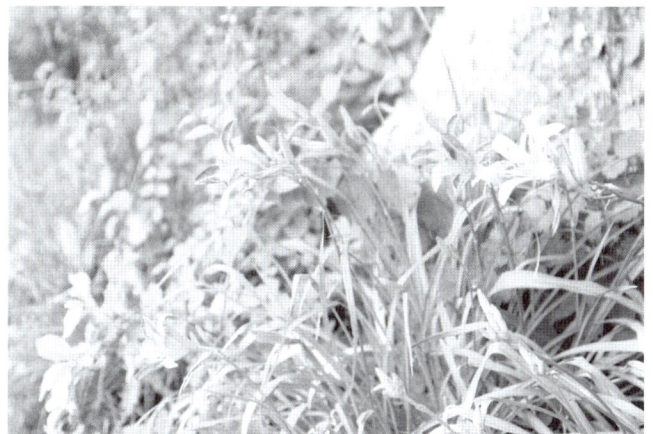
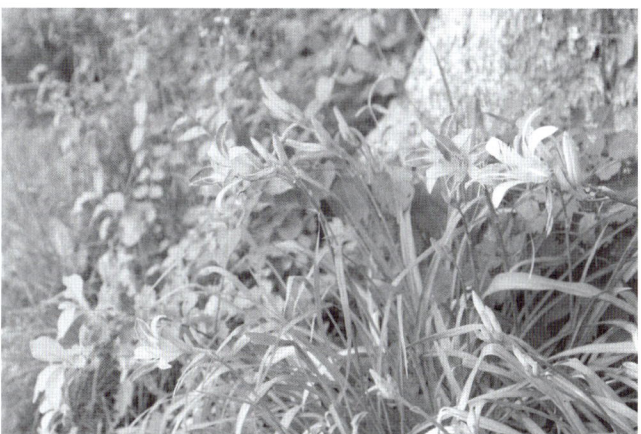
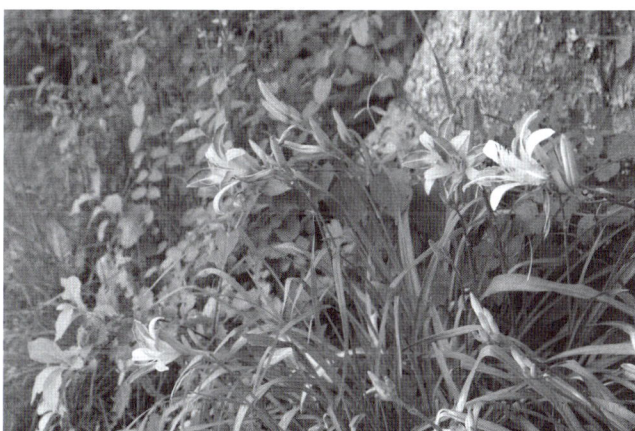

visual meaning you are seeking. A built-in light meter on all video cameras can trigger an **auto iris** function (also called **auto exposure**), which will take the average meter reading for your scene and automatically set the camera's aperture. However, exposure control is such a crucial area of aesthetic impact that you will want to be very discerning about when you allow the camera to automatically set your f-stop and when you want to set it yourself. With digital cameras, a small difference of even a quarter or half of an f-stop can have a big impact on the image in terms of shadow detail, color saturation, and overall feel. In addition, only you know which part of the frame should be set for optimum exposure. See Chapter 12 for more on controlling your aperture and exposure.

All professional and industrial-grade cameras and many (but not all) consumer cameras have manual override capabilities. Digital cameras often offer a **manual aperture override** (also called "push auto iris") function on your camera (Figure 9.23). This function allows you to turn the auto iris on briefly to get an average exposure, and then turn it back to manual to fine tune.

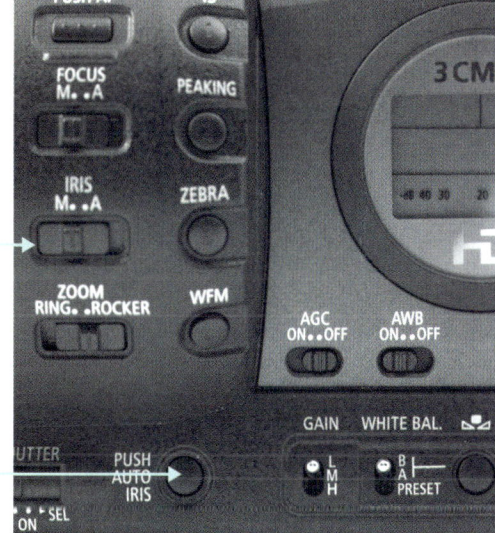

■ **Figure 9.22** These three images suggest how light values can fall along the range of possible exposures. The top image was shot at f/4, the middle image (which has the fullest range of light values) at f/5.6, and the bottom image at f/8.

■ **Figure 9.23** A close-up of the aperture controls on a Canon XF300. In this case there is a manual/auto switch (A), and then a button that temporarily engages the auto-iris function to give you a baseline exposure (B).

Lens Speed

The ability of a lens to gather light is determined by the largest possible aperture opening of that particular lens. We refer to this ability as **lens speed**. A **fast lens** can open up to allow more light than a **slow lens**. A lens with a maximum aperture of f/1.4 is a very fast lens and can register a readable image with very little light. Why are some lenses faster than others? What limits the ability of a lens to gather light are the optics: the number, size, and quality of the glass elements. Generally, wide-angle lenses are faster than telephoto lenses. Zoom lenses tend to be slower than prime lenses, as their construction requires many more elements. In fact, a maximum aperture of only f/3.5 or f/4 is not uncommon for a zoom lens.

DEPTH OF FIELD

Beyond the question of exposure, the selection of your f-stop plays an important role in determining the look, tone, mood, and visual content of each and every shot in your film. This is because f-stop impacts the **depth of field (DOF)**. As we discussed earlier, the **plane of critical focus** is the point at which the lens focus is actually set, and there can be only one setting for any given situation. However, when we look at an actual photographed image, we notice that there is always an area, both in front of and behind this plane of focus, that also appears to be in focus. This range of apparent focus along the z-axis is called the DOF. The relative depth or shallowness of this area is not fixed. It can be as shallow as a few inches or as deep as infinity (Figure 9.24).

For any given scene, depending on lighting, filters, and other factors, there may be a range of f-stops that will give an acceptable image. Therefore, the decision of which f-stop to use is often made based on the desired DOF, and boils down to the questions: What do you want to communicate with this shot? Which f-stop will create the image that best expresses your idea? What are the possibilities of your shooting situation in terms of lighting?

Creating a frame with a **shallow depth of field** makes your subject stand out from the environment and gain prominence in the frame, because objects both in front of and behind the subject are out of focus and indistinct. Adopting a **deep depth of field** (also called "deep focus") increases the amount of information we see along the z-axis and gives environmental detail that can provide more context. In addition, a deeper DOF makes it easier to keep your subject in focus.

In terms of f-stop, the larger the aperture opening (smaller f-stop numbers), the shallower the DOF will be. The smaller the aperture opening (larger f-stop numbers), the deeper the DOF will be. That is why scenes shot in very low light situations have such a shallow DOF that we sometimes can see an eye in focus, but the ear, just a few inches back, is soft. Conversely, scenes shot in brightly lit environments can have a DOF so deep that everything in the background is in focus. Sometimes, when shooting in bright light, cinematographers will add **neutral density** (ND) filters to cut down the amount of light, allowing them to open up and decrease the DOF.

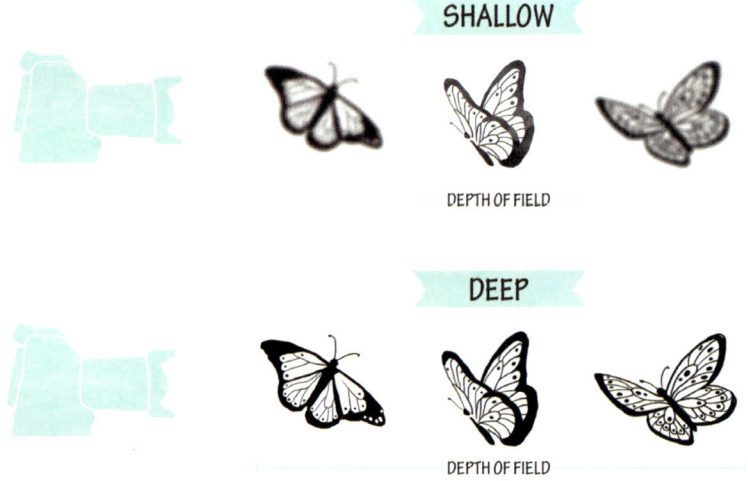

■ **Figure 9.24** Shallow vs deep depth of field (DOF).

■ DEEP FOCUS VS SHALLOW DEPTH OF FIELD

In this scene from Alan Berliner's *Nobody's Business* (1996), Berliner used an extremely long lens with its very shallow DOF to isolate his father from the people around him, emphasizing the feeling of a "lonely man in a crowd" (Figure 9.25). Note how the lens also compresses the space along the z-axis, making the people in front of and behind Berliner's father seem closer together.

In *Helvetica* (2007), a documentary by Gary Hustwit about the Helvetica font, deep DOF allows us to see detail on the widest possible range of signs in Times Square (Figure 9.26). This is important because at this point in the film, Hustwit is making the point that Helvetica is everywhere, so ubiquitous that we don't even notice it.

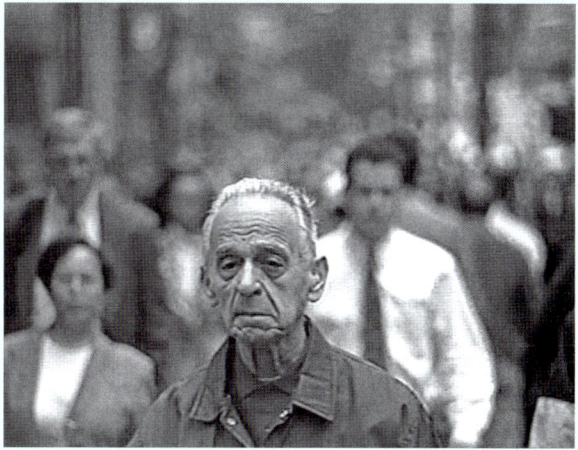

■ **Figure 9.25** Shallow depth of field in *Nobody's Business*.

Whether to use deep or shallow DOF in documentary depends as much on the situation as on your aesthetic goals. As cinematographer David Alvarado says,

> *If it's not heavy action and I'm outside, and I want it to be pretty with shallow DOF, I can shoot at f1.4, but if there's heavy action I wouldn't want to shoot so shallow. It would be hard to follow the action and keep the right things in focus. So I would decide to shoot at f3.5 or f5.6.*[3]

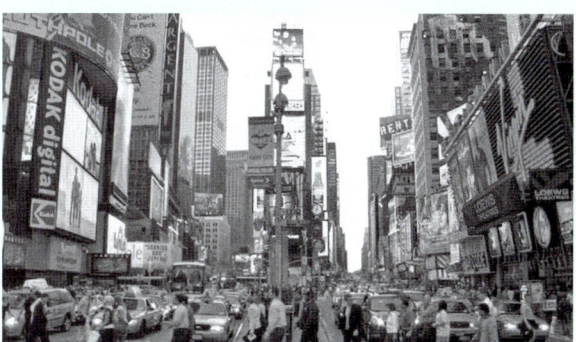

■ **Figure 9.26** Deep depth of field in *Helvetica*.

Other Factors Impacting Depth of Field

Another primary factor in determining DOF is the size of the image sensor. The smaller the sensor, the deeper the DOF tends to be. It is harder to get shallow DOF on a camcorder that has a 1/3" (8.4 mm) sensor than it is with a DSLR, which may have a full 35mm sensor. In fact, many filmmakers chose to shoot with large sensor cameras because they like the look of a shallow DOF.

There are two other variables that determine the actual range of DOF over which we have some control:
1. The focal length of the lens. The longer the focal length of the lens, the shallower the DOF will be. The shorter the focal length of the lens, the deeper the DOF will be. So, in documentary work, it is good to remember that it is much easier to keep subjects in focus when shooting with a wide-angle lens than a telephoto (or using the wide end of the zoom lens range).
2. The focus point setting. The closer the subject is to the camera, the shallower the DOF will be. This is why, in documentary interviews, if you place the subject too close to the camera, you risk having them go out of focus if they lean forward or backwards even a little bit. Conversely, the farther away you place the subject from the camera, the deeper the DOF will be.

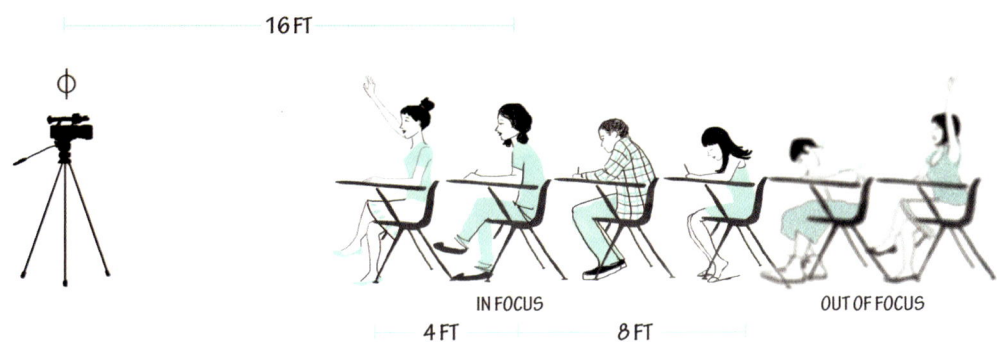

■ **Figure 9.27** The 1/3–2/3 rule showing the range of focus in front and behind the subject. In this case, the depth of field is 12 feet. If the focal point is on the student in the second row, this will put the students in the first, third, and fourth rows in focus as well.

The 1/3–2/3 Rule

Regardless of your actual DOF, the **1/3–2/3 rule** for DOF tells us that two-thirds of the depth range along the z-axis is behind the focus point and one-third is in front. Let's say you are filming several rows of students in a classroom, from the front of the room. If you want the first four rows to be more or less in focus, you should focus on the second row, which means that the one row in front and the two rows behind will also be in focus (Figure 9.27).

■ CONCLUSION

While you might think that, with documentary shooting, you have the job done when you have clear focus and adequate exposure, nothing could be further from the truth. Harnessing the power of focus, aperture, and focal length will allow your shots to resonate deeply with meaning. Do you want the environment you are depicting to feel expansive, or claustrophobic? Do you want to isolate your subject, or present them in a context that gives the viewer additional information about who and where they are? These are just a few of the questions you can ask yourself when working with the variable components of your lens.

CHAPTER 10

Camera Support

Deciding if your camera should move during a shot and how you want it to move are critical to the tone, style, and meaning of your film. Whether you're panning, tracking, tilting, or staying absolutely still, choosing the appropriate camera support is vital. You need to understand the equipment you have available to you and the expressive potential of each piece of gear, so that you can achieve your aesthetic goals.

Let's say during preproduction you decide that your film would best be told as a series of meticulously lit and composed static compositions where the camera barely moves, as in *Our Daily Bread* (2005), Nikolaus Geyrhalter's documentary about industrial food production. Or perhaps you want your film to open with a 7-minute tracking shot of a Chinese electronics factory, like *Manufactured Landscapes* (2006) by Jennifer Baichwal. Or you choose to invoke hard realism and intimacy through a restlessly moving camera, as we see in a film like *A Lion in the House* (2006), Julia Reichart and Steven Bognar's documentary about children with cancer and their families.

Each of these choices was perfectly suited to the content and concept of its respective film, and each one required a different kind of camera support. You need to ask yourself what camera support system will allow you to achieve the particular look and style you are after, and if you have or can afford the equipment needed to achieve it. Let's take a look at some options.

THE HANDHELD CAMERA

The cheapest and most readily available method of camera support is the human body. "Going handheld" means using your hands and arms for holding small and lightweight cameras, or carrying a larger camera on your shoulder and bracing it with your arm (Figure 10.1).

Handholding always introduces some instability into the image, because the camera reflects the human movements of the operator. No matter how steady the camera operator

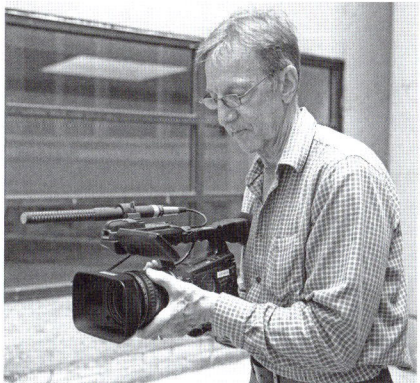 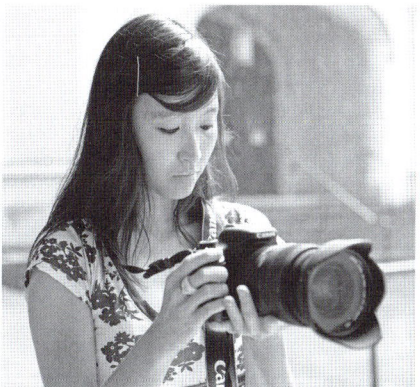 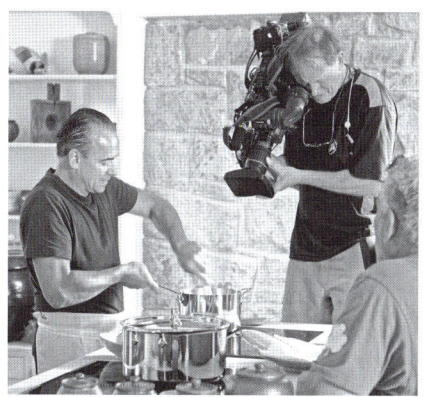

Figure 10.1 Handholding a camera can be fairly easy for short periods when using a small camcorder (left) or DSLR (center), but for extended shooting a larger shoulder-mounted camera may present an easier solution (right).

is, a handheld camera is never as stable as one mounted on a tripod, nor should it be. The handheld camera is a staple of much documentary filmmaking, for several reasons. First, a handheld camera can respond more effectively to unplanned events, making it a particularly appropriate choice for observational documentaries that require the cinematographer to follow unscripted action. In addition, the movement obtained with a handheld camera has an aesthetic quality that adds a feeling of immediacy and **realism**, and thus **authenticity**, to the documentary image. It may also go so far as to imply a certain ethical stance, characterized by the filmmaker's decision to observe and document, as opposed to shaping, the reality in front of the camera.

For all of these reasons, the handheld camera has been popular with documentary filmmakers since the advent of portable 16mm film cameras during the 1960s, and the corresponding birth of the **cinéma vérité** and **direct cinema** movements (Chapter 2). In fact, these advances in portable handheld technology produced major changes in the documentary form.

Using a handheld camera is not as easy as simply slinging a camera on your shoulder and shooting. We've all seen plenty of home movie footage that's so jittery it makes us nauseous. Techniques for handheld shooting require a great deal of body strength and control to keep the image from looking haphazard or sloppy, and must be practiced. In many ways, small ultralight cameras are more difficult to control than larger cameras because the weight of a camera, especially when mounted on a shoulder, provides some stability. If you decide to go handheld, your movements should be as controlled as possible while still feeling natural. Don't worry that it will look like a tripod shot; it won't. Controlled imperfection is the aesthetic point.

Once upon a time, a "handheld" camera always sat on the user's shoulder and was supported in front by the right hand, which would also control the servo zoom control and start and stop recording. The left hand was then free to adjust focus, aperture and other camera controls. Since many cinematographers are now filming with small cameras that don't sit on the shoulder, the term "handheld" now often refers to literally holding the camera in your hands, supporting it with a shoulder mount (more on shoulder mounts below) or working with a camera big enough to sit on your shoulder.

■ TIPS FOR SHOOTING WITH A HANDHELD CAMERA

- **Camera movement comes from the body**, not just the hands. Use your entire body: feet, legs, torso, arms, and hands.

- **Keep your knees bent and loose**, like a skier, for shock absorption.

- **Stay toward the wide angle end of the lens**. A telephoto lens only magnifies the jitter and instability of the frame. If you need to get closer, move in closer.

- **Breathing should be long and steady**. Don't hold your breath or you will find the need to gasp for air in the middle of a shot, causing an inevitable jerk of the frame.

- **Don't hold the camera rigidly**. Rhythm, grace, and controlled movement are key.

- **Take advantage of the pivoting LCD screen and the light weight of palm-held camcorders** to go beyond eye-level shots. These cameras allow you to see your compositions even when the camera is dangling low from your arm or held aloft far over your head.

- **Practice, practice, practice**. Like any other creative skill, you get better at handholding a camera by doing it over and over again. Great handheld cinematographers are great because they've handled a camera nearly as often as a great pianist has touched the piano keys or a tennis pro has swung a racket. No great skill is acquired without effort, learning, and practice.

■ SHOULDER MOUNTS

Larger camcorders, common before the advent of small digital and DSLR video cameras, had the advantage of being heavier and shoulder-mounted. While this would not necessarily seem to be an advantage—after all, shooting is hard work, and more muscles are required to support a heavier camera—the image from a camera mounted on an operator's shoulder tends to be more controlled and smoother than one from a small handheld device. The lens of a shoulder-mounted camera also rests at approximately the same level as the eye of the cinematographer, creating what may feel like a more natural perspective for the viewer than a camera held at torso-level, where many small cameras are more comfortably held.

For these reasons, many cinematographers working with DSLR and other small cameras prefer to use a **shoulder mount** (Figure 10.2). When choosing a shoulder mount, it is important to consider what type of camera you are using. Some rigs can accommodate several types of cameras, while others are suited to one model. It is also important to ask yourself what types of additional equipment you will need to attach to your mount. Common add-ons include a **monitor** (Chapter 8), **external drives**, **follow focus** systems (Chapter 9), a **matte box** (Chapter 11), and **receivers** for **wireless microphones** (Chapter 13).

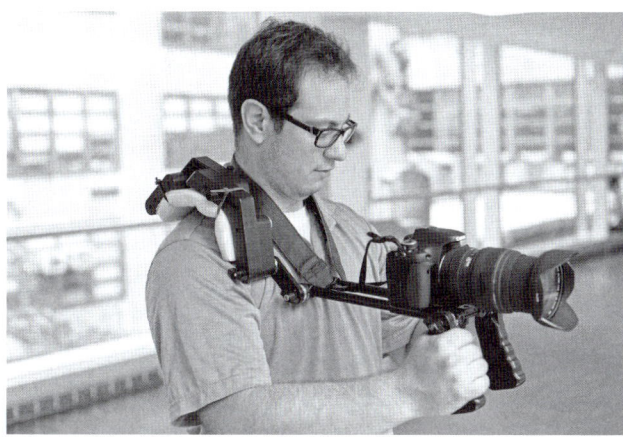

■ Figure 10.2 A simple shoulder rig for a DSLR.

With larger cameras, it is critical that your shoulder rig be properly balanced. Proper balance means that when you are not supporting the mount with your hands, it should sit on your shoulder without pitching forward or backward, or to one side. Commonly, weight will need to be added to the back of the rig to balance the weight of the camera at the front end. An improperly balanced shoulder rig will force the camera operator to use their arms to hold up the front end, which is very difficult for long filming periods and likely to produce back injuries. Adding battery packs or weights to the back of the shoulder mount allows the operator's body to do the work of supporting the camera, and gravity helps the camera stay balanced. Importantly, a well-balanced camera and rig will allow the operator to use one hand to adjust focus or change the focal length of the lens. It is worth mentioning that the added gear that is likely necessary to make a DSLR or small mirrorless camera useful for documentary will add significantly to both the cost and the weight of your equipment package.

THE TRIPOD

After handholding, **tripods** are the most common form of camera support in documentary. A tripod is a three-legged support designed to hold the camera steady for precise subject framing and also to allow for fluid pans, tilts, and **compound moves**. Professional filmmaking tripods are designed with **pan heads** that are different from the static heads used in still photography. These are highly adjustable, allowing a filmmaker to frame and maneuver with a precision and fluidity not possible with a handheld camera.

In documentary, tripods are commonly used for formal "sit-down" interviews. An interview can last an hour or longer, making it impractical to handhold the camera. In addition, using a tripod gives the interview visual continuity that can both help focus attention on the subject and make editing easier. Tripods are also extremely common in news gathering (Figure 10.3), where the camera must often be far away from the speaker, making handheld shooting very difficult, and where shooters must wait for long periods for the action to begin.

Tripods may also be used for shooting establishing shots and other elaborate visuals that require a controlled camera. For example, in Patricio Guzman's *Nostalgia for the Light* (2010), there is a shot of a pre-Colombian carving in Chile's Atacama Desert, high up on a cliff. Cinematographer Katell Djian does a slow zoom from a long shot to a close-up of the carving (Figure 10.4). Although it would be possible to shoot this handheld, we wouldn't be able to absorb the detail of the carving because the final close-up would be at the telephoto end of the zoom range and would be shaking too much. The tripod also

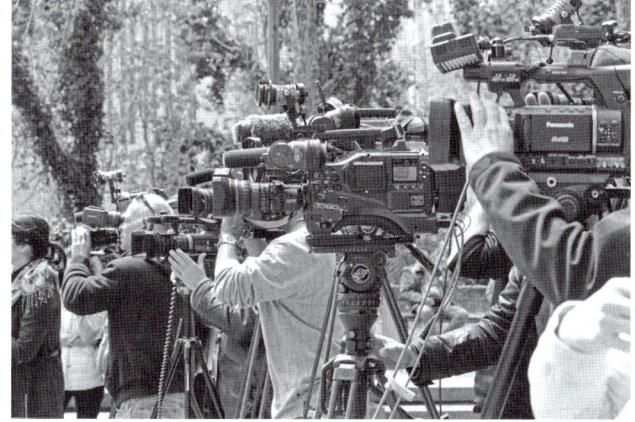

■ Figure 10.3 News shooters often use tripods, especially when covering press conferences or speeches. Photo courtesy of VOCAL-NY.

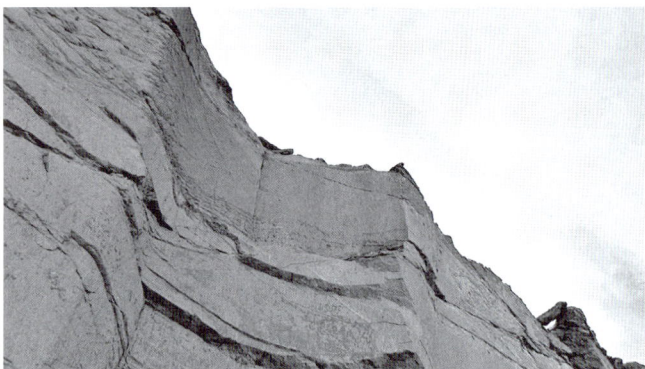 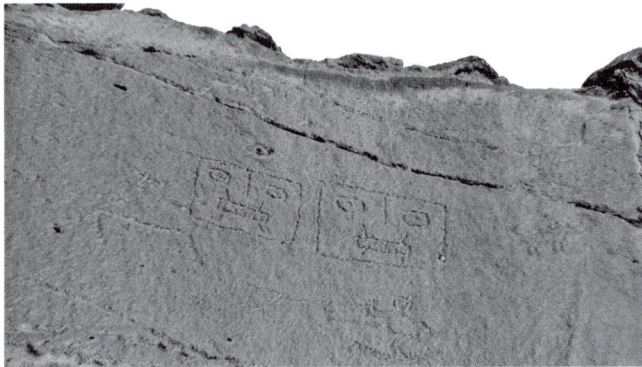

■ **Figure 10.4** This shot from *Nostalgia for the Light* begins with a long shot (left) and zooms in to a close-up (right). This type of shot is best taken using a tripod because of the stability and precision needed.

lends this shot a controlled, meditative feel that would be diminished by the observational realism associated with a handheld camera.

Finally, for any kind of **time lapse** photography, where a long time period is condensed to a short period by speeding up the footage, you will need to use a tripod.

The design of the tripod has remained essentially unchanged since the earliest years of cinema (Figure 10.5). A tripod can be broken down into two major components: the **head** and the **legs** (also called **sticks**). Some less expensive tripods are constructed with the head and legs in one unit, but the most flexible tripods are those that are designed as systems, so that each component is separate and interchangeable to fit a variety of production situations (Figure 10.6).

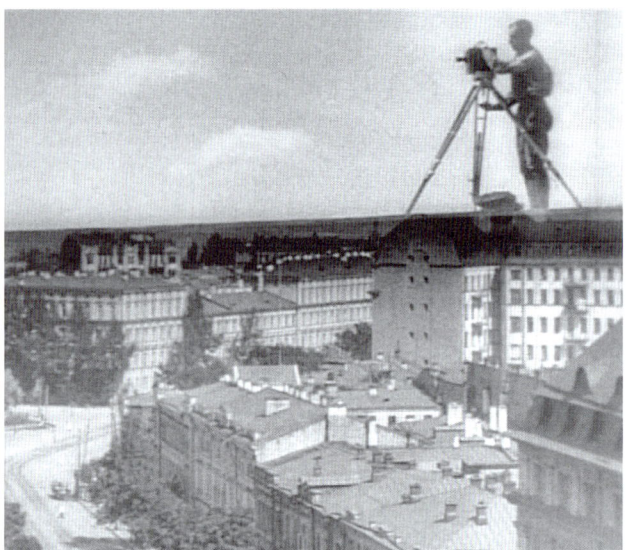

■ **Figure 10.5**
The tripod has been used since the early history of filmmaking, as seen in Dziga Vertov's *Man with a Movie Camera* (1929).

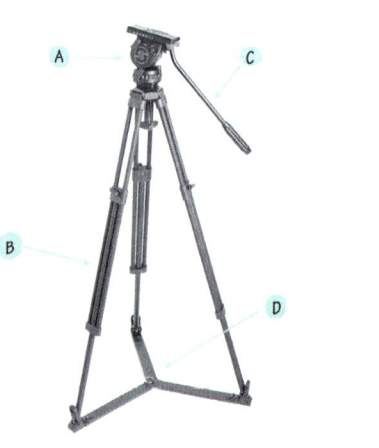 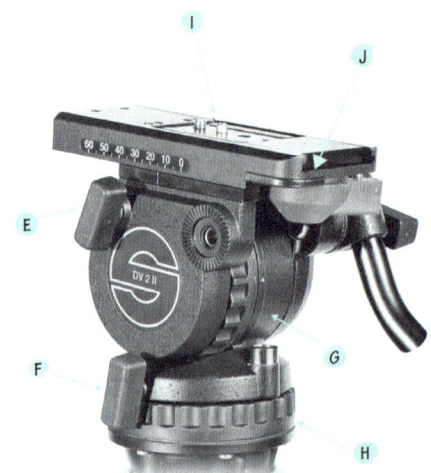

■ **Figure 10.6**
A tripod system will commonly have a head (A), extendable legs (B), a pan handle (C), and a removable spreader (D). A professional tripod head, like this Sachtler DV-2 fluid head shown in close-up on the right, has a tilt lock (E), a pan lock (F), tension (drag) adjustments for the tilt and pan controls (G, H), a camera mounting plate (I), and a quick release lock for the base plate (J).

Tripod Head (A)

In terms of movement precision, the most important component of any tripod is the **head**. The tripod head is where the camera is mounted, and is the component that swivels left and right for panning, as well as up and down for tilting. The quality of the head greatly affects the smoothness of the camera moves executed using the tripod. Tripod heads come in different sizes to accommodate various camera weights. A small head, like the Sachtler DV-2, is designed specifically for small cameras (Figure 10.6). Larger heads, like the Miller Compass 15, are built to accommodate the bulk of large video camcorders weighing up to 20 pounds. You can find out what weight your tripod head can handle by checking the manufacturer's specifications. Since tripods themselves tend to be both bulky and a rather heavy burden on a shoot, it is very important to match your tripod's weight capacity with the actual equipment you plan to mount on it (Figure 10.7).

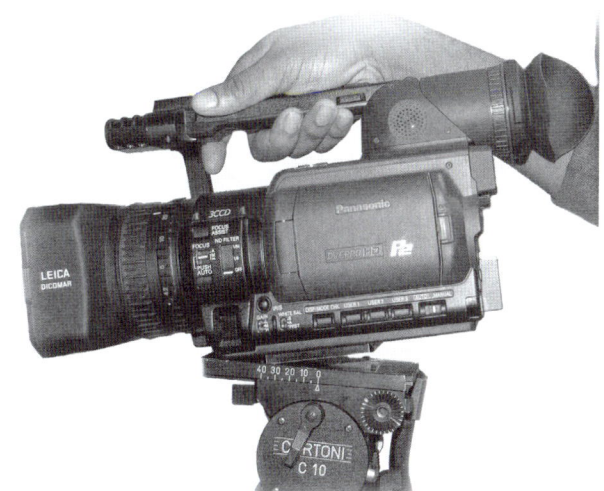

■ **Figure 10.7** Picking the right tripod for the job. For smooth, controlled camera moves, convenience and safety, the tripod should match the weight rating of the camera being used.

An important factor determining the quality of the tripod's panning and tilting abilities is the **resistance mechanism**. Smooth moves with a tripod are accomplished by adjusting the resistance of the tripod head against the weight of the camera and the speed of the move. A very slow pan, for example, is smoothest with heavy drag on the pan mechanism. The two types of resistance mechanisms you're likely to come across are **fluid heads** and **friction heads**. Fluid heads use pressurized hydraulic fluid to provide the adjustable drag necessary for smooth camera moves. Friction heads use the surface friction between internal plates, sometimes lined with cork, to create movement resistance. Fluid heads are more expensive, but they give you much more precise and varied adjustments to facilitate your camera moves, and they generally have a smoother and more even action throughout the panning and tilting range.

There are several features on a tripod head that are common to all professional tripods, and you should locate these right away (Figure 10.6).

Pan and Tilt Locks (E & F)

Pan and **tilt locks** completely lock down the head mechanism, keeping the tripod from pivoting at all. The most important lock for you to locate is the tilt lock. If your camera is slightly unbalanced on the tripod (from the addition of a heavy battery, for example) and the tilt lock isn't tight, the camera can tilt forward or backward all the way, even sending the camera crashing to the ground. The standard procedure to avoid this catastrophe is to tighten the tilt lock between takes and never leave the tripod and camera unattended.

Pan and Tilt Dampers (G & H)

Pan and tilt dampers adjust the amount of resistance for their respective movements. Generally speaking, the more slowly you wish to execute a move, the more resistance you want, and vice versa. This assures smoother motion and greater control. The amount of resistance is usually characterized as **drag**, and many tripod heads will have as many as ten levels of drag.

Pan Handle (C)

The **pan handle** is used to control the movements of the camera. On most tripods, the angle of the pan handle can be adjusted for various tripod heights and personal comfort. Many tripods allow you to mount the pan handle on the left or right. Take the time to adjust the handle for maximum comfort and control. An important cautionary note here is that you should never carry a tripod by the pan handle. Pan handles are usually made of lightweight aluminum and the adjustment threads can easily strip or break off.

Camera Mounting Plate (I)

Finally, all tripod heads have a **camera mounting plate**, which attaches the camera to the tripod head. Cameras are secured to the mounting plate with a threaded mounting screw. Most professional film and video cameras use a 3/8" mounting screw, and small video cameras use a smaller 1/4" mounting screw. Make sure the mounting screw matches the threads on the underside of the camera before you leave for your location.

You might be wondering why we mention a tiny detail like the size of the camera mounting screw. In documentary production, every little detail is crucial. We have had students who have gone on location with tripod heads that had the wrong-sized mounting screw. They arrived on location with everything in place—crew, subjects, permissions—but had no way to secure the camera to the tripod. Instead of shooting on a tripod, they had to handhold an entire hour-long interview. Since this didn't match their other footage (not to mention the difficulty of holding the camera steady that long), the look of the project was seriously compromised, all on account of one little screw.

It's also important to note that many tripods have adjustable mounting plates. An adjustable mounting plate will slide slightly forward and backward on the head. This allows the camera operator to precisely balance the camera on the tripod. Ideally, you should be able to take your hands off the camera, without the tilt lock engaged or any drag on the mechanism, and the camera will remain level. This way, the operator doesn't fight gravity while executing a camera move. In addition, you will typically find a **quick release feature** (J) on the mounting plate. The quick-release feature allows you to pop the camera on and off the head of the tripod quickly, making it easier to move from one location to another quickly. You should never carry the tripod around with a camera attached. The quick release also lets you quickly remove the camera from the tripod to go handheld and then pop it back on again for tripod shots. Don't forget to remove the quick release plate from the camera and stick it back on the tripod at the end of the shooting day!

Head Mount

The head mount is at the base of the tripod head and is where the head mounts to the tripod legs. With modular tripod systems, the head can be used with a variety of different legs. Most quality tripods have claw ball or ball-and-socket mounts, which can be loosened to freely adjust the angle of the tripod head in any direction to achieve a level base no matter where the tripod is standing. It is much easier to level a tripod by using this adjustment than by varying the lengths of the three legs. Tripods with adjustable heads also usually have a **bubble leveler** to assist in leveling of the head (Figure 10.8).

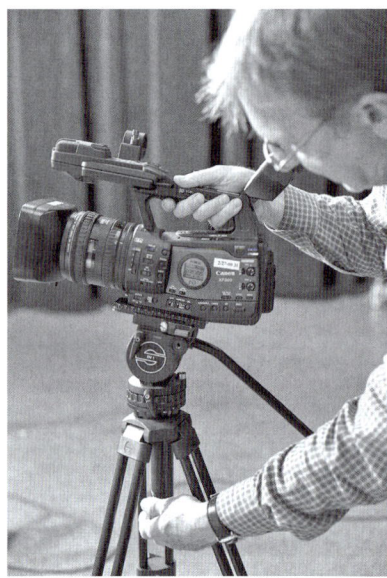
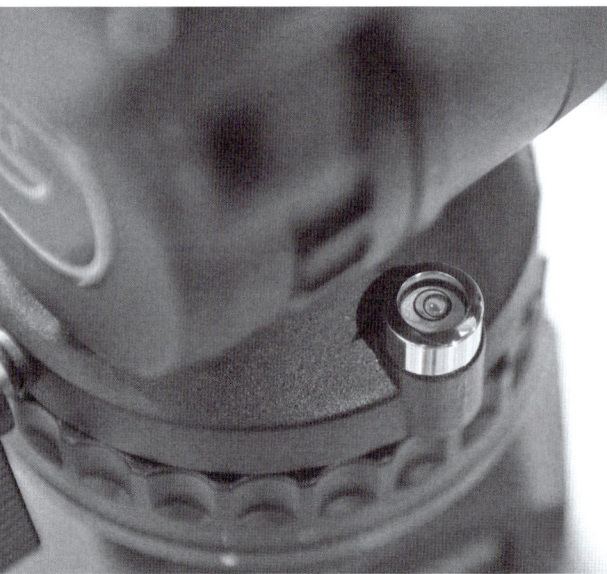

■ Figure 10.8
Here the camera operator is adjusting the level of the tripod head (left) using the bubble leveler (right).

The legs (or "sticks") of a tripod are adjustable so that the tripod height, and therefore the camera height, can be easily changed from shot to shot. Also, because the legs are independently adjustable, they can provide a firm footing on uneven terrain, like a hillside or on stairs (Figure 10.9).

Some tripod systems offer legs in different heights, on which the same head can be used interchangeably. Typical **standard legs** have three stages of extension, and can position the camera between 3 feet and 6 feet high. Another option are two-stage legs, which have additional length for extension and can offer even higher angles. On many professional tripods, the legs are allowed to open out freely to any width for a stable base of support. To keep the legs from completely sliding out from under the camera, a **spreader** is often used. Some tripods have a built-in spreader, while others require a separate unit. The feet of some tripod legs have spikes that can be pushed into the ground in exterior locations, but these spikes will obviously slip on hard surfaces or destroy wooden floors, so you must use a spreader in these situations.

For shots lower than 3 feet we often use **baby legs**, which have a height range from less than 1 foot to about 3 feet (Figure 10.10).

Many documentary cinematographers forgo bringing a set of baby legs on location because of the weight and hassle of carrying a lot of extra equipment. You need to make sure you have the equipment you need, while remembering that a large equipment package is the enemy of the spontaneity so often required in documentary production. And documentarians are great at improvising! Sometimes a rope tied around the tripod legs can replace a spreader and allow the tripod to get very low to the ground. It is not uncommon to see documentary filmmakers using a pillow or a folded up jacket to support the camera in an unusually low or awkward position.

THE MONOPOD

With the advent of lighter-weight digital camcorders and DSLR shooting, as well as the ubiquity of the one-man-band crew, the **monopod** (once a tool used only by still photographers) is becoming increasingly popular with documentary shooters. A monopod (Figure 10.11) is a single pole that can be used to reduce camera shake in the vertical plane, allowing for smoother handheld shooting. While it is not as stable as a tripod, and cannot support a camera independently, the monopod is more lightweight and portable than a tripod. In POV's 2013 Documentary Equipment Survey, the Manfrotto 516B monopod emerged as a popular camera support for filmmakers. One said,

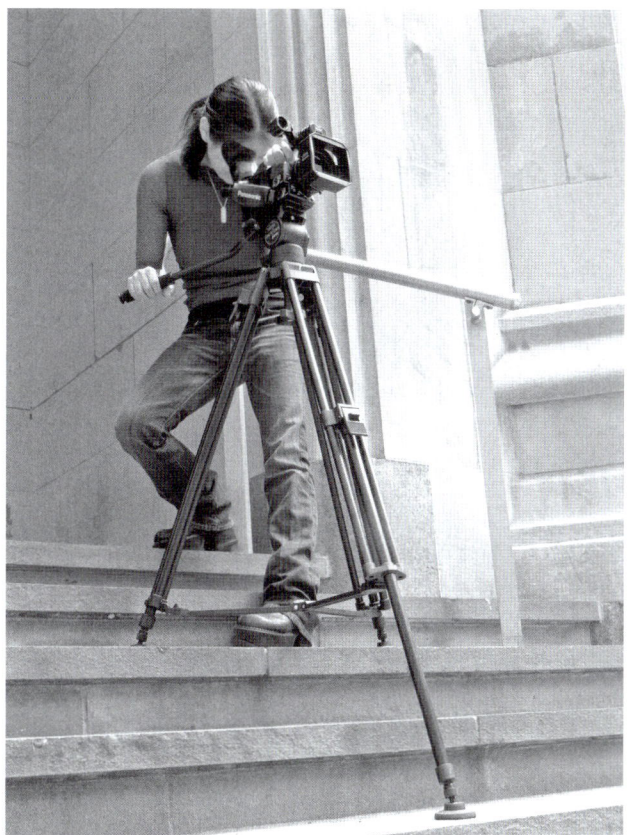

■ **Figure 10.9** The individually extendable legs of a tripod make it possible to get stable support on uneven surfaces, such as a staircase.

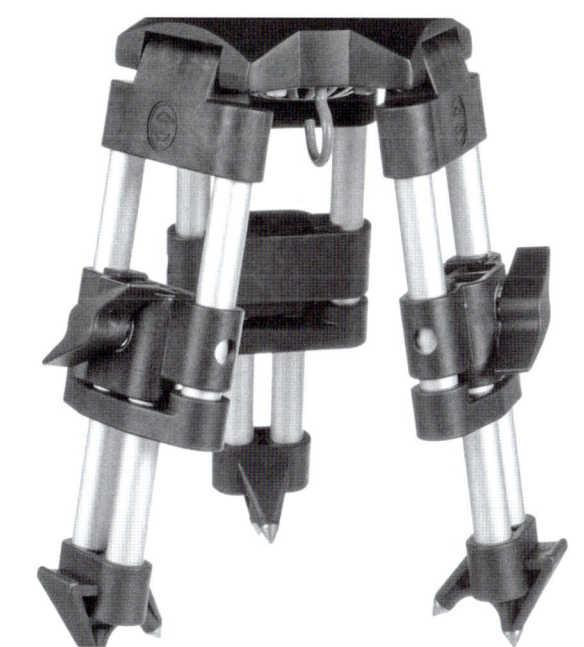

■ **Figure 10.10** This "baby legs" tripod gives a height of up to about 10 inches.

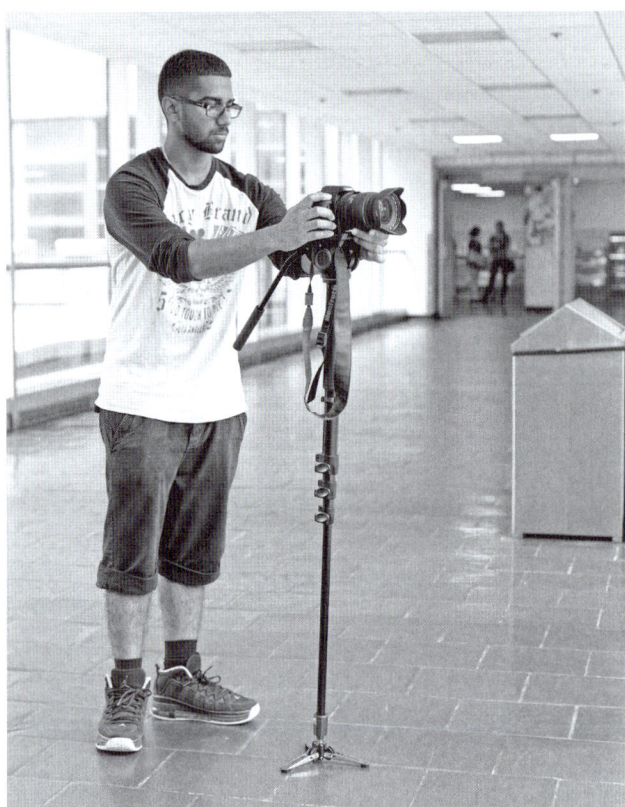

Figure 10.11 A monopod can be used, in lieu of a tripod, to reduce camera shake.

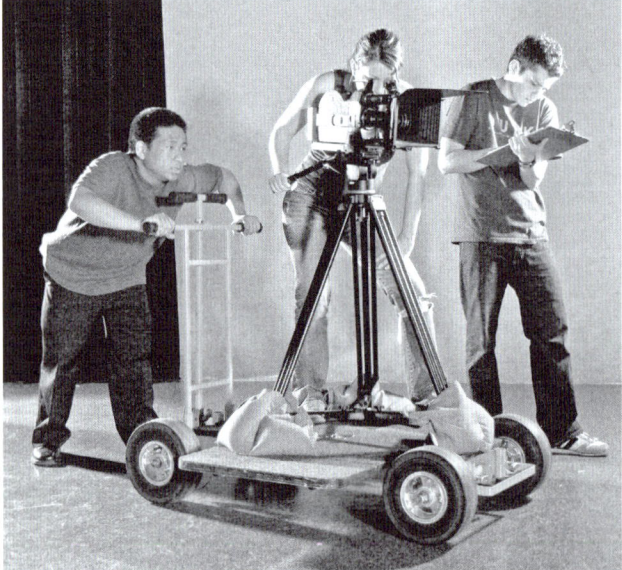

Figure 10.12 A "doorway dolly" has inflatable wheels that allow for a smooth transit and do not require tracks.

Figure 10.13 Dollies that use tracks can create extremely smooth moving shots, even over rough terrain, but their setup is a time- and labor-intensive endeavor.

[It] is a fantastically useful and versatile piece of equipment. It has a ball joint at the bottom and three little flip-out feet, so it offers stability and movement in a very light package. It's strong enough to hold the Canon C-300 as well as any DSLR.[1]

Remember that a monopod is a stabilizer, not a substitute for a real tripod in situations where a pan or tilt is required.

THE DOLLY

A **dolly** is a camera support on wheels that is used when your shot requires a **dynamic move** (Chapter 7) and you want it to be smoother and more controlled than what you can achieve with a handheld camera. Dollies are relatively rare in documentary, with notable exceptions including the opening shot of Jennifer Baichwal's documentary *Manufactured Landscapes* (2006). For that shot, the cameras moved on a dolly through a factory for more than 5 full minutes, revealing the incredible size of the plant. Many types of dollies are available, from expensive to inexpensive, and extremely heavy to relatively portable. Some dollies have soft, inflated rubber tires and require a smooth, even floor (Figure 10.12). Other dollies run on tracks that are laid out in straight or curved sections along the desired path of the camera movement.

Laying dolly track creates extremely smooth camera moves, but it is a time- and labor-intensive task that requires the careful placement of wooden shims to even out the dolly's movement. For this reason, students often think twice about using dollies on tracks. Professional dollies provide a post for you to mount your fluid head so that you can execute smooth pans and tilts while the camera is being moved around, while inexpensive dollies require that you mount the entire tripod on the base (a substantially less stable arrangement). There is no doubt: dynamic moves with dollies are wonderful, but you need to be aware that using a dolly can be a time-consuming addition to your production schedule (Figure 10.13).

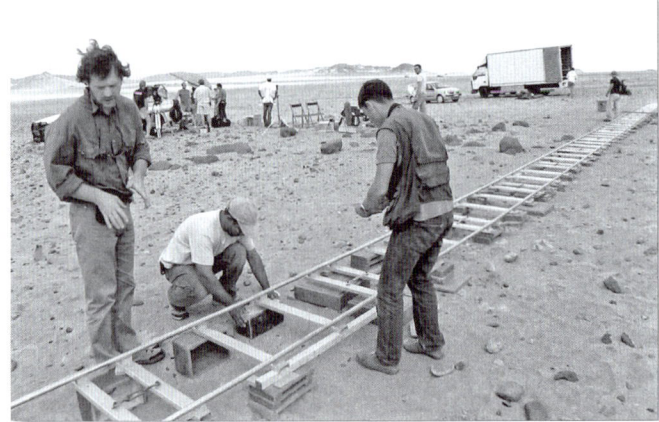

As the saying goes, necessity is the mother of invention, and many people throughout the history of filmmaking have used their ingenuity to achieve their ends with minimal resources. One of the most common dolly-like devices is a wheelchair. The cinematographer simply sits in the wheelchair and is pushed.

■ CAMERA SUPPORT IN THE IMMORTALISTS

David Alvarado and Jason Sussberg used a variety of innovative camera support systems in their documentary *The Immortalists* (2013), about the science of life extension. One of their interviews with Bill Andrews, a marathon runner, was shot from a van while Andrews was running (Figure 10.14, above). "We used a $60 tripod and weighted it down with rocks," says Alvarado. "It worked because we didn't need to do any moves [that needed a fluid head]."[2]

Alvarado and Sussberg used a slider to introduce one of the film's main characters, scientist Aubrey de Grey, because they wanted a dynamic moving shot (Figure 10.14, below). De Grey most often does his work in a pub with a pint of beer in hand. Alvarado says:

> *Aubrey has a 3-foot long red beard, he's a mythic looking character. We had shot a lot of handheld vérité material, but we were trying to introduce him in this bar, so we used sliders because we needed to give the audience a chance to sit there and stare at him. He just drank his beer and did his computer work, and we got shots of it. It's just a bit more kinetic than a still shot.*

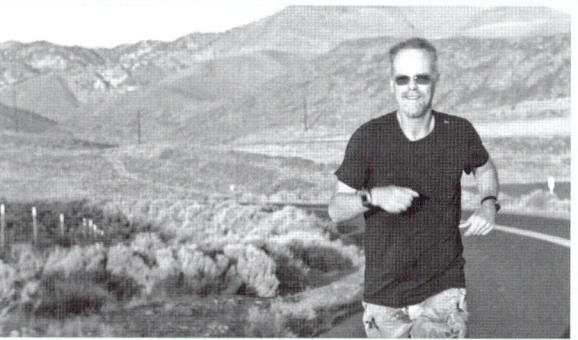
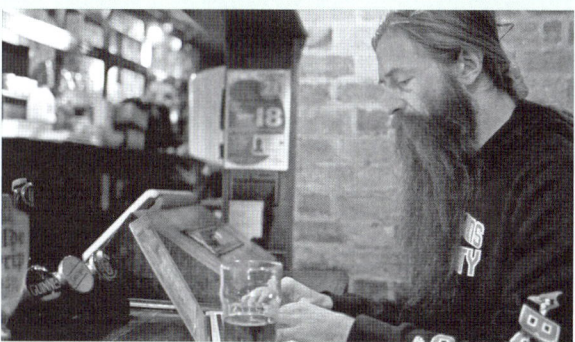

■ **Figure 10.14** Shots filmed from a moving car (above) and with a slider (below) in *The Immortalists* (2013).

Much of *The Immortalists* is handheld, but Alvarado never used his cameras (a Canon C-100 and a Canon 5D) without a weighted shoulder mount (Figure 10.15). He says,

> *I never hold the camera in my hands. When you do that, the camera moves in ways that we don't do with our heads. We don't look at the world from that position or with that kind of shakiness. And it gives the viewer a sort of disturbed sensation, even if they're not aware of it. For me it's very important to put a weight, hopefully equal to the camera, on the back of a mount like the Redrock, and have a comfortable shoulder pad. Even with a DSLR, it allows the camera to move the same way we move with our normal bodies. You have to have a lot of upper body strength to do that, so I work out to have good upper body strength.*

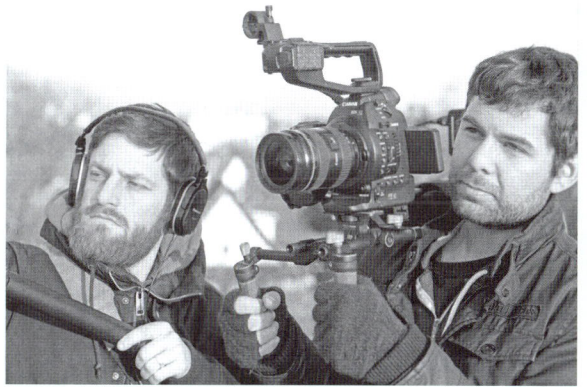

■ **Figure 10.15** David Alvarado (right) using a Redrock Micro shoulder mount with a Panasonic C-100 camera on *The Immortalists* (2013). Co-director Jason Sussberg is on the left. Photo by Erika Kapin.

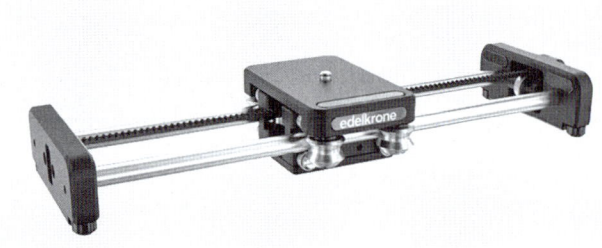

■ **Figure 10.16** A slider can be a less expensive alternative to larger dolly systems, especially if you are using a small camera like a DSLR.

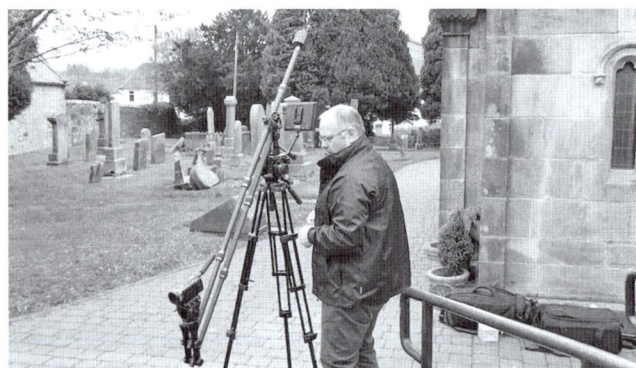

■ **Figure 10.17** A jib arm like the Glidetrack Carbon Crane can be used to get boom shots, even on location. Photo by Philip Johnston/www.hdwarrior.co.uk.

Sliders

A less expensive and time-consuming alternative to large dolly systems is the slider (Figure 10.16). A slider is a small apparatus, usually from 1½ to 3 feet wide, that you can put on stands or on a tripod (or between two tripods). By mounting a small camera on a slider, and pushing it left to right (or right to left), you can create a move that feels like a dolly but requires much less effort and preparation.

For those on a tight budget, a quick Internet search produces many examples of homemade sliders for DSLR and other lightweight cameras, many involving roller skate wheels or skateboards.

JIB ARMS AND CRANE SHOTS

As we learned in Chapter 7, lifting the camera up and down is called **booming** (you "boom up" or "boom down"). On big budget fiction films, this is done with a crane that holds both the camera operator and the camera. In documentary these shots are relatively rare, but when they are done the cinematographer generally uses a **jib arm** that can attach to a tripod. You sway its long arm up and down and side to side to give the camera a smooth, controlled movement (Figure 10.17).

One advantage of the smaller digital and DSLR cameras is that their light weight has opened up possibilities for camera support that weren't possible with heavier cameras. Sometimes filmmakers will rent a small crane or jib arm for one day to get a number of shots that can be integrated throughout their documentary to give a particular aesthetic and raise the production value.

STABILIZING ARM SYSTEMS

Invented by cinematographer Garrett Brown in the 1970s, the Steadicam stabilizing system combines the mobility and ease of use of a handheld camera with the smooth and controlled movements of a dolly. The downside to Steadicam systems for students and low-budget filmmakers has always been the cost and complexity of the system. However, since the advent of lightweight video cameras, we've experienced the emergence of a whole range of far less expensive and less cumbersome stabilizing systems (Figure 10.18).

Most stabilizing systems are ultra-lightweight handheld units that use a simple system of counterweights to smooth out the movements of the operator as they move with the camera through space. With practice, you can get wonderfully smooth tracks, dollies, and arcs with these systems.

More recently, a variety of powered stabilizing systems using **gyroscopes** and **gimbal mounts** for cameras have emerged (Figure 10.18, right). These typically involve one person holding the camera, while another controls pan and zoom remotely using a computer or smartphone. The stabilizer can correct for tilt, roll, and pan movements, and can even be set to deal with issues such as engine vibration in a helicopter.

CHAPTER 10
Camera Support

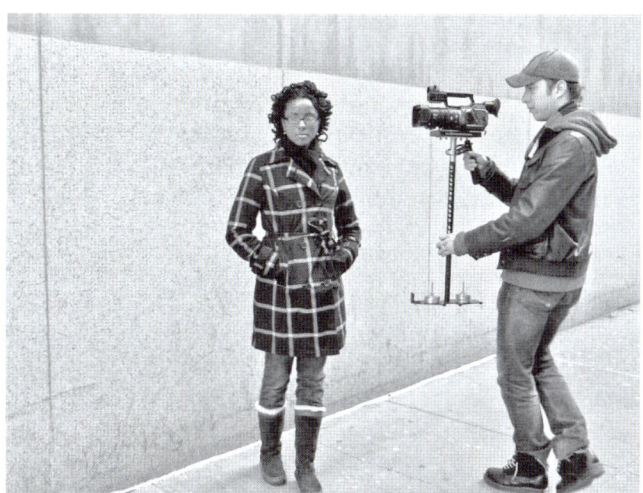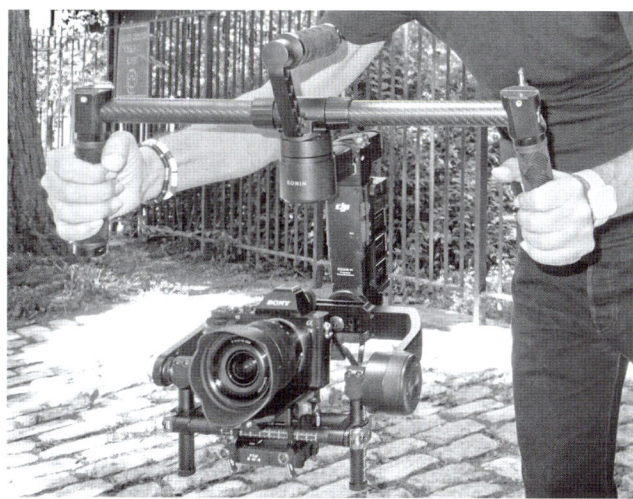

■ **Figure 10.18** The emergence of small video and DSLR cameras has prompted the creation of lighter, cheaper stabilizing systems, like this Glidecam (left) being used for a moving shot. Gimbal stabilizers use computer controlled motors, like this DJI Ronin-M (right, shown here with a Sony A7S camera). Gimbal photo by Shari Sperling.

DRONES

No discussion of camera support systems would be complete without a discussion of **drones**. Once upon a time, an aerial shot was a complex and very expensive option that involved renting a plane or a helicopter, and working with someone specializing in aerial photography. Today, small drones—flying devices that mount tiny cameras—allow for shooting in an amazing number of situations (Figure 10.19). Typically, these systems allow the images to be transmitted via Wi-Fi directly from the air, so you can monitor and control your shooting carefully. Many drones come equipped with stabilizing systems like gimbals (see above) so that extremely smooth aerial shots can be filmed. Note that legal issues around drones are still being worked out. Make sure you have any necessary permissions before putting anything in the sky with a camera on it. Drones are also prone to crashing, so use with care.

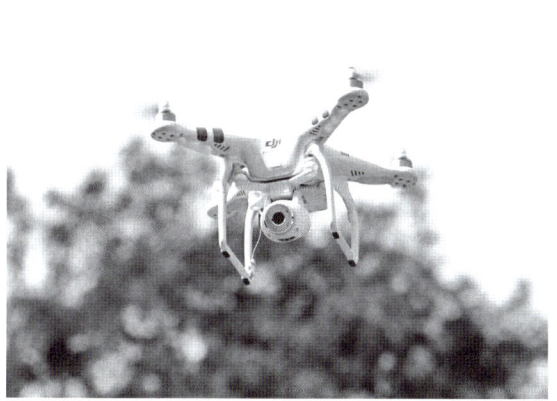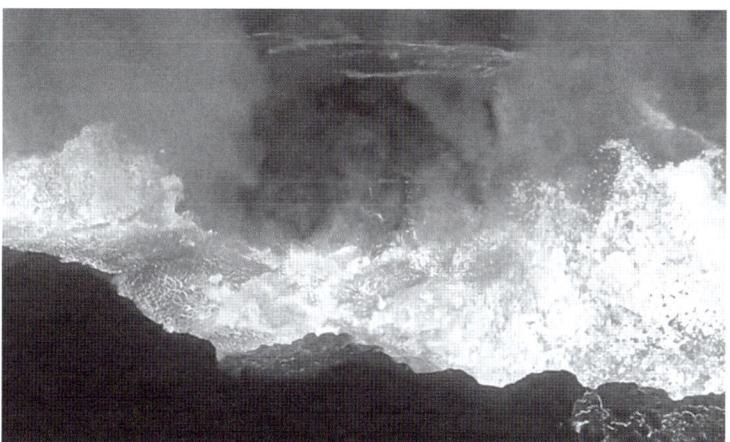

■ **Figure 10.19**

A small drone (DJI's Phantom Series) used for aerial cinematography. Drones can be used to take images in places humans cannot go, like this shot of an erupting volcano in Iceland (right). Images courtesy of DJI.

UNDERWATER PHOTOGRAPHY

A specialized area of documentary is underwater cinematography. Manufacturers offer a professional option in the form of underwater housings for a variety of cameras, which are great if you have your scuba gear and know how to dive. Now the availability of a variety of inexpensive waterproof cameras, and even the advent of new underwater drones, means that the water's surface is no longer a great barrier to a documentary maker.

CONCLUSION

From the super-controlled fluidity of a gyroscopic gimbal stabilizer to the edgy movement of the handheld camera to the formal pivot of a tripod, different camera supports offer different "feels." There is no system that is better or worse—there is only what is appropriate for the conception of your film, and for your schedule and budget. Often, within a single film, there will be scenes that work best with a handheld camera, and others that require the stability of a tripod, while a signature transition shot may call for a slider or a jib arm. But whether you handhold a camera, put it on a tripod, or wheel it around on a dolly, both the movement of the camera and the fashion in which it moves must be motivated by the story you're telling and style you are using to convey it.

CHAPTER 11

Basic Lighting for Documentary

> *Everything can be transformed, deformed, and obliterated by light. Its flexibility is precisely the same as the suppleness of the brush.*
> **Man Ray, *La Photographie N'est Pas L'art*[1]**

Film is a visual medium, yet for many documentary filmmakers, lighting is a secondary concern. Unlike fiction film, where "painting with light" is part of the standard process and actors are paid to wait on the lighting crew, documentary makers depend on the cooperation of their subjects and borrowed time. In addition, modern digital cameras are highly light sensitive, able to produce an image with **available light** in many situations. The addition of a bulky kit of lights, difficult to carry and laboriously time-consuming to set up, can seem like an imposition that limits spontaneity and gets in the way of the creative interaction with reality that is central to the documentary process. Yet an understanding of film lighting principles, and perhaps even more centrally an awareness of light itself—what it does and how it works its magic on the human eye—is indispensable for any documentary filmmaker. The more you know, the more you can develop your own approach to lighting, one that suits your own shooting style, your own sense of **production value**, and the basic expressive needs of the particular film you are making.

A look at the work of great documentary filmmakers will reveal a wide variety of approaches to lighting, some boldly stylized and others assiduously naturalistic. Some makers work with cinematographers who are renowned for their work on fiction films, others are do-it-yourself shooters who rely on a couple of tried and true lighting instruments and techniques. In all cases, understanding the essential properties of light and basic lighting techniques will make you a more flexible, efficient, and expressive filmmaker.

WHY LIGHT?

The most rudimentary reason for lighting is to ensure exposure so the camera can register a visible image. But there can be many reasons to light a scene, or to control the available light in your shooting situation. They include:
1. Getting an exposure
2. Adding depth, dimension, and aesthetic interest to the image
3. Developing visual emphasis
4. Setting tone and mood
5. Creating visual consistency, both within a scene and for the project as a whole

The best lighting approach is one that does all five of these things at the same time.

In documentary, we tend to think of a camera as "capturing" the reality in front of it, but the instrument we're using has a serious limitation: it is representing a three-dimensional world on a two-dimensional screen. On that flat screen, light and shadow are key ways we define objects and understand depth as well as texture. In addition to the clues that help us perceive the image, there are larger questions about how the look serves the intention

DOCUMENTARY LIGHTING TO ENHANCE MEANING

Ellen Bruno's short documentary *Split* (2013) is a deeply personal exploration of how six young people process their parents' divorce. The lighting, by award-winning cinematographer Ellen Kuras, supports the director's goals for the film. While the interview setup looks simple, just putting a camera in front of the subject in this situation would not give an effect at all like what we see (Figure 11.1).

The light is soft, gentle, and restrained, seeming to come from only a single source, allowing us to feel we're in intimate contact with the young person who is revealing her feelings about the way her life has been altered. The **low key** (Chapter 12) quality of the light adds to the intimacy by de-emphasizing the space surrounding the subject, adding an almost somber note. The soft light, which falls away quickly, also emphasizes the physical presence of the subject. She seems to almost "pop out" of the frame. The saturated colors create a consistent look both within the scenes, and across the film as a whole. Even the details, which look "natural," are carefully controlled. The window light in a dark room is typically much brighter than the interior and can typically only be used by applying neutral density (ND) gel over the window, as was likely done here. Another thing to note is how the subject's eyes are unlit. This is unusual in documentary interviews, and adds to the sense of the subject as someone of unseen depths, depths that we hope to explore.

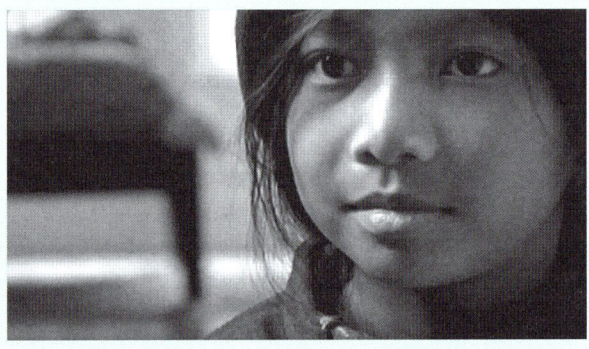

Figure 11.1 In *Split*, subtle yet expressive lighting by cinematographer Ellen Kuras develops an intimate mood in this "kid's-eye" view of divorce.

of the film. Even a cinéma vérité filmmaker dedicated to a strictly "fly-on-the-wall" approach defines their style by the way they treat light levels. The blown out exposures of gritty black and white film are a signature of authenticity in the great observational documentaries of the 1960s (Figure 12.8). The highly stylized reenactments in Errol Morris's *The Thin Blue Line* (1988), with their carefully controlled studio lighting, offer another approach that uses lighting to emphasize the constructed nature of what we call truth.

Lighting also picks out detail, emphasizing one aspect of a situation and de-emphasizing another. Mood in documentary is also heavily affected by lighting. The inclusion or elimination of shadows, the range of colors in a scene, the hardness or softness of the light, and the direction the light comes from—all of these lighting choices have a profound impact on the emotional tone that will be communicated to the audience. Finally, consistency is a key goal of any lighting strategy. In a documentary shooting situation, it is easy to have one shot very dark and the next very bright, or one blue and the next orange, just from natural variations in the light. These differences, if not dealt with carefully, will affect a viewer's ability to see the images as part of the same scene.

Lighting as Respect

Another almost contradictory way of understanding lighting in documentary is exactly in its role as a sign of moviemaking. Sometimes setting up lights signals to your subjects the seriousness of the enterprise, helping to create the unspoken contract that underlies their participation in your project. This can be particularly true for interviews, which are such a key part of documentary lighting that they get their own section in Chapter 12. Another way to think about this has to do with how people are treated by filmmakers. A democratic approach to making films would suggest that all of the subjects in a film be treated as "authorities" or experts in the conditions of their own lives, and given the same level of concern and respect by the camera, regardless of their place in social hierarchies outside of your film. There is no inherent reason that a senator in their office should get more production value in terms of lighting than a factory worker on the job or a housewife in her home.

CHAPTER 11
Basic Lighting for Documentary

ELEMENTS OF EXPOSURE

What does it mean to get an **exposure**? It's all about light: how much of it is bouncing off your scene, into your lens, and registering on your imaging device. But how do we control exposure? In filmmaking, every exposure you make involves an intricate interrelationship between all of the variables that produce, transmit, control, transform, or record light. Here are the primary elements along the path, beginning at the light source and ending at the imaging device:

1. **The light source**. Whether you are shooting under the sun or with artificial lights or a mixture of both, the aesthetic and technical properties of your lighting source have the biggest impact on the look of your image. Of central importance for exposure control is the **intensity** of light, meaning how much light is falling onto your scene, but also significant are the **quality** and **color temperature** of the light.
2. **The scene**. What are the visual dynamics of your scene? Or more specifically, what are the physical properties of the space, the reflectivity of the objects, the volume of the area, the colors and shadows, and movement? All these need to be considered when lighting and creating an exposure.
3. **Filters**. **Lens filters** are often employed in documentary production to alter the quality, color, or intensity of the light entering the camera. We don't always use filters, but when we do, they affect many of the other exposure elements.
4. **The lens and aperture**. As we mentioned in Chapter 9, all of the light exposing your imaging device passes through the lens. The lens aperture determines the amount of light that is allowed to pass through to hit the sensor. Aperture control is one of the most flexible variables for creating the best exposure for each image (see Chapter 9 for more on aperture, **f-stops**, and exposure).
5. **Frame rate, shutter speed, and gain (ISO)**. The camera's frame rate (60i vs 24p, for example) has an impact on the duration of each exposure. The amount of gain (or, in the case of DSLR cameras, the ISO setting) and shutter speed are also important factors (Chapter 8).
6. **Imaging device**. Whether you're using CCDs or CMOS sensors, understanding and factoring in your imaging device's particular and unique sensitivity and response to light is essential in getting the shot the way you want it.

In documentary production, where you almost always have less time than you want to set up lights, or gel windows, there is always going be a tension between your creative desires and the concrete reality of the situation you are in. Imagine you have 2 hours to do an interview. Do you want to spend 90 minutes setting up and 30 minutes on the actual interview, or the reverse? On the other hand, if you are going to film someone driving, it

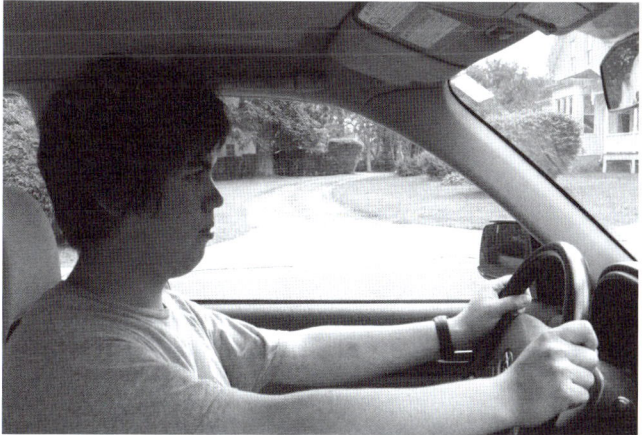 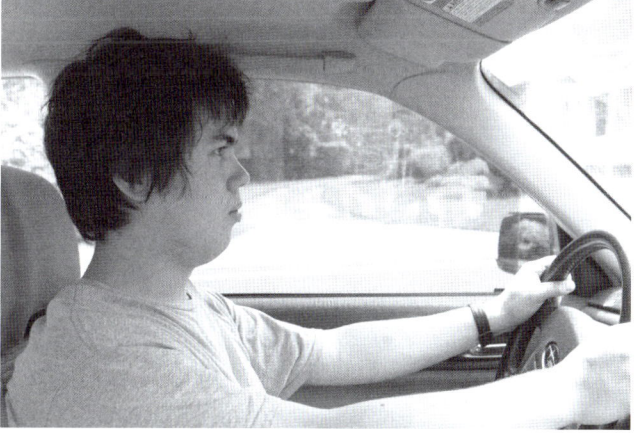

■ **Figure 11.2** Combining sunlight with shade means a broad (and difficult to work with) range of exposure values. On the left, a correct exposure for the exterior means the subject is in silhouette. On the right, ND 0.6 over the side window brings the exterior light down two stops, making it possible to open up and expose the driver properly (Figure 11.20).

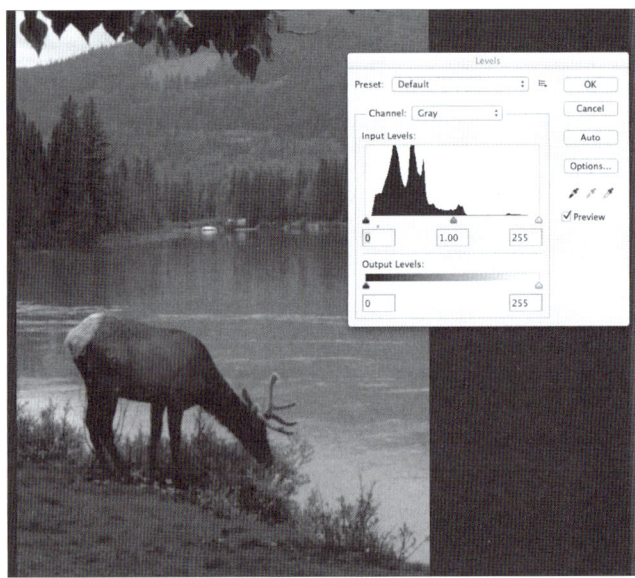
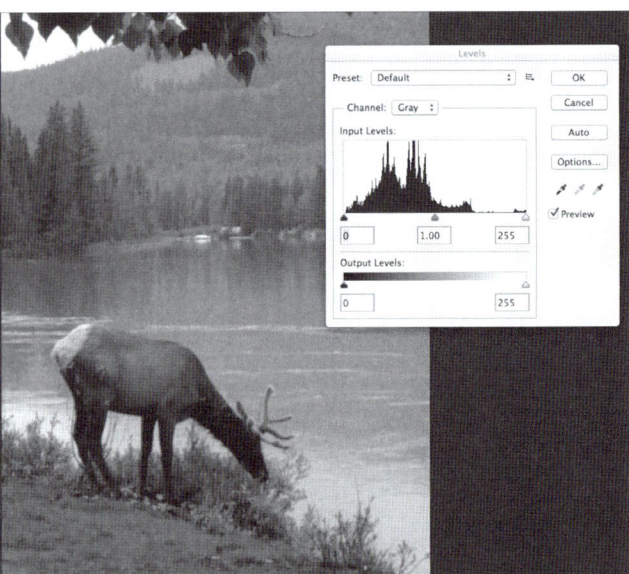

■ **Figure 11.3** A histogram (created in Adobe Photoshop). In the image on the left, you can see that most of the pixels in the image are clustered towards the low end of the spectrum, telling us that the image doesn't have very much brightness. On the right, we have adjusted the image so that light and dark values are more evenly distributed. This is reflected in a more "stretched out" histogram with more light values.

may be worth inconveniencing the subject and mounting a small light over the dashboard, or putting ND gel on the side window to balance the interior and exterior light. The difference could be between a haphazard image and a highly expressive professional looking one (Figure 11.2).

Monitoring Exposure

With many cameras and monitors, you can view exposure range directly via a **histogram** on the screen. Figure 11.3 shows an image with a superimposed histogram. The histogram tells us the light value of every pixel registered by the sensor. This is useful information. You can see whether you are taking advantage of the full range of dark and light values in the scene, and whether you are under- or overexposing. You can also see if your camera is "clipping," or overexposing, parts of the image. In this image, the values are clustered in the dark part of the histogram, meaning that there isn't a lot of brightness in the picture as it is being captured.

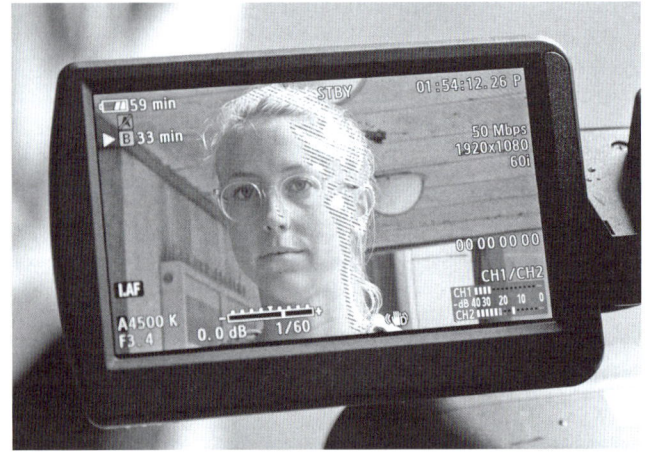

■ **Figure 11.4** Zebras indicate parts of the image are over a certain luminance level, in this case 100 IRE units.

Another useful tool for monitoring exposure is the **zebra function** (Figure 11.4). The zebra can be set for various levels, but probably the most useful is to set it so that the viewer image is overlaid with the zebra pattern when the exposure is above 100 IRE units, or "full white." This still allows you to overexpose, but reminds you to check carefully when you are approaching the exposure limits.

■ THE FUNDAMENTAL SOURCES OF LIGHT

Anything that gives off light, from the blazing midday sun to a candle, can be used as a lighting source in a scene. **Natural light** refers to light coming from nature, a source that is not artificial. Usually we mean the sun when we talk about natural light, but the term also applies to light that comes from nonelectric sources that aren't naturally occurring, like campfires, candles, and fireplaces. **Artificial light** is any light source that generates light through electricity. Artificial lights can be as big as a 10,000-watt light or as small as a flashlight.

The term **available light** refers to light sources that ordinarily exist in any given location. For example, if you walk into a grocery store with your camera and simply shoot by the light of the fluorescent fixtures overhead, or if you shoot in a bedroom illuminated only by the sun streaming in from a window, you are shooting with available light. **Mixed lighting** refers to combining available sources and artificial lights to achieve the look you're after. It's very common to use the sun as one light source and artificial lights as another.

Very often, natural or available light sources are not powerful enough to create an exposure, but we nonetheless want the audience to feel like a particular source is illuminating the scene. For example, imagine a subject is curled up in her living room reading a book, and we want the audience to believe that the 25-watt reading lamp is the only light illuminating her face. The lamp's wattage is unlikely to be strong enough to get a good exposure. In this situation, you might bring in an artificial light to duplicate the color, quality, and direction of the ostensible light source, but at a higher intensity.

This strategy of using additional lights to enhance or duplicate light, which would logically be emanating from an existing light source in the scene, is called **motivated lighting**. Motivated lighting is a central strategy for creating **naturalistic** lighting designs (Chapter 12). These are **realistic** lighting setups where the light source, intensity, and texture can be logically derived from what the viewer knows about the shooting situation.

The simplest lighting setup is one that uses available light, whether sun through a window, an overhead fixture, or a lamp on a table. Sometimes you can create enough control of the available light by opening or closing a curtain, or turning off the overhead lights, to create the lighting effect you feel is appropriate for the situation. More typically, however, you will find yourself using one or more lighting instruments. Controlling your tools properly requires knowing how light works.

THREE ESSENTIAL PROPERTIES OF LIGHT

Light sources don't simply give off generic light. Every light source emits a light that has specific characteristics that contribute to the look of your scene. Three of the basic properties of light that give any light source its distinctive character are **intensity**, **quality**, and **color temperature**.

Intensity

Light **intensity** is the strength of the light emitted by a source. Direct sunlight is obviously a very intense source of light, although the actual intensity changes depending on its angle at various times of day. With artificial light, intensity depends largely on the **wattage** of the lamp used (500 watts, 1,000 watts, etc.). When we speak of lamp wattage, we use the symbol "K" to stand in for "thousand." So a 1,000-watt light is called a 1K ("one kay") and a 2,000-watt light is called a 2K. (Do not get this K mixed up with the "K" symbol used for degrees Kelvin, which relates to color temperature.)

The intensity of light hitting your scene is also greatly affected by the light-source-to-subject distance. The farther away an instrument is placed from the subject, the weaker the light is on that subject. This diminishing intensity as the unit is moved away follows the **inverse square law**, which says that the intensity of light falls off by the square of the distance from the subject (Figure 11.5). Obviously, the converse applies as well. When you bring a light in closer, you increase its intensity. If the inverse square law seems like a lot of calculation to do on the set, you can simply apply this rule of thumb: if you double the distance between the lighting unit and your subject, say from 10 feet to 20 feet, the strength of the light will be reduced four times and will be only one-quarter the intensity compared

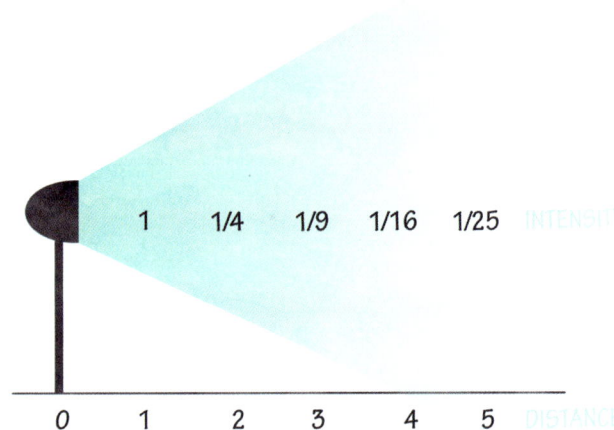

■ **Figure 11.5** The inverse square law. Doubling the distance from the light source to our subject means that the illumination is spread over four times the area and is therefore only 1/4th the intensity. Likewise, tripling the distance means cutting the light to 1/9th of its original intensity.

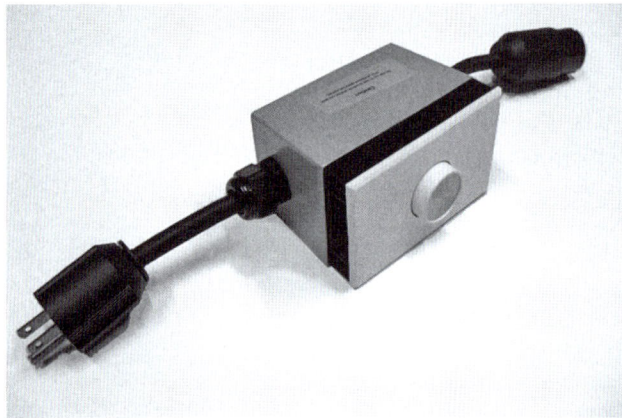

■ **Figure 11.6** This simple in-line dimmer can be plugged into any circuit (less than 1,000W in the case of this model from Mole-Richardson) to add an extra level of control.

to the original position. If you halve the distance between the subject and the lighting unit, you will increase the light intensity four times.

You can also change the intensity of a light in a variety of other ways. Adding a **scrim** to the light will reduce its intensity. Some lights have dimmers, and dimmers can be added to any power cord (Figure 11.6). In addition, spotlights have different reflectors that can be inserted behind the bulb to vary the intensity of the light. Many lights will have a **flood/spot control** (where the flood is less intense) as well. These last two alter the quality of the light along the hard/soft spectrum as well as the intensity, as we will discuss next.

Quality

The texture of a light—how hard or soft its beam is—is referred to as its **quality**. The bulbs for the most commonly used film lights involve a wire filament. That glowing filament becomes the **point source** of the lamp's illumination, creating a highly directional beam. Light that travels directly from a lamp to the subject is referred to as **hard light** or **directional light**, because the light rays, which travel straight and parallel to each other, all fall on the subject from a single angle, causing sharp shadows and bright highlight areas. Lighting units that do not illuminate directly from the bulb, but instead bounce the light off a reflective surface, emit a **diffused** or **soft light**. The reflecting surface scatters the light rays in a variety of directions, disturbing their parallel paths (Figure 11.7). Diffused light rays do not hit the subject from the same angle and therefore create softer shadows and smoother highlights. Other lights that do not generate light from a point source, such as fluorescent lights, also create a soft light. It's important to note that the larger the area of the diffused bounce surface, the softer the light.

Understanding this principle, you can see that it is not difficult to soften the light from a hard lighting instrument by simply bouncing it off any diffusing surface, like a

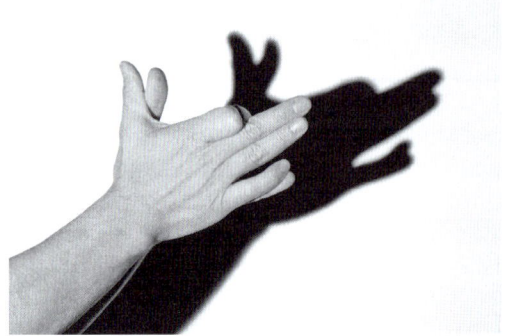 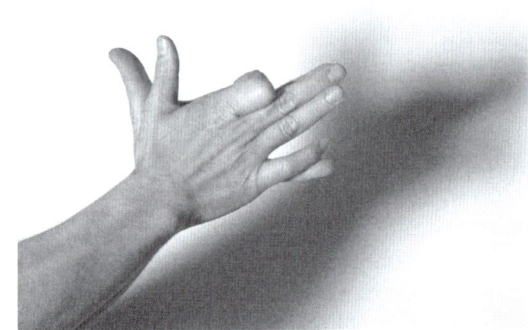

■ **Figure 11.7** Hard light creates sharp shadows (left) because the light beams maintain their parallel direction. Soft light (right) creates diffused shadows because the scattered light beams hit the subject from many directions.

white wall or a white **bounce card** or **reflector** (Figure 11.8). You can also soften light from a hard lighting unit by placing **diffusion media** in front of the beam (Figure 11.28). Diffusion media scatters the light rays in a way similar to that achieved by bouncing light off a diffusing surface. Be aware, however, that diffusing light always decreases its intensity. As with so many other things, the choice is based primarily on applying the appropriate aesthetic choice for the content of your film.

Hard light, which travels directly, tends to travel further, giving a **long throw**, and is easier to control. It also creates hard shadows. Soft light by its nature tends to spread, giving it a **short throw** and making it more difficult to control. Soft light makes for few shadows, and gentle ones.

Color Temperature

Light comes in a variety of colors, from purple to red. In daily life, our brains compensate for these differences and we don't notice them much. However, different sources emit light of different frequencies, and the camera registers these as different colors. The tonality of a light is called its **color temperature** and it is measured using the **Kelvin scale** (Figure 11.9). Average daylight is 5,600K (quite blue or "cool"), but the sun can change color temperature dramatically over the course of the day. The most common artificial lighting instruments for documentary production are **tungsten-halogen lights** (also called **quartz lights**), which have a color temperature of 3,200K (quite "warm" or orange). Newer LED light panels often come with a color temperature control which allows you to dial up different temperatures between daylight and tungsten standards (Figure 11.10).

As discussed in Chapter 8, with the **white balance** function you can set your camera to see a specific color temperature of light as "white." Generally, your goal is to achieve a consistent and fairly neutral color temperature.

Combining lights with various color temperatures in one scene can present challenges. Ways of compensating for differing light color values include adjusting the white balance function on your camera, and using color conversion gels on light sources (p. 179).

■ CONTROLLING LIGHT

Once you have an idea of what light's qualities are, it is time to think about how to control it to get the images you need to tell your story. Unless they encounter an obstacle, light waves travel in a straight line. Anyone who goes out on a clear night can see the light traveling from galaxies millions of light years away, simply because there is nothing blocking its path. If light hits a reflective surface, it will change direction. If it shines through a

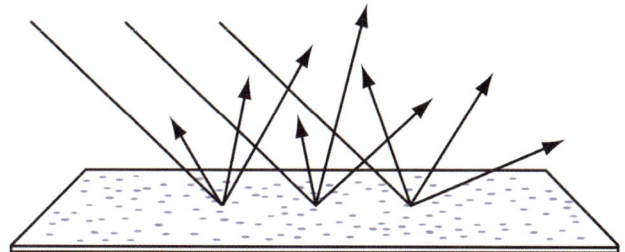

■ **Figure 11.8** A diffused surface, like a show card or a reflector, scatters the light rays, changing the quality of the light from hard to soft.

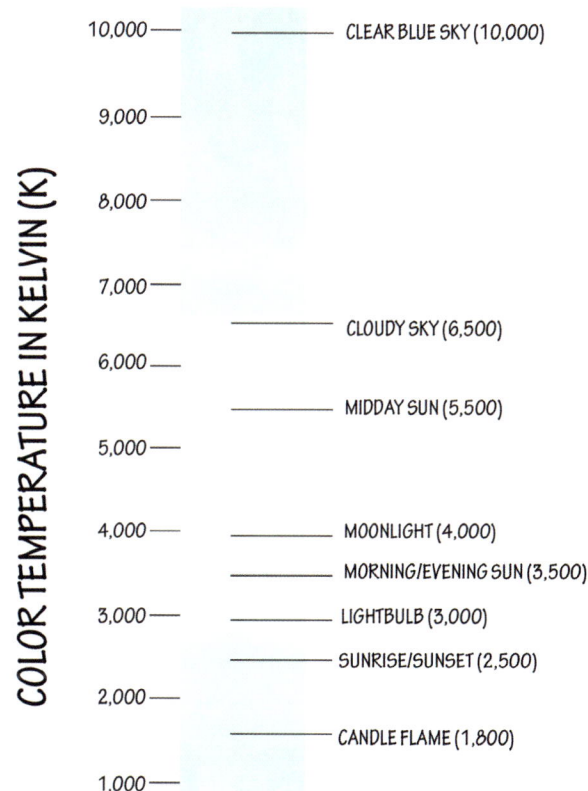

■ **Figure 11.9** This chart shows the color temperatures of various common light sources measured in degrees Kelvin. (See plate section for color.)

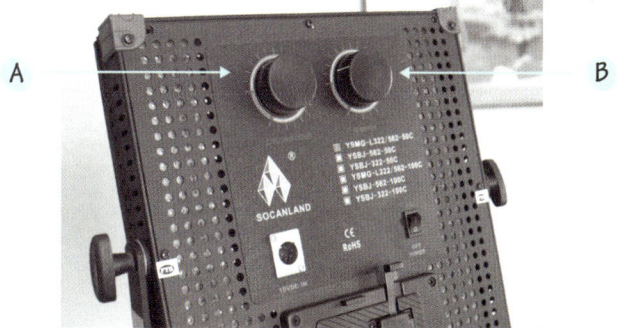

■ **Figure 11.10** The dial on the upper left on the back of this LED light controls color temperature (from a blue 5600K to an orange 3200K) (A), while the one on the right is a dimmer to adjust light intensity (B).

translucent material, it will soften or change color. These behaviors of light are the foundation of any lighting strategy. Let's review them:

1. **Blocking light**. A fundamental way to control light is to block it. On a lighting instrument, this is accomplished with **barn doors**. On a set, this can also be achieved with **flags** mounted on stands (Figure 11.29). On location, this might mean closing the curtains or blinds. However you do it, blocking light is a strategy that will help make sure that the light is where you want it, illuminating significant parts of your scene, and not where you don't want it.
2. **Bouncing light**. **Reflecting** or **bouncing** light offers an important approach to putting light where you want it. While **reflectors** and **show cards** are designed to reflect light, a light-colored wall or ceiling will often be adequate for a location shoot. Remember that bouncing alters the quality of light as well as the intensity, giving you light that is softer than the original source.
3. **Filtering light**. **Filtering** light by putting it through something that will alter it gives you control not just over the amount of light, but over other qualities as well. **Gels** or **diffusion** can make hard light soft, but can also change the color of the light. Filtering can work over a light source, whether a window or a lighting instrument, or over the camera lens for a variety of special lighting effects.

BASIC LIGHTING EQUIPMENT, FILTERS, AND GELS

Lighting Units

There is a dizzying array of lights available for documentary production, with new ones being developed all of the time. It would be impossible to present them all in this book, but the following sections present some lighting units that are commonly used.

Open-Faced Lights

Open-faced lights are units that consist of an open lamp (no lens) and a **specular** (mirror-like) reflector behind the bulb. Open-faced lights are a hard light source and act primarily as **key lights** and **set lights**. The **open-faced spot** is a common unit that has a movable lamp, allowing you to focus its throw from a broad to a more narrowly defined area (Figure 11.11, left). If you have a small light kit, an open-faced spotlight is a sturdy and efficient light to include. **Broads**, which are open-faced lights with no spotting capability, simply deliver a hard, efficient bright light (Figure 11.11, right). Both lights come in a variety of intensities, from 250 to 2,000 watts.

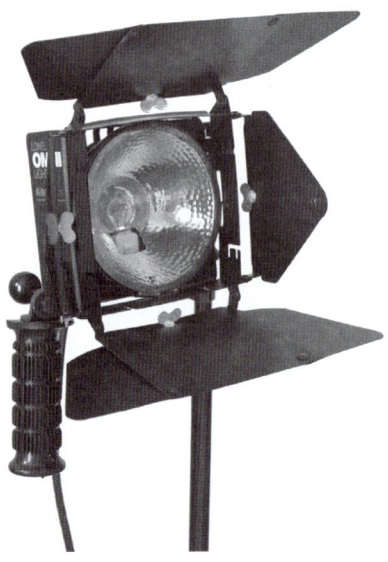
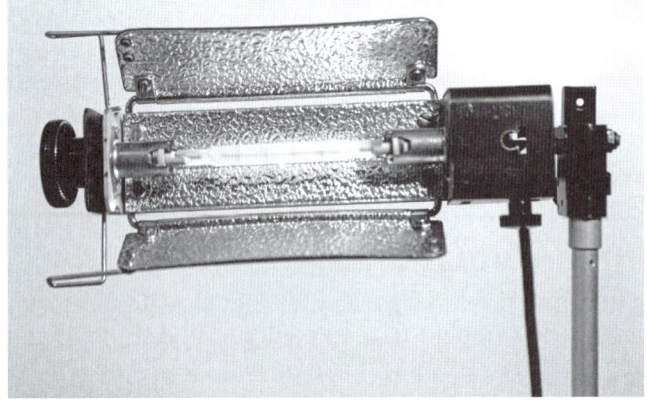

■ **Figure 11.11** The light on the left is Lowel's Omni, a versatile 500 W open-faced light whose small size and portability make it useful for documentary field production. The light on the right is a mini-broad (Lowel's Tota), which offers a lot of very hard light in a small package.

CHAPTER 11
Basic Lighting for Documentary

Fresnels

Fresnels are one of the most versatile lighting units you will find in a location light kit. What distinguishes a Fresnel is its unique lens and its movable lamp, which allows it to spot its beam with fair precision while not having the harder edge associated with a spotlight (Figure 11.12). The lens also gives this light a very long throw, so it can be set up quite far from the subject. Though the textured lens does soften the light somewhat, Fresnels are still considered hard lights. Fresnels are named after Augustin-Jean Fresnel, the French physicist who designed the shape of the lens, originally to send the beam of an oil lamp far out to sea from coastal lighthouses.

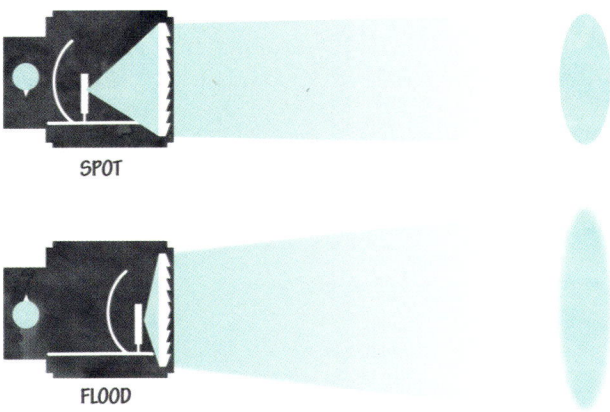

Figure 11.12 Fresnels have lenses that focus the beam more effectively than open-faced lights. In the spot position (top), the bulb and the reflector are farther from the lens, creating a sharp beam. In the flood position (bottom), the bulb and reflector are brought closer to the lens, creating a wider throw.

Fresnels come in various sizes and wattages. The medium wattages (300W to 650W) (Figure 11.13, right) are commonly used to light people and are a good **key light** source (Chapter 12). A small Fresnel (100W to 200W) like the Pepper light (Figure 11.13, left) is commonly used on location for **eye lights**, **backlights**, and **kickers**. They are almost always equipped with barn doors (Figure 11.30) which allow you to block part of the beam.

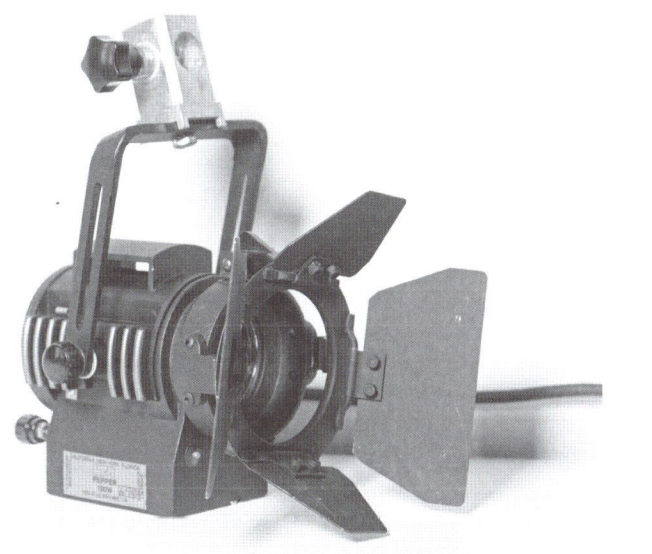
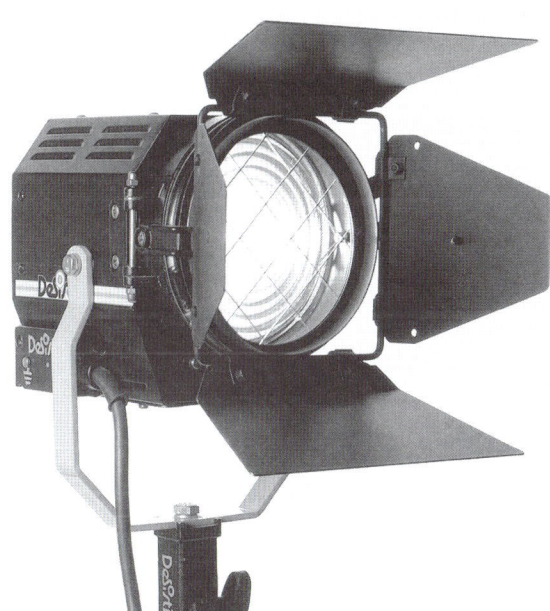

Figure 11.13 The LTM 100/200W Pepper Light (left) is a typical small Fresnel used for back or eye light. The De Sisti 650W (right) is a typical medium wattage Fresnel offering hard light with a long throw.

Soft Lights

Soft lights are units that do not throw the light beam directly from the lamp. Rather, they are a soft, even source. In documentary, soft light is generally created by bouncing a hard light off an umbrella or enclosing a hard light in a nylon shell (Figure 11.14). Soft lights are popular in documentary because the diffused light looks less artificial than hard light. In addition, the lack of shadows means soft lights are kind to the human face, making them ideal for interviews. Soft lights come in a variety of intensities, and common wattages are 500W, 1K, and 2K. Keep in mind that a 500W soft light will be quite low intensity, compared

Figure 11.14
This Chimera softbox (left) is a typical folding soft light used for documentary location lighting. The Lowel Pro (right) uses a reflector umbrella to create a portable soft light.

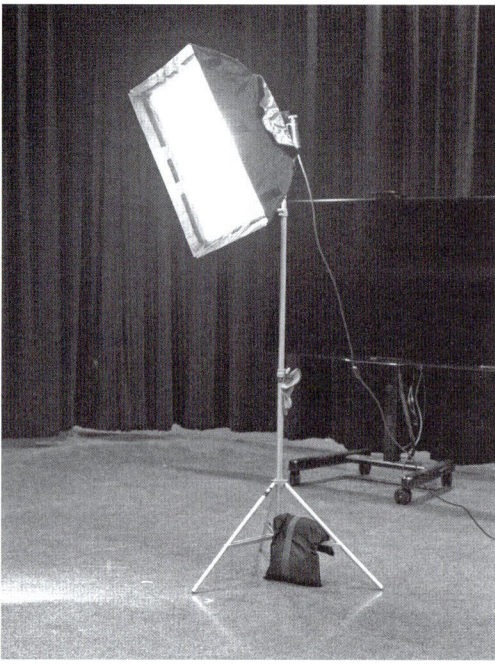
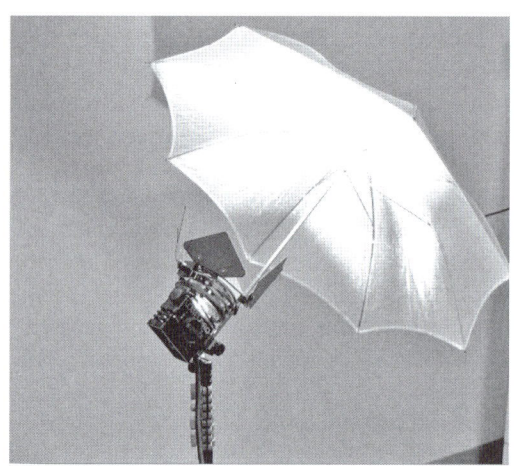

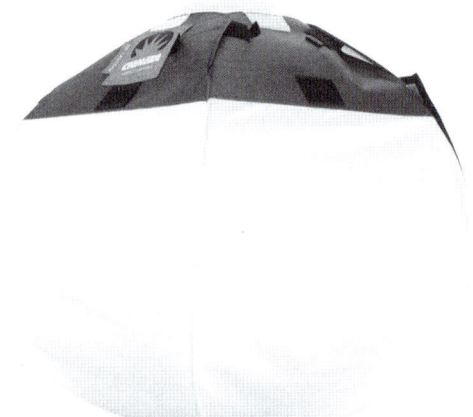

Figure 11.15 Chinese lanterns, this one by Chimera, throw a soft even glow. Some cinematographers use the paper ones that are readily available at low cost, but be careful they don't catch fire.

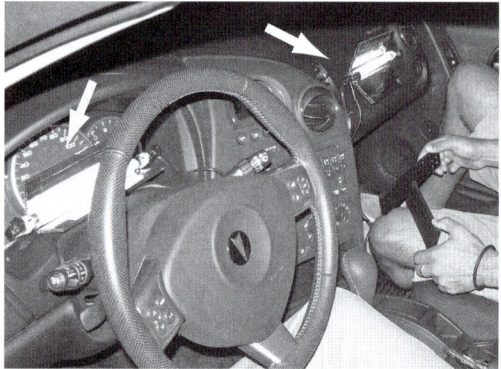

Figure 11.16 Using a small fluorescent lamp to add light to a car interior.

to a 500W hard light. While a 1K hard light might be more light than you need for almost any documentary situation, a 1K soft light might give the perfect soft illumination required for an interview.

While softbox units that fold up for packing are very popular, some filmmakers prefer to create their own soft light source by bouncing light from a hard light unit off a reflector umbrella, a show card, or even a white wall. Also popular in documentary are **Chinese lanterns** which throw a soft even glow in all directions (Figure 11.15).

Fluorescent Lights

Fluorescent lights generate their illumination by passing an electric charge through mercury gas trapped within a hollow tube, causing it to glow. Because of this construction, fluorescent lamps give off a very soft light that can be flattering. In addition, they are lightweight and draw very little power. Fluorescent units come in a wide variety of sizes, from large banks holding ten 48-inch fluorescent tubes to tiny nook fixtures holding a single 9-inch fluorescent lamp capable of being tucked into the dashboard (Figure 11.16). Fluorescent lights burn cool, and the units are collapsible, making them a good choice for location shooting. Fluorescent lighting units can also be rebulbed with lamps of various color temperatures. The downside is that they are rather delicate. Note that fluorescents used for film production are different from the types typically found in schools and office buildings, which can create problems both from unflattering color and potential for flicker. A common fluorescent light for documentary field production is the Kino Flo Diva, which comes in small banks of 200W each.

LED Lights

Light Emitter Diode (LED) lights are relative newcomers to the world of documentary lighting, but they are becoming very popular in a variety of situations. LEDs are built from sets of tiny individual cells, which are highly efficient and run on DC power, which means they can be powered with batteries. LED lights can be found in a huge variety of configurations, from tiny units designed to be mounted on a camera to large light panels that generate a soft even light (Figure 11.17). These units are also highly controllable, typically offering both a dimmer switch and a color temperature control. Their portability, versatility, and ease of use guarantee that, as their cost comes down, LEDs will play a larger and larger role in the world of documentary lighting.

HMI Lights

Hydrargyrum Medium-arc Iodide (HMI) lights are mercury vapor lights that were developed as an alternative to tungsten lighting. They are common in film and television as large (5K or 10K) lights. Because they are daylight balanced (5,600K), HMIs are often used to illuminate exteriors. They require a ballast, or transformer, to produce the high voltages they need to function. Small portable HMI kits do exist, but they are expensive. In general, HMIs are not common for documentary production.

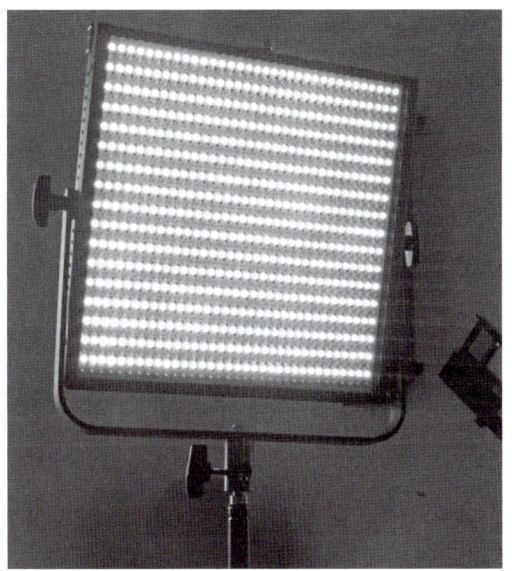

■ **Figure 11.17** This 12"x12" LED light can operate on batteries or AC current, and provides a cool and controllable fill light.

Reflectors

Reflectors are not lighting units per se, but we discuss them here because, as an illumination tool, they are as essential to a cinematographer as any lamp. Reflectors are lightweight, portable surfaces that bounce light. Reflectors usually have two sides with different reflective qualities: a diffused surface (white) that simultaneously bounces and diffuses a hard light source, and a specular side (silver or gold) that reflects and maintains the hard quality of the source. While reflectors are available as hard **show cards** or **bounce boards**, the reflectors typically used in documentary production are flexible ones with a metal band sewn into fabric with a reflective coating. These reflectors can be folded into a fraction of their full diameter and whipped out as needed, for instance to fill shadows in a daylight exterior interview (Figure 11.18).

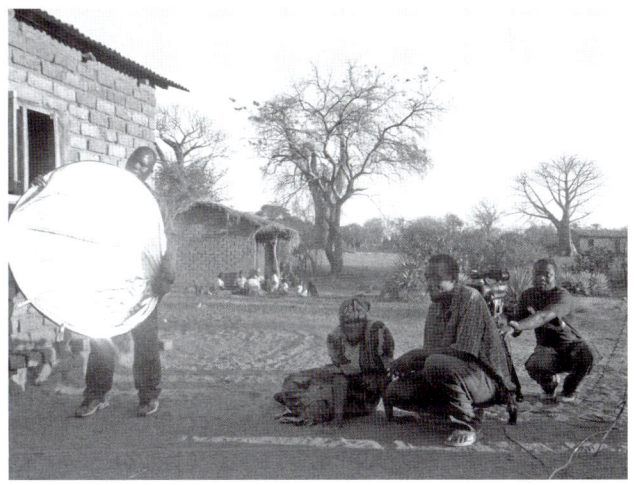

■ **Figure 11.18** This daylight exterior shot under the hot African sun (and far from any electricity) gets much needed fill from a reflector. Pictured here is cinematographer Mike Kambalame for Story Workshop's production *Okoma Atani* (2010).

Camera Filters and Lighting Gels

Camera filters and gels are key tools for subtle control of your lighting. They are both used to change the quality and/or color of light in a scene. The fundamental difference between the two is that **camera filters** are glass or hard plastic elements mounted on the camera, in front of the lens, to change the quality of the light from all sources entering the camera. **Gels** (short for gelatin from which they were originally made) are sheets of material that are used in front of a lighting unit (or over a window) to alter the quality and/or color of that particular light source *before* it falls on the scene.

Altering Light with Filters

Camera filters are mounted in front of a lens in two ways: they either screw directly onto the front of the lens or are held in a **matte box**. Filters that mount directly onto the lens are usually glass in a metal mounting ring (Figure 11.19, left). These filters come in a wide

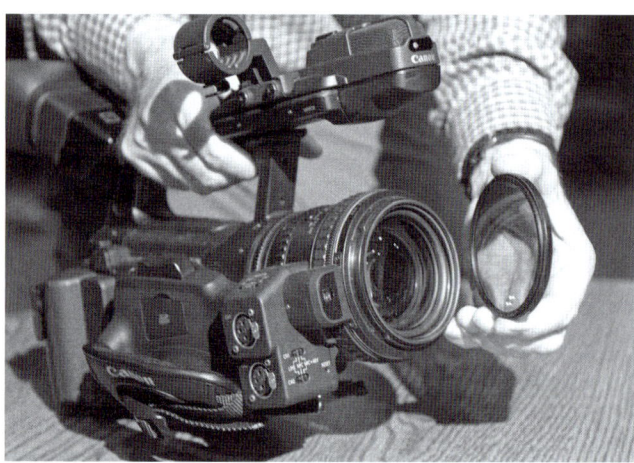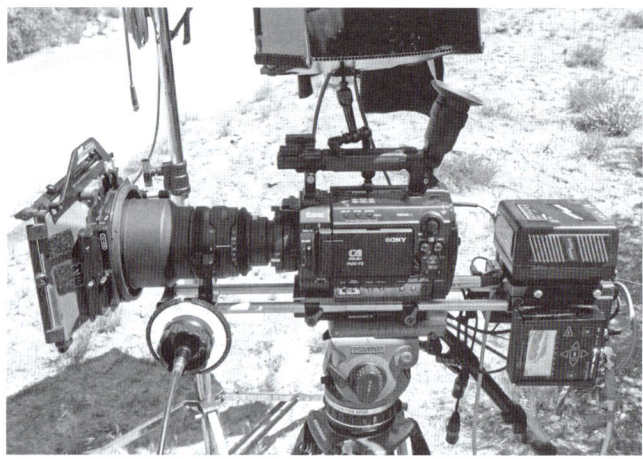

■ Figure 11.19
A filter that screws directly onto the lens (left), and a matte box that holds filters and is mounted over the lens housing (right). Matte box photo by Curt Pair.

variety of sizes to match the diameter and mounting threads of various lenses. Matte boxes attach to the front of the camera and extend out from the lens to prevent **lens flare** (Figure 11.19, right). They have filter holders and slots for holding several rectangular glass or plastic filters independent of the lens. Different matte boxes are designed to hold specific filter sizes (2 × 2, 3 × 3, or 4 × 4 inches). Make sure that you have the proper size filter for your particular matte box.

There are literally hundreds of different filters on the market that accomplish a wide range of different effects. Camera filters break down into three broad categories: **color correction**, **exposure control**, and **special effects**. It's not possible to cover every filter available, but the following sections cover a few of the most common and indispensable filters for filmmaking.

Neutral Density Filters

Neutral density filters (or **ND filters**) are gray-tinted filters that simply cut down the amount of light entering the lens (Figure 11.20). Filter manufacturers have different systems for

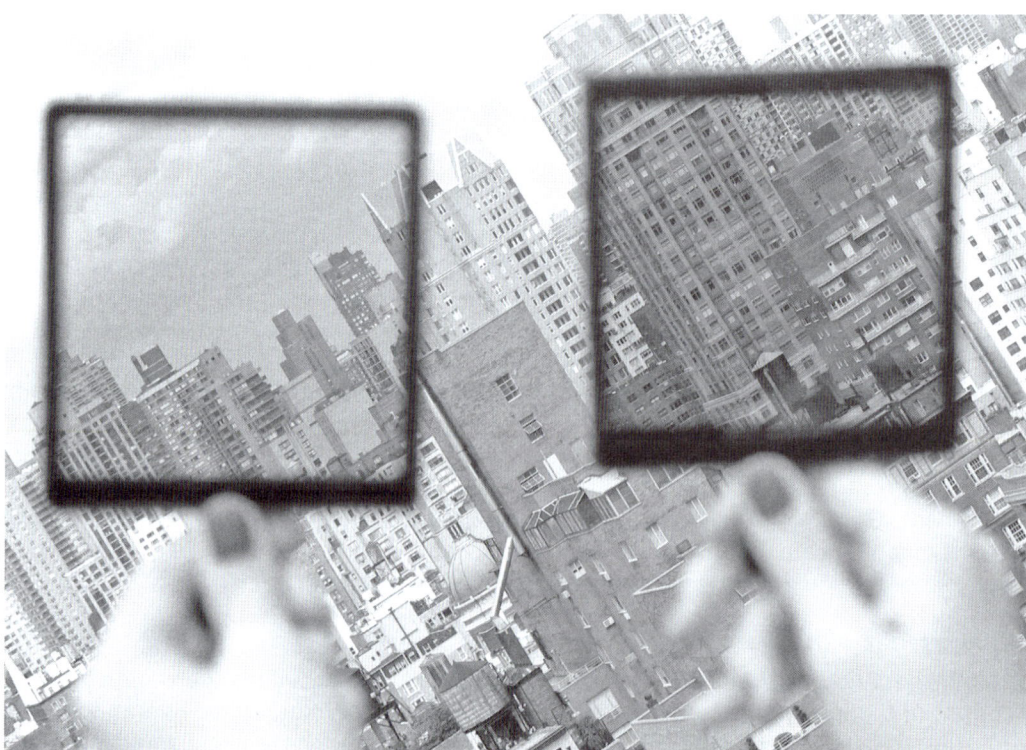

■ Figure 11.20
Neutral density filters cut the amount of light entering the lens without changing its color. ND 0.3 (left) reduces light by one stop and ND 0.6 (right) cuts the light by two stops.

indicating the light blocking capabilities of a specific filter. In the system used by Lee and Tiffen, a filter capable of blocking one f-stop worth of light (cutting the light in half) is a ND 0.3 filter. Hoya and B+W use the term ND2 for the same filter. For simplicity, we will stick with the former system.

ND filters are exposure control filters and do not affect color at all. An ND 0.3 filter cuts the amount of incoming light in half, or one full stop; an ND 0.6 cuts down two stops, and an ND 0.9 cuts down three stops. ND filters are useful if you find yourself shooting on a sunny day, and in fact many cameras will give you a warning when you need to add an ND filter. This filter is also used when you want to decrease your depth of field without changing your lens focal length, as it allows you to decrease your f-stop, or open your aperture (Chapter 9). This is especially important when shooting with a smaller image sensor, as the depth of field tends to be very deep. Many cameras have ND filters that are built-in and accessible either through menus or on a filter wheel behind the lens (Figure 8.31). Also popular are variable ND filters, which can be set in increments from 1 to 8 stops, allowing for precise control.

Diffusion Filters

Diffusion filters are special effect filters used to soften an image while maintaining sharpness of focus. Exactly how and how much they soften the image depends on whether the filter uses a white or black diffusion effect, as well as on the degree of diffusion. **White diffusion** creates a soft haze, from the subtle refracting of white highlights, and **black diffusion** softens the image by delicately flaring the shadow areas of the image. The degree of diffusion is designated by a scale beginning with the fractions 1/8, 1/4, and 1/2, and then going from 1 to 5. In documentary, diffusion is mostly used to soften wrinkles on an interview subject. Some shooters feel that the unfiltered digital video image can be excessively harsh and will routinely employ a very light, black diffusion to slightly soften the image's "electronic" edge.

Polarizing Filters

When light reflects off shiny surfaces, specifically nonmetallic surfaces like glass or water, it scatters and vibrates in many directions, causing glare. A **polarizing filter** reduces or eliminates the obstructing glare, as well as reflections coming off transparent surfaces like glass and water. A polarizing filter is made of either one glass element that rotates, or two elements, where one is fixed and one rotates. Each element is manufactured with tiny parallel lines. These lines block light that is off-axis, allowing only light waves that are parallel to one another to pass through the filter (Figure 11.21).

Polarizers offer a great amount of creative control because you can easily see, as you rotate the filter, exactly how much glare and reflection you are eliminating (Figure 11.22).

Polarizers are also handy for darkening blue skies to make cloud formations stand out vividly. For this use, the angle of the sun to the filter is important. Darkening blue skies works best when the sun is not directly overhead. This means the effect works better in the morning and later afternoon. A polarizer does not alter the color tonalities of your scene, but it does take a toll on exposure. Most require a compensation of 1.5 to 2 stops. Also remember that polarizers work through the precise angles between the light and filter elements, so moving the camera by panning or tracking can visibly change the polarizing effect.

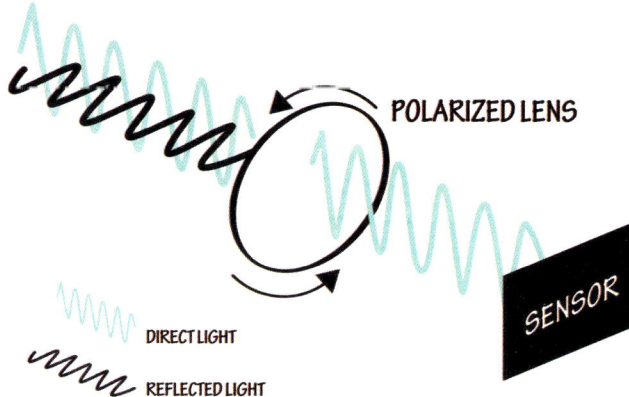

■ **Figure 11.21** When shooting shiny, transparent surfaces, the reflected and direct light travel together toward the lens. To stop the reflected light, the polarizer is rotated until it blocks the off-axis light rays, allowing only direct light to pass through.

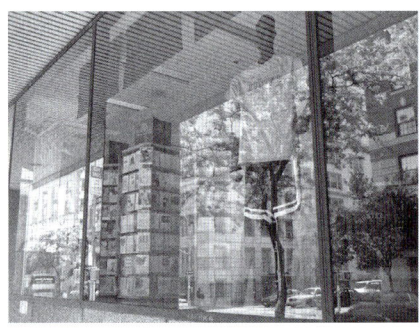 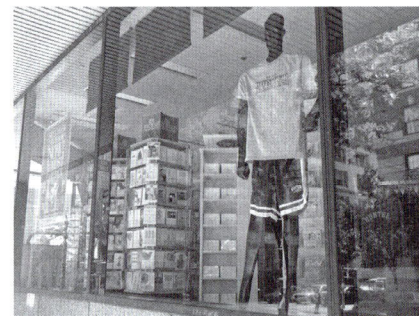 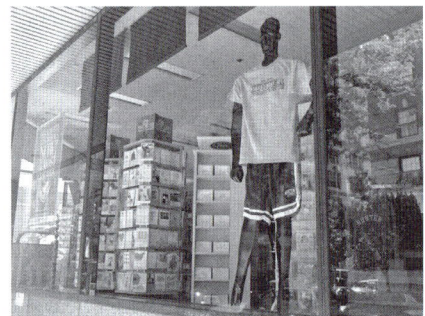

■ **Figure 11.22** Glare on the window makes it difficult to see through (left). Turning the polarizing filter shows the gradual reduction in light reflecting off the window's surface (center). At its most effective angle, the polarizer can almost completely eliminate glare (right).

Graduated Filters

Graduated filters incrementally introduce a filter effect into only a portion of the frame, leaving the rest of the frame unaffected (Figure 11.23). A graduated ND filter, for example, may incorporate a noticeable ND effect at the top of the frame to darken the sky, but the ND effect will taper off and disappear by the center of the frame, leaving the bottom half of the image completely unchanged.

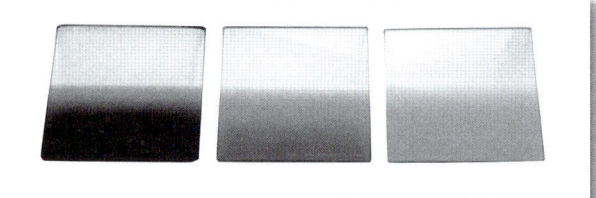

■ **Figure 11.23** Graduated filters gradually introduce a filter effect into a portion of the frame. Shown here are (left to right) ND 0.9, ND 0.6, and ND 0.3 graduated filters.

Graduated ND filters are popular because they reduce the contrast range in an image by bringing down the brightness of the sky so that the exposure more closely matches that of a shaded area on the ground. Graduated color filters are also popular, especially those that affect the color of the sky. Examples include the sunset graduated filter, which warms up the sky with an amber tint, and the blue graduated filter, which deepens blue skies. Color graduated filters need to be used with some caution, as they are not the most subtle effects you can apply to your image.

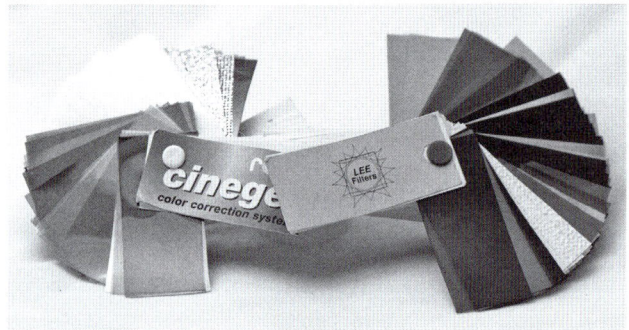

■ **Figure 11.24** Gels come in hundreds of colors and intensities. (See plate section for color.)

Altering Light with Gels

While filters are mounted on the camera, gels are positioned in front of a specific light source to change the color or quality of that particular source's output. There are several different manufacturers of lighting gels offering literally hundreds of different colors, shades, and effects to choose from (Figure 11.24). In documentary, cinematographers use these gels extensively to change the color temperature of light in a scene, as well as to flatter a subject or "perk up" a background.

Color Conversion Gels

Color conversion gels are used to change the color temperature of a light source, and they come in two basic flavors: **CTO** for "color temperature orange" (Figure 11.25, right), and **CTB** for "color temperature blue" (Figure 11.25, left). CTO gels convert daylight (5,600K) into tungsten color temperature light (3,200K).

Full CTO converts 5,600K light directly into 3,200K, but 1/2 blue CTO converts 5,600K daylight to 3,800K (a little bluer) and 1/4 CTO converts 5,600K daylight to 4,500K (even bluer). These gels allow the cinematographer a high degree of control in shifting the color tonalities of light sources. These are commonly put over windows to bring the daylight into the range of tungsten lighting.

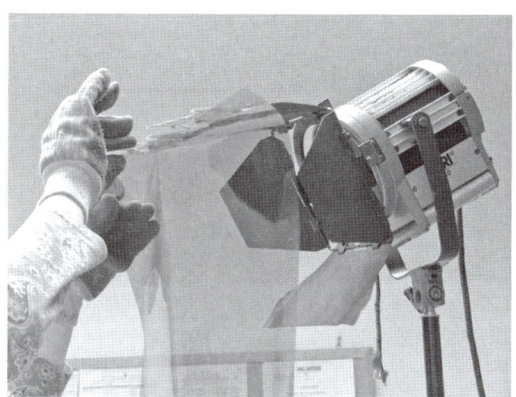 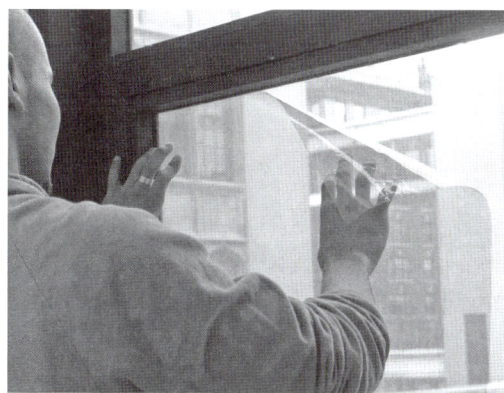

Figure 11.25 CTB filter being placed on a light to make it "daylight" (left). CTO filter being placed on a window to convert the daylight to "tungsten" (right). (See plate section for color.)

CTB gels convert a tungsten light source to daylight color temperature and are mostly used directly in front of lighting units. **Full blue** converts 3,200K light into 5,600K, but CTB also comes in various conversion degrees. For example, 1/2 blue CTB converts 3,200K to 4,100K (less cool) and 1/4 CTB converts tungsten to 3,500K (even warmer).

Color Conversion Gels and Mixed-Lighting Situations

CTO and CTB gels are indispensable for situations in which you have lighting sources with different color temperatures in one location. Let's say you are lighting a subject with tungsten light (3,200K) but there is a window with daylight streaming in (5,600K) close-by. If your camera is balanced for daylight, the subject will look as orange as a carrot. If you balance for tungsten, the window light will turn an unnatural blue. What to do?

There are two ways you can balance the light in this situation. You can cover the window with orange gel and white balance the camera to tungsten light, and all lighting sources will be tungsten color temperature. However, the difficulty with this approach is that it's not so easy to cover a window with gel, especially a large one. Lining windows requires that you carefully tape the gel to the window frame, making sure that there are no wrinkles that will refract light and reveal the gel. It can certainly be done, but it takes time and practice.

The other, more common, option would be to cover your tungsten lights with blue gel (CTB), so that they match the color temperature of the sunlight, and white balance your camera to daylight (Figure 11.26). Although putting a gel in front of a light is easier, there are drawbacks to this approach, too. Using a gel on your lights cuts the light intensity and creates greater contrast between the tungsten areas and the bright sunlight areas.

Both solutions work, though, so choosing one depends on your specific situation. The principle to remember is to use gels to change the color temperature of one source to match the other.

Also, remember that 1/2 and 1/4 color conversion allow you to subtly control the color. Let's say the image you are shooting is a winter scene and you want it to feel like it's cold outside but warm inside the house. You might choose only a **half blue** gel for the interior lights, which would convert them only partially to daylight, maintaining the warmth of your interior sources.

Neutral Density Gels

Like ND filters, **neutral density gels** cut down the intensity of a light source without affecting the color. ND 0.3 cuts intensity by one stop, ND 0.6 by two stops, and ND 0.9 by three stops (Figure 11.23). Because these gels are very often used on windows to

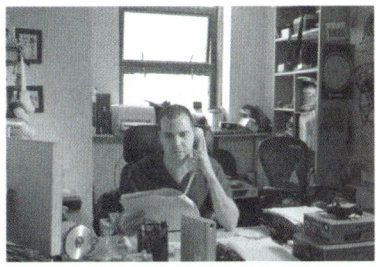
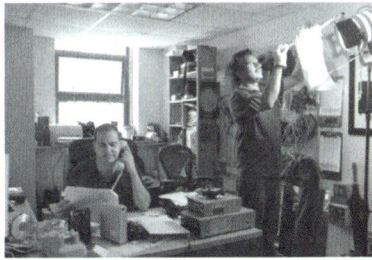
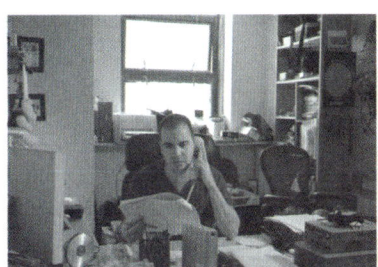
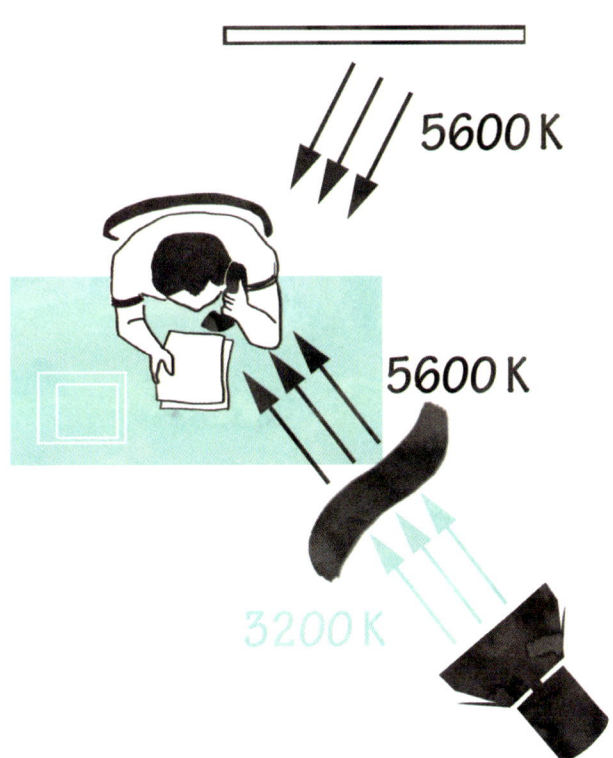

■ **Figure 11.26** Shooting with a camera balanced for daylight will make the daylight from the window appear white, while the light from the tungsten light will look orange (top). Placing a CTB gel over the tungsten light changes it to daylight (middle), matching the color temperatures of all sources (bottom). (See plate section for color.)

■ **MIXING LIGHT TEMPERATURES**

Sometimes, rather than putting gels on lights or over windows to even out the color temperature of the light sources in a scene, cinematographers choose to keep the color temperature of the various lights as they are. In the example below, from Christian Frei's *War Photographer* (2001), the cinematographer has lit the subject (Christiane Amanpour) with artificial lights (3200K) while balancing the camera closer to the color temperature of the daylight outside (5600K). The resulting difference helps pull Amanpour out of the background and gives her a warm intimate feel (Figure 11.27).

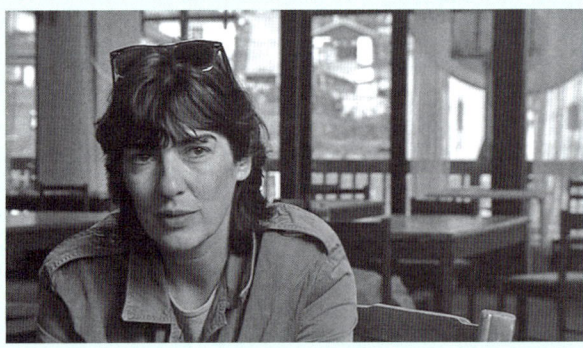

■ **Figure 11.27** Using mixed light for aesthetic effect in *War Photographer*. (See plate section for color.)

moderate the intensity of light pouring into interior scenes, you will often find ND mixed with CTO in a single gel. A CTO ND 0.6, for example, will change the color temperature of the daylight to 3,200K and will reduce the intensity of the window almost three stops.

Diffusion Media

Diffusion media are used to soften the output of a hard light source, like an open-face spotlight. Diffusion can be used as a single layer or doubled or tripled to increasingly soften the light. Using a spotlight with diffusion creates light that is less harsh than a spot, but still more controllable than that of a soft light. The trade-off is that diffusion can cut light intensity drastically, but this can also be an advantage. Diffusion is not called a "gel" because there are many different kinds of diffusion, made from a variety of materials. **Tough spun** (made of spun glass), **tough frost**, **grid cloth**, and **tough opal** are some common diffusion materials. The designation "**tough**" on any gel indicates that it is heat resistant and can be placed on lights—with caution, of course (Figure 11.28). Like color conversion gels, diffusion comes in varying strengths, with full diffusion cutting your light exactly one f-stop, and half and quarter diffusion offering gentler effects.

Basic Grip Gear

Documentary productions rarely have enough crew for a separate person to deal with lighting. Lighting falls under the responsibilities of the cinematographer, but whether you are the director, the sound recordist, or the associate producer, you may be called on to chip in. For this reason, everyone on set should have a basic understanding of the tools of the lighting trade. There is too much specialized grip equipment to cover all of it here, but these are some of the most commonly used grip tools you'll encounter on documentary productions.

Stands

Light stands are what we usually position lighting units on, especially in field production. They are collapsible three-legged stands that have a telescoping center pole to raise and lower the light as necessary. **C-stands** are your all-purpose holder, used for hanging, holding, or positioning flags, scrims, or just about anything that needs hanging (Figure 11.29). They are heavy and awkward to transport, but their flexibility makes them indispensable in many situations. Combined with a **gobo head** and **gobo arms**, C-stands become infinitely adjustable and versatile.

Gear for Light Control

When lighting, we want to be able to carefully control where the light falls and where it does not. Blocking light to keep it from falling where you don't want it is called **trimming** the light, and it's easy to do with hard light. Soft light, on the other hand, is difficult to trim. Because its light rays scatter in all directions, soft light will not create the sharply defined shadow edge necessary for precise trimming. Light that falls where it should not is called **spill light**, and soft light tends to spill.

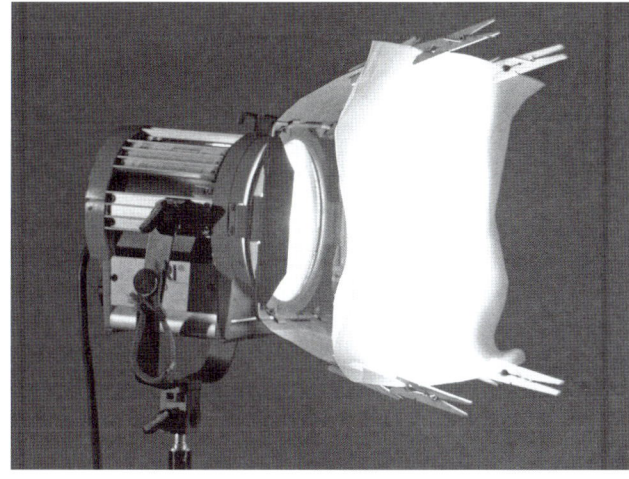

■ **Figure 11.28** A layer of tough frost diffusion attached to barn doors to create a softer light.

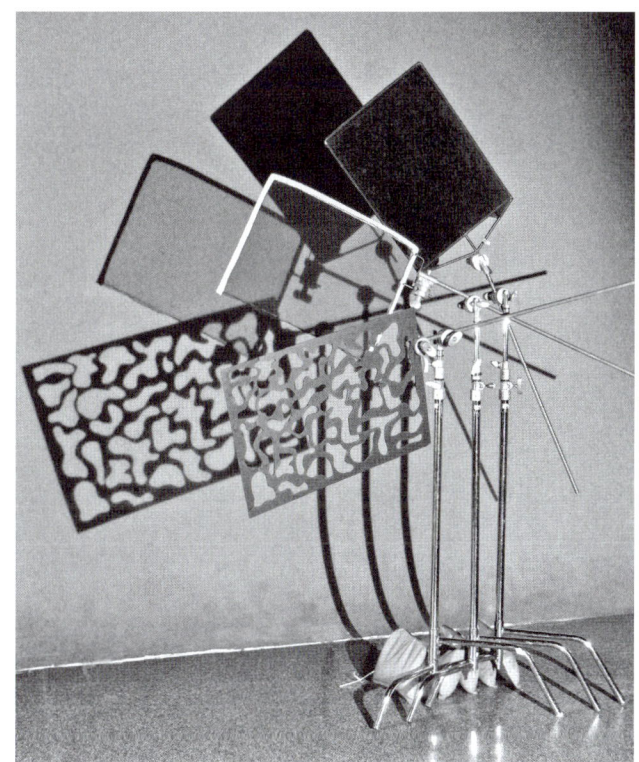

■ **Figure 11.29** C-stands are all purpose holders used on film shoots. Here a C-stand is shown supporting (from left to right) a cookie, a scrim, and a flag.

Barn doors are a standard addition to almost every hard lighting unit and are designed to help control where the light falls, and to control **spill**. Barn doors fit onto the front of the lighting unit and consist of two or four foldable black metal leaves (Figure 11.30). When precise trimming is called for, we often use **flags**, which are free-standing frames covered with black felt, to sharply define where the light falls and where it doesn't.

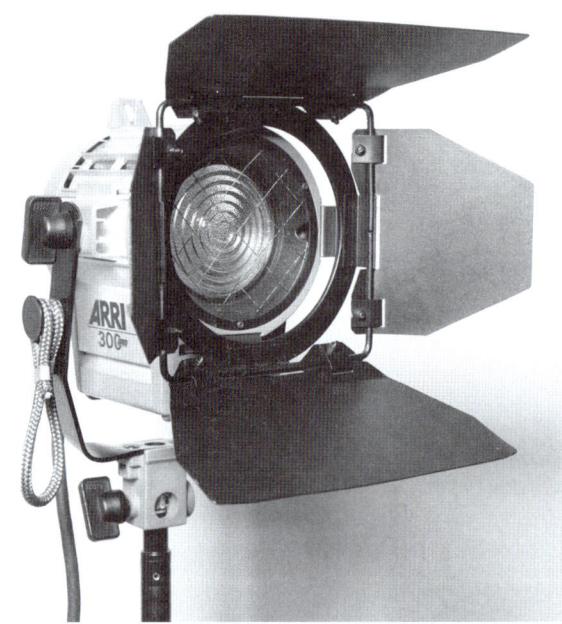

Figure 11.30 Barn doors are used to keep light off areas of your set where you don't want light. They come on both Fresnels and open-faced spots. The hexagonal wire is for safety, not light control.

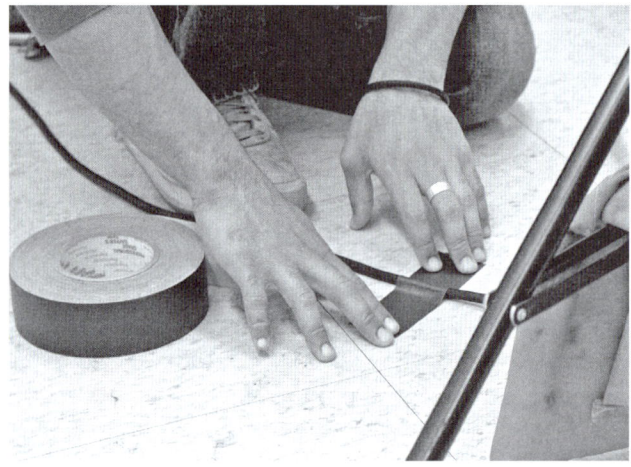

Figure 11.31 Securing cables with gaffer's tape to prevent people from tripping on them.

Various other tools are used to cut the amount of light without using diffusion. **Scrims** fit right behind the barn doors on a light to reduce the intensity of the light. Scrims are wire mesh screens that fit directly in front of the lighting unit. The denser the wire mesh, the more light it cuts. A single scrim cuts the output of the unit by half a stop and a double scrim cuts it by one full stop. You can use multiple scrims to achieve the intensity you need.

Nets are netting material stretched across a frame and, like flags, are usually supported by C-stands. Nets are used purely to cut the intensity of light, by one, two, or three stops. Obviously you can reduce the intensity of light simply by moving it, but by placing the net over *part* of the beam, you can cut intensity on only a part of the scene. **Silks** are like nets, but the material is partly opaque, which not only cuts the light intensity, but diffuses it as well. **Gobo** is the general name given to anything that comes between a light source and the scene and throws a shadow pattern. One specific kind of gobo is a **cookie** (short for **cucoloris**), which is metal or foam core that has had shapes cut into it to create patterns on a wall, floor, or other surface (Figure 11.29).

Clamps

There are all sorts of clamps used to hold things on a film set, but there are two that can be of special use when it comes to placing lights. **Gator clamps** are heavy-duty spring clamps with rubber teeth to ensure a very tight grip on things like doors and tables, and **mafer clamps** are designed to lock onto pipes. Both clamps are built with posts to which you can attach a small light. These clamps allow you to position or hide small lights by attaching them to a door, a bookcase, or any place you can find a grip.

Miscellaneous Grip Gear

A few of the other important items in a grip package would include the **stinger**, which is the on-set name for an extension cord, **splitters** for plugging multiples devices into one outlet, and **3-to-2 adapters** for plugging three-pronged plugs into two-pronged outlets. Be careful when doing this; see Chapter 16 for more on electrical safety. **Sandbags** are placed over the legs of light stands to keep them from toppling over. One indispensable item is **gaffer's tape**. Gaffer's tape rips easily into any width and length strip you need, it holds well, and it leaves no adhesive residue behind. It is especially useful for taping down cables (called **dressing cables**) to prevent people from tripping (Figure 11.31). Do not substitute common duct tape for gaffer's tape, even though it is much less expensive. Duct tape is designed to be permanent and will leave gum all over your equipment and anything else it touches. And of course, don't forget a pair of **gloves**, preferably leather that won't burn. A typical bulb has a surface temperature measured in the thousands of degrees.

Never set up a light, lay a cable, add a gel, or plug in a stinger without considering all the safety issues involved. In the context of documentary filmmaking, where you are often setting up equipment in locations full of nonprofessionals, careful placement of lights, cables, and stands is extremely important.

The Ditty Bag

A **ditty bag** is a filmmaker's general utility tool kit and is filled with items you might find useful on the set. Ditty bags are built over time, but here are a few standard items to get you started:
- Lens cleaning fluid/tissues
- Jeweler's screwdriver set
- Screwdrivers: various sizes, regular, and Phillips
- Pliers: regular and needle nose
- Sharpies
- Allen wrench set
- Canned air
- AC plug adaptors (three-prong-to-two-prong with ground loop)
- Tape measure
- Cable ties
- Tweezers
- Extra batteries (AA, 9-volt, and whatever your microphones use)
- Pencils and small note pad
- Small scissors
- Flashlight
- Leather grip gloves
- AC circuit tester
- Leatherman tool or Swiss Army knife

With all of these tools, there is really only one way to gain expertise. Even with the best kit in the world, documentary filmmaking is a continuous series of improvisations and unplanned lighting situations. Practice is the best guide, but in the next chapter we will explore some common approaches that can help you get started.

Lighting and Exposure—Beyond the Basics

CHAPTER 12

In this chapter, we explore lighting and exposure more deeply. We will look at concrete strategies cinematographers use to light a variety of common documentary situations, as well as aesthetic factors that filmmakers consider and some of the technical challenges that cinematographers face while trying to achieve a specific look.

When you first start out, movie lighting can seem somewhat mysterious and tremendously time-consuming. Once you have learned to control your image through lighting and exposure though, countless expressive possibilities become available to you. And the more you work, the greater your technical and aesthetic repertoire.

Basic lighting setups represent the building blocks of the cinematographer's craft. Knowing these fundamental setups, which combine directionality, quality of light, and function, will help you to understand how to create certain visual effects and also help you determine an answer to the most basic question: Where do I put this light?

Once in a particular location, one of the first things to consider is **directionality**. Where is the light coming from? And where do you want it to appear to be coming from? Even when you are simply shooting an interview on the street, with no artificial lights, you can control the light by positioning the interview subject to face one way or another so the sunlight falls on them in a specific way.

It is always helpful to remember that the range of light placement options is three-dimensional. You can place your lights anywhere in the imaginary globe that surrounds your subject: in front, behind, along the side, high above, below, near, far—at any angle and any distance, as long as the lights stay out of the frame of the shot (although this, too, is not an absolute rule). Here are a few basic lighting angles, with an indication of the resulting effect created by each one. Remember, don't just look at the direction of the light but at the throw of shadows as well (Figure 12.1).

a. **Frontal light** is illumination that comes essentially from the angle of the camera. Because the light rays duplicate the camera's angle of vision, most of the shadows are not visible to the lens as they fall straight back. Frontal light has a flat look resulting from this absence of shadows.

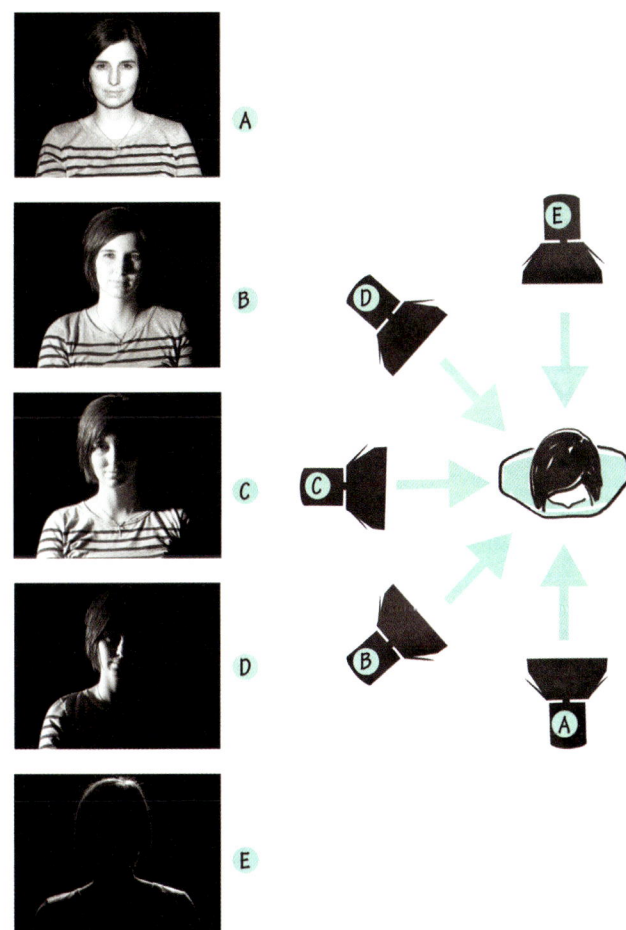

■ **Figure 12.1** The placement of lighting units determines the angle of illumination and the angle at which shadows fall. Pictured are five standard angles along the same horizontal plane: frontal (A), 3/4 front (B), side (C), 3/4 back (D), and back (rim light) (E).

b. Move the light along an arc, away from the camera, and shadows start to appear and become more prominent as the light moves farther from the camera position. A 3/4 **frontal light** is a lighting unit that is positioned at 45° from the camera. Notice the shadows cast by this light. This light position is often raised vertically by 45° as well. The presence of some shadows that create facial modeling makes this a useful light position for interviews.

c. Move this light another 45° away from the camera so that it is now positioned at a 90° angle from the camera and we have a **sidelight**. This light comes directly from the side of the subject and has the effect of dividing the illuminated object in half, with one side lit and the other in shadows. Sidelight maximizes shadows and therefore texture as well.

d. Moving this light another 45° away from the camera, we have a 3/4 **backlight**. The area that this position lights is mostly hidden from the camera, but we do see bright highlights on the top and side edges of the subject. Notice how this angle causes the light to illuminate the shoulder and hair, and cuts the light side of the figure out from the background while allowing the other side to blend into the shadows. This placement for a backlight is so common that it even has its own nickname, a **kicker**. This light is also commonly raised vertically by 45° to catch slightly more of the hair and shoulders.

e. Finally, move this light another 45° from the camera and the light is now 180° across from the camera, illuminating the subject's back. The camera can see only a small sliver of illumination around the top of our subject, as the front falls completely into shadow. This light is commonly called a **rim light**, and must be placed carefully to avoid **flaring** the lens.

In addition to the horizontal angles, you need to consider the dramatic changes in shadow and mood as you adjust the lighting unit's **height** (or **vertical angle**) from **high angle** to **low angle** (Figure 12.2).

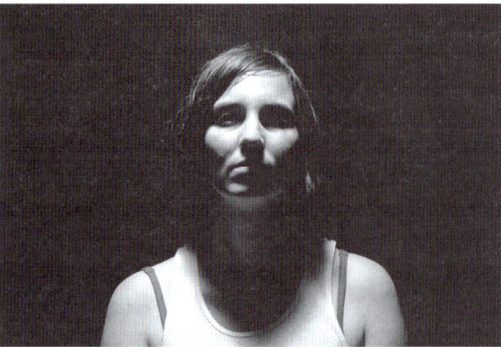 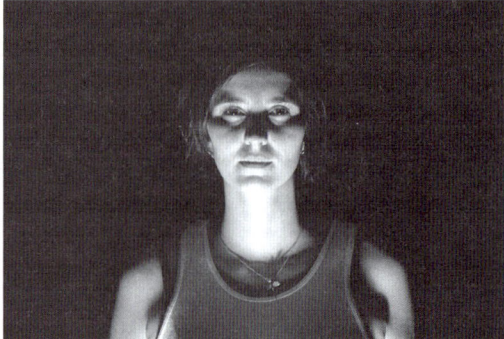

■ **Figure 12.2** The vertical angle of a lighting unit can dramatically change the look of a subject. Pictured are a high-angle frontal (left) and a low-angle frontal (right).

Let's look at a few basic setups documentarians commonly face, and at some strategies they use for lighting them.

LIGHTING INTERVIEWS

One area in documentary where lighting plays a large role is the interview. The documentary interview can take many forms from highly formal to "off the cuff," in locations from a bedroom to a studio with a full lighting grid. Most approaches use some aspect of a strategy known as **three-point lighting**.

Three-Point Lighting

While the term three-point lighting refers to a specific lighting setup commonly used in interviews, in a more general way it is a good guide to the role different lights can play in any lighting situation. In any three-point lighting setup, the **key light** provides main illumination of the scene, the **fill light** takes care of shadows, and the **backlight** will help separate the subject from the background. The function of the lights is more significant than their specific placement. Sometimes two of the three will create the lighting effect you want, and at other times available light from, for example, a window can take on one of the three roles. Three-point lighting in its classic form employs a key light (positioned at 30° to 45° from the camera and at a 45° vertical angle), a fill light (usually opposite the key), and a backlight (usually a 3/4 back) (Figure 12.3).

While it's a useful formula, it is important not to think of three-point lighting as a rule that must be observed in every shot, and it's especially problematic to think that one should *always* light people with the three-point lighting scheme. It is useful, however, to understand how each of these lights functions in more detail.

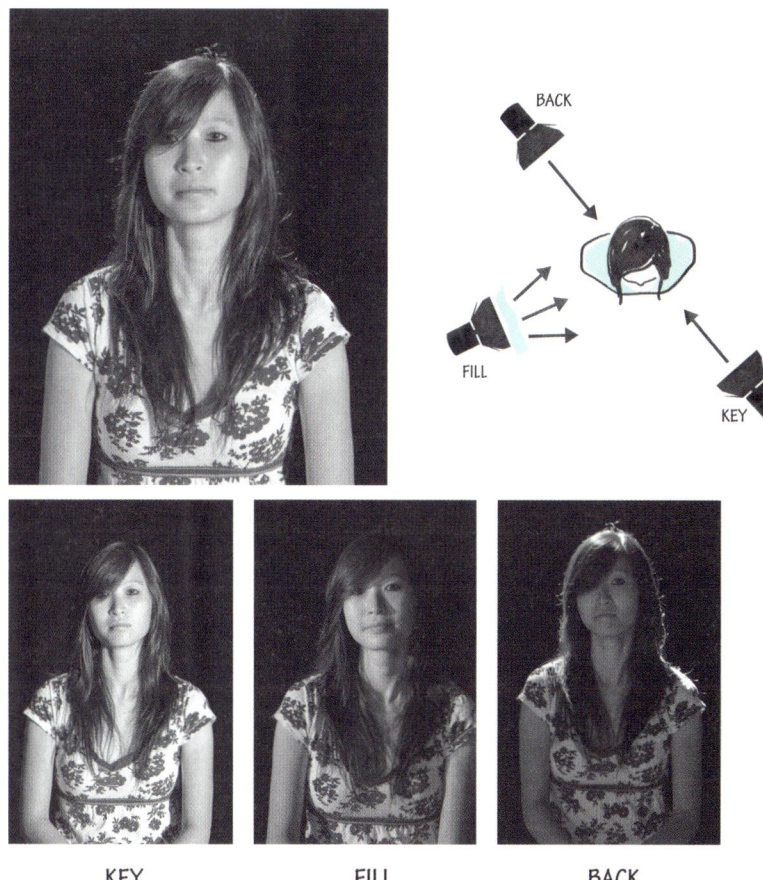

■ **Figure 12.3** A typical three-point lighting setup consists of a key light, a fill light, and a backlight. On the bottom you can see the effect of each light in isolation.

Key Light

The key light is the primary source of illumination in your scene (Figure 12.3, bottom left). Often the key light is a hard and bright light source, but it's not uncommon in documentary to see soft keys, where the gentler shadows are kinder to the human face. The job of the key light is a base illumination, and to create depth by casting shadows (known as **modeling**). For formal "sit-down" interviews that look more constructed, the audience will not expect realistic lighting quality or placement. For scenes in which a more realistic look is needed, for example an observational scene where the interview is more impromptu, the key light should be a **motivated light source**, which means that when positioning this light you should consider the logical "real" source within the scene for that illumination. It might be that you actually use the sun streaming in through a window for your key light, or you might place a light to simulate the sun streaming in from the window in a naturalistic way.

Fill Light

As you can see in the directionality examples (Figure 12.1), a hard light (like most key lights) casts sharp and dark shadows. When lighting people, a hard key light will create nose and chin shadows and sunken eyes. A **fill light** is a soft light that is positioned to fill in some, but not all of, the shadows created by the key light (Figure 12.3, bottom middle image). Using a fill light is not mandatory, but it is commonly used in most lighting setups. Often in documentary interviews, the fill light is provided by a reflector bouncing the light from the key back onto the subject (Figure 12.4).

Typically the fill light should be placed at an opposite angle to the key light, which makes sense, given that it has to fill in the shadows that fall exactly opposite the illuminated area.

The degree to which you decide to fill in those shadows varies depending on the look you are after. You can choose to keep shadows quite dark, but fill in just enough to see some

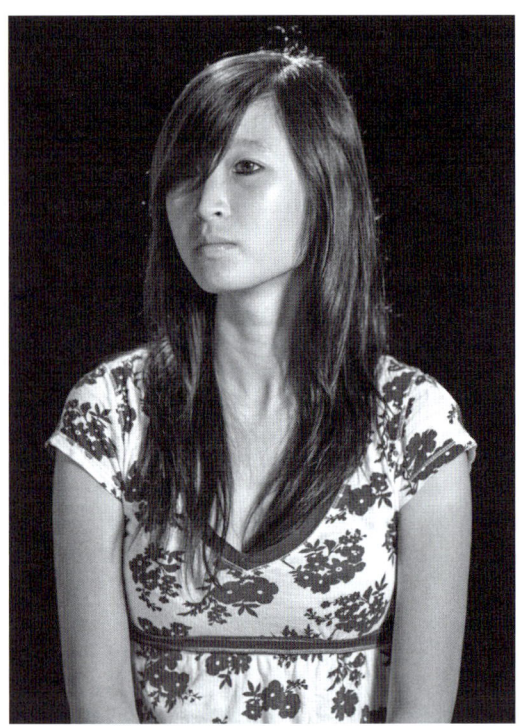 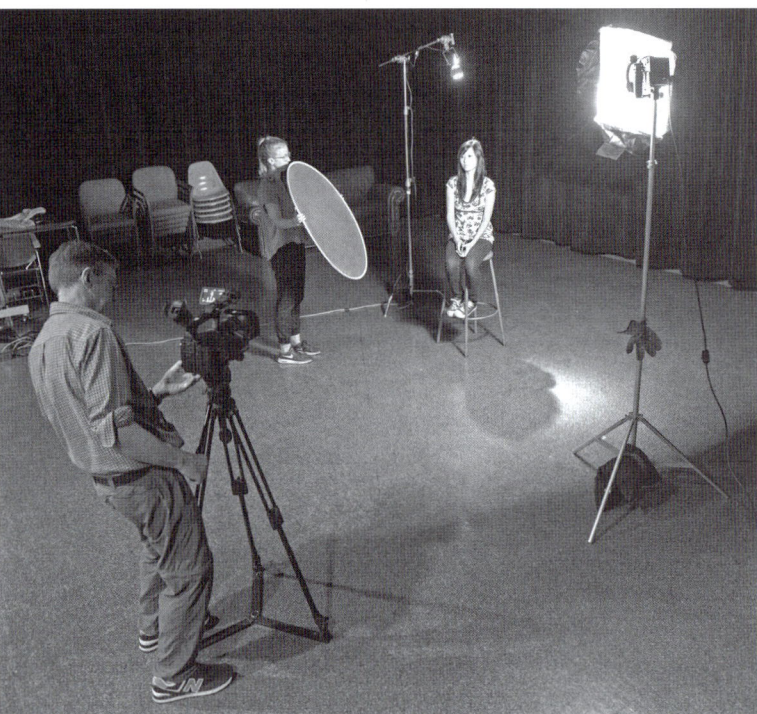

■ **Figure 12.4** This interview uses a softbox light (a Chimera) as a key, a reflector for the fill, and a small Lowel Pro as a backlight. The result is a softer look than in Figure 12.3.

detail in the shadows, or you could almost completely fill the shadows with soft illumination, flattening out the image to create a bright image in which almost everything is visible. The critical factor in determining the density of the shadows is the intensity of the fill light. The stronger the fill light, the less prominent the shadows will be.

Backlight

A **backlight** is a light that separates the subject from the background by positioning a somewhat lower intensity light at a high angle behind the subject (Figure 12.3, bottom right). The backlight can be either hard or soft. It creates, along the edge of the subject, a rim of light that clearly traces the edges of the figure and helps create depth in the frame. When lighting people, this light is often a 3/4 backlight (or kicker), positioned opposite the key, which illuminates the hair and shoulders of the subject. Obviously the color of the subject's hair is a factor in determining the intensity of the backlight. Blonde hair tends to thin out and create a halo when intense backlights are used. Dark hair or clothing against a dark background will benefit from being backlit. Backlight is so common in interviews that viewers expect it, and may even find shots without the separation from the background a backlight provides dull or hard to read. On the other hand, overly intense backlight that seems to come from nowhere can give your shot a highly artificial feeling.

There are many variations on three-point lighting. Figure 12.4 shows a setup where a softbox is used for the key light and a reflector provides the fill.

▪ LIGHTING STYLES

Looking at sample documentary interviews reveals that even within a three-point lighting strategy, there are ways to create very different effects (Figure 12.5). Consider the interview below, from Ken Burns' film *The War* (2007). Cinematographer Buddy Squires has created a very **stylized** look, meaning that the image has carefully modulated areas of light and dark intended to create a dramatic feel. A counter example would be the interview in Ross McElwee's *Sherman's March: A Meditation on the Possibility of Romantic Love in the South during an Era of Nuclear Weapons Proliferation* (1986). This interview is more **naturalistic**,

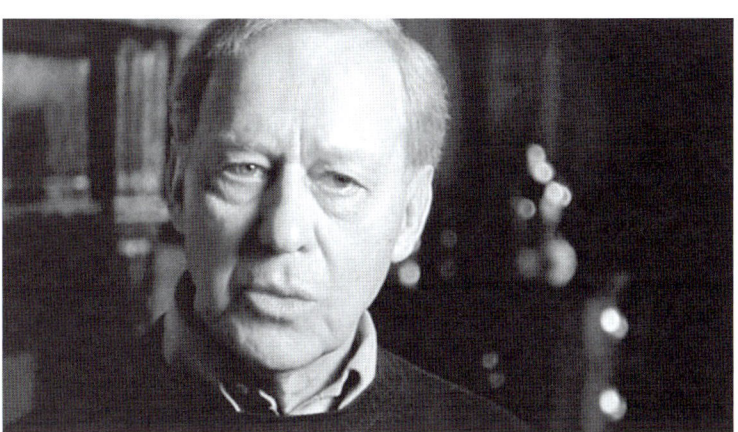 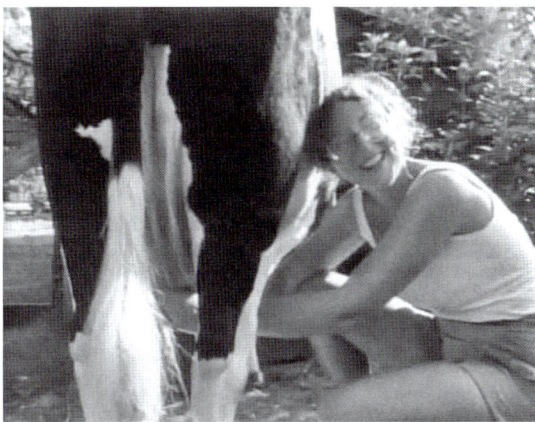

■ **Figure 12.5** Stylized and naturalistic lighting. On the left, Billy Squires created a mood of somber significance for an epic historical documentary, *The War*. On the right is a more naturalistic approach in *Sherman's March* that conveys a feeling of spontaneity.

meaning that it appears less intentionally constructed, as though the filmmaker just happened to show up and no special effort was made to light the character. It is important to note that a naturalistic look does not mean that the subject has not been lit. The use of strictly available light does not always translate into what the human eye "naturally" sees, because no digital sensor sees light quite the way the human eye does. So in an effort to duplicate what an audience expects to see naturally, films employ considerable and careful technique in lighting.

In the world of documentary, where the relationship with the real world is central, one might imagine that more naturalistic or realistic approaches to lighting would prevail. This is true, by and large, but there are many exceptions. The documentary interview, as suggested above, is often highly stylized. But you must always keep in mind that there are not two strictly delineated approaches or polar opposites—in fact, naturalistic and stylized lighting designs exist along a highly flexible continuum of aesthetic possibilities, and these approaches are often also mixed within the same documentary. That said, for our introduction, we'll discuss the unique principles of each lighting philosophy in discrete terms.

Lighting Ratios

Through lighting control, we can easily create an image with relatively few shadows, or one in which shadows dominate the composition. These communicate very differently to an audience. Broadly speaking, prominent shadows tend to create a more dramatic mood. A look with fewer shadows feels more realistic than stylized, and speaks to a world where information can be readily conveyed. **Lighting ratios** (also called **key-to-fill ratios**) are the way you measure the relative intensities of the major light sources illuminating your subject: the key light and the fill light. The ratio between the key and the fill lights is expressed as **key + fill : fill**. If you are a cinematographer, you will probably have a light meter, and can measure the key-to-fill ratio in **foot-candles** (p. 191). If you don't have a light meter, you can zoom in to a specific area of the frame and use the auto-iris control on your camera to get a reading for the isolated key (on the brightest side of their face) and the isolated fill (the other side). The key here is *relative* readings. If you get an f5.6 from the key side, and an f4 from the fill side, you know the ratio is 2:1 (remember, every setting in the f-stop scale doubles or halves the amount of light entering the lens). A lighting setup with a *low* key-to-fill ratio, like 2:1 or 3:1, means that the fill light is filling in shadows until they are quite light. A ratio of 1:1 means that both the key and the fill are the same intensity and there are no shadows at all.

A lighting setup with a *low* key-to-fill ratio overall, not just on the face of a subject, is called (somewhat confusingly) **high-key lighting** (see Figure 12.15 for an example). High-key lighting ensures visibility in all parts of your scene with an overall bright and even illumination. High-key lighting minimizes shadows, texture, and dimensionality. Conversely, a high lighting ratio like 16:1 (4 f-stops) will yield very dark and prominent shadow areas. This occurs when the intensity of the fill light is considerably lower than the key. A lighting setup with a *high* key-to-fill ratio is called **low-key lighting**. In the Buddy Squires interview (Figure 12.5), a low-key effect is achieved by creating alternating vertical bands of light and dark. The left side of the subject's head disappears into shadow, while the other side is framed by a dark patch as well. A **practical** and a window on the right add another band of light.

EXPOSURE CONTROL AND METERING LIGHT

Digital cameras all use some form of **through the lens (TTL) metering** to figure out what the correct exposure should be for a shot. A TTL meter is a **reflective light meter** that calculates the exposure by averaging out the light from a scene after it has entered the lens. A reflective meter measures light bouncing off of a surface, as opposed to an **incident meter**, which can read light falling directly on a source. A reflective reading is taken at the object you're lighting rather than in the camera. Exposure is actually a combination of the light reflecting off the scene, the sensitivity of the sensor (or gain, which can be varied; Chapter 8), and the f-stop, which is also variable (Chapter 9). It is important that you know how your particular camera "reads" the scene to figure out the exposure. Often cameras use **center-averaging**, basing exposure on light values at the center of the image. This is fine if you want to expose for the center of the frame, otherwise it's problematic. In other cases, a camera will weigh the light values across the scene and give you an average. This is also a problem. Imagine a room with a window. If the camera exposes for the bright sunlight outside, your scene inside will be shrouded in darkness. Conversely, if someone is in front of a very dark background, like a curtain or a blackboard, the camera may overexpose them.

The first thing you must do to take control of exposure is find out how to turn off the automatic iris function. Look for the **manual aperture override** (also called "manual exposure") function on your camera and turn it off. Second, you need to know how to tell what the f-stop setting is at any given time. Only some high-end professional cameras actually have the f-stop scale etched on the iris ring. Many cameras, if you turn the auto-iris function off, display an f-stop scale on their LCD screen or viewfinder. Typically, you will see an f-stop displayed in the viewfinder. Consumer cameras often have no scale at all, requiring you to judge exposure by eye.

Manual Exposure Control

Determining your "best" exposure requires using a combination of the zoom lens, the in-camera meter, the automatic iris, and the manual override functions (Figure 9.23).

Here are the standard steps for finding the best exposure for your shot:
1. Decide which part of the frame you would like exposed correctly. This is an aesthetic decision based on the composition, mood, and story.
2. With the camera on auto-iris, zoom in tightly to that portion of the composition, preferably so that it fills the frame, and let the auto-iris select the "correct" exposure for that small portion of the total scene.
3. Turn off the auto-iris by switching to manual override. This will lock in that exposure.
4. Zoom out and compose your shot. It doesn't matter where in the frame you place your subject, or how bright the background is, or what might pass in front of the lens during the take. Your exposure is locked in and will not change.
5. Finally, tweak the manual iris to finesse the exposure by looking at the final result in your viewfinder or on a high-quality field monitor.

Keep in mind that you can zoom in to any portion of the scene and lock in the exposure there to check out the effect of various apertures. This will give you a clear sense of the exposure possibilities for your scene.

Sometimes you will want to use a light meter to augment the camera's internal metering. This can be particularly useful when setting up the lighting for an interview, where the relative light values should be important to you. If you want a specific key-to-fill ratio, for example, you can measure the value of your key light in foot-candles and then talk to your cameraperson about what they need to do to give you, say, a 4:1 key-to-fill ratio without having to keep the cameraperson busy zooming in on the left and right sides of someone's face. You know that a reading of 200 foot-candles from the key dictates a reading of 50 foot-candles from the fill side. By the same token, if you are trying to create a lighting setup for an observational shoot where you may need to evaluate the light throughout a whole house, or a school building, a light meter can give you a sense of some of the things you may need to do to control exposure, whether lowering the blinds on a window or turning on overhead lights, and so on.

The Incident Light Meter

The **incident light meter** is the most common and versatile meter used in media production (Figure 12.6). It measures the intensity of light falling on a particular part of a scene. This meter is simple to use and gives a consistent reading from shot to shot. All incident meters have a half-globe light diffuser, called a **photosphere** (or "lumisphere"), which fits over the photosensitive cell. The photosphere, held near the subject and pointed toward the camera, gathers the light falling on the subject from the front and sides, and averages out these light intensities to arrive at an overall incident light intensity reading.

The actual measurement taken by a meter is in foot-candles in the United States, or **lumens** in the metric world. The meter takes that number, along with ISO information and shutter speed, and calculates an appropriate exposure. One of the problems with using a meter to derive an actual f-stop is that most video cameras don't use the ISO system to define their light sensitivity (remember they use gain instead). So you need to figure out what the ISO equivalent is of, say, 0 dB or +3 dB gain. DSLRs use ISO numbers, and hybrid cameras like the Canon C100/300 series can be set to use either gain or ISO numbers, making accurate external metering easier.

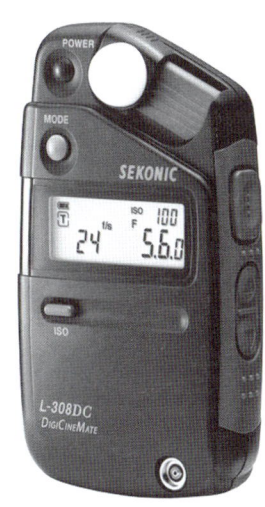

■ **Figure 12.6** This Sekonic L-308DC light meter is designed for use with video cameras, and gives accurate readings to small portions of an f-stop.

Another aspect of newer cameras is their ability to shoot in an **extended dynamic range** or **log gamma** mode (p. 203). The added dynamic range means extra f-stops and added picture information, which is great. It also means that for the first time with video cameras, what you see in the viewfinder is NOT necessarily what you get. The image you see when shooting in an extended dynamic range or log gamma mode will often look washed out. In these cases, using a light meter to check light values may offer you reassurance that the ultimate results are going to be what you want (Figure 12.18).

The Gray Scale

One other useful tool for controlling exposure is the gray scale. The gray scale is a chart calibrated in steps from black to white (Figure 12.7). Each step halves and doubles light in a way that corresponds with a camera's f-stops. These different steps are often called "zones" based on the work of American photographer Minor White.

The most important zone for us to consider, in order to understand how light meters work, is the one right smack in the middle, between pure black and pure white. Zone V has a reflectance value of 18 percent and is also known simply as "middle gray." All light meters, incident or reflected, are calibrated to the middle gray tone. In other words, they tell you what kind of exposure they think you need, to make sure that a middle gray in a scene

0	I	II	III	IV	V	VI	VII	VIII	IX	X
3.5%	4.5%	6%	9%	12.5%	18%	25%	35%	50%	70%	100%

Black velvet	2%	Midgray 18%	Caucasian face	36%
Black face	10%		Light grays	70%
Green leaves	14%		Off-whites	80%
Brown face	16%		White chalk	96%

■ **Figure 12.7** Minor White's Zone System uses a gray scale divided into eleven steps, or "zones," which can be used to assign an exposure to a subject according to predetermined reflectance values.[1]

will give you a middle gray in the reproduced image. Of course, it is up to you what you want to do with that information. As we suggest, this is only a place to start from. In fact, if you take a picture of either a gray scale or an 18 percent gray card using the camera settings you are using to expose your scene, it will give you a way to cross-check your exposures later. If you are doing serious lighting or shooting with an extended dynamic range, you will also probably want a chip chart, which gives you a reference set of light and color values. Filming the chart will create a record of your exposure and color settings that can be used to calibrate the color grading in postproduction (Chapter 22).

LIGHTING OBSERVATIONAL SCENES

A political convention, a meeting at a school, a busy household. As we discussed in Chapter 2, much documentary filmmaking is observational. People are doing something and you are filming them. When you approach lighting for an observational scene, the first thing you need to ask yourself is what is important in the scene. What do you need people to be able to see? Then, what kind of feel are you going for? While the goal of reaching the basic exposure levels needed to film in a particular location may be easy, it is *how* you light your scene that will define your approach to filmmaking. A key factor is how aware your viewers are of your lighting efforts. A light that appears to come from a natural source such as the sun, or an overhead light in a room, is called **motivated**. Motivated lighting gives a realistic effect. What reality actually consists of is a question for philosophers, but for filmmakers it's important to remember that **realism** is a style, one that you may have to work to achieve. For most observational filmmaking, an approach that does not call attention to itself, but serves the larger goal of presenting us with a look at a real situation, will prevail. Another name for this approach is naturalism, literally "making things look natural."

A **naturalistic** approach strives to appear as plausible and harmonious with the real environment as possible. Lighting direction and sources are always motivated, lighting continuity is observed from shot to shot, and the relationship between the various light sources duplicates what we would expect in a real-life situation. For this reason, the impact of naturalistic lighting is subtle, unobtrusive, and realistic. Obviously, one way to obtain a raw, naturalistic look is to use no artificial lighting but, rather, to use only available light.

The **direct cinema** and cinéma vérité films of the 1960s, which used new high-speed film stocks such as Tri-X and 4-X, allowed shooters to follow subjects pretty much anywhere without adding light (Figure 12.8).

Naturalistic lighting, however, does not necessarily mean that a filmmaker uses only available light. Documentary filmmaking offers an endless variety of shooting situations and many of them are interior spaces not designed with filmmaking in mind. Often filmmakers

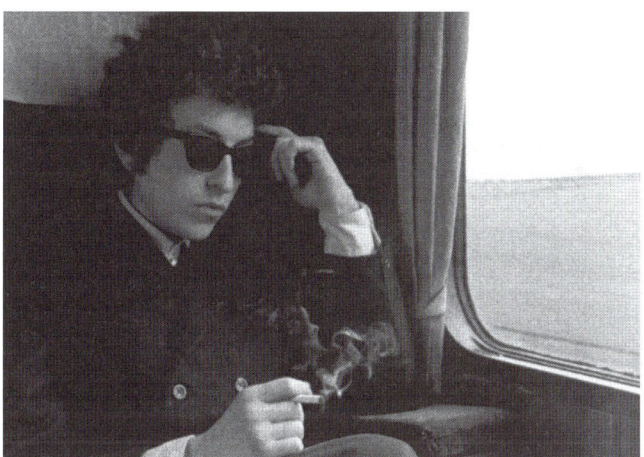 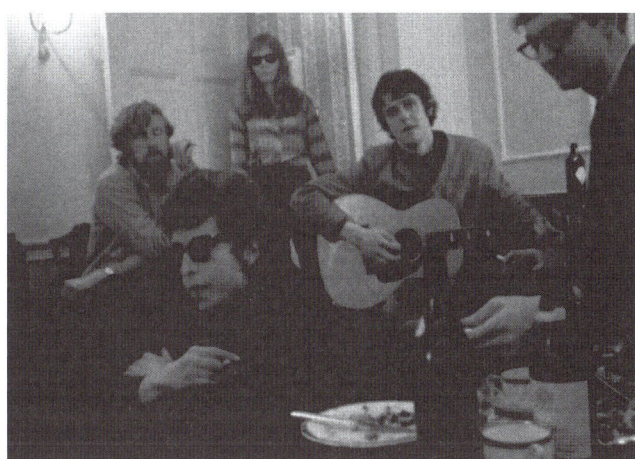

■ **Figure 12.8** With images like these from *Don't Look Back* (1967), D.A. Pennebaker redefined documentary naturalism. In the medium shot on the left, Dylan's torso disappears into the background, while in the group shot on the right, the available light is all on the background, leaving Bob Dylan, Donovan, and their pals in the murk. Every shot is a claim of authenticity that cries out, "We didn't manipulate the lighting here!"

will bounce a hard light off a ceiling, or hang a paper lantern or two from the ceiling, to raise the light levels of a space in general. While you will develop your own approach, there are a few things to think of. If you have to light a large room with many occupants very quickly, say to film a public meeting where you don't have control over who moves where, the easiest thing to do may be to bounce a hard light or two off the ceiling (especially if the ceiling color is light). Another approach is to do some kind of **180° lighting**, with lights at two ends or sides of the space. This kind of **cross lighting** means both lights act as key or fill (or front light and backlight), depending on which light your subject is closer to. You will also get modeling on your subjects in a way that will help separate them from the background.

Lighting an observational situation, like a house that people will be walking around in unpredictably, calls for another strategy. A few lights placed in strategic locations, perhaps the kitchen where people tend to gather, or hung on bookshelves and in doorways, may give you enough light while keeping your lighting instruments off-screen. The trick here is to avoid having light stands that might appear behind a subject at an inopportune moment. Clamps and hangers, to keep lights off the floor, are essential. Sometimes a light on a fire escape, or in the yard pointed in through a window to simulate daylight, can also be helpful.

Today, with highly sensitive imaging devices that can offer a very broad range of exposures, a naturalistic strategy that uses only available light is also quite possible. As filmmaker and cinematographer S. Leo Chiang says,

> I don't like using what feels like artificial light in an observational situation. And also, this camera (the Canon C100) does so well in low light that I don't find myself needing to add light. With my previous camera, sometimes I would go into a room and put up a couple of paper lanterns, china balls, just to bring the ambience of the room up. But now I try not to use anything additional if I don't have to.
>
> For indoor situations during the day, I always try to move the subjects out of the spot in front of the window, so I can be in front of the window and they won't be backlit. I have this weird technique. I don't ask people to move, but if someone is standing somewhere I don't want them to be, I will actually go next to them, pretending I'm shooting, and they will move away from me.[2]

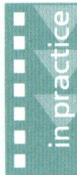

DEALING WITH WINDOWS

One of the most common issues you will face, especially if you are working with available light, is windows. The problem, as you can see in Figure 12.9 (left), is the high contrast ratio between the bright scene outside the window and the face of a subject inside the room. While you could spend time putting artificial light on the subject, or putting ND gels on the window, a quick solution is to simply move the subject away from the window, as in Figure 12.9 (right). This allows you to take advantage of the light from outside, as opposed to fighting it.

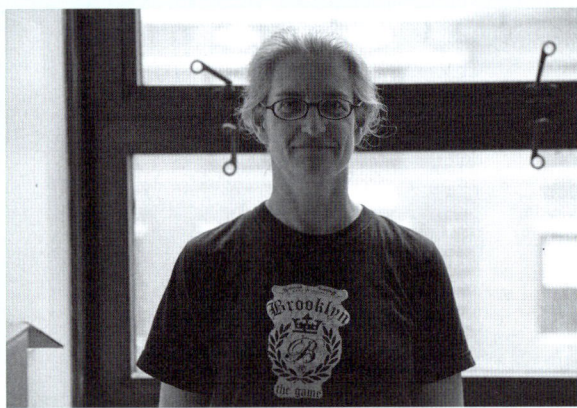 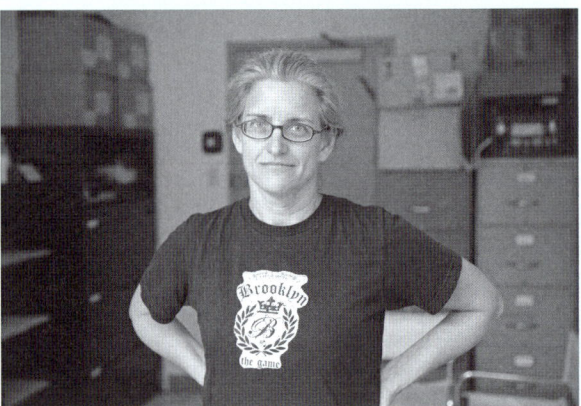

■ **Figure 12.9** If a subject is standing in front of a window (left), it is wise to move them so that the cameraperson has his back to the window and the subject is facing him (right).

SET LIGHTS, SPECIALS, AND PRACTICALS

There are several specialized lights used for lighting interiors, and like other lights we have discussed they are described by their function. **Set lights** are used to light the larger areas of the set: the architecture, furniture, set dressing, and so on. In interview setups, a set light is often used to illuminate part of the background behind the subject.

Specials are low-wattage, unobtrusive lights used to "kick up" the illumination on a specific object or a small area of the frame. For interviews, one of the most common types of specials is an **eye light**, a very small light carefully narrowed by barn doors to just put a bit of sparkle into the eyes of a subject.

Lights that are part of your location, such as household lamps and overhead fixtures, are called **practicals**. In some cases, they can provide useful illumination, but often they are not powerful or controllable enough for a good exposure. At other times, they may be too bright for what you want them to do. A common practice in documentary is to rebulb such lights (with either higher or lower wattages) so they work better in the scene, or to put them on dimmers.

STYLIZED LIGHTING

Stylized (or **expressionistic**) lighting approaches are designed to draw attention to the aesthetic components of the image. Lighting placement, color, and exposure can be unmotivated, or motivated by a logic other than the plausible illumination of the particular physical environment. For example, a stylized lighting scheme might be motivated by the dramatic logic of a scene, by character psychology and point of view, or by the need to create a specific emotional tone or additional thematic layer. Stylized lighting is often associated with nonrealistic film genres, like fantasy films, or films that intentionally invoke an overtly theatrical tone. At first glance, this might seem to put stylized approaches firmly outside of the world of documentary. But documentary is not one thing. In Isaac Julien's

LIGHTING FOR OBSERVATIONAL SHOOTING

In *Casting the First Stone* (1991), a documentary about women on both sides of the "abortion wars," Julie Gustafson worked in her typical highly observational style, an approach that means spending large amounts of time with her subjects over days, weeks, and months. Outdoors she depended on available light, and the fact that she would film in the same situations several times (Figure 12.10). She also makes a point of arriving ready for anything, with her camera and sound gear already rigged to roll. She carries a light with her, typically a Lowel Omni, in a small backpack with its own stand and extension. This means she is literally "ready for anything" whether an exterior or a trip to a dimly lit diner or office. For interiors where she will be returning more than once, such as the home of a subject, she uses a naturalistic lighting strategy. This doesn't mean foregoing lights, however. As she explains,

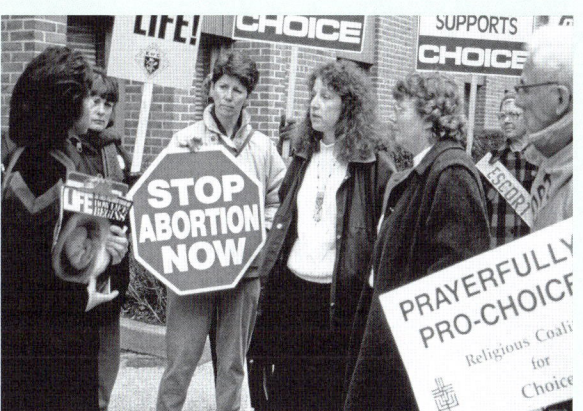

■ **Figure 12.10** *Casting the First Stone* (1991) director Julie Gustafson's observational approach depends on spending large periods of time with her characters in all sorts of situations.

> I do "zone lighting." I go into the location, wherever it is, before I'm going to shoot, and I look around. I observe where most of the movement in the house is. I have a meal with the family, and I see that they tend to be at the stove, the sink, and the table. I ask myself, which side of the table are people most likely to sit, where are they most comfortable? Sometimes you have to ask people, sometimes you can tell by the way things are set up. If there's a lot of stuff on one side of the table, you know they don't sit there. Sometimes someone will say, "That's so and so's favorite chair." And then you say, "Well, where do you usually sit when you talk with him?"
>
> Once you know where people are likely to be, you have to decide where your basic camera stance is going to be, so that you can set what is essentially your key light. And you can set any other fill lights that you might want to use.
>
> I try to see where I can put up two—usually not more—750 to 1000 watt lights. I use a lot of practicals. If there's an overhead light with a porcelain socket, I'll remove the existing bulb and I put a heavier photoflood bulb in it. You have to put diffusion on it, and you have to be careful that it's not too hot, and not throwing a lot of shadows, but the idea is that when the subject goes into the kitchen and flips on the light, it's bright enough for you to get a good image.
>
> Basically, you figure out where people are going to be, and you look for the most attractive ways to set the lights where there's some subtlety, not just a wash of light. I really hate that video look where everybody's nose blends into their face.[3]

Even though 1K lighting units may not be necessary for modern HD cameras, the principle of observation and **zone lighting** strategies remain essential today.

Frantz Fanon: Black Skin, White Mask (1996), about the psychiatrist and postcolonial theorist Frantz Fanon, the filmmaker uses highly expressive lighting for dramatic effect (Figure 12.11). The low-key look, with its many shadows, emphasizes all that is unknown in the human psyche. In more dramatized tableau sequences, light is used to separate and emphasize various parts of the scene. There is much use of cookies to create a "prison" effect of projected bars on the actors in these reenacted sequences.

In addition to the lighting, filters that affect the entire frame can be deployed to create a stylized effect. Barbara Hammer's *Resisting Paradise* (2003) is a richly layered examination of the artist's and individual's role in times of conflict (Figure 12.12). It focuses on Henri

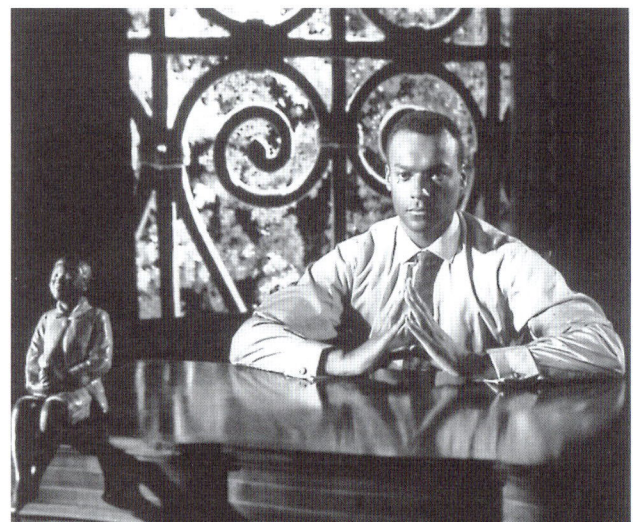

Figure 12.11 In this shot from Franz Fanon: *Black Skin, White Mask*, the expressionistic lighting helps convey a sense of life in the shadows of colonialism.

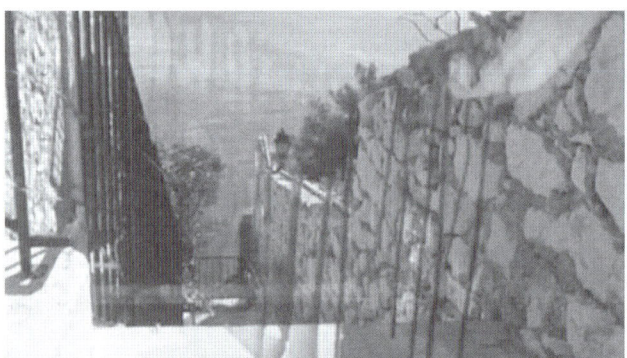

Figure 12.12 Barbara Hammer's *Resisting Paradise* (2003). This exterior, shot through a painted glass surface, gives an impressionist flavor to reality and emphasizes the role of color and light in the mind of the painter.

Matisse and Pierre Bonnard's artistic efforts in the south of France during World War II, while also examining the world of Matisse's family and others in the French Resistance movement. To give a sense of how Matisse, primarily a colorist, saw the world, Hammer actually films scenes through washes of colored paint on glass.

EXTERIOR LIGHTING

Shooting outdoors does not mean simply accepting the light nature has to offer. Here, time of day, weather conditions, and geographical latitude are key factors. When lighting exterior scenes, you must be crafty about the way you control your light sources, whether the sun during daylight hours or available artificial light at night. The following sections offer a few tips.

Location Scouting and Time of Day

When lighting is crucial, take the time to scout your location to figure out what time of day has the best light, and try to schedule your production around that time. Remember, the sun is constantly shifting, so when timing is critical make sure to schedule your call early, allowing for setup time so you'll be ready to shoot when the light is just right. If your schedule doesn't allow flexibility and you are required to shoot whenever you can get the location, you should try to scout the location at the time you anticipate shooting so that you have a good sense for the angle of the sun at the time you will be shooting. Typically, the more directly overhead the sun is, the less flattering it is to subjects, and many filmmakers will try to avoid filming exteriors during the middle of the day. Shooting in the shade can be an option, but the contrast between shady and bright sections of the scene can offer other difficulties.

Check the Weather

To be fully prepared, regularly check a weather service to determine if it will be sunny, partly cloudy, or overcast. You should also be clear about the exact sunrise and sunset times. The degree of cloud cover drastically changes the tone and mood of an exterior image. Overcast days diffuse the sun, creating a soft, high-key look. Depending on the thickness of the cloud cover and the angle of the sun, there can be more or less directionality to this soft source. Sunny days produce a hard and bright light, which creates a very high-contrast situation. Exposures and lighting ratios have to be carefully considered on these days. Partly cloudy conditions, especially on windy days when the sun plays hide-and-seek, are particularly challenging because exposures can shift dramatically from one shot to the next or even within a single take.

Subject and Camera Positions

Just as with shooting indoors using artificial lights, your first lighting consideration when shooting exterior shots is where to place the key light. In this case, you cannot move your key (the sun) to change its directionality, but you *can* move the orientation of your subject and camera to get the angle you desire (Figure 12.9). In a street interview situation, this can mean "clocking" around the person you're speaking with until the sun is in the most

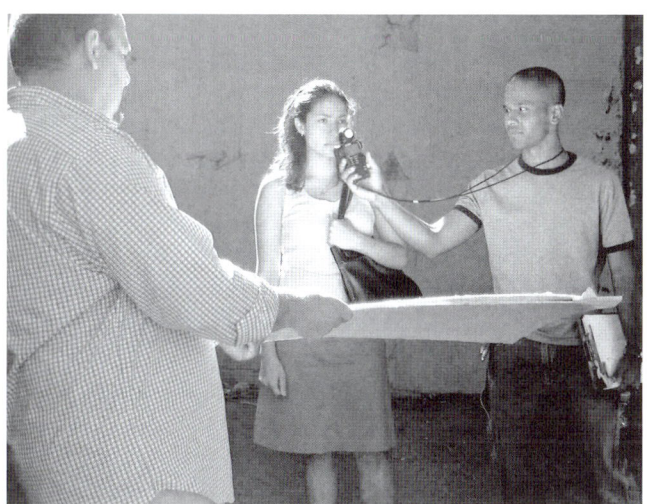 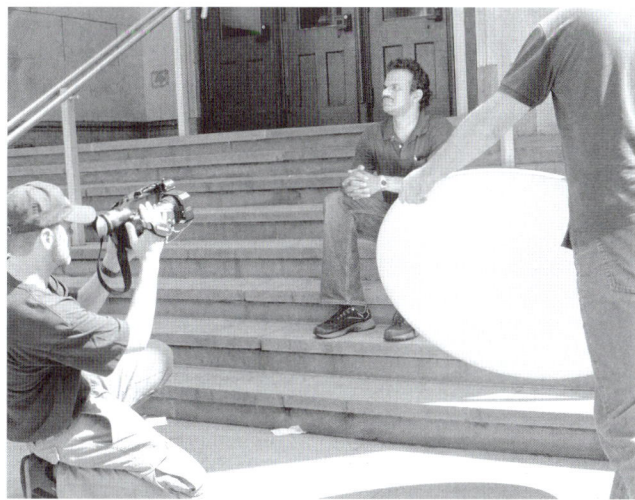

■ **Figure 12.13** Direct sun is used as a hard backlight and also bounced back onto the talent to provide a soft key (left). When subjects are in the shade (right), a reflector can bounce sunlight back onto the subject to get a better exposure and contrast range.

desirable position, usually behind you and illuminating him/her. However, as you rotate around your subject to find the optimum lighting angle, always keep an eye on what this is doing to the background of your composition.

Sun plus Bounced Light

Perhaps the most useful lighting instrument for exterior shooting is the **reflector** (p. 175). If you use the direct sun as your backlight, then you can place a reflector (diffuse side up) opposite the sun, to soften and bounce sunlight to provide a soft key light. A typical placement would put the reflector low on the other side of the camera, filling shadows under the subject's chin and adding eye light. One light source (the sun) thus becomes both a key and backlight (Figure 12.13, left).

Shade plus Bounced Light

When the direct sun is too intense, you can move your subject into the shade of a tree or a building. Heavy shade, however, can flatten out the image. In cases where this is not appropriate, you can always use the mirrorlike specular side of a reflector to bounce some of that hard sunlight onto your subject in the shade to add dimensionality to the image (Figure 12.13, right).

Using a reflector is a common strategy for changing the subject-to-background illumination ratio when you have a subject in shade and there is sun close enough to use as bounce light, making your subject brighter than the shaded area around him. This makes him stand out from the background, or "pop."

Dusk-for-Night

Sometimes you want to shoot images of a location at night, but once night falls there is too much contrast between lit areas of the frame and unlit ones. A solution is to shoot at dusk. Just after the sun has set, there is still ambient light in the sky but streetlights, car headlights, and building lights start to turn on, creating a sense of evening while it is still light enough to shoot. Another concept worth mentioning here is **magic hour**, sometimes called "golden hour." This is a period just before sunset when there is still enough light to film, but the strong shadows of normal daylight are missing. Although it is misnamed, as magic hour may be less than half an hour long, this period offers real cinematic "magic."

Shooting at Night

Given the startling developments in camera sensitivity, it is more possible than ever to actually shoot nighttime scenes using available light and small portable lighting units for

MAKING A DOCUMENTARY IN THE DARK

For her documentary *Border* (2004), Laura Waddington spent months filming Iraqi and Afghani refugees at a Red Cross camp in northern France as they played a nightly game of cat and mouse with police trying to prevent them from hopping on trucks headed for England (Figure 12.14). The exposure levels were at the limits of what the small camera was capable of. Lighting mainly with car headlights, the occasional camera-mounted light, or the light of the dusk sky, Waddington was able to capture images of refugee life, efforts to flee punctuated by moments of police violence. Ultimately, the visual qualities of night shooting became the aesthetic core of the film. As one critic noted, "Shot secretly, the shutter wide open, almost in slow motion, the images create an aesthetic experience of fear, of terror, as if fallen out of a nightmare, peopled with out of focus figures."[4]

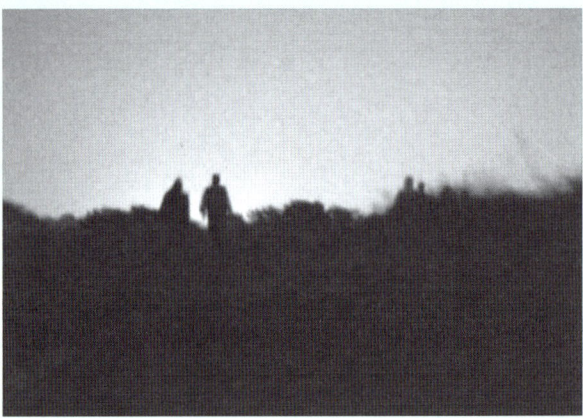

■ **Figure 12.14** Laura Waddington's *Border* (2004) is shot almost entirely at night using a mix of headlights, on-camera light, and available light.

highlights and emphasis. You cannot shoot a scene in a farm field under moonlight and expect to get an exposure, but in an urban context, if you keep your frame tight, shop window lights and bright street lamps can give you acceptable exposures. You can then augment these available sources with small, battery-powered lights. Nighttime shooting is tricky, and tests are especially recommended.

Camera-Mounted Lighting

One common lighting solution for difficult situations, especially those that involve a roving camera and a lot of subject movement, is a small camera-mounted light. In a dark setting with unpredictable lighting a camera-mounted light can make the difference between getting a scene and not. One of these lights will give needed exposure for a face in a nighttime crowd, or an object in an unlit room. However, the "sun-gun" look, reminiscent of the battery-powered lights of a television news crew with its tendency to create hotspots and heavy shadows, may give your shot a crude "newsy" feel you don't want. If you have assistance, a battery-operated portable light held *above* camera height will give a more natural look by dropping shadows toward the bottom of the frame. LEDs, or other lights that have a dimmer, provide a big advantage in camera-mounted situations.

■ EXPOSURE: BEYOND THE BASICS

Now that you are familiar with the issues that come up when lighting a scene, we can turn our attention to slightly more intricate issues related to lighting your scene, and the interpretation of that light through the camera's electronics. We need to look a little closer at how the sensor actually responds to the various light values in a scene, beyond just its general sensitivity. Three additional concepts are essential to a more advanced understanding of lighting and exposure for video: **contrast range**, **characteristic exposure curve**, and **dynamic range**.

Contrast Range

Contrast range, also called "luminance range," is the difference between the brightest and the darkest areas of the scene you are shooting. Remember, "bright" and "dark" consist of a combination of incident light intensity and reflected light values (p. 167). Even in a high-key scene, there will be tremendous variations in light levels. Contrast range can be expressed either in terms of a ratio, or in terms of the difference in f-stops between

CHAPTER 12
Lighting and Exposure—Beyond the Basics

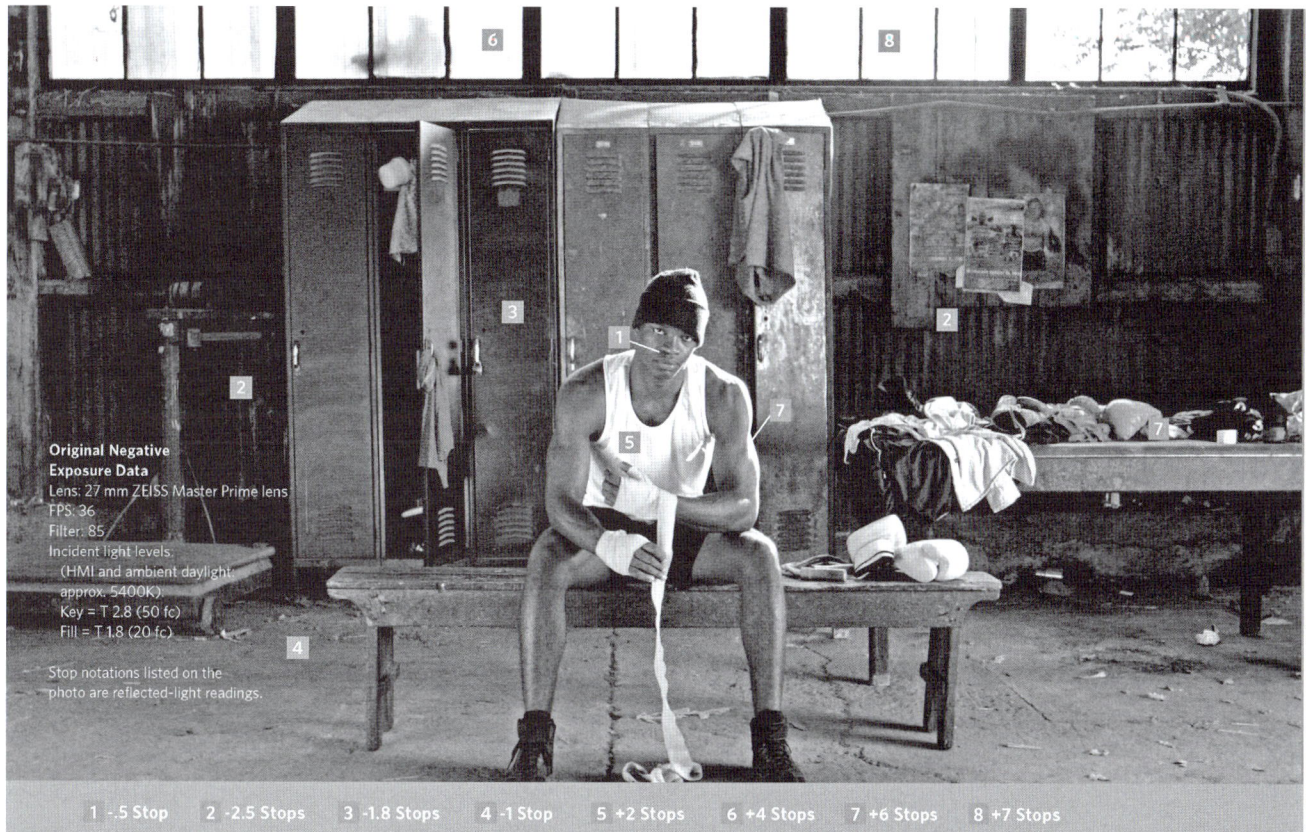

Figure 12.15 Film is still the gold standard for its ability to handle contrast in an image. This scene from Kodak shows the contrast range in f-stops, from the dark wall to the left of the lockers (-2.5 stops) to the bright windows above (+7 stops) of their Vision 3 500T negative stock, a total of 7.5 stops.

the two luminance extremes. For example, it is not unusual to discover, through multiple light meter readings, that a scene's lightest area is 16 times brighter than its darkest area. We can express this as a contrast *ratio* of 16:1 or as a contrast *range* of 4 f-stops. Why? Remember that each stop is a halving or doubling of brightness, so 4 stops from darkest to brightest is 2 × 2 × 2 × 2 = 16. If the darkest area of your image reads 20 foot-candles, then the brightest parts will read 320 foot-candles. It should be noted that four stops is a relatively narrow contrast range. It's not unusual to have a contrast range of 256:1 (8 f-stops) or even more (Figure 12.15). One central question concerns how much of this contrast range your camera's sensor can faithfully reproduce.

Dynamic Range

Broadly defined, **exposure range** (also called **dynamic range**) is the range of luminance values your specific imaging device can render with detail before falling off into complete overexposure (**blown out** or **clipped whites**) or complete underexposure (**crushed blacks**), where no image detail is visible. Exposure range is expressed in terms of the range of f-stops within which the imaging device will see detail. It is often the case that the contrast range of a scene exceeds the exposure range of your imaging device, which means that visual detail will be lost either in the brightest or darkest parts of your scene, or both. Cameras vary in their ability to render detail in bright or dark areas of the image. For example, an inexpensive consumer video camera can handle 7 or 8 stops, while a higher-end camera like Sony's A7S can handle about 12 stops. So if you want to truly control your image, it's important to know both the contrast range of the scene you are shooting and the ability of your imaging device to render those exposure values. Once you know these facts, you can use camera controls and lighting to selectively bring areas of your scene into or out of the exposure range of your imaging device to create visual emphasis and interest.

In addition to the camera's ability to record a broad range of light levels, there is its ability to monitor those levels. In many cameras, the viewfinder, particularly if it is a flip-out LCD viewscreen, deals with contrast poorly. For this reason, many cinematographers will use a good-quality field monitor to give a better idea of what is going on with the lighting.

Shooting with Dynamic Range in Mind

As we've suggested, dynamic range refers to the camera's ability to reproduce light and dark aspects of a scene. When looking at a real situation, you will have to make choices about what is important to you in the scene. Do you care about the shadow detail, like the folds in a dark garment, or the curls in someone's dark hair? If so, you can open up your aperture and let the highlights in the scene be overexposed. If what is happening in the brighter parts of the image are important to you, like how the clouds look in the sky, then you can stop down and sacrifice the detail in the shadow areas.

Although there are specific limits to what a particular camera can do, the ability of sensors to handle wide dynamic range is improving regularly. The gold standard historically was film, where the dynamic range (expressed as "latitude") could be as high as 14 stops. Because of the demand for digital cinematography to replace film, many manufacturers offer ways to extend the dynamic range of their video cameras. We will explore some of these options below.

Characteristic Curves and Gamma

In addition to the range the camera can handle, there are significant differences in the ways different cameras reproduce the light within that range. For example, two cameras might have the same range of 8 stops, but respond quite differently. That difference is represented graphically in the **characteristic curve** (Figure 12.16). In a sense, the characteristic curve represents a camera's personality, how the sensor responds to the light hitting it. Imagine a medium level gray that a camera sees. It can represent that gray as it is, or as a bit darker or lighter. Another camera will respond differently. These differences

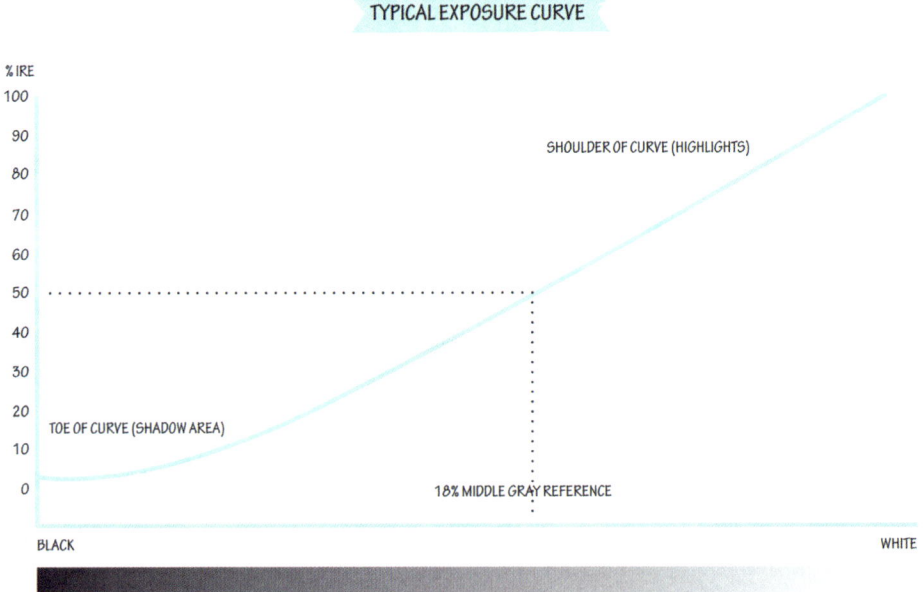

■ **Figure 12.16** This figure shows a characteristic curve for a video image. The y-axis represents the light in the scene from dark on the left through a medium 18 percent gray to a bright 100 percent white on the right. This represents the input, or the light entering the camera. On the x- (horizontal) axis you can see the output, the amount of luminance in IRE units generated by the camera in response to this incoming light. The slight curve at the bottom of the image is the "toe" and indicates that the shadow detail falls off gently. The lack of a curve at the top or white end suggests that there will be no emphasis on detail in the white part of the exposure curve.

in characteristic curve mean that one camera may offer more shades of gray at the dark end, adding shadow detail, while another may show more of the differences in highlights. This can be a bit complicated at first, and it is much easier to visualize when you actually start comparing cameras.

In many cameras, you can influence the characteristic curve of the camera's imaging by changing settings, most notably the **gamma**. Gamma represents the capacity of an imager to differentiate between the various luminance tonalities (shades of gray) in a scene and is represented by the angle of the straight-line portion of the curve—in other words, the steepness of the slope. The ideal angle for a straight line would be a perfect 45°, meaning a perfectly proportional increase in density to exposure. This would faithfully duplicate all of the subtle shifts in the gray scale (Figure 12.17). However, the human eye does not work the way a video sensor does, so a "perfect curve" doesn't necessarily look pleasing to the viewer.

Changing your camera's gamma setting allows you to choose which part of the curve you want to expand or compress. Canon, for example, offers nine different gamma settings. Cine 1 "softens the contrast in darker regions and emphasizes gradation changes in lighter regions," while Cine 3 provides a "stronger contrast between light and dark regions, and greater emphasis on black gradation changes."

Black Stretch, Knee, and Log Gamma
An additional detail of the characteristic curve that is greatly affected by the angle of the curve slope in the **toe** (the dark end of the curve) and the **shoulder** (the bright end). Video circuitry creates a signal with no toe and no shoulder, which means a hard clipping of **whites** and an abrupt plunge into inky blacks when the exposure approaches the extremes of under- and overexposure. Without the curved toe and shoulder at the ends of the exposure limits of the imaging device, the video image not only fails to duplicate the film's gradual tapering off of detail toward total black or total white, but it also loses out on a few stops of usable exposure range.

Black stretch is a setting that can extend the sensor's sensitivity in the darkest parts of the image so that you

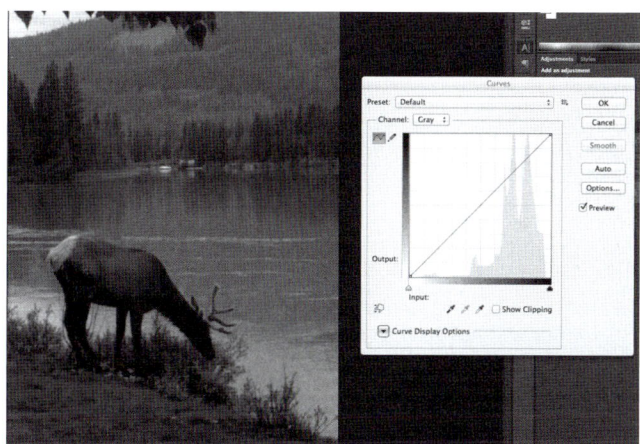

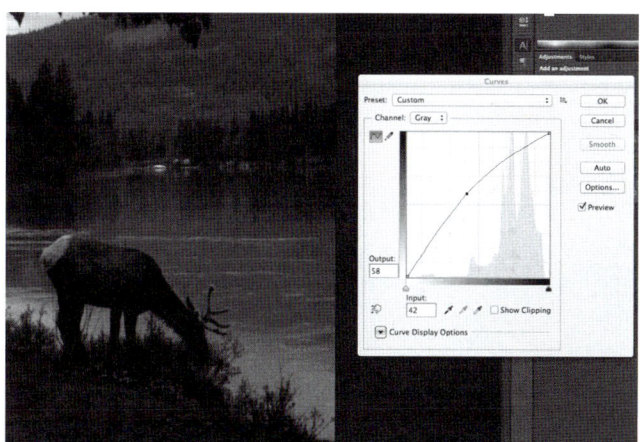

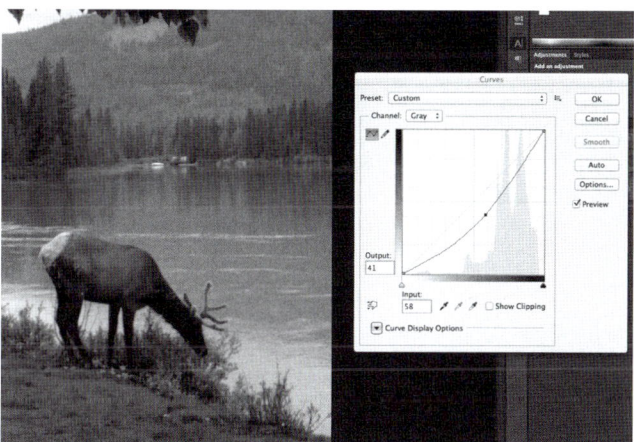

■ **Figure 12.17** Here the same still image is shown with no changes in gamma (top), with a gamma curve that minimizes contrast in the midrange (middle) and one that emphasizes contrast (bottom). The graph next to the picture represents the characteristic curve for each image.

are able to see somewhat more detail in the shadow areas of the shot. Engaging black stretch is the equivalent of creating a "toe" in the characteristic curve. You will see a little taper to the extreme underexposures, which means that things at the darker end of the light range fade off gently, offering more shadow detail, and you gain about one stop at the bottom end. Black stretch is like a video gain function that selectively boosts only the darkest portions of the image. As with video gain, you need to be careful that you don't overdo black stretch because you can introduce video noise into an area that was otherwise clean, or you can create **blacks** that are not rich (called **milky blacks**) in all portions of your image that are black. Some of the work of black stretch can be more accurately and safely accomplished in two ways: careful lighting of the dark areas of the image (when you have lights) so that you bring those areas into your dynamic range or through postproduction color correction (pp. 364–365).

Video is especially vulnerable to overexposures that commonly show up in two circumstances: highlights on prominent areas of a subject that reflect the key light, like cheekbones or foreheads, and in situations of extreme contrast ratio, like bright windows visible in a dark interior location. This overexposure, called **clipping**, can be avoided by the careful use of **zebras** (Chapter 11), but even without overexposure, bright highlights can cause an extreme and uneven loss of color saturation and detail in the image. **Video knee** is a signal compression adjustment that is the equivalent of creating a "shoulder" in the signal's response to intense exposures. Many HD cameras allow for manual setting of the upper signal levels (near the ultimate white clip level), allowing more detail to be visible as you approach total overexposure. Attenuation of extreme white levels can be set at 80 percent (low), 90 percent (mid), and 100 percent (high). The earlier you set knee to kick in, the more detail you'll see in your highlights. The drawback is that setting knee at 80 percent can make your whites look gray. Many cameras now have an easily accessible automatic pre-knee setting, called **auto-knee** (also called **auto highlight control**), designed to give you maximum detail depending on the highlight values of the particular image in the frame. Auto-knee is one of the few auto settings that you might consider leaving on while you shoot, but it works best with static frames. A shot that pans across bright areas will reveal the processor adjusting as it detects highlights and corrects on the fly.

As mentioned above, many cameras now offer gamma settings that give video a more filmic look by softening the top and bottom of the exposure curves, meaning that the camera's exposure eases into shadow and highlight areas. One of the most common signal tweaking functions is **CineGamma**. CineGamma (aka Cine-like, Cinematone, or Film Rec) electronically flattens the straight-line portion of the video signal's characteristic curve and introduces a shoulder to the highlight areas. This accomplishes two things simultaneously: it slightly extends the dynamic range of the camera, and reduces the contrast of the image, thus ameliorating the video's "crispy" electronic look. With CineGamma, you'll see more detail in the shadows and highlights. The drawback of this setting is that the overall reduced contrast of the image can, in some cases, create washed out midtones and colors (Figure 12.18).

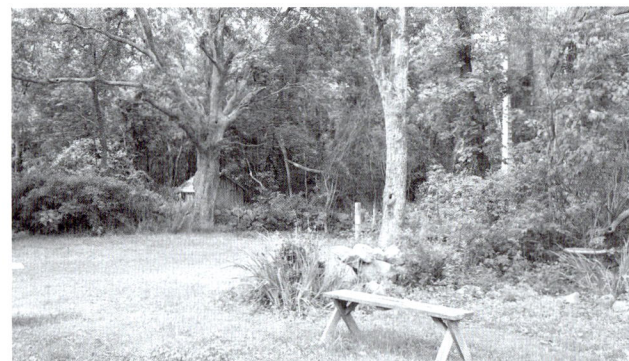
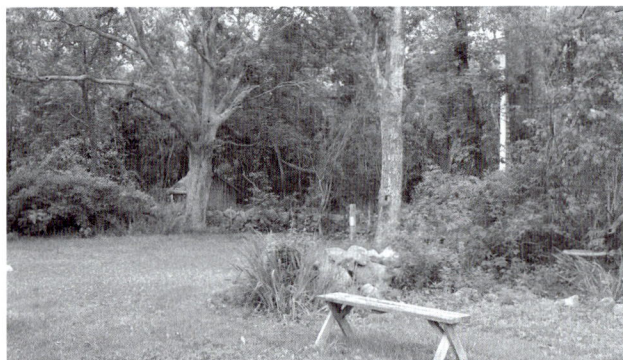
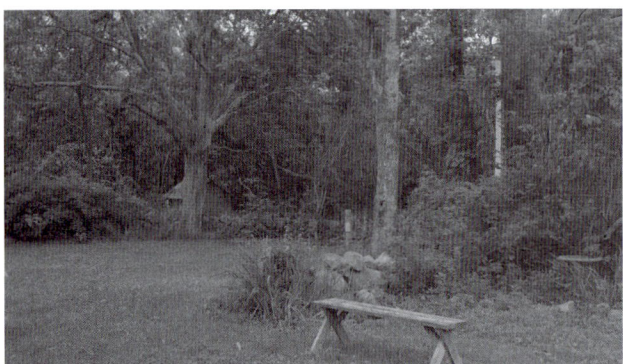

■ **Figure 12.18** This woodsy yard is represented in three of the different gamma modes available on the Canon C100. The top image is standard mode, which looks fine but risks burning out the highlights, such as those on the bench in the foreground. The middle image was shot with Wide DR to add several stops to the exposure range. The image looks darker here, but has much more picture information in the highlights. The bottom image was shot in the Canon Log mode, creating an image that looks murky to the eye, but will respond well to color grading in postproduction.

Log gamma settings stretch the dynamic range of the image to the maximum the sensor is capable of, which can mean going from 10 or 11 to 12 or more stops (Figure 12.19). The resulting image has lots of highlight and shadow detail, but looks flat and quite unnatural until it is corrected in postproduction. In fact, another name for this approach is **shooting flat**. Shooting with log gamma means that your workflow in postproduction will have to include **color grading** (Chapter 22). For documentary work, one alternative is an **extended dynamic range** setting (Wide DR in this case), available on some cameras, that demands less work in postproduction (Figure 12.18, middle).

Always use caution and moderation when you use any of these settings. Altering the electronic signal of your camera can have unintended consequences. If you're interested in using black stretch, video-knee, or Cine-Gamma, make sure you shoot tests before going into production. Also remember that adjusting the signal is not a substitute for careful, sensitive, and creative attention to lighting and exposure.

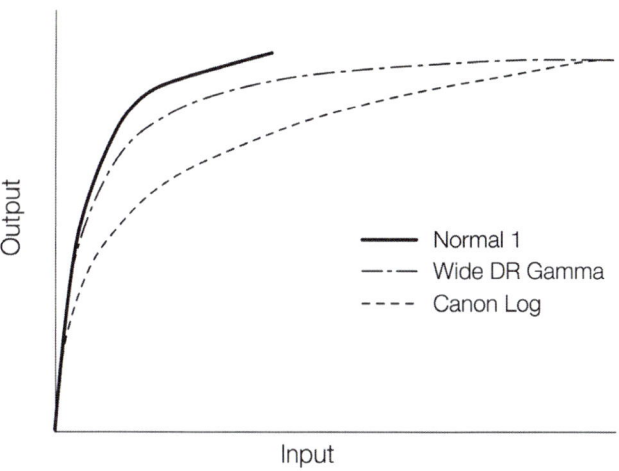

■ **Figure 12.19** Log gamma (Canon Log in this case). Like many manufacturers, Canon offers two options to create a broader exposure range. Wide DR and Canon Log modes offer several extra f-stops, indicated by the longer curves.

Color Settings

Video cameras also typically have a color "look." People will argue about the warmth of one camera's image vs the naturalness of another. Most cameras now have a variety of color settings, which affect how the camera reproduces color. A discussion of these is outside the scope of this book, but if you have a particular idea about color reproduction, you should investigate these settings on your camera.

■ CONCLUSION

As you've seen, documentary lighting isn't just a matter of throwing light onto a scene so that we can make out the physical subject. Lighting is communicating visual ideas and inflecting the film with a mood, a tone, and a visual context. The approaches we've explored in this chapter should give you a solid sense of how you can get started in creating the lighting approach that best suits the story you are telling.

… CHAPTER 13

Sound Basics and Equipment

> *The cinematic or televisual experience is as sensuous aurally as it is visually. Just as the picture transforms the spectator's experience of the sound, the sound transforms the spectator's experience of the picture.*
> **Ilisa Barbash and Lucien Taylor, *Cross-Cultural Filmmaking*[1]**

THE IMPORTANCE OF SOUND

It is an unfortunate reality that the visual aspects of film and video are given priority over the sound aspects in most filmmakers' minds, and in most film schools. We call it "film school," after all, and not "sound school." Perhaps not surprisingly, then, sound is often a blind spot for filmmakers, especially those just starting out. All too often, a lot of time, money, and preparation go into the production of the images, but filmmakers begin to think seriously about sound only after they try to work with the terrible audio they recorded during production. Yet, in the final experience of watching a documentary, viewers will forgive an out-of-focus or shaky image much more easily than a soundtrack with a loud buzz or inaudible dialogue. In addition, a well-constructed soundtrack can do much more than convey content. Good sound adds tone and mood, contributes information about a place, and can foreshadow events and accentuate their impact. Like a well-lit image, good sound can add perspective and depth to your shots and scenes.

A documentary soundtrack is made up of many elements (Chapter 21). Some, like narration and musical score, are recorded after production when editing is underway. Many of the most critical sound elements of a documentary, however, are recorded on location while you are filming your images. These include **synchronous sound**, **wild sound**, and **ambient sound**. Capturing these sounds accurately is extremely important, and you often only have one chance to get it right. Despite the prevalent idea that you can "fix it in post," correcting problems in your recorded sound is expensive and the results are often far from what you would have gotten if you had recorded it right in the first place. The production sound team, those people who record sound in the field, are therefore the unsung heroes of the documentary production world. When they do their job perfectly, no one notices them; when the sound is bad, they are cursed. Good sound people are invaluable, and smart filmmakers understand that getting clean sound during production means a stronger sound design, more creative options in editing, and time and money saved.

SOUND RECORDING TODAY

The digital revolution has not revolved around the shooting, editing, and presentation of images alone. Since the beginning of the twenty-first century, there has been a veritable sea change in the tools and techniques of recording, mixing, and replaying audio as well. Sound recordists have gone from recording sound separate from the camera on magnetic tape, to recording an analog and then digital signal in-camera, to recording separate sound again on tiny cards in digital audio recorders!

On the reception end, there was a time when distribution on video or through broadcast TV meant that people would be listening to your film on little 3-inch built-in speakers. Today people are fast equipping their home theater units with super-high-fidelity, digital **surround sound** audio.

Whatever the changes in technology and equipment, though, the end goal is the same: to gather the cleanest and most accurate possible sound in the field during production, isolating the **signal**, the sounds we want to hear, from the sounds we don't, the **noise**. In order to do that, you need to understand what sound is, and how it behaves under various conditions.

UNDERSTANDING SOUND

Picture the way a pebble thrown into a pond creates waves that ripple out in concentric circles. Similarly, a **sound wave** is a pressure wave, consisting of an alternating pattern of high pressure (**compression**) and low pressure (**rarefaction**), that travels through the air (or water, for that matter). The vibrating source of this pressure can be a guitar string, the contact between a baseball and a bat, or human vocal chords. These sound waves are eventually received by some sensitive membrane, like an eardrum or microphone diaphragm, which duplicates the vibration patterns of the original source.

There are four basic properties of sound that are essential to understanding audio and the techniques of microphone placement and recording for documentary production:
- Pitch (frequency)
- Loudness (amplitude)
- Quality (timbre)
- Velocity (speed)

We plot these sound wave characteristics on the graphs shown in Figure 13.1. The common sine wave graph measures the compression of the air molecules caused by a particular sound. With this graph, we are able to see certain properties of any sound.

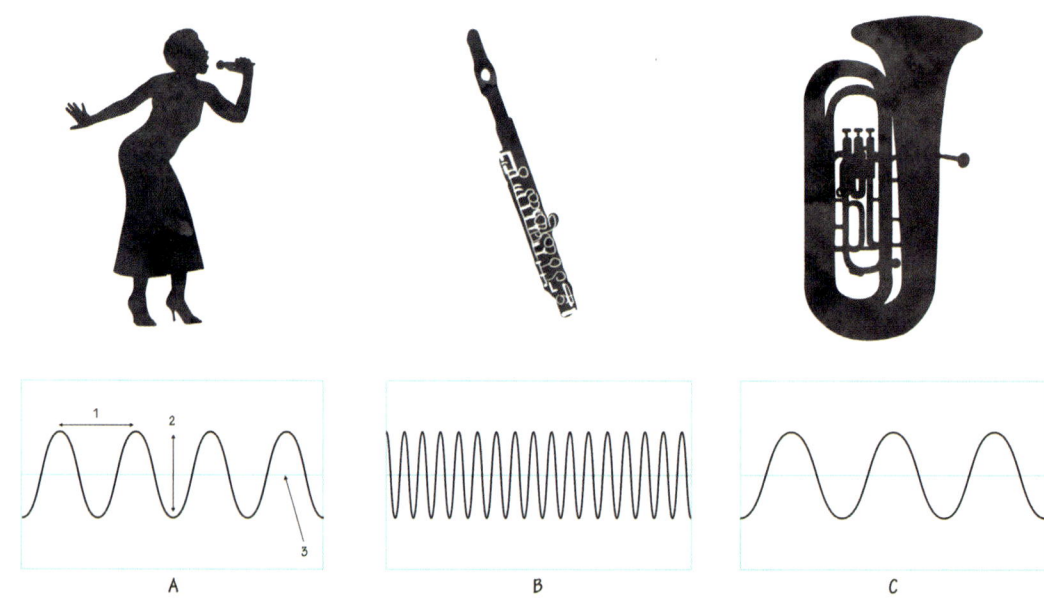

■ **Figure 13.1** A simple sound can be understood in terms of its wavelength (1), its amplitude (2), and the degree to which it deviates from normal air pressure (3). In terms of wavelength (1), the number of waves per second determines the pitch of a sound. The human voice has midrange frequencies ranging from 150 Hz to 2,000 Hz (A). A piccolo can reach a frequency of 5,200 Hz (B), and a tuba can create sounds as low as 45 Hz (C).

Frequency (Pitch)

We all know that certain sounds are "high," like a kettle whistling, or "low," like the rumble of thunder. These properties of sound are commonly referred to as its **pitch**, and are caused by the **wavelength**, or the **frequency**, of the sound waves. Wavelength and frequency are two ways of measuring the same basic phenomenon: the length of one cycle, from peak to peak. A wavelength is plotted from one highest pressure point to the next highest pressure point. The number of these waves that pass a fixed point over the course of one second is the measure of the frequency of the sound wave. This measure of **cycles per second** is referred to as **Hertz (Hz)** and is measured along the graph's x-axis. Sound waves travel in fairly consistent **wave cycles**, meaning that the pitch doesn't change much even as sounds get quieter over distance.

A sound that generates 10,000 wave cycles every second has a frequency of 10,000 Hz, also written as 10 kiloHz, or 10 kHz. The fewer the cycles per second, the lower the pitch of a sound; the more the cycles per second, the higher the pitch (Figure 13.1).

Neither the human ear nor a microphone can perceive all sound frequencies. The range of detectable pitches for a given apparatus or organ is called its **frequency range**. An average, healthy human ear can distinguish pitches from 25 Hz to 20 kHz. Dogs can hear frequencies beyond 20 kHz (this is why they can hear high-pitched dog whistles that humans cannot). The frequency range that a microphone or a sound recorder can duplicate in a useful way is a common measure of equipment quality, and is called its **frequency response**. In terms of microphones, a typical "mic" used by a news reporter in the field would have a much more limited frequency response than one used to record an orchestra.

Amplitude (Loudness)

Each peak high and low pressure point has a specific height, or **amplitude,** which is a measure of the **loudness** of a sound and is measured on the graph's y-axis (Figure 13.1). The higher the amplitude peak, the greater the displacement pressure of the sound wave, and the louder the sound. Loudness is measured in **decibels (dB)**. Because the human ear can register a vast range of loudness levels, the decibel scale is a logarithmic one. We won't go into the complexities of logarithms here, but basically this means that a small adjustment in dB can be reflected in a huge change in loudness. Another way of looking at it is that it takes an increase of 3 dB to double the loudness of a sound, and a decrease of 3 dB to halve loudness of a sound. Note that the actual decibel measurement is a pressure measurement, but the result, a measure of what we hear, is subjective.

The loudness range that the human ear can distinguish falls between the **threshold of hearing** (0 dB) on the lower end and the **threshold of pain** (120 dB) on the upper end. A normal conversational tone is approximately 55 dB. A whisper is around 25 dB and a scream is around 75 dB. At 150 dB, eardrums will rupture. In most recording situations, the loudness of your source fluctuates. Sometimes the range between the quietest and loudest sounds is minor, while at other times it can be extreme. For example, listen to the opening of Richard Strauss' symphonic tone poem *Also Sprach Zarathustra*, Op. 30 (which was used in Kubrick's *2001: A Space Odyssey*). The piece begins with the softest, barely audible drone of the double basses and builds to an all-out, full orchestra fortissimo—led by crashing cymbals, blaring horns, and pounding tympani—in only a minute and a half! The range of different loudness levels in a scene, or musical sequence, is referred to as its **dynamic range**. *Also Sprach Zarathustra* has an extremely wide dynamic range. Comparatively, a song like the White Stripes' *Fell in Love with a Girl* has a narrow dynamic range because it remains at the same loudness level throughout. A conversation that goes from a whisper to screaming has a wide dynamic range, whereas a politician's speech delivered in a monotone has a narrow dynamic range. Wide dynamic ranges can be challenging for both the sound recordist and the recording equipment.

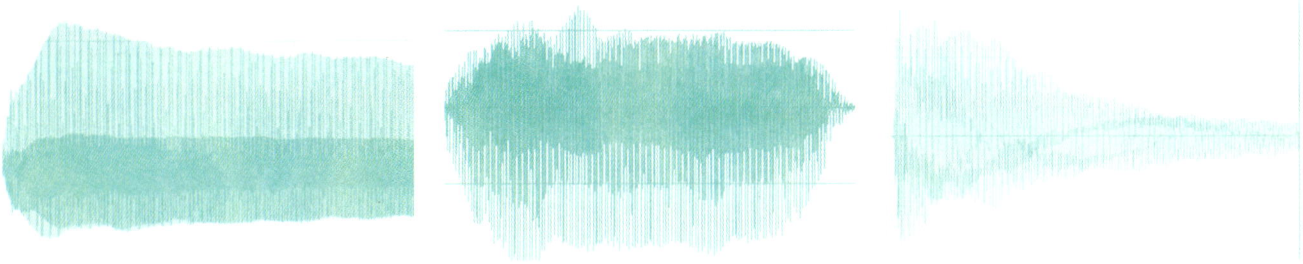

■ **Figure 13.2** Waveforms for a piano playing middle C (left), a violin playing middle C (center), and a human voice singing middle C (right).

Inverse Square Law

The amplitude of a sound wave diminishes according to the **inverse square law** as it travels through space, which means that the intensity of a given sound decreases by the square of its distance from the sound source. This is the same law that governs the drop-off of light intensity as one moves away from the source of illumination (Figure 11.5). You can measure it by the same rule of thumb: doubling the distance from the source results in the loudness diminishing four times, and halving the distance from your source will increase the loudness four times. Knowing that sound intensity drops off quickly as one moves a microphone away from the audio source is essential when determining microphone placement.

Quality (Timbre)

The sound waves shown in Figure 13.1 represent pure, electronically generated tones with no character or aberrations. The waves of sounds from the real world are not quite so uniform, as they lack a smooth curve and perfectly symmetrical peaks and dips. Most naturally occurring sound waves include characteristic irregularities in the overall shape, which dictate the particular quality of that sound.

The central and dominant shape of the wave is called the **fundamental tone**, but every fundamental tone also resonates with a series of imperfections and coinciding waves that are known as **overtones** and **harmonics**. These elements constitute the **timbre** of a sound, its unique tonal composition and characteristics of that sound (its richness, harshness, or resonance, for example). Timbre allows us to easily distinguish different instruments playing the same note. For example, middle C on a piano sounds quite different from middle C played on a trumpet, or on a guitar, or when sung by a human voice (Figure 13.2).

Velocity

As a wave that travels through air, sound has both directionality and speed. At a temperature of 60 degrees, the **speed of sound** is 1,117 feet per second (about 762 mph). This is very slow compared to the speed of light (which is 983,571,056 feet per second). This is why, when you're watching a fireworks display, you see the big flash of light first and hear the boom of the explosion seconds later.

■ PRODUCTION SOUND

There are several names for it—**production sound**, field recording, and audio gathering—but the name of the game is the same: get the best quality sound possible. The sound team on a documentary is generally just one person, and their responsibility is to get as clean and strong a sound recording as possible, and to keep the different types of sounds from a location separate so you can combine them later to your taste. Getting great production sound means understanding the physics of sound, knowing your equipment, and practicing good recording technique (Chapter 14).

Production sound breaks down into two rough categories: **synchronous sound (sync sound)** and **wild sound** (also called **nonsync sound**).

Sync Sound

Sync sound is recorded with the image, so sound and picture correspond with frame accuracy, and are said to be **in sync** (Figure 13.3). Sync sound could be an interview, a conversation between people at a dinner table, or the sound of a door closing—anything in which the sound emanating from the scene is recorded simultaneously with the picture.

Sync sound can be recorded using a **single-system** or a **double-system** process. In single-system, audio and video are gathered at the same time, with the same apparatus (the camcorder), and are recorded in sync on the same media (videotape or memory card). In **double-system** recording, sound is recorded on a separate audio recorder and combined with the picture in postproduction.

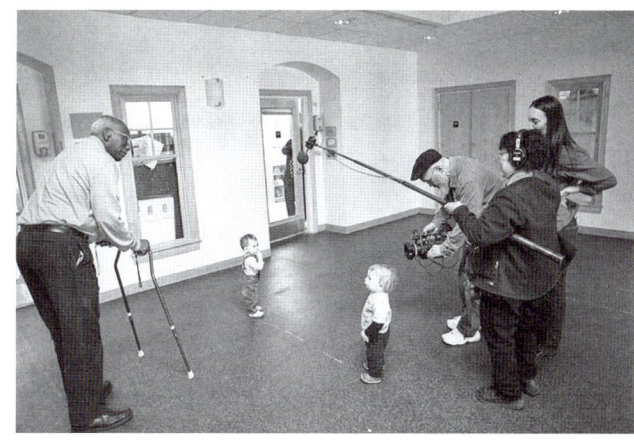

■ **Figure 13.3** The documentary sound crew often consists of one person who is in charge of recording sync sound. Here, sound recordist JT Takagi is working with Director of Photography Michael Chin and Director Megan Mylan on the short documentary *My Little Friends* (2013). Photo courtesy of Principe Productions/PrincipeProductions.com.

Most digital video cameras have the capability to record both audio and video, ensuring that sound and picture are automatically and always in sync. Film, on the other hand, is a double-system sound medium, meaning the film camera records the image, and a separate sound recorder gathers the audio. Historically, documentarians working in video used single-system, and the sound recordist would send the audio signal to the camera via a **breakaway cable** (Figure 13.4, left). Double-system is now used frequently with DSLR shooting (Figure 13.4, right) because of the audio limitations of many DSLR cameras. DSLRs, created for the consumer market, are equipped with miniplug connectors for microphone inputs. These are notoriously unreliable, as well as **unbalanced** (and therefore more prone to interference), and are replaced on more professional cameras with the sturdier XLR inputs.

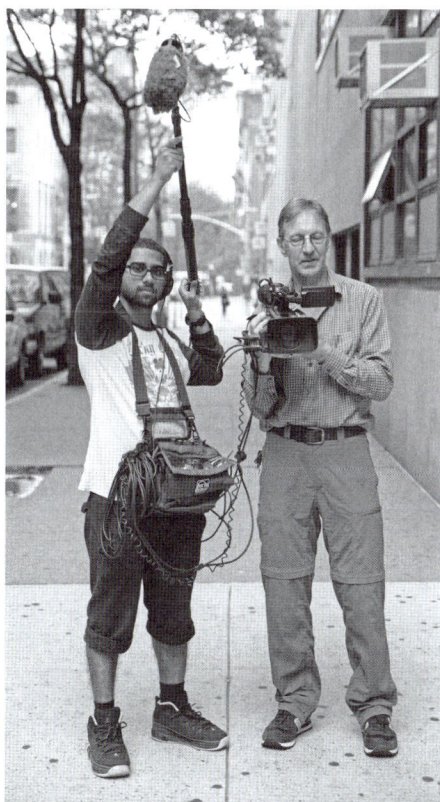
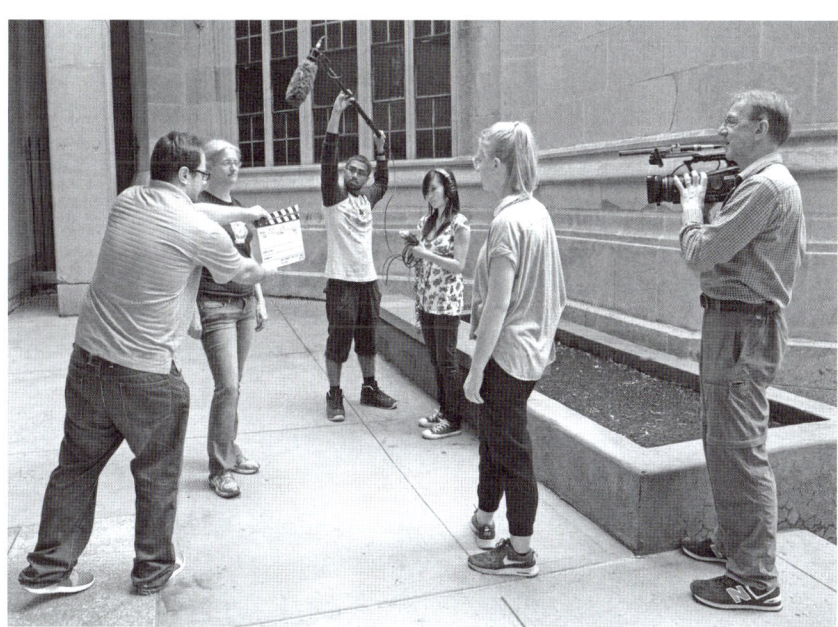

■ **Figure 13.4** In single-system recording (left), cables connect the audio and video equipment. With double system sound (right), the audio recorder is separate from the camera. Because the sound recorder and camera work independently, a slate is used so that picture and sound can be synced in postproduction.

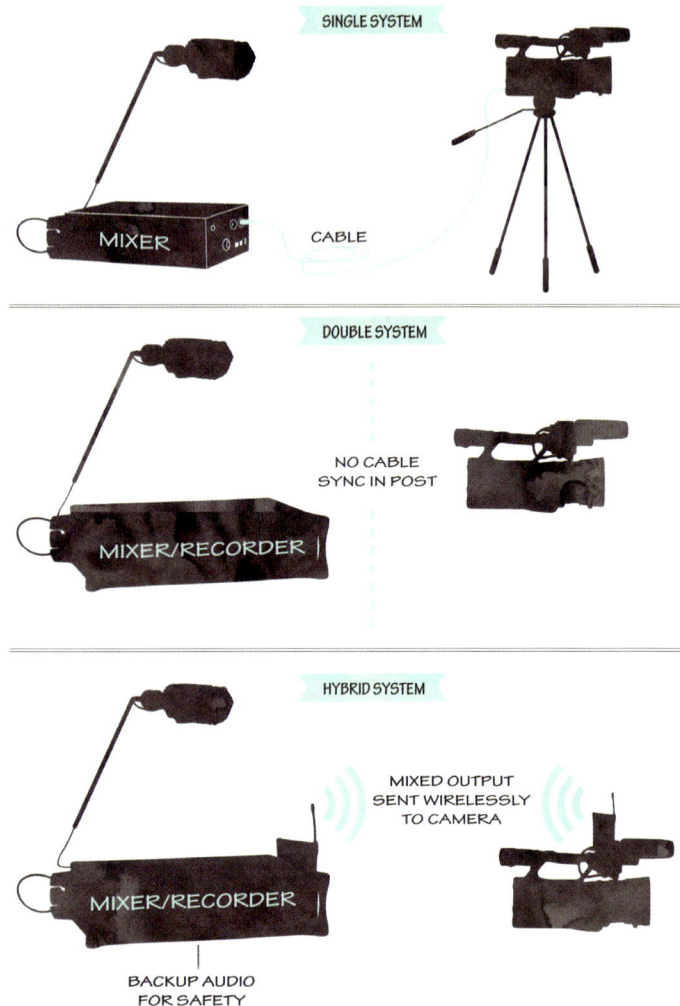

■ **Figure 13.5** Audio signal path for various documentary sync sound recording setups.

In documentary practice today, the line between single- and double-system sound is further blurred by the use of wireless technology. To avoid having the camera and sound recordist connected by an unwieldy cable, many sound recordists send the signal from their portable field mixer or recorder (p. 219) to the camera using wireless technology. This is single-system sound, but because they will usually run a backup digital audio recorder as well, it can be considered a hybrid setup (Figure 13.5).

Double-system sound always requires the additional step of syncing audio to the picture in post-production. This has traditionally been done through the use of a **slate**. The slate is used to create a one-frame, easily identifiable reference "moment" with which to line up the picture and sound. That moment is the sharp closing of the slate, which is recorded by the camera and the audio recorder at the beginning of every take. Later, in your **nonlinear editing system** (NLE), it is easy to find the exact frame where the slate closes. Then, you simply line up the clap image with the corresponding audio and everything after that point, for that take, should be in sync (Figure 13.6). There is more on syncing picture and sound in Chapter 17.

Many professional audio recordists prefer to work double-system because, as mentioned earlier, they are freed from having to be connected with the camera by a cable. Many work with time code-equipped digital audio recorders, like the Sound Devices 633 field mixer/multi-track digital audio recorder. By syncing (or **jamming**) the **time code** of their recorders with the time code on the camera at the beginning of the shoot, the picture and sound can be easily synchronized in the editing room.

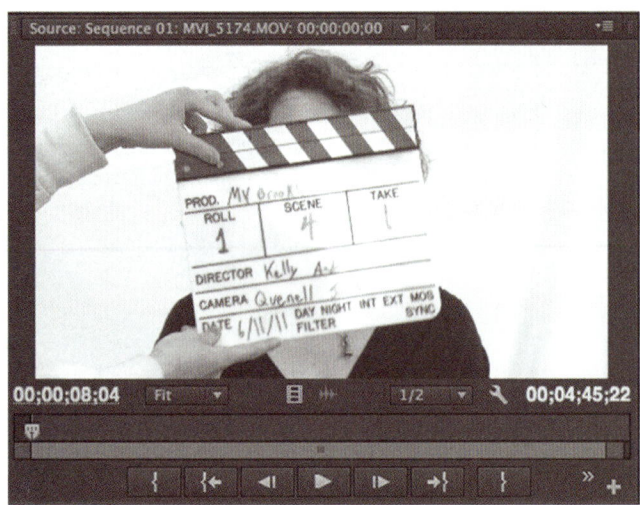
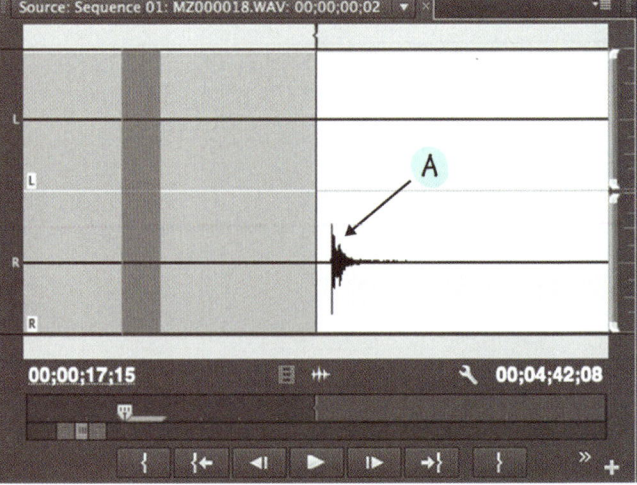

■ **Figure 13.6** A properly shot and recorded slate is the perfect audiovisual point of reference in postproduction. The frame where the slate is clapped is marked in the video file (left), and then in the sound file (A). The clips can then be merged into a new clip with video and audio in sync.

For students and others without budgets for expensive recorders and wireless transmission systems, shooting single-system is still safer and quite common. If at all possible, use a **breakaway cable** that sends two channels of audio to the camera and then brings the output of the camera back to the sound person so they can monitor the recorded signal through headphones (Figure 13.7).

There are advantages and disadvantages to shooting single- or double-system sound. With single-system, the difficulties of slating and syncing the audio with the picture in postproduction are avoided. On the other hand, single-system requires that the sound recordist be physically connected with the cameraperson via a cable (or use an expensive wireless transmission system). In addition, single-system means that you need to be mindful of the input levels on the camera itself. Unless you are working with a **portable field mixer** (pp. 219–220), this places an additional burden on the cameraperson, whose main job is to be concentrating on the image (not the audio levels).

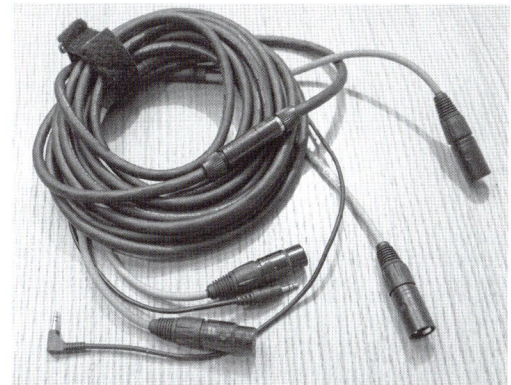

■ **Figure 13.7** A breakaway cable allows two channels of audio to travel from a field mixer into the camera, and brings an audio signal back so the sound recordist can monitor the output of the camera. A "quick release" connector allows the sound recordist to separate quickly from the camera operator.

Double-system recording allows the sound person more mobility in finding the best microphone placement, and to set their own **recording levels** (Chapter 14). Syncing sound in postproduction is also becoming easier because of software programs, like Singular Software's PluralEyes, that allow for rapid and fairly mechanical syncing of sound and picture.

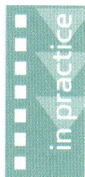

■ CHANGING SOUND RECORDING SETUPS

Daniel Brooks (Figure 13.8) is a sound recordist who has worked on more than 100 documentaries and TV programs over the past 25 years. He summarizes the history of double- and single-system recording this way:

> When I started (in the 1980s) we still had Nagras with open reel magnetic tape, and you could only record 11 or 13 minutes on a 5-inch reel, and then you had to change it. And every time you started and stopped you had to sync with the camera. It was really not conducive for any sort of vérité or reality shooting because you had these very small windows. With video it became single-system, and we sound people became the "pull-toys" of the camera operators because we were cable-connected to them. Now wireless mic technology has gotten much better and we are using radio transmitters and receivers to send the sound to the camera, while recording backup in audio recorders we carry on us. So we've gone back to double-system, which is very exciting for me because it allows sound to not be attached to the camera, and to go where the sound is, instead of where the camera is. Now I can roll when I hear something good, and I don't have to run over the camera person and say "Roll!" and have him say, "I'm still focusing, I'm not ready yet." If I have the great soundbite recorded the editor can cover it with a cutaway, and build a scene around it. It's great having the ability to be autonomous.[2]

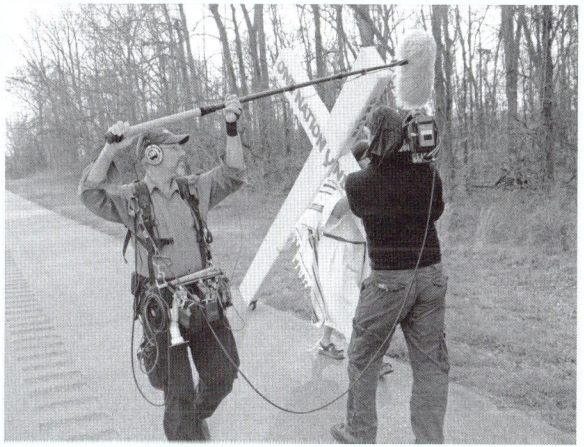

■ **Figure 13.8** Sound recordist Daniel Brooks carries a six-channel mixer/recorder on a harness, with wireless mics and a shotgun on a boom. Here he is shown shooting single-system sound on location for Holly Hardman's *Good People Go to Hell, Saved People Go to Heaven* (2013).

Wild Sound

Wild sound is audio that is recorded on location, but not simultaneously with the picture. The most common type of wild sound recorded on a documentary shoot is **room tone**, which is the **ambient sound** of a location when nobody is talking (Chapter 14). Another type of wild sound is **wild sound effects**. Often when recording dialogue or interviews, sound recordists will try and create the quietest environment possible in order to get the "cleanest" recording of the dialogue. Later, they will record sounds from the environment that can be added in to help build a richer, more complex soundtrack. JT Takagi, a filmmaker and sound recordist who works with Third World Newsreel (a progressive alternative media center that trains, distributes and produces media by and about people of color and social justice issues) explains:

> *Say we're shooting a family at home, and we're interviewing the mom at the kitchen table. There are kids playing in the next room, the TV is on, and someone is cooking at the stove. That's reality, but we don't record it that way. We send the kids out with someone to get ice cream. We turn off the TV, and the fridge, and the stove. And then once we've done the interview, we'll record the extra sounds of someone cooking in the kitchen, the TV show they've been watching (or something similar), and we'll bring the kids back and let them play and record that. It might be while the camera crew is packing up in the hallway, or while everybody else is having lunch. In postproduction, those sounds will be layered back in, and it will sound like reality!*[3]

From time to time, you might be unable to get a specific sound because of microphone placement, or simply because you missed the opportunity to record the sound when it occurred. In these cases, a sound recordist will often rerecord specific sounds from the scene as wild sound so the editor can insert them in postproduction. For example, in a documentary interview situation, when the sound of a plane overhead or a car passing interferes with the recorded sync sound, the sound recordist will often wait until the interview is over and then ask the interviewee to repeat certain words or phrases and record them wild so they can be inserted during editing.

Sometimes wild sound can be recorded and used as a **sound design element**. For coauthor Kelly Anderson and Allison Lirish Dean's film *My Brooklyn* (2012), about a lively commercial area in Downtown Brooklyn, the filmmakers recorded wild sound of the location—people selling cellphones, hip-hop emanating from storefronts, conversations on the street, buses passing by—that could be layered on multiple tracks in postproduction to add specificity and character to the representation of the place (see Chapter 21 for more on sound design).

Room Acoustics

Sound recorded in a loft with hardwood floors and big windows will be quite different than sound recorded in a carpeted room with window drapes. An environment with hard surfaces is called **live** and is undesirable for sound recording because a microphone will pick up the audio directly from the source as well as the audio bouncing off the walls and floor. The result is a boomy or echoey sound as the signal duplicates itself over and over again, creating **reverberation** (or **reverb**). The carpets and furniture in the second room, however, are poor reflective surfaces and serve to absorb sounds after they leave the source. This is known as an acoustically **dead** recording space. Sound recordists often use sound blankets (or comforters or rugs) to create a deader environment for recording. You can't get rid of "boominess" or reverb in postproduction, but you can always add it to a track later on. So the goal during recording is typically to record under the deadest conditions possible.

Another factor that affects acoustics is room size. A small tiled bathroom is a very live space, but the reverberation intervals will be shorter than in a studio loft, where the sound

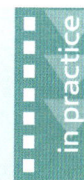

■ WORKING IN LIVE ENVIRONMENTS

Sound recordist Daniel Brooks (Figure 13.9) tells about a time he had to record in a very live room for a documentary about the architecture of telephone buildings:

> *The only place we could shoot the interview was in a big empty room that had metal floor plates and hard walls and glass windows, and it was super live.*
>
> *Over the years, I've acquired these sound absorbing panels that you can put in your home recording studio. I found some of those in a dumpster, and I glued them onto some corrugated plastic. I brought those to the telephone building and put them up, as well as sound blankets, and it sounded great! It had been an utterly unrecordable space before, and then, by knowing what direction the person was going to be speaking in, and putting sound panels to catch the sounds before they hit the walls and bounced to the ceiling and hit the floor, I was able to make it quiet.*[4]

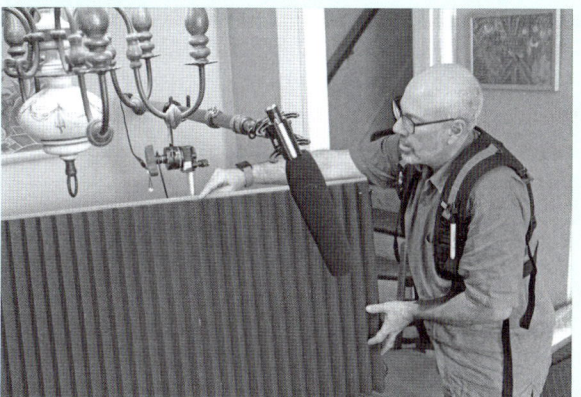

■ **Figure 13.9** Daniel Brooks' alternative to sound blankets is a homemade sound panel made of studio foam baffle mounted on a lightweight backing.

travels a greater distance to a reflective surface and back to the microphone. What this means for sound recording is that in the bathroom, the reverb will be less problematic, though it may still be noticeable.

■ DIGITAL SOUND RECORDING

The Basic Signal Path

Let's look at the basic signal path of a sound in a particular digital audio recording situation. Sound starts out as an acoustic source, which is transformed into an analog electronic signal, then turned into digital data, only to be transformed back into acoustic sound again (Figure 13.10):

1. Sound recording begins with the **source** of sound, which emits acoustic energy (sound waves).
2. These sound waves enter the microphone, which converts the acoustic energy into fluctuations of electrical voltage that are analogous to the original sound waves. The electronic signal is analogous, or like the original sound wave, in two ways. When the sound is loud, the electronic voltage goes up. When the sound is high pitched, the electrical waves' frequency will increase correspondingly. This fluctuating voltage created by a microphone is called a **microphone** (or **mic**) **level signal,** which is sent to the digital audio recorder (or a camcorder) via a microphone cable.
3. The relatively low-voltage mic signal first passes through a **preamp,** where the signal is boosted, and then goes to an **analog-to-digital converter** (**ADC**), which **samples** the analog audio information and translates it into binary code (a series of 1s and 0s). The binary data represents the characteristics (frequency, amplitude) of the source sound.
4. The digital information is stored as a file on some form of recording media (this could be a hard drive or memory card, depending on the recorder you use). In the case of

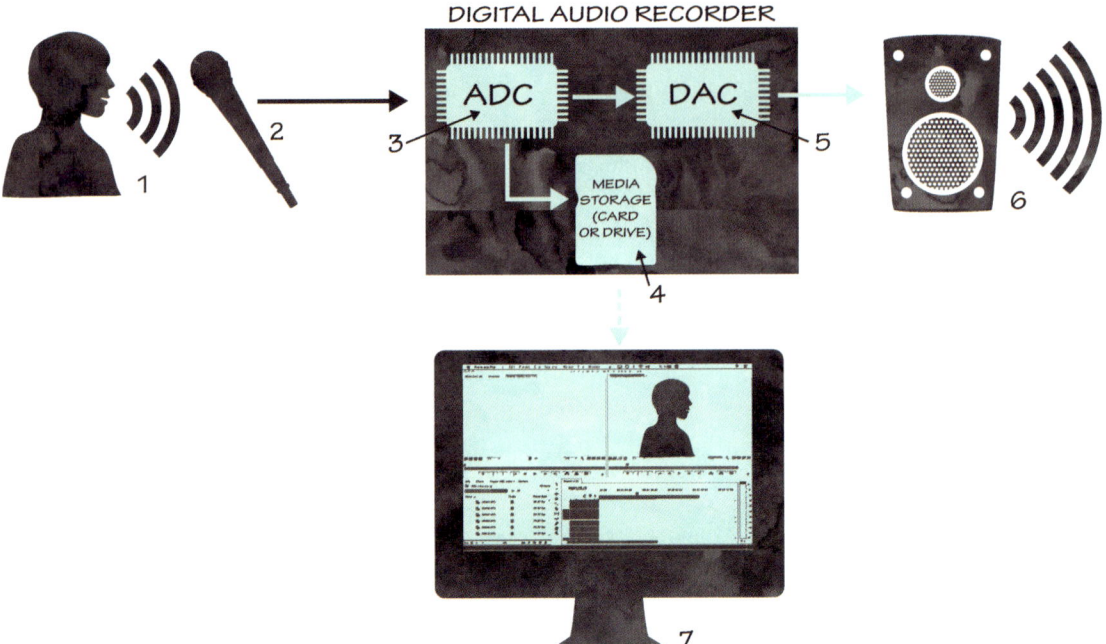

■ Figure 13.10
The basic signal path of sound in digital audio recording.

camcorders, the audio is recorded onto tape or memory cards and is linked to the picture files.

5. When playing the audio back, the data is sent to a **digital-to-analog converter** (**DAC**), which changes it back into electronic energy and outputs a **line level signal,** which is the audio signal used between audio devices such as cameras, mixers, and amplifiers.
6. The audio line signal can then travel to speaker amplifiers or headphones, which convert the signal back into sound waves that travel through the air and are received by our ears.
7. The audio data can also be sent digitally to the hard drive of a digital editing system.

Balanced vs Unbalanced Audio Signals

An important characteristic of the sound flowing through your cables and connectors is whether it is **balanced** or **unbalanced**. A balanced audio signal runs through a three-wire cable: two wires for the signal and a hum-resistant shielding cable, which is usually grounded. The signal can travel long distances with no quality loss, and is relatively impervious to distortions like hum and RF (radio frequency) interference. A balanced signal usually travels through **XLR connectors**, which are found on all professional digital video equipment, including microphones.

Unbalanced audio, on the other hand, is found in consumer cameras that use a **miniplug** connector for audio input. These are highly unstable (because they can easily pull out) and prone to interference and hum. (See p. 216 for workarounds for cameras with miniplug connectors.)

Digital Audio Quality: Sampling Rates and Bit Depth

Regardless of your recording medium, you will have choices about what **sample rate**, **bit depth**, and even file type to use when you are recording sound. These parameters affect recording quality and are important factors in ensuring a smooth high quality workflow through postproduction. These settings define the ADC process, especially as it relates to how thoroughly and accurately the analog information is measured before it is recorded digitally.

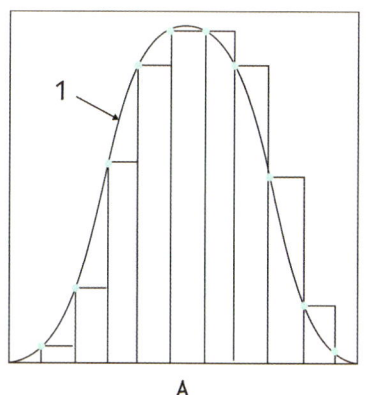 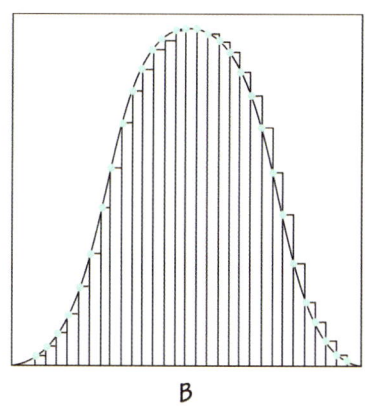

■ **Figure 13.11** The process of converting analog sound (1) to a digital format involves sampling the signal at regular intervals. The lower the sampling rate (A), the less accurate the digital version will be; a higher sampling rate (B) creates a more faithful reproduction of the original sound.

Audio sample rates determine how many times a sound is measured or "sampled" per second. One **sample** is a single measurement of the sound wave, like a snapshot of a piece of that sound. The more the samples (the higher the sample rate), the more accurate the reproduction will be because amplitudes will be measured more often, giving a better picture of both amplitude and frequency variations (Figure 13.11). Higher sample rates produce better quality sound, but they take up more space on your storage medium. The most common sample rate for recording audio on either a camcorder or a digital audio field recorder is 48 kHz (that is, 48,000 sample measurements per second). As a point of comparison, the standard sample rate for audio CDs is 44.1 kHz (you'll find this sample rate on some recorders and camcorders). On high-end audio recorders, you'll find sample rates up to 96.096 kHz or even higher. For most documentary situations, 48 kHz should be more than adequate.

Bit depth is a measure of the accuracy and detail of each audio sample, determined by the number of binary digits (**bits**) assigned to each sample; this is also known as the **sample size**. The greater the bit depth, the better your audio quality will be because the sound wave, in all of its complexity, is more accurately defined. Imagine having a ruler that is divided into 1/4-inch units. If any measurement falls between the 1/4-inch marks, it will be rounded up or down. This ruler doesn't give you particularly accurate measurements. Now imagine a ruler that is divided into 1/48-inch units and another that is divided into 1/96-inch units. These rulers will measure far more accurately because measurements that fall between markings need to be rounded only slightly. Bit depth works the same way, with a sound being measured more or less accurately, through the number of sampling "levels." A 4-bit sample will measure 16 possible levels, an 8-bit sample will measure 256 possible levels, and a 16-bit sample will measure 65,536 possible levels. With each bit you add, you double the number of values that can define that sound, so with 24-bit audio, there are 16,777,216 possible levels! With greater depth, a more accurate picture of the original audio wave can be rendered. For areas of the wave that are not measured directly, the equipment will round up or down in a process called **quantizing**. With more bits, you reduce the **quantizing error** of the recording. In the field, you will often encounter 12-bit audio (substandard), 16-bit audio (good quality), 20-bit audio (better quality), and 24-bit audio (superior quality generally only found on professional equipment).

The mechanism for converting an analog signal to digital data via sampling is called **linear pulse code modulation (LPCM) audio**. LPCM audio is an uncompressed encoding method, and it is by far the most pervasive digital recording process for professional audio field recorders and video camcorders. The most popular audio file formats for audio field recording, **.WAV** (PC standard format) and **.AIFF** (Mac standard format), use LPCM encoding. So, to summarize, the **standard sample rate** and **bit depth settings** for high-quality media production audio are 48 kHz and 16-bit, but if you have the capability and storage space to go to 48 kHz and 24-bit, then by all means use those settings.

PRODUCTION SOUND TOOLS

Sound Recording on Video Camcorders

Despite the increasing popularity of double-system recording, many documentary filmmakers are recording single-system sound with their camcorders, and you can get great audio this way. Devices that use tape as their record medium write LPCM digital audio along with the picture signal. Cameras that use file-based media create picture and sound files simultaneously. While most camcorders appear on paper to have excellent audio specifications, there are mitigating factors that can present problems, particularly with lower-end equipment.

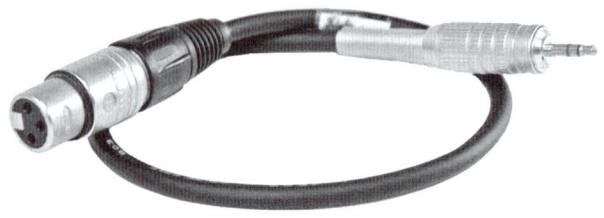

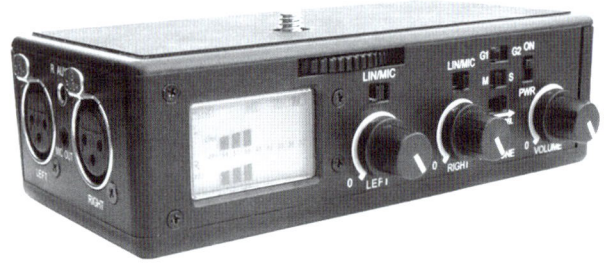

■ **Figure 13.12** Although it is possible to get an XLR-to-mini cable (top) to use professional microphones with 1/8-inch microphone inputs, a mountable adaptor like the Beachtek (bottom) provides a sturdier solution.

Miniplug audio inputs are especially a problem with low-end camcorders, as well as for DSLRs. These connections are fragile and prone to poor contact, and the cables are unshielded and unbalanced. Some people use an **XLR-to-mini adaptor** (called a **pigtail**) so that they can use professional external microphones. This, of course, is better than nothing, but the problem with this solution is that it converts your lovely balanced, shielded audio into an unbalanced signal, vulnerable to interference and noise. We have had the experience of shooting with a professional microphone connected to the camera with an XLR-to-mini adaptor, only to find that AM radio was being picked up on our tracks.

Many people use camera-mountable adaptors with preamps and XLR connections for cameras that have only miniplug audio inputs (Figure 13.12). These adaptors allow you to use XLR cables, and some even provide a shielded cable to the camera. However, where you find miniplugs, you may also find cheap preamps and audio circuitry, which will add system noise to your signal.

Professional cameras with XLR connectors will have two microphone inputs with independent **level controls**. This is important as you will often be using two microphones to record different sync sounds at the same time (by having one mic on each person in a two-person conversation, for example). You want to make sure you have the ability to record these as separate tracks and that you can set and monitor their levels independently. In Chapter 14, we explore in detail the proper method for setting levels manually.

Controlling the record levels of your audio carefully is a key to good sound. Unfortunately, the preset for many consumer-grade cameras is **automatic gain control (AGC)**, which automatically sets your record audio levels. As with autofocus and auto-iris, in most instances you should turn off this blunt tool and set your levels manually. The problem with AGC is that it tries to bring every sound to a middle volume, regardless of whether it is a shout or a whisper. It is constantly responding to peaks and pauses in audio, adjusting levels up when there is quiet and down when a loud noise occurs, however briefly. The background sounds, too, rise and fall very noticeably with each auto adjustment. Like any prescriptive advice, though, this recommendation can be ignored at times. If you are going as a one-man-band to a noisy demonstration, you should probably set your audio level to automatic and concentrate on your shooting.

The Digital Sound Recorder

If you are shooting with a DSLR camera, or want to record double-system sound as a backup for wireless transmission to the video camera, you will be using a **digital sound**

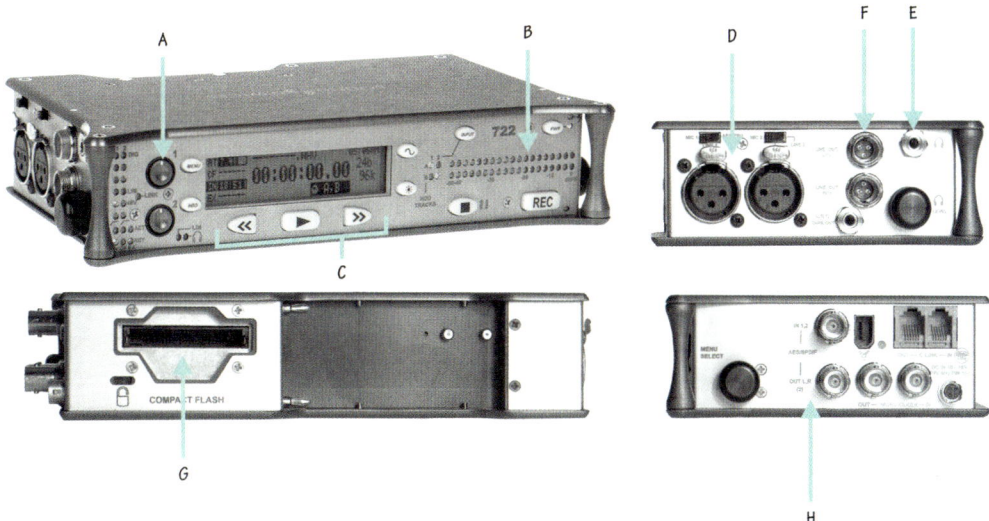

■ **Figure 13.13** Professional sound recorders have the same features: level control potentiometers (A), a peak meter (B), controls for record, play, and searching (C), analog/digital audio inputs (D), headphone jack (E), audio outputs (F), record media bay (in this case compact flash memory (G), and digital audio inputs and outputs (H).

recorder to record your audio. All portable digital sound recorders used for documentary production record LPCM audio and are essentially the same in their basic features and operation (Figure 13.13). These features include microphone inputs, record level controls and meters, recording quality settings, and audio outputs. Increasingly, digital sound recorders are also mixers, capable of handling and combining up to a dozen or more sound inputs.

Microphone Inputs

True XLR microphone inputs are essential for documentary production. XLR connectors are the professional standard connector for microphones and mic cables. If it's possible, stay away from any recorder with miniplug inputs. Portable field recorders typically have between 2 and 12 separate microphone **inputs**, which record to separate **channels**. Each channel can be monitored, controlled, recorded, and transferred as a distinct audio track.

Preamps in the recorder boost the mic input signal. The quality of your audio depends not only on the sampling rate and bit depth settings, but also on the quality of the components inside the recorder. Cheap preamps can be a major source of unwanted system noise and will "dirty up" your 48 kHz, 16-bit audio so much that it sounds terrible. **System noise** is electronic junk that contaminates the audio signal you want to record. The specifications for the system noise of any particular recorder are measured by its **signal-to-noise** (S/N) ratio, which is the ratio between the audio that we want to record (the signal) and unwanted interference (the noise) that contaminates that signal. Signal-to-noise ratio is measured in decibels, and the higher this ratio is, the "cleaner" your audio signal will be when it's recorded. For example, an audio recorder that has a signal-to-noise ratio of 55 dB (55:1) means that 1 dB of noise will be detectable when a signal of 55 dB is played back after recording. A signal-to-noise ratio of 95 dB (95:1), however, means that the playback signal can be as high as 95 dB before we detect any noise at all. Professional digital field recorders should have an S/N ratio of 80 dB or higher.

Level Controls and Meters

Adjusting and monitoring the strength of your audio signal is at the heart of the sound recordist's craft. The term **levels** refers to the strength of your audio as it enters the

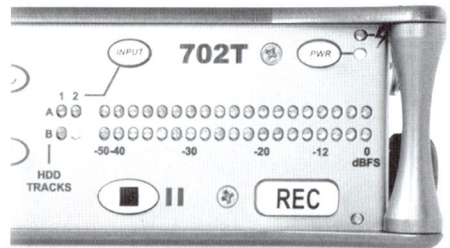

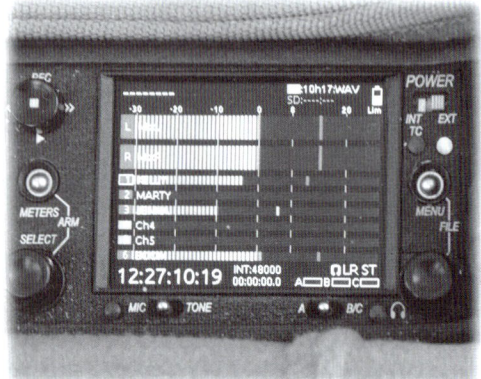

■ **Figure 13.14** Peak meters are essential for monitoring the strength of the signal being recorded. They can be LED based (top, showing a two-channel meter) or LCD based (bottom, showing a six-channel meter with two outputs at the top.)

recorder, and the degree to which you boost or lower that audio with manual **level controls**, sometimes called **gain controls** or **pots** (short for **potentiometers**). This adjustment determines the strength of the recorded audio signal and is called **setting levels**. On professional recorders, you will have one level control for every microphone channel, allowing you to adjust the levels of each microphone independently. Setting levels is aided by a **peak reading meter** (Figure 13.14). The peak meter is a highly sensitive instrument that measures and indicates the level of every sound entering the recorder. Each mic input will have its own corresponding peak meter. Meter displays can be quite different from machine to machine—they can involve pivoting needles, colored LED lights, or backlit LCD displays. Whatever indicators they use, all displays are calibrated in decibels that run from –∞ dB on the extreme low end, through –40, –30, and –20 dB, and so on, to 0 dB on the high end. At –∞ dB, there is no signal at all and you will record only system sound. If your signal strength approaches 0 dB, you are already recording at too high a level and your sound will be distorted. This can be confusing, as 0 Db would seem to refer to silence, not an optimal sound level. We will discuss the reasons for the difference, and more about setting record levels in Chapter 14.

Playback, Controls, and Outputs

All recorders have Play, Record, and Stop buttons that control the starting and stopping of audio recording and playback. A **headphone jack** with its own volume control is standard. Be careful that you do not mistake the headphone volume level for the record volume level! Headphones are used to monitor the quality of your audio, *not* the audio levels as they are being recorded. The only way to monitor your record levels is by looking at the peak meter on your recorder. Many students shooting their first films have their headphone volume turned all the way up while the record levels are extremely low. The result is audio that is unusable because it is recorded "in the mud," or too low or "in the mud".

All recorders also have **audio outputs** to send the recorded signal to other devices, including to your camera (as an analog signal) or to your computer (as a digital signal). The number and type of outputs varies.

Digital Recording Media

An important aspect of digital audio recorders is their **recording media format**, which refers to the media they use to store the audio data. Most audio field recorders record in the .WAV file format, but how they store these .WAV files differs. Digital recording formats come and go as technology evolves, but there are a few standard ones that you are likely to encounter.

Flash Memory Recorders

Sound recorders using **non-volatile flash memory cards** are a popular and relatively inexpensive choice. Almost every major sound recording equipment manufacturer has developed portable flash recorders. These recorders do not have internal hard drives. Instead, they record audio directly to **data cards**, typically either CF or SD cards. From these, the sound can be transferred onto computer hard drives for storage, and the cards can be reused again and again. Compact flash cards also contains no moving parts, which means they are reliable in extreme conditions (Figure 13.15).

Hard Drive Recorders

Hard drive recorders write their data directly to a hard drive. Most portable units intended for media production use a 2.5-inch solid-state drive (SSD) with a capacity of up to 250 GB or more. Depending on the size of the hard drive, these recorders can store many hours of audio.

Hard drive recorders also interface with computer editing software seamlessly and have a reputation for being quite robust because temperature, humidity, and motion have little effect on their functions and recording. The benefits of hard drive recorders come at a price, however, as they are notably expensive. Ultra-high-end, professional hard drive recorders include simultaneous secondary media recording to flash memory or a tertiary storage device, like an external hard drive. The Zaxcom Zax-Max can even send a wireless signal to a camera or other external device (Figure 13.16).

Portable Field Mixers

Portable field mixers (also called **microphone mixers**) are small audio consoles that allow for independent level control of multiple microphone inputs (usually from one to four). You can combine the inputs in various ways and output two channels of sound to your camera (Figure 13.17).

Many sound recordists working with single-system setups find portable mixers an indispensable tool, because camcorder level controls are located right on the camera and it can be very awkward to have the sound recordist hovering around the camera setting levels. Using a field mixer enables the sound recordist to monitor and control levels at a distance from the camera. A mixer also allows the recordist to use multiple microphones and select which signals to send to the camera. The output of a field mixer can connect with the camera via XLR cables, a breakaway cable or via a wireless connection. It is vital, however, to calibrate the gain levels of the mixer and the camera so that you maintain audio level consistency. This process, called **setting tone**, is discussed in detail in

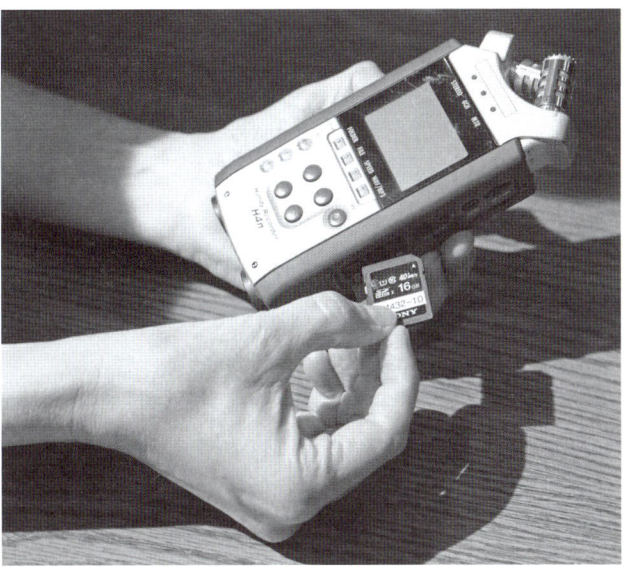

■ **Figure 13.15** Compact flash memory cards allow for small, yet sturdy digital recorders like this Zoom H4n.

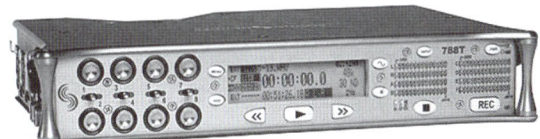

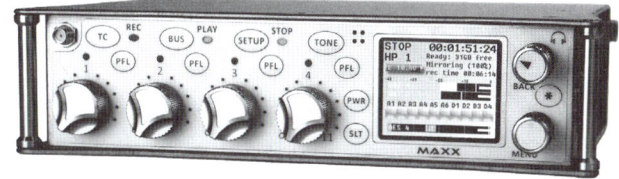

■ **Figure 13.16** Some high-end digital sound recorders like the Sound Devices 788T (top) store data directly to an internal solid state drive as well as to flash memory cards. The Zaxcom Zax-Max (bottom) sends a wireless signal directly to a camera or other external device.

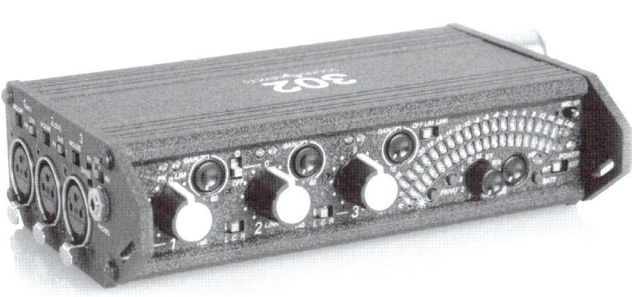

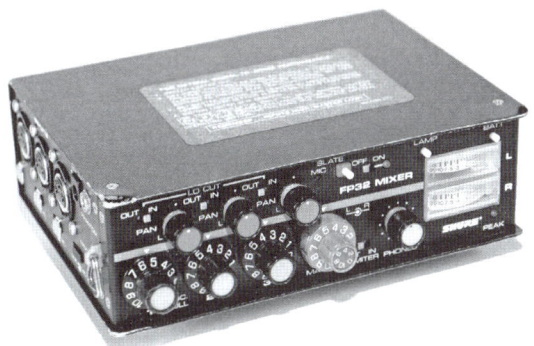

■ **Figure 13.17** Field mixers allow precise control over the recording levels of several inputs. Pictured are 2 three-channel mixers, the Sound Devices 302 (left) and the Shure FP33 (right).

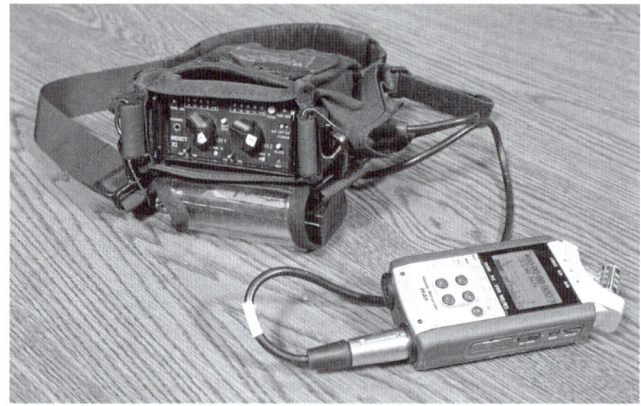

Chapter 14. Located in the signal chain between the microphones and the camera audio input, field mixers are small enough to be worn in a carrying case over the shoulder.

While mixers and audio recorders were traditionally separate devices (Figure 13.18, top), a recent development is the integration of the mixer and the digital audio recorder, as seen in the Sound Devices 664 recorder (Figure 13.18, bottom). These allow the recordist to both control levels and record audio files. They can also send audio to the camera via cable or wireless. They can record up to 16 channels of audio and are becoming quite standard in professional sound for documentaries.

Microphones

Simply put, a microphone is a device that converts acoustic energy (sound waves) into electrical energy (electrical signals). All microphones are constructed with a **diaphragm**, a thin membrane that is extremely sensitive to the vibration of air particles. The vibrations of the diaphragm, which correspond to the sound waves buffeting it, are translated into fluctuating voltage. One of the ways we identify different microphones is by the method they employ to make this conversion.

Dynamic, Condenser, and Electret Condenser

A common type of microphone for field production is the **dynamic microphone**, which generates a signal through electromagnetic principles. This microphone is sometimes called a **moving coil microphone** because the diaphragm is connected to a wire coil with a permanent magnetic charge. This coil is called the **voice coil** and is suspended around a permanently fixed magnet. As the diaphragm responds to a particular sound source, the coil moves up and down with the vibrations of the diaphragm. Each movement of the coil through the electromagnetic field that surrounds the magnet produces an electrical current that is analogous to the original acoustic vibrations (Figure 13.19, top).

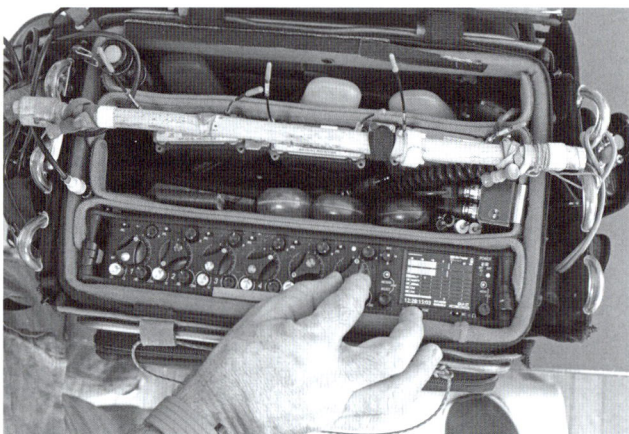

■ **Figure 13.18** A modest audio recording setup involves a portable field mixer and separate audio recorder (top). Another approach is to use a combination mixer/recorder like this Sound Devices 664, which can mix six channels to two as well as record each channel separately (bottom).

Dynamic microphones are renowned for their rugged construction, which makes them a favorite for shooting in rough weather, high humidity, or around heavy machinery. They are also less expensive than other types of microphones. As a general rule, dynamic mics are faithful to the original sound, and also have a fairly good frequency response that is especially appropriate for the human voice. In close mic situations, they are more than adequate, which is why news reporters, who

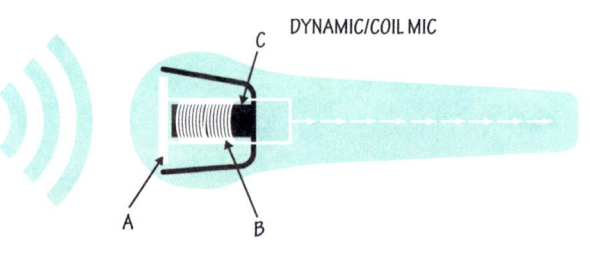

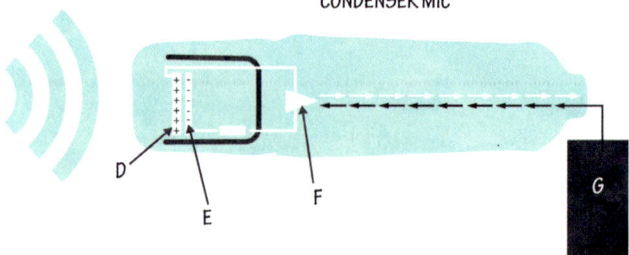

■ **Figure 13.19** A moving coil microphone (top) works by converting the movement of a diaphragm (A) into an electrical charge when the coil (B) attached to it moves up and down while suspended around magnets (C). A condenser microphone (bottom) uses a positively charged diaphragm (D) and a negatively charged back plate (E) to form a capacitor; the movement between these two electrically charged plates creates voltage fluctuations that are sent to a preamp (F). In order to keep the backplate charged, this mic requires a power supply (G).

don't mind having the mic in the shot, usually use these mics. When the microphone needs to be further away from the subject, or greater frequency response is necessary, recordists usually turn to the condenser (or electret condenser) microphone.

Condenser microphones use a diaphragm to translate the sound waves into electrical energy, but instead of using a magnet they use a **capacitor** to create the electrical signal. The capacitor, or condenser, is made of two round plates oriented parallel to each other, with a very narrow space between them called the **dielectric**. One plate is the microphone's diaphragm, a movable acoustically sensitive membrane; the other is a fixed plate called the **back plate**. Both of these plates are charged with polarized voltage. When the plates are close, they can store a certain amount of electricity. When they are further apart, they can store less and the current drops. When sound waves move the diaphragm, the voltage relationship between the plates creates the electrical signal. Because there is no heavy magnet to move, the resulting signal is more sensitive, especially when recording higher frequencies. The output signal of this capacitor is very low, however, so condenser microphones have a **preamplifier** ("preamp") built into the microphone (Figure 13.19, bottom).

In order for the microphone's capacitor to work, both plates require some source of power to provide the necessary polarizing voltage, and the preamp also requires some power. Condenser mics can be powered through the use of **phantom power**, which is power provided by the camera, audio recorder or mixer, delivered to the microphone via one of the three XLR cable prongs, or through the use of a battery power source, which is usually located in an intermediary capsule connected to the microphone (Figure 13.20).

Electret condenser mics offer a less expensive alternative. Though not quite as sensitive as condenser mics, they are still superior to dynamic ones in terms of sound quality. The electret is a piece of electrically sensitive ceramic that generates its own electricity when squeezed. This means their condenser is permanently charged and they need only a small amount of power for their preamp. This is usually provided by a small battery located in the microphone itself (AA, or the smaller N battery, or the even smaller LR44 1.5 volt). The low power requirements allow for a more compact design, which is always welcome in field production. Price-wise, electrets occupy a middle ground between condenser mics, which are expensive, and dynamic mics, which are less expensive. They are the mics most likely to be used on student or lower-budget productions.

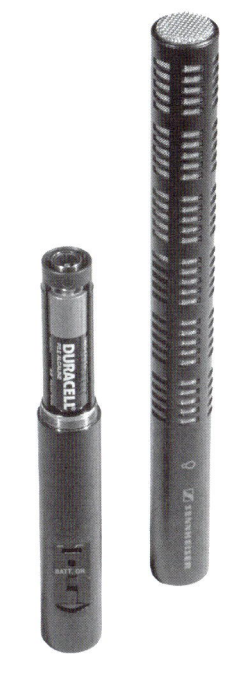

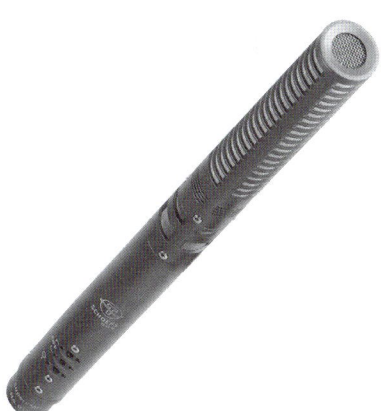

■ **Figure 13.20** This Sennheiser ME66 electret microphone (top) uses a battery to provide the power necessary to charge the capacitor. The Schoeps SuperCMIT2U condenser microphone (bottom) needs to pull phantom power from a field mixer or other source.

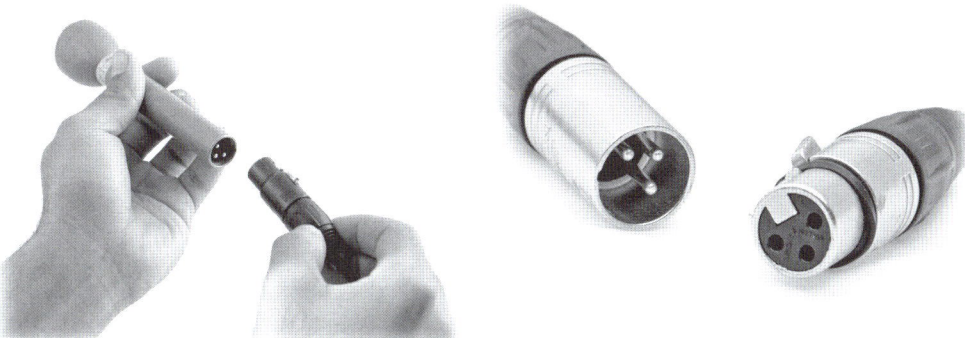

■ **Figure 13.21** The standard professional audio cable is the XLR, a tough and inexpensive solution for sending balanced, distortion-free audio between microphones and recorders (including cameras).

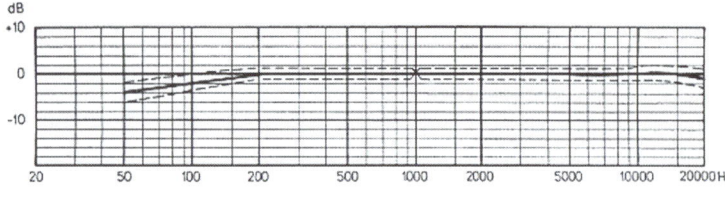

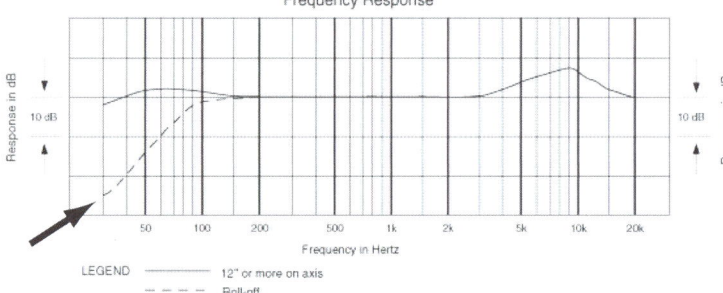

■ **Figure 13.22** A frequency response graph plots how sensitive (measured in dB, on the x-axis) a microphone is to a range of frequencies (measured in Hz on the y-axis). Note that the Schoeps MK41 microphone (top) has a very flat response, meaning that it favors all frequencies equally (except extremely low ones). The Audio Technica AT803b, an omnidirectional lavalier microphone (bottom), has a "brighter" high end to emphasize voices, and a "roll-off" option that cuts out low frequencies at the arrow.

Most professional-quality microphones send a **balanced output** utilizing the standard **XLR** professional microphone connector (Figure 13.21). This shielded connection greatly protects the signal from interference caused by AC, fluorescent hum, or radio frequencies. The other advantage of XLR connectors is that they are rugged, and the male end of the connector fits with the female end through a tongue-and-groove fit and a spring lock, providing for a strong and stable connection that cannot be inadvertently pulled loose.

Microphone Frequency Response

Frequency response refers to the sensitivity of a given microphone to the range of high and low frequencies in the sound spectrum. This measurement is represented by a **frequency response graph** (Figure 13.22). The x-axis on this graph measures the microphone's response in dB, and the y-axis measures the frequency of the recorded sound. A perfect microphone would have an equal response throughout all frequencies of the sound spectrum, resulting in a flat line. This is known as a **flat response**. For all mics, however, the response dips at the extremes of their capabilities. All professional microphones come with a spec sheet that will indicate the instrument's frequency range.

Some microphones come with a **low-end roll-off** switch that makes them less sensitive to low frequencies. This can be useful in situations where there is wind or traffic noise in the field. A roll-off switch usually has two symbols (Figure 13.23), and it is critical that you check your microphone before shooting to see which setting it is on. Documentary, which presents many challenges for the sound recordist, requires that you use your judgment when deciding whether to record "flat" or use the roll-off setting.

Microphone Directionality

An additional way of defining microphones is by their **directionality** (also called **pickup pattern**). A microphone's pickup pattern dictates the area and range within which the microphone will respond optimally. In simple terms, some microphones record sound all around them, while others favor the sound in a particular direction. Directionality is sometimes described as a microphone's **angle of acceptance**.

Omnidirectional

An omnidirectional microphone (Figure 13.24) picks up audio from all directions equally. This microphone is a good choice for recording general ambient sounds (like crowd noises) or for recording a scene where sound emanates from a number of different directions (e.g., four friends gathered around a table for dinner). This is a good choice for interviews in which you want both the interviewer and the interviewee to be recorded equally.

■ **Figure 13.23** Some microphones have a low-end roll-off setting (B) that makes them less sensitive to low frequencies, usually caused by wind or machine noise. If you prefer to record the full range of frequencies in your environment, record "flat" (A).

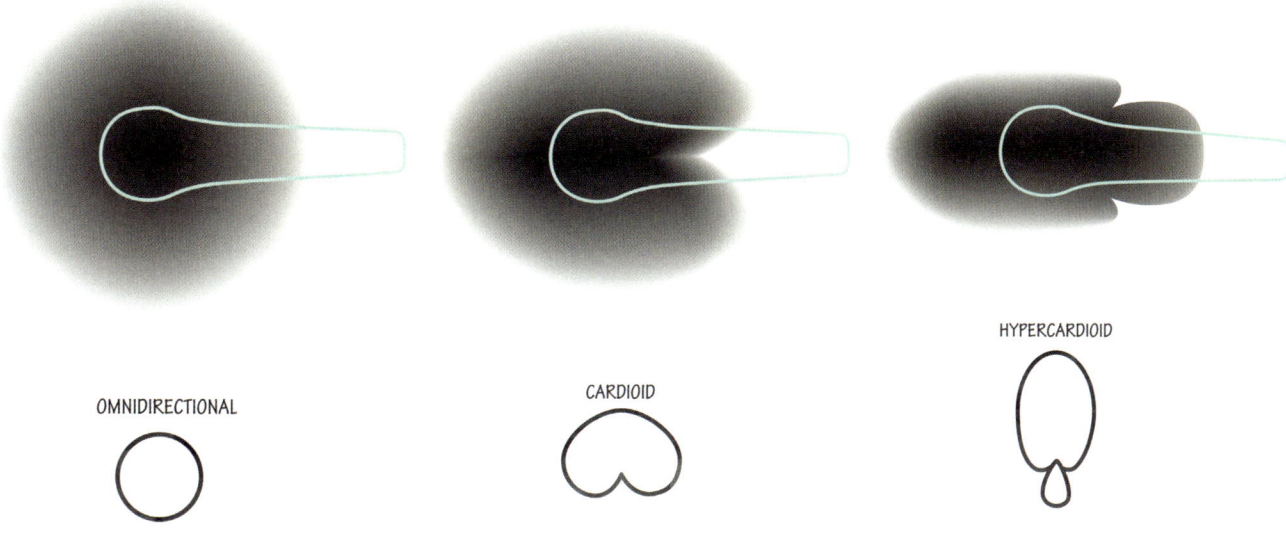

■ **Figure 13.24** The pickup pattern of an omnidirectional microphone allows it to capture sound equally from all directions.

■ **Figure 13.25** A cardioid microphone has a pickup pattern that favors sound coming from the front and sides, but not from behind.

■ **Figure 13.26** A hypercardioid microphone pickup pattern has a narrow range of acceptance and increased sensitivity. It greatly favors sound coming from the front and not from the sides or back.

Cardioid

The pickup pattern of a **cardioid** microphone (Figure 13.25) is just as its name suggests: heart shaped. The pickup pattern is somewhat directional, so the mic can be aimed specifically at the source of the audio. This mic minimizes extraneous noise while providing a natural ambient feel. Its sensitivity is primarily in front, with some sensitivity to the sides, but the mic picks up very little from behind, which is usually where the equipment and crew are. This is one of the most common microphones used in documentary production.

Hypercardioid and Shotguns

Hypercardioids and **shotgun mics** (also called **supercardioid** or **unidirectional**) duplicate the heart-shaped pickup pattern, but these mics are considerably more sensitive to sound directly in front of them (Figure 13.26). Their pickup patterns are highly directional, meaning that they are considerably narrower than a cardioid and can be held at a greater distance. A full shotgun mic is extremely sensitive and the most directional of the two. Often recordists will use the hypercardioid, which is directional but more forgiving if your placement is slightly off, and a lot shorter and hence easier to use and less imposing. There are drawbacks, however, to using both of these microphones. Because these mics are so sensitive, you must be careful when using them indoors. Not only will they pick up the sound directly from the source, but they can also easily pick up the reflections of that sound, resulting in audio with a "boomy quality." These mics are quite successful outdoors, but here, too, you must be careful about sounds within the mic's direct pickup pattern that might not be noticeable to your ear. For example, a camera-mounted shotgun or hypercardioid mic will pick up not only the voice of the subject it is pointed at, but also the truck that is half a block away behind them.

Microphone Usage Types

Microphones are also characterized by their form and function. Here are a few common types.

Handheld

They are commonly used by news reporters and others who don't mind if the mic appears in the frame. Generally dynamic, they usually have an omnidirectional or cardioid pickup pattern. It's a good idea to have one of these sturdy options in your kit as a backup.

Shotgun

A shotgun mic is a mic designed to be supported by a **shock mount** on a **boom pole** or a **pistol grip** (Chapter 14). A narrow pickup pattern and excellent frequency response makes these mics the workhorses of documentary field production. Both mics in Figure 13.20 are shotguns commonly used in documentary. We will explore techniques for using this mic in Chapter 14.

Lavalier

Lavalier microphones (also called "lavs") are tiny clip-on mics that can be attached to a lapel or tie, or easily hidden under a collar (Figure 14.4). They usually have an omnidirectional pattern and are the typical mic solution for an interview where the subject won't be getting up and moving around. These are electret condenser mics, and their power supply and preamps are in a capsule separate from the actual microphone head (Figure 13.27).

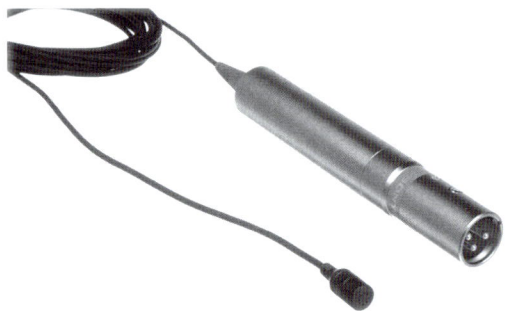

■ **Figure 13.27** The Sony ECM-44 lavalier is a commonly used microphone for interviews where the subject isn't moving around a lot.

Lavs are often used with wireless transmitters for observational shooting as they free the subject from either a cable connection or a boom while their position close to the subject's mouth provides a high signal to noise ratio. They also allow the subject to be very far from the cameraperson, when booming is impractical because the boom would appear in the shot. In Ilisa Barbash and Lucien Castaing Taylor's *Sweetgrass* (2009), for example, wireless lavs were used extensively to capture the voices of sheepherders at distances of up to a mile from the sound recordist and camera person (p. 349).

Wireless Microphones

Wireless microphones (also called **radio mics**) consist of a small pocket-sized transmitter to which a microphone (very often a lavalier) is attached. The transmitter sends the electrical audio signal via VHF or FM frequencies to a receiver that is connected to the input of the digital audio recorder or the camera. Wireless lavaliers are extremely common in documentary because they allow close miking of subjects while maintaining freedom of movement (Figure 13.28). Wireless microphones are also especially advantageous to the one-man-band shooter, who will put wireless lavaliers on one or more subjects and feed the signal directly into the camera (Chapter 14).

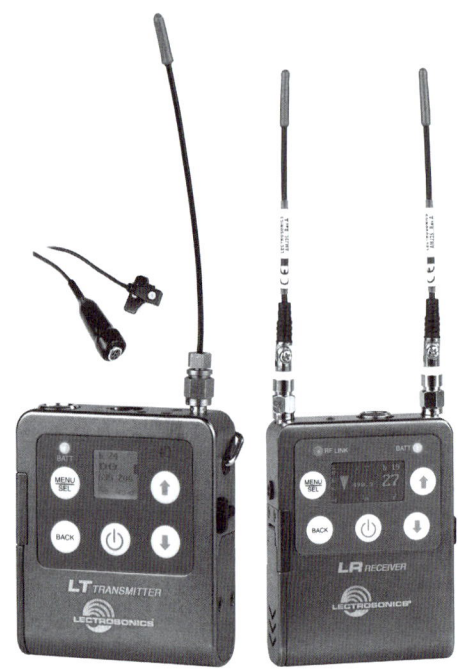

■ **Figure 13.28** This Lectrosonics L series hybrid digital wireless microphone system includes a transmitter (left) and a receiver (right) and features an M152 lavalier head.

If there is a downside to wireless microphones, it is that they are expensive and vulnerable to interference, especially as the transmitter is moved away from the receiver. Some systems use a "diversity" mechanism that is constantly searching for the clearest transmission path. As with most things, the more expensive the microphone, the less prone to interference it is. You should always have a hard-wired solution available as backup.

Pressure Zone Microphones (PZMs)

Pressure zone microphones (**PZMs**), also known as **boundary mics**, are specialized mics mounted on a plate, typically metal (Figure 13.29). One of the main advantages of this mic is that it records in a way that eliminates reverb in situations where many people are speaking from different parts of a room. PZMs are often used to record a meeting around a table, or they can be taped to the wall in the back of a room full of activity (like a performance). A lavalier can be mounted on a piece of wood or metal to create an impromptu PZM.

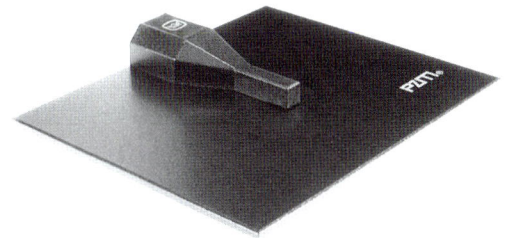

■ **Figure 13.29** Pressure Zone Microphones (PZMs) are mounted on a plate and are useful for recording multiple voices around a table or in a room.

Onboard Microphones

Another microphone that should be mentioned is the **onboard microphone** or **camera microphone** (Figure 13.30). These microphones are typically of very low quality and should be avoided. Professional cameras allow you to mount your own microphone, which is fine as a backup but has disadvantages even when it is of high quality. Using an onboard mic as your only microphone can be problematic. Since often your camera will be pointing at something besides the source of the audio you want (at a cutaway, or a reaction shot, for example), it is best to allow a sound person to control microphone placement and give the cameraperson the freedom to shoot without having to consider the audio being recorded by the onboard mic. Finally, camera microphones often pick up noises from the camera operator and from camera mechanisms like the servo zoom.

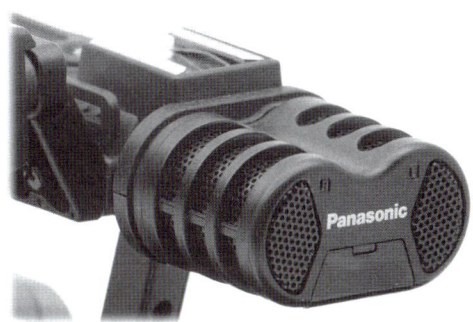

■ **Figure 13.30** Camera-mounted microphones are commonly found on even the cheapest video cameras, but the inability to control their position in relation to subjects makes them of limited use.

Microphone Support

While documentary filmmaking stresses mobility, there are occasions where a microphone stand can be a lifesaver (Figure 13.31). One example is that a stand can take the place of a non-existent boom operator during an interview. Mic stands come in both free-standing and desk models. Most sound kits include at least a small folding desk mic stand.

The Importance of Headphones!

It is impossible to overemphasize the importance of wearing good-quality headphones and using them to monitor your recorded audio signal. Unfortunately, this is an error we often see (or hear) in documentary production classes: a great scene with no audio, or audio that is rendered unusable by interference, hum, or some problem in the environment. Earbuds are great for listening to your tablet or phone, but for documentary production invest in a pair of high quality headphones that can isolate your recorded audio from the sound in your environment.

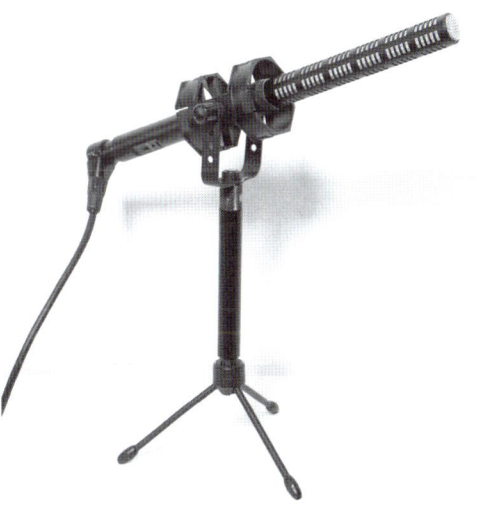

■ **Figure 13.31** A desk stand like this Quik Lok is small, light, and can be incredibly helpful, especially for a "one-man band" shooter.

CONCLUSION

A thorough understanding of the nature of sound and of sound recording equipment (Figure 13.32) is essential for any serious documentary filmmaker. But the single most effective factor in good sound isn't related to the money spent on equipment. Rather, it's good listening, microphone placement, and troubleshooting problems that count. In the next chapter, we look at techniques used by sound recordists for capturing the best possible audio in a variety of documentary situations.

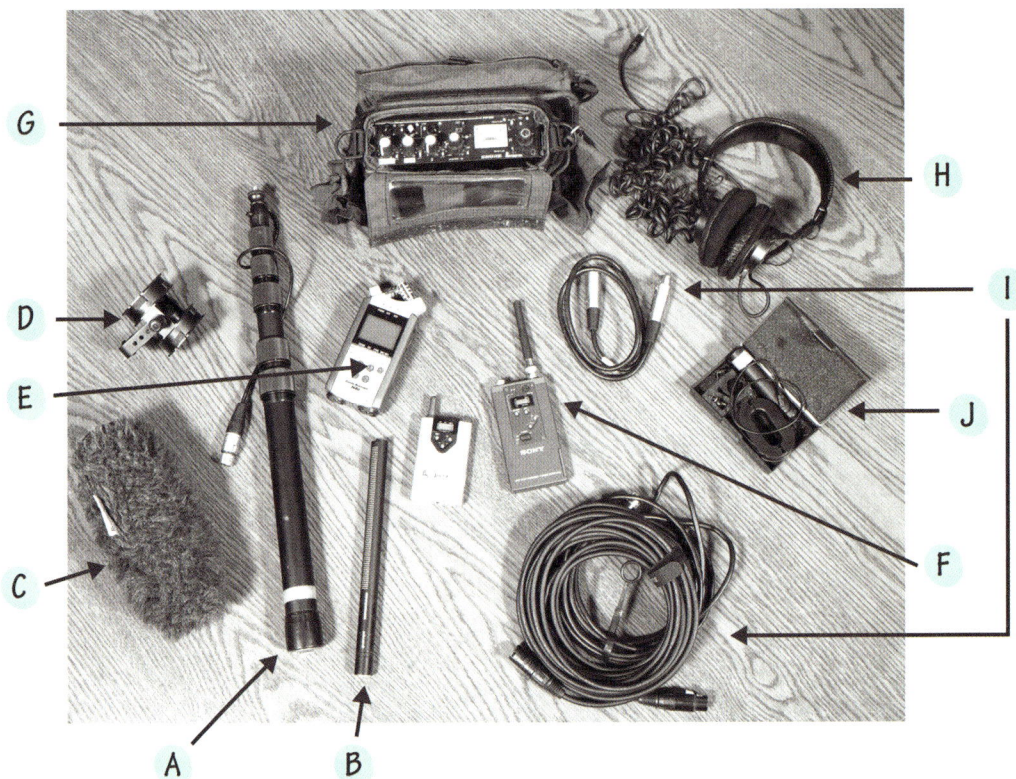

Figure 13.32 A sound person's basic arsenal: boom pole (A), shotgun mic (B), windscreen (C), shockmount (D), zoom recorder (E), wireless transmitter and receiver (F), portable field mixer (G), headphones (H), XLR cables (I), lavalier mic (J).

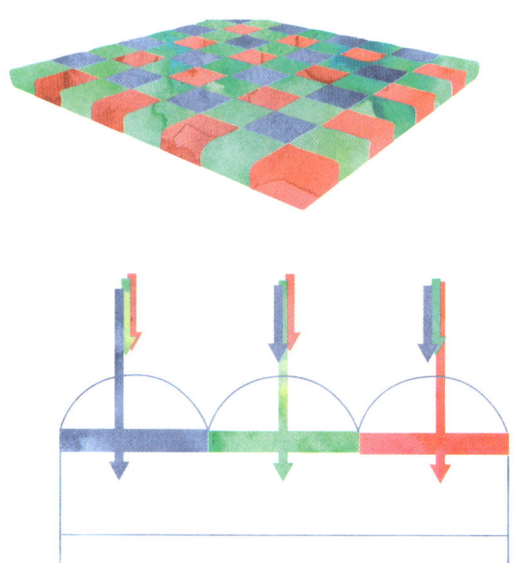
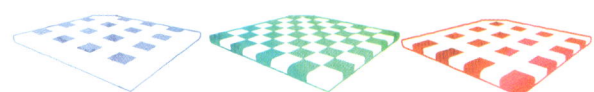

■ **Figure 8.29**
A Beyer Pattern Filter separates light into three different colors in a mosaic pattern. The red pixels are on the right, the green (which predominate) are in the center, and the blue are on the left.

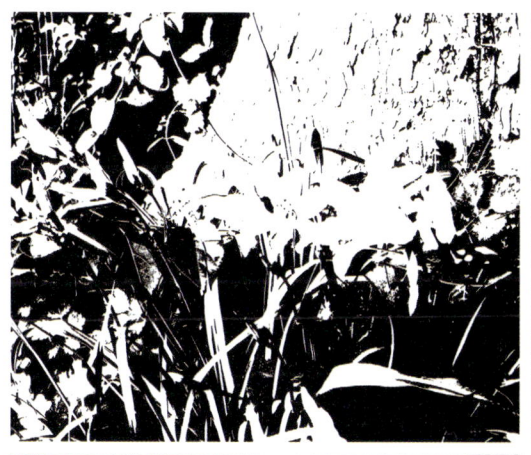
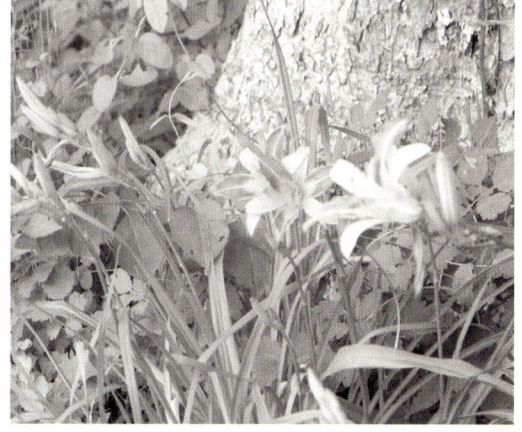
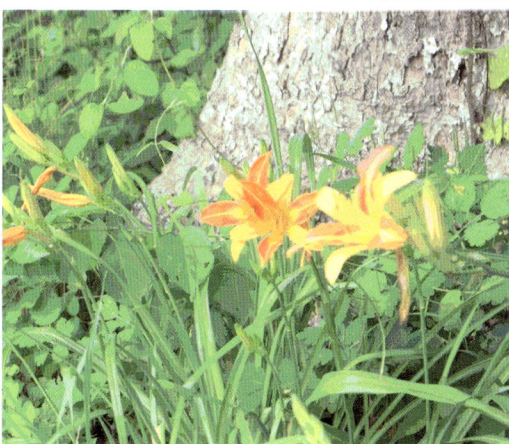
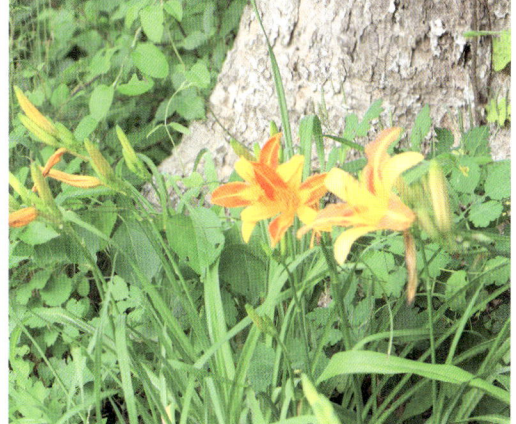

■ **Figure 8.32**
Bit Depth is an important aspect of the digital image. Shown here (clockwise starting with the upper left image) are 2 bit (black and white), 4 bit (16 shades of gray), 8 bit color (256 colors), and 24 bit color (16.7 million colors).

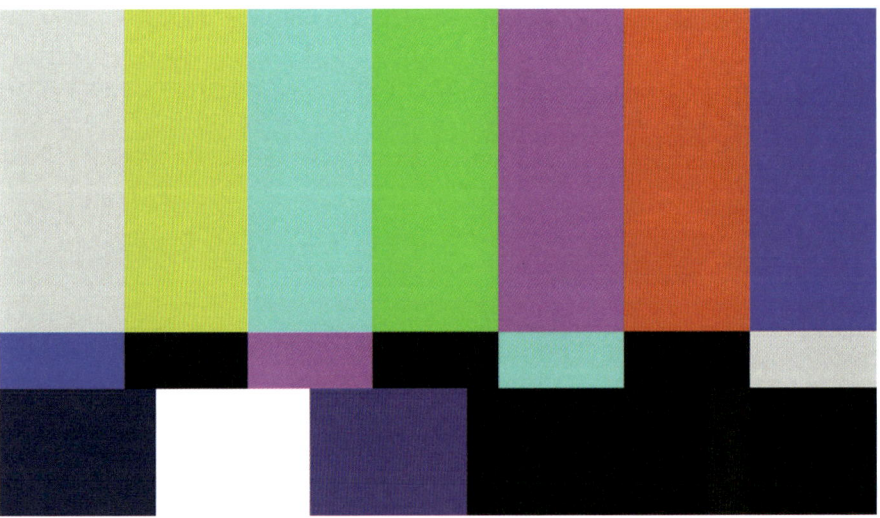

■ **Figure 8.36** In this window you can see a representation of the Rec. 709 color space, with the small x marking the spot where a neutral white can be found.

■ **Figure 8.37** This image shows a color bar display properly set for white, black and chroma levels.

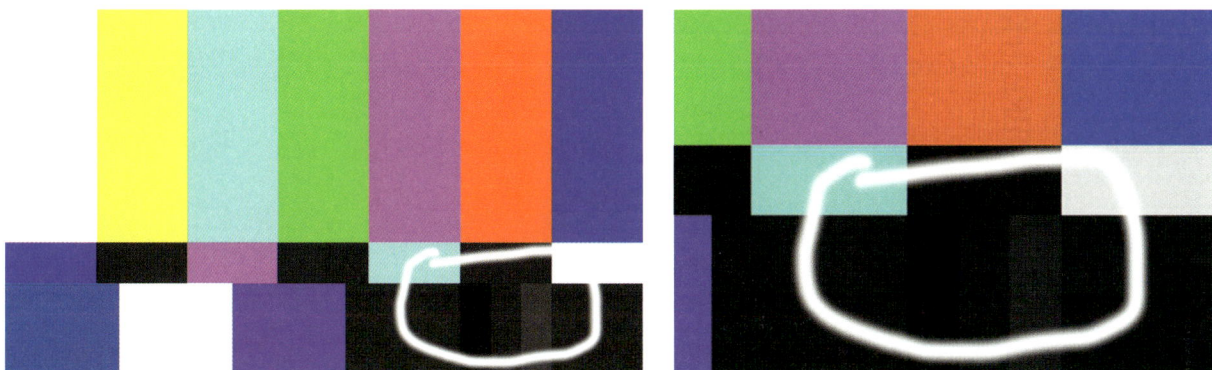

■ **Figure 8.38** In this typical color bar display, the brightness of the three small bars on the lower right (called the pluge, from picture line-up generation equipment) can be used to set brightness level. In the closeup section of the bar display (right), the setting has been adjusted so that the difference between the two bars on the left of pluge almost disappears.

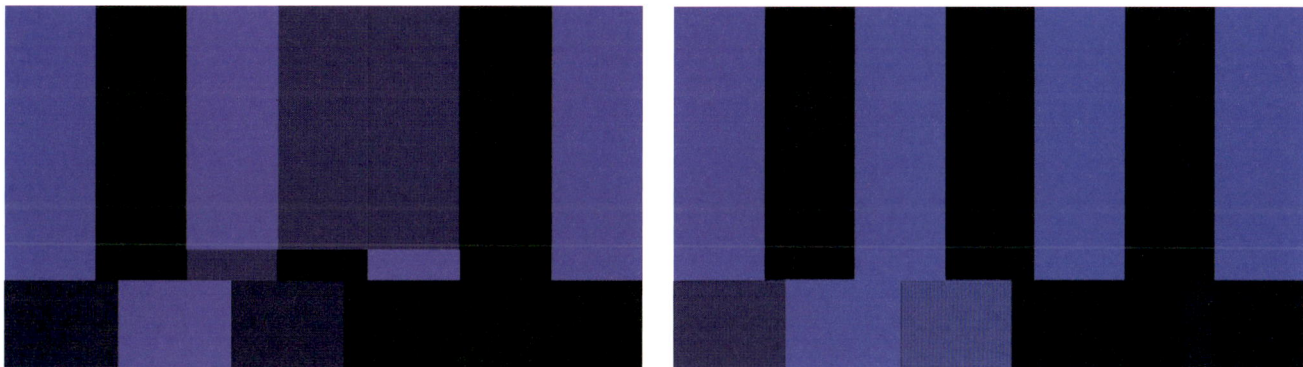

■ **Figure 8.39** Setting up a monitor with a blue gun. Adjust the chroma level on the display until you're looking at solid, alternating bars of equal value. The image on the left shows an incorrectly adjusted chroma because the third and fifth bars show small stubs at the bottom. On the right, the chroma has been set properly.

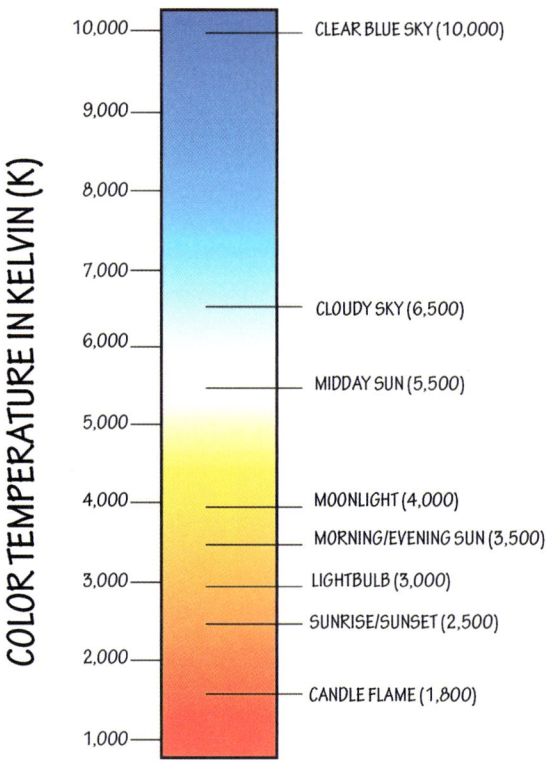

■ **Figure 11.9** This chart shows the color temperatures of various common light sources measured in degrees Kelvin.

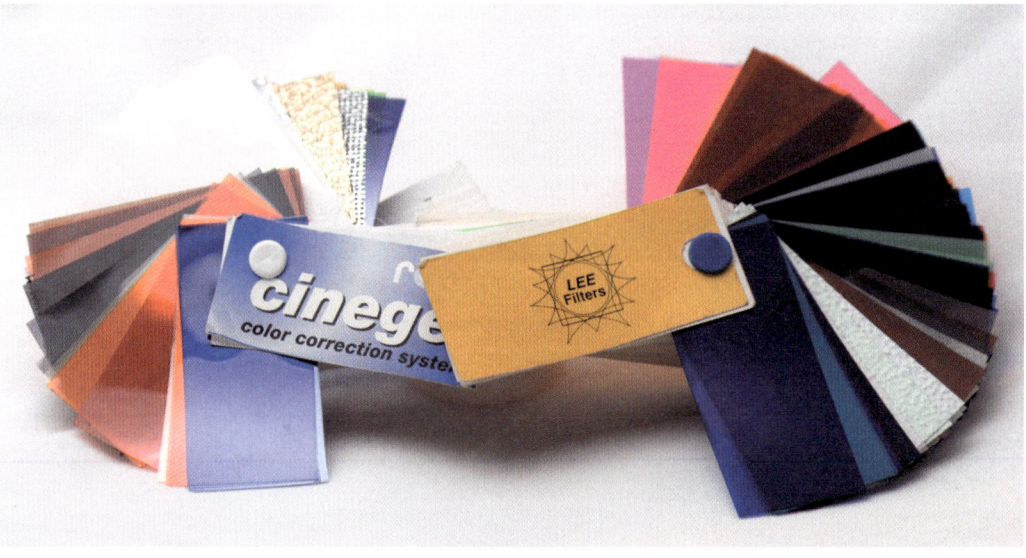

■ **Figure 11.24** Gels come in hundreds of colors and intensities.

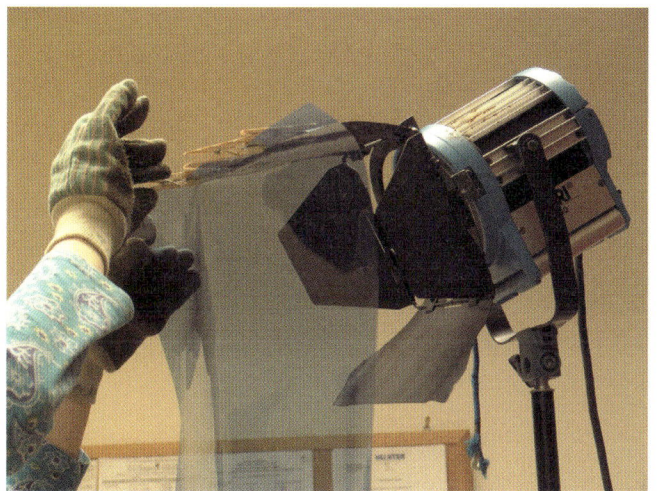 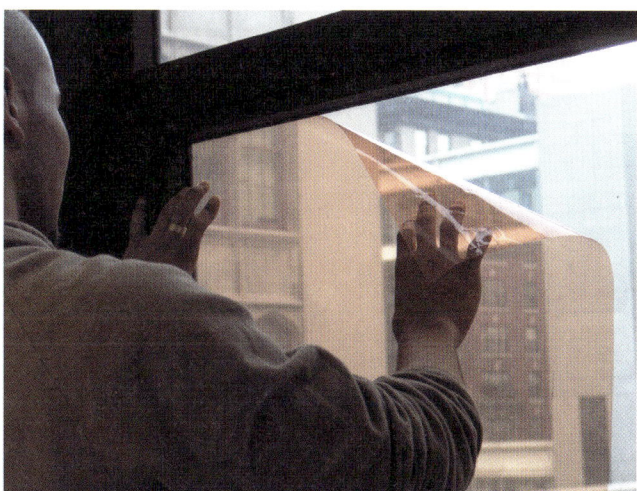

■ **Figure 11.25** CTB filter being placed on movie light to make it "daylight" (left). CTO filter being placed on window to convert the daylight to "tungsten" (right).

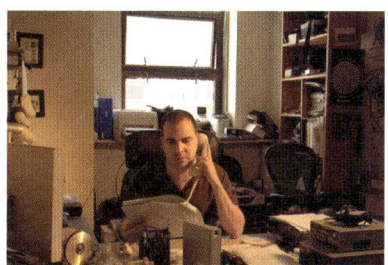
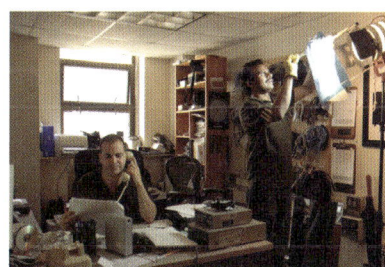
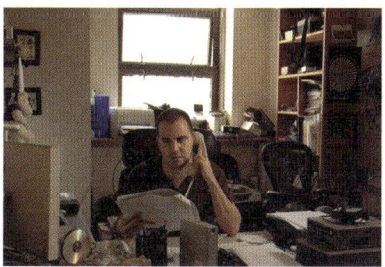
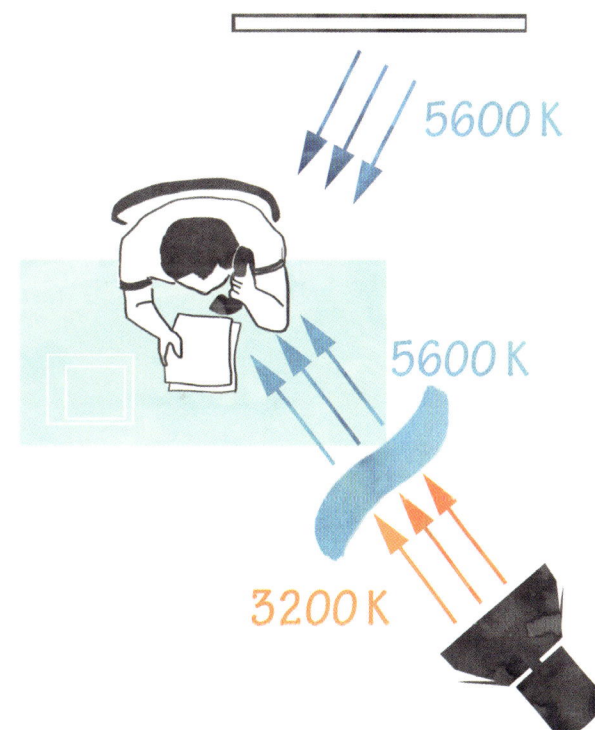

■ **Figure 11.26** Shooting with a camera balanced for daylight will make the daylight from the window appear white, while the light from the tungsten movie light will look orange (top). Placing a CTB gel over the tungsten light changes it to daylight (middle), matching the color temperatures of all sources (bottom).

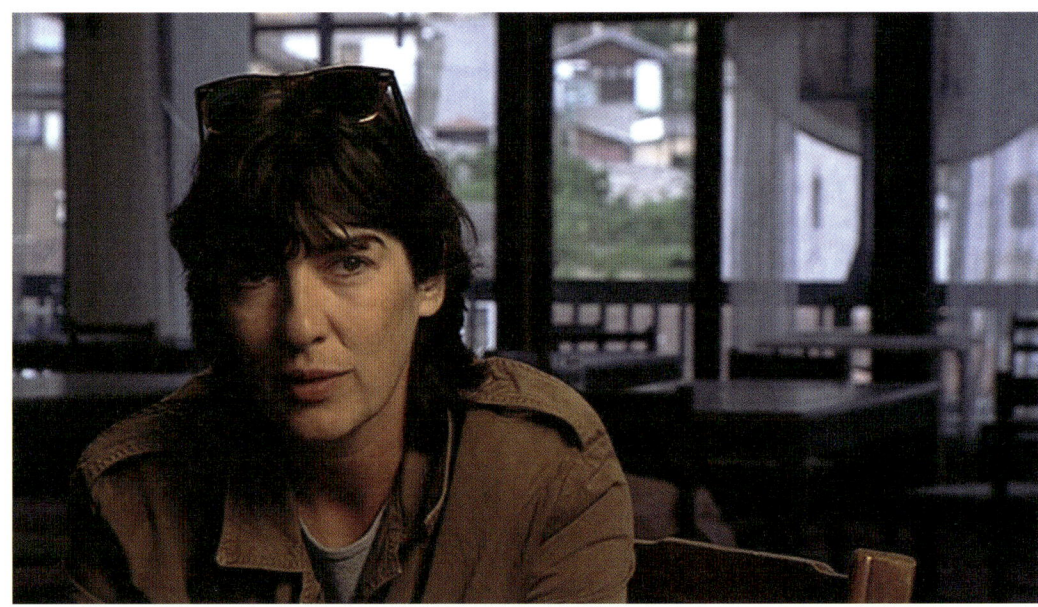

■ **Figure 11.27** Using mixed light for aesthetic effect in *War Photographer*.

■ **Figure 22.4**
Adjusting hue and saturation using the Fast Color Corrector in Premiere Pro. The dot in the middle of the color wheel (A) is in the center before the image is adjusted. In order to reduce the blue tint, and add orange, you drag the dot slowly away from the blue side of the color wheel and towards its opposite, orange (B). As you can see, the result is a warmer image.

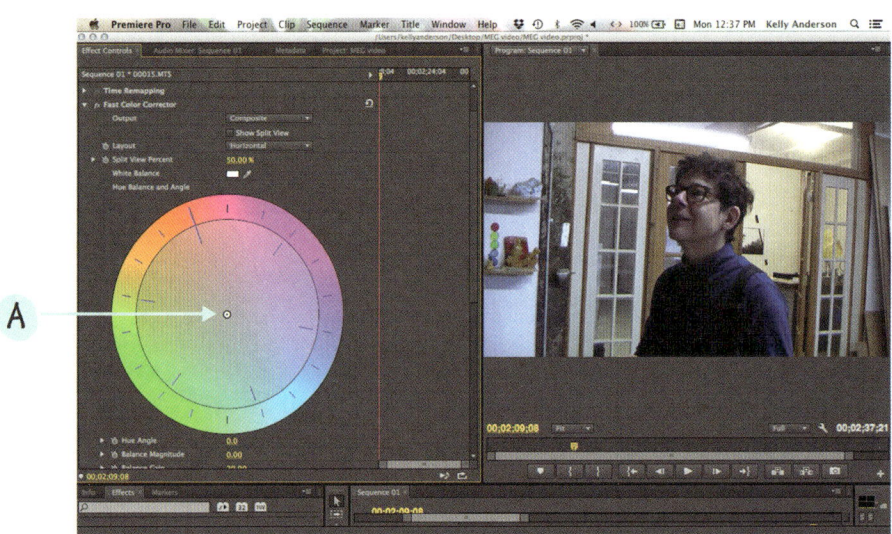

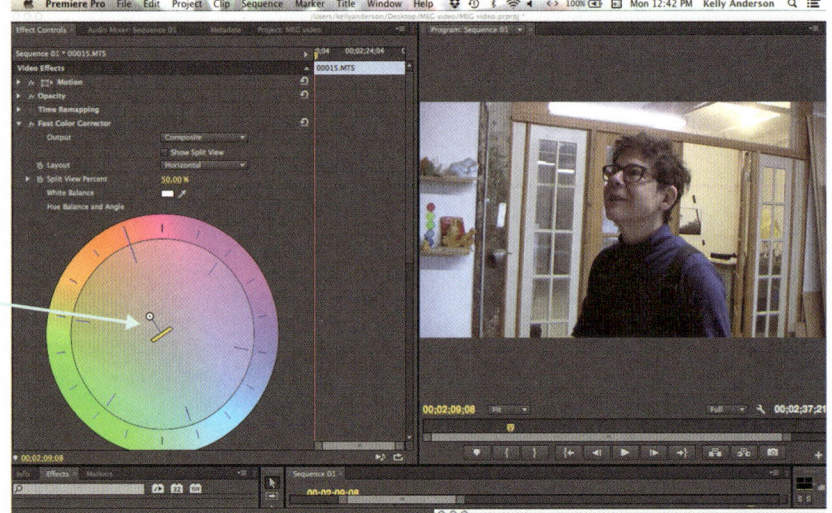

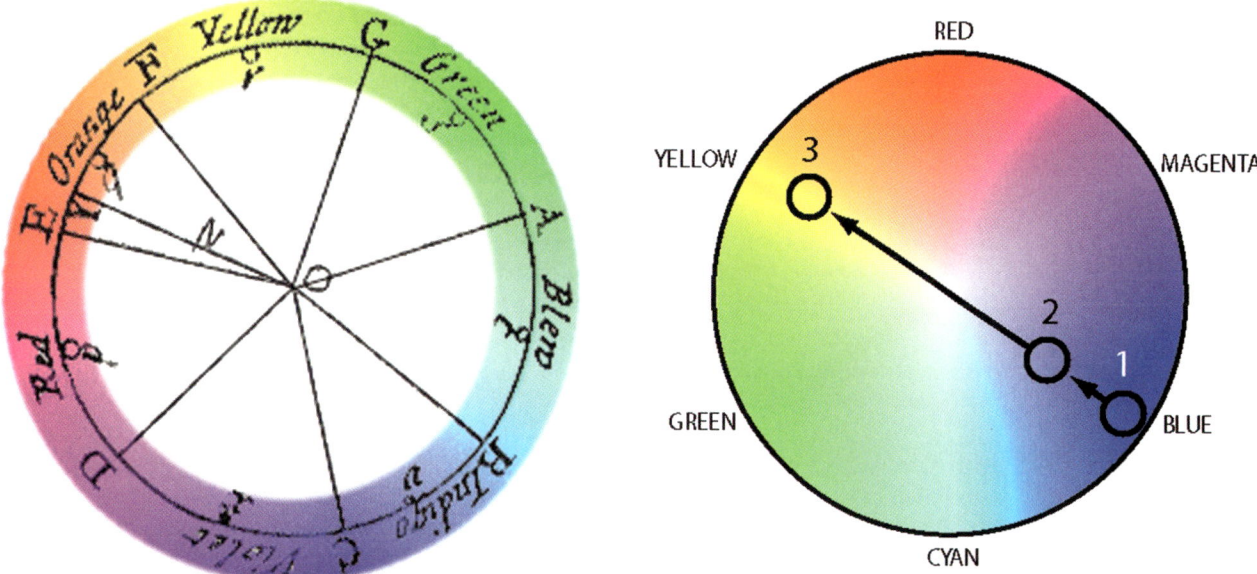

■ **Figure 22.5** The first color wheel is attributed to Isaac Newton, who in 1706 arranged red, orange, yellow, green, blue, indigo, and violet into a natural progression on a rotating disk (left). As the disk spins, the colors blur together so rapidly that the human eye sees white. The color wheel in many color correction programs follows the same principle (right). As you reduce the amount of blue, for example, you increase the amount of its complementary color, yellow.

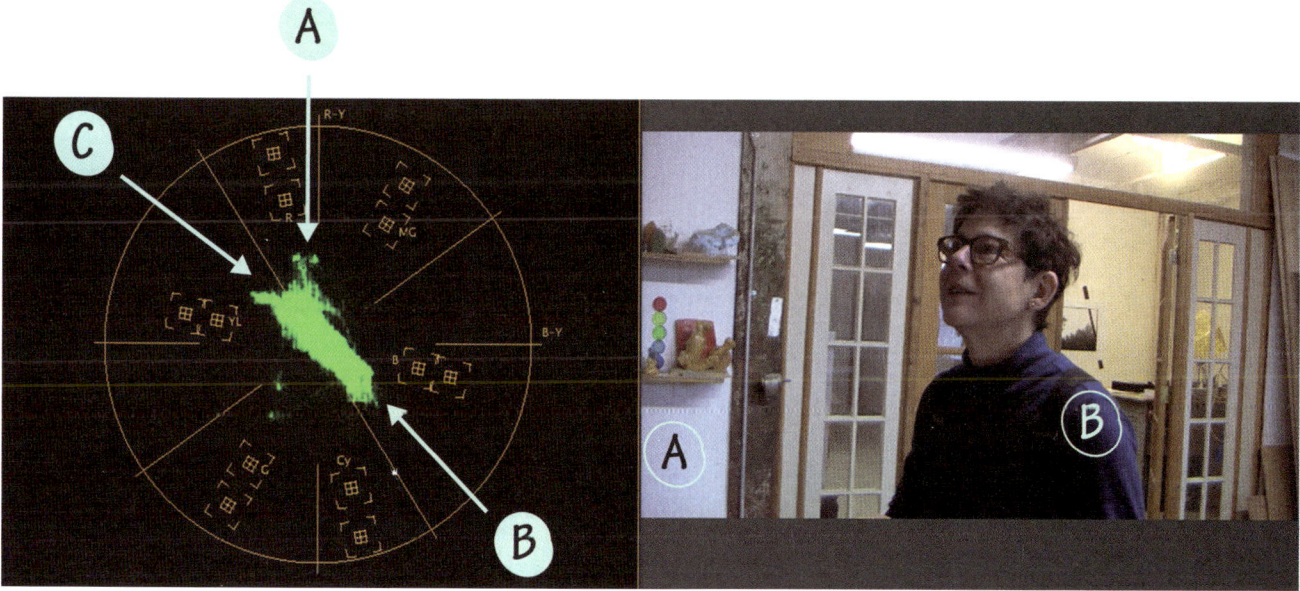

■ **Figure 22.6** The Vectorscope represents the saturation level of the various colors in the image. The red object on the shelf (A) creates a spike on the "red" area of the vectorscope (A). Similarly, the blue shirt (B) registers strongly in the "blue" area of the vectorscope (B). The (C) line represents skin tones, and is a valuable reference point when correcting people's faces. Because what registers is the color of the blood, not the pigment of the skin, all skin tones should register along this exact line.

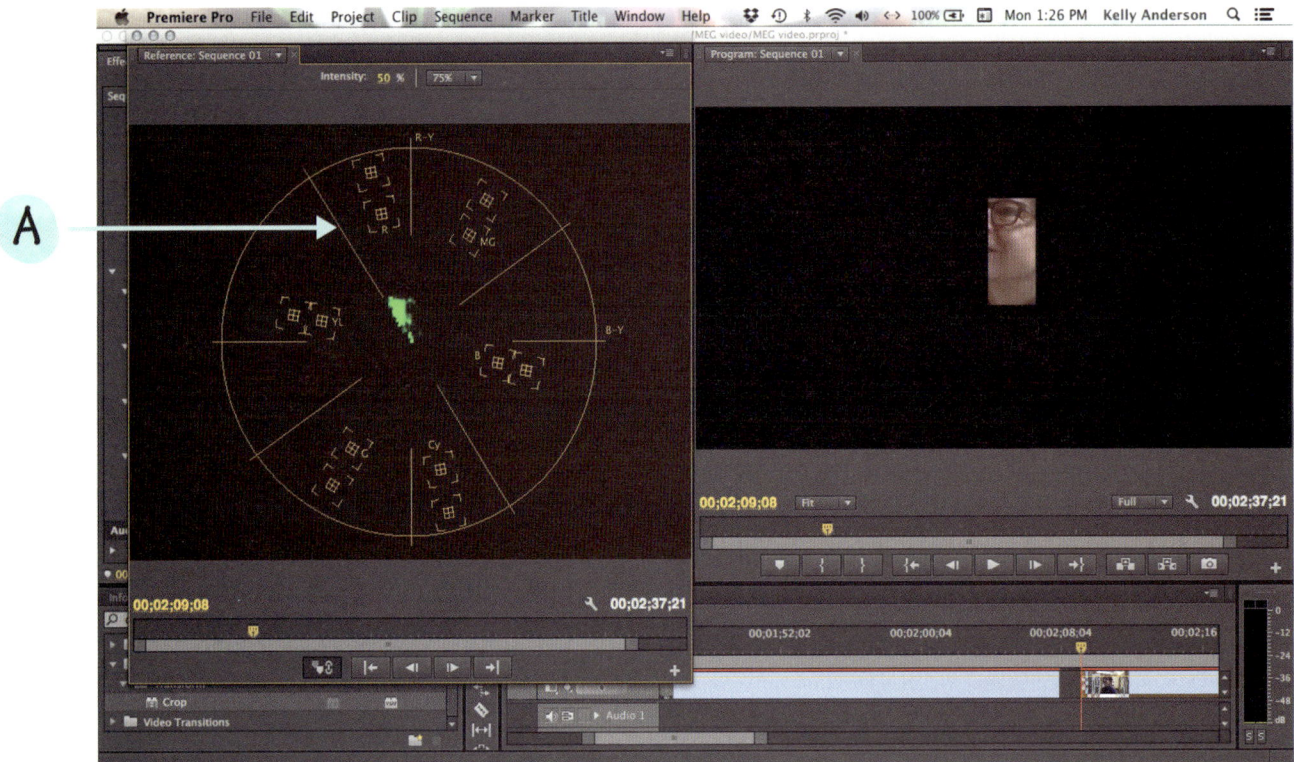

■ **Figure 22.7** The vectorscope's Flesh Tone Line. Cropping the program panel image to reveal just the face of the subject illustrates how skin tones, when they are corrected properly, fall along the vectorscope's flesh tone line.

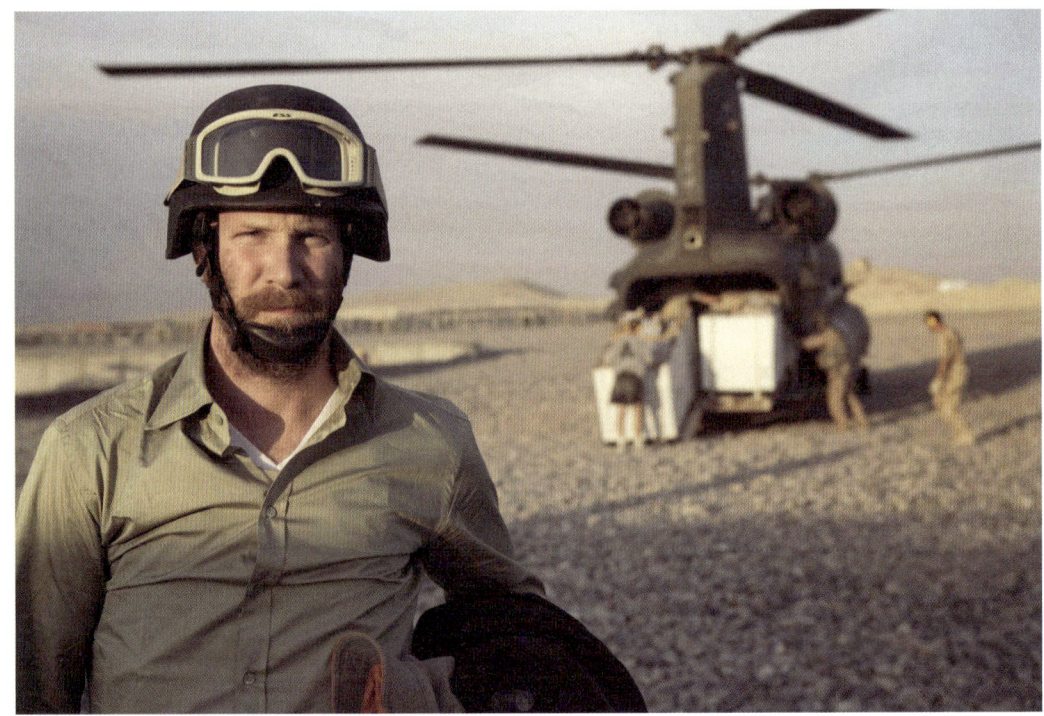

■ **Figure 22.8** In this scene from Morgan Spurlock's *Where in the World is Osama Bin Laden* (2008), color grading brings out the subtle colors and textures of the Afghani landscape.

CHAPTER 14

Location Sound Techniques

THE SOUND RECORDIST'S JOB

The basic and most common production team on a documentary consists of a cinematographer and one **sound recordist** (Figures 13.3 and 14.1). The sound recordist is responsible for getting the best quality audio onto the recording format, and this is a big job. These responsibilities include:

- Scouting locations when possible, and doing a location sound survey
- Understanding the acoustics and ambient qualities of a given location, and controlling them as much as possible
- Understanding, as much as is possible, who and what is going to be filmed
- Choosing the most appropriate microphones for the situation
- Placing microphones, whether on people, handholding, on a boompole, or on a stand
- Setting record levels on the camera (for single-system recording) or on the audio recorder (for double-system recording)
- Monitoring the recorded sound during filming, and stopping production if necessary
- Delivering the sound in the appropriate format and configuration for postproduction
- Creating and delivering sound reports indicating key information about what was recorded using which microphones

The sound recordist has to do all these things while keeping the microphones out of the frame, wrangling cables, and staying out of the way of the cameraperson and equipment on the set. This is skilled and difficult work that takes much practice. If you are recording **single-system** and are cabled to the camera, the job is made all the more difficult because you need to make sure you don't let the cables pull on the camera while getting your microphones as close to the subject as possible. If **double-system**, you need to ensure that the sound will sync with the picture (there are a variety of ways of doing this; see Chapters 13 and 17). Despite the importance and difficulty of the job, sound recordists are generally underappreciated by all but experienced filmmakers, who practically worship the ground a good sound recordist walks on. One bit of good news in all of this is that if you understand sound recording and do it well, you will likely always have a job in production.

SOUND AND THE DOCUMENTARY CREW

Because sound recording is so important, we can't advise beginners (or even seasoned documentary practitioners) to try to do everything on their own. A two-person crew, where one shoots and one does sound, is a tried and true combination, and produces great results even with its small size. There are times, however, where a filmmaker chooses to forego using a sound recordist in order to preserve the intimacy of a situation. If you are highly experienced with shooting, and with sound, this can work. David Alvarado, one of the directors of The Immortalists (2014), has this to say:

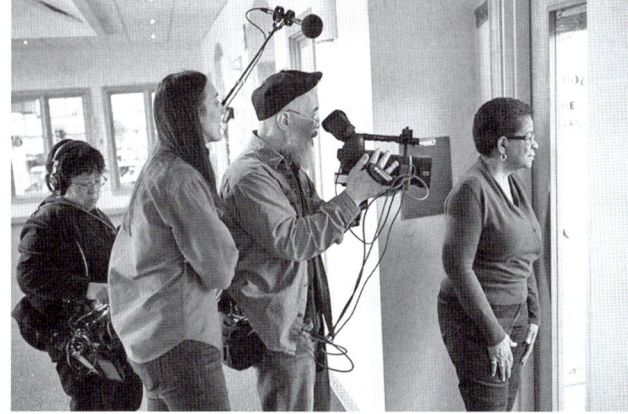

■ Figure 14.1 A typical documentary crew. Sound recordist J T Takagi, Director Megan Mylan, and Director of Photography Michael Chin filming the short documentary *My Little Friends* (2013). Photo courtesy of Principe Productions/PrincipeProductions.com.

> *I was shooting on The Immortalists, and Jason Sussberg did sound. But there are about 5 or 6 one-man-band scenes in the film that I shot on my own. I had a digital audio recorder with four inputs on the back of the Redrock (shoulder mount, see pp. 154–155), and literally everyone on the set had a wireless microphone on them. And then I put a really good, $3,000 Schoeps microphone on top of the camera. I just set the levels to get the dialogue in the right range, and let the limiter (pp. 237–238) do the rest. It's not advisable, but for some scenes we did it that way. (See Figure 6.1 for a picture of David shooting as a one-man-band crew.)*
>
> *It depends on the scene. If it's a vérité event where a person's going to be going around talking to different people who aren't miked, there's no way around it. If you want good sound you have to have a boom operator in there (pp. 239–241), and they have to have the philosophy of any good recordist, which is "I'm going to get as close as I possibly can without getting into the frame." And they're fighting for inches, you know, because every inch you get is better than the inch before it.*[1]

As David suggests, one-man-band shooting relies on a cameraperson who knows a lot about sound and can keep their eye on many variables at one time. In addition, if you are going to want to record good audio for anybody who is not miked, you will need a sound recordist with a boom. Finally, the cost of multiple good wireless mics may make the configuration David describes impractical for many filmmakers.

BEFORE THE SHOOT: PREPPING AND SCOUTING

As veteran sound recordist Daniel Brooks says, "The thing that differentiates a good sound person from a mediocre sound person is the *proactive anticipation* of what is going to happen." This means that much of the work of sound recording happens before filming. The first step in prepping for a shoot is a conversation between the sound recordist and the director.

Ideally, here is the information a sound person should know in order to be fully prepared:
- What is the topic of the film?
- What style is it? For this particular shoot, will you be filming sit-down interviews, or is it observational? Or a combination?
- What is the location for the particular shoot? Has anybody scouted the location with an ear for sound? If not, is it possible for the sound person to scout (or at least arrive early)?
- How much control do you have over the location? If it's a restaurant kitchen, for example, can you schedule the shoot at a time when the dining room is empty?
- What camera is the cinematographer using?
- Is this **double-system** or **single-system** recording?
- Is there anything particularly sensitive about any of the people you are filming? Are there any restrictions in terms of how the participants can be miked?
- What is going to happen? How many people will be part of the action, and need to be recorded?
- How much prep time will there be on set before the camera rolls?
- What will the daily workflow be in terms of transferring files, etc.?
- What are the specifications for the **deliverables**: audio file type, record settings, and media format?

Whenever possible, the next step is to scout the location where shooting will take place. On documentaries, for budget and scheduling reasons, it's rare that the sound recordist will be asked to scout. But if at all possible, somebody who understands sound should do a scout before the shoot, or the sound recordist should plan to arrive on location early enough to evaluate the aural environment.

As sound recordist and filmmaker JT Takagi explains:

> *Make sure whoever does the location scout is thinking about sound. And you have to ask about that, because if they aren't thinking about sound, it can be a disaster. You end up on set, and you can't hear anything initially, because everybody is setting things up, clanging things around and yelling, and when you actually do roll, that's the only time you get quiet, and it's at that point you realize, "Oh, what's that horrible buzzing noise?" or "They're doing construction down the hall?" All of which could have been addressed ahead of time.*[2]

Common problems in a location include loud highways or traffic nearby, lawn mowers, noisy neighbors, barking dogs, construction, airplane flight patterns, loud HVAC—if you can name it, a sound recordist has probably had to deal with it. While these cannot always be controlled—you would be hard-pressed to find a New York City location without traffic noise, or an office without HVAC—scouting ahead of time can help you figure out whether you can live with the sound problem, mitigate it, or need to find another location. The person doing the scout will complete a location survey (Figure 14.2).

Before arriving on set, sound recordists should also ensure that they understand the technical specs, record media, and delivery details expected for their audio files. Different edit systems, editors, and sound designers prefer their **sound elements** in various formats or recorded at specific settings (frame rate, sampling rate, bit depth). Also, increasingly deliverables include **isolated tracks** from all microphones as well as a 2-channel output mixed on the fly by the sound recordist.

■ LOCATION SOUND PROBLEMS

We once had some students who were making a short documentary about the renovation of Hunter College's Roosevelt House, a landmark building where Franklin and Eleanor Roosevelt lived in Manhattan. The students badly wanted to film the Hunter College president in front of the actual building, but when they returned to the classroom with their recorded interview, the sound of construction on the street completely drowned out the sound of the President speaking, rendering it unusable. Unfortunately, it was the type of interview that could only be scheduled once.

What should they have done? Wait until construction was finished, or talk to the workers to see if they could take a break for 15 minutes anytime soon. Or, move the President! As it turned out, the shot was framed tightly enough that you couldn't really tell Roosevelt House from any other brownstone building in the neighborhood. The students were devastated, but they and everybody else in the classroom that day learned a valuable lesson.

■ ON LOCATION: THE SHOOT

On the day of a shoot, the sound recordist's job is to:
1. Evaluate the location
2. Figure out a microphone placement strategy in consultation with the director and the cinematographer
3. Prepare the location and set up equipment
4. Place and test microphones
5. Set levels and tone if possible
6. Record the audio
7. Deliver the audio files

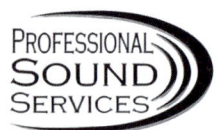

NEW YORK • NEW ORLEANS
www.pro-sound.com

Location Scout Check List

Script Location: _____

Actual Location: _____

Noise	Location Of Noise	Material/Method of Attenuate
Refrigerators/Compressors		
Pipes/Fans/Heat/AC/Radiators		
Florescent/Neon/Practical Lighting		
Windows/Doors		
Floors/Acoustics		
Mirrors/Reflections		
Air/Road Traffic		
Telephones/Alarms/Door Chimes		
Neighbors/Dogs/Children/Generators		
Genie Placement/Cable Thru		
Other Noises/RF		
Cart Placement		

New York: 311 West 43rd Street, Suite #1100 • New York, NY 10036
Tel: 212.586.1033 • Toll Free: 800.883.1033 • FAX: 212.586.0970

New Orleans: 1515 South Salcedo Street, Suite #130 • New Orleans, LA 70125
Tel: 504.309.7112 • Toll Free: 855.309.7112 • FAX: 504.309.7138

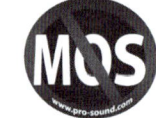

■ **Figure 14.2** This location survey from Professional Sound Services offers a typical checklist of potential sound problems.

Evaluate the Location

On the day of production, the sound recordist should arrive early to listen for any noise-makers at the location, like refrigerators, fans, fluorescent lights, and radiators. What about room acoustics? Will sound blankets be needed?

It is common to unplug refrigerators, but make sure you turn them on again after the shoot! A common trick is to put your keys in the refrigerator so you will have to go back and get them before leaving, which will remind you to turn the fridge back on. Also turn off electronics like computers, answering machines, and phone ringers. Make sure everybody on the set turns off their cellphones.

Finally, the sound person will work to make the location as dead as possible (Chapter 13). For a sit-down interview, this might involve hanging sound blankets outside the frame. For an observational scene, it could involve dragging an area rug into a room with wooden or tiled floors to reduce the number of reflective surfaces.

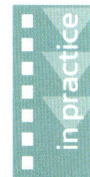

■ DEALING WITH UNEXPECTED SOUND ISSUES ON LOCATION

Sometimes, despite the best scouting, there are sound issues that arise on the day of shooting. In addition to all their required production skills, sound people often end up having to be skilled negotiators. JT Takagi explains about one film she did sound on:

> The producer and director loved the look of the house, and they had done a scout, which was good. Then they found out, luckily before we shot, that there was a daycare center next door. So they had to find out what times of day the children came outside to play, and we planned to restrict the time we did the interview so it wouldn't be during those times. The day we went to shoot, of course, they broke their schedule. So then we had to send someone over to negotiate, which sometimes means saying, "Let's all go and get ice cream!" to get people out of the way. You do things like that. Sometimes it's an unpleasant neighbor who usually isn't home during the day, so when the place was scouted it was quiet, but they decided not to go to work that day, and the stereo is on very loudly. Then you have to see who is on the crew who seems the nicest, kindest, or most gorgeous, or whatever, to go negotiate that situation. And once in a while it also involves cash.[3]

Devising a Sound Recording Strategy

Daniel Brooks explains how much of sound recording is asking the right questions before the camera even rolls:

> Once the scene starts, you can't really do anything invasive like putting a microphone on, rearranging a microphone, or (depending on what the lighting situation is) even adjust the boom much. So you have to think about all these things before you actually start shooting. It's a constant process of grilling the director. "Who is going to be in the scene?" "What are they going to do?" "Oh, they're going to talk to somebody else?" "Who's that other person?" "Can we put a mic on them?" And then, "Oh, then they're going to go into a car? So are we going to shoot it in the car, or are we just going to let them drive away?" Understanding all that stuff allows you to do things like put the microphone in a position where the seatbelt doesn't land on top of it and blow out your sound for that scene. If you know that this person is driving, you will put the lav on the right side of them instead of the left side, because the shoulder strap is a killer. So knowing how to ask the right questions, and then processing that information, and thinking of all the variables that could happen, allows you to prepare for them so that

when the scene plays out, you are mostly covered. And inevitably somebody will stop and turn to somebody on the street that you haven't miked, and say "Hey, so what do you think about such-and-such?" So you always have a boom (pp. 239–241). No matter where I go, I always have a boom and it's always plugged in, and if something happens it's just a matter of extending it. It could be that a battery dies on the wireless, or that the mic gets ripped from its position, or that the subject turns and talks to somebody who wasn't supposed to be in the scene. The boom is really essential to cover that kind of stuff.[4]

A combination of factors will determine whether you record single-system or double-system audio. When dealing with observational situations, most sound people prefer to record double-system so they can find the best possible microphone placement without having to worry about being cabled to the camera. For students, who typically work without time code capable equipment or expensive transmitters, this setup will require a good audio recorder and slating in the field to allow syncing in postproduction. When working this way, you should use the onboard camera mic to record **reference audio** so you can sync more easily in postproduction (Chapter 17). There are also many situations where having the sound recordist connected to the camera isn't a big problem. For sit-down (formal) interviews, a single-system setup is perfectly appropriate and an even simpler solution.

The next step in your strategy will involve setting up your microphones. Documentary productions usually record sync sound from at least two microphones. You keep these sounds as separate tracks on your recording media, so that in postproduction the sound editor can favor the best channel, or combine the two. For example, if you are shooting a sit-down interview, a hard-wired lavalier should be placed on your subject, and a boom mic (usually a hypercardioid) should be used as well. In addition to providing backup when the interviewee touches their chest and creates noise on their lavalier (as invariably happens at the most emotional or important part of an interview!), the mic on the boom will capture more of the room **presence**. Often the lav and the boom mic will be mixed together in postproduction to create an ideal balance between the close sound of the lav and the more full sound of the person speaking in a room with ambience.

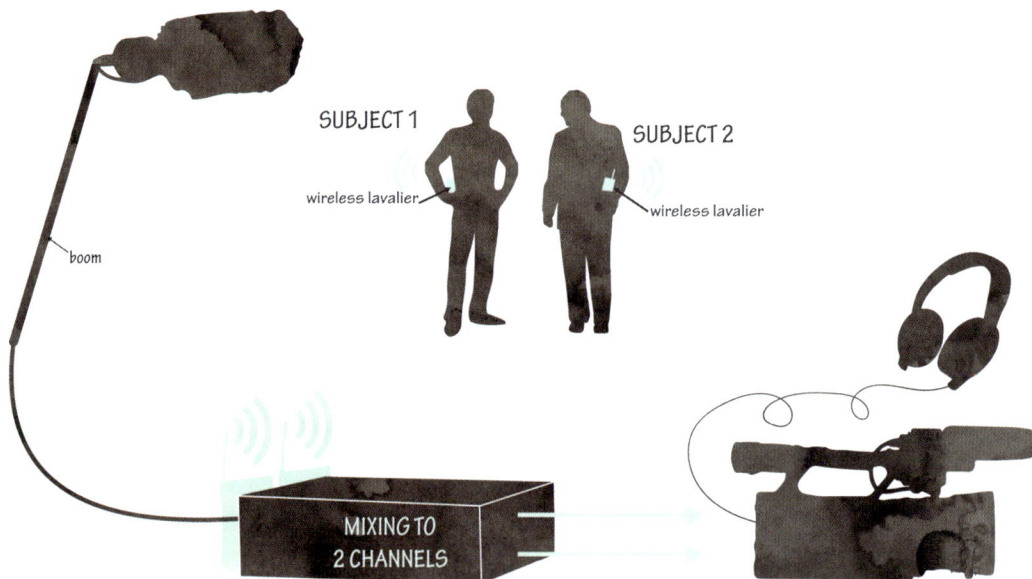

■ **Figure 14.3** A typical setup for recording documentary sound: wireless microphones are placed on two subjects, and a boom is used to pick up all other sounds. All three microphones are fed into the mixer, and the sound recordist mixes a two-channel output for the camera. They may also record isolated tracks (ISOs) and deliver those.

For observational scenes, you will likely be using a combination of a shotgun mic on a boom, and wireless lavs placed on one or more subjects. The number of wireless mics available to you will largely be determined by your budget, but it is also important to figure out how many people in the scene will be speaking. Often it will be enough to have one wireless lav on your main subject, and a boom to capture any other important audio. This is a common setup for a **walk-and-talk** scenario, where the main subject walks around a neighborhood or some other location, and speaks mainly to an off-camera director or the cinematographer. If they encounter someone along the way, the boom can be used to capture the audio of the person they speak with.

For observational situations where it is important to record more than one subject, multiple wireless mics can be used. Many reality TV shows routinely wire up six or more people. But be aware that your mixer and/or audio recorder will only be able to record so many channels of audio (2, 4, 6, 12, or 16, depending on the model), and at a certain point it becomes impossible for one person to monitor and mix them adequately. Also, concealing wireless mics takes time and a bit of expertise, and will add substantial prep time to your setup (Figure 14.3).

Regardless of the number of wireless mics you are using, a boom mic is always essential. A boom mic records richer sound than a lav, and because of its narrow pickup pattern a sound recordist can have a great deal of control over what it records. The boom allows the sound recordist flexibility in mic placement. As long as it's out of the frame, a boom can be above, below, or next to the subject. Resist the temptation to rely solely on wireless, or to put a mic on the camera and leave it at that. The boom is your safety blanket, and will often be the source of your best sound.

For most documentary situations, between one and four wireless mics will be sufficient. Sometimes the sound recordist will record **isolated tracks** (called iso's) for each mic, as well as a mix they create "on the fly." For the beginning documentary sound recordist, keeping it simple by recording two sources on separate channels is advised. See Figure 14.3 for an overview of a common setup.

Setting Up Your Equipment

Sound recordists typically move around with all the equipment they need on their body. You will need your recorder and/or mixer, with all of your wireless receivers in one bag. Always carry headphones. If you are booming, you will need to mount your boom mic and wrap your cables so that you can move quickly without problems. Keeping your cables coiled and neat, while remaining prepared to let cable out and coil it back up as needed, is a skill learned with time.

A final step in setting up your equipment is making sure that everything has fresh batteries and is working properly. Change batteries every day to avoid creating problems on set. Interrupting a shoot to change batteries is disruptive and will not be appreciated if it can be helped. Some equipment will need new batteries even more often, and a cable can go bad at any time, so be aware.

Be tactful when putting lavalier microphones on people. Most documentarians want microphones to be invisible, so putting a microphone on someone inevitably involves putting the mic and wires under clothing. Explain to people what you are doing, and ask for their permission before reaching inside their clothing or touching them. It can be helpful to allow them to run the mic up under their shirt or pants and then hand it to you for securing. If you need to plant a mic on a minor, always make sure their legal guardian is present.

■ **CONCEALING LAVALIERS**

For sound recordist Daniel Brooks, concealing a lavalier microphone starts with setting the microphone head in a cocoon made of **moleskin,** which has an adhesive backing and is designed to stick to human skin. The next step is to ask the subject to drop the cable down under her shirt. Daniel then removes the protective plastic from the back of the moleskin and tacks it on the subject's chest, asking her to pat it down to make it stick properly. He then connects the transmitter at her waist. The result is a firmly attached and trouble-free microphone, which is relatively impervious to clothing noise (Figure 14.4).[5] To see a video of this in action, visit our companion website (www.routledge.com/cw/Anderson).

Setting Levels

Getting optimum audio levels depends on a combination of microphone placement and manual audio level adjustment on your recording device. The term **setting levels** refers to controlling the loudness of a signal as it enters the recorder or mixer, which in turn determines the strength of the recorded audio signal. All professional recorders offer manual level controls. The craft of the sound recordist centers on the ability to find proper levels, which generally means setting the loudest possible record level without **overmodulating**. The most important tools for monitoring and setting audio levels on a digital recorder or video camera are the **peak meter** (found primarily on cameras and sound recorders) and the **VU meter** (found primarily on field mixers).

Setting Levels on a Peak Meter

Peak meters are calibrated in decibels, from –∞ on the low side to 0 dB on the high side. If your audio level approaches 0 dB, your audio will become **overmodulated** or **overloaded**, which means the signal is too strong to be sampled accurately and the result is distorted sound. Sudden and loud transient sounds, like a car door slamming shut, which spike above 0 dB, are especially a problem, because even these brief noises can cause crackling on the soundtrack. You cannot fix overmodulated sound in postproduction, so it's better to record low than to overmodulate.

On the other hand, if you record a level that is too low, you will be required to boost the sound level in postproduction. By turning up the volume of the recorded signal, you also turn up the volume of the unwanted audio **noise** and the result is greater background and system noise. Recording too low is called recording "in the mud." Recording too low is different than recording soft sounds, which sometimes, appropriately, barely register on the peak meter.

To make sure you obtain a good, strong signal, but protect yourself from overmodulation, you should set your levels so that the loudest audio in the scene peaks at –20 dB on the peak meter. It can be hard to set levels in a documentary situation, as you don't know what will occur during filming, but getting a good sense of how loud various people speak in regular conversation is a good guide. The range between –20 dB and 0 dB is called **headroom** and it gives you a buffer for any unforeseen and sudden audio spikes, like people suddenly yelling or slamming a door (Figure 14.5).

When setting record levels, it is best to avoid extremes on the level control knobs. You never want to have your level control set all the way to its loudest setting or too close to its lowest setting. These extremes usually mean there is either something wrong with your microphone placement or you have some technical problem along the signal path. Also remember that not all sounds need to be recorded at –20 dB. Very low sounds, like papers rustling as someone studies in the library, are fine to record at a low level like –40 dB or –30 dB. Trying to get this soft sound to peak at –20 dB will force you to increase the level to its maximum, which will increase the extraneous room noise (ambient sound) and system noise to an unnaturally high level. If a fairly strong source, say a person speaking, is registering very low on the meter, then it's preferable to move the microphone in closer than to boost the recording levels too high.

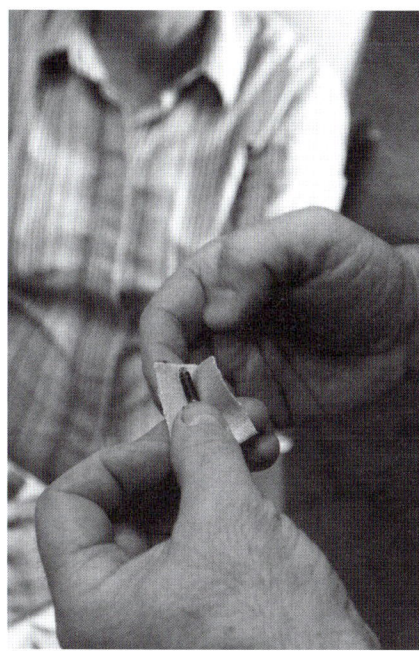
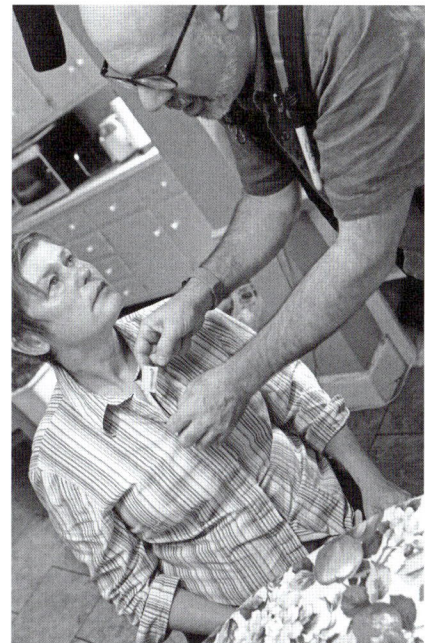
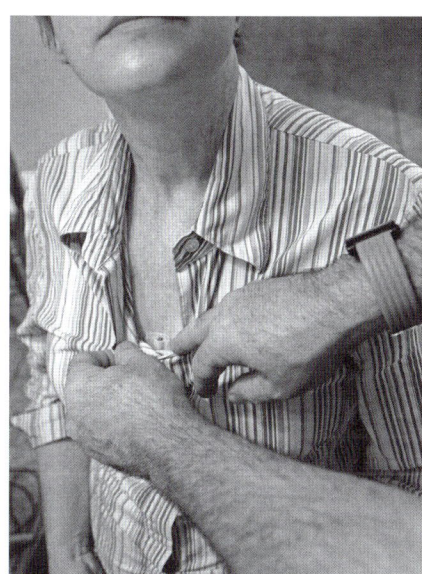
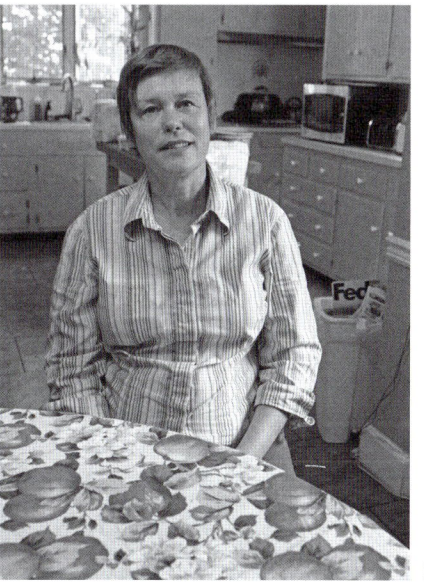

■ **Figure 14.4** In (A) we can see the tiny Countryman B6 lavalier in its nest of moleskin. In (B) the microphone is being placed. In (C) Brooks is showing the microphone placement on the subject's chest. In (D) we can see the subject with the microphone concealed, ready for her interview.

■ –12 OR –20?

In professional recording situations, audio levels are expected to peak at –20 dB. Confusion is created, however, by the fact that some prosumer and consumer cameras set their internal standards to –12. This may be adequate but keep in mind that you risk overmodulation by setting your level at –12.

Also, some cameras don't have numbers on their meters at all! Instead, their peak meter is green or white, and turns to red on the upper end where sounds are likely to be overmodulated. In these cases, make sure to keep your sound level well below the red zone. When in doubt, play back your recorded sound and listen for any distortion.

Another strategy is to use slightly lower recording levels on the second of your two audio channels. So if your audio is peaking at –12 on one channel, lower the level on the other channel so that it is peaking at –18 or –20. This will only work, though, if you are recording the same audio on both channels. And there is no harm in testing a sound file in your NLE if you can.

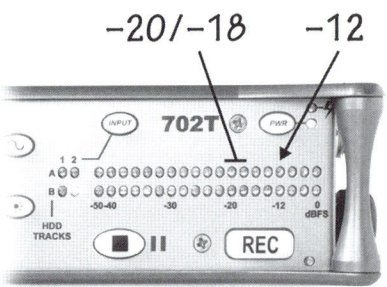
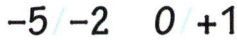

Figure 14.5 Normal dialogue should be recorded to peak at −20 dB.

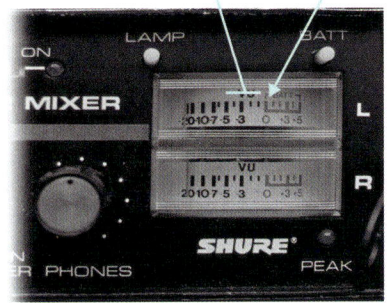
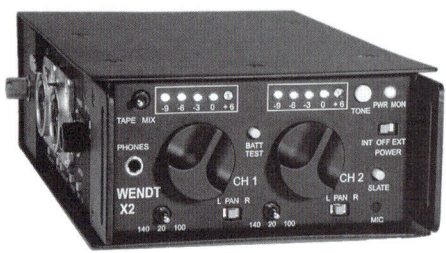

Figure 14.6 The scale of a VU meter is different from that of a peak meter. The loudest signal should peak between 0 dB to +1 dB, with normal dialogue registering between −5 dB and −2 dB. On the top is a needle-based gauge on the Shure FP33 field mixer. On the bottom, the Wendt X2 portable field mixer features an LED level indicator.

Setting Levels on a VU Meter

If you use a field mixer for setting levels, you will likely encounter the **volume unit (VU) meter**, which monitors your incoming audio signal differently than a peak meter. While peak meters respond to all sounds directly entering the recorder, the VU meter indicates an average sound level. It is, therefore, not highly sensitive to short, sharp, percussive sounds. For example, a slamming door in the middle of a moderately quiet scene will cause the needle to jump a bit, but not to the true decibel level of that slam, because the noise is too brief for the needle to respond accurately. In addition, although the VU level range is calibrated in decibels, it has a different scale than the peak meter. The VU meter's indicators run from −20 on the low end to +3 on the high end, with 0 dB as the optimal level. The point on the scale from 0 dB to +3 is highlighted by a thicker, red bar on a needle scale or red lights on an LED scale (Figure 14.6).

As a general rule, the loudest sounds in a given recording situation should peak at 0 dB. Occasionally, the reading can peak in the red zone but should not spend too much time there, and in no situation should the VU meter needle "pin" against the +3 side of the scale. Normally spoken dialogue is set to average around −3 dB so that any sudden, loudly expressive moments might peak between −1 dB and 0 dB. Very low sounds, like paper rustling in the library, can be set to register around −10 dB. If you read in the previous chapter that 0 dB is the quietest sound audible to the human ear, you may wonder what is going on with this scale. The fact is, the dB scale used for metering is a different one, whereas 0 dB is a defined reference level of sound volume.

Setting Tone

Reference tone is a 1 kHz pure tone that is used to calibrate a chain of audio devices in the field. Let's say you are plugging your microphone into a field mixer (with VU meters) that you will use to set and monitor levels during the shoot. The audio signal will go from the

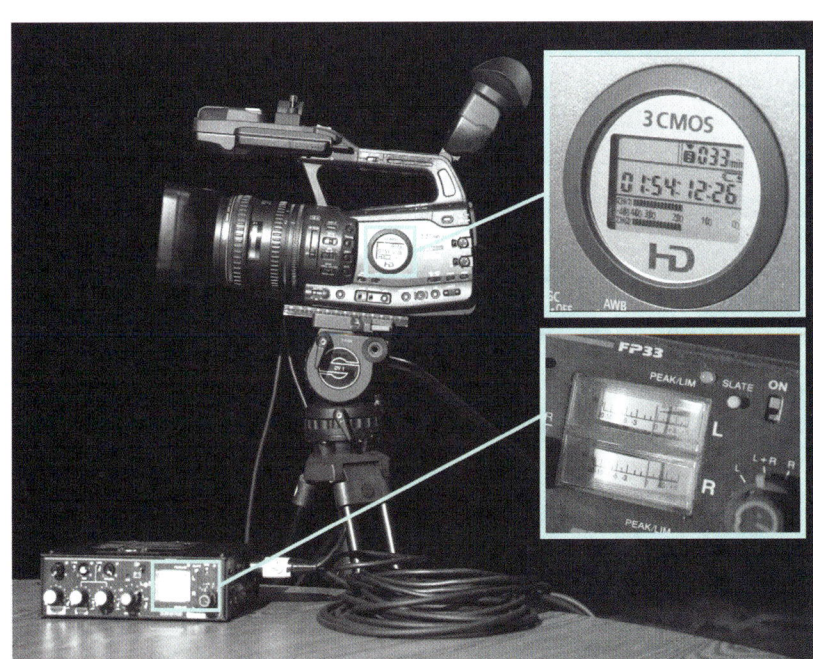

Figure 14.7 Setting tone. A 1 kHz reference tone is used to calibrate the output of the mixer with the input of the camera. The mixer's VU meter reads the tone at 0 dB (bottom insert), whereas the recorder's peak meter should be set to register the tone at −20 dB (top insert).

mixer into either the camera or a sound recorder. This is a very common audio chain, but how do you know where to set your level controls on the recording device so that the recorded audio will match the optimized levels you set on the mixer? All field mixers have a button that will generate the 1 kHz reference tone, which allows you to set the record levels so that what you see on the mixer during the shoot will match what the camera is recording. If you set up your mixer so that the 1 kHz tone registers exactly as 0 dB, and then output the tone to the camera and set its level at –20 dB, you will know that if your levels look good on your mixer, they will be good on the camera as well (Figure 14.7).

It is standard practice to record 30 seconds of **reference tone** at the head of your record media, often accompanied by color bars if you are recording single-system and your camera can generate them. This ensures that audio transfers and levels in postproduction can be calibrated with the original audio recording. This is called **bars and tone** and it assures the postproduction team that what they are hearing and seeing is exactly what was recorded.

RECORDING YOUR AUDIO

Once filming is underway, the sound recordist's job is to monitor the sound, hold mics, adjust levels, and be the "ears" of the production. Just as a cinematographer is trained to see every light source on the scene, a sound mixer is trained to hear every sound on the location that might wind up on the recording. Knowing when to interrupt production because of unwanted sound problems is difficult and subjective. It is the sound recordist's job to make sure the audio is clean. On the other hand, there are situations where interrupting what is going on is inadvisable, and it would be easier to "pick up" (rerecord) a particular line later on. You should discuss with the director ahead of time whether he wants you to interrupt production for sound issues. Often, unless it's a disastrous interference or there is no sound, he will want you to signal to him that there is sound interfering with recording and he will decide whether to stop filming.

Riding the Gain during Recording

When you initially set levels for dialogue, this "normal" dialogue level is only your first reference. As the shooting situation unfolds, it is the job of the sound recordist to make adjustments to audio levels to accommodate the changes in volume that are part of a real-world soundscape. Raising or lowering the record level as needed is called **riding the gain**, or **riding levels**.

A word of caution is in order here. The difference between the loudest and softest sounds in any single recording situation is called the **dynamic range**, and setting levels for a sound situation with a wide dynamic range is a mixer's greatest challenge. Riding levels too often or too extremely causes unnatural fluctuations in the background noise and can cause unanticipated sounds to spike above 0 dB or fall "into the mud." A range of loud and soft sounds is natural. It's important to capture a strong audio signal, and certainly important that dialogue be intelligible, but if you constantly raise and lower the levels so that every sound records at the same level, the effect is terribly unnatural. Use judgment and caution, and listen to your recorded audio to learn what strategies are working for you and which can be tweaked.

As mentioned in Chapter 13, it is critical that you disable Automatic Gain Control (AGC) and adjust your recording levels manually.

Limiters, Microphone Attenuation, and Frequency Filters

While AGC is not recommended, there are other automatic audio controls that you will encounter on cameras, recorders, and field mixers that can be useful. **Limiters** are volume controls that only come into effect when an audio signal reaches overload (Figure 14.8). At this point, the limiter suppresses the loudness by **clipping** the sound before it can peak.

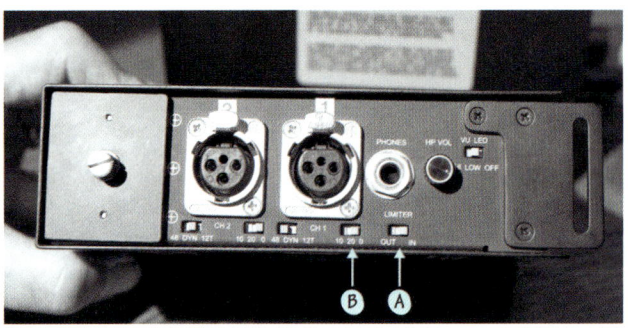

■ Figure 14.8 Limiter (A) and Attenuation (B). On this mixer each input has the option of −10 and −20 dB attenuation.

The danger with employing a limiter is that it can be difficult for an operator to tell if the levels are properly set, as volume extremes never peak when the limiter is turned on. In controlled audio situations, try not to use the limiter at all, though it can be useful when a single person is both booming and setting levels and you anticipate some erratic loud noises in the scene. In these cases, set the levels for the most common audio first, then employ the limiter. Another tool on your mixer or digital recorder is a **microphone attenuation** or "pad" switch, which cuts the overall volume of incoming audio by 10 or 20 dB (Figure 14.8). This can be very useful in loud sound environments where a sensitive microphone will send a signal that can overload the mixer's inputs.

Frequency filters automatically remove unwanted portions of the frequency range. The most common filters found on field mixers and recorders are designed to cut off low frequencies and are variously called **bass**, **bass roll-off**, **low-pass**, or **low-frequency attenuation filters**. Bass roll-off is common because we often encounter wind noise (wind hitting the microphone diaphragm), traffic noise, and low machinery hum (like rumbling HVAC systems) in the field. For example, perhaps we are filming in a factory where there is a constant, low-frequency machinery hum that is making dialogue difficult to record. A low-frequency filter will automatically suppress frequencies below, say, 50 Hz (the specific frequencies "rolled off" are variable depending on the system). Use frequency filters with caution—the equalizing capabilities in postproduction are far more sophisticated and precise.

Headphone Monitoring

In the field, sound monitoring is always done through headphones. Headphones with **isolation pads** are essential so the sound recordists can be certain that what they are hearing is only the audio being recorded. Earbuds or small headphones do not prevent sound coming directly to your ears, making it impossible to tell what you are hearing directly and what you are recording (Figure 14.9).

In addition to monitoring for sound problems (like loose connections or signal interference), headphones are also used to evaluate other aural qualities of the recording situation, like background noises or the acoustics of the recording location. This is important because if there is a sound issue, like a car passing by outside your location, you need to make a quick decision whether that noise affected your recorded tracks or not. The recorded sound might be quite different from what people in the room experience with their bare ears.

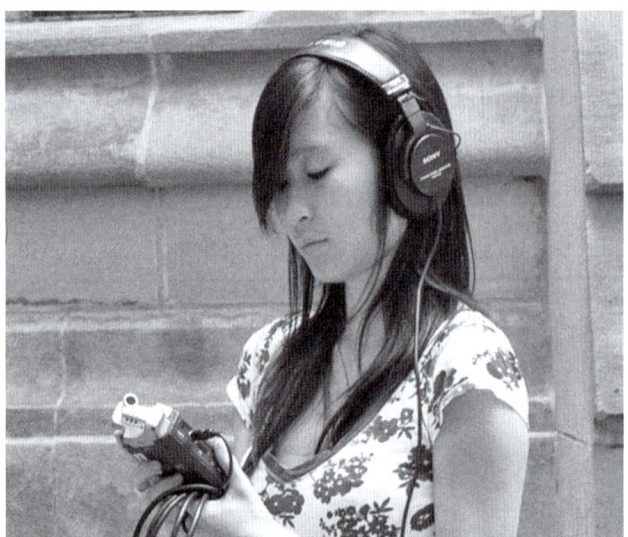

■ Figure 14.9 Large headphones that completely cover the ears should be used to monitor audio, because they block out noise.

Once record levels are set, the sound recordist can use her headphones to double-check the accuracy of her microphone placement, being sure to keep it on-axis and the subject-to-mic distance consistent (p. 239).

It is also important to listen to the output of the sound at the last point in the audio chain. It is entirely possible that your audio will sound great when it leaves the mixer but that there will be a problem in the camera, or on the way to the camera or recorder. For this reason, whenever the output of the mixer is being sent to the camera via wireless transmission, the recordist will always create a backup recording on a portable audio recorder. If you are hard-wired to the camera with a breakaway cable, you can monitor the actual output of the camera through the breakaway cable's headphone return. As a last resort, plug your headphones directly into the camera—it's better than not listening!

Microphone Technique

Booming: Clean Sound, Consistency, and Being On-Axis

The key to getting good audio in the field is recording clean and consistent sound. By "clean," we mean the desired sounds with as little background mixed in as possible. Key to this is choosing a mic with the best "pickup pattern" for the job. In addition, getting the microphone as close to the subject as possible is essential, because the stronger the signal from your desired sound source, the lower you can set your record levels and the lower the extraneous noise will be. Background sound in recording is like salt in cooking: you can always add a little more later, but you cannot take it out if you've put in too much.

Consistency means making sure that there are not identifiable differences in the sound as the scene unfolds. This means maintaining more or less the same distance between your microphone and the subject. It is also important to place your mic correctly in relation to your audio source. Mics should be pointing at the mouth of a person speaking, not the top of their head. Also make sure that your target is in the microphone's optimal sensitivity range. Correct placement is referred to as being **on-axis** (Figure 14.10). As a rule, the sound recordist needs to be constantly double-checking that the mic is in its best position as the subject moves around. Then they adjust levels on the recorder to get a strong signal. Remember, boosting the input gain to compensate for a badly positioned microphone will yield poor results.

One indispensable tool for microphone placement, and a common sight on any film production, is the **boom pole**, which allows you to position a mic as close as possible to the source but still remain outside the boundaries of the frame (Figure 14.11). A boom pole is a long, lightweight pole that telescopes out to various lengths. At one end is a **shock mount** that holds the microphone in place. Shock mounts come in many different styles but the principle is the same for all of them. The microphone is held securely in place by a series of rubber bands or other mounting that absorbs any vibrations or handling noise from the boom pole (Figure 14.12).

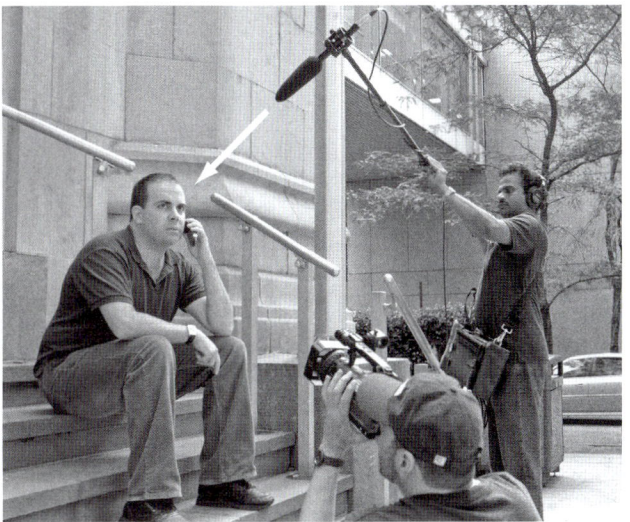

■ **Figure 14.10** Microphones should be positioned "on-axis." Note how the microphone is pointing directly at the subject's mouth from above and slightly in front.

The boom pole allows the operator to suspend the microphone precisely over and in front of the speaker, and to position it so that it records the audio as it is coming out of their mouth. Sometimes, it is advantageous to hold a boom below the talent and angle the microphone upward, but this can be tricky, as you may pick up background noises from above, like airplanes flying overhead if you are outdoors or fluorescent lights buzzing if you're inside.

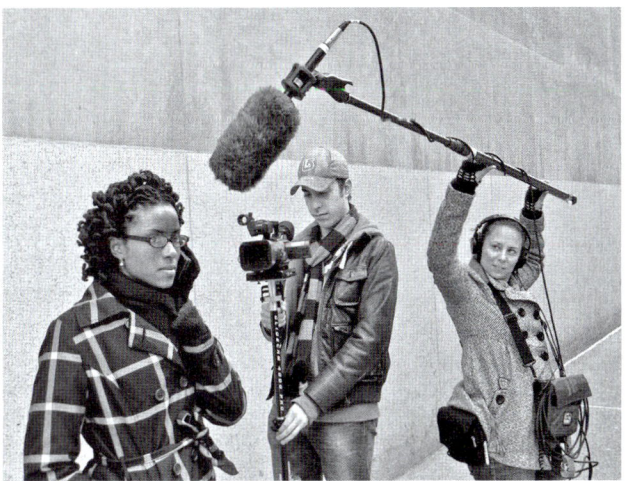

■ **Figure 14.11** A boom pole is essential to keep microphones as close to the subject as possible while keeping the mike and boom person off frame.

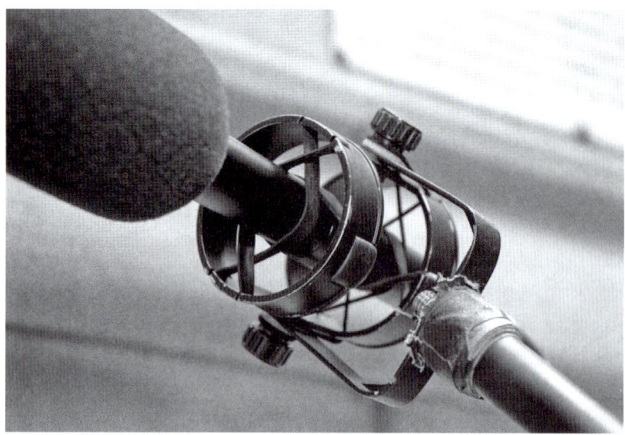

■ **Figure 14.12** A shock mount keeps the microphone secured and prevents it from picking up vibrations or handling noise from the boom pole.

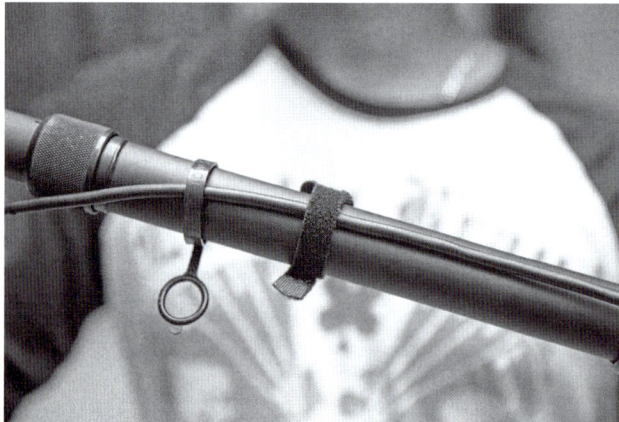

■ **Figure 14.13** Plastic (left) or velcro (right) ties can be used to secure your cable to your boom pole.

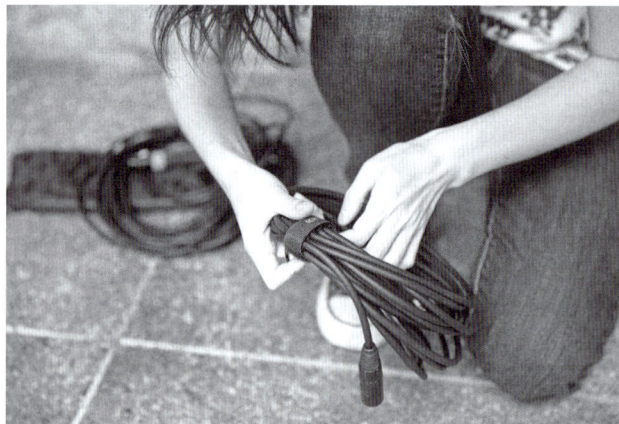

Figure 14.14 Learn how to coil cable properly and keep your cables well organized.

Boom Technique

Using a boom requires careful technique and a lot of practice. Here are a few tips:

1. Consistency is essential. A boom operator must maintain both a consistent distance between the speaker and microphone and the proper on-axis mic angle during a take. Pulling the boom away from a speaker, even a few inches, or repositioning the microphone even slightly off-axis will drastically change the quality of the audio and shift the balance between the audio you want and the background noise.
2. Boom poles should be handled gently to reduce vibration on the pole, which can be transmitted up to the microphone. Take off all rings that can tap against the boom pole. Use your body and fingertips to change the angle of the microphone and keep subjects on-axis.
3. The boom operator should communicate with the camera operator to determine the limits of the frame. While you should not interrupt the cameraperson during shooting, you can try and assess the expected framing of an interview ahead of time, and set your boom position accordingly. A camera operator will let you know when you are in the frame! Try not to have it happen often.
4. Care must be taken not to cast a boom shadow over the set or onto the subject. Usually, the boom operator sets up after everything is ready to go and fits in around the existing camera and lighting situation.
5. Often boom operators are called upon to follow moving subjects. Sometimes this means pivoting the body; at other times it may mean walking alongside the subject and camera operator. Care must be taken to move quietly, stay on-axis, and maintain consistent subject-to-mic distance. It is also essential to watch where you are going so you don't walk into a fire hydrant or light post! Often a production assistant will be assigned to help the camera person, but the sound person is usually on their own to navigate the physical environment, often while staying connected to the camera.
6. Some boom poles are made so that the mic cable runs inside, but in cases where the mic cable is free, the cable should be wrapped a few times around the pole to avoid having it slapping against the pole or drooping into the frame. Many sound recordists use velcro or plastic ties (Figure 14.13), or hair bobbles, to attach cables to boom poles.
7. Learn how to coil cable (there is a technique for making it loop and lie flat) and keep your cables organized (Figure 14.14). You will have to be able to wrangle your cable (let it out, gather it back up again) quickly as the distance between you and the camera person changes. Don't let cables lie on the floor

where people can trip over them. Conversely, don't keep them so short that you are pulling on the camera's connectors. This takes practice.

8. In situations that are too tight for a boom pole, it is also possible to mount a microphone on a small handheld device with a shock mount, called a **pistol grip** (Figure 14.15).

Recording Room Tone

When you are using multiple microphones, it is inevitable that the background noises (or **ambient sound**) will shift from shot to shot. In postproduction, sound editors and mixers will attempt to create **audio continuity** between your shots so that there is a seamless sound transition between them. In addition, dialog is often cut up in editing, and you can end up with noticeable gaps, which must be filled.

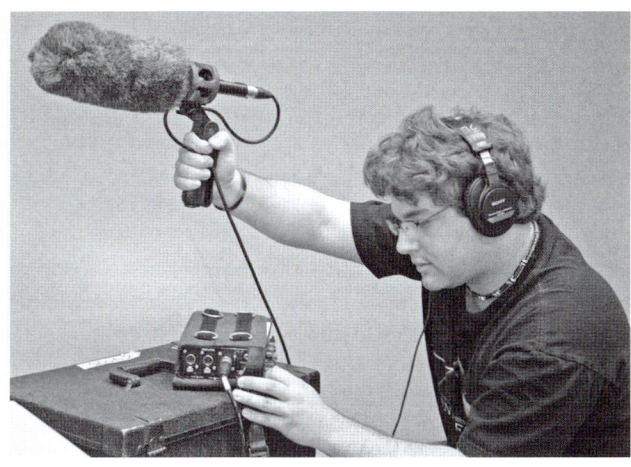

■ **Figure 14.15** Recording sound in close quarters can make handling a boom cumbersome; for these situations, a pistol grip is more convenient.

To help with this process in postproduction, you should always record one minute of **ambient sound** (or **room tone**) at each and every location. This is often done when filming is about to wrap. Before anyone starts packing up equipment, the sound recordist asks everyone to "be quiet for room tone." The mic is then opened at the normal, speech level and the recordist announces the sound take by stating (1) the production title, (2) the location, (3) the date, and announcing "one minute of room tone." Then everyone stands still while one minute of general ambient sound is recorded. The recordist then calls "End room tone" and wrapping can begin. It is important to do this while the crew and equipment are still on the set. Remember they, too, were part of the ambient atmosphere during each take. Room tone should be recorded even before turning off any lights, because they will make little pinging noises as the metal cools.

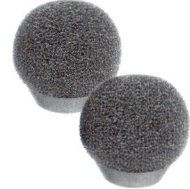

Wind Noise

A final common sound challenge, especially outside, is **wind noise**. Microphones are particularly vulnerable to wind noise because the wind buffets the highly sensitive microphone diaphragm. High winds can sound like a freight train, but soft winds, too, can contaminate sound by generating a low-frequency rumble. **Windscreens** dampen the effects of the wind on the diaphragm without altering the incoming sound waves. Thankfully, there are many windscreens on the market that fit the head of almost any microphone, even lavaliers, and you should always bring one with you for each mic that you plan to use (Figure 14.16).

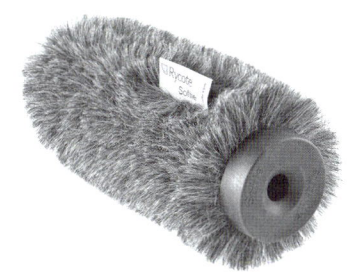

Doing a Sound Report

The day's filming is over, but there is one more task for the sound recordist. What a particular production will need in terms of a sound report can vary widely but it is always important to create some kind of documentation of your day's work. Of key importance will be

■ **Figure 14.16** Windscreens come in many sizes and levels of effectiveness. Here we see small foam windscreens for lavaliers (top), and a Rycote Softie provides reasonable protection for a boom mic (center). On the bottom a Rode zeppelin being covered with a "dead cat" for heavy duty weather.

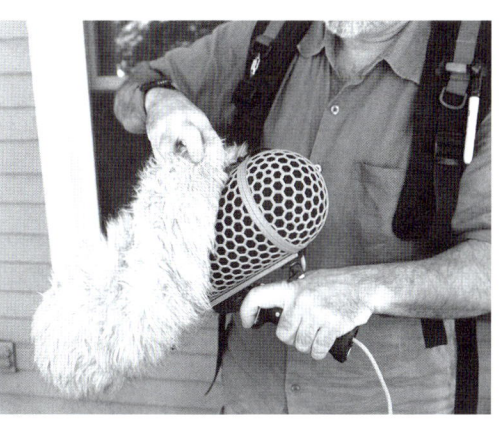

MONO VS STEREO RECORDING

Mono recording refers to a setup where each sound source has its own recorded channel. **Stereo recording**, on the other hand, dedicates two channels to each sound source. Each channel captures the sound from a different perspective in an effort to reproduce the dimensionality of human hearing. Stereo recording is most common for music and sound effects that involve motion, like a train or bird passing by. Detailed information about stereo recording is beyond the scope of this book, but it is increasingly popular.

Because of the need to retain left-right spatial relationships, stereo recording is best done with a stand rather than on a boompole. There are different types of placement, but the X-Y placement (Figure 14.17, left) is the easiest and most common. The two microphones are close, almost touching to avoid **phase error**, which occurs when sound waves arrive at different times from the same source, canceling each other out. In addition, the microphones are not particularly close to the source, as close proximity would not give a good sense of the stereo dimensionality (Figure 14.17, right).

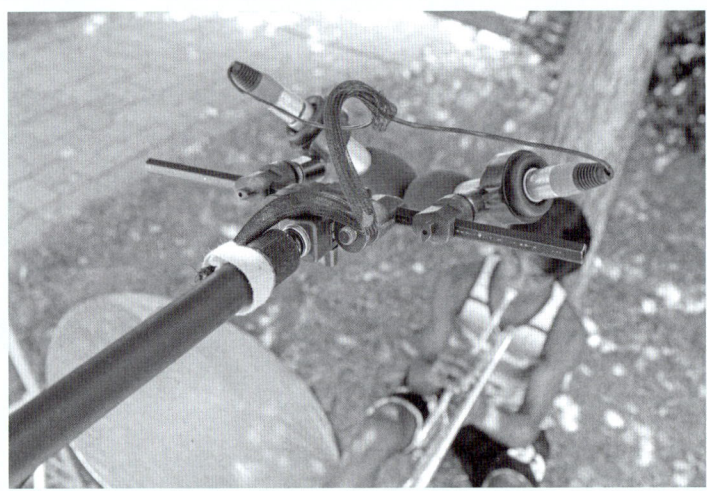
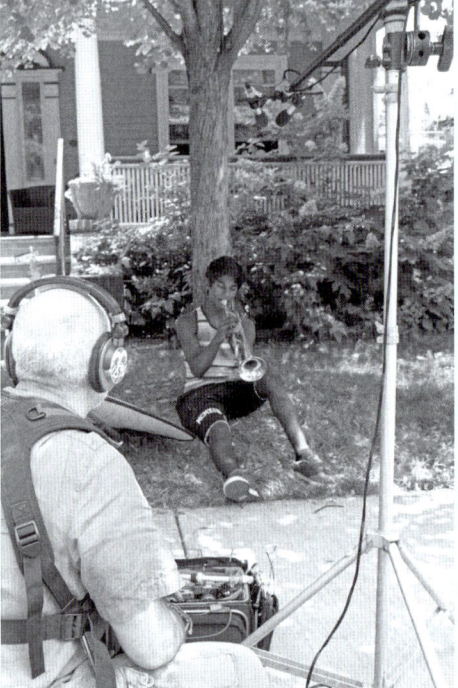

Figure 14.17 Stereo recording demands careful placement of microphones to achieve the desired audio dimensionality and perspective.

noting which microphone and/or subject was on which input during recording. Also, did you do any wild recording? There is no visual record, so your notes are essential. Also note the location of any room tone, and any specific problems in the tracks. If you are working single-system, it's a good idea to ask the cameraperson for time code numbers when you start or end a scene. If you are working double-system, you may or may not have time code, but you will definitely have file names and/or numbers. For a typical printed sound report, visit our companion website (www.routledge.com/cw/Anderson).

CONCLUSION

Each location and each miking situation is unique and poses a variety of challenges. To a large extent, that's the fun of this job! As a sound recordist, you need to understand the capabilities and limitations of your equipment, and be resourceful and creative in devising strategies to obtain the best possible audio under any circumstances. Often an entire scene can be created around a special piece of sound, and a rich soundtrack can truly heighten the experience of "watching" a documentary.

Interviewing and Working with Subjects

CHAPTER
15

At its core, documentary filmmaking is about relationships with people. Many documentary directors will tell you that the human exchanges at the heart of the process are why they do this work. Securing access, building trust, and maintaining relationships with your subjects are a central aspect of a documentary filmmaker's work. And the interview—one of the core elements of documentary filmmaking—is an opportunity for deep communication that can be extremely meaningful and is often emotionally intense. Forging and maintaining relationships with your subjects requires skill, patience, and time. But as many filmmakers have said, documentary films are only as good as the relationships they are built on.

BUILDING AND MAINTAINING RELATIONSHIPS

There are different kinds of relationships you can have with your documentary subjects, and they require different levels of commitment. There are times when you will preinterview someone on the phone, schedule an interview, show up at their office or home to do the interview, and not see them again until your film premieres, if ever. This is common with experts and others who play a limited role in your film. At other times, particularly if you are making character-driven observational films, you will spend much time getting to know your subjects and building trust. This time invested not only gains you access, it can change the quality of what you get on screen.

Sometimes building a relationship means spending time without filming, or putting the camera down in the middle of a shoot and going out for a meal or a walk with your subject. If you and your subject share a commitment to the issues in your film, this relationship can be easier to forge. For example, filmmakers Tami Gold and coauthor Kelly Anderson were participating in protests over the shooting death of Amadou Diallo, who was unarmed when he died in a hail of 41 police bullets, before they decided to make their film about police brutality, *Every Mother's Son* (2004). Their presence at these events eventually convinced the main subjects of the film, mothers whose sons were killed by police, that they were doing something more in-depth than the news reporters who would show up one day and disappear the next.

Zach Heinzerling spent years getting to know Ushio and Noriko Shinohara, the main characters in *Cutie and the Boxer* (2013):

> *The scenes that I feel are the core of the movie are these very casual conversations, mostly over meals. I could only film a scene like that when they weren't thinking about why or what I was filming. When you start a film, the person you are shooting is always hyper-aware of the camera. I always tried to make it really, really hard for them to tell what particular aspect of their life was important to me. So over time all aspects of their life had the same importance, whether they were cooking, or talking about rent, or about art, or about their relationship. They couldn't decipher what I wanted them to talk about, and then play into it, or avoid talking about it, or whatever it would be that might affect the naturalistic nature of the environment. People are always acting on some level, even if it's documentary; when the camera is in the room, it's a*

performance. My goal was to allow a more naturalistic performance. And it took a long time to reach that point. I'm not sure if it's the most efficient way of making a documentary, but I think efficiency is something that you throw out when you make documentaries.[1]

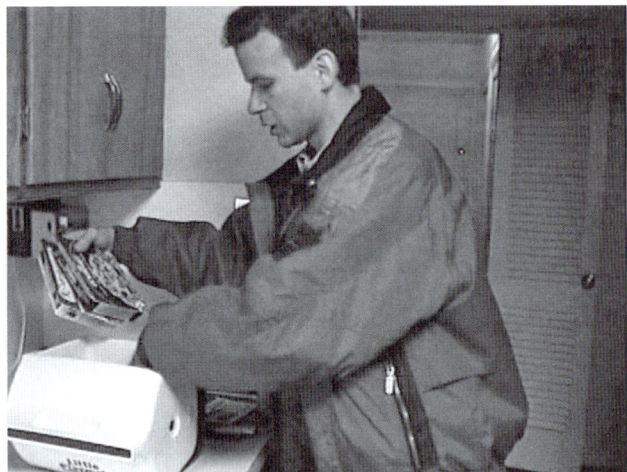

■ **Figure 15.1** In *Out At Work*, the filmmakers' intimacy with Ron Woods allowed them to capture key everyday moments, like this one of Ron packing his lunch.

Spending time with your subjects also allows you to understand their environment, their home, their neighborhood, their habits, and their relationships in ways that almost always provide a deeper understanding of who they are. When coauthor Kelly Anderson and Tami Gold filmed with Ron Woods, an auto worker who is a main character in their documentary *Out at Work (1997)*, about workplace discrimination against lesbians and gay men, they asked Ron if they could stay with him while they were filming. As a result of being in Ron's home, they were able to see up close what the details and conditions of his life were. There is a scene in the film where Ron is getting ready for work, and packing his lunch. He opens the freezer and there is nothing there but a stack of frozen dinners. He grabs two and puts them in his lunch box (Figure 15.1). The solitude of the moment is heartbreaking, and it's a detail the filmmakers wouldn't have uncovered if they had stayed in a motel and filmed for a few hours one day.

Many documentaries take years to unfold. It's common to "check in" every once in a while to find out how your subjects are doing, what is going on in their lives, whether there is anything you should film, or just to say hello. In the best case scenario, the relationship is such that the subject will call you to let you know something is happening that you might want to film. Don't count on it, though. Stay in touch if you want to avoid missing important parts of your story!

While developing trust and intimacy can be beneficial for a film, it can also create false expectations and blurred boundaries in terms of responsibilities. See Chapter 5 for more on ethics as they relate to your relationships with your subjects.

ON-CAMERA INTERACTIONS WITH SUBJECTS

Interviewing

Most of your on-camera interactions with the people in your film will take the form of interviewing. Interviews can feel dull and canned, which is why they are often referred to as **talking heads**. A good interview can also be a riveting instance of personal transformation where we witness the subject remembering, realizing, or reexperiencing something significant. A great interview isn't just determined by the subject's level of charisma. It's also a product of the quality of the interviewing techniques used. Good interviewing requires planning as well as the ability to listen profoundly, to surrender to the moment, and to improvise when unexpected and important material emerges.

Preparing for the Interview

You should decide early on in your filmmaking process whether your voice will be an **element** in the final film. If it is, you will have to make sure it is recorded as you ask questions. If it isn't, think of ways of framing your questions that will require your subject to answer in a full statement that will make sense to the viewer. Questions that result in a "yes" or "no" answer should be avoided.

Before you interview someone, write up a list of questions. If you are interviewing someone who has written or spoken widely about your subject, make sure you have read or watched at least some of what they have written or said. This will give you a sense of their perspective. It's also important for you to have a sense of how they might fit into the film as you understand it at that moment. Will they be confirming your hypothesis? Giving a counter opinion? While they may surprise you, having an idea of their role in your film will help you avoid asking questions that are too broad or unlikely to provide useful material. If you are doing a film that is more investigative and your interviewee is likely to try and dodge difficult questions, you will need to have hard facts on hand.

Some questions will be designed to elicit factual information you need to tell your story, particularly if you aren't planning on using narration for exposition. Other questions will be designed to draw out more analytical points, or emotional content. As a general rule, start with the easier questions and work your way up to the material that is likely going to be more difficult for your subject to talk about.

Finally, think *storytelling*. Try to get your interviewee to tell you *stories about what happened*, not just opinions about issues. Here it is useful to use the distinction Louise Spence and Vinicius Navarro make in their book *Crafting Truth: Documentary Form and Meaning*[2] between primary and secondary sources in documentary. **Primary sources** are people who directly experienced an event you are dealing with in your film. They are often participants or eyewitnesses. From them you want the story of what happened, what they saw, and how they felt. Their opinion of the issue may be important, but try to get an account of the actual experience first. People often feel more comfortable giving opinions than telling you what happened and how they felt about it. **Secondary sources** are often experts, like academics or policy makers. They are more likely to contribute opinion and analysis to your documentary. This is valuable as well. It can be useful to ask them to speak personally as well as in their expert capacity. An example is coauthor Kelly Anderson's interview with Craig Wilder, a historian, in *My Brooklyn* (2012). Craig's role in the film is to explain the concept of redlining, the process of mapping urban neighborhoods by race and denying access to credit to those occupied by African-Americans. In the interview, however, she asked him to speak personally about his experiences growing up in Brooklyn, yielding material like this interview bite:

> *For me, Downtown Brooklyn is just filled with memories. Even now, when I walk down there, I kind of see past the stores that are there, and I'm looking for Abraham and Strauss. We loved Abraham and Strauss. It just seemed like you had walked into a museum. There were flowers everywhere, and there was that woman who stood in this information booth, which was actually a big marble thing that looked like a vase, and we stared up at her and asked her questions. We wanted to talk to her all day long.*

Moments like these add humor and warmth to Wilder's character in the film, making him a primary as well as a secondary source. If you are having a hard time coming up with questions, Storycorps has a great list to get you started (storycorps.org/great-questions).

Interview Location

Remember that the setting of an interview, whether a cluttered lawyer's office, a perfectly arranged home, a factory floor, outside a prison, or on a boat, adds context and can speak volumes about your character. Also remember that if you can't hear your character over the ambient sound in the location, or the ambience is distracting, you are better off in another place.

Your choice of location for your interview will also depend on the style of your documentary. If you are shooting an observational documentary without formal interviews, you will likely

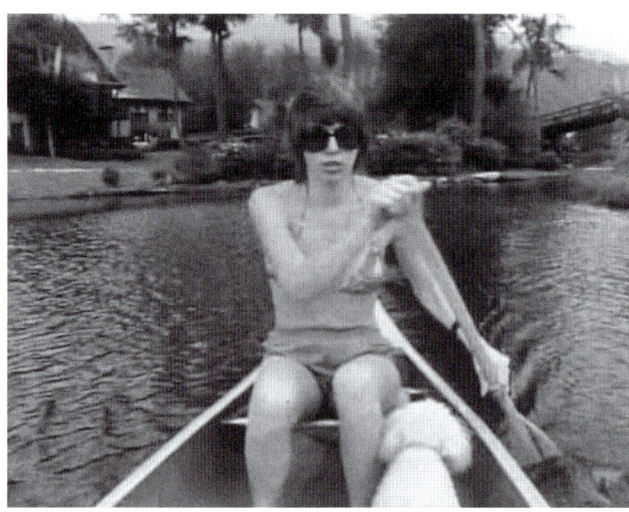
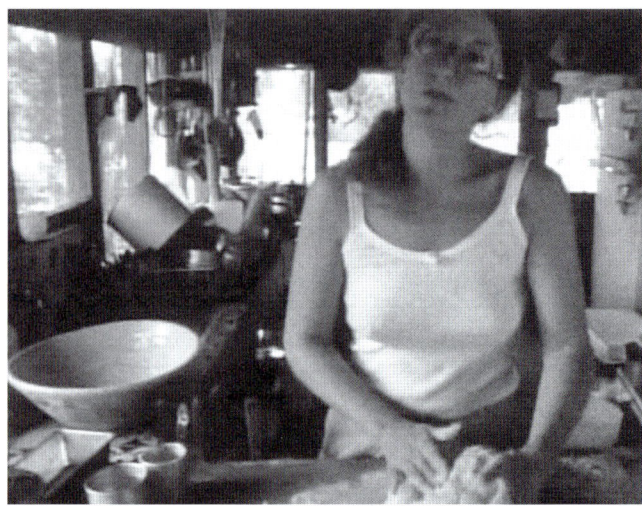

■ **Figure 15.2** In *Sherman's March: A Meditation on the Possibility of Romantic Love in the South During an Era of Nuclear Weapons Proliferation*, director Ross McElwee interviews his sister while they are canoeing, and a former girlfriend as she is making bread.

be interviewing your subject in a setting directly related to their everyday life, say at the kitchen table or sitting on the couch. Having your interviewee do a simple activity while talking can work wonders in terms of relaxing them. In fact, a common approach to stilted acting in theater and narrative film is to give the actors something to do while they say their lines.

In *Sherman's March: A Meditation on the Possibility of Romantic Love in the South during an Era of Nuclear Weapons Proliferation* (1986), director Ross McElwee takes us on a journey that is ostensibly about General Sherman's march of destruction through the South during the American Civil War. As this wry documentary unfolds, though, it becomes about McElwee's quest to find a romantic partner. This director takes an unusual approach to interviewing: he interviews people as they are engaged in unusual daily activities, from milking a cow to making bread to canoeing. The result is visually interesting, provides additional information about each character and the environment, and relaxes the subject so that they speak more spontaneously (Figure 15.2).

Another version of this approach is the **walk-and-talk** interview, where the camera follows the subject as they show us around a particular location. This setup has all the advantages of the above approaches, with the added benefit of allowing the subject to *show* us what they are speaking about. An example is an interview with historian Craig Wilder in *My Brooklyn*. Wilder walks around the Bedford-Stuyvesant neighborhood of Brooklyn, NY, as he describes the history of the area (Figure 15.3). The approach adds movement and dynamism that can be a nice alternative to a formal seated interview.

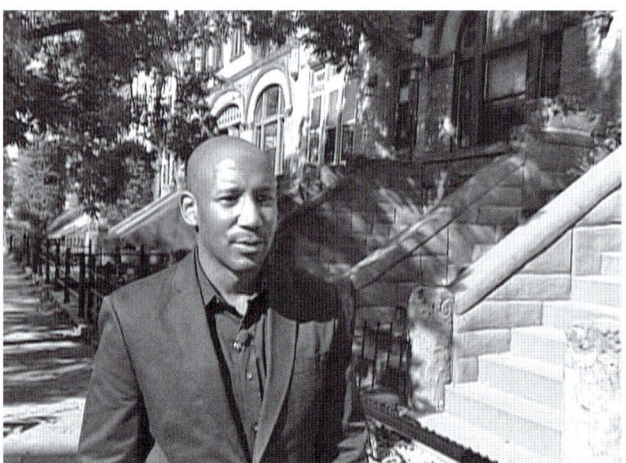

■ **Figure 15.3** Craig Wilder speaks about his neighborhood as he walks down the street he grew up on in this "walk-and-talk" interview in *My Brooklyn*.

There are times, however, when a more formal approach to interviewing is appropriate, and this is still the most common approach for documentary interviews. By "more formal," we mean a setup where the subject has been deliberately asked to sit or stand in a particular location, time has been spent lighting the setup (usually a **three-point lighting** setup, as explained in Chapter 12), and they answer questions. Generally, the person conducting the interview is off-screen, though this is not always the case.

CHOOSING THE RIGHT BACKGROUND

Interviews are the bread and butter of documentaries, but doing them well and maintaining interest is far from easy. Charles Ferguson's Academy Award®-winning *Inside Job* (2010) is a close investigation of the role of the financial sector in the 2008 global economic crash. Cinematographer Svetlana Cvetko creates a variety of interview setups that differ widely while still offering an elegance, an attention to background, and rich lighting. All these factors emphasize both the power position of the interview subjects and the scrutiny to which they are being subjected (Figure 15.4).

Sometimes a director will place a subject in a situation that is particularly evocative for both the audience and the subject. As Michael Rabiger says in his book *Directing the Documentary* (Fifth Edition), "Settings shake loose many emotion-laden memories. The fact is that we are not fixed in whom we are . . . the context to each exchange and the personality of each interlocutor always draws something a little different."[4]

In *Hiroshima Bound* (2015), coauthor Martin Lucas takes Hiroshima survivor Clara Yoshida to the Hiroshima Peace Memorial at Ground Zero in downtown Hiroshima City. The locale, a tourist spot, might seem an overly predictable or generic place to conduct an interview with a survivor. Initially, Ms. Yoshida offers a fairly typical first-person account of her memories of August 6, 1945. Ultimately, though, the location provokes an intriguingly unexpected response:

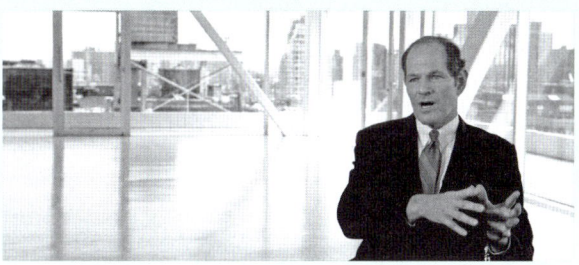
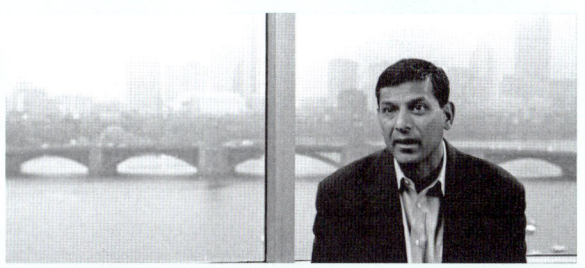
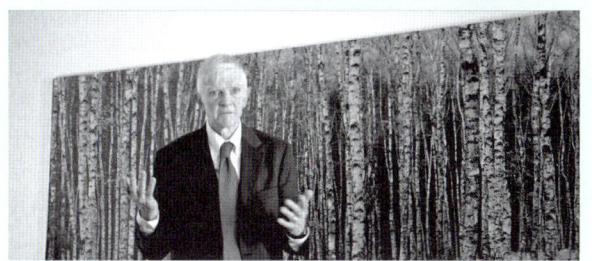

■ **Figure 15.4** In *Inside Job*, cinematographer Svetlana Cvetko's approach ensures the interviews avoid being generic. Here, shots bounded by glass and steel, million dollar views, and fake forest wall coverings give a flavor of the corporate world, while the medium shot chosen for the interviews gives a feel for the subjects' body languages and fashion senses.

> **Lucas:** *This is a place that people come to from all over the world. But how about for you? Is this a place that you visit in your own life?*
> **Ms. Yoshida:** *Yes. Once in a while I visit, but even if I take my visitors—you know, people from foreign countries—I take them here. But I wait outside. I don't want . . . It's very hard for me to look again and again, you know, at the same thing. So I just ask them to look at it by themselves.*

The tone of Ms. Yoshida's voice, her hesitations, and the expression on her face when confronted with the location convey to the viewer the immense pain that, even after 60 years, this experience has caused her (Figure 15.5).

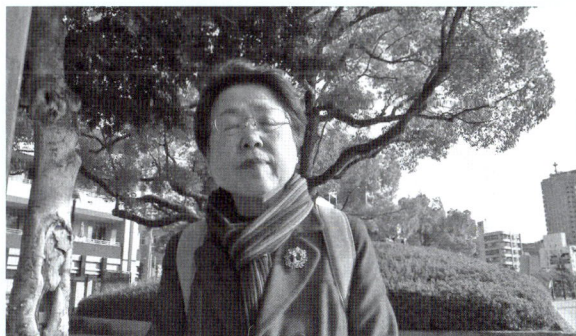

■ **Figure 15.5** Ms. Yoshida stands in the park outside the Hiroshima Peace Memorial in *Hiroshima Bound*.

A formal interview gives the director and crew much more control over the lighting and sound aspects of the location. It also gives both the interviewer and the subject the ability to be focused. In an era of short sound bites, an extended interview allows people a chance to explain complex or nuanced ideas. There may also be ethical reasons one would choose to do a formal interview. Filmmaker Tami Gold explains why she and coauthor Kelly Anderson chose to do formal interviews with the three main characters of *Every Mother's Son*:

> *When you sit someone down to do an interview, you are giving them the right to think deeply about the questions you are asking. You aren't forcing them to be spontaneous and candid. If they don't like their answers they can start over again. And that feels really important to me, not just because you get detailed information and more of a narrative, but it's also really important because it's respectful. Pundits on television, spokespeople who represent different political parties or organizations, are always sitting down, so why should a worker not be sitting down and allowed to think? Why should a mother whose child was killed by police not be able to sit down and reflect?*[3]

See Chapters 6 and 14 for more on the importance of selecting the best locations for your interview.

Setting Up the Interview: Visual Considerations

In addition to choosing a revealing location, creating strong visual compositions, and recording clean sound, there is the important question of where to place the interviewer relative to the person being interviewed, and to the camera.

Eyeline and Subject Placement

Eyeline in filmmaking refers to what the subject appears to be looking at. In documentary, this will generally be an off-screen interviewer. The critical issue is *how close the interviewer is to the camera's lens*. Because the lens is a surrogate for the audience, there is a strong emotional and psychological component to eyeline. When the person being interviewed looks directly into the lens, she appears to be speaking to us (the viewers). The further her eyeline moves away from the lens, the more distant we are from her, and the more aware we are that she is speaking to another person who is in the room. In an observational scene that involves two or more people, the off-screen person may be another key player in the scene. In an interview, however, you generally want maximum rapport between the person being interviewed and the audience, as that is what will keep your audience engaged. As with anything, you can break this rule and "trouble" this engagement for your own ethical or aesthetic reasons, but know the rules before you break them, and break them for good reason!

In documentary interviewing, we generally avoid having interviewees look directly into the camera lens as they are speaking. Why? Whether or not the audience is conscious of it, documentaries are generally expected to be authored by a person, the filmmaker. Speaking directly to the audience in the **direct address** used by news anchors is therefore awkward and out of sync with the documentary tradition. In addition, interviewees tend to speak more comfortably when they are making eye contact with a person instead of looking into a camera lens.

Having your subject's eyeline as close to the lens as possible, without looking into it, means placing the interviewer right next to the lens. Whether the interviewer is to the right or left of the lens will depend on the composition of the frame, and is something you should discuss with your cinematographer before they set lights. Generally you will place your subject on the left side of the frame if the interviewer is sitting to the right of the camera, and vice versa. This creates appropriate lookspace and a more dynamic frame (Chapter 7). Often directors will have half their subjects placed on the left side of the frame, and

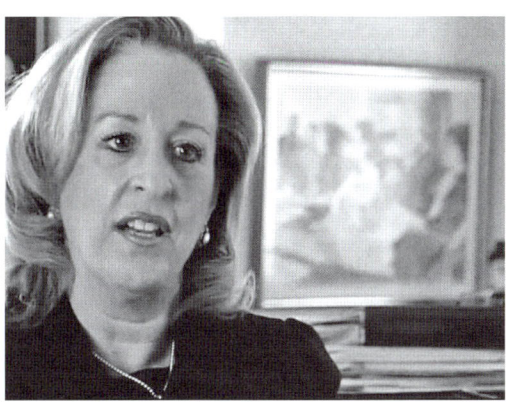 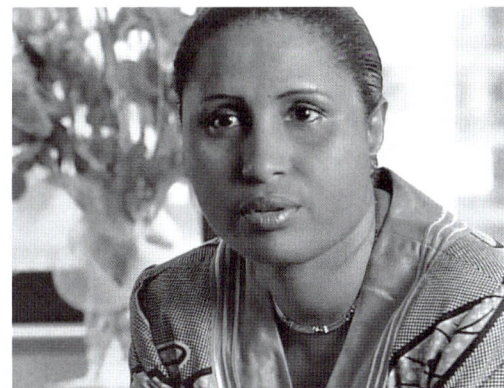

■ **Figure 15.6** Eyeline and subject placement. In *Every Mother's Son*, the directors placed their subjects (attorney Susan Karten, left, and Kadiatou Diallo, right) on the left and right sides of the frame, respectively. They are speaking to an interviewer positioned on the opposite side of the camera, close to the lens, creating an intimate rapport with the viewer.

the other half on the right, resulting in what feels more like a natural conversation than a series of individual statements. If two characters are likely to be intercut a lot, it is common to try and place them on opposite sides of the frame so they will balance one another out in the final film (Figure 15.6).

A notable exception to the eyeline rule is filmmaker Errol Morris' interrotron, a complex teleprompter-type device that projects an image of the interviewer right in front of the lens, allowing the interviewee to speak to a person while looking into the camera's lens. The result is effective and unsettling for the audience (Figure 15.7). Another exception is the **video diary** that has become part of many documentaries, especially as technological developments have put cameras in the hands of pretty much anyone. In the video diary, subjects speak to the camera directly. The effect is highly intimate because we assume there is no interviewer there, and we are experiencing the unmediated confessions of the person speaking (Figure 15.8).

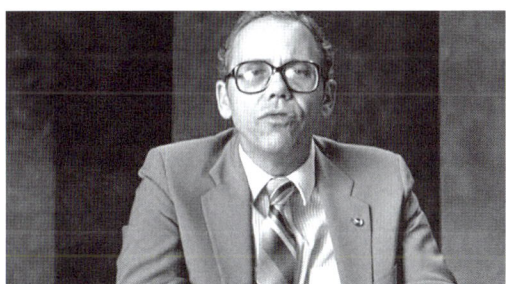 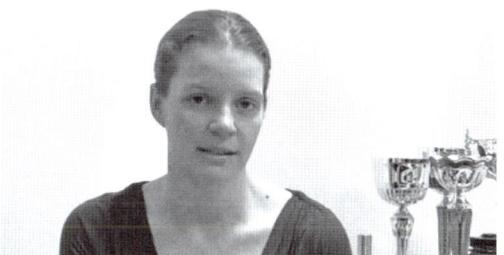

■ **Figure 15.7** Errol Morris' interrotron encourages the interviewee to look directly into the lens, to unsettling effect. This image is from *Mr. Death: The Rise and Fall of Fred A. Leuchter, Jr.* (1999).

■ **Figure 15.8** The video diaries in Mark Levinson's *Particle Fever* (2013) have a direct "into the camera" eyeline, creating intimacy.

In addition to making sure your interviewee is close to the camera lens, make sure they do not sit or stand higher or lower than the lens unless you are making a specific aesthetic statement. It is a common mistake to have subjects' eyelines looking down or up, creating a distracting confusion for the viewer, who is left to wonder who they are looking at. This is a common occurrence when one person is handling the camera on a tripod and doing the interview at the same time, as they are often standing higher than the lens if the subject is sitting. The exception, of course, is the handheld cinéma vérité interview with a shoulder-mounted camera, where the cameraperson is by definition at eye-level (see examples from *Sherman's March* on p. 246).

Framing Considerations

Generally, interviews are framed in medium or close shots, though occasionally people will be interviewed in a wider frame that shows more of their environment for context. As a general rule, the closer the shot, the more intimate the connection with the audience, so even if you love the wide shot keep in mind that the viewer will feel more connected to your subject if you frame them more tightly. Many cinematographers will change the framing between interview questions so that the editor can cut between them more easily without breaking continuity (Chapter 19). Also common, but not to be overused, is a slow zoom in during a very emotional or otherwise significant moment.

Conducting the Interview

Once you are on location, you can put your subject at ease with light conversation while the crew is setting up, or allow them to do whatever makes them comfortable on their own. Take care not to tax them with difficult conversations, as you want them to have energy when you start filming! Also try not to talk with them about material that is part of the interview content. It's fine to say, "That's a great story, can you wait and tell me about it on camera?"

Lighting an interview always takes time, so avoid tiring out your subject by having her sit under hot lights while the crew sets up. Have a production assistant or somebody else sit in the interviewee's seat until the setup is almost finished, and then your subject can sit in for some last minute tweaking. Finally, a bit of foundation and face power, and a tissue or paper towel, can be useful in reducing any shine from perspiration on their face.

Before rolling, prepare your subject by reminding her what you want from them in broad terms. People generally want to please you, and will do better when they know the general focus of the interview. Let them know you will be editing the interview, so they are welcome to stop and start again if they don't like how they phrased something. Also tell them you may interrupt and refocus them. If your questions are not going to be part of the film, you will need to ask them to speak in complete thoughts. This is sometimes a difficult thing for subjects to grasp until you demonstrate it for them with a quick rehearsal. Often it goes something like this:

Director: Where did you grow up?
Subject: New England.
Director: Actually, I need you to say a full sentence, like "I grew up in New England."
Subject: Okay, I get it.

Once they get the hang of it, you will interrupt them less and less.

During the interview, remember to position yourself as close to the camera lens as possible, and maintain eye contact with your subject. You can remind her to look at you, especially if she is looking around at other crew members. It is a good idea to ask sound people and other crew to stay out of the subject's line of sight, or at least refrain from making eye contact with the subject, so she isn't tempted to keep looking away while talking. As your subject is talking, give nonverbal encouragement by nodding or through your facial expressions. Do not, however, fall into the common novice trap of saying "Yes," or "Uh huh," or "Right," while they are talking. Your voice will end up on the soundtrack and make it incredibly hard to edit the dialogue.

It is our recommendation that you prepare a solid list of questions that covers everything you think you might need for the film. Bring the list with you, and *put it away during the interview* so you aren't tempted to look at your paper instead of maintaining eye contact with your subject. At the end of the interview, you can consult your list of questions to make sure you haven't forgotten anything.

The single most important thing you can do while interviewing someone is to *listen*. This is easier said than done, as you may find yourself nervously thinking about the next question instead of listening to what is happening in the moment. Listening is important because *the best interview questions are almost always follow-up questions.* If you are really listening to someone talk, they will say things that are clues to deeper content. When a subject offers you a hint of something meaningful and relevant to your film, and you are really listening, you can ask them a follow-up question. Here's an example from *Every Mother's Son*:

Iris Baez: I was in the upstairs kitchen when the call came.
Director: What do you mean the upstairs kitchen?
Iris Baez: We have two kitchens—the upstairs kitchen is for the early eaters, and the downstairs kitchen is for the late eaters. It's because there are 17 kids in the house. Five biological, four that I adopted, and the foster kids.

A director who wasn't listening might not have picked up on the "upstairs kitchen" reference, yet it was the key to unlocking an important detail about Iris that reveals much about her character.

Other follow-up questions that work well are things like, "Why?" or "What do you mean?" Just asking someone to go deeper, or to clarify, will often get to something more emotional. Sometimes just saying something empathetic, like "It sounds like that was really difficult" can be effective.

When interviewing, resist the temptation to fill in silences too quickly. Nobody likes awkward moments, but they can be useful in an interview. Sometimes your subject will pause, and if you just stay silent, they will fill in the silence, often with something valuable. Also, allow them time to reflect, recall, and then add more. The silent pause at the end of a statement can also be powerful, and you can destroy that moment by speaking too soon. On the other hand, if your interviewee is going off on a tangent about something you know you won't use, feel free to gently but firmly interrupt him and redirect him. In addition, not all interview subjects are created equal. If you are interviewing a spokesperson for a cause, or a public relations person, he will have specific training on how to shift the agenda in a direction that suits him. Keep an eye out for answers that feel rehearsed, and be ready to reapproach an issue from a direction that might get a more genuine or spontaneous answer. Letting someone run away with an interview is not good directing!

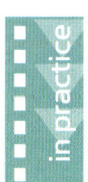

TIPS FOR INTERVIEWING

- Prepare questions but leave them aside during the interview.
- Prepare your subjects for what they can expect during the interview before you start.
- Listen!
- Listen for "keys" that will unlock deeper content. Ask follow-up questions.
- Maintain eye contact; give nonverbal affirmation.
- Don't be afraid of silence or awkward moments!
- Don't step on their answers or interject verbal exclamations while they speak.
- Feel free to ask what you think might be a stupid or naive question.
- Don't let the subjects run away with the interview. It's okay to ask them to answer in a complete sentence, to repeat something more concisely, or even redirect them.
- Keep it specific. Ask people to tell a story, or relive an event. Specific experiences resonate more than opinions or vague statements.

At the end of the interview, it's good practice to ask subjects, "Is there anything else you'd like to say?" You might also ask the crew if they have any questions to add. If they have been working on the project for a while, they are often likely to think of something you have overlooked. And don't forget to get a signed release (Chapter 5)!

Directing Participants in Cinéma Vérité Scenes

If you are shooting observational scenes, you will likely want to interact with your subjects at least some of the time. One of the hardest tasks a director faces is knowing when to throw in a question that will catalyze a scene, and when to stay quiet and let things play out on their own. The way you deal with this balance will be at the core of your stylistic approach. Some directors, like Frederick Wiseman, never ever intervene, but he also shoots massive amounts of footage until he gets the necessary revelatory moments. Others intervene frequently. With time, you will develop your own approach.

Similarly, some directors will never ask a subject to repeat an action so it can be filmed better, or from a different angle. Other directors have no problem asking a subject to walk through a door, or down a set of stairs, again. Some even orchestrate entire scenes that wouldn't have happened if the film wasn't being made. The important thing is that you

DIRECTING CINÉMA VÉRITÉ

Filming cinéma vérité involves knowing when to intervene in a scene, and when to keep quiet. Filmmaker Tami Gold (Figure 15.9) discusses how she used both approaches in her film *Looking for Love: Teenage Mothers* (1982).

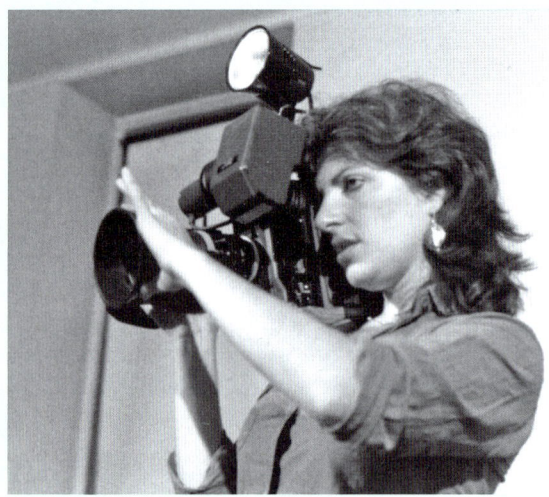

■ **Figure 15.9** Tami Gold filming *Looking for Love: Teenage Mothers* in 1982.

One of my dear friends, Gloria, became the main subject of the film when her daughter Audrey got pregnant at 14. I went to their house to film, and Audrey wasn't there even though she knew I was coming. The baby was there, and Gloria was really embarrassed that I was there waiting for her daughter. I didn't say anything. All I did was film. Gloria was upset, and trying to feed her granddaughter, who was crying, and Gloria turned to the camera and said something like, "See what I mean? I have to be the father, the mother. I have to take care of everything, and I have to think for everybody." That wouldn't have happened unless I was absolutely quiet.

Then the daughter came home, and they sat in the living room. Gloria was still mad at Audrey, and she said, "Where were you?" Audrey said, "I'm trying to get a job at Wendy's." And the mother said, "You can't get a job, you're in school." They proceeded to have a fight, and I'm filming it. And at one point, Audrey started to cry. And finally I talked, and I said to her, "What's wrong?" And she said, "She thinks I'm a kid. I'm not a kid, I'm an adult. I have a child. I'm angry." And I waited a few very painful long moments, and asked, "Why does that make you angry?" She said, "Because I'm not a kid," and she then went into a powerful emotional statement about what having a child meant for her.

We don't go into situations with a list of questions and start checking them off. We have to go into every setting with an understanding of who we are filming, why we are filming, and introduce profound effective listening because that will inform everything we do, and allow us to play into what's happening, rather than imposing onto what's happening.[5]

WHEN TO INTERVENE IN A DOCUMENTARY

One of the most difficult questions in a documentary is balancing your personal relationships with the needs of the film. For his feature documentary *Last Train Home* (2011), Chinese-Canadian documentary maker Lixin Fan spent three years following the Zhang family as the parents toiled in the garment factories of coastal Guongzhou and made the arduous annual trek home to be with their children for Chinese New Year in Sichuan Province, some 1,200 km away.

A dramatic high point of the film comes when the family have returned to the countryside after an exhausting three-day trip. The relationship between the parents and their sullen teenage daughter Qin, who resents their almost total absence from her childhood and their prodding to graduate from high school, falls apart completely as she decides to drop out of school and go to the coast to work. The film is shot in a highly observational style, but as Qin lashes out she turns to the camera. "This is the real me!" she states defiantly. The situation presented Fan with a dilemma:

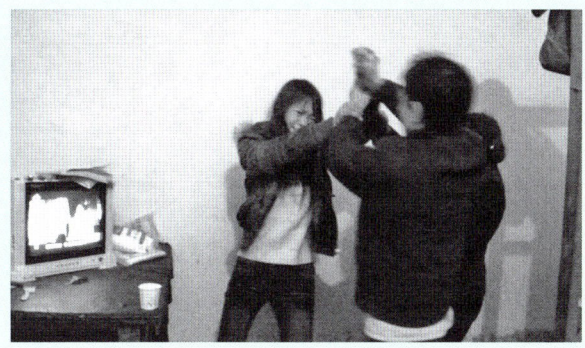

■ **Figure 15.10** When a family reunion in *Last Train Home* turns into violence between Changhua Zhang and his daughter Qin, director Lixin Fan must decide whether to intervene, and how.

> When they started, I was not there. I was in the next room, changing a light bulb. And then I heard the yelling. I immediately ran over and she saw me standing in the doorway. So she turned and yelled at me. That was a really tough and sad moment for me. That was all the family conflict, the family tension, between the father and the daughter . . . I'm a director, and I'm supposed to keep myself objective. But on the other hand, I feel a part of the family. And then I started to debate: I want this scene, it's a great scene. It reveals all the conflicts in the story, in society! I almost could not afford to lose it. Fortunately, my cameraman and soundman were still rolling, and they didn't stop. But on the other hand, how can I stand there and not do anything? I actually went in. It's not in the film, but I went in and I separated them. Qin said the f-word again and the father was trying to hit her and throw her on the ground. I [could] not just see them fight and selfishly keep my scene in my little film. Afterwards, I sat down with the father, because I felt it was a very awkward position for me to be in. We talked for hours. I needed to do some damage control, because it was really messing up the dynamic between me and my subject, and also between the father and daughter . . . My editor helped me to make the decision to ultimately edit that footage out of the film.[6]

figure out where you draw the line and how to get the best material you can, given the limits you have set for yourself.

CONCLUSION

Few things are as central to documentary filmmaking as the relationships you will build and maintain with the people in your films. Sometimes these will last a lifetime, while at other times they will live on only in the film. Perhaps more than in any other art form, the foundation of a documentary is built on someone else's reality. Proceed with caution, care, and intelligence and never forget that engagement with other people is a privilege and a joy. You will learn much from these interactions as you develop your documentary filmmaking practice.

Production Procedures, Etiquette, and Safety

CHAPTER 16

ON THE DOCUMENTARY SET

With small crews in real-world locations and situations that can vary from a quiet living room to a war zone, the documentary set would appear to have little of the hierarchy visible on fiction film sets. Very often, there will be no more than three or four people collaborating on a project. But don't let the small size fool you! Good documentary filmmaking is not about "shooting from the hip." When you are on location, in the middle of other people's lives with your cameras, microphones, and lights, it is extremely important to have a clear idea of who does what, and who, quite literally, "calls the shots." A smart director will share her vision with her crew in advance, work out a few ground rules, and consult regularly to ensure that everyone is working toward a common purpose.

Even though the director and producer are the last word on any project, on a documentary set they will often depend on the cinematographer and sound recordist to have their own ears and eyes, to work independently at times, and to chip in with ideas or solutions to problems. From the cinematographer you might hear, "Let me get a few shots of the stuff on the mantelpiece." Or from the sound recordist, "I need some ambience to cover those long shots." For this reason, documentary filmmakers often work with collaborators they can depend on to share their vision and working methods, and often work with the same people over and over again. Most crews develop subtle forms of communication to let each other know that they did or didn't get what they needed, or whether they think the interview subject has said everything that they're going to, or even that there is a better shot than the one they're taking if they just move the camera slightly. In other words, every member of a documentary crew is always on their toes and sensitive to the reality and the possibilities that are unfolding around them.

A film location is an exciting, intense, and often pressure-packed environment with energetic people who are focused, driven, and usually working with limited time and resources. In this environment, there is often a temptation to cut corners to get the job done quickly. But cutting certain corners can be counterproductive—or worse, downright foolish and dangerous. Remember, a documentary set is usually other people's property, and often a personal space where they live their lives. The following sections cover essential set etiquette and safety issues that should always be observed so that your production experience is safe, productive, and rewarding for all involved.

SET ETIQUETTE: HUMAN AND MATERIAL RESOURCES

Everyone on a documentary set should be treated with respect. All crew members must respect each other, as well as the people, both on- and off-camera, at any location. This brief code of conduct outlines the standards of behavior for members of a production team:
1. *Do your job, whatever that job is, to the best of your ability.* Documentaries are created by a small, coordinated, and collaborating group of individuals. One person slacking off places an unfair burden on someone else who has their own job to do. Doing your job well also means knowing your job well. If you sign on to be the sound recordist on someone's film, then you had better know how to be an excellent sound recordist. Learn what you need to know to be exceptional at your job, whatever that job is. Doing

your job well also means staying alert and being ready when you are needed. Sometimes, there are periods of downtime on a shoot. Keep your ears and eyes open for anything that needs doing. Lulls in activity are not invitations to go wandering off to get snacks or make personal phone calls. In documentary, reality proceeds at its own uneven pace. You never know when you may need to jump into action, and the last thing you want is for a producer or director to shout, "Anybody know where the hell [so-and-so] is? We are ready to shoot!" If you are a knowledgeable, conscientious, reliable, and effective worker, people will want to work with you again and again. Every project contributes to the reputation you establish for yourself.

2. *Always be on time, which means be early!* The media production world places a very high premium on promptness. Being late shows a phenomenal lack of respect toward the other people who arrive on time ready to work. In other words, when you are late, you waste other people's valuable time. Location shooting often means a tight travel schedule, or dealing with interview subjects who have limited time windows. If you have a reputation for being late, you simply will not work much.

3. *Maintain a positive "can-do" attitude.* Documentary film productions involve lots of problem solving: rigging a light in a bathroom where there is no space, extended hours to get just the right content, recording usable audio in noisy environments. A production thrives with people who love a challenge and are innovative when it comes to solving a problem or working in less than ideal circumstances. A lot of times, this means going above and beyond a narrowly interpreted call of duty and keeping a smile on your face.

4. *Respect the team structure.* Even in a small documentary crew, people have specific roles and responsibilities. This does not mean you can't help out. Very often the director will end up holding a microphone, or the cinematographer will ask interview questions. The trick is to do so when called upon, and to respect the expertise of the individual crew members. You may be the sound recordist, and notice that it looks like a light needs adjusting. Don't go and adjust it yourself, or complain to the director about it. Depending on the situation, you may have a quiet word with the cinematographer, or make an offer to make the adjustment if you can see they are tied up. Sound recordist Daniel Brooks talks about how using his eyes is an important part of his job:

> *Being a sound guy, you end up having these ongoing relationships with people. You get to know their aesthetic and you're able to assist them. A lot of times, especially in documentaries, the camera person is looking at a 30° or 15° field of view through the camera. And so part of my job, as a sound recordist, is to see the other 330° and observe what is going on outside the frame. If he's focused on something and I see something amazing happen, I can say "Hey, pan to your left, there's a really cool thing happening." And so the sound recordist acts as a team member.*[1]

5. *Treat everyone with courtesy*. If you treat people well, they will treat you well. Listen to people. Give praise where praise is due and do not take credit if it is not yours to claim. Learn people's names. Don't criticize negatively or humiliate people if mistakes are made. Don't get in the way of the work other people have to do. Crude comments or jokes about race, gender, sexual orientation, disability, religion, or specific people on the set are not appropriate. Raucous behavior in general can throw everyone's concentration off. Stay cool, calm, and focused.

All this does not necessarily mean every shoot is a total love-fest. In fact, you will surely find yourself on sets where you don't like some of the people you're working with. But when you sign onto a production (paid or not), you have a personal obligation to do your job as well as you can and see the shoot through successfully. Once it's all over, you can vow never to work with certain people ever again, but for the duration of that film shoot you must do your job.

There are also many people on a documentary set who aren't crew members, and they must be respected as well. Documentary subjects let you into their real lives, and they are not paid. The delicate relationship, not just with the director but with the entire crew, is built on trust and respect, and sometimes this is earned over months. It's terrible when that relationship is shattered by an off-hand rude comment or a breach of privacy.

Often you will be shooting in public places like parks, sidewalks, beaches, and neighborhood streets. These places are not your private film set, so you must treat the public with respect and try not to disrupt their lives too much. In other words, keep as low a profile as possible. This includes not making excessive noise, not parking in a way that obstructs other people's access, being conscientious about litter, and not taking up more space than is necessary. Think of yourself as an ambassador for filmmaking in general.

Respect and Protect the Location

Making documentaries involves locations that are ordinarily not film sets. While there are situations where you need to be firm and push to get what you need for your project, remember you are often in someone's home or their place of work. The unwritten rule in these cases is that, like a backpacker, you should leave a location in exactly the same condition you found it, or better. This requires that everyone on the team be careful to protect the location. Since filming on location can involve quite a bit of rearranging, moving sofas, turning off appliances, removing pictures from the wall, putting gels on windows, or tying back curtains, you should be clear about what you've done, and how to undo it. You may also find yourself having to plug in a light that has a much higher wattage than the typical home fixture. Did you ask if it was okay? Did you find out where the fuse or breaker box is? In fact, if there is a fuse box, did you bring a couple of extra fuses in case of a blowout (pp. 263–265)? If it is an office, you may need to be in touch with building staff. A circuit breaker blown on the 14th floor that needs to be reset by someone you don't know how to find, can be extremely aggravating for all concerned, and may result in you losing the cooperation of a subject.

A few extra precautions are standard:
1. Carefully assess the electrical distribution so you don't overload internal wiring.
2. Designate a single place for the production team to dispose of garbage.
3. Place delicate objects well out of harm's way, and ask the location owners to secure their valuable items in another place.
4. Be aware of the placement of hot movie lights, as they can blister paint and burn drapes.
5. Invest in a roll of real **gaffer's tape**. Be careful about using tape directly on walls as it may peel paint off. Tape cables down or run them under rugs. Tape down and/or **sandbag** light stands.
6. Assign someone the job of monitoring the condition of the location. If necessary, this person can suggest that the crew take some time to clean up the space afterwards.
7. Take photographs before you move furniture and objects around so that you know exactly where everything belongs when it comes time to return the space to normal.

From time to time, an accident will occur and the location may sustain some damage. For example, you accidentally gouge the wall while moving a light stand. Don't try to hide the damage and get away with it. Tell the owner of the property and offer to fix it. If one of their possessions gets broken, finding a replacement on eBay or sending them a gift certificate for a nice dinner can go a long way toward making everyone feel better.

Respect Your Equipment

Media production is highly technical. In documentary, you depend on your equipment to function for long hours in all sorts of climates and weather conditions, often very far from any source of replacement or repair. Neglecting, manhandling, or misusing your equipment will undoubtedly hurt you because your gear will either not function properly or cease to

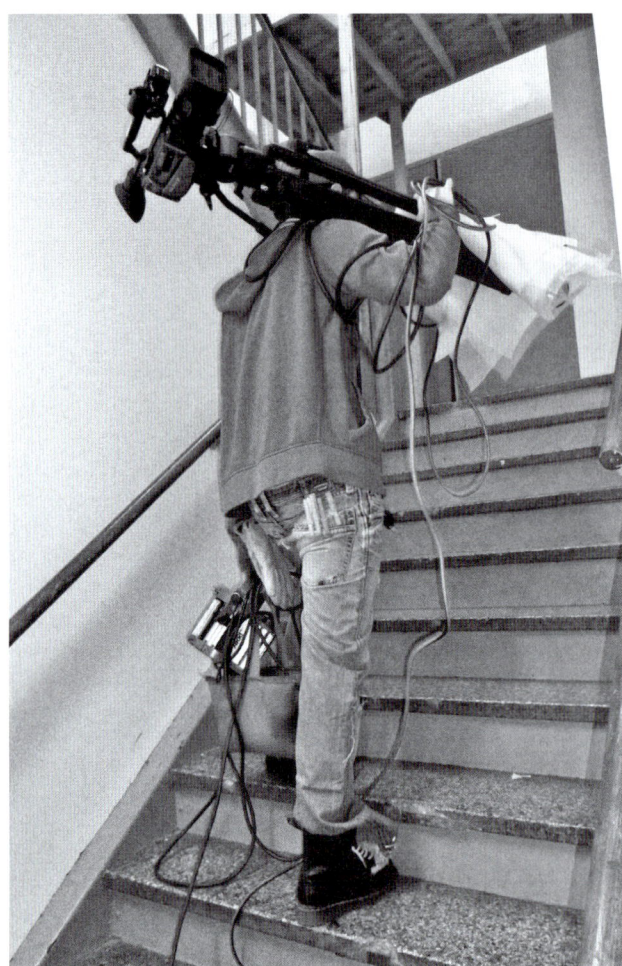

Figure 16.1 Careless handling of equipment will result in damage, production delays, and even injury. This guy is doing everything wrong. By carrying too much gear and dragging improperly coiled cables, not to mention the camera slung recklessly over his shoulder, he's tempting a production calamity.

function at all. In the case of electrical equipment, misuse can be especially dangerous and even deadly. Respecting equipment includes educating and training yourself in the proper use of your gear long before you get on location, using the specific item for its intended use only, handling all gear with care, not physically modifying or customizing equipment that is not yours, maintaining an orderly location and **staging area**, packing equipment away properly, and using common sense at all times (Figure 16.1). Obviously, when you are renting equipment, you will be charged for damages. In a school situation, where all students rely on the quick turnaround of common and properly functioning equipment, your man-handling of gear can not only result in a fine or loss of privileges. It could also jeopardize other students' ability to complete their work, and therefore their film and their grade is put at risk.

Food and Breaks

Ten- or twelve-hour work days are not unusual on a documentary production. When a crew finds its groove and a good scene is playing out, you can get caught up in the moment and lose all sense of time. The body, however, knows when it's been working hard for hours. To maintain the morale and physical stamina of the crew, well-timed breaks for food and hydration are essential. Giving people meal breaks will only make them a happier, healthier, and more productive crew.

Because film shoots are long and hard, and food is essential, you should take any dietary issues of your crew seriously. A producer should know before ordering food who is a vegetarian, or if people have any food allergies. Don't feed the crew pizza every day!

Film work is physically strenuous and sets can get hot, so you must have plenty of water on hand to keep your crew hydrated. This is especially critical for hot days. And it only stands to reason that if you want your crew to drink water to stay hydrated, you'd better make sure that there are bathrooms conveniently available. Part of preproduction is securing the necessary facilities.

PRODUCTION SAFETY AND SECURITY

The information in this section is designed to alert you to some of the major issues concerning production safety and security and to prompt you to take them very seriously. These guidelines are here to help you avoid risk of death, injury, arrest, equipment loss and damage, lawsuits, project collapse, and a bad reputation. Absolutely nothing else in this book means anything if your project is not a safe one and catastrophe occurs. This discussion, however, is in no way comprehensive, nor can it address the safety concerns of every production and circumstance. For this reason, we urge you to do further research into the specific safety contingencies of your particular project and to check with all applicable labor union, state government, local government, location, and school safety regulations and procedures before you start rolling the camera.

Don't be a hero; be an intelligent filmmaker. Get permission to enter property. Get permits when they are required (Chapter 6). Getting a high-angle shot by shimmying up a light pole or hopping a fence onto private property are risks and need to be treated as such. The first step in avoiding stupid accidents is to acknowledge that we are all capable of poor judgment and therefore must remain vigilant, stay smart, follow rules, heed warnings, and listen to others who have the experience and expertise to tell us how things should be done and when we're being unwise and reckless (Figure 16.2).

Prepare for Safety

A great deal of the effort and attention for ensuring a safe production process happens in preproduction. Don't think that your project is so small or so blessed by the filmmaking gods that you can get away with avoiding these steps:

1. Research, study, and follow all safety regulations and guidelines that apply to your specific project. This may include guidelines from the state or local governments and law enforcement, regulations of the specific location where you are shooting, and the safety guidelines established by your school or department as well as the production parameters expressed by your instructor (in the syllabus or verbally) for the class.

2. Everyone on the production team is responsible for safety. Documentary filmmaking is inherently unpredictable. Always be clear about who is responsible for which areas of safety. As you are planning your production, you should be clear about the big picture risks going into any location or situation. As a director or producer actually on location, you are the one responsible for safety decisions. The cinematographer is responsible for safe deployment and rigging of equipment and placement of camera crew.

3. Location surveys should include looking for and noting any safety concerns in the specific location. These should include a careful assessment of electricity capabilities, structural conditions, hazardous materials, potential fire hazards, weather exposure, proximity of high voltage lines and traffic, dangerous natural terrain, neighborhood crime trends, hospital proximity, and so on. Also note all emergency exits, fire extinguishers, and access points. The goal is to anticipate and address specific safety concerns before the shoot occurs.

4. Everyone on the film team should have the emergency contact information for the police, fire department, and emergency medical service. It's a good idea to put this information right on the call sheet, which everyone gets (Chapter 6).

5. Schedule reasonable hours. Allow enough time for the crew to rest between shooting days, and schedule enough time to allow your crew to do their jobs thoroughly and thoughtfully. Don't cram so many things into each day that everyone is rushing and cutting corners just to stay on schedule.

6. Everyone must know how to operate their gear before they go on location, especially large and potentially dangerous items like dollies and generators. Never try to operate equipment that requires training and certification level expertise unless you have that training or certification. Hire a certified operator.

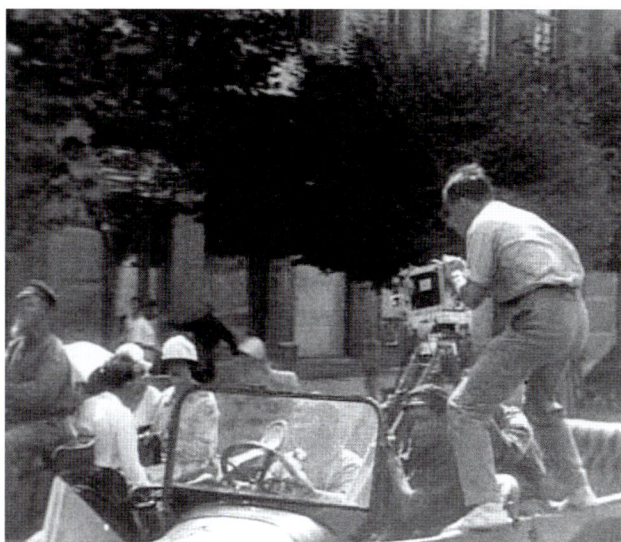

■ **Figure 16.2** This is an exuberant idea for an improvised traveling shot filmed at a time when cars were rare and car mounts nonexistent. These days, though, you'd likely get in serious trouble for a move like this. This is one of the rare times we will tell our readers, "Do not do what this master filmmaker is doing!" From Vertov's *Man with a Movie Camera* (1929).

■ THE THREE COMMANDMENTS OF FILM PRODUCTION SAFETY

1. Every filmmaker has a moral and legal obligation to keep their subjects and crew, and the public, safe. Lack of funds is never an excuse for poor safety practices.

2. Safety is everyone's responsibility. You are first responsible for safety in your specific area, but if you see something dangerous or excessively risky anywhere else during a shoot, you must mention it.

3. Learn and follow all safety regulations and guidelines that apply to your specific project (government, school, location).

Production Insurance

Production insurance is key regardless of the size, scale, or budget of your production. Insurance protects the project from catastrophe should there be any injury caused by the production, not to mention damage to the equipment. Many rental houses require proof of insurance (some rental houses will provide insurance on equipment for an extra fee). In addition, you will need to show proof of insurance coverage in order to be allowed to shoot in many locations, including in parks, on bridges, and more. Don't wait until the last minute. You need to find an insurance company, determine what kind of insurance you need, complete the application process, and wait for it to be binding, so give yourself plenty of time. If you're a student, your department should have information about where and how to acquire production insurance. There is more about insurance coverage in Chapter 6.

Employment Rules and Workman's Compensation

For good reason, most municipalities have strict rules about worker safety. If someone is injured working for you, it is your responsibility. Historically, in the film world, this responsibility has been avoided by calling the crew "independent contractors." More recent legal decisions suggest that this is a poor defense. Many producers deal with this issue by paying crew members through a payroll service. This will cost you a bit more in the short run, but it means that the requisite deductions have been made, and that you will have a clear paper trail for the government. Most importantly, it means that if someone does get injured on your production, they will be able to get the medical treatment they need.

International Travel

If you are traveling to the far side of the planet to do your shoot, you may want extra travel insurance. For example, if you are shooting scenes in rural Africa, in a country with only one hospital (as coauthor Martin Lucas did in Malawi), it makes sense to have special medical evacuation (medevac) insurance to fly an ill or injured crew member out of the country. In addition, an **International Driver's Permit** is a good investment if you plan to drive in a foreign locale. Most national drivers' associations issue them (in the United States, you can use the American Automobile Association).

Another thing to think about before heading abroad is having your crew take a trip to a doctor or travel medicine specialist. Aside from ubiquitous dangers like tetanus, in many parts of the world you may need to consider diseases like malaria, hepatitis, or other less common diseases that are specific to certain regions. Some immunizations require a series of shots, others a course of pills that you need to start taking before you start your trip. You should also have a basic first aid kit with you at all times. Even a scratch or a bite can develop into something serious if not treated quickly.

It's worth pointing out that even not knowing the language well enough can cause problems. Coauthor Martin Lucas was working on a documentary in Lebanon during the 1982 Israeli invasion. The local fire patrol showed up in a red hook and ladder truck and told the crew to leave the area they were shooting in. The crew politely ignored them, figuring they were not the police or the army, so why should they listen? It turned out they had been tasked with destroying a big pile of leftover battlefield explosives, and a few moments after they left a big explosion deafened the crew and rained shrapnel down on them.

Documentary makers try to mitigate these risks by hiring a **fixer**. A fixer is an assistant who speaks the language and can double as a driver, run interference with local authorities, and offer insight into local conditions. On the way to a shoot for a health clinic in the slums of Dhaka, Bangladesh, coauthor Lucas was surprised to be taken by one of the clinic staff to a public fountain where a large man in shorts and a body decorated with knife scars held court. It turned out he was the "boss" of the neighborhood, and nothing happened in it without his blessing. This vital piece of information was something only a local, in this case one of the subjects, could know.

Another precaution worth taking when working far from home is to arrange some sort of backup in case your equipment breaks down, is damaged, or is stolen. One approach is to arrange for a rental house at home to stand by with a camera they can ship to you quickly. A second approach is to bring a second camera, like a small HD camera or an inexpensive DSLR with you, and leave it in a safe locale while you are out on location.

Finally, electricity can vary in voltage from place to place, and is unstable in many parts of the world as well. Be clear that you know the standard voltage where you are going. Some countries can surprise you. Japan, for example, has both 110V and 220V. Make sure you have adaptors that match the outlets where you are going. In addition, plugging a lightbulb for 110V into a 220V or 240V circuit can blow out the bulb as well as the circuit.

When you travel, make sure you have bulbs for the appropriate voltages, as well as plugs or adaptors. More and more equipment these days, including camera and computer chargers, is set to handle a broad range of voltages, but other equipment may not be so flexible. Transformers and voltage converters are designed for very specific circumstances. You need to look at your equipment and your workflow carefully before taking any equipment to another country.

Common Sense

By far, the preponderance of accidents that happen on location occurs because people forget to use common sense. No one on a film shoot should do or request anything of anyone that would even remotely jeopardize their safety. Asking a camera operator to climb up onto a steep rooftop to get a panoramic shot constitutes a willful and dangerous lack of common sense, as does jury-rigging a structurally unsound and untested camera mount to a moving car. Both cases constitute negligence, which is defined as conduct that falls below the standards of behavior established for the protection of others against unreasonable risk of harm (Figure 16.3).

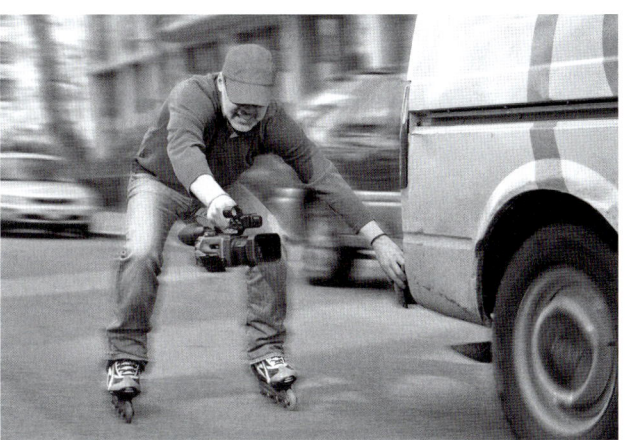

■ **Figure 16.3** No amount of liability insurance or skating prowess will ever make this kind of thing a good idea.

You should also avoid distractions, like pets, visitors, and the reigning king of all distractions: the smartphone. Ask your crew to keep their phones off until break time. One of the coauthors once visited a student film set and saw someone trying to set up a big 2K soft light while talking to a friend on a cellphone squeezed between their ear and shoulder. Bad idea!

Although this next point should be obvious, it must be stated in no uncertain terms. No drugs or alcohol on any shoot. Also, it's up to each crew member to dress appropriately for their particular role on the set. This is especially important for crew who work with or around heavy equipment and electrical gear. Leather palmed gloves to protect your hands from scorching lights are obvious, but it should be equally obvious that high heels or open toed shoes are not appropriate footwear if you're required to move equipment, or work in a jungle, either concrete or tropical. Always wear shoes or boots that protect your feet. You should also wear pants that cover your legs. Finally, it's important for safety's sake to keep your set neat and orderly with room for movement. Use your staging area; put things away that are not being used. Don't leave gear where people can trip on it and never ever block emergency exits with equipment.

Rest and Health

Filmmaking on any level is strenuous work. Keep yourself healthy and mentally sharp by getting enough sleep and eating well during your production period. Also, allow your crew to do the same. Without rest, your thinking and coordination will be blunt and you'll lack the energy to deal with the general intensity level of filmmaking. No one is an exception. Also, be sensitive to driving times. If you're shooting 250 miles from home and expect to wrap at midnight, arrange for hotel accommodations; do not ask anyone to drive 4 hours to get home after a 12-hour workday.

Weather

The entire production team must be aware of the expected weather conditions and dress appropriately. In cold conditions, wear warmer clothes than you would normally wear on a cold day. When you are working in low temperatures for hours, the cold eventually seeps in. Have a plan for somewhere to warm up, even if only a car with a good heater. In extremely hot weather, lots of drinking water is especially crucial and if you're outside, protect your crew from sun exposure. This means providing sunblock and shade in the form of tarps and umbrellas, which also protect equipment from direct sun. Finally, don't shoot in hostile weather just to stay on schedule. Ice storms, rainstorms, heavy snow, and gale force winds not only make for a miserable experience and compromised footage, but are simply dangerous. Don't risk injury to personnel and damage to equipment; just reschedule. If you are shooting somewhere such as a sea coast or a mountain top where extreme weather is a real possibility, make sure to double check with the national weather service (www.weather.gov in the United States; https://weather.gc.ca/ in Canada), and check for coastal flood advisories or storm warnings before heading out.

Risky Locations

If, during the location scout or survey, you discover that a location is not structurally secure, that there are hazardous materials on the site (asbestos, flammable or toxic compounds), or that the electrical wiring presents a danger, then simply look for another location. It's also best to avoid dangerous locations like steep cliffs, soft riverbanks, and busy highways. When you must shoot in neighborhoods with high crime rates, your best bet is to find out from local organizations where it is safe to be and when, and have other crew with you.

Water

If you are shooting on a boat or near any large body of water, do not use 120/240V electricity at all. Rather, since you'll be outdoors, use bounce boards or battery-powered lights. Additionally, life vests and safety lines are mandatory. Don't use "tippy" boats, and don't overload boats. While waterproof housing exists for cameras, most equipment will sustain serious damage if it gets wet.

Air

Another area where safety is a concern is the sky. If you are planning an aerial shot, your best bet will probably be someone at a local airport who has worked with camera crews before and has a special camera mount. An aerial shot can add something special to a documentary, but must be prepared for carefully. Sometimes the best way to get a shot is by removing the door of a plane, for instance. This means the cameraperson and equipment must be tied in very carefully. In addition, aerial photography may involve special permissions. By and large, this type of shooting is out of the range of this book, but in an age where a few hundred dollars will get you a drone with a camera mount, the future of aerial cinematography is destined to grow in unexpected ways that offer new thrills and accompanying dangers. If you plan on using a drone, make sure you check with the Federal Aviation Administration (FAA) (in the United States) or the Civil Aviation Authority (CAA) in the United Kingdom, to find out what the laws are, and think very carefully about the safety issues involved in sending up a drone where you plan to.

Security

In addition to safety, you must think about the security of people, equipment, and personal belongings when you are shooting, especially on location. Theft of equipment and the personal belongings of cast and crew is a common problem on film sets. A producer must ensure that the staging area for equipment is secure and that everyone has a safe place to store their personal belongings while they are on set. This is especially challenging when you are shooting in a public exterior location. In some cases, you may need to assign a person the job of locking away and watching over people's belongings. Never leave valuables and equipment in a car. Cars get broken into all the time. One colleague tells a story of driving home from a long shoot with her cinematographer and stopping to have a bite to eat. They tried to find a bonded (insured) parking lot because they had some equipment in the van, but they couldn't find one so they parked on a fairly busy street. When they returned to the van, all the locks had been popped off and the equipment was gone. In this instance, she was lucky on three counts: (1) she had paid extra for theft insurance when she rented the van, (2) the cinematographer did what any professional would do: he took the camera into the restaurant with him, and (3) the thieves were not interested in all those DigiBeta tapes in the van and left them behind. These contained all the footage they had shot up to that point!

Gear also gets stolen when there are not enough people loading or returning equipment. One person must be assigned the job of watching the vehicle while others take equipment inside or out. Loss also often happens on messy, disorganized sets, or when set striking is rushed. Leaving equipment in a hallway while the entire crew is in the apartment shooting is asking for it to get stolen.

Security also means providing a safe way to get to and from the location. If people must travel home late, drive them or pay for a cab.

Electricity and Safety

Documentary production's lighting needs can mean adding thousands of watts of power to systems that usually handle much smaller loads. Electricity is dangerous stuff and must be treated properly. A few safety principles and a bit of common sense are all it takes to ensure a safe and successful production experience.

How Much Electricity?

Before you start plugging lights in, you need to determine how much electrical power you have at your location and how it's distributed. This will help you figure out how many lights you can work with, and where they can be set up and plugged in. Below is a simple procedure that can be done during your **location survey** to determine how much power you will have, and where it is. This will save you a lot of time and labor by keeping you from lugging more lights than you could possibly use to the location, or by keeping you from having to completely overhaul your lighting scheme when you discover the lighting plan you envisioned isn't possible given the true electrical situation at the location.

1. Locate the **breaker box** (or **fuse box**) for your particular location (Figure 16.4). A breaker box brings the raw power from the utility company into a building and breaks it out into various circuits distributed throughout the rooms. Each circuit is rated in **amps** (short for "amperes") and has a dedicated **breaker switch** (or **fuse**) with the amp rating written right on it. The amp rating tells us how much electricity can safely flow through that circuit. Common circuit ratings found in homes and apartments in the United States (and any country where 120V power is standard) are 15 amps (most rooms) and 20 amps (rooms that use heavy-draw appliances, like kitchens and bathrooms), but you'll need to check your breaker box to be sure. If you exceed the circuit's rating by plugging in too many lights, the breaker will trip and cut the electricity. With a fuse, a metal filament embedded in the fuse melts and breaks the connection, and it must be replaced. If a breaker trips, you can simply reset it with the flick of a switch, but when you do so you must make very sure you reduce the amount of electricity you are drawing on that circuit or it will trip again. The purpose of breakers and fuses is to keep the building from burning down. Excess electrical load causes the internal wiring in the walls to heat up so much that the insulation melts, leaving super hot and exposed wires to short circuit and possibly start a fire.

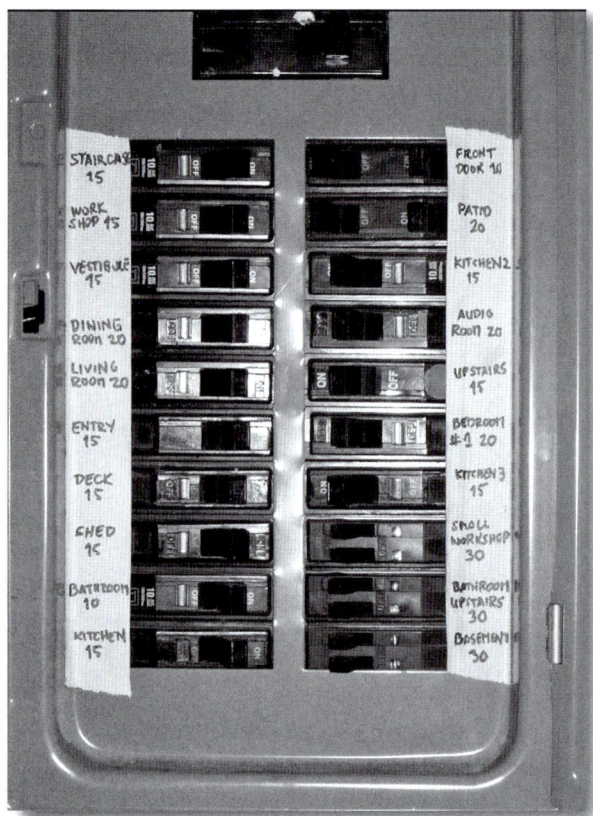

■ **Figure 16.4** Electricity on location. A lighting crew has carefully labeled this household breaker box after determining where each circuit is located and what the amperage rating is.

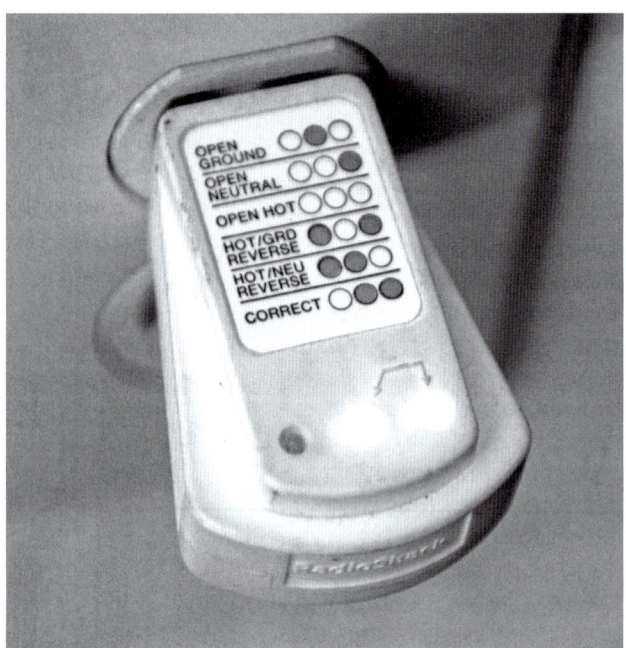

■ **Figure 16.5** Circuit testers will tell you whether the circuit is properly wired, with a "hot," a "return," and a ground. Many circuits are improperly grounded or wired.

2. The next step is to determine which wall outlets are on which circuits. To determine the distribution, simply turn on one breaker at a time and plug a small lamp or a circuit tester (highly recommended) into each outlet (Figure 16.5). Take note of which breaker controls which outlets throughout your location. Occasionally breakers will be labeled "kitchen," "living room," "master bedroom," etc., but these labels are often wrong, so it's best to simply figure out for yourself which outlets are connected to which circuit.

3. Calculate the amount of electricity you can draw from each circuit. To determine how many watts of lighting you can plug into any single circuit, use the following formula: **watts = volts x amps**. We already know what amps are and their rating can be read straight off the breaker of each circuit. The next step is to know the voltage of your system. Volts (voltage) are the measure of the electromotive force of the electrical current. In the United States, a normal AC outlet will vary from 110 to 120 volts. To give ourselves some margin for safety, it's always best to use the conservative figure 110 volts for our calculations. So in a situation where the circuit breaker is listed for 15 amps we can do the following calculation: **110 (volts) x 15 (amps) = 1,650 watts**. This means we can plug in up to 1,650 watts of light on each 15-amp circuit. For a 20-amp circuit breaker, it would be: **110 (volts) x 20 (amps) = 2,200 watts**.

If you're using 220V power, and a 10-amp circuit, the equation would go: **220 volts x 10 amps = 2,200 watts**. However, it is not safe to go right up to the limit of any circuit. As wires start to heat up, fuses can blow. Also, be careful to take into account or unplug any appliances at the location that draw power. It's easy to forget that the refrigerator is plugged into the kitchen's 20-amp circuit. If lights adding up to 2,100 watts are plugged in while the refrigerator compressor is off, invariably the fridge will kick back on just in the middle of an interview, and BLAM!—the breaker trips and the lights go out.

Electrical Loads and Time

The length of time that lights are on is another factor that can push a circuit to the breaking point as cables heat up. A provision in the National Electrical Code states that if an electrical load is run continuously for more than three hours (as we often do on a location) then it must be considered a "continuous load." A circuit that has a continuous load must be de-rated to 80 percent of the posted protection. So if we plan to power our lights on a 20-amp circuit for more than three hours continuously, we must rate that circuit (and do our calculations) at 16 amps (**110 x 16 = 1,760 watts**). For a circuit that is ordinarily 15 amps, our continuous load calculation must be made with a 12-amp rating (**110 x 12 = 1,320 watts**).[2]

CHAPTER 16
Production Procedures, Etiquette, and Safety

The math sounds complicated, but the point is to be careful, especially keeping film lights operating for long periods of time. A good practice is to turn off lights any time you are taking a break from shooting.

Splitting the Load

If you do not have access to the breaker or fuse box, then you will need to be extremely cautious when you plug in lights. If you blow a fuse, it's "lights out" for the rest of the shoot. The best strategy is to bring plenty of heavy-duty extension cords so that you can "split the load." That means that you may be shooting in the living room, but you've plugged the key light into the kitchen circuit while your fill is powered from a different circuit in the bedroom.

Lighting Safety Tips

1. The first rule of safety is to use common sense at all times. Things can become quite hectic on a shoot, but you should always take your time and do things correctly. Never cut corners on safety to save time and don't try to get away with untested, unsafe jury-rigging.
2. Never attempt to do things that require the expertise of a trained and certified electrician. This includes doing repairs on high wattage lights, opening up breaker boxes to "tie into the mains," and rewiring outlets.
3. Maintain a professional attitude toward your equipment. Abused and manhandled gear will break and, in the case of lighting equipment, can give you a severe shock. Keep an eye out for fraying cables or loose connectors.
4. Lights get very hot and can burn everything from hands to walls. Keep flammable items away from them. When bouncing lights off walls, keep them back far enough that they will not blister the paint. Be aware of all flammable materials on the set, such as curtains, and keep lights clear. Always wear leather-palmed grip gloves when handling hot lights. Never put gaffer's tape in direct contact with the unit's housing or even the

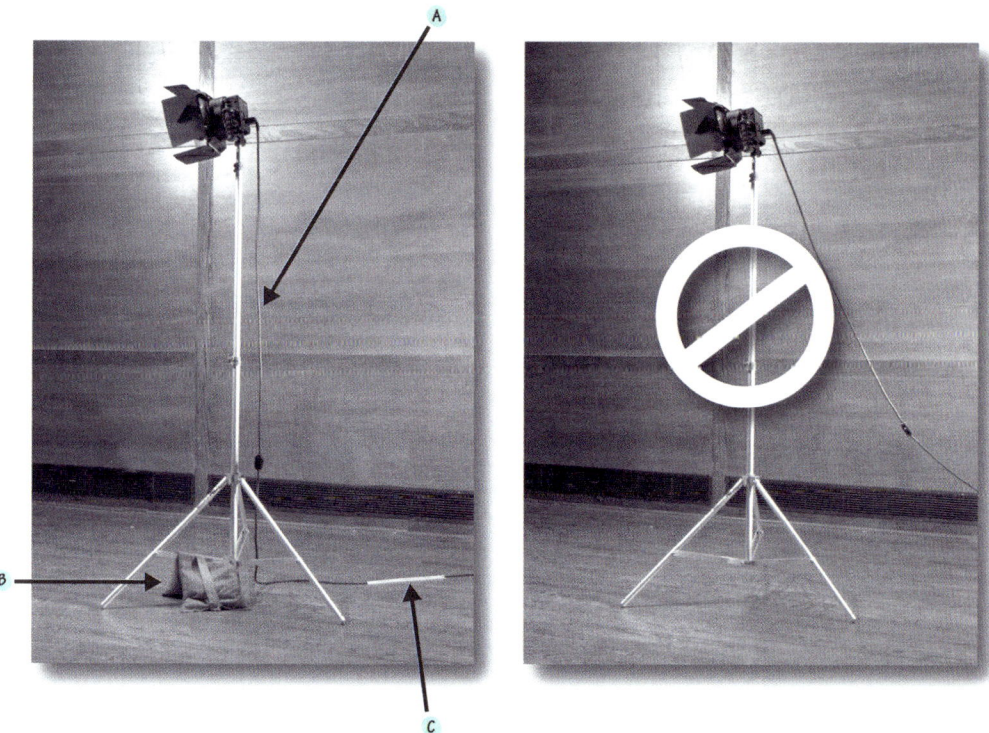

■ **Figure 16.6** Lights should always be set up with the cable flush against the stand (a), stabilized with sandbags (b), and cables taped to the floor to prevent accidents (c).

barn doors, as it will melt. Use clothespins or clamps instead. When you are hanging lights from the ceiling, be very careful where you place them. A hot light can set off the automatic sprinkler system for a whole room or building!

5. Gels designated as "tough" (tough spun, tough blue, etc.) are flame resistant and can be used near lights but will melt if not mounted properly. Also, carefully handle any **scrims** that are used on lights (Chapter 11), as they also get super hot.
6. Always turn off lights when they are not in use. After a shoot, turn them off and let them cool down completely, on their stands, before you pack them away.
7. Never touch the bulb of a professional light, even if it is cool. Lamps get extremely hot and can obviously burn you, but touching a cool lamp with your bare fingers is also dangerous because your fingers leave oil on the bulb. The oil cooks when the lamp is turned on and eventually it can cause the bulb to explode. Always use the plastic or paper sheath provided with a new lamp to handle the bulb.
8. Electricity and water do not mix. When shooting scenes involving water, like bathtubs and swimming pools, it's best to go with available light. If you must use lighting for interior bathroom scenes, use battery-powered lights and do not set up lights where they could fall into the water.
9. When setting up a **light stand** or a **C-stand**, try to keep the weight as evenly distributed as possible to avoid having the stand topple over. Use a sandbag to stabilize every stand (Figure 16.6, left).
10. Do not use home extension cables for your film lights. Typically they are not rated properly for heavy use. Make sure you have heavy-duty industrial extension cables that are rated for the amperage you are using.
11. Keep your cables neat. Use extensions so that cables fall straight down from the unit to the ground rather than stretching out diagonally to reach an outlet (Figure 16.6, right). Tape down your cables with gaffer's tape (called "dressing cables"), and always coil unused cables and put them out of the way, safely in the staging area.
12. All hanging lights, barn doors, and any other item rigged overhead should be secured with a safety chain.

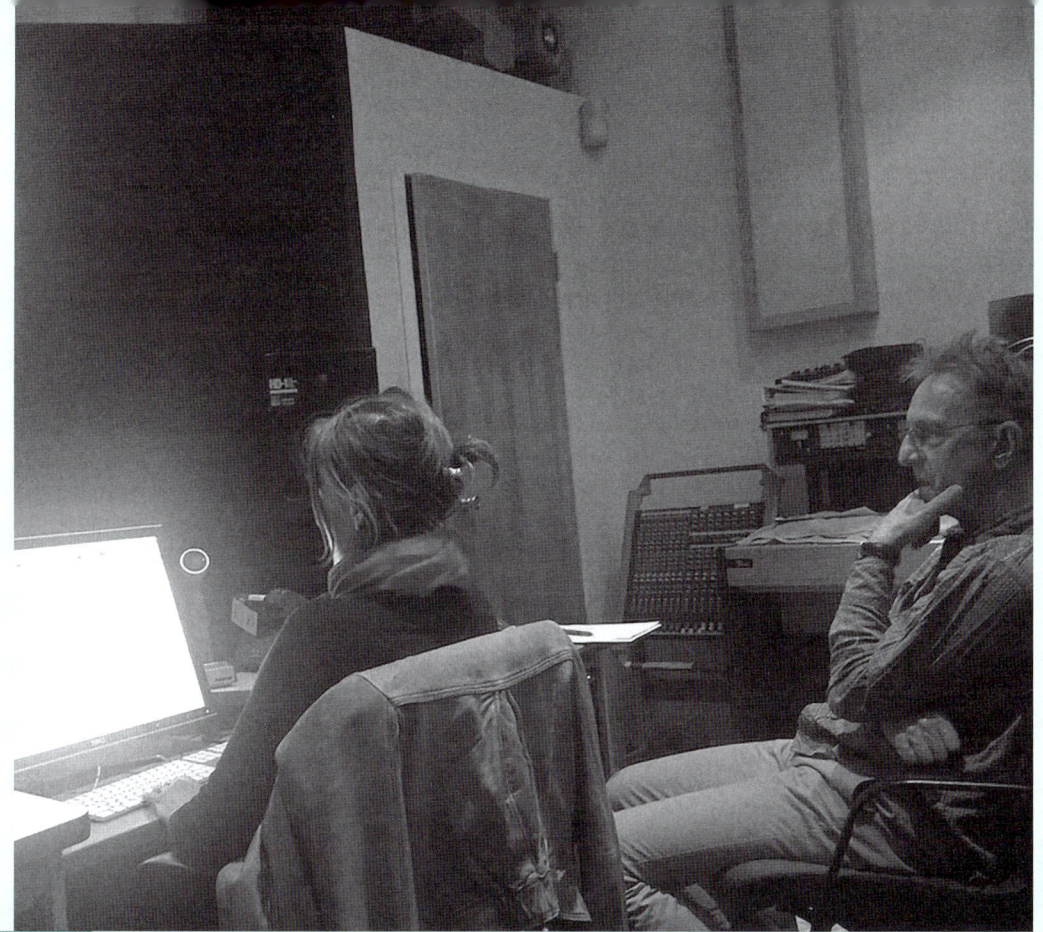

PART 3 POSTPRODUCTION

Postproduction Workflow and the Process of Digital Editing

CHAPTER 17

Your shooting is done. Your digital media is "in the can." What's next? This is the first of a series of chapters about the postproduction phase of documentary production. In this chapter, we will look at the technical, organizational, and craft aspects of postproduction. In Chapter 18, we will consider the role that writing plays in creating a finished documentary. In Chapter 19, we will look at the conceptual and aesthetic issues involved in editing.

■ POSTPRODUCTION OVERVIEW

Postproduction encompasses all of those creative and technical processes that go on after the shooting stops—but it's never quite that neat. While the goal is to complete shooting before you start editing, on a documentary it is not uncommon to find yourself shooting more material as you refine your story during editing. In addition, for many documentaries, you will be adding a variety of other materials in postproduction that will greatly affect your final film. These include **archival footage**, **stock footage**, **still photos** (all covered in Chapter 20), **graphics**, **narration** (Chapter 18), and additional sound elements including effects and music (Chapter 22).

The key people involved in postproduction are the director, the producer, the editor, and the assistant editor. Many documentary filmmakers edit their own films, and if you are a student making a short documentary for class, you probably will too. In fact, when you are starting out, it's a good idea to do as much of the postproduction as possible yourself so that you gain a hands-on understanding of how it all works, as well as a conceptual understanding of the expressive power and flexibility of editing. On a larger project, the entire process may be overseen by a **postproduction supervisor** who ensures that things go smoothly and that time and money aren't wasted by making choices at the beginning of the process that have undesirable effects later on in the postproduction chain.

There are a variety of specialists who can bring fresh conceptual perspectives, imaginative energy, and technical expertise to your film during this stage. Writers, **sound designers**, composers, **sound editors**, and **rerecording**

THE BASIC PHASES OF POSTPRODUCTION

1. Lay out a systematic **workflow**, if you haven't done so already (p. 270).
2. Create a **master list** of footage.
3. **Transfer** and/or **transcode** footage for **ingest** into your edit system. Make sure you have a strategy for naming clips before you begin ingesting (p. 274).
4. Organize your material by **logging** and **transcribing**, either in your editing system or on paper (p. 284).
5. In your editing system, organize your clips into **bins** based on character, date, theme, or whatever works for your particular project. Bin columns are also versatile and useful for project organization (p. 284).
6. Create **paper edits** or other organizing documents (p. 289).
7. Edit the picture and sound into **rough cuts** (p. 290) using temporary graphics, low-resolution **archival materials**, and **scratch** music and narration.
8. Create a **fine cut** (p. 292); check availability of all licenses for footage, stills, and music.
9. Lock picture.
10. Incorporate final graphics and cleared, high-quality archival footage and stills.
11. Record final narration, if you are using it.
12. Get the final version of the musical score from composer, or existing music you have licensed.
13. Edit and mix sound (Chapter 21).
14. Correct color (Chapter 22).
15. **Master** the project and create **submasters** for distribution (Chapter 22).

mixers (Chapter 21), and **colorists** (Chapter 22) can add an amazing amount of creative value to your film. If you are working on a low budget, don't assume you can't find people who can contribute to your postproduction process. A composer who is also starting out, for example, may be willing to work on your project for little or no money in order to develop his/her own sample reel.

Postproduction Workflow

Workflow is the technical path your project will take from sound and image acquisition to exhibition. This includes choices about the shooting format, the editing format, editing software, finishing processes, your mastering format, and your final distribution formats. Filmmakers can easily lose their way in the workflow stream, with unexpected and often expensive results. A little bit of research at the very beginning into the ways various production and postproduction phases and formats interface with one another will go a long way toward minimizing nasty surprises. Doing some tests using the various types of footage you will be working with and taking them all the way through postproduction is advisable. At the very least, talk to other filmmakers and postproduction professionals, including any facilities you'll be working with, before you begin postproduction.

The postproduction workflow is to some extent based on decisions you've already made in production, including what camera you used, what format you shot in (and what format other footage such as archival material comes to you in), and how your sound was recorded (**double-** or **single-system**). Your postproduction workflow is also based on an understanding of your desired distribution venues (Chapter 23).

At this point in the evolution of the medium, there are a wide variety of postproduction pathways one can take, and each option has a significant impact on the budget of the film, your work process, your documentary's look and sound, and ultimately on your range of exhibition possibilities. We are also at a time of big transitions in terms of available digital **nonlinear editing (NLE)** software tools. A few years ago, Apple's Final Cut Pro (FCP) and AVID's Media Composer dominated the documentary editing field. Today, with Apple's move to the more consumer-friendly Final Cut Pro X, documentary makers and editors who used FCP have been migrating, often to Adobe's Premiere Pro or to Avid's Media Composer. For the near future, things will continue to be in flux, but a good grasp of postproduction basics, as we are providing below, will help you make the best decisions for your project regardless of the specific system you're using. For the purposes of this book, we will use examples and figures from both AVID's Media Composer (Avid) and Adobe's Premiere Pro (PP).

When devising your workflow, you should have answers to the following questions:
1. What was the film shot on: SD, HD, 2K, or 4K? What codec, resolution, and frame rate? Did you shoot single- or double-system sound? (Chapter 8)
2. What editing software will you use? Will you be using specialized ingest software (p. 274) or syncing software (p. 277)?
3. Will you work at highest resolution throughout, or save space and RAM by using lower-resolution versions of your files (**proxies**) and linking back the higher-resolution footage at the end? (p. 276)
4. Do you want to transcode all your footage to a single editing format at the beginning of editing, or will you work with mixed formats and standardize at the end? (Each approach has advantages and disadvantages; see p. 275.)
5. Will you edit and mix sound within your editing system, use specialized software to do it yourself, or rely on a specialist to finish the soundtrack? (Chapter 21)
6. Will you do the **color correction** (also called **grading**) on your own, or do you plan to use a professional colorist? Will you need specialized third-party software if you do it yourself? (Chapter 22)
7. How do you want to **master** the project? (Chapter 22)

8. Do you want your master to be **mono**, **stereo**, or **surround sound**? (Chapter 22)
9. How do you want to distribute the project (Chapter 23) and what media types will be required for exhibition?

Finally, if you are delivering the program to a broadcaster or other type of distributor, you need to make sure you understand what their specifications are so you deliver everything correctly.

Let's look at a typical low-budget project shot on HD that aims to finish on one of the HD digital video formats with the intention of screening at festivals and streaming on the Internet (Figure 17.1).

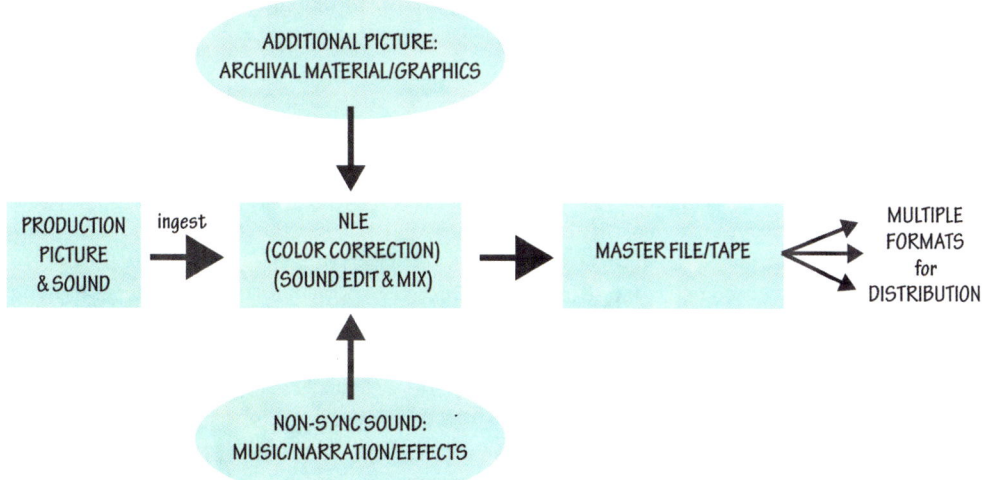

■ **Figure 17.1** Low-budget workflow. Shoot HD video, edit and finish in your nonlinear editing system (NLE), master as a file for festivals, DVD, and web. Master audio is stereo.

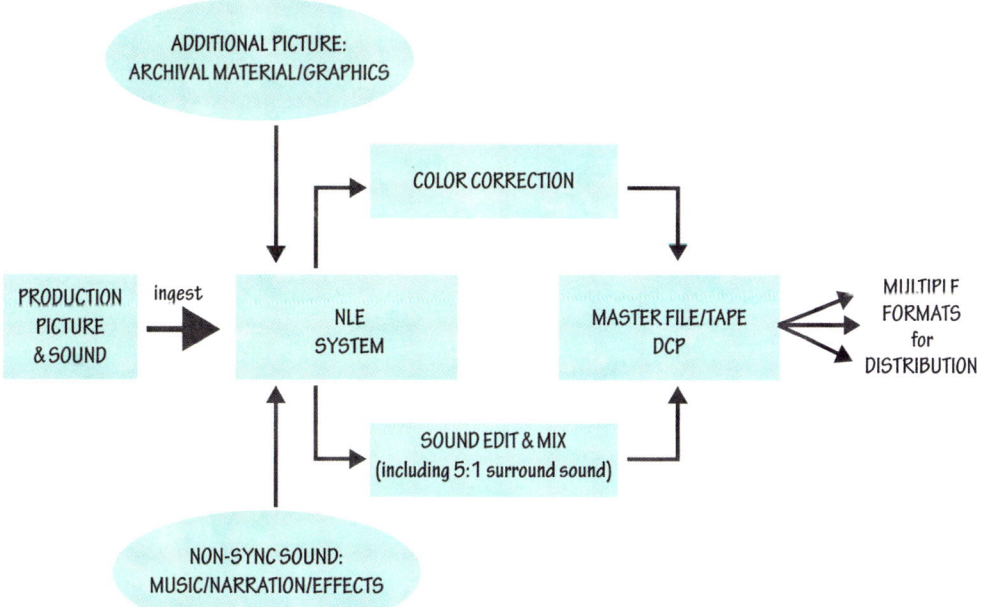

■ **Figure 17.2** Medium budget workflow. Shoot HD video, edit and lock picture in your nonlinear editing system (NLE), send to professional sound edit and mix, and professional colorist. Master as a file for festivals, DVD, and web. Includes surround sound for Digital Cinema Package (DCP).

For a low-budget or student project, you will likely do some of your own color correction or sound finishing in your NLE. For a higher end project, more suitable for broadcast or theatrical release, you will actually be exporting both sound and picture and taking them to a mix session and a color correcting session, respectively (Figure 17.2).

THE PROCESS OF DIGITAL EDITING

Virtually all documentaries are edited on a digital **NLE system**. Editing in the digital domain means that all visual and sound components of the project, no matter what their original form (film, analog audio, or video), must be converted into digital data in the form of **media files** and brought into a computer running specialized editing software. Any piece of visual footage, or any piece of sound, can be instantly accessed through a computer's **random access** capability and easily labeled, organized, duplicated, cut, arranged, trimmed, mixed, and manipulated.

Digital NLE is "non-destructive" editing, which means that any cutting, arranging, and effects you might perform occur only virtually. Your original media files are not altered in any way (Figure 17.3). All editing is done via **media file indicators**, which use **time code** (Chapter 8) and clip names to "point" to the original data without ever changing the underlying media files themselves. For example, let's say you have a camera take that is 10 seconds long and you want to use 2 seconds from the middle of that file in your cut. You simply indicate the time code numbers where you want the shot to begin (the **in-point**) and end (the **out-point**). Then you edit that portion of the shot into the program sequence. As you do this, however, you are in fact not cutting any actual media. Rather, your in-point and out-point numbers tell the computer what piece of that media file to play back at a particular point in your cut. This is why it's easy to make or trim a shot a few frames longer or shorter, or try numerous versions of a **sequence** using the same shots in different order. You are simply altering data indicators, not the underlying media files.

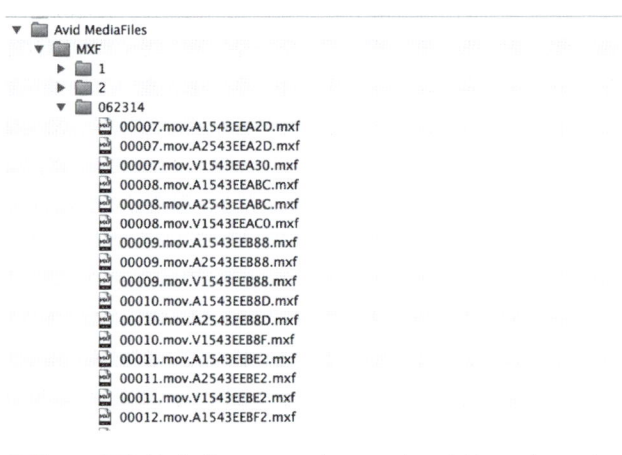

■ **Figure 17.3** Media files are saved on an external drive and are not actually altered during editing. Pictured are the .mxf files for a project in Avid Media Composer, located in a file called "Avid MediaFiles" on an external hard drive.

All of the editing decisions you make—length of shots, order of shots, layering of audio, and so on—constitute your **edit decision list (EDL)**. The EDL is one of the major components of your **project file**. The project file will have an extension based on the NLE program you are using, like .prproj for Premiere Pro, or .avp for AVID Media Composer. Unlike media files, which are big, project files are small because they only contain the EDLs for your various sequences, source media information, **user preferences**, and **settings**. Because they are small, project files can be sent easily from one computer to another. It is not uncommon, therefore, to have multiple people working on the same project in different locations. As long they each have a set of hard drives with the identical source media files on them, they can email the project file back and forth.

Learning an NLE program can be overwhelming. The best way to approach your software is to learn the basic functions first. Learn how to choose the shots you want, how to perform cuts, and build a simple sequence. Rearrange the shots and trim them longer or shorter as you need. Learn how to layer a few tracks of audio and adjust sound levels, keeping your footage in sync. Maybe try a dissolve or two. That's all you really need at first. Focus on what you need to know to tell your story. As soon as you discover that you truly need to use a particular transition or effect, look it up and learn how to do it. There are tutorials online for pretty much everything you will want to learn, often created by the NLE's manufacturers.

The Basic NLE System

There are purely consumer programs, like Apple's iMovie and Sony's Vegas, which are inexpensive and relatively easy to learn. These programs are not flexible enough, though, for anyone who seriously wishes to make accomplished documentary films. The more professional programs, like Avid's Media Composer and Adobe's Premiere Pro, are more expensive but have much greater capability in terms of editing sound and picture, handling large projects, and integrating with professional finishing workflows for color correction and sound mixing. All professional NLE programs tend to work on the same basic principles and use similar interfaces.

The Hardware Setup

While small projects can be completed in on a laptop computer (Figure 17.4), most editing setups use a desktop computer. The hardware for a typical NLE station consists of a computer and monitor(s) (Mac or PC) running NLE software, **external hard drives**, a **media transfer device** (camera or card reader), speakers and/or headphones, and a comfortable chair (Figure 17.5). Editing requires a fairly powerful personal computer. Many editing setups will use two monitors, with one (often an HD monitor) dedicated to a full-screen display of the program.

External hard drives store your media files, and connect to your computer using either Thunderbolt or USB 3.0. Most NLE software instructions recommend not putting media files onto the internal drive of your computer, where your software resides. This is a speed issue and also a convenience issue. Media saved on a portable hard drive can be used with any editing station running the same software. Keep in mind that media files take up a lot of space, so you must calculate storage needs before you start working with your footage. Storage space depends entirely on your editing format. Five minutes of 1080/60i HD footage in codec like Apple ProRes HQ will require 5 GB of drive space, while 5 minutes of AVCHD footage takes up much less room. Any number of free format/storage calculators can help you figure out the storage needs for your format's codec and data rate (p. 132).

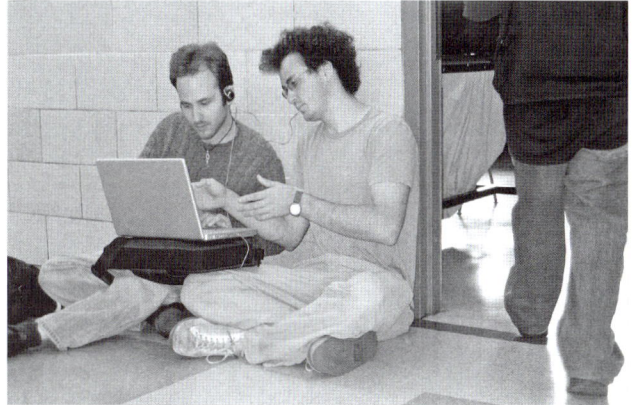

Figure 17.4 The convenience of today's editing software. Two students do some last-minute cutting in the hallway before their class begins.

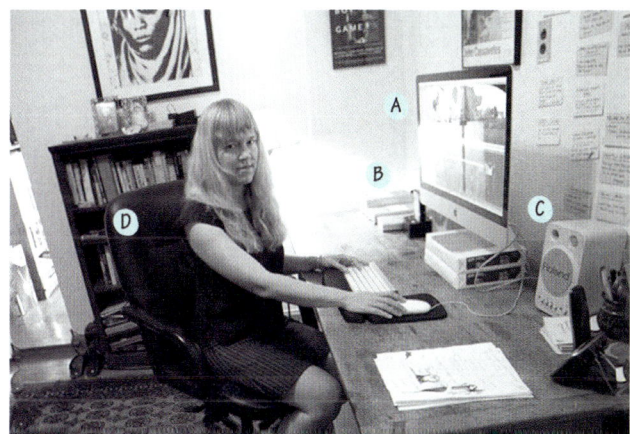

Figure 17.5 A typical NLE system setup (in this case, Annukka Lilja editing Deirdre Fishel's *Care*): computer (A), external hard drives (B), speakers (C), and a comfortable chair (D).

In addition to holding your original media files, your NLE system will create new media called **render files** for a variety of reasons. It's essential that you have plenty of extra space for these files. It's also important that your hard drive have a spindle speed of 7200 rpm. Many less expensive drives run at the slower 5200 rpm speed, which is inadequate for playing back HD footage. Currently a new type of **solid-state drive (SSD)** can offer even higher data transfer speeds, but the high price and small size makes this less likely to be found in an editing context.

A **media transfer device** is used to download your footage into the NLE system. Again, this depends on your shooting format. If you're shooting on HD tape, then you'll require a deck interfacing with the computer, or you can use your camera. If you are shooting on memory cards, you'll need your camera or a card reader. Note that some computers come with a reader installed. Often footage will be transferred or transcoded onto a drive in the field by a **Digital Imaging Technician (DIT)**.

A good set of speakers is important to get a true sense of your audio. If you are working in a room where there are other people, you'll be forced to edit with headphones. Headphones are fine while you're constructing the rough cuts of your movie, but the final soundtrack mix should always be done with high-quality speakers to get an accurate sense of how the balance and presence of the audio will sound to an audience who will be listening to your documentary through speakers. In particular, problematic bass sounds that you will be unaware of listening to headphones will become obvious when your tracks are played through good studio speakers.

A comfortable chair is a must. Editing requires that you remain inside an editing room, sitting on your behind, in front of an NLE system for days on end. Under these conditions, it's not uncommon for repetitive stress injuries to occur. For this reason, an adjustable ergonomically correct chair is important.

Setting Up Your NLE Project

When you create a new project in your NLE, you will need to set it up so that the program understands the basic parameters of your project. One of the most important settings is your **format**, which relates to the format of the material you will be importing and how you want it to be converted when you bring it into your NLE (Figure 17.6). Your **scratch disk (PP)** or **capture drive (Avid)** determines where your NLE will put any files it creates while importing or during editing. It's important to set these correctly every time you edit, or you run the risk of spraying footage throughout your system and ultimately losing files. Finally, your **sequence settings** determine the format of any new sequence you create.

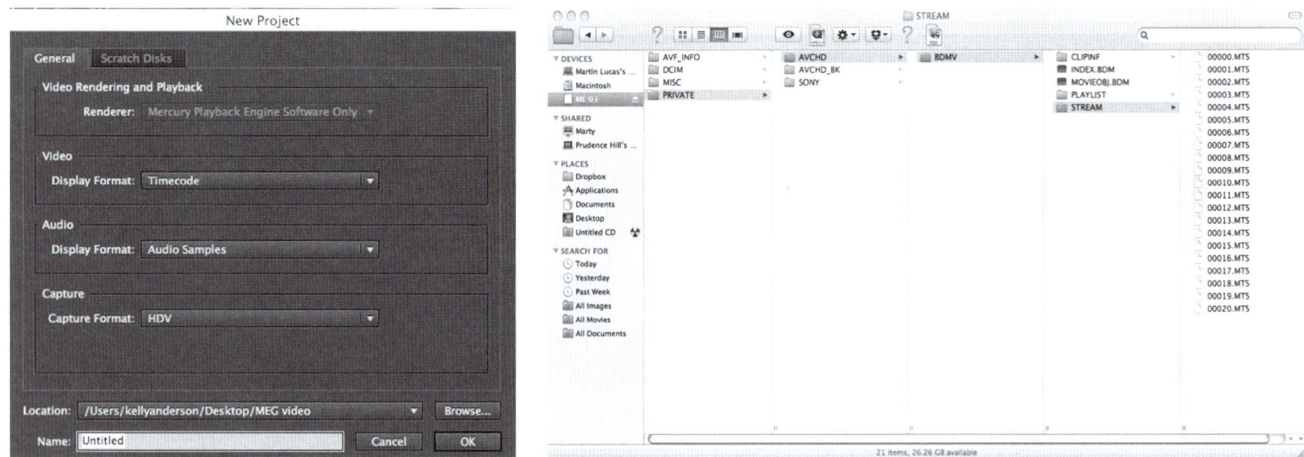

■ **Figure 17.6** Settings dialog box in Premiere Pro (left) and Avid (right). Here you can see the choices available for setting up a project in a variety of formats.

Ingesting Your Video

These days, you will most likely be shooting on memory cards (SD, CF, P2, or SxS) or onto a hard drive. You will bring your material into your NLE environment via a process called **ingesting**. Once you've inserted a card into your computer or card reader, you have several options. One is to use the computer's operating system to copy the entire contents of the card, including its file structure, onto your hard drive. You can then bring the media files right into the NLE working environment, or convert them into another format for editing using your NLE software or another application. In other situations, manufacturers will provide software that reads the file structure on the card, and copies the files onto the hard drive, **wrapping** them in the process. An example is the Canon XF utility. Wrapping involves putting the media into a **file format** that the NLE can understand and work with, without changing the original shooting format encoding. Premiere Pro prefers files wrapped in Quicktime or **.WMV** (the Windows container format) wrappers. Avid, on the other hand, saves all media in the **Material Exchange Format (.mxf)** container format.

COMMON SOURCE MEDIA FORMATS

Many cameras that shoot in the AVCHD format use a file structure based on the one developed for Blu-ray discs. Material shot in this format is actually not saved as discrete files, but as **streams**, which lack the structure of normal files. Some of the information, like time code, is actually stored in a separate folder (Figure 17.7). This means that the media typically has to be wrapped in a **container format**—in other words, turned into individual files (.mov for Premiere, .mxf for Avid). Different cameras generate media with different file structures, and they may also have to be rewrapped or transcoded for use. NLE and camera manufacturers make it their business to offer updated software add-ons and plug-ins that will allow the newest camera files to be ingested. Before you start trying to bring in any media, you should make sure your software is up-to-date and set up to bring in the media you are working with.

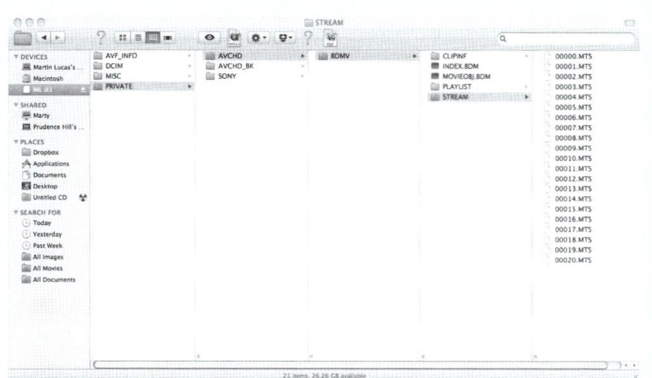

Figure 17.7 The file structure of an AVCHD disk. The media is on the right in the Stream folder as .mts files.

Depending on our workflow, your media may be need to **transcoded**. Transcoding means converting the media to a new codec that the NLE is optimized to work with (from AVCHD to Apple Prores, for example).

Once your material has been ingested, it will appear in your NLE as clips (p. 284).

Working Natively vs Transcoding

Increasingly, NLEs (including PP) can handle a variety of codecs **natively**. This means that they can be ingested as they are, without transcoding. When you determine your workflow, you will need to decide whether to work natively or transcode all of your footage so that it is in one consistent codec. Documentary editors often face a "codec salad," meaning that some footage was shot on one camera, other footage on another, archival material is in another format altogether, and so on. Avid will always convert to its own proprietary codec and wrap in an .mxf container.

The advantage to working natively is that you don't have to spend a lot of time early on transcoding to a single format. The disadvantage of mixing formats is that long sequences can bog down your computer as it tries to process the many codecs in real time. Your finishing may also be more complicated and can reveal unsuspected problems. There is no consensus among editors at this time as to which approach is better. We suspect that, as software and processing speeds improve, working natively will become more common.

Frame Rate Considerations

If you are working in NTSC, you will have shot your footage either at 24 fps (actually, 23.97 in most cases) or 30 fps (actually 29.97). Hopefully you will not have combined both in one project! You now have to decide whether to edit in 23.97 or 29.97. The important thing is to work backwards from your intended delivery formats. You cannot mix frame rates within one sequence, so you will have to either convert your 24 fps material to 30 fps, or vice versa.

When video cameras capable of shooting 24 fps first came on the market, they were incapable of actually recording at anything except the broadcast standard of 29.97 fps. This problem was solved using an approach inherited from the days of film-to-video transfers, called **3:2 pulldown**. The DSP in the camera would repeat certain fields (half a frame, remember!) so that the 24 frames filled the 29.97 timespace. Today, many HD cameras have the capacity to shoot 24p native (24Pn). XDCam and AVCHD, for instance, both include Pn formats. The implications of this can be a bit complex. The most important thing to think about is your workflow, which can go a couple of different ways for productions that shoot 24Pn. One alternative is to edit in 24P and do a pulldown at the end to create a 29.97 fps master for broadcast. Alternatively, you could do the pulldown right away, and edit in 29.97 fps to make a broadcastable master. Then you can reverse the pulldown process to make 24 fps versions of your show for DCP or Blu-ray, both of which support that frame rate.

BACKING UP YOUR MEDIA

One of the biggest problems with modern digital media, in comparison with earlier forms such as film or analog video, is that it is totally virtual. The cards and hard drives that cameras record on are erasable and reusable, so the media you've imported is all you've got. It is very easy to lose your whole show in a hard drive crash or other computer disaster. You need to develop a backup system for your media, and use it rigorously. A standard approach is to simply copy each card that you import into your NLE system onto a second backup drive, so that there is a second copy that you can access if your main drive fails. Some ingest software will automatically make backups as it imports your material.

Working with Proxies ("Off-Line" and "Online" Editing)

Not many documentaries are shot on high-resolution formats like 4K, but this is likely to change in the near future. And even in HD, many documentaries have more than 100 hours of footage, resulting in terabytes of needed hard drive space. Sometimes, your NLE will have a hard time handling your high-resolution files. In any of these cases, it may be advantageous to create **proxies**, which are lower resolution versions of your high-resolution media files. Proxies take up less storage space and are less demanding in terms of computing power. The idea behind proxies is that you edit with them, and then can easily go back to the high-resolution original files and cut them in after you have finished making your editorial decisions and your cut is locked (p. 292). Using proxies for editing is also called **off-line editing**, which refers to an earlier time period (before about 1995) when all editing was done this way. Similarly, recreating your cut using the high-resolution footage is called **online editing** or **conforming**.

INGESTING WITH SPECIALIZED SOFTWARE

Many workflows involve using special software, either in the field or as a first step toward setting up postproduction. These software systems allow you to ingest clips, transcode footage, create subclip markers, add metadata, and even back up your material while importing your media into your NLE system (Figure 17.8).

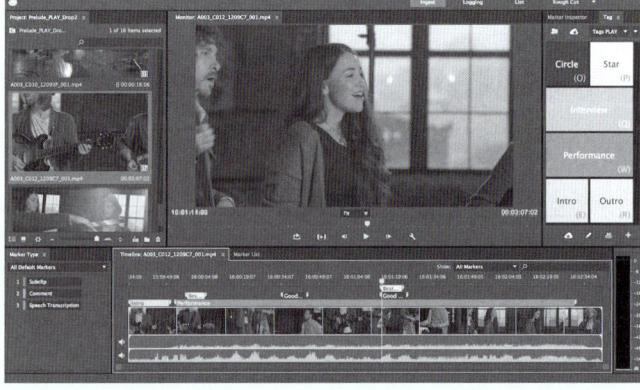

■ **Figure 17.8** Adobe Prelude is a software companion to Premiere Pro that allows for ingest, transcoding, and logging in the field.

If you are working with AVID, the system will automatically transcode your source material into the AVID DNxHD proprietary format. You can select from a variety of compression levels, expressed as bandwidths (Mbps). A high quality level would be DNxHD 220 (10-bit, full image quality, with a 220 Mbps bandwidth), while a compressed proxy could be DNxHD36 (8-bit, lower image quality, with a 36 Mbps bandwidth).

Cameras are increasingly capable of shooting high-bandwidth files (4K, for example) that are too big for edit systems to handle, so the use of proxies will likely continue for the near future.

Ingesting Audio

Ingesting audio may seem easy, but in fact there are several things you need to be aware of to avoid problems. The first is to make sure that you are ingesting at the same sample rate that you are using in your project's main sequences. If you recorded single-system, it is likely that your audio will have a sample rate of 48 kHz. But some cameras have other options and if you are using a separate audio recorder, you may have elected to record at a higher sample rate, such as 96 kHz, and your editing software may or may not be capable of converting this on the fly. Stereo is another key issue. If you recorded in stereo, you need to make sure the import settings match this. If you didn't record in stereo (Chapter 14), you don't want to import your two channels of audio as a stereo clip. All nonsync audio sources, music, and sound effects must also be ingested with care. If you bring in a music track, which will often have a sample rate of 44.1 kHz, the NLE may handle it, and it may sound okay in the sequence, but cause trouble when you go to a mix. In addition, sound effects downloaded from the Internet may be in a compressed file format such as MP3, which you should also plan to convert before importing them. In fact, MP3 files are generally problematic for use in a documentary soundtrack, so try to avoid them where possible. The best formats to use are the two uncompressed digital formats, .wav and .aiff.

Syncing Picture and Sound

If you have shot single-system, then the audio will be captured in sync along with the picture. However, if you have shot double-system, then your audio was captured separately and stored as .wav or .aiff files. Now, each scene must be **synced** in your NLE system. There are different ways of doing this:

1. **Using a Slate to Sync**

   Open the image clip in the viewer and find the exact frame where the clapper arm on the **slate** closes. Place an in-point on that frame.

   Open the corresponding sound clip. You will see a sound wave representing the audio on that clip. Find the exact point where the "clap" occurs (looking at a waveform of the sound clip will help tremendously) and mark an in-point. Audio scrub, which allows you to hear frame-by-frame audio as you drag the viewer playhead, is also helpful.

   Select the video and audio tracks and, using the **autosync** (Avid) or **merge clips** (PP) command, create a single synced clip. Be sure you select the dialogue box that tells the program to use the in-point as a sync-point.

2. **Syncing When Your Picture Files Include a Single-System Scratch Track**

   Often, when you are shooting double-system, your camera will have recorded audio that is not good enough to use in your soundtrack, but which can be useful for syncing. (This is often the case with DSLR shooting, for example). If you do have a **scratch track**, just expand the vertical height of the track to make the waveform more visible and line up the waveform of the double-system track with the waveform of the single-system scratch track. Play the track. If it sounds "reverb-y," it's not quite in sync. Once the clip plays back without any echo or reverb, it's in sync and you can merge the clips.

3. **Using Time Code to Sync**

   If you are fortunate enough to have shot with a camera and sound recording device that had locked time code (p. 116), you will be able to use the time code on the clips to sync your audio and video.

4. **Using Pluraleyes to Sync**

   Pluraleyes is a software program by Singular Software that synchronizes audio and video clips automatically without the need for time code or slates. It integrates with Premiere Pro and AVID Media Composer.

The NLE Software Interface

In standard editing mode, most NLE systems divide the edit environment (or desktop) into four main windows (Figure 17.9): the **project window** (Avid) or **project panel** (PP), (A); the **preview monitor** (Avid) or **source panel** (PP), (B); the **timeline,** (C) ; and the **sequence monitor** (Avid) or **program panel** (PP), (D). The names may differ, but their function is basically the same regardless of the particular NLE program you are using.

The Project Window (Avid) or Project Panel (Premiere Pro)

The **project window** or **project panel** is the main window for storing, organizing, and accessing all of your project's visual and audio elements. Your media files are called **clips** and are organized in folders called **bins**. Each type of sound and picture element has a particular icon that identifies it (Figure 17.10). Remember, these are just reference information, not actual media—they simply point to the actual media files that are stored on an external hard drive. Another element you will find in this window is the **sequence**, which refers to your edited material as represented in the timeline (see below).

You can create as many bins as you need. Most NLE systems provide great flexibility for customizing, organizing, and identifying project elements. Clip information can include the date filmed, log notes, description, in and out time code numbers, duration, number of audio channels, frame rate, compression, codec, pixel ratio, and so on. You can customize how you see this information, and use it to sort your clips and sequences (Figure 17.11).

The Preview Monitor (Avid) or Source Panel (Premiere Pro)

This window is where you view your source clips, and then set in-points and out-points to delineate the exact piece of footage from the longer shot that you want to edit into your film (Figure 17.12).

The Timeline Window

Once you've decided on the specific parameters of the shot you'd like to insert into your film, you place it into the **timeline**. The timeline is where you truly edit your movie by inserting, deleting, arranging, rearranging, and fine-tuning your clips as you build your documentary one cut at a time.

The timeline is divided into discrete **video and audio tracks** for maximum creative flexibility. A typical timeline will automatically provide one video track and two audio tracks when you start a project, but you can add as many tracks as you need. You have the option to cut, rearrange, or apply effects to only the picture, or only the sound, or any combination of picture and sound tracks. Audio tracks can be layered to create complex sound design. Multiple video tracks can be used to create superimpositions and other layering effects (Figure 17.13).

CHAPTER 17
Postproduction Workflow

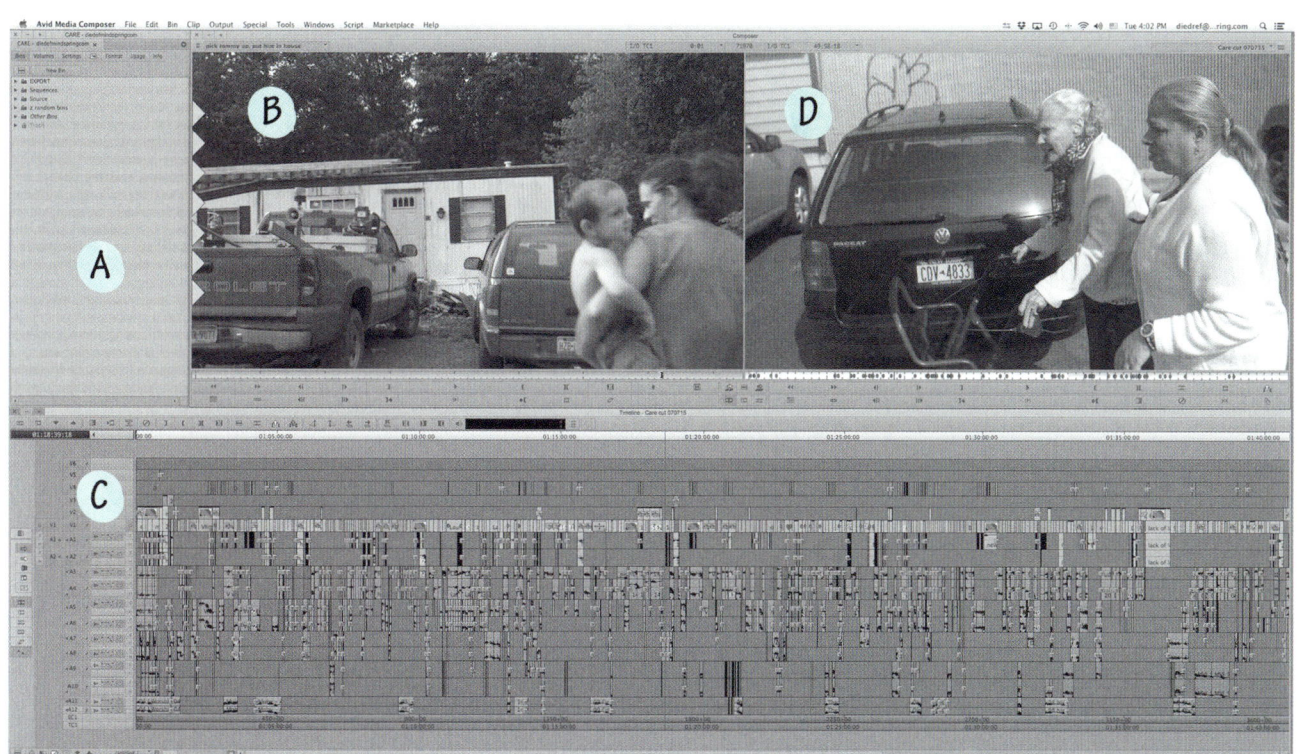

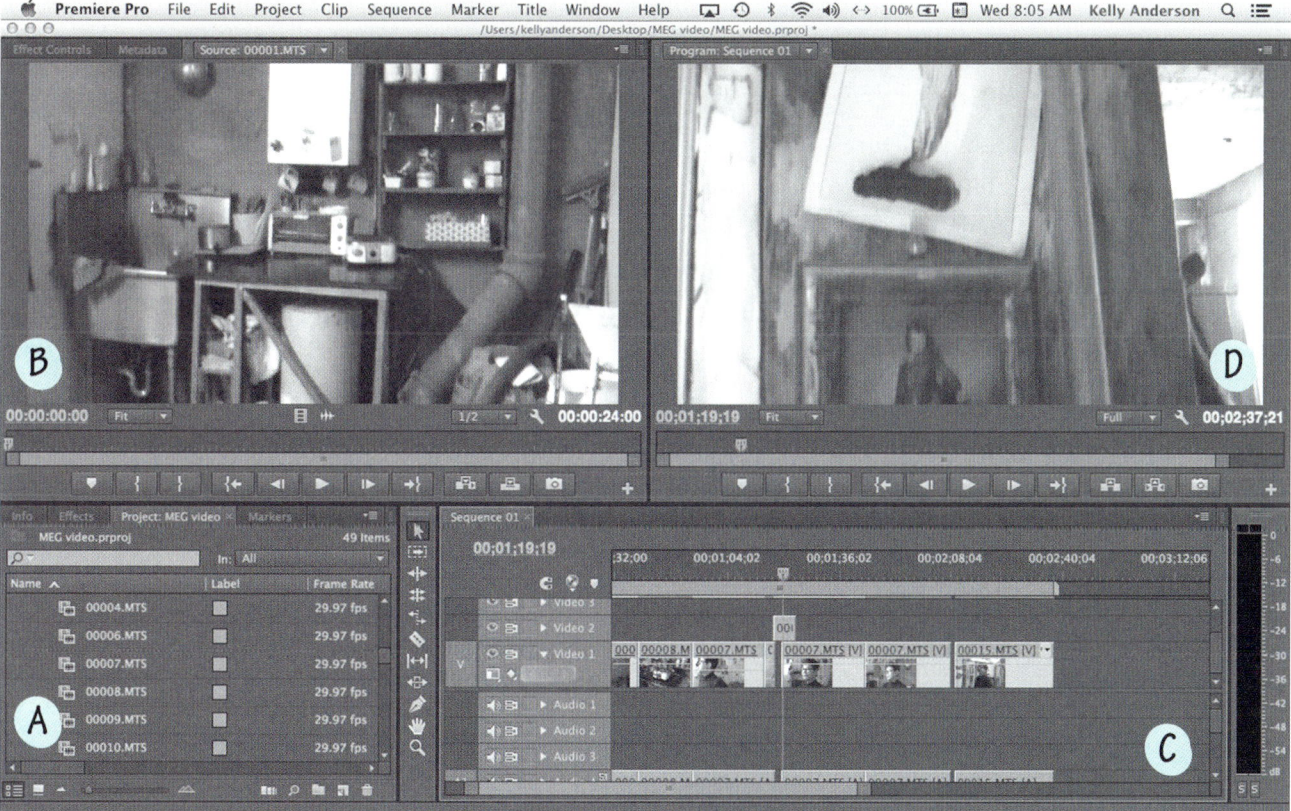

■ **Figure 17.9** The four main editing windows are essentially the same in Avid (top) and Premiere Pro (bottom): the project window (Avid) or project panel (PP), (A) ; the preview monitor (Avid) or source panel (PP), (B); the timeline, (C); and the sequence monitor (Avid) or program panel (PP), (D).

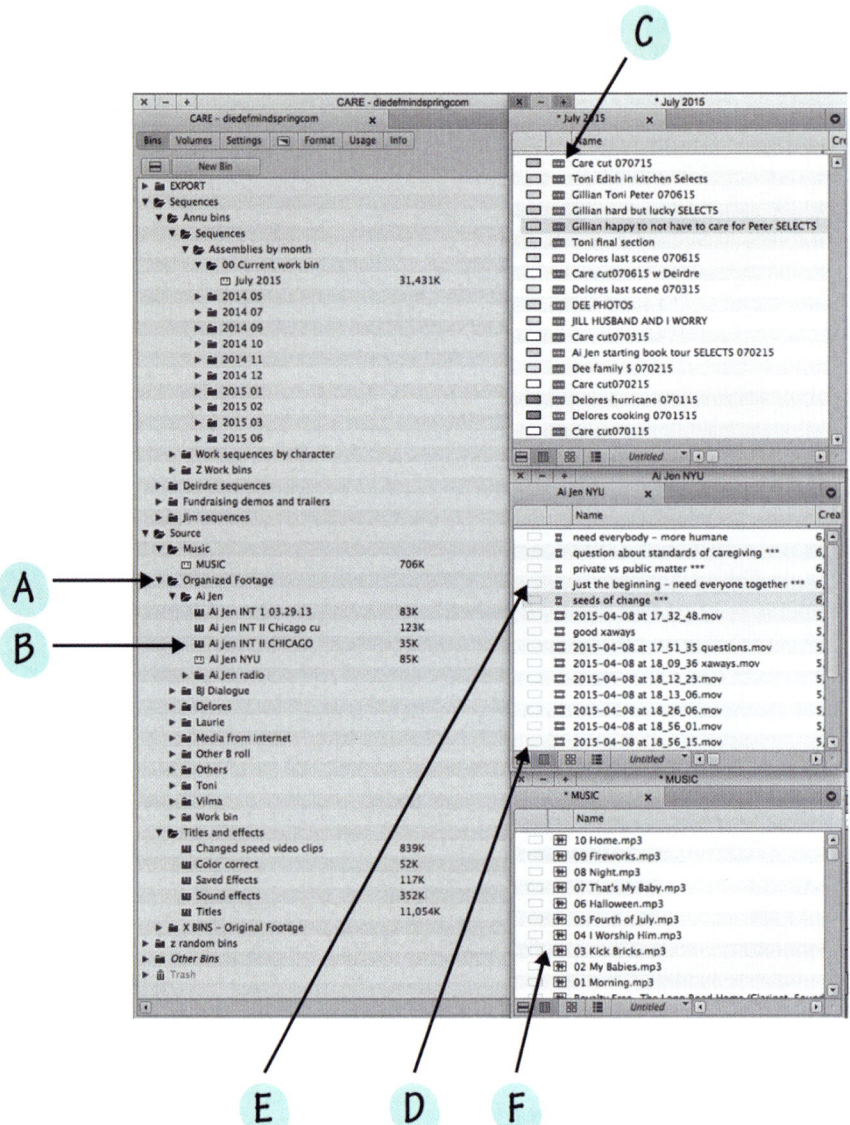

■ **Figure 17.10** The organization of project files in Avid Media Composer. The Project Window contains folders (A) for project organization, and bins (B) which hold sequences (C), clips (D), subclips (E), audio files (F), and other elements.

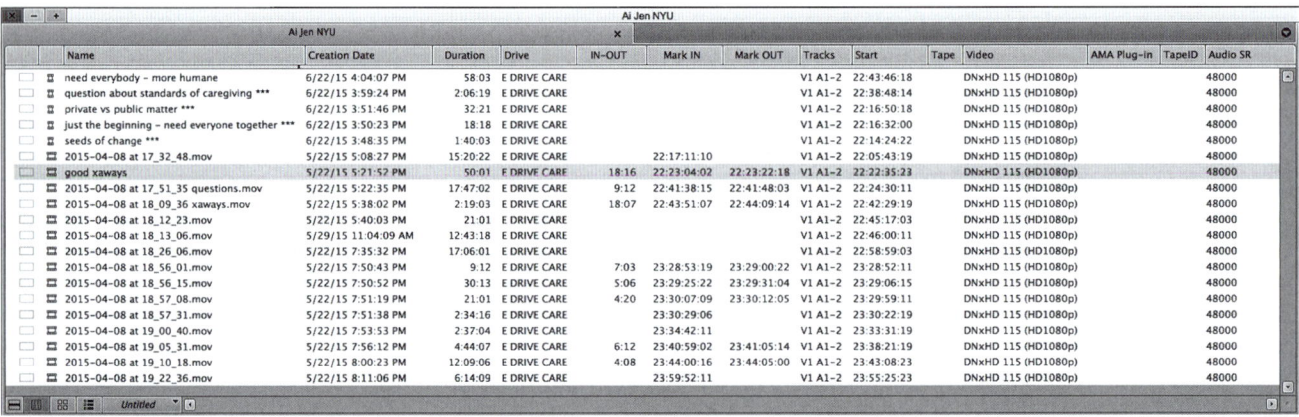

■ **Figure 17.11** Bins have many columns that contain useful information for organizing and finding clips. This example is from an Avid project.

CHAPTER 17
Postproduction Workflow

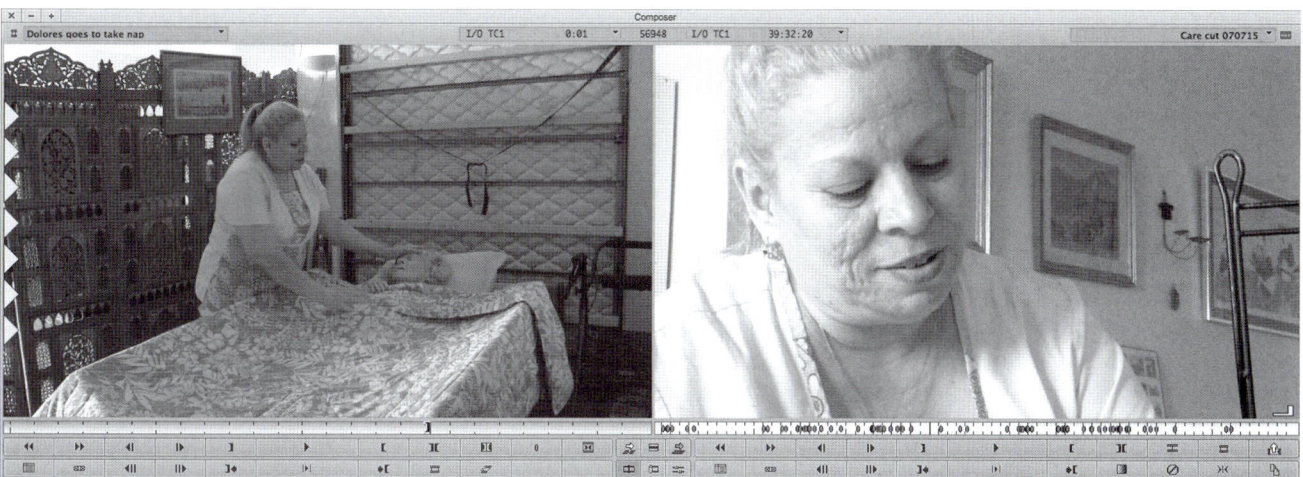

■ Figure 17.12 The preview monitor in Avid is the left half of the composer window (shown in its entirety here). This is where you view your source clips, and set in-points and out-points.

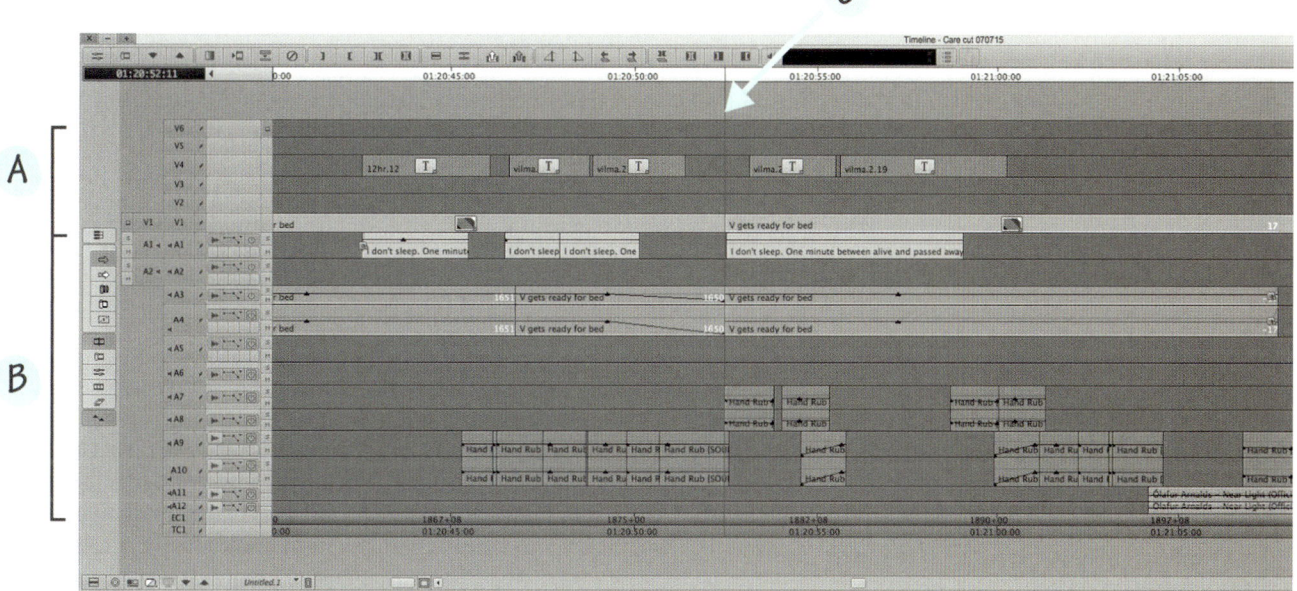

■ Figure 17.13 The timeline consists of the picture track(s) (A), sound tracks (B), and playhead (C).

As you lay down clips in the timeline, you are creating a **sequence**, which is a graphical representation of your edited movie. Sequences are saved in the project window or panel, along with your clips. Sequences should be clearly named and saved frequently. One of the great advantages of digital editing is that you can create multiple sequences, copy sequences, create versions of sequences, and even insert part of a sequence into another sequence.

Inside the timeline is a **playhead**, which is a horizontally scrolling vertical line running through all edited tracks. The playhead tells you where you are in the timeline and is used to move through your sequence quickly. You can also use the playhead to determine where edit points are placed and where shots are inserted. If you hit play, the playhead moves across the sequence in real time.

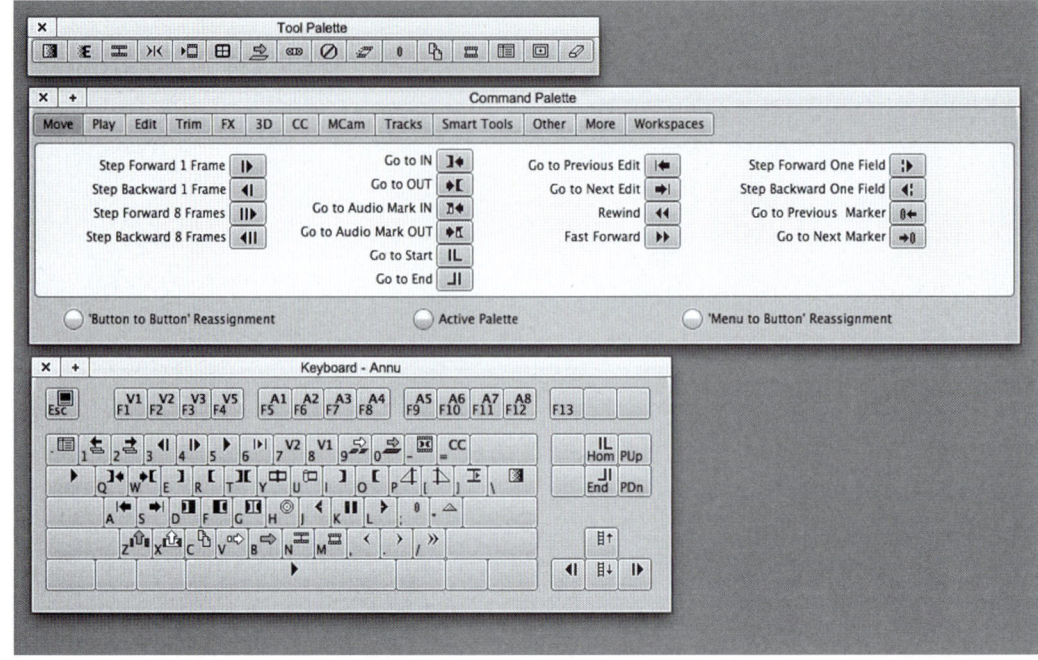

■ Figure 17.14
Avid's Tool Palette (top) allows you to access commonly used tools for editing, and the command palette (center) allows you to map functions onto your keyboard (bottom) for faster editing.

In all NLE programs, the number of tools and the possibilities for working in the timeline are staggering. Some capabilities, like the ability to trim shots shorter or make them longer with frame accurate precision, are essential tools for editing. Other timeline functions you will use only rarely. It is not possible to cover the functions in detail in this book, so we refer you to the software instruction manuals. All NLE systems have a Getting Started manual, which is the best place to begin. Also, there are many online tutorials, user forums, and books readily available.

The Sequence Monitor (Avid) or Program Panel (Premiere Pro)

This window is where you watch your sequence as you build it. Wherever the timeline playhead rests, that frame of video is viewable in the **sequence monitor/program panel**. You can move through the sequence in real time, slowly or quickly, or frame by frame using the transport control buttons at the bottom of the window. You can also drag the playhead to move around the sequence extremely quickly. The playhead in this window is a duplicate of the playhead in the timeline window. See the right half of Figure 17.12 for an image of Avid's sequence monitor.

In addition to the four main windows, there are other auxiliary windows that you can include on your desktop for the sake of convenience. One in particular is the **tool palette**, which allows you to access timeline tools with the click of your mouse. You can also map tool functions onto your keyboard so you can perform tasks easily without needing a mouse or keypad (Figure 17.14).

Menu, Icon, or Keyboard: Take Your Pick

One thing you'll discover on all NLE systems is that there are usually three ways of doing exactly the same thing. You can find any given command inside **pull-down menus**, or you can trigger the same command by clicking an **icon** on the desktop or using a keyboard **shortcut**. For example, in Premiere Pro, setting in- and out-points on a source clip can be accomplished three

■ **SUMMARY: THE FOUR BASIC NLE WINDOWS**

1. **Project Window (Avid)/Project Panel (PP)**: This is where you store and organize your editing elements: video clips, audio clips, graphics files, and sequences.

2. **Preview Monitor (Avid)/Source Panel (PP)**: This is where you preview clips and determine in-points and out-points for your shots.

3. **Timeline**: This is where you edit and arrange your image and sound files to create a sequence.

4. **Sequence Monitor (Avid)/Program Panel (PP)**: This is where you view your edited sequence and mark in-points and out-points on the timeline.

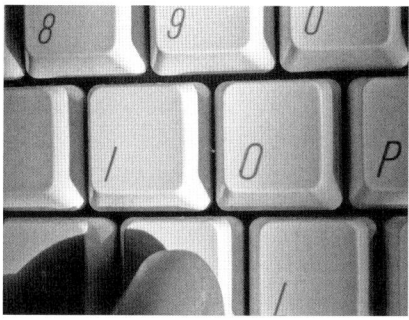
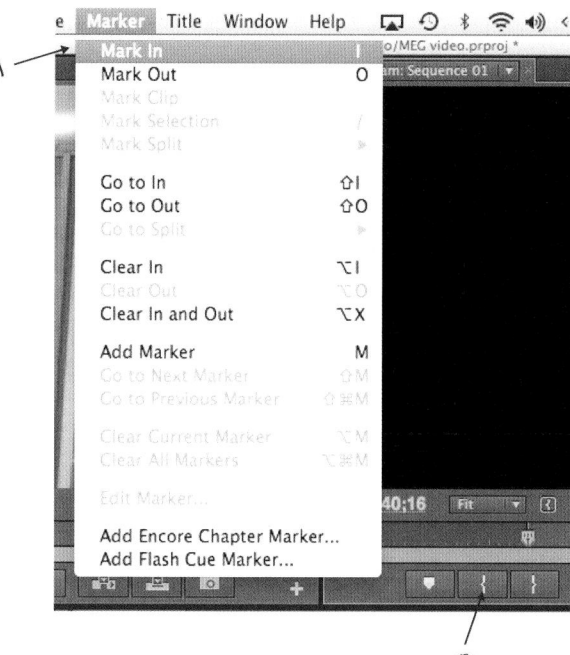

Figure 17.15 Many functions can be accomplished in multiple ways. For example, you can set in- and out-points on the keyboard (left), through a menu (A), or by clicking icons (B).

ways: by hitting the "i" or "o" button on the keyboard, by clicking on the mark in/mark out icons in the source panel, or by scrolling down the "mark" menu to the "mark in" or "mark out" command (Figure 17.15). You don't need to memorize all three ways of doing every task. Professional editors tend to use more keyboard commands as they are the quickest, but most people use a combination. Customize your process, and find the easiest and most comfortable route for yourself.

There are two special keyboard functions that are extremely handy to know:
1. The J, K, and L buttons are universal transport control buttons. J plays in reverse at normal speed, K is pause, and L is play forward at normal speed. Pressing J and L multiple times increases or decreases the play speed from normal speed (one press) to 2x to 4x to 8x (four presses). Holding the K and pressing J or L will give you slow motion.
2. The command-Z keystroke combination instantly undoes your last action. Inevitably, as you edit, you will click a wrong icon or drag and drop something where it doesn't belong, or even accidentally delete an entire sequence. If you've made a mistake, simply hit command-Z, and all is put back where it was before your blunder.

MAKING SIMPLE EDITS

The more you edit, the more tools, edit modes, and shortcuts you will incorporate into your routine. The best way to learn software is one function at a time as the need arises. The place to start is making simple cuts. Let's go through the process of using the basic windows in Premiere Pro to make some simple but very common edits.

For this exercise we will use a footage shot of Harley "Inspector Collector" Spiller, an artist and educator in New York City whose work is based on his passion for collecting things. If you want to load the raw footage into your own Premiere Pro project and follow along, the files can be downloaded from our companion website (www.routledge.com/cw/Anderson).

ORGANIZING YOUR FOOTAGE

Good organization is the basis of all good editing. Unfortunately, many inexperienced editors, awash in the anticipation of seeing their footage in the context of an edit, begin to capture their media without thinking through the organization of their material. This is a critical stage, especially with file-based media. If your material is not named and organized well, you can actually lose track of it quite easily. Clip naming conventions should be figured out *before* you begin ingesting footage, as it becomes riskier to change them after you have established a relationship between your media file indicators (clips) and the underlying media files they point to. In addition, good organization makes it easy to see what you have and find things you need. When you have only a few hours of footage, it might be possible to wade through it and find a golden moment you remember from production, but when you are dealing with dozens or hundreds of hours of material, you will never be able to keep things sorted in your mind. Developing good habits now will pay off throughout your career, and will save you time and money on any documentary, big or small.

The basic stages of organization are:

1. Create a **master list** of footage shot and acquired.
2. Develop a consistent and systematic strategy for naming and describing (**logging**) clips in your NLE system.
3. Develop a consistent and systematic strategy for organizing your footage into bins.
4. Transcribe interviews and cross-reference with clips in your NLE system.

The Master List of Footage

This might seem obvious, but many students never create a list of what they have shot! Your **master list** of footage is a list of all your **elements**, with the date created and a short description of the material. It's like an overview of your project in a couple of pages you can review at a glance. In former times, this would have been a list of tapes. Nowadays, it is more likely to be a list of folders. Naming conventions can vary, but one strategy is to name your folders according to the date they were shot, as well as the card number for that day (1, 2, 3, etc.). Next to the name, include a short description of the material. For example:

01_15_14_Card_1	Roger at work
01_15_14_Card_2	Roger at work, Roger interview Pt. 1
01_15_14_Card_3	Roger interview Pt. 2
01_17_14_Card_1	Visuals of Detroit, Maria at home
01_17_14_Card_2	Maria at home, Maria Interview

The specifics of your naming convention matter less than the principle: you should be able to know what you have to work with, as well as when it was shot, and be able to go through it at a glance quickly and easily to remind yourself what material you have. It is very important that you remain consistent with whatever system you use. In the master list, you should also include archival material, stills, graphics, and audio elements.

Naming and Describing Clips

Depending on your workflow, you may name your clips before you import them or rename them once they are in your NLE. Either way, avoid having multiple clips with the same name because it will make it hard to keep track of your footage. Even if the NLE system assigns a more randomly generated series of numbers (like the name "20140305173352" assigned to a clip by Canon's XF utility), many editors prefer to give their clips descriptive names (like "CU Roger writing," or "WA Maria w groceries"). The advantage of giving your clips descriptive names is that the clip's name in the browser, and in the timeline, will give you an indication of what it is. Dangers of renaming clips include not being able to **re-link** clips if they go **off-line**, which means that the relationship between the media file indicator (the clip) and the underlying media files has broken for some reason. If you are using proxies, be especially careful about renaming clips, as you will have to go back to your high-resolution media when you are finished editing. Make sure you think through your workflow carefully before you start to rename clips!

Using Bins to Organize

One very useful approach to organizing your material works like this: in the project panel or window, you should create a bin for each day of shooting, and within those bins, create bins for each card, using the same names you gave your original media folders in your master tape list. You can then duplicate the clips from each card and sort them into other bins based on character, event, theme, and so on. This is just one way of organizing your material. If you develop another system that allows you to find your material easily, then by all means use that.

Within your bins, you can use columns to organize your material as well. For *My Brooklyn*, for example, coauthor Anderson created a bin for still photographs, within that bin columns for "theme" and "source." It was then possible to find all the clips for a particular theme, like "1930s," or "architect renderings" simply by sorting the bin by that column. "Source" is a useful category for third-party elements that may need to be cleared, as it can remind you at a glance where a particular image came from. You can even add a column where you keep track of which images are free to use and which will require licensing (Chapter 20).

However you organize your bins, it is a good idea to export the information in them to a spreadsheet. Print these up, along with your master list of footage and **transcripts,** and keep everything in a **postproduction binder** so that you can access the documents easily as you work.

TRANSCRIPTS—ARE THEY REALLY NECESSARY?

Every student we have ever directed to make **transcripts** has reacted with horror. It's true that creating a word-for-word transcript of your interviews is time-consuming. Until voice-recognition programs get better, you are likely going to be transcribing yourself or paying someone else handsomely to do it for you. However, there is no better way to keep track of the content that is in your interviews. Once you have spent a half hour looking for a particular sound bite you remember but can't locate, you will start to understand the value of a transcript that can be perused and searched easily.

A transcript is a word-for-word typed script of *every word* a speaker says. That includes "ums," "ahs," false starts, and asides. Transcripts should be done for all interviews. They are also very useful for observational scenes that include a lot of dialogue.

When the transcript is complete, devise a system for cross-referencing your transcript with the clips in your NLE. One way to do this is to put **markers** on your clips, and then name them something that you can write on your transcript as a reference. (Some editors use the initials of the character plus a number, like "RW1," "RW2," and so on.) Whatever system you come up with, the idea is to be able to code your transcripts so that when you want a particular piece of media from an interview, you can find it in an instant.

Some NLEs, like Premiere Pro, claim to be able to transcribe your interviews using voice recognition. Quality varies, and is much improved by uploading a text file of the transcript. AVID's ScriptSync will allow you to upload a transcript and sync it with clips so that you can find any piece of footage easily using a transcript or using a word-based search.

For the purposes of the exercise, we will assume that you have already created a project in Premiere Pro and organized it. You have four bins in the Project Window: "Raw Footage," "Interview Subclips," and "Harley apt. visuals." There is also a bin for sequences.

We are going to edit a short scene, in which Harley introduces us to his bottle cap collection and talks about collecting being important to him. We will start with a medium shot (MS) of Harley seated at a table talking, then cut to a close-up (CU) of his bottle caps, then back to a MS of Harley talking about collecting being important to him. Because he is standing in the last shot and sitting in the other two, we will finish by putting a **cutaway** shot of a Chinese menu over the beginning of the standing shot so that we don't break continuity.

The bins and clips we will work are:

Bin: Interview Subclips
   HS 1 intros beer cap collection
   HS 3 collecting identity

Bin: Harley Apt. Visuals
   CU bottle caps
   kitchen cutaways

Double-click on the sequence in the "Sequences" bin to open it up in your timeline. Then open the "Interview Subclips" bin. Double click on the clip "HS 1 intros beer cap collection." You will notice that the clip appears in the source panel window (Figure 17.16). Use the transport controls to play the clip, then set an in-point right before Harley says "This is my beer bottle cap collection" (at time code 02;43;26;25). The time code is displayed on

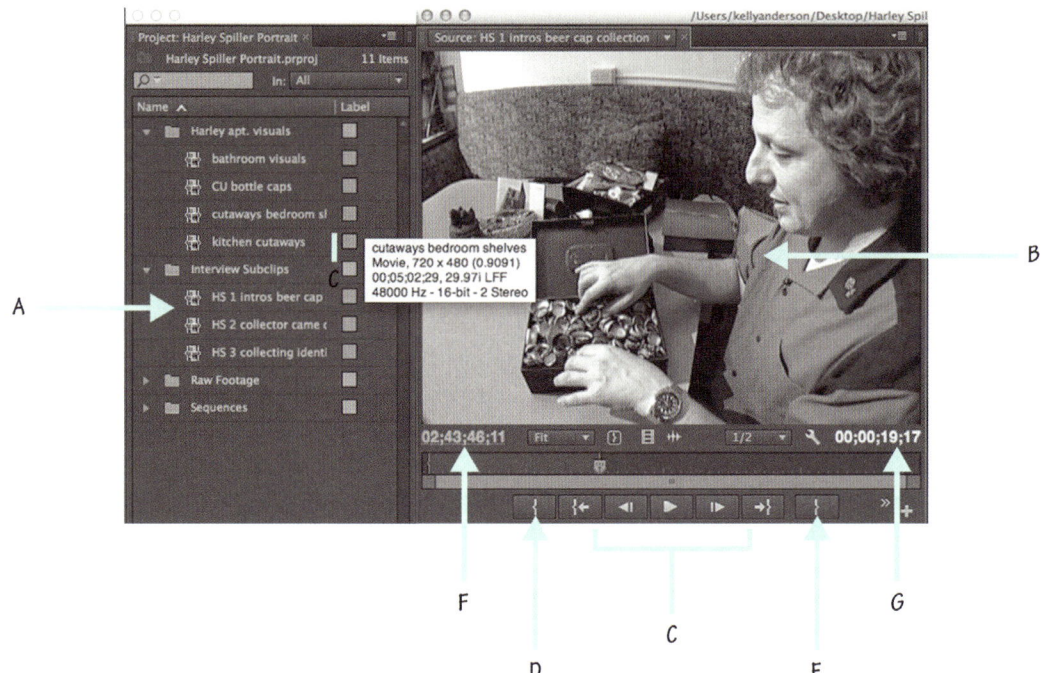

■ **Figure 17.16** Double-click the clip "HS 1 intros beer cap collection" (A) to load it into the source panel (B). Use the transport controls (C) to play the clip. Use the "i" key or the "set in-point" button (D) to mark an in-point at 02;43;26;25. Use the "o" key or the "set out-point" button (E) to mark an out-point at 02;43;46;11. Your time code is displayed on the left side of the panel (F), and the clip duration is on the right (G).

the bottom left of the source panel window, just under the image. Set an out-point right after Harley says ". . . that are different" (at 02;43;46;11). You will notice that the area in between the in-point and the out-point is highlighted in the source panel's scroll bar, and that the clip duration is 19 seconds and 17 frames.

Now click and drag the clip from the source panel to the program panel and let go. You will see the clip appear in your timeline. Congratulations! You have made your first edit. You can play your sequence (which consists of only one shot at this point) using the transport controls on the program panel, or you can drag your playhead through the timeline to review the shot (Figure 17.17). Pushing the spacebar always starts or stops playback.

Next we want to add a second shot. Double-click the subclip labeled "CU bottle caps" and select an in-point at 02:57:18:16 and an out-point at 02;57;33;02 (the duration will be 14 seconds and 17 frames). Go to your timeline window and make sure "snapping" is turned on (the magnet icon). You can then simply drag your shot into the timeline and place it next to the first shot. Because **snapping** is turned on, the shot should automatically fall right into place.

Now let's make a **3-point edit**. Let's say you play the sequence and decide that you want the next shot to come in right after Harley drops the blue and white bottle cap (TC 00;01;46;04). Find that frame and set an in-point *on the program panel side* this time, using the "i" key or the mark-in button (Figure 17.18). This tells Premiere Pro where to put the next shot you add to the sequence. Load "HS 3 collecting identity" into the source panel and set your in-point right before Harley says "Collecting is a big part of my identity" (00;03;34;09) and an out-point right after he says "it's the information that you put in here that really counts" (00;04;12;10). Now drag the clip onto the program panel. The clip appears in your timeline, but instead of starting at the end of the previous clip, it starts at your in-point, covering up the end of the "CU bottlecaps" clip. This is called a 3-point edit

CHAPTER 17
Postproduction Workflow

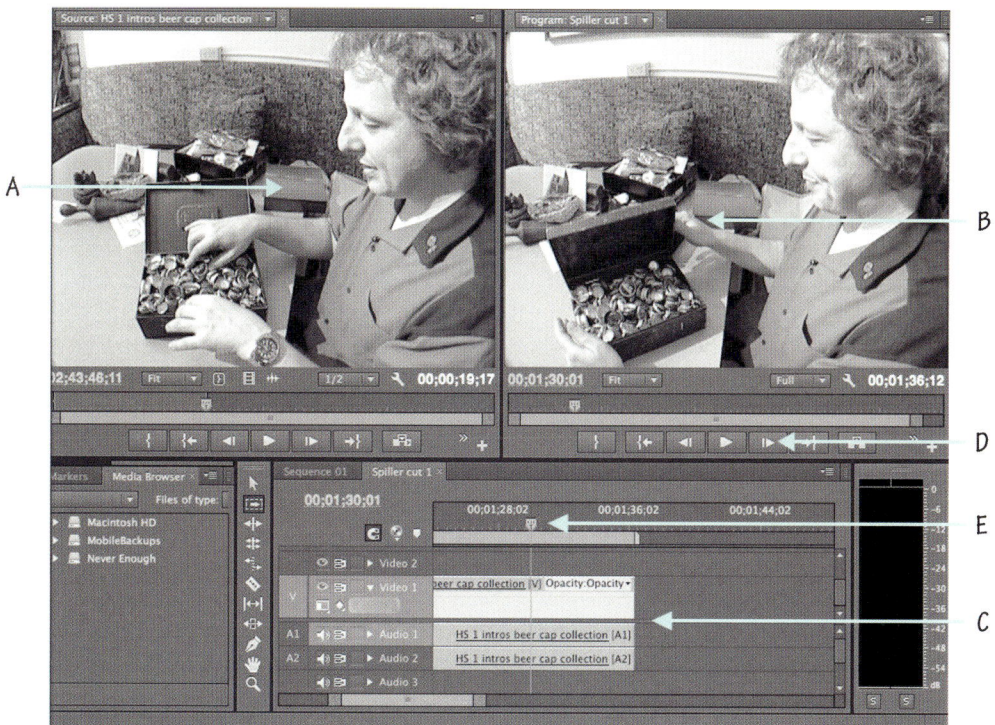

Figure 17.17 Make your first edit by dragging the image from the source panel (A) to the program panel (B). Your clip will appear in the timeline (audio and video) (C). You can review your sequence using the transport controls in the program panel (D) or by dragging the playhead through the timeline (E).

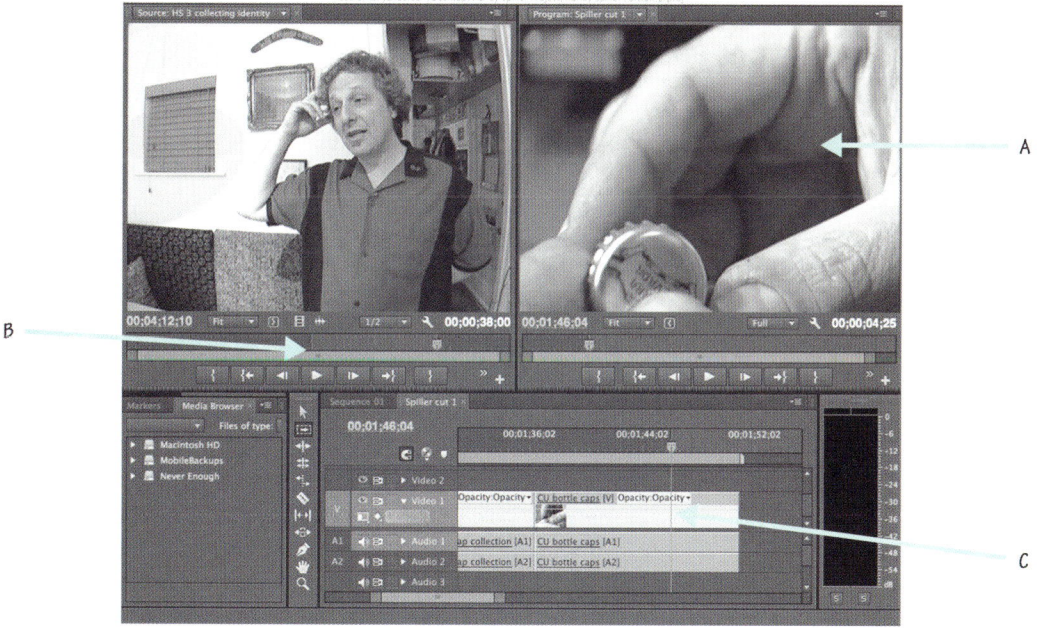

Figure 17.18 Make a 3-point edit by selecting an in-point in the program panel (A), and an in-point and an out-point in the source panel (B). This tells Premiere Pro to put the new image into the timeline where the playhead is (C), covering up the end of the existing shot.

because you are selecting a total of 3 in- and out-points—two in the source panel and one in the program panel. This type of edit gives you precise control over not only which section of your source footage you want to use, but where you want it to go in the sequence you are building.

You may have noticed that when you made the edit, an overlay appeared in the program panel that said "Drop to Overwrite; use Cmd to Insert." There are two basic types of edits in all NLE programs: **overwrite** and **insert**. Overwrite edits cover up whatever was in the timeline before the source material came in. All the edits we have made thus far in this exercise have been overwrite edits. Insert edits are different in that they open up a space in the timeline for the new clip, and push any existing material further down the timeline. You might want to try the previous edit using insert instead of overwrite, to experience the difference.

There are times when, instead of adding things to the timeline, you want to delete material. Let's look at our cut. You will realize that in the third clip, there is a long pause right after Harley says "it's what you know about the stuff that really counts" (00;01;59;15 in the timeline). Let's mark an in-point there on the program panel, and an out-point right before he says "I've been collecting Chinese menus since 1981 (00;02;02;18 in the timeline). Now under the "sequence" menu, go to "extract" (You can also use the apostrophe key: '). Premiere Pro will take the material you have selected out of your timeline and close the gap. This is called an **extract** edit. A **lift** edit is similar, except that instead of closing the gap, it leaves a space in the timeline where the deleted material used to be.

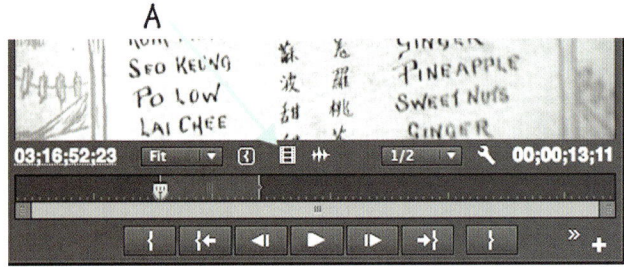

■ **Figure 17.19** Using the "video only" icon (A) to bring video into the timeline without its accompanying audio.

■ SUMMARY: EDITING BASICS

These sample edits cover most of what you will need to make a basic sequence and start editing. To review, they are:

- loading clips into the source window
- marking in- and out-points
- making insert edits
- making **overlay edits**
- making three-point edits
- lifting
- extracting
- making audio only and video only edits
- making split edits

There are many, many other tools, functions, and capabilities in your NLE. You will no doubt become familiar with them as you need to use them.

When you play the sequence now, you will notice two problems with **continuity** (Chapter 19). First, at 00;01;46;04 the shot jumps from a bottle cap in Harley's hand to Harley standing. There is a second, more obvious, **jump cut** at 00;01;59;14. One way to fix this is to find a shot or two that we can put over the image in this section, leaving the audio intact. If you are following along using the footage from the companion website, you can look through the clip called "kitchen cutaways" and find a shot that is at least 13 seconds and 11 frames long. In the source panel, I will mark a tilt down a Chinese menu with the in-point 03;16;52;23 and the out-point 03;17;06;05. Now be careful when you make the edit! You want to replace the video in the timeline, but not the audio. To do this, use the **video only icon** (Figure 17.19) to drag the picture directly into the timeline, and place it right where you want it. Now watch your sequence and give yourself a pat on the back for learning the basics of editing in Premiere Pro!

Split Edits

In the exercise above, we relied exclusively on **straight cuts**. These edits cut the picture and sound on the same frame, at the beginning (also called the **head**) and end (the **tail**) of each shot. In many instances, documentary editors combine sounds and images in more complex ways. Many of these fall into the category of **split edits**. In an **L-cut**, the picture cuts to the next shot first, and the audio cut occurs later. An example would be an interview that starts in sync, but as the person continues to talk we see images unrelated to their location. These cuts are useful when you are condensing dialogue, as you can use the incoming images to conceal cuts in the interview and avoid a visual **jump cut**. The **J-cut** is the opposite: the audio cuts out first, while the picture plays a bit longer before cutting to the next shot. The timing of these edits depends on a number of factors, some creative and some practical. A split edit can seem more "natural" than a hard cut, perhaps because it mimics the way we often perceive real events, hearing something first, and then turning our heads to look. It is a useful exercise to take a sample documentary scene and take it apart conceptually so that you can understand how split edits contribute to the whole. There is an example of a documentary scene that uses split edits on pp. 308–310.

EDITING STAGES

The documentary editing process is extremely flexible, but there are stages that all projects must go through.

Reviewing Raw Footage

Everything you shoot in production constitutes your **raw footage**. While you will likely review your material as you shoot it, your first task when you begin postproduction is to sit down and watch it all again. As you watch your footage, you are evaluating each and every scene *as though you are seeing it for the first time*. As you view your material, take detailed notes on which shots you think you might use. These are called **selects** (shots you won't use are called **outtakes**). You need to develop your own shorthand for note-taking. There are various tools available in your NLE, including color coding and markers, or as previously explained you can use columns in the project window to make notes. Often documentary cinematographers shoot long continuous takes. Although your material comes as clips, these may or may not need to be further broken down. Some editors like to break these down into **subclips**, excerpted sections of the original long take that act as independent clips. Some editors create "selects" sequences by shoot day or topic. These are good to look at for a quick reminder of what you thought was good material when you first reviewed it.

As you review and evaluate your footage, you should also be keeping notes with any ideas for structure, themes, or relationships relevant to your project, or even ideas about how shots or scenes may work together. These notes are rough and spontaneous, but they help you make connections and identify the storytelling potential of your footage. Even if you have transcripts of your interviews, you should be watching that footage with the same fresh set of eyes. Sometimes sound bites seem great on paper, but the way they are delivered is less compelling.

Another thing worth mentioning in an era when many people edit their own films is that, as an editor, you are wearing a different hat than you did as a director. You need to be detached, even ruthless. Ask yourself, "What is significant about what I have here?" and "What story can this material tell?" The film that can be made at this point is very often different from the one you had in your mind while shooting. Try and see this as an opportunity instead of as a disaster! Every editor, on every project, confronts this reality.

Paper Edit

Once you have a sense of what material you have and what story it might tell, you can start to conceptualize a structure. A **paper edit** is one tool that allows you to organize your documentary on paper before you start actually editing. It can save you much time and effort. Here is one way to approach creating a paper edit.

Consider the bare-bones structure of your story. What is a possible beginning, middle, and end? Consult the dramatic arc in Chapter 3, and think about possible themes and takeaways from your film for the audience. Then, look through your **observational material** and find the scenes or events could become potential building blocks. A **scene** is something that unfolds in one place at one time. If you shoot at a location for half a day, there may be a dozen incidents that could be the basis of a scene, but which one you choose depends on the story you are telling. Say you've been shooting in a middle school classroom. You might have a few moments that stand out as being interesting: a meltdown by a student, a learning moment with some shared reading where the teacher shines, or a personal interaction at the end of class with a student who is having trouble.

If your film is about the fairness of evaluating teachers by their students' test scores, the most significant scene might be the one where the teacher shines, because it shows that learning happens in ways that aren't reflected on tests. Or the meltdown might be useful, as it could show the challenges teachers face in the classroom.

Whichever scene you choose to develop, it's important to understand that a scene generally has some type of conflict, and ends when that conflict is resolved, even in a small way. So, with the hypothetical meltdown, the scene will end when the student calms down, or when the teacher decides he needs to be brought to a counselor's office. Also important to consider is how the scene might contribute to the progression of ideas and information in your film.

The reason we start with observational scenes, if we have them, is that interviews are almost always better used when married to a concrete unfolding situation than as stand-alone elements. In addition, the vast majority of student documentaries suffer from an overabundance of talking heads and a shortage of other types of material, so it makes sense to focus on finding your best observational material first.

We suggest putting each scene you have identified on an index card. Include the content, the characters involved, and what you expect the scene to deliver in terms of an "event" or point delivered. Arrange these cards into some kind of order with an eye to the dramatic arc of your film. You should be able to identify a beginning, a climax, and a conclusion. Now add interview bites, ideas for montage sequences, text cards, animation, or voice-over on additional cards and you have a paper edit!

Your paper edit can be taped on a wall, laid out on the floor, or put into a notebook. It is a roadmap for your editing.

Rough Cuts

Now that you have a solid idea of how you want to structure your documentary, you can start to build a rough cut, following the structure you developed on paper. Start with the opening of the film and work from there. As you build the film, your main characters and events will come to life. You will get a clear idea of which interviews work really well and which don't. It is guaranteed that some ideas that seemed great on paper will not work at all. There may be glaringly obvious ways to rearrange the material to improve your storyline and thematic threads. All this is good and part of the process. Paper edits are written on paper, not in stone. As you put the film together, take advantage of the evolving connections and chemistry that happen when you actually put your material together, and feel free to reorganize things along the way. You can expect this rough cut to be longer than your final film, but with practice it will give you a fairly clear idea of what that final length might be.

At this point, you should use the basic tools available in the edit system, like straight cuts instead of dissolves. Avoid complex split edits (p. 288). It is important not to over-polish the film at this stage. It may be irritating to view material that isn't perfectly finessed, but you want to feel free to be able to move material around, and complex transitions between shots will only get in the way. There is another danger to overcutting: sometimes the magic of a fine-tuned cut will make you think something is working on a structural level when, in fact, it is not.

If you are planning to use narration, here is where you begin writing it. It is a good idea to start actually inserting **scratch narration**, whether recorded straight into the edit system or from a separate recorder. You will record final narration as part of your sound mix, so don't worry about the quality or performance at this point. Graphic elements like titles and animated sequences should also be scratch at this early stage. You can insert title cards as placeholders to indicate any footage or scenes that remain to be filmed.

You will edit several rough cuts of your film, reorganizing things to improve the flow of the story with each version. Rough cuts are where you spend the majority of your time and do most of your creative thinking. There is a lot of cutting and recutting during this stage as you discover the final style, shape, and rhythm of your film.

When you are in rough cut stage, it is a good idea to transcribe your cut periodically. This makes it easier for you to talk through your structure with your editor or other people who give you feedback.

Rough Cut Screenings

It is hard to maintain a fresh eye when you spend months editing your documentary. For this reason, it is important to have **rough cut screenings** for sample audiences. These can be trusted friends, larger groups of people who are similar to your intended audience, or other filmmakers who you believe may have constructive criticism or helpful contributions to make. It can also be useful to screen rough cuts for experts on your subject matter, to make sure you aren't misrepresenting things or framing issues in a way you ultimately won't be comfortable with. If you expect your film to be used widely by a certain group of people like, for example, doctors, then pulling together a screening for a group of doctors is an excellent idea.

Rough cut screenings can be harrowing for directors and editors. Try to listen, take notes, and refrain from arguing with the audience. Remember, not everybody's comments will be useful or on target. More often than not, people suggest solutions that are incorrect, but are pointing to a real problem that you may solve by other means. Take some time to digest and evaluate all of the feedback you received from the screening before running back to the cutting room and pulling everything apart. You do not need to use all of the suggestions, but you should use whatever can make your film stronger. And remember to thank people for their important contribution to your work.

Building Your Soundtracks

In the rough cut stage, working with sound is just as important as working with picture. As you develop your cut, you should plan to keep your sequence audio split out into tracks that reflect the main sound sources you've recorded. As an example, you could create four tracks for interviews, four tracks for ambience and audio from observational scenes, two tracks for music, two tracks for narration, and so on. Any scene will have its original sound, often on more than one track. Keep as much production audio as you have in the timeline, even if that means muting it temporarily so you can hear other sounds. If you are working with a composer, they may give you sketches of music you can lay in to figure out what they should develop further. More commonly, you will place **temp music** pulled from any source (regardless of whether you have the right to use it), just to get a feel for the style and tone that will work for the scene. Later, the composer will create something that works in a similar fashion, or you can acquire other music that you have rights to use (Chapter 21).

For screening rough cuts, you will have to create a **scratch mix**. This means getting your audio levels into a comfortable range without spending too much time developing a full mix.

The Fine Cut and Picture Lock

Once you're happy with the structure of your film, and all of the sequences are working the way you want them to, and you've determined that there will be no more big changes to the film, you can start to fine-tune the rough cut. The **fine cut** involves finessing all of the edits one by one. This is the time to make those small adjustments to, for instance, get that cut on action just right, add the dissolve between two scenes, or trim a few frames off a shot to get the timing just perfect. The fine cut is also where you replace temporary graphics, archival footage, and stills with high-resolution versions that you have cleared the rights to. At this stage, make sure you have a complete and accurate list of **lower thirds** (IDs) and **end credits** (Chapter 22).

This stage is also where you add additional sound elements like sound effects, extra ambiences, final music, and final narration. Once the placement of all your elements is perfect, all of the editing decisions have been made, and you've decided you will not trim a single frame more, you have arrived at **picture lock**.

Finishing

Picture lock does not mean all of the creative work is over. The film still needs finishing, which means that you turn your attention to three areas: **sound design**, **graphics**, and **color correction**. Depending on your workflow, you may handle these within your NLE system, as in Figure 17.1. Alternatively, you may plan to export your sound and picture for mixing and color correction with outside professionals (Figure 17.2). Professional sound design is covered in Chapter 21, and color correction and graphics are covered in Chapter 22.

HIGH-END FINISHING WORKFLOWS

Shooting on high-resolution formats like 4K is still relatively rare in documentary, but this is a growing area of production. Godfrey Reggio's documentary *Visitors* (2013) consists of 74 shots of mostly human faces staring back at the audience (Figure 17.20). It was shot on 4K in order to show the faces in extremely high detail, and exhibited using a digital 4K projector.

Considering the workflow for a project like this is a useful way to consider how to deal with the massive file sizes that 4K generates. In these cases, filmmakers often edit with proxy files instead of the original media (p. 276). Once picture is locked, they go back and **conform** the film using the original 4K files. The output can be anything from a Digital Cinema Package to a hi-resolution file to a Blu-ray or DVD or stream for the web (Figure 17.21).

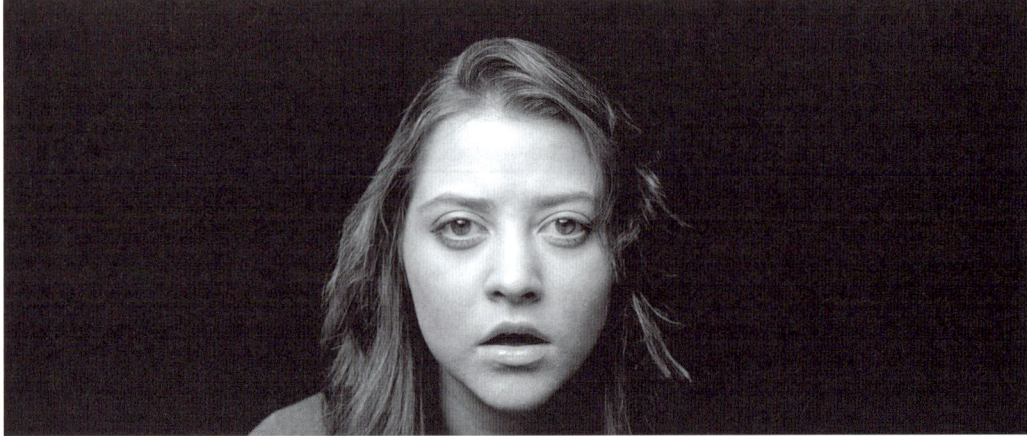

■ **Figure 17.20** Godfrey Reggio's 4K documentary *Visitors* consists of 74 shots of mostly human faces staring back at the audience.

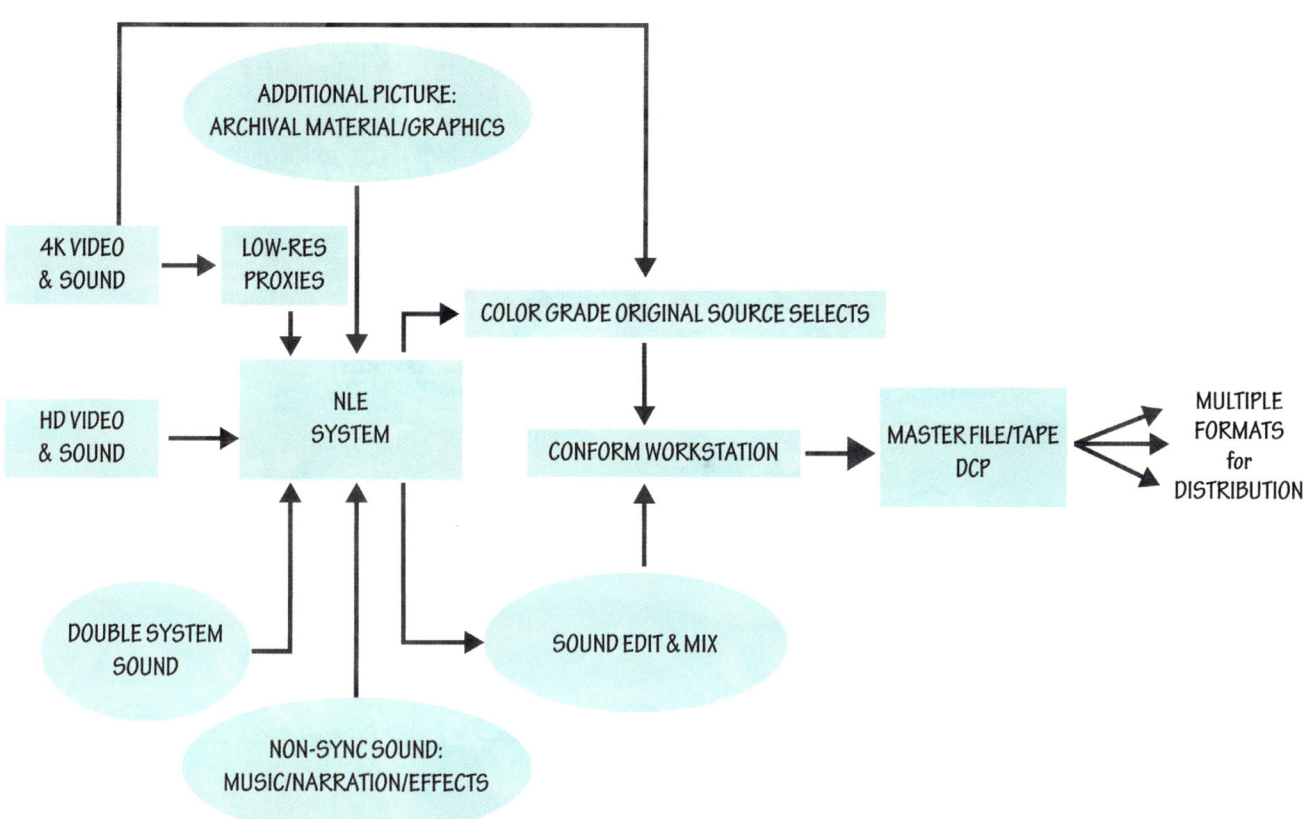

■ **Figure 17.21** Picture and audio paths for a 4K workflow. Shoot uncompressed 4K video and HD video; create low-res proxies for editing; conform back to Hi-Res source; Master DCP and various formats. Audio is surround sound.

Mastering

The final step in the editing process is to master the film. This means outputting the final film to a sturdy, archivally sound digital form from which distribution copies can be made. Although most NLE systems offer a wide range of output options, you will, no doubt, want to master to a format that does not involve any further video data compression. These days some people continue to master on digital HD tape, while others retain files on a hard drive that is backed up. And, of course, many do both for safety.

OVERVIEW OF EDITING STAGES

1. Develop clip naming conventions
2. Ingest audio and video, transcoding as necessary
3. Sync sound and picture (if necessary)
4. Log and transcribe media, create bin structures in NLE
5. Develop paper edit
6. Edit rough cuts (multiple)
7. Rough cut screenings
8. Edit fine cut
9. Cut in final, cleared archival material and music
10. Lock picture
11. Color correction (grading)
12. Sound edit and mix
13. Create master
14. Create submasters for distribution on various platforms

■ EDITING ELEMENTS (IN PROJECT WINDOW/PANEL)

- **Master clips**. A master clip references the media file. Clips are trimmed, altered, and manipulated during the edit session, but because they are only "pointers" to the media file, all edit decisions occur only virtually, leaving the media unaltered.
- **Subclips**. Smaller clips made from, and referencing, the master clip. Subclips do not reference the media file; if you delete the master clip you will lose the subclip information and it will not play.
- **Audio clips**. A clip with no picture will have a different icon, but otherwise acts the same as other clips.
- **Graphics**. Graphics files with multiple layers (like Photoshop) will import with the layers separated. Alpha channels (which define transparency) will import as well.
- **Sequences**. The edited sequence of video, audio, and graphic clips arranged in the order you need to tell your story. Clips used in the sequence are essentially a playlist of the information from the master clips, and therefore they directly reference the underlying media files.

■ ORGANIZATIONAL ELEMENTS

- **Project**. A top-level folder (located in the project window/panel) that includes all of the elements of the movie, including sequences, bins, clips, graphics, and stored effects.
- **Bins**. Second-level folders that are used to organize audio and video clips and graphic files. You can create as many bins as you need.
- **Scratch Folder (PP) or Capture Drive (Avid)**. This is the folder on the external hard drive where all of your media files and all of your render files will be stored. This is referenced by the editing software, but accessed through the computer's operating system.
- **Backup File Folder**. These are copies of the project file created automatically by the software.

■ BACKING UP YOUR PROJECT AND SEQUENCES

It is important to **back up** your project at the end of each day of editing. If you are editing with your project file on your local computer, simply drag a copy of the project file (extension .prproj, or .avp) onto a separate drive. While dragging, the project file will make a copy onto the destination drive. *You do not need to make a new project file every time you edit*—this may confuse things as you will be likely to open up the wrong project at some point. Periodically you should archive a copy of your project file, with the date included in the file name, in case your project becomes corrupted. It is important to remember that copying your project file doesn't back up your media, only the work you've done with it.

As you build your edited program, you will likely want to save copies of sequences before rearranging or deleting material. Many editors make a practice of creating a new sequence every day they edit. A good practice is to give your sequence a name that includes the date. When you want to save a version, simply highlight the sequence icon in the project window and duplicate it. You can then rename the new sequence with the current date, and start editing on that one. The old sequence will be preserved, and named with the date it was created. You should keep all these sequences together in a bin titled "Sequences."

As you edit, you should save your project frequently. Your NLE system will also create automatic backups and store them in a folder. You should make sure this is on a separate drive from your main project file to protect yourself in the event of a crash. If you do have a system crash, you can find the most recent backup on the other drive and most of your work can be rescued.

Writing and Structuring the Documentary

CHAPTER 18

> *There are millions of different ways to make material work. You can make the material serve what you see as the truth of the situation. It's really in your hands. You have to decide what you think happens in this footage; then you have to take, say, an hour and a half of film of a particular event and make it into a three-minute scene that communicates what you think happened in that hour-and-a-half event. It's the only way you can proceed. You're trying to distill. That's essentially what you're doing in this whole process, distilling the truth, as you perceive it.*
>
> **Tom Haneke, Documentary Editor**[1]

> *Documentary films are written four times. The first time you write it is when you conceive your [interview] questions because those questions have to lead to a narrative. You have to know that the answers of your subject are going to start piecing together the film. The second part is when you get the transcripts back. I highlight them and start to puzzle all the different bites together. Where there is a break and it needs to be redirected, you write the voice-over. That is the third part of the process. The fourth time you write is when you are in the edit bay and you look at the footage. You do it all over again. It is really about taking your subjects' voices and giving them narrative.*
>
> **Stacy Peralta, WGAW Nonfiction Writers Caucus**[2]

What is "writing" to documentary filmmakers? We think of documentary makers filming actuality and piecing it together. But as the quotes above suggest, writing is part of the documentary process from beginning to end. If you've read previous chapters of this book, especially Chapter 3 (Structuring the Documentary) and Chapter 4 (The Documentary Proposal), you'll have a clear idea of how writing plays a key role from the very beginning of any documentary project. Writing allows you to work and rework the broader structure of your documentary. On paper, you can easily piece together the flow of ideas, experiment with the order of scenes, and decide what specific contribution each of the film's components will make to your narrative strategy. Also, as the second quote above suggests, writing plays a specific role in planning your interviews, as well as editing them. And on top of all of this is the writing you do that will actually be in the film—whether in the form of narration, titles, or graphics.

As Tom Haneke suggests, there are many stories hidden in every batch of footage. Now that you are in postproduction, you have to figure out how to assemble your material into scenes that will carry your narrative arc, however you define it. In this chapter, we will explore the "big picture" aspects of structuring and writing your documentary in postproduction. A more detailed look at building sequences, and how meaning is produced when shots are placed next to one another, follows in Chapter 19.

WHERE TO BEGIN?

It is our sincere hope that you have been thinking about questions of style (Chapter 2) and structure (Chapter 3) throughout your production process. It is likely that your initial ideas and assumptions have been revised, along with your **hypothesis** (Chapter 1), many times as you have been shooting. At this point, you should have at least a provisional sense of what elements you will incorporate, including whether you will be building observational scenes, using narration, creating animation or graphics, and so on. You may also already have a sense of the overall story arc and how different characters and events will fit into the trajectory of your film. But as you'll see below, postproduction is an opportunity to rethink that structure. Here are some guidelines based on our experiences editing our own work and helping students structure their films.

STORY ELEMENTS: CHARACTER, EXPOSITION, AND PLOT

As we discussed in Chapter 3, the momentum of any film is generated through conflict. People have goals. Obstacles stand in the way. Their effort to overcome these obstacles and achieve their goals moves the story forward. Layered with the characters' stories is the presentation of issues and the audience's unfolding understanding of the situation, whether it is a global financial crisis, a lack of affordable housing, or an artistic career that has stalled.

You, as the filmmaker, know everything (in fact, much more than will ever be in your film). But structure is *how* you will tell the story: the flow of ideas, the revealing of details one at a time to make a compelling narrative. Structure is also about creating mystery, suspense, or a "need to know" before you give the viewer pieces of information. It's a bit like playing a hand of cards. You have an ace. Your best approach to the game is rarely to lay it out during the first round. Similarly, as a filmmaker, you should consider what the most compelling points you have to make are, and plan to bring those in judiciously, at strategic moments over the course of the film.

When you get to the edit room, you have already done your best to film compelling characters, events, and interviews that you hope will deliver a strong story. Now it is time to think about how you will weave those elements together, and craft your dramatic arc in the most specific way you can. Classic screenwriting texts talk about the three elements of story: **character**, **exposition**, and **plot**. While this idea comes from dramatic writing, and many documentaries seem more about information than drama, the idea is useful. However you conceptualize the people and events you're focusing on, you will always need a balance between these story elements. Ideally, any sequence in your film will contain all three. **Character** refers to the personality, aspirations, and internal conflicts of the people in your film. In some cases, this will include the filmmaker. **Exposition** is information the viewer needs in order to follow the story. This background information is often essential, but you always run the risk of stopping the flow of the film when you introduce it. A key aspect of good storytelling is figuring out how to fit in exposition without impeding the forward momentum of your story. And **plot**, the actual "what happens," is at the heart of dramatic storytelling. In a documentary, of course, the events are not ones that you dream up while sitting at your laptop. They come from the real world, as do the subjects you are filming. While certain other elements, like reenactments, can be created, by and large these real people and their real actions define what you have to work with.

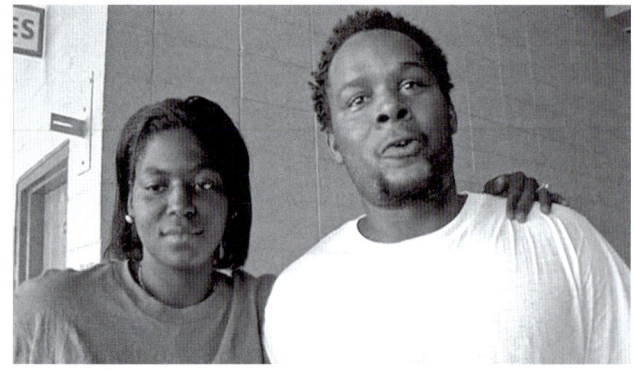

■ **Figure 18.1** Kim and Scott, the main characters of *Trouble the Water*, as we first meet them at the New Orleans Superdome two weeks after Hurricane Katrina.

Trouble the Water (2008) is an Academy Award®-nominated documentary by Tia Lessin and Carl Deal. It follows two residents of New Orleans' Ninth Ward, Kim and Scott Roberts, as they deal with the aftermath of Superstorm Katrina and the institutional racism and indifference that threaten to destroy their lives and those of their families and neighbors. The film has all the basics of a good story: characters who want something, barriers that get in the way, conflict, and high stakes. What is valuable to see in this film is how elegantly its combines its plot, its characters, and its exposition.

The film starts with the crew meeting Kim and Scott at the New Orleans Superdome, a sports arena turned refugee shelter, shortly after Hurricane Katrina has destroyed New Orleans (Figure 18.1). It then flashes back two weeks to home footage taken by Kim as she documented the arrival of the storm with a new video camera.

One of the reasons *Trouble the Water* is such a gripping film is because of the way it deals with character. The main subjects—Kim, Scott, and Kim's brother Larry—are presented as people with rich and complex inner lives, as well as people who are facing severe external conflicts. They come to terms with themselves as they deal with Katrina. We see them rescuing people from the water and giving them shelter. We see them concerned about pets. We see them "borrow" a truck and evacuate a large group of elderly people and children to an area in the north part of the state where they can get help. We find out that their struggles in life began long before Katrina. Kim's mom was a crack addict who died of AIDS when Kim was 13. Both Kim and Scott dealt drugs. Part of their struggle is with their own past history, and it is a struggle they embrace. The filmmakers feed us this information slowly, allowing us to judge these people by what they do before we learn about their personal histories. For example, we only learn about Kim and Scott's history of drug dealing toward the end of the film, when they see the possibility of a better life for themselves. This makes a powerful point in terms of the larger story, which seeks to portray the Katrina disaster as linked to a legacy of racism and poverty.

Although the film is strongly character-based, it depends heavily on contextualizing Kim and Scott's story within the larger catastrophe of Katrina. In the opening of *Trouble the Water*, we hear Kim as she shoots a home video and talks to her neighbors about whether they will stay for the storm or evacuate. This material is intercut with exposition in the form of television news material (Figure 18.2). We see a TV weather radar image of the storm swirling across the Gulf, and a shot of the jammed highways leading out of the city. There is a press conference with New Orleans mayor Ray Nagin, where he urges citizens to evacuate. Then the filmmakers place a title over Nagin that says, "No public transportation is organized to evacuate the city." The title is a rare example of the filmmakers using their own words to provide background information, and it gives us a clear sense of the film's critical point of view. Then we return to Kim as she bicycles around the neighborhood. More news material

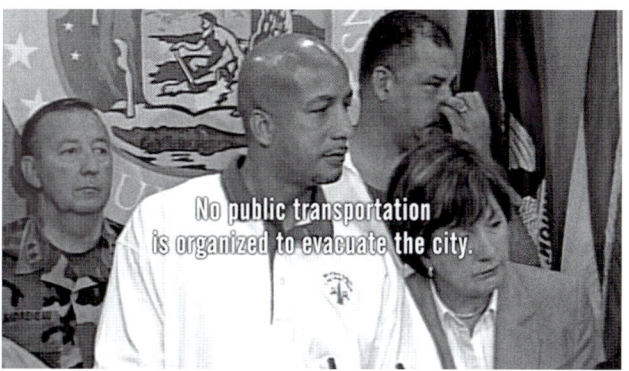

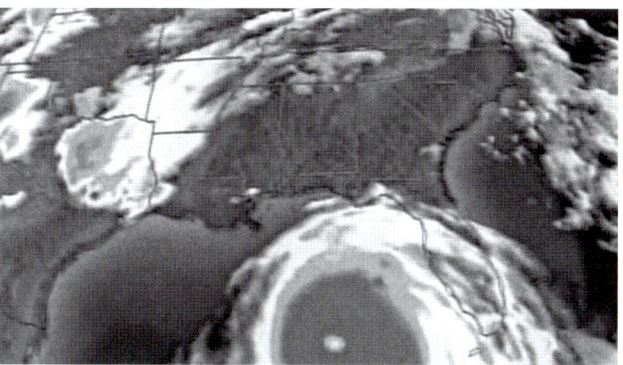

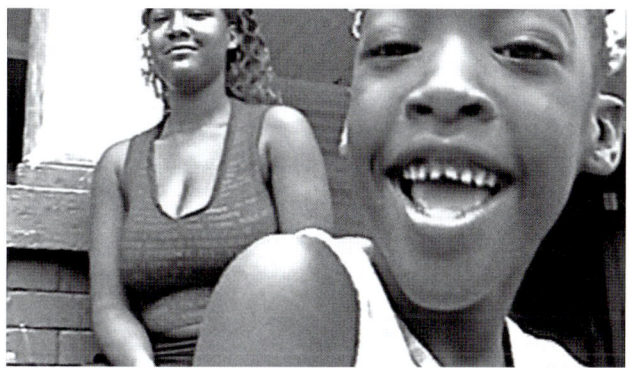

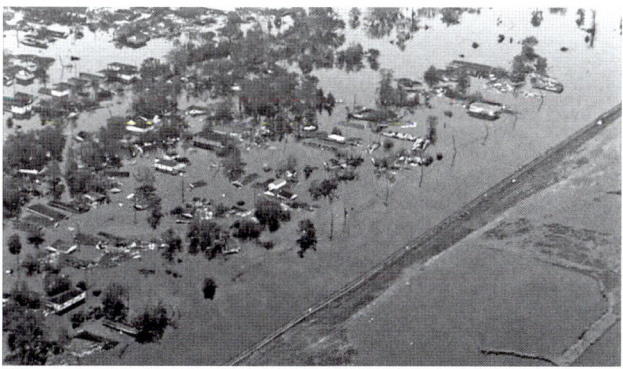

■ **Figure 18.2** In the opening sequences of *Trouble the Water*, images of the mayor of New Orleans, radar image of Hurricane Katrina, and an aerial shot of the flooded city from news give exposition and contextualize the personal home video chronicle of the main subject, Kim.

indicates that there are some 100,000 residents who can't get out of the city. Then we go back to Kim's erratic camerawork and lively commentary. The contrast between her wildly swinging camera and the staid news material with its professional commentary both adds to a feeling of urgency and gives a sense that authorities are out of touch with the potential scope of the coming disaster.

This adroit mix of television news footage, Kim's video, and the filmmakers' own documentary material continues throughout the film. The combination makes it clear that this is not just a story of two people coping with a natural disaster; it is also a tale of how the natural disaster plays out in the society at large.

One good example of the relationship between plot, exposition, and character involves Kim's grandmother. At the time of the storm, this elderly woman was in Memorial Medical Center, where the staff left the patients in their beds to die. The hospital story was major news nationally at the time of the storm, but it only enters the documentary's storyline when Kim and Scott learn of the grandmother's death from an uncle in another part of the state. Rather than front-loading the film with this information, the filmmakers let us find out about it as Kim and Scott do, making the film's condemnation of this official negligence all the more powerful. This scene fills all three narrative functions—plot, character, and exposition—at the same time. On the level of plot, the film only reveals the grandmother's story as Kim explains to a prison official that she needs to get her brother out of jail for the funeral. At this point, we find out not only about the grandmother's death, but that Kim's brother and other inmates were also trapped, in their cells without food, for days. This is brilliant plotting. On the level of character, Kim's emerging strengths are visible in her concern for her brother, and her efforts to maintain family solidarity by getting him bailed out for the funeral. Finally, the scene gives major support to the overall theme: the official abdication of any responsibility for the welfare of the least powerful citizens during and after Katrina (Figure 18.3).

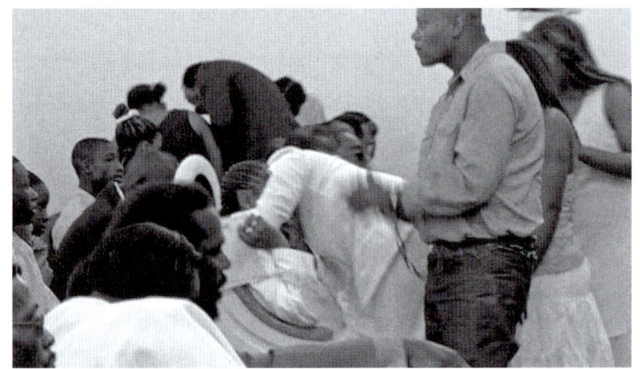

■ **Figure 18.3** In this scene from *Trouble the Water*, Kim's incarcerated brother is allowed to attend the funeral of their grandmother who died of neglect in a hospital abandoned by its staff, but only in chains.

Character and plot can function in many ways. Some films follow one character, while others follow multiple threads. Sometimes it's best to tell each character's story from beginning to end before embarking on another character's journey. At other times, you will want to interweave the stories, cutting back and forth to reveal similarities and differences, allowing the stories to resonate with one another and contribute to a larger narrative. The important thing to recognize is that characters becomes plot as they deal with obstacles and try to achieve goals. How will she handle this moment? Will he even survive? Will the group break up in the face of crushing difficulties? Once we are invested in the characters' lives, the answers to these questions become important and draw us into the world of the film.

▌ STRUCTURAL ELEMENTS: OBSERVATIONAL SCENES, INTERVIEWS, AND VISUAL EVIDENCE

Once you've defined the big picture of your basic story, you'll need to evaluate how to tell the story in the most cogent and poignant manner. This gives urgency to the need to evaluate your elements based on what you've learned about your material during the **paper edit** process (Chapter 17). As you build your film, you will find that some main points can be made using **observational** scenes, while others will be expressed through the **interviews** and the **visual evidence** you've collected. When you can, show rather than tell. Allow audiences to come to their own understanding by watching and evaluating the footage, rather than telling them the story and what it means. Other key information can be brought out through narration or text on screen. Remember, no one of these elements acts independently. Figuring out how they will interplay is key to structuring your work. Let's look briefly at how different types of material play into structuring and writing your film.

Observational Scenes

Something is happening: a contentious town hall meeting, a firefight in the mountains of Afghanistan, a cargo plane taking off with a load of African carp, a couple fighting over the bills. Observational scenes like these are powerful because they put the viewer in the center of the action, as close to direct experience as you can get in a film. Observational scenes are the heart of many documentaries, and their presentation of events as they unfold allows the viewer to look at an aspect of the world and draw their own conclusions. These scenes can be handled in myriad ways, but *how* they reveal meaning is in your hands. Once you have a clear grasp of your story arc, you can start to make decisions about what the point being made by each scene will be, and start to cut to highlight that event and elucidate its meaning. Remember every scene will contain its own mini-drama that contributes to the whole. That doesn't mean it is super-dramatic or intense, though it could certainly be. It does mean that it has new information that moves your story forward while offering a new perspective on a topic, and a chance for viewers to see your subjects in action. Just because something happened and you recorded it, is not a reason to put it into your film. Ask yourself, "What exactly is this scene about?" You should be able to answer that both in terms of what is happening literally, as well as be able to articulate its role in the larger argument or arc of your documentary. A scene that does not contribute to the overall meaning of the story, as charming as it may seem to you, or as difficult as it was to shoot, simply doesn't belong in your film.

Lixin Fan spent several years filming with Zhang Changhua and Chen Suqin, the Sichuan couple whose life as migrants working in the sweatshops of Guangzhou is at the heart of the story of *Last Train Home* (2009). Their struggle to survive symbolizes that of millions of other Chinese peasants whose sacrifices keep the Chinese economy afloat. A key event, as the title of the film suggests, is the annual railroad journey from the coastal factories back to the rural provinces that are home to some 130 million migrant workers. It is the largest human migration on the planet. The moment is key, because it is here that the lives of the couple who are the film's main subjects are linked visibly to the destinies of the other millions of workers that share their experience. Fan shot this event twice. The first time the couple tries to take "the last train" starts with a short scene about 8 minutes into the film. There are no tickets available (Figure 18.4) Then we see Changhua and Suqin eating a meal and discussing how tough it may be to get tickets. The feeling is subdued. We cut to a scene of the children and grandparents in the country waiting for

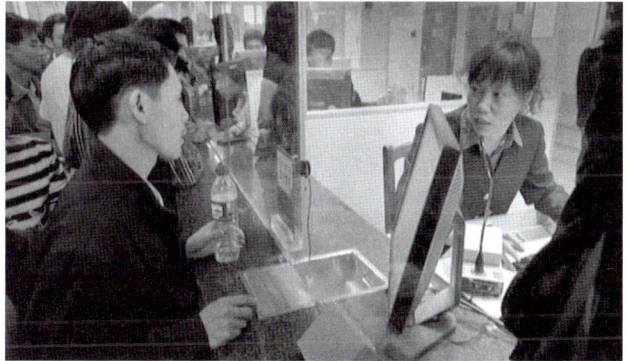
■ **Figure 18.4** Zhang Changhua learns that there are no tickets available for a Chinese New Year's trip to his home village in an early scene from *Last Train Home*.

them to arrive. Then, with only a few days left in the holiday period, we see Changhua checking at the cancellation office, and finally getting two returned tickets. Only at this point do things heat up, as the couple make a mad dash to get themselves and their luggage packed with presents onto the train.

The next year, the couple's recalcitrant daughter Qin has now joined her parents working on the coast. Once again the New Year arrives with the need to travel home. We think we know what to expect, but the station, which the year before was relatively quiet, is now surrounded by vast crowds. More and more people pile in, but no one leaves. There are police, then soldiers. People are crushed by the crowd. It becomes clear that there are hundreds of thousands of people at one train station, and not a single train is leaving.

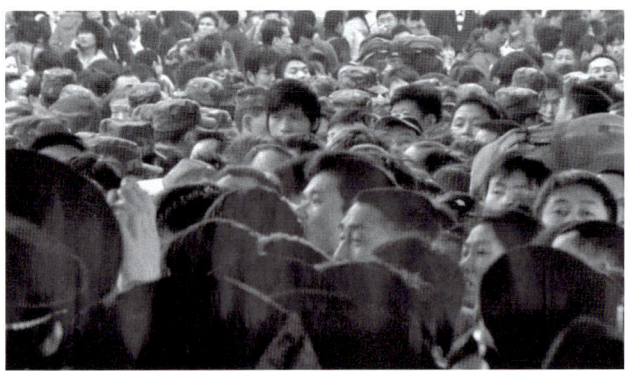

■ **Figure 18.5** One of the climactic moments of *Last Train Home*, when the main characters find themselves stranded in a stampeding crowd of over half a million people waiting for trains at Guangzhou Station.

Over half a million people are stranded, and the family we are following, and the film crew, are stuck in the middle of this hell. Even though there is no real dialogue the camera offers us a window onto the world of the characters, and allows us to experience with them the vast scale of the human disaster as it unfolds (Figure 18.5). These two scenes, of the same event as it plays out very differently in two different years, reinforce one another and create the drama of the film. This is observational filmmaking at a high level.

While the value of some observational scenes may be obvious at the time of shooting, many scenes carry story in a way that may only become clear in postproduction. When you review your footage, stay attuned to small situations or moments that reveal underlying psychological drama. Sometimes something as small as a look or a comment muttered under someone's breath can end up speaking volumes and provide the key event of a scene.

Interviews

The interview, as discussed in Chapter 15, is a unique formal element of the documentary. It is with interviews that you can offer viewers much of the informational strength of your story very efficiently. Interviews frame information with the authenticity of the eyewitness or the authority of expertise, and invite the viewer's interest, their sympathy (or lack of it), and their judgment. While it would be wrong to put words in your interviewees' mouths, you will be able to pick and choose from the material you've recorded, streamlining accounts and highlighting emotional reactions or key points. Sometimes a film can be built almost entirely of interview material. Erroll Morris's *Fog of War* (2003), for example, is essentially an extended interview with former Secretary of Defense Donald McNamara, and contains only a sprinkling of archival footage to offer context. Charles Ferguson's *Inside Job* (2010) unpacks the 2008 financial crash through a series of interviews with financiers and deal makers. More often, though, interview material is intercut with observational material to reinforce a point your film is trying to make in an elegant and credible way. Remember, your interview subjects become characters in your film. Each one should offer a new and useful point of view. You are unlikely to need two experts on constitutional law to offer viewers background, unless they sharply disagree! And because they are characters, it is almost always helpful to give viewers a sense of your interview subject with some material of them doing something besides just talking to your camera. Even if you're meeting someone in their office, a bit of footage of them interacting with others in their workspace can prove invaluable. By the same token, if you have a person appear once in your film, it is probably a good idea to have them reappear. A strong interview subject, once introduced, becomes a familiar character to viewers over time.

Visual Evidence

We've discussed the way that visual evidence works in other parts of this book, but remember that it is something to be thinking of all of the time as you build your story. An accumulation of detail enriches your film and helps build the case you are making.

In *Trouble the Water*, as the storm builds, we see the deserted Ninth Ward and get poignant visual details: children trying to play, and the first shingles getting ripped off a roof (Figure 18.6). As the rains come, we see the trees swirl and hear Kim pray. Then the camera goes to black. The next shot is accompanied only by the sound of moving water. It is an aerial shot of the broken levee, and it pulls out to reveal a city underwater, then it fades again to black, ending what is essentially the first act of the film. This series of images, which start out very small and local and end up with an aerial overview of the massive levee breach, make the point that the failure to evacuate has created a human disaster of

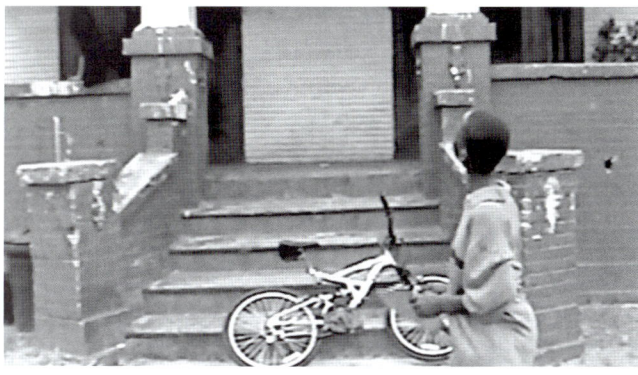 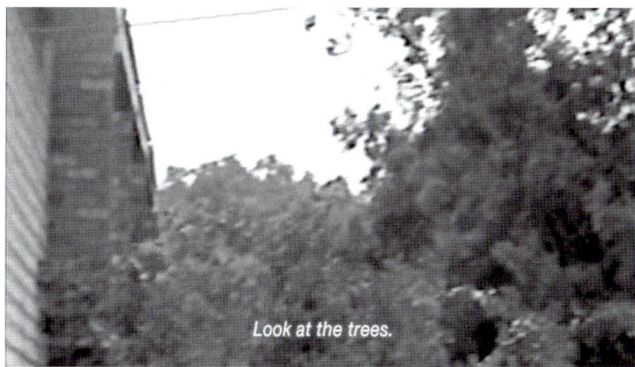

■ **Figure 18.6** A boy holds a shingle that has just blown off the roof of his house. Trees start to swirl in the strong wind. These small details add up to powerful visual evidence for the arrival of Hurricane Katrina in this scene from *Trouble the Water*.

unprecedented magnitude. Because visual evidence is just that—evidence—it works best when presented at the right moment, one in which the viewer is looking for real-world confirmation of a claim.

CHRONOLOGY: HOW TO HANDLE TIME

One big decision in structuring a documentary is the question of time. Will you present the events in the order they unfolded in reality, or will you shuffle them around? And if you do rearrange the timeline, will your audience understand what you are doing and what is happening? A classic example of a straight chronological structure would be Robert Drew's *Primary* (1960), which follows the campaigns of senators Hubert Humphrey and John F. Kennedy as they vie for the Democratic nomination in the 1960 Presidential election. The two men are doing equally well in the polls, and the primary election is in a few weeks. This film takes a straight chronological approach, unfolding as the events do, without cutting back or forward in time. It ends with a Kennedy victory. This adherence to linear time works well for a story about an election with a tight timeframe and a clear winner, but it may not be the most compelling approach for every film. *Trouble the Water*, for example, starts two weeks after the Katrina catastrophe and develops its story through flashbacks to the days before and during the storm. This allows the filmmakers to show us the same characters and locations at two different points in time, which adds drama to the story. It also allows us to view the events of the storm with more information than we would have had at the time.

While you may have ideas about flashbacks or starting at the end and working your way back through time, you are typically better off starting your editing process by assembling the story in a linear way. Once you have a sense of your sequences, you can start to contemplate more complex approaches to the chronology.

Sometimes the idea of linear chronology is used, even if the events are not presented in the order they were shot. In Fred Wiseman's film *High School* (1968), the documentary is structured around a school day. The film starts with a PA address from the principal, and a boy gets sent to the dean. A teacher walking the hall to monitor students looks into the gym and we move into an exercise sequence. Although the film was actually shot over the course of months, this "day in the life" formula highlights the sense of boredom, isolation, and arbitrariness that characterize a schedule-driven public institution.

Some films, of course, explore topics in a way that doesn't depend on chronology at all. As discussed in Chapter 3, documentaries that are more rhetorical are structured more like a trial, with evidence and opinion presented as they are needed to develop and maintain the flow of ideas. An example would be Eugene Jarecki's *The House I Live In* (2012), which looks at America's 40-year War on Drugs through a series of interviews. Various interviewees detail the failures of US drug and criminal justice policy. The presentation of ideas has little to do with when things were filmed, or even when they occurred.

Alternatively, your main timeline may be built around your investigatory efforts as the filmmaker Michael Moore's work is typical in this regard. *Roger and Me* (1989) follows Moore's journey to understand the closure of General Motors' auto plant in Flint, Michigan, Moore's hometown. Moore's film raises another interesting point about chronology. While you are free to rearrange events for dramatic effect, it's important that you not mislead your audience or oversimplify things. In his efforts to indict General Motors for Flint's troubles, Moore added events into his film and through their placement made it seem like they happened after the plant closed when in fact they occurred before. There was a big debate at the time about whether his actions were justified. Just be forewarned that you need to be careful about implying causation through your handling of time.

Very often, documentary filmmakers will have more than one timeline or chronological trajectory in a film. In Marco Williams' 2006 documentary, *Banished: How Whites Drove Blacks Out of Town in America* (2006), about four US communities that violently forced African-American families to flee their homes in late nineteenth and early twentieth century America, there are two main timelines that interweave. One is Marco's own efforts, with the help of a local journalist, to uncover these long-hidden stories. The other is the devastating history of dispossession and racial violence that occurred from the 1880s through the 1920s.

WRITING NARRATION

Narration can be an extremely useful tool in the kit of a documentary filmmaker. The kind of Voice of God narration, associated with the monolithic thinking of educational and propaganda films of another era, gave narration a bad name. In addition, filmmakers often want audiences to discover things for themselves, rather than be told what they are seeing. But narration can take many forms and, when skillfully used, it can add an important dimension to a documentary project. For some types of films, it is essential. Narration can quickly provide information and context that interviews and observational material may not offer on their own. It can also be more efficient than using complex editing maneuvers to make your interviewees say everything that needs to be said. Finally, narration can also set the tone of a film. Will it be humorous, hard-hitting, ironic, or contemplative?

When writing narration, do many rewrites to make sure it is clean, does not repeat itself, and avoids clichés. Editorializing, or emotional manipulation, should generally be avoided. If you are using narration, put it into your cut early in the editing process so you can to see how it works against the picture and other sound elements.

Third-Person Narration

A third-person statement of facts is by far the most common form of documentary narration. When you write in the third person, you take on an omniscient position. The third-person narrator speaks from outside the actions and events of the film, stating what are meant to be taken as facts. Use this power wisely. Don't claim as fact something that is subjective. If you editorialize or promote an opinion, you may lose the trust of your audience. The advantage of putting narration in a documentary is that anything that you can bring to writing can be brought into our film. Your own sensitivity to nuance, your grasp of poetic imagery, and the depth of your research can all be used to enrich your film.

First-Person Narration

With first-person narration, the filmmaker speaks directly to the viewer from the "I" subject position. This very direct mode of address establishes the stakes that the filmmaker has in the unfolding story. It can also reveal the purpose behind the film's creation, and even some of the process of making it. In this type of narration, the filmmaker becomes a character in his own film, though not necessarily an on-screen one. Eugene Jarecki's *The House I Live In* (2012) situates the story in the personal experience of the filmmaker, who starts the film with the voice-over "My family came to America fleeing the Holocaust in Europe." We see family photos, and hear Jarecki speaking in the first person. The narration doesn't make this a film about Jarecki, but rather serves as a perspective funnel to bring the viewer into the film through the eyes of a filmmaker who is personally impacted and concerned about the situation documented in the film (Figure 18.7).

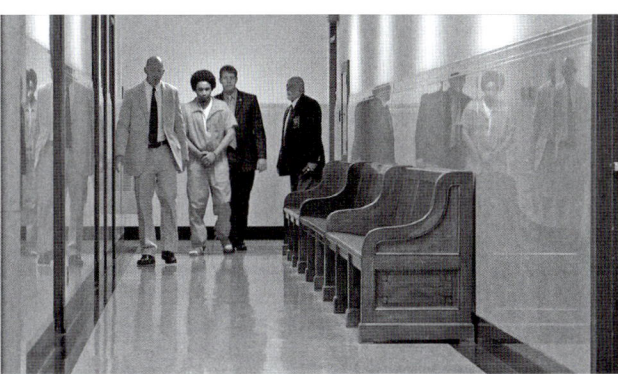

■ **Figure 18.7** In *The House I Live In*, director Eugene Jarecki takes a critical look at America's 40-year War on Drugs. While most of the film documents the criminal justice system at work, he starts the film with a personal narration that situates himself as someone growing up in a white family who sees black acquaintances pulled into an ongoing nightmare. Courtesy of Samuel Cullman.

Writing Narration

One approach we recommend is to write and record **scratch narration** as you build your cut. One reason we suggest developing scratch narration as you go along is that it allows you to approach the writing of a documentary scene in an organic way. The rhythm of the words, and of the pauses, can evolve with the other elements of the scene. One important thing to think of here is, what kind of information can be carried on the soundtrack, and what is better left to interviews or the visuals?

The key is to write and rewrite, trying to pare down what you are saying to a minimum. Screen time and your audience's attention are very precious, and you don't want to use three words where two will do. It's up to you to develop a style, whether formal or informal, poetic, or matter-of-fact, that suits the project you're making.

Useful as narration may be, it can't solve all your problems. Non-fiction books are well suited to giving readers a complex understanding of a situation with a solid basis in fact and theory. Movies are great communicators, but the information must be embedded in a real-life context. Narration may be providing useful information, but it also a step away from the reality on screen, and can be less engaging than observational material or even than an interview. Use it wisely.

■ **WRITING NARRATION: TIPS**

- Don't repeat in narration what is expressed by the images, interviews, or observational scenes.
- Rewrite and trim as much as possible.
- Work with scratch narration so you can see how it works with picture and other sounds.
- Maintain a consistent voice and POV.
- Keep the language elegant and direct.
- Avoid the passive voice!
- Avoid overly complex sentences. Express one idea at a time!

Styles of Narration

Many films have a very straightforward journalistic approach to narration. But you should keep in mind that since the first sound films, documentary has offered a wide variety of approaches to narration. One of the early documentaries of John Grierson's team at the British General Post Office (GPO), *Night Mail* (1936), is a tour de force (Figure 18.9). A simple factual narration that details the movement of the mail train on its route is interlaced with a poem W.H. Auden wrote specifically for the movie:

> Thousands still sleep and dream and have nightmares.
> They are asleep in Glasgow, asleep in Edinburgh.
> They dream on, but they hope that when they awake they will have letters.
> Their hearts will pound when they hear the knock on the door of the postman,
> for "who can bear to feel himself forgotten?"

NARRATION AS COUNTERPOINT

While making *In Whose Honor?* (1997), about the use of Indian mascots at the University of Illinois, director Jay Rosenstein shot a typical Saturday crowd of sports fans fooling around and having a good time before a football game. The narration offers us a fresh and specific perspective on events, so that images that might otherwise go by unnoticed, like a logo on a sweatshirt or a handshake between two local businessmen, start to take on a new significance.

In Whose Honor? uses narration to establish a tone, a position, and a point of view on the issue of Native American mascots in sports. The main voice in the film is that of Charlene Teters, a Spokane Indian whose campaign is against Chief Illiniwek, the University of Illinois' beloved mascot. Because of her experience and her identity, Teters has an authenticity that provides a moral backbone to the film.

The other main voice is that of a third-person narrator. That person offers us a sympathetic yet objective perspective that is closely tied to the visual evidence presented. Take, for example, this sequence near the film's beginning.

Let's look closely at some of the opening narration of the film. The first voice we hear in the film is that of Teters, who explains how difficult it is for her to see her people and their sacred traditions used for halftime foolery. Then we go to narration and accompanying visuals:

(Shots of a football parking lot crowd).

Narrator: It's a Fall Saturday afternoon at the University of Illinois.
Guy roasting wieners: Great Day for Football!
Narrator: Fans come from all around to support the home team, the Fighting Illini.
Fan with beer in each hand: Go Illini!
Narrator: It's a mix of business and pleasure . . .
Three guys in white shirts: Hi, Chuck, Ron. How are you?

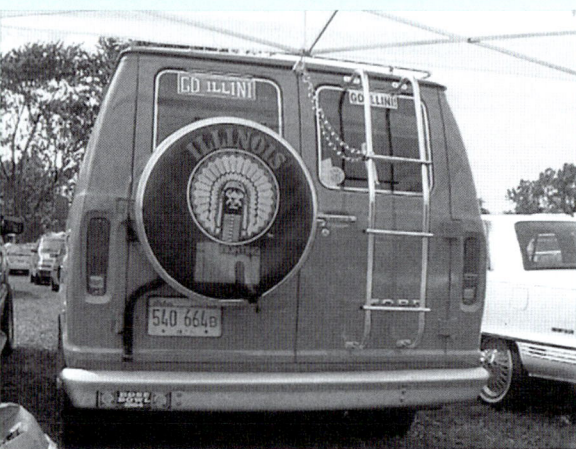

■ **Figure 18.8** In *In Whose Honor?* visuals work in conjunction with narration to create an effective illustration of the sports culture at the University of Illinois.

Narrator: Politics and local celebrities. And everywhere is the symbol of the University of Illinois, a fictitious American Indian character named Chief Illiniwek.

Shots of mascot on cars, tee shirts, stores, a guy in an American Indian outfit dancing around with cheerleaders (Figure 18.8).

Narrator: Chief Illiniwek has been part of the University of Illinois for seventy years. Dancing at halftime in home football and basketball games, the Chief has become a crowd favorite.

The narration explains how deeply embedded in local culture and tradition Chief Illiniwek is. And it does in conjunction with a skillfully edited montage sequence, in 50 seconds. While not completely neutral, the narration does not condemn or editorialize. It establishes the narrator as a trustworthy guide, capable of taking us as viewers on a journey to explore whether Teters' point is valid or not. And this narration helps give the film's dramatic engine a strong start.

Auden's incantation invites viewers to a much more personal and subjective stance in relation to the idea of getting or sending a letter. It is imbuing the images of post office workers sorting and bagging the mail with our deepest hopes and fears. The poetry is read to a building tempo that works closely with the music of Benjamin Britten and the pace of the editing to create an effect that still has emotional punch some 80 years later.

Writing the Essay Film

One final form worth mentioning is the **essay documentary**. The essay film is typically organized around a poetic or personal voice-over. This form is freed from the constraints of chronology and the documentation of events in real time, and largely free from the need to educate the viewer using facts. The essay film takes up the project of "making visible theoretical ideas," as film theorist Nora Alter writes.

> One can jump throughout space and time . . . from the objective representation to the fantastic allegory to an acted out scene. One can represent dead or living, artificial or natural things. Using everything that exists and that allows to be invented—just as long as it can serve as an argument for the visualization of a basic idea.[3]

One of the great masters of this form is Chris Marker. His film *The Last Bolshevik* (1993) is structured as a series of letters to Russian film director Aleksandr Ivanovich Medvedkin (1900–1989) (Figure 18.10). *The Last Bolshevik* is a tribute from one filmmaker to another, an archeological expedition into film history that reveals new cinematic treasures, prompting us to reflect on the relation between art and politics in the former Soviet Union. The film uses archival film footage, observational material shot by Marker, and iconic images (including a sculpture of a horse rotating on a pedestal), all tied together by Marker's poetic voice-over.

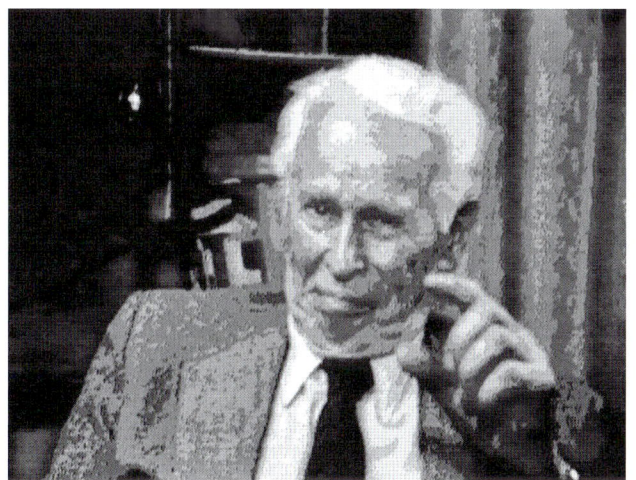

■ **Figure 18.9** In this scene from *Night Mail*, the narrator recites poetry that is accompanied by the sound of the train coming up through the hills that separate England and Scotland.

The film starts with an interview with an elderly man speaking Russian, filmed in a medium close-up. Over it, we hear Marker's voice-over:

> Aleksandr Ivanovich Medvedkin is a Russian filmmaker born in 1900. Tired fathers carve notches on the furniture to measure their children's growth. The century carves such notches on Medvedkin's life. He was five, and then in rode What Has to Be Done. Seventeen, and he knew. Twenty, the Civil War. Thirty-six, the Moscow Trials. Forty-one, World War Two. Fifty-three, Stalin's death. And when he himself dies in 1989, it is on the crest of Perestroika. In one of his last interviews, he berated me as usual. "You lazy bastard. Why don't you ever write? Just a few lines, like this."

■ **Figure 18.10** *The Last Bolshevik* is structured as a series of letters from director Chris Marker to Russian filmmaker Aleksandr Medvedkin.

Medvedkin holds up his hand with a small space between thumb and forefinger. The film freezes on the shot (Figure 18.10), and the narrator continues:

> Dear Aleksandr Ivanovitch, now I can write to you. There were too many things to hush up then. Now, there are too many to say, and I will try to write them, even though you're not here to listen any more. But I warn you, I'll leave much more space than there is between your two fingers.

This starts a narration that carries viewers through the entire film with language that works against the typical realism of documentary, creating instead a rich field of metaphor and historical appreciation for a world where imagination is as important as fact.

CONCLUSION

While we think of filmmaking as a visual art with the camera as its main tool, after reading this chapter you should have a sense that writing is central to every documentary film project, and that it is much more than just putting pen to paper (or fingers to keys). We write to develop the flow of our film, to organize and rework our storytelling strategy, to convey information, and to give our documentary a point of view and a tone. While this may seem daunting, remember that every word you write or scene you cut will help you focus more clearly on what your film is about and how to communicate its heart (and hopefully your own) to an audience.

CHAPTER
19

The Art of Documentary Editing

Today, the idea of editing—juxtaposing images with one another, and with sounds—is so much a part of our media experience that it can be hard to even notice the cuts between shots in a documentary. It is worth stopping to remember, however, that the very first films, the Lumière Brothers' snapshots of life at the end of the nineteenth century, consisted of only one shot. These "actualities" ran about a minute long, and did not have any edits, but they did accurately document everyday activity, events, and places of the time. *Le Repas de Bébé* (1895) consists of one shot of Auguste Lumière, his wife, and baby daughter having breakfast in the countryside, while *Barque Sortant du Port* (1896) consists of a single shot of a boat leaving the port, being rowed into rough seas by three men (Figure 19.1). It wasn't long before people discovered that new and more complex meaning could be created by cutting the film and rearranging the order of shots, and a language of film editing quickly evolved. Documentary is an integral part of that history, and continues to push the formal language of film editing forward.

There are two basic concepts that form the foundation of all documentary and fiction film: **juxtaposition**, which relies on the contrast between shots to create filmic meaning, and **continuity**, a system that assures us that individual shots, when cut together, will give the illusion of smooth and continuous time, movement, and space, no matter when or in what order the shots were taken.

Fiction films, which commonly attempt to create a sense of unified time and space, rely heavily on continuity style shooting and editing. **Observational** documentary films are the closest relatives of the fiction cinema because they also rely on a sense of unified time and space in which the action unfolds more or less as if the camera wasn't there. Prior to the 1960s, though, observational documentaries were difficult to make because of the lack of portable equipment that could record sync sound. The result of this was that documentary came to rely less on continuity, and more on the ways ideas could be conveyed through the juxtaposition of images and sounds using techniques drawn from the arenas of rhetoric, propaganda, or artistic experimentation.

▪ EDITING EXPOSITORY FILMS

As discussed in Chapter 2, many early documentaries were created with primarily educational goals. From Depression Era films like *The River* (1938) and *The Plough That Broke the Plains* (1936) to propaganda films like the World War II *Why We Fight* series, many early documentaries relied heavily on third-person narration (Chapter 18). Accompanying visuals contributed meaning, but most of the messaging was conveyed through an omniscience and authoritative spoken text (Figure 19.2). While this range of documentary style has broadened since then, many documentaries still take the expository form. Not all expository films use narration, as interviews may do much of the job of delivering content (along with the visual evidence and graphic elements). In general, though, a hallmark of expository documentaries is that the verbal elements carry much of the film's story or arguments.

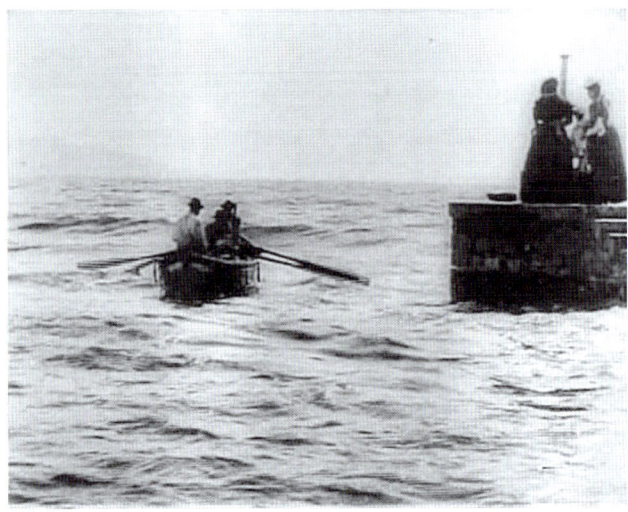

■ **Figure 19.1** *Barque Sortant du Port* (1896) like all Lumière Brothers' films, consisted of a single shot.

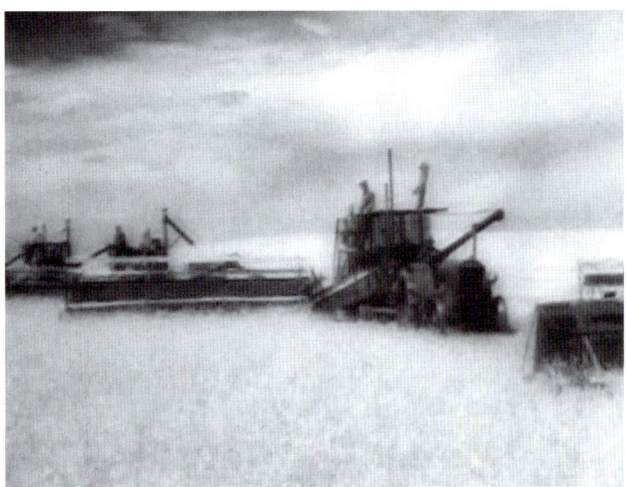

■ **Figure 19.2** In expository documentaries like Pare Lorentz's *The Plough That Broke The Plains*, about the destruction of the Great Plains by uncontrolled agricultural production, an omniscient narrator tells us what the filmmaker wants us to know: "We turned over millions of acres for war . . . the world was our market!"

Most documentaries today take a less obviously didactic approach than the documentaries of the 1930s and '40s, but they likely rely on a combination of an authoritative third-person narrator accompanied by strong supporting visuals. Take, for example, Marco Williams' documentary *Banished: How Whites Drove Blacks out of Town in America* (2006), edited by Kathryn Barnier, about the forced expulsion of African-Americans from three Southern towns in the early twentieth century. The film opens with a narration that is illustrated, literally, through original drawings (Figure 19.3).

The narrator tells us, "In 1864, in Washington County, Indiana, White residents made a very simple proposal to the Black community: leave or die." We see hand-drawn images of white men attacking black men, and of lynchings. The images reinforce what we are hearing.

Later in the film, documents, photographs, and archival footage accompany what is being put forward in the audio track, lending authority to the speaker and to the film's arguments. One of the main characters in *Banished* is Elliot Jaspin, a reporter at Cox Newspapers who has been researching the expulsion of Blacks from towns during the Reconstruction era (circa 1865) (Figure 19.4). In an interview setting, Jaspin recounts, "The only conclusion you can come to, after you look at all this, is that Blacks feared for their lives and they fled the county."

We see Jaspin in the interview setup for only a few seconds, however. The rest of the time we see images of newspapers from the 1860s, with headlines like "Negro Residents in Panic" and "Crowd Whips Several and Orders Them to Leave" (Figure 19.5, left). These images are more than illustrations; they are powerful **visual evidence** that helps persuade us that what we are hearing is true.

Banished also puts images of Jaspin at work over the audio from his interview (Figure 19.5, right). These observational shots provide us with a deeper sense of who this man is. Piles of papers and files all over his desk tell us he is a meticulous and dedicated investigative reporter.

This sequence is an example of the ways more expository elements like interviews and narration work hand-in-hand with more observational elements in many contemporary documentaries. It is quite common to see observational scenes that play out in "real time" followed by narration or an interview with one of the film's characters. Often, observational scenes play out partially, and then the sound drops down or out and we hear narration or interview voice-over as we continue to see the scene unfold.

For example, *Banished* presents us with a powerful observational scene from a 1987 march in Forsyth County, Georgia, where civil rights activists were confronted by white supremacists (Figure 19.6). We hear sync sound from the event, which at times fades down to allow us to hear the sound from an interview, recorded later on, providing perspective or recounting the events.

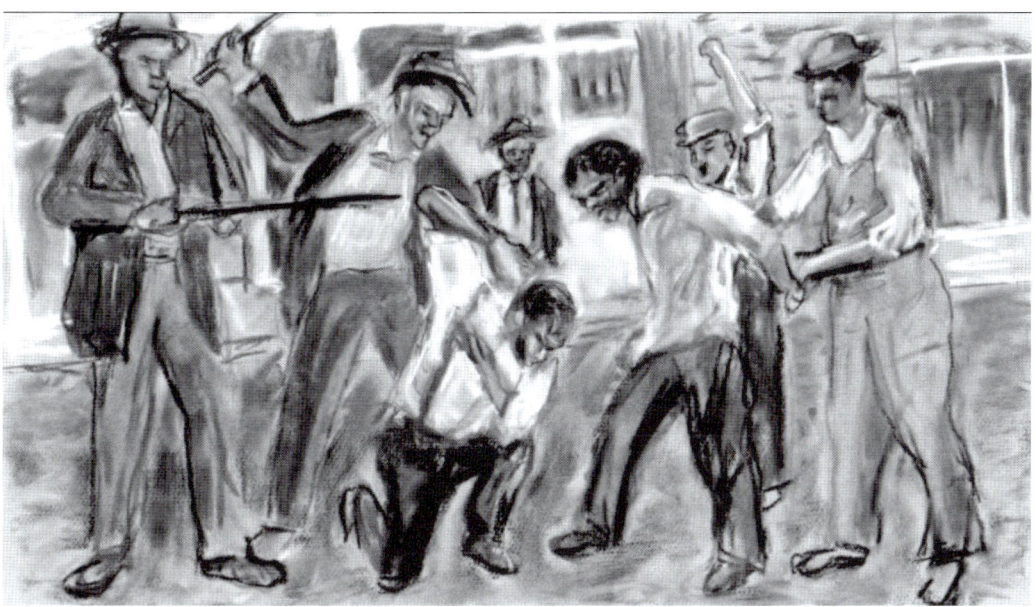

■ **Figure 19.3** Marco Williams employs charcoal drawings like this one in the opening sequence of *Banished: How Whites Drove Blacks Out of Town in America* to provide visual support for the unknown history of expulsion of blacks from towns across the country.

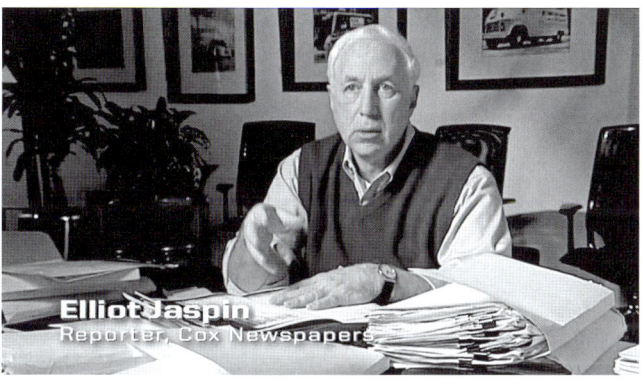

■ **Figure 19.4** Reporter Elliot Jaspin in an interview setup in *Banished*.

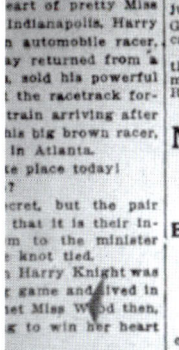
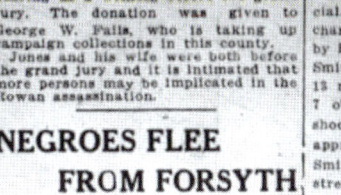
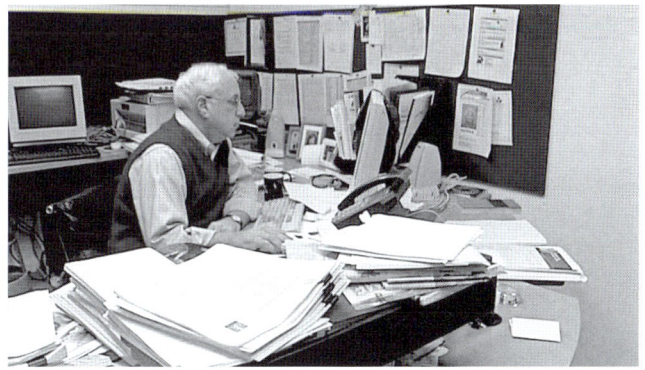

■ **Figure 19.5** Newspaper headline (left) and Elliot Jaspin at work (right) in *Banished*.

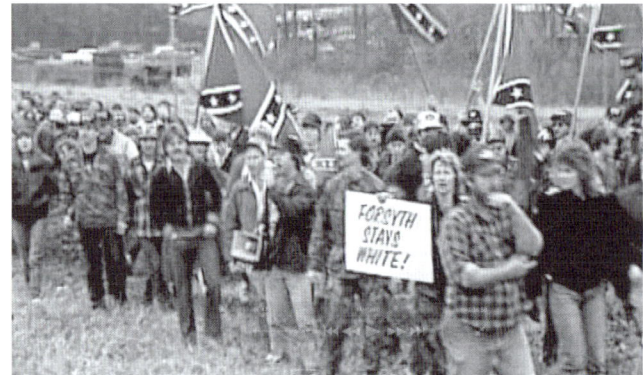

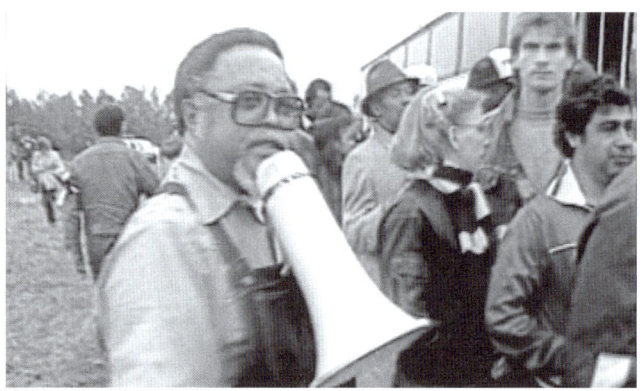

All expository documentaries treat the combination of interview, narration, observational, and other elements in their own way. Observational footage and eyewitness accounts can give expert analysis an experiential human touch. A narration may be illustrated by graphics with facts and figures. Music can contribute to the emotional tenor of a sequence. Editing is a matter of coordinating all of these elements in the best way you can. Each element carries its own burden of meaning, and ideally they all support one another to achieve the film's goals.

EDITING IMPRESSIONISTIC FILMS

Another approach to documentary editing that has contributed to its form today is more **impressionistic** and poetic. Consider an early film like Joris Ivens' 1929 film *Regen* (*Rain*), discussed in Chapter 2. The story is of a passing rain shower in the Dutch city of Amsterdam and is told through a series of shots that explore the graphic and compositional aspects of the frame. Though the film presumably shows one passing rain shower (it was actually shot over several weeks), the order and arrangement of the shots are determined less by continuity of action than by continuities or contrasts of pattern, movement, and composition from shot to shot (Figure 19.7). The effect is to open up meanings, inviting the viewer to consider the relationship between the shots. It also relies more heavily on emotion and impression than argument.

Watching Ivens' film today is a startling reminder of how the same formal and poetic impetus drives much documentary editing today.

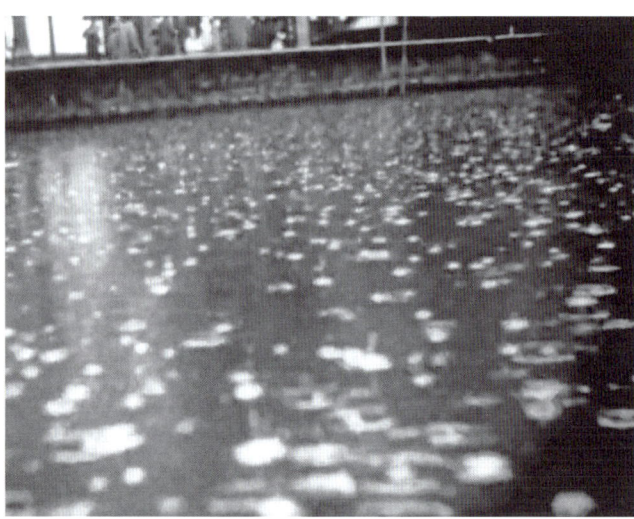

■ **Figure 19.6** An observational scene from *Banished*. The sync sound is brought down at times so we can hear context and analysis provided by interviewees like Rev. Elisabeth Omilami, one of the participants.

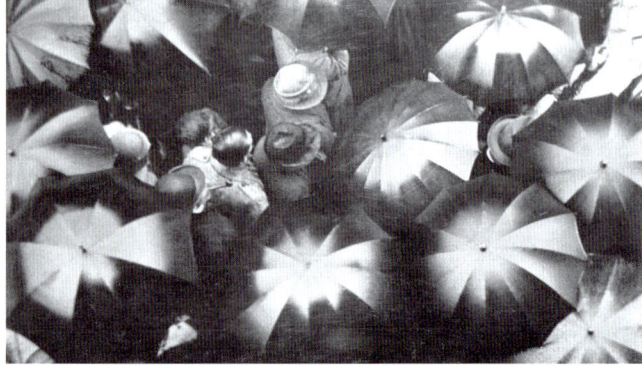

■ **Figure 19.7** Consecutive shots in *Regen* (*Rain*) show how editing is used to explore the relationship between shots of raindrops falling on water (left) and a crowd with umbrellas (right).

Associative Editing

Ivens' film, and many documentaries, make use of **associative editing** techniques. Broadly speaking, associative editing works by comparing or contrasting the content of the shots to create an association that is not contained in the individual shots. The connecting content can be either formal (color, shape, movement) or more thematic and metaphorical. The idea is that by juxtaposing shots that don't have an immediate, direct, or obvious narrative connection, new meaning is generated.

Associative editing relies on theories of montage developed by Soviet filmmakers in the early part of the twentieth century. These filmmakers, including Dziga Vertov and Sergei Eisenstein, saw the cinema as a potentially revolutionary art form that could wake up the masses to the reality of life around them and create a new form of citizen who would be highly engaged with their social reality. They were interested in the power of conflict and juxtaposition, both within individual frames and between shots.

In his essay "Methods of Montage," Eisenstein attempted to define the various relationships that could exist between shots.[1] These included:

- **Metric montage**, where the cut point is based on the duration of the shot.
- **Rhythmic montage**, where the length of the shot depends on what is happening in the frame. Length can vary, and effect can be obtained by changing the length of shots. In this type of montage, changes in rhythm create new meaning.
- **Tonal montage**, which uses the emotional meaning or "mood" of the shots to determine their placement relative to one another.
- **Overtonal/Associational montage**, which is the combination of metric, rhythmic, and tonal montage properties in a sequence.
- **Intellectual montage** (the highest form, according to Eisenstein) juxtaposes shots to create a new intellectual meaning.

While these categories might seem abstract and unrelated to documentary practices today, they are in fact quite present in most documentaries. In *Nostalgia for the Light* (2011), Chilean filmmaker Patricio Guzman uses a variety of these tactics to bring seemingly unrelated elements into relationship with one another. The film documents astronomers who use high-powered telescopes in the Chilean desert to see into outer space, as well as a group of women who comb through the desert sand in search of the remains of their loved ones who were "disappeared" during the brutal military dictatorship of General Augusto Pinochet. One particularly devastating sequence uses several of Eisenstein's montage categories to bring these seemingly disparate topics into relationship to one another (Figure 19.8).

A shot of the universe as seen through a telescope dissolves into close-ups of the surface of the moon and asteroids. The shots are

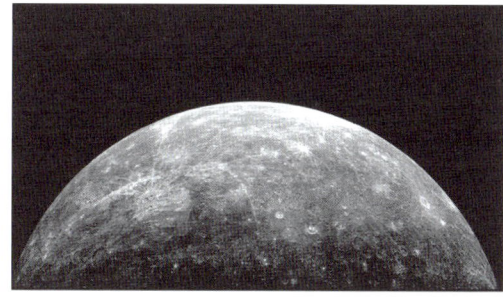
A

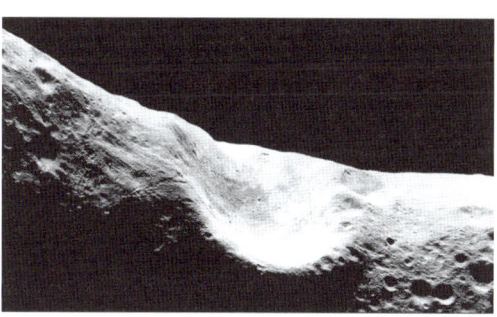
B

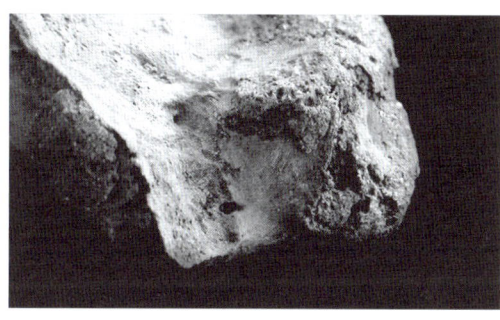
C

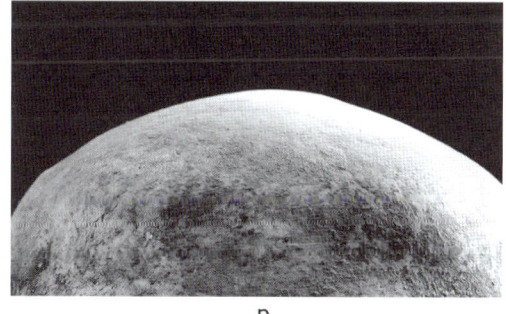
D

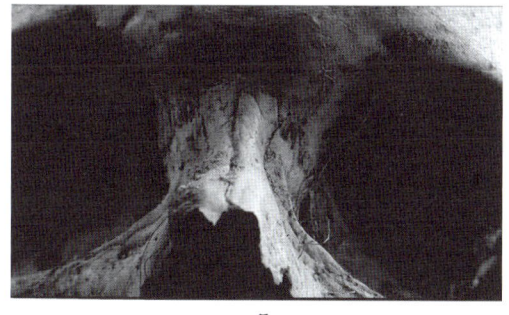
E

■ **Figure 19.8** Montage in *Nostalgia for the Light*. The moon (A), asteroids (B), human bones (C), and a skull (D), which matches the moon in shot (A). The camera tilts down to reveal that this is a human skull (E).

ASSOCIATIVE EDITING IN THE OPENING OF *THE MOST DANGEROUS MAN IN AMERICA*

More commonly, documentaries employ some version of associative editing in an **opening montage**. An example is the opening sequence of *The Most Dangerous Man in America* (2009), a documentary by Judith Ehrlich and Rick Goldsmith about the Pentagon Papers, secret documents leaked by military analyst Daniel Ellsberg that exposed the extent of US involvement in the Vietnam War (Figure 19.9). In the first two minutes of the film, we see the juxtaposition of at least six types of footage: maps of Cambodia and Vietnam in a vintage photocopying machine, stylized re-enactments of a man sneaking documents out of a file cabinet and into a briefcase, archival footage of aerial bombing, official State Department documents, interview clips, and archival footage of Richard Nixon, Secretary of State Henry Kissinger, and Daniel Ellsberg himself.

This rich assortment of images and the accompanying sounds draw the viewer in through a series of juxtapositions. The past is seen next to present-day interviews, which gives us a sense that we will be viewing historical events through a contemporary lens. Footage of aerial bombing superimposed on official State Department documents creates a sense that policy formed in Washington has an impact on actual lives on the ground in Vietnam. There is also the juxtaposition of the perspectives of government officials like Nixon and Kissinger, who say things like, "If entire file cabinets can be stolen and given to the press you can't have orderly government anymore," with that of Daniel Ellsberg, who is seen saying to reporters, "Wouldn't you go to prison to help end this war?"

In addition to the more thematic and content-related associations, there is a juxtaposition of styles at work. The dramatically lit reenactments feel like a spy thriller, but their theatricality is undermined by the gritty 16mm news footage that follows. The film is telling us that although this has all the suspense of a Hollywood thriller, it is a story based in reality. This raises the stakes for us as viewers.

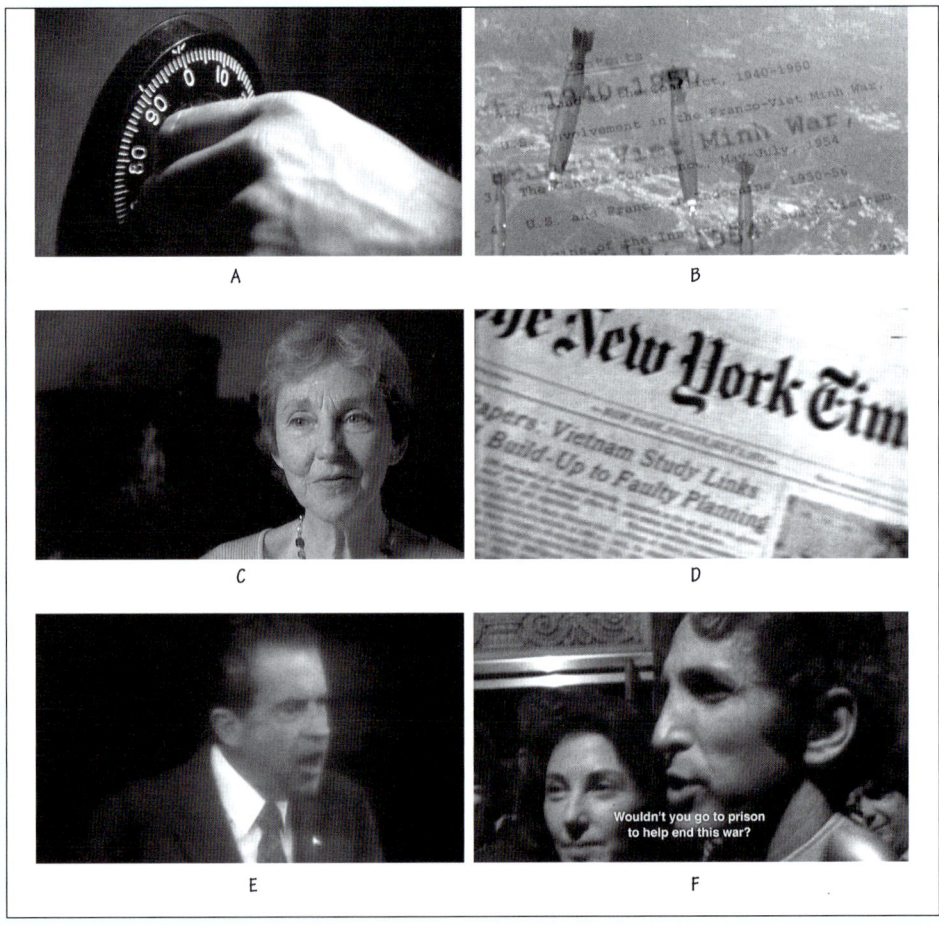

■ **Figure 19.9** Associative editing in *The Most Dangerous Man in America*. Stylized "spy thriller" reenactments (A) are juxtaposed with archival footage and documents (B). Mrs. Ellsberg tells us this will be a private story (C) but it is also very public (D). And the film's central conflict: government secrecy (E) vs the public's right to know (F).

approximately four seconds long each (metric montage) and have similar lighting, color palette, and texture (tonal montage). The ambient audio, which sounds roughly like air blowing in a tunnel, plays under all the shots, joining them together. These shots of space are followed by extreme close-up shots of human bones, which look astonishingly similar in texture, color, and shape to the surface of the moon and asteroids. The last of these shots is almost identical in shape to the first shot of the moon (this is called a **graphic match** because of the compositional similarities between the shots). The camera then pans down to reveal that what we are viewing is in fact a human skull.

This beautiful and emotional sequence is the essence of Eisenstein's intellectual montage. Questions of scale and context collapse, and the viewer is left to experience the contrast between the dead mineral composition of the moon and the organic nature of the bones that just recently held flesh. We are left asking what the relationship is between outer space and the most inner anguish, and how do humans find purpose in a world with such unknowability and injustice?

OBSERVATIONAL DOCUMENTARIES AND THE CONTINUITY SYSTEM

During the 1960s, with the advent of sync sound and the possibilities afforded by portable equipment, the idea of showing a story in "real time" began to take precedence in documentary. Observational filmmakers like Frederick Wiseman, Robert Drew, and the Maysles filmed events as they unfolded, and cut them together using the dominant convention of the fiction cinema: **continuity editing**.

The hallmark of continuity style is to render each edit, the link from one shot to another, as seamlessly as possible. In order to cut a film in this style, the filmmaker has to shoot it with an understanding of the conventions of continuity so that the editor will have the right shots to work with. Although the principles of the continuity system can, at first, seem a bit like a needlessly complex jigsaw puzzle, they are, in fact, quite simple and intuitive once you are aware of them. Here are a few of the basic rules of continuity, as well as an exploration of how they are used in some documentary films.

FOUR BASIC PRINCIPLES OF CONTINUITY EDITING

1. Continuity of mise-en-scène (shared shot content)
2. Continuity of performance, actions, and placement
3. Continuity of spatial orientation
4. Avoiding "too similar" shots

1. Continuity of Mise-en-Scène (Shared Shot Content)

Let's start with two shots connected by one single edit (Figure 19.10). We want to cut shot A with shot B as seamlessly as possible. Shot A is a long shot of two men at a chess table in the park starting a game. Shot B is a medium close-up of the player with the white pieces making his first move.

Mise-en-scène is a term derived from film studies that refers to everything that appears before the camera and its arrangement. In documentary, this means our subjects and their environments. The first rule of continuity—preserving continuity of mise-en-scène—means that the clothes our character wears, the things he touches, and his surroundings need to remain the same from one shot to the next. Because in real time our chess game might last an hour, it's not uncommon that two shots like these might not actually be shot one right after the other. Perhaps as the day gets colder, our character puts on a jacket. Preserving continuity means that a shot with the jacket off will not cut seamlessly with a shot taken later on, when our subject is wearing the jacket. Similar issues come up around anything that changes noticeably over time, including plates of food being consumed, drinks, cigarettes, clocks, or even the position of the chess pieces on the board. Coauthor Kelly Anderson was once the coproducer on a TV program where Character A was washing

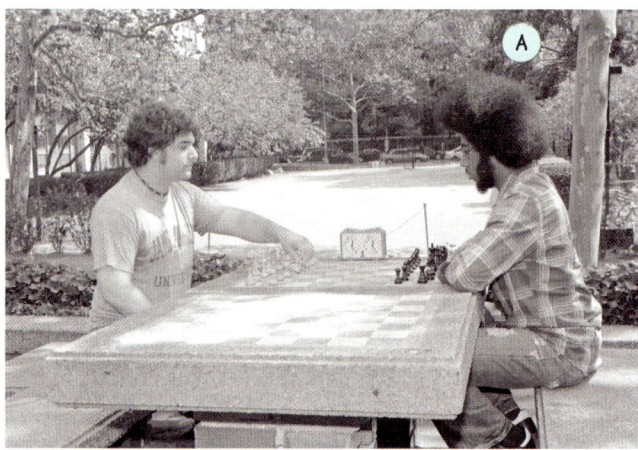
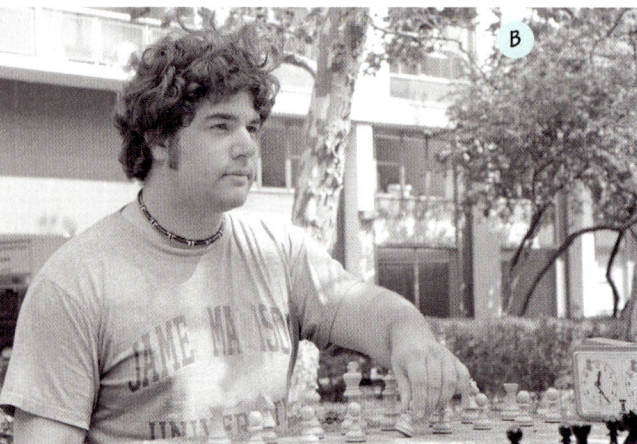

Figure 19.10
A simple edit. Cutting from a long shot (a) to a medium close-up (b).

a frying pan at the kitchen sink. When the scene was edited, the shot was cut next to a shot of Character B listening to Character A speaking. It took the filmmakers a while to realize that the frying pan being washed was also seen, full of scrambled eggs, on the stove next to Character B. Many jokes about this being a "2-frying-pan-family" ensued. The audience likely never noticed the continuity error, but it's a good idea to keep these things in mind when shooting and editing. The idea of the observational style is to allow the audience to experience what is going on with the characters in the moment, without being distracted by reminders that images were actually shot at different times.

The angle and quality of the light must also be consistent if you want to edit shots together and create the illusion of continuous space and time. Documentary audiences are more likely than fiction film viewers to forgive small changes in lighting between shots, and color correction in postproduction can help you match different lighting setups, but joining images shot at noon with others shot at dusk will likely present problems if you want the audience to experience them as occurring in a continuous time.

2. Continuity of Performance, Actions, and Placement

In the chess game above, if we are to cut shot A seamlessly with shot B, then the placement and physical actions of our performers must be consistent. In the example of the chess game, our character moves the king's pawn with his left hand in the long shot, so he must move the same chess piece with the same hand in the medium close-up. This ensures that the visible actions in the two shots match. Also, our character is sitting upright with his right hand in his lap in the long shot, so he cannot be leaning forward, resting his chin in his right hand in the medium close-up.

Consider these two shots from Zachary Heinzerling's Academy Award®-nominated film *Cutie and the Boxer* (2013), discussed in Chapter 7 (Figure 19.11). The long shot on the left shows Ushio wetting craft paper and hanging it on a clothesline. This is followed by a medium shot of the same activity. Even though the second shot was probably taken later, the two shots cut together relatively seamlessly because the setting, lighting, and Ushio's wardrobe, as well as the position of the paper and of his hands, match between the two shots.

Unlike in fiction filmmaking, where the editor will have multiple takes of a scene shot from many angles to work with, the documentary editor will comb through the footage looking for shots that can be edited together seamlessly to convey the action of the scene. This is not always easy. For example, in the sequence above, a close inspection reveals that there is actually more paper hanging from the line in the second shot, but the match is close enough that audiences don't notice the difference and the edit is "good enough" to pass muster. In certain cases where even a "good enough" match cannot be found, one

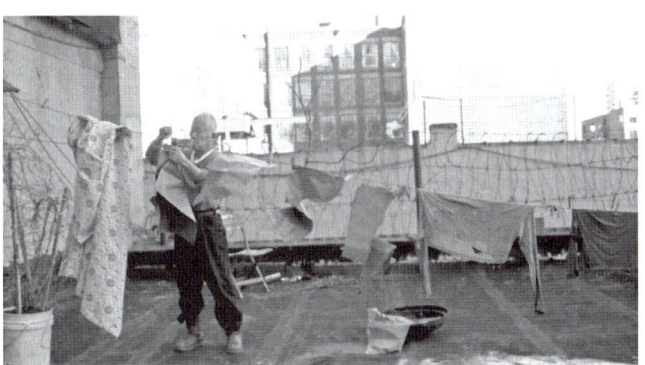
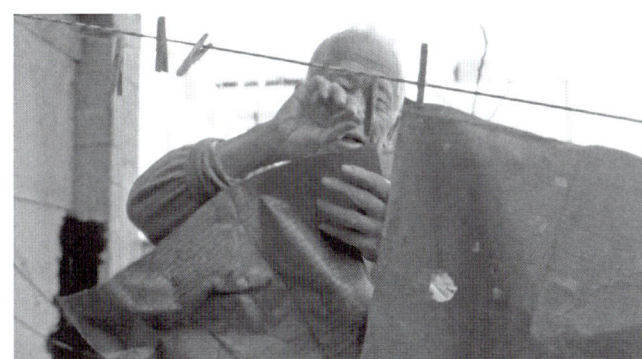

can always use a **cutaway** between two shots of action, creating a "bridge" that maintains the illusion of continuous actions (p. 317).

■ Figure 19.11
Continuity of performance and action in *Cutie and the Boxer* (2013).

3. Continuity of Spatial Orientation

For the viewer to understand the physical space of the scene and the relationships between characters and objects in that space, we need to maintain coherent and consistent spatial orientation. Spatial orientation begins with the **180° principle**, which, in basic terms, means that you must shoot all of the shots in a continuity sequence from only one side of the action. In other words, when a scene begins with a shot taken from one side, you cannot cut to shots taken from the other side because the perspective of the viewer will be reversed and create disorientation. See Chapter 7 for an analysis of how this plays out in a scene from *Cutie and the Boxer*.

Using our chess game as an example, this means you can cut from shot (A) to shot (B), but not from shot (A) to shot (C) (Figure 19.12). When you begin shooting, the man playing with the white pieces is to your left. When he looks at his opponent, he faces left to right.

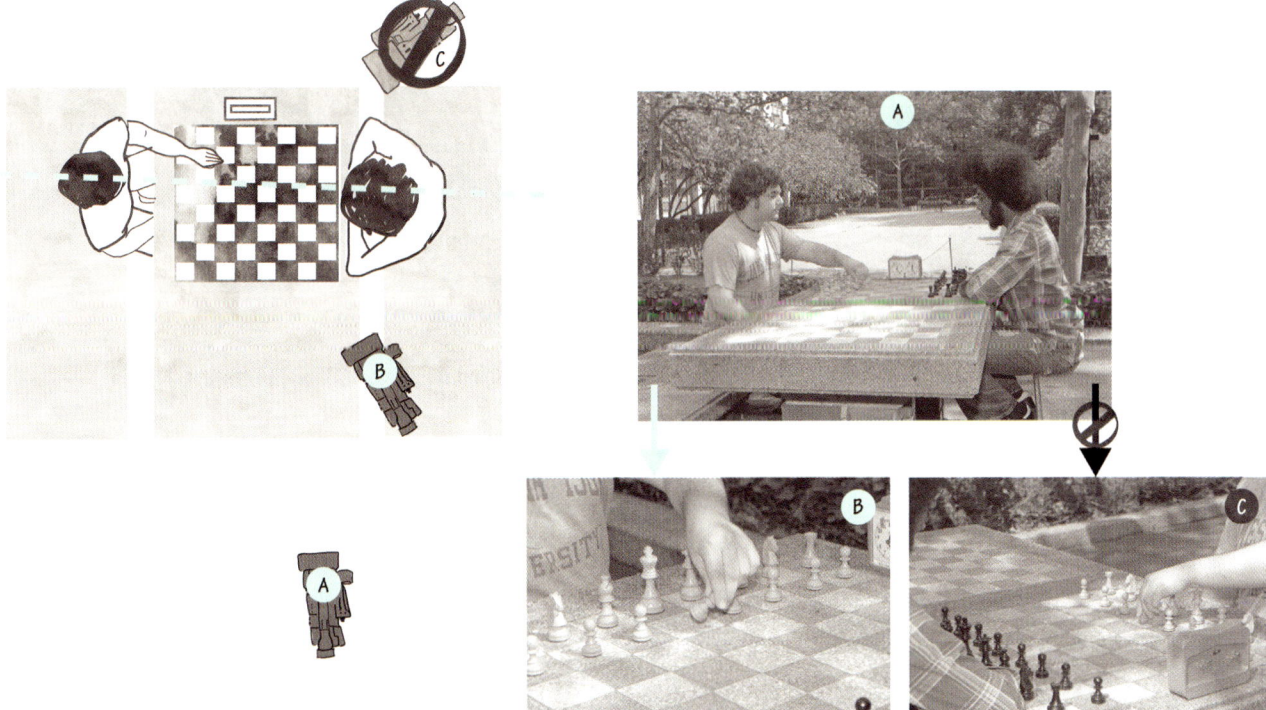

■ Figure 19.12 Continuity of spatial orientation. Character sightlines establish the 180 degree line of action and shot (A) establishes on which side of that line the camera must remain. Shot (C) crosses the line and you should not use shots from that camera position.

The opponent playing the black pieces is to your right and he faces right to left. This is the spatial orientation from your side of the table. However, for the onlooker who is watching the game from the other side of the table, across from you, everything is reversed. When we make a film, the camera is the spectator, and to shoot this scene we cannot take some shots from one side of the table and others from the opposite side because that would reverse the direction and position of the players' faces.

Notice in shot (C) that our character now suddenly faces screen left, and is positioned on the right side of the frame. This shot will not cut with the first shot without causing spatial confusion for the viewer. The viewer might think that the players, for some reason, suddenly changed places and the total shift in background and the position of the clock will seriously throw off the illusion of continuous activity.

4. Avoiding "Too Similar" Shots

The too-similar-shot rule (our own term) states that, when we cut from one shot of a subject to another shot of the same subject, we need to make sure that each shot is a distinct composition in terms of frame size or camera angle. If we try to cut together two shots of the same subject when the frames are very similar, then the viewer has the feeling that a single shot has simply lurched forward a little bit. This is called a **jump cut**, and the awkwardness of the edit calls attention to itself. In some instances this may be a desirable aesthetic approach, but if you are trying to create a sense of seamless time and space it won't work. Basically, this rule tells us that in order to cut from shot (A), the men sitting at the chess table, to shot (B), white making his first move, we must significantly change the angle or the size of shot (Figure 19.13).

In documentary interviews, you can often see this principle in action. Since most people talk in a more long-winded way than most documentary directors find economical, it is common to edit together various pieces of an interview to make a statement clearer or shorter. Often a cinematographer will vary the shot size while the interviewer is asking each question to give the editor more options for cutting between parts of the interview.

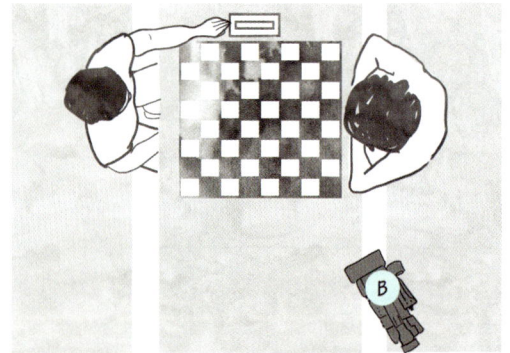
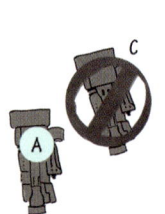
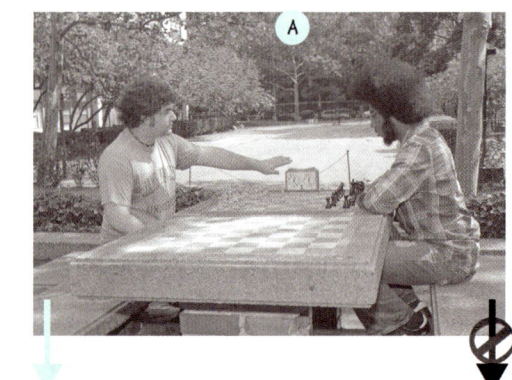
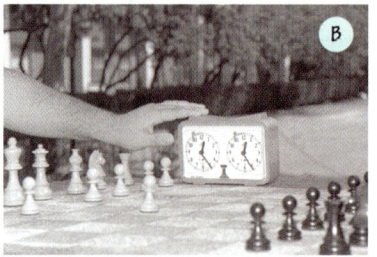
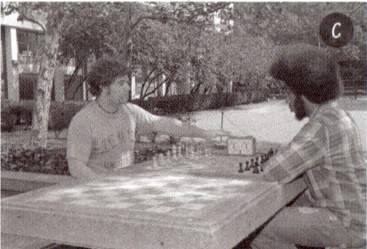

■ **Figure 19.13** The "Too Similar Shot" rule. Two shots of obviously different sizes and angles such as shot (A), a long shot profile shot, and shot (B), a close-up frontal from a frontal three-quarter angle cut together smoothly. Two shots that are nearly identical in framing, such as shot (A) and shot (C), will cause a jump cut when edited together.

CHAPTER 19
The Art of Documentary Editing

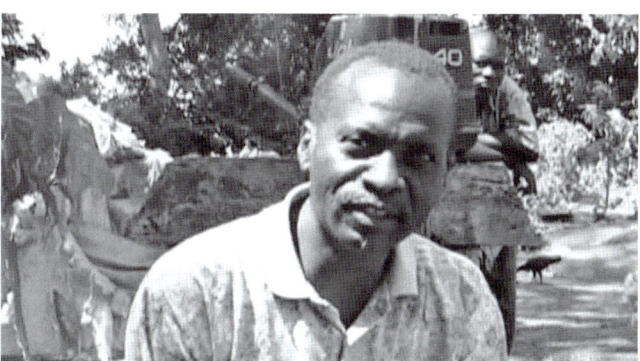
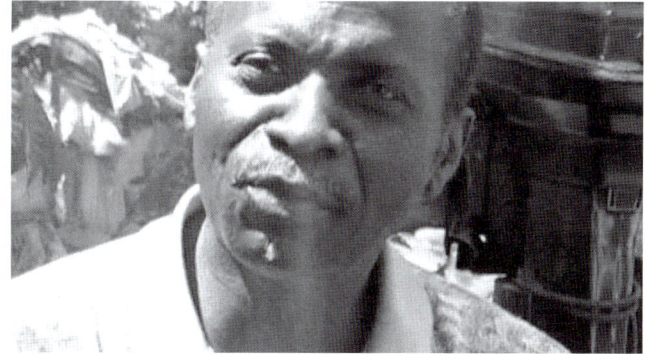

■ **Figure 19.14** A medium shot of an interviewee, cut next to a close-up shot. These two shots cut together without creating a jump cut because the framing is significantly different.

Figure 19.14 shows an example from Hubert Sauper's *Darwin's Nightmare* (2004), which explores the impact of the globalized trade in fish and guns on the people who live around Lake Victoria in Tanzania.

In the scene, we see an interview subject talking in a medium shot, then there is a cut to a close-up of the same person in the same interview setup (Figure 19.14). The cut feels seamless because there is enough of a change in the shot size.

5. Cutaways

Later on in the same interview sequence, there is another cut in the interview. In this case, the editor employs another standard documentary convention: the **cutaway**. A cutaway is a shot of a detail within your scene other than the main action. Here, the cutaway is a shot of a young boy with a distended belly, a sign of malnutrition, walking on the beach (Figure 19.15).

A word of caution is in order here. Cutaways can create strong associations and can alter the meaning of what is being conveyed in the scene. The interview we are discussing concerns the globalized competition for natural resources in Africa. As the interviewee asks, "Who is to gain, and who is to miss?" the film cuts to the shot of the boy on the beach. This creates a powerful statement that Africans, in particular the most vulnerable, are losing out. The film provides powerful evidence that this is indeed the case, but it is worth remembering that we have enormous power as documentary filmmakers. In actuality, we don't know who this child is, why he is starving, or whether it was shot the same day or even on the beach the interview was shot on. Because of the power of continuity conventions, the audience will probably assume these things are happening simultaneously. All documentary filmmakers deal with the challenge of creating a representation of an event after it occurred. You will find your own ways of delivering on the trust your audience invests in you.

In addition to being a staple of interview editing, cutaways can also be extremely useful in observational scenes. In S. Leo Chiang's *Mr. Cao Goes to Washington* (2012), analyzed in Chapter 7, a cutaway of some campaign materials tells us that Cao is the first Vietnamese-

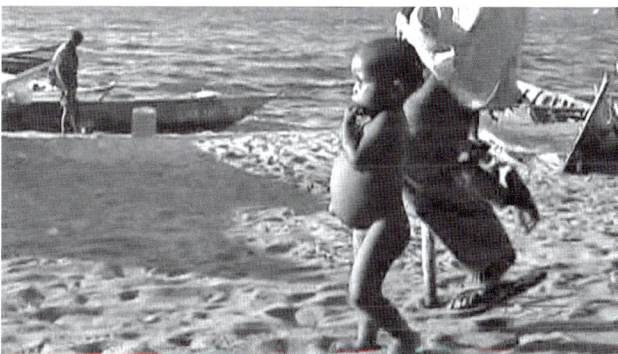

■ **Figure 19.15** A cutaway in *Darwin's Nightmare*.

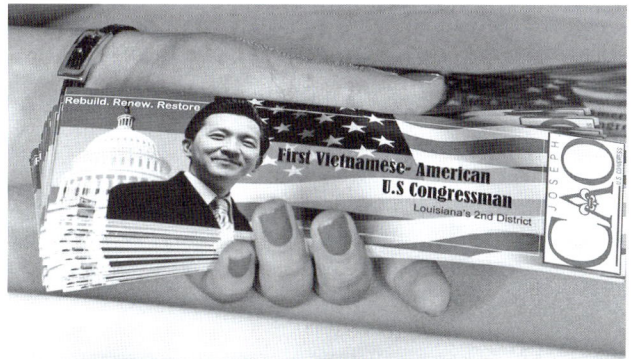

■ **Figure 19.16** Significant detail in *Mr. Cao Goes to Washington*.

American Congressman in the history of the United States (Figure 19.16). Without this cutaway, this critical information would have had to be delivered through interviews, narration, or text cards. This shot could also be called a **significant detail** shot.

TIMING, RHYTHM, AND PACING

Another way of thinking about editing refers to questions of **timing**, **rhythm**, and **pacing**. As you get into the nuts and bolts of editing, you will find yourself pondering some of the following questions:

- What is the best place to put my in-point for the shot I am about to cut in?
- How long should I hold the shot before cutting to something else?
- Is there a "best place" to cut out of a shot?
- Should my shots overall be short, or longer?
- Should I vary the length of the shots in my sequence, or keep them about the same duration?

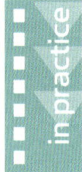

JUMP CUTTING INTERVIEWS

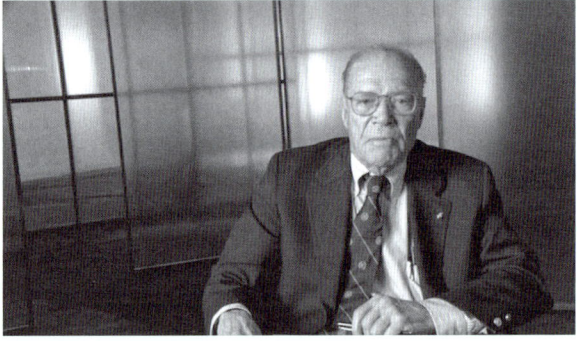 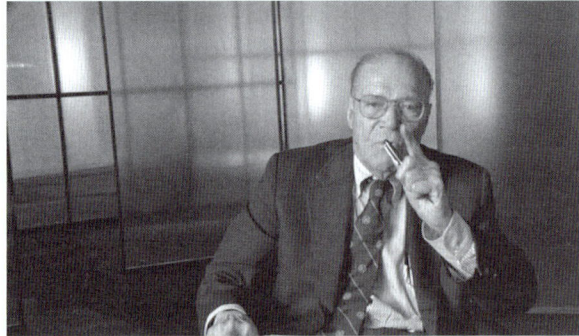

■ **Figure 19.17** The left frame is cut next to the right one in *Fog of War*, producing a jump cut because McNamara's position in the frame changes only slightly and his hand is raised in the second shot.

The use of intentional jump cuts directly challenges the precept of invisible edits by tossing out concerns like the 180° line of action, the too-similar-shot rule, and the use of cutaways to hide edits. The key to using jump cuts in your film is to utilize them as an intentional technique, a stylistic choice around which you plan and organize your shooting.

Errol Morris' *Fog of War* (2003) is based largely on an interview with former Secretary of Defense Robert S. McNamara. Morris edits the interview and does not cover the cuts with any other visuals, resulting in jump cuts (Figure 19.17). He explains:

> I have always heavily edited my interviews . . . In all of my previous films, I have tried to cover my tracks. I put images over the cuts in the soundtrack, and I hide all of the cuts.
>
> McNamara has a way of talking where he endlessly qualifies what he's saying. He says X, and then he stops and he qualifies X. And then he qualifies the qualification. And then often qualifies the qualification of the qualification. And so on in some infinite regress. Not quite infinite. But often confusing. And also long-winded. (Of course, it could be argued that it is precisely these extended qualifications that give us a deeper understanding of McNamara's personality. Yet, I think that's there's enough of them left in the movie to give the general idea.)
>
> I wanted to hear him talk, but I also wanted the essence of what he was saying.
>
> In this film, for whatever reason, I liked leaving them raw.[2]

The effect is to let us in on the process of fabrication, to tell us that this portrait of McNamara is authored and emanates from a filmmaker with a point of view. Morris wants us to know that there was more said, but that he has decided to cut it out.

In other words, *what makes a good cut*? The answer to this question is subjective, and you will find your own approach and style for each film, but what follows are some thoughts about how other filmmakers have approached these issues.

Timing

Timing refers to the specific placement of a shot within the sequence, meaning the precise moment you cut to a new shot for maximum impact. Good editors have a sixth sense for timing: it seems to be in their bones. The rest of us experiment—we try an edit and then trim it until it feels right. A few tips:

- Know when to cut away from an interview or a subject. There are moments when a person's facial expression, or body language, is more important than their actual words. Don't reduce the power of a moment by inserting a cutaway over some of your best material. The reverse is also true—to minimize an impact you don't like, you can cut away to another shot.
- In some cases, the moment after someone finishes speaking is extremely powerful. Perhaps they have just said something they didn't expect to say, or have more to say but are holding back. Don't lose the moment by cutting away too quickly.
- If your shot includes a camera move (a zoom or a pan, for example), let the shot begin a frame or two before the move starts, and let it "land" before cutting away from it. This is especially true if you are cutting to another still shot. If you need or want to cut while the camera is moving, try cutting to another moving shot.
- If a person, car, or other object is moving through the frame, let them leave the frame before you cut out of the shot. Similarly, be deliberate about where you cut in or out of an action or gesture.

Rhythm

Rhythm within a sequence refers to the duration of the shots relative to each other, and the patterns of emphasis, or pulses, these durations create. If you consider an edited shot as a pulse or a beat, like a musical beat, then you will be able to manipulate the duration of these image "beats" to create regular, irregular, or syncopated visual rhythms.

In documentary, we often confront questions of rhythm when cutting a montage to music. Should you cut on the beat, holding every shot for the same amount of time, say four or eight beats of music? Or should you vary it, cutting several shots together on the beat, and then holding several shots for longer? Either approach can work. Watch a wide variety of films to get a sense of how their editors tackle this question and find your own approach.

Pacing

Pace (also called "tempo") is, of course, related to rhythm, in that it is determined by the duration of shots next to other shots. But pace refers specifically to the rate of speed that a scene, or sequence of scenes, plays out. A fast-paced editing approach can suggest intensity, excitement, energy, or even confusion or chaos, depending on the context. Slowly paced editing can lend a feeling of casualness, contemplation, or even torpor or stasis to a movie. In *Nobody's Business* (1996), an experimental documentary by Alan Berliner about his father, Berliner uses pacing extensively to create mood and meaning (Figure 19.18). During a sequence where he is researching family birth and death records, shots of what appear to be fragments of official records go by extremely quickly (3–5 frames each), emphasizing the sheer number of records and how overwhelming it must be to go through them all on a microfilm reader. Finally, the sequence ends with a 6-second wider shot with the name "Rigrod" in the center, which is the town Berliner's grandparents were from.

An example of a slower-paced film is Nicolas Philibert's *Etre et Avoir* (2002), about a one-room schoolhouse in rural France. The film begins with three shots of farmers herding cattle in a snowstorm. The shots are quite long (12 to 21 seconds each), but the scene feels frenetic because the cows are panicking, the farmers are nervous, and the snow is

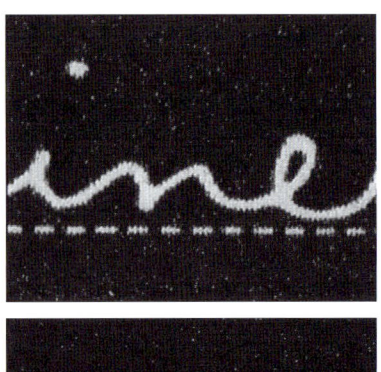
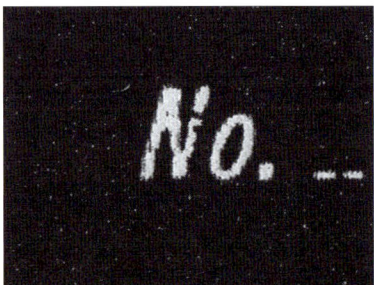
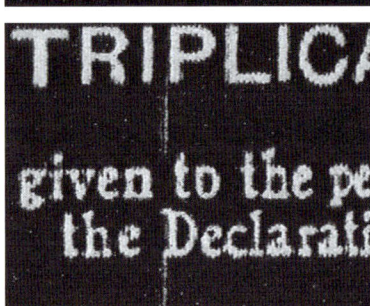
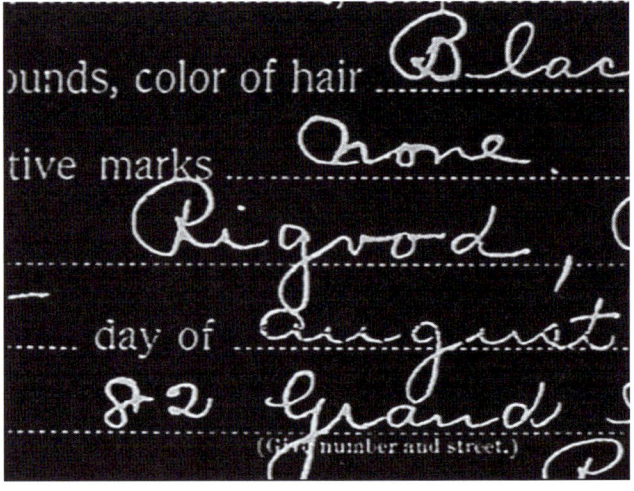

■ **Figure 19.18** Pacing in Alan Berliner's *Nobody's Business* (1996). Fragments of documents (left 3 images) are cut together so quickly they are barely readable. The sequence lands and holds on a wider shot of the document that shows where his grandparents are from (right).

coming down hard. Then the film cuts to a shot taken from inside the school, through the window. The snowstorm is raging outside but inside it is quiet. Then we see desks with chair piled high: an empty schoolroom. Suddenly a turtle enters the frame, then another. For a full 33 seconds we watch the same wide shot, without any camera movement at all, as the turtles make their way across the floor. Through its pacing, the film is telling us that things are going to move, quite literally, at a turtle's pace, and that we should settle in to appreciate what can be discovered in the stillness (Figure 19.19).

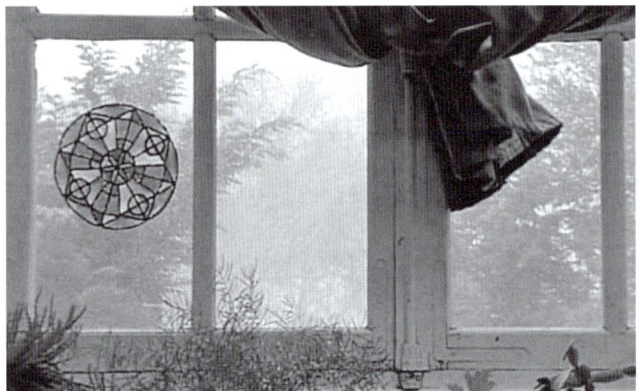
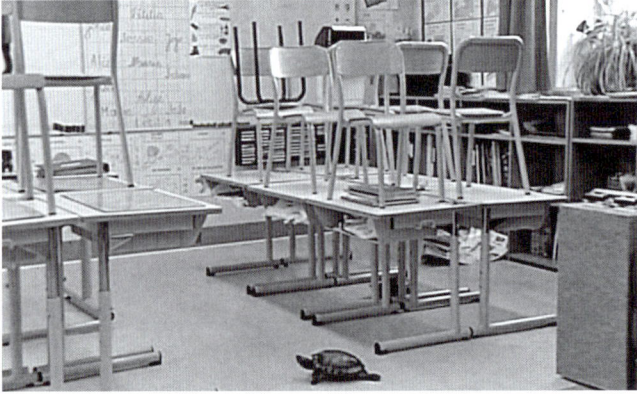

■ **Figure 19.19** In *Etre et Avoir*, pacing is used to tell us that things move slowly in a one-room schoolhouse, and that we should expect to spend time discovering the beauty in the stillness.

In many films, the pacing is determined by the subject matter, or by the style the director or editor chooses. However, very few films strictly maintain a single pace from beginning to end. Contrasting the pace of scenes is an important tool for creating narrative emphasis and overall story shape.

EDITING PATTERNS

Try and approach each scene with a strategy. Perhaps you will start with a long shot (LS) to establish the location, then move to a medium shot (MS), and then a close-up (CU) of the specific action going on. Or, start with a CU, cut to a MS to reveal its local context, and then to a LS to tell us where we are. You don't need to use the same pattern each time. In fact, varying your editing patterns can keep your film feeling alive and interesting.

In *Nostalgia for the Light*, Guzman begins a scene about his childhood with the following sequence of shots (Figure 19.20). The first shot is so close up it is abstract, sparking our curiosity about what will follow. The shots that follow progress from CUs to MSs to a WA, mimicking the expanding consciousness of childhood, which begins with the intimate objects in the home and ends with the wider world outside.

Try to avoid extremes of focal length from one shot to the next. An important part of editing is to establish a sense of space, and this means not disorienting the viewer. Avoid going from an extreme long shot (ELS) to an extreme close one (ECU). Instead, try cutting from a LS to a MS, and then to the close-up. As with all rules, you may break this one for a desired effect.

Try to come in and out of a scene, and certainly in and out of your film, with a bang. Look for intriguing, well-composed **transition shots** for your openings and closings. Often the opening and closing shots can serve as "bookends" for the content in between.

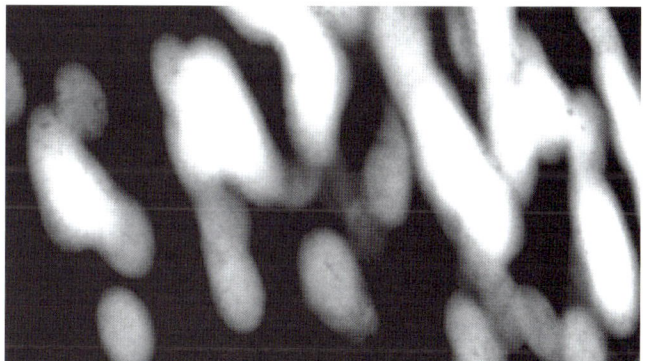 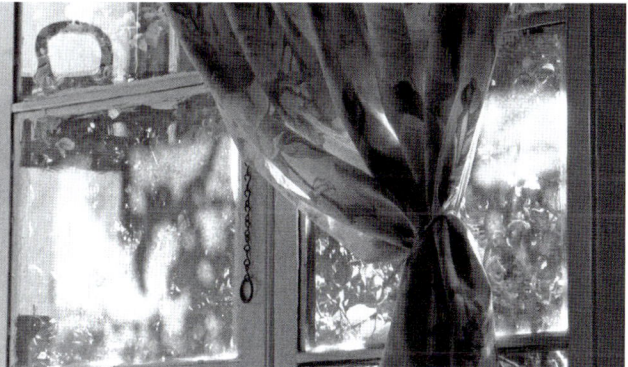
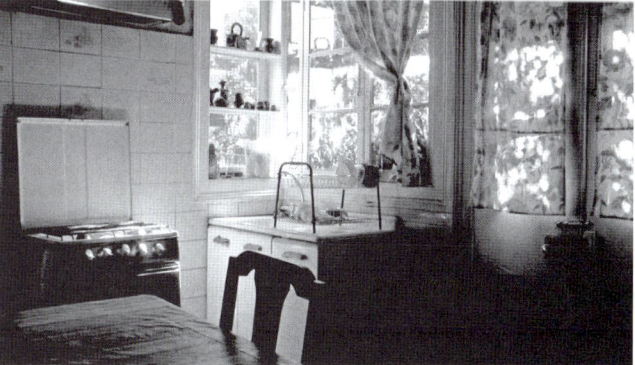 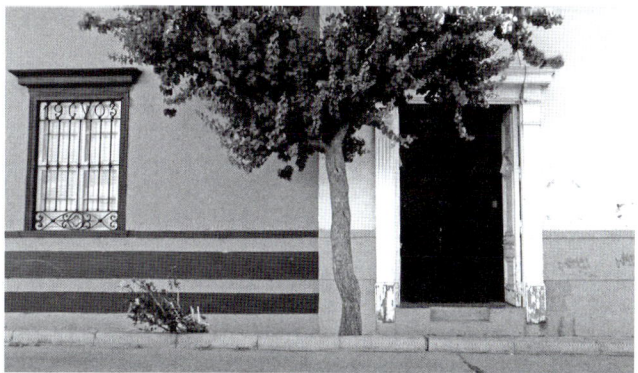

■ **Figure 19.20** Selected shots from a sequence in *Nostalgia for the Light*. The sequence begins with an extreme close-up (top left), moves to a medium close-up of the window (top right), then a medium long shot of the kitchen (bottom left), and ends with a long shot of the exterior of the house (bottom right).

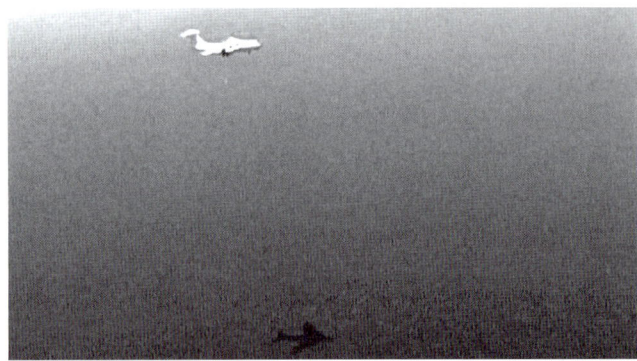
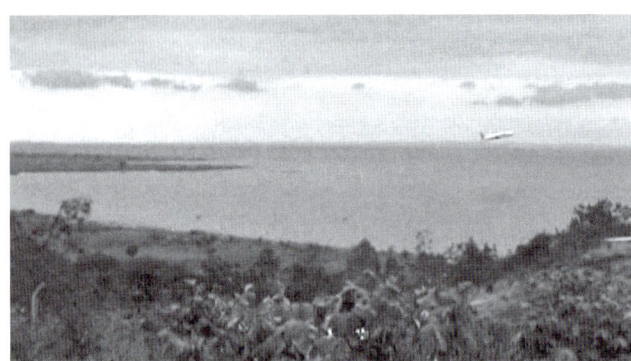
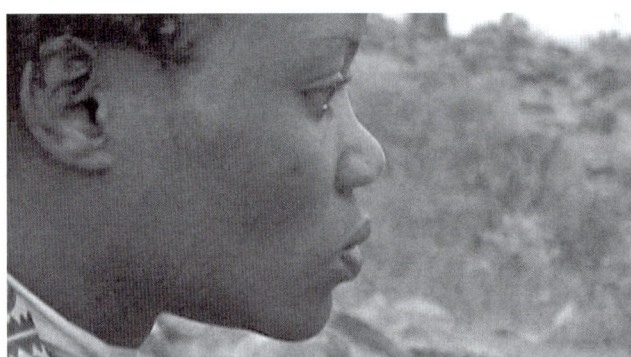

■ **Figure 19.21** The opening (top) and closing (center, bottom) shots of *Darwin's Nightmare* bookend the film and remind us of globalization's human consequences.

In *Darwin's Nightmare*, the opening shot is of a cargo plane landing, suggesting that the story is beginning (Figure 19.21). Throughout the film, we learn that these planes not only pick up fish, but deliver weapons to some of Africa's most conflict-embroiled nations. These trades devastate the local communities in many ways, including promoting disease and drug use. The film's last shots are of a plane leaving, which is reminiscent of the opening, and a final shot of a local woman watching the plane depart—reminding us that some people can leave the nightmare but that others are stuck to endure the consequences of globalization run amok.

IMAGE TRANSITIONS

There are many ways to get from one shot to another, but in the world of documentary filmmaking, there are really only three transitions that are widely used: the **cut**, the **dissolve**, and the **fade**.

The Cut

For the most part in this chapter and in the previous chapters, we're exploring the function, power, and versatility of the cut, which is the joining of two shots such that the last frame of the first shot is directly replaced by the first frame of the next shot. The visual shift in a cut from one shot to the next is sequential, instantaneous, and complete. The cut is the most efficient and unobtrusive way to move through the images and moments in your film, and they are by far the most effective technique for creating clear, sharp, meaningful juxtapositions. In Jennifer Baichwal's *Manufactured Landscapes* (2006), there is a powerful cut from a shot of an iron being made on an assembly line to a shot of a similar iron that is rusting away in a trash dump. The cut emphasizes a central theme of the film: the endless cycle of consumption and waste our economic system creates, and its environmental impact (Figure 19.22).

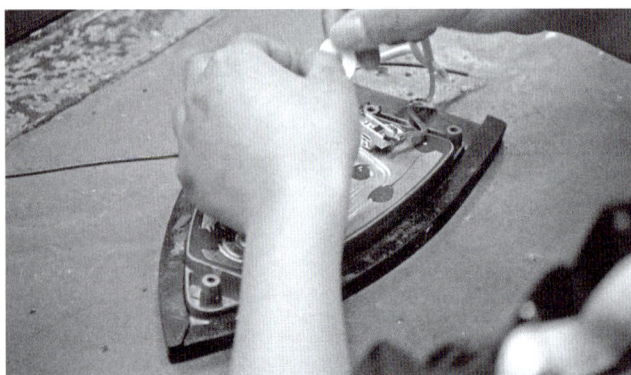
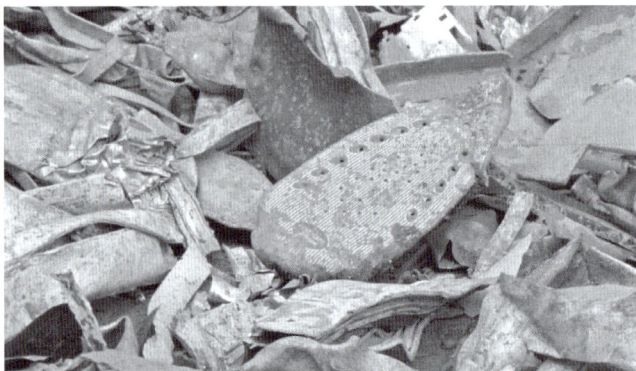

■ **Figure 19.22** A powerful cut in *Manufactured Landscapes*.

The Dissolve

In a dissolve, the first shot gradually disappears as the second shot gradually appears. With a dissolve we see, for a moment, both images on the screen simultaneously (Figure 19.23). A dissolve can have any duration the filmmaker needs, from a few frames to many seconds. A long dissolve becomes a **superimposition** (two images layered over one another) before giving way to the second shot entirely. A dissolve invited the viewer to think about the deeper relationship between two shots. Dissolves are often used to imply a significant change in time, space, or theme. As such, a dissolve is a promise. It says, "Look at these two images merging, something significant is happening." For this reason, it should not be overused. Students often throw dissolves in everywhere just because they can. Finally, if two images don't cut together well, dissolving between them won't fix the problem!

The Fade

The **fade-out** is a slow disappearing of an image into a color, and a **fade-in** is the slow appearing of the image from a color. Most commonly, one sees a fade to (or from) black, and less frequently, a fade to (or from) white or another color. The duration of the transition, and the amount of solid color between the images, can be short or long. Very often a fade-out and fade-in are used back-to-back as a transition from one image to another. In the language of film editing, this technique is frequently used to signal a time ellipsis or to punctuate a major shift in the dramatic direction of the movie. There is a strong sense of closure after a fade-out, and if followed by a fade-in, the audience feels a sense of a new beginning.

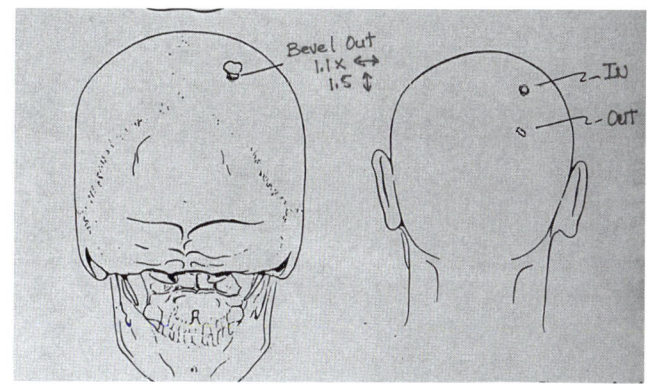
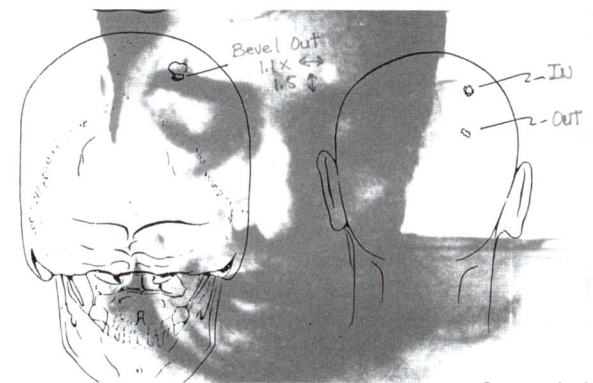
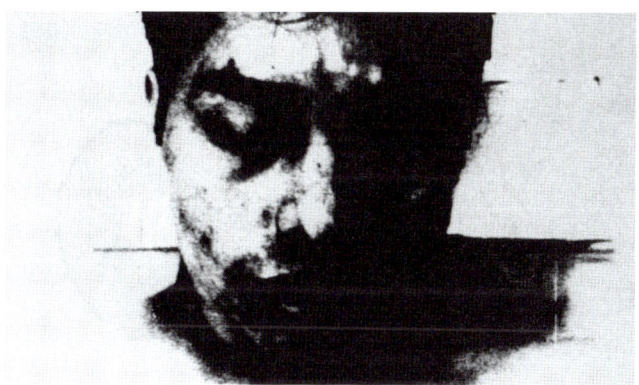

■ **Figure 19.23** This slow dissolve from Errol Morris' *The Thin Blue Line* (1988) takes us from forensic drawings to the morgue photo of a fallen police officer, reminding us that there are real beings behind abstract figures.

CONCLUSION

As we've seen in this chapter, it is in the editing room that documentaries take their true shape. We've looked at a variety of approaches and a broad array of considerations you need to keep in mind as you develop your film. With such a big arsenal, it may be tempting to use as many of the tools mentioned here as you can. But remember it is the story that comes first. It's often said in the editing room that "less is more." Be economical with your editing, and make sure every shot serves your story and moves your film forward. Just remember, putting the right two shots together can take people's breath away. Getting that right will take you a long way.

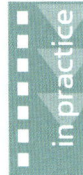

COMBINING IMAGES IN A SINGLE FRAME

Any discussion about the way images work together would be remiss without a consideration of **compositing**. Compositing is the combining of visual elements from separate sources in a single frame. This technique is often used in fiction films, usually for special effects (Superman flying over the city skyline, for example). Compositing is less common in documentary, but there are filmmakers who have explored the possibilities of layering distinct images to create a new, more multiplicitous, film language. One in particular is Edin Velez, who speaks about layering images in Chapter 1. When asked why he began putting images together in his experimental documentaries during the 1980s, he says:

When you look at a painting, you can sort of scan the painting and create your own narrative. You can look at a figure in the foreground, or the background, or the painting as a unit. When I started trying to layer images, it was to try and get away from the tyranny of the single frame, because I thought film and video were so linear. We need to watch one image, followed by another image, and so on. I wanted to try and create a more "interactive" experience. That term didn't quite exist yet, but I wanted to try and create a video screen in which there were a number of different elements that were all moving the story forward. So you could look at the moving image screen, almost as one looks at a painting, and in a weird sense re-edit every scene to your liking. It was about trying to create an alternative film grammar that could tell a linear story with more options.[3]

Figure 19.24 shows how Velez used keyframes and mattes to block out part of each image so it could be layered over or under the other images. While the technical aspects of compositing are beyond the scope of this book, we include an example here because it is a technique that is important to some makers and we want you to be aware that it exists.

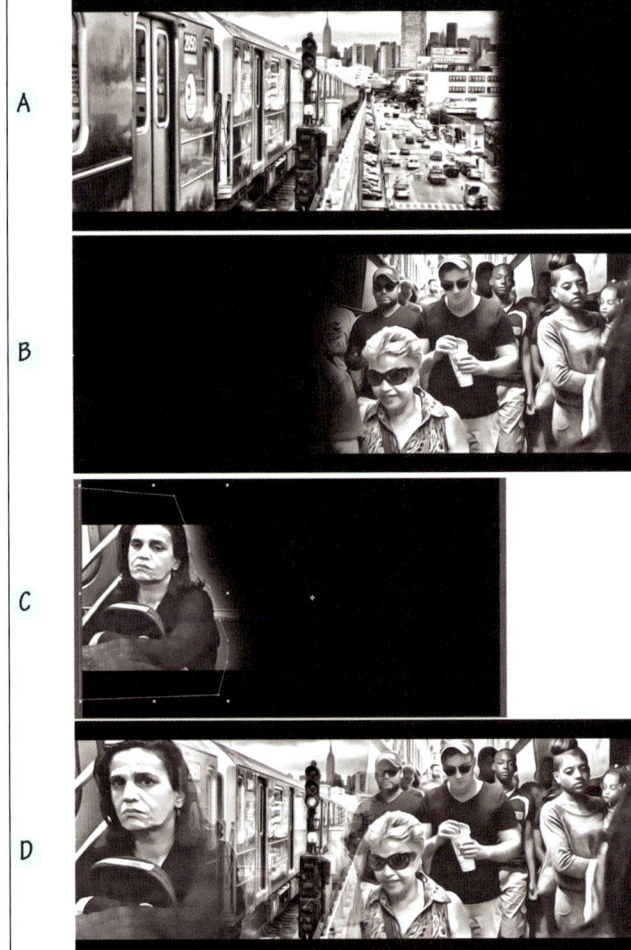

■ Figure 19.24
Compositing in Edin Velez's *State of Rest and Motion* (2015). Images (A), (B), and (C) are separate images that are layered into the final image (D) using mattes. Frame (C) shows the keyframes used to create the matte.

CHAPTER 20

Archival Storytelling

Documentary filmmakers often find themselves using **archival material**: historical footage or stills that someone else produced. This might be moving images shot in film or video, or still images like photographs, newspaper articles, event programs, or court documents. This kind of material can enrich a film, add texture and dimension to our understanding of the events and the period, and provide compelling evidence for the filmmaker's vision and argument. In fact, more than a few documentaries are made using nothing more than archival material. Finding the right archival material can be a daunting task. This chapter will explore some of the reasons for using archival material, and some of the strategies professionals employ for locating it. We will also take a look at the nuts and bolts of how to keep track of archival material, and how and when to obtain legal rights to use archival material in a documentary project.

For archivist and documentary producer Ann Bennett, archival material is integral to documentary storytelling:

> *For me, archival storytelling can take you to a different time or place. It gives context and provides texture. It becomes another voice—it can give any moment, scene, story or entire film a whole different vantage point. Just like your interview subject is your witness, your archival materials are your evidence. They help explain and share what your story is and why it's significant.*[1]

As Bennett suggests, for some films, archival material may play a small role—spice in the stew, as it were. But for other films, archival footage can play a major role.

ARCHIVAL RESEARCH

The first step in beginning to do research is to know what your documentary is really about. This is related the film's **hypothesis** (Chapter 1). It is important to get as specific as you can. Otherwise, your historical footage risks seeming generic, and will add little to the story. As Bennett says,

> *It's important to at least have an idea from the director or producer, of what is the goal for the story, what are the main themes? If you can get at the mission of the film, that will help you as you start to work out your methodology.*

Once you have a clear idea of what your story is and what role archival material plays in it, you can develop a research strategy and start looking for material. While a quick search using an Internet search engine may be a first step, it will only scratch the surface. The next step is to get a real sense of the historical situation you're dealing with, and this requires deeper research and detective work. Who were the major players? Where did the events take place? Who was covering the story at the time? Who or what group was involved or affected by the events? What were the lasting ramifications? Often your local library is a good starting point. Are there good books that deal with the subject you are focusing on in your film? Read the book, or at least the relevant chapters. Definitely look at the bibliography, where you may find the sources of actual photos, documents, or moving images that you may be able to feature in your film. Archival research can be thought of as a spiral or a series of concentric circles, getting both deeper (gathering more detail) and wider (learning new aspects related to your topic) as you explore the territory. You will find yourself constantly returning to older sources armed with new perspectives that can take you closer to your goal.

Your local public library is only the first of a broad spread of public institutions that can be sources for a vast array of material. After the library, you can move on to city and state historical societies, and national collections such as the Library of Congress and the National Archives in Washington DC. The advantage of these archives is that many of their materials will be in the **public domain** (p. 333) and can be used for free. Public university and museum collections can be good sources as well.

Every country has some sort of government archive where scholars, journalists, and documentary filmmakers can conduct research for archival materials. More and more, these collections are available online. One example is the European Film Archives online database (www.filmarchives-online.eu), which focuses on a broad cross section of non-fiction material including documentary and educational films, newsreels, and travelogues from half a dozen European sources including the British Film Institute and sources in Germany, Belgium, Italy, Switzerland, and the Czech Republic. The French Cinématèque (www.cinematheque.fr), started by the legendary archivist Henri Langlois, offers the largest collection of audiovisual media resources in the world. How you access these resources, and what uses of the materials are allowed, varies widely. The US National Archives, for example, is committed to putting a variety of material online that can be downloaded and used in documentaries without paying any rights or having to visit Washington DC. A more comprehensive list of archival sources is included on our companion website (www.routledge.com/cw/Anderson).

In addition to public institutions, there are several major **stock houses** with large collections of archival footage and stills. These are large corporations, such as Corbis and Getty Images, that are in the business of collecting and licensing images. While their collections are large, so are the prices they charge. A producer on a medium- or low-budget documentary will typically try to keep the amount of commercially obtained material to a minimum.

Another significant commercial source will be the archives of television networks and local TV stations. *Trouble the Water* (2008), discussed in Chapter 18 in detail, depended heavily on this sort of material to give a broad historical context to the story of its main characters during and after Hurricane Katrina. This type of material is found by contacting the networks directly, and it can also be very pricey.

The third important group of archive sources are nongovernmental cultural institutions, such as art museums, historical societies, private universities, and special collections focused on particular content areas. These include collections such as the Walter P. Reuther Labor Library and Archive, housed at Wayne State University in Detroit, the GLBT Historical Society in San Francisco, and the Film Stills Archive at the Museum of Modern Art.

While newspapers are commercial enterprises, their back issues can often be accessed through libraries and through online databases such as Lexis Nexis. Large newspapers like the *New York Times* are obvious resources, but local newspapers, the community press, and even defunct publications can offer material that is sometimes more relevant to the events you're researching.

While any research should include these types of sources, it is important to remember that for the particular story you are telling there often exists a trove of valuable historical material found in personal archives like family photo albums, vacation videos, ephemera, or other documents or objects. Local institutions, such as schools, churches, and community centers, may have their own archival collections as well. These unofficial sources, exactly because their contents never been seen before in a film, will have greater impact than footage that has been in a dozen other documentaries.

It's critically important to look at other films on your subject. You may want to actually license some of their footage (or **outtakes**) for your own film. More often, you will see what archival material they found, and can consult the list of archives in their end credits to get a sense of where you might go to find what you need.

Talk to Somebody!

Another key aspect of doing research is to actually engage with people face-to-face. While online search engines can do a great job, they can never suggest lines of inquiry you haven't thought of, and they will never ask you follow-up questions. A librarian, an archivist, a scholar in the field, or even a neighborhood resident or unofficial community historian can suggest routes to imagery (not to mention potential interview subjects and more). The knowledge actual people have may extend way beyond the limited information on a catalogue entry. Much archival material is also in **lots** or boxes with only the vaguest of references to what they contain (Figure 20.1). Often the librarian is the person who knows what the archive holds beyond the bare catalog descriptions, and speaking with her can open doors to visual evidence and information that speak to the heart of your story.

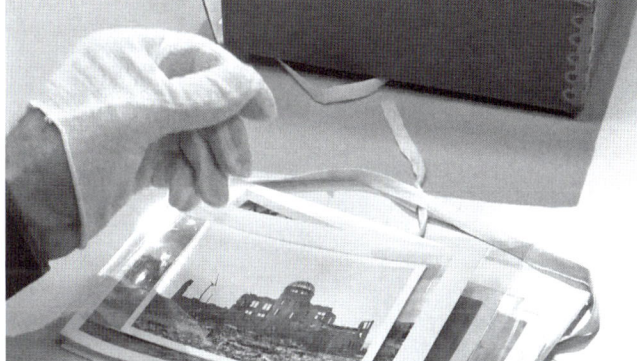

■ Figure 20.1 Coauthor Martin Lucas doing archival research at the International Center of Photography for his historical documentary *Hiroshima Bound* (2015).

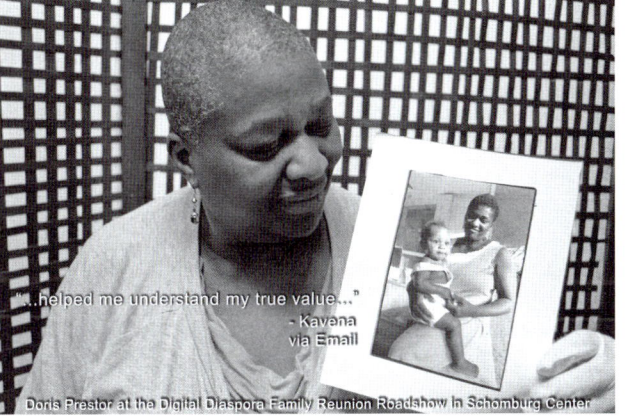

■ Figure 20.2 This image from the Digital Diaspora Family Reunion event, held at the Schomburg Center for Research on Black Culture in New York, suggests the value of the "crowdsourced" archival approach used by the *Through a Lens Darkly* team. Photo by Natalie Shmuel for Digital Diaspora Family Reunion, LLC

WAYS OF USING ARCHIVAL MATERIAL

Documentary films use archival material for a variety of reasons. Probably the most common is that archival materials—whether still images, documents, moving images, or audio—provide visual evidence to back up your storytelling goals. This combination of visual imagery from archival sources and a knowledgeable narration is the "bread and butter" of many historical docs.

But history is not fixed, and in fact is constantly being rethought, reevaluated, and recontextualized. Documentary films are often at the forefront of debates about the meaning and significance of historical events. In a strategy that uses humor to devastating effect,

GETTING CREATIVE WITH ARCHIVAL RESEARCH

In the Trenches with Archivist and Producer Ann Bennett

Ann Bennett has done archival research and producing for more than a dozen documentaries, including *Soul Food Junkies* (Byron Hurt, 2012), *Africans in America* (WGBH, 2008), and *People like Us: Class in America* (Center for New American Media, 2001).

We talked with her about her work on *Through a Lens Darkly: Black Photographers and the Emergence of a People* (2014), directed by Thomas Allan Harris (Bennett was also a producer on the film). *Through a Lens Darkly* explores the role of photography in helping to shape the identity of African-Americans from the time of slavery to the present. Based in part on the pioneering work of Deborah Willis, particularly her book on black photographers, *Reflections in Black*, the film is built around a rich history of hidden and forgotten images. It complements these images with interviews with important African-American visual artists including Carrie Mae Weems and Lorna Simpson.

Bennett says there were several important lessons learned during the process. One was the value of a **crowdsourcing** approach to find images and documents that have never found their way into an official archive.

> As we began research, we found that black photographic content within mainstream institutions was sometimes nonexistent, very inconsistent, and certainly not as thorough as we would have liked. But we knew that within black communities, in addition to having a black doctor, mortician or business leaders, there was always a photographer. And even people with modest means had photographs taken. So you have to go to the people who actually commissioned work from those photographers, and say, "Do you have a photograph of when you were in school?" "Do you have wedding photographs? Births? Funerals?" That's how we started the Digital Diaspora Family Reunion project (http://1world1family.me/category/tald/). We realized we had to take another tack and speak to individual scholars and librarians and community members who were helping us tell our story anyway, and ask, "Are there images that could help us understand this story?" The people who have images are very proud of them, so once you put the word out, people will come to you. When we did our first event in Atlanta, there was one woman who literally came in with a steamer trunk full of photographs![2]

While many documentary films have a website, for *Through a Lens Darkly* this actually meant creating an Internet-based archive that has a life independent of the film. And as Bennett suggests, it has meant not just putting the word out, but doing events including a Digital Diaspora Family Reunion Roadshow in Atlanta, GA. Director Harris projected scans of the photographs that people had brought to the event, and audience members reacted with their own insights and observations (Figure 20.2). While involving the public in this way is unusual, it was essential for creating an archive of images that otherwise might never have been seen and shared. And it certainly provided rich visual evidence for the film.

Doing Thorough Research

According to Bennett, one key to finding great archival material is to strive to know your story intimately, and to keep thinking imaginatively about your search. For Catherine Arnaud's film *Sidney Poitier, an Outsider in Hollywood* (2008), Bennett was able to locate an image of the actor Sidney Poitier and singer Harry Belafonte delivering bail money for jailed marchers in the Selma civil rights marches of 1965, led by Martin Luther King (Figure 20.3):

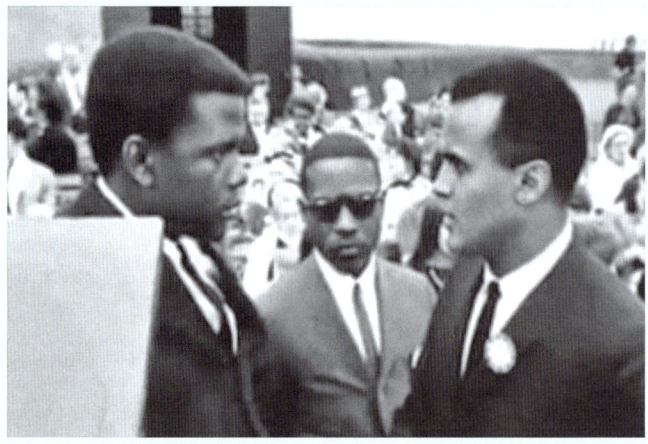

■ **Figure 20.3** Sidney Poitier and Harry Belafonte in *Sidney Poitier: An Outsider in Hollywood*.

> The producers were looking for images from this event where Poitier and Belafonte had gone down South to deliver some bail money. The filmmakers knew that Poitier and Belafonte had given a press conference right before or after they had come from delivering the bail, but they couldn't find any visual material. The only way I was able to identify it was by going to a written history of the civil rights movement, and I found a written history of the civil rights movement, and I found a reference to Poitier and Belafonte going to deliver this money. It was a 1,000 page book, but in it I was able to find the details of the date, the location and the airport where

they'd given the press conference. Only then was I able to go to NBC and find the footage. So it's all about knowing your story and your subjects thoroughly. That will help inform you when you have to broaden your search and to really dig deep.[3]

Thinking Historically about Categories

When thinking about archival footage, it's essential that you understand the people, places, and events in their historical context. Sometimes the names by which events are known today are not what people called them at the time. The same is true for social categories. For example, before the 1930s, the term "unemployment" was not a social category. People would be termed "without means of support" or perhaps "jobless." So a search for images of the unemployed from an earlier era should reflect the categories of the period. This means putting your own mind back into another era. As Ann Bennett explains:

Oftentimes what you're looking for may not be listed under the name of the event as it's become known. Now we have the "March on Washington" or "Watergate" or the "Tet Offensive." But they didn't have titles when they happened! We were looking for content to help us illustrate black LGBT culture for Through a Lens Darkly and I found, at the Drama Library at Yale, they had a collection of African-American culture, and within that there was a small vaudeville collection. In this collection there is all of this amazing stuff of different acts, but a good chunk of those acts were drag acts, material from the '20s, '30s and '40s. It wasn't just one guy in a dress—there was a lot of material! Finding that really informed all these other searches for things that we now call "gender and identity." It's been there all along, but it just wasn't categorized as such.[4]

Jayne Loader and Kevin and Pierce Rafferty's *Atomic Cafe* (1982) repurposes educational and propaganda material from the Cold War to paint a compelling and darkly funny picture of a nation caught up in a "nuclear fever" that needs to be experienced to be believed. Burt the Turtle, in order to train children to crawl under their desks as soon as they see the bright light of an Atomic blast, demonstrates how he ducks and safely covers himself inside his shell whenever a firecracker explodes nearby (Figure 20.4). The framing of this cartoon with footage showing the terrible devastation of the bombing of Hiroshima shows the vast gap between the dangers of nuclear technology and the way it was framed for the public. The film helped define a genre characterized by its appropriation and repurposing of archival material for social commentary. It also contributed to a contemporary dialogue about national priorities during the Reagan Era.

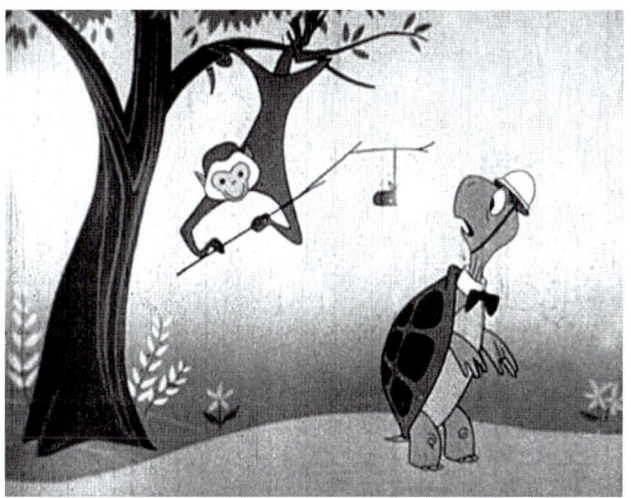

■ **Figure 20.4** *Atomic Cafe* repurposes an archival Civil Defense film to ironic effect.

Some filmmakers have used archival material to explore the complex links between collective history and personal memory. An example is Rea Tajiri's *History and Memory: For Akiko and Takashige* (1991), a personal essay about the Japanese-American internment during World War II. The film uses footage of the Pearl Harbor attack from the fiction film *From Here to Eternity* (1953) to launch a complex narrative that counterposes national wartime jingoism with the traumatized silence of her own family in the postwar era, creating a critique of an American society that implicitly condones a racist policy. In the film, she finds government footage of internment

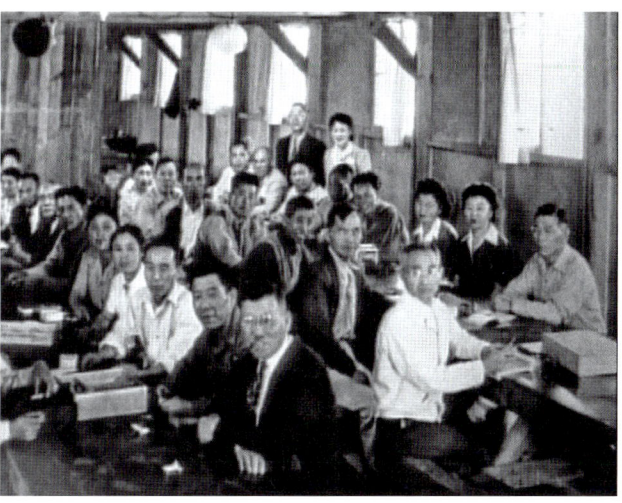

■ **Figure 20.5** This archival still from the National Archives, featured in the documentary *History and Memory: For Akiko and Takashige*, shows interned Japanese-Americans including filmmaker Rea Tajiri's grandmother.

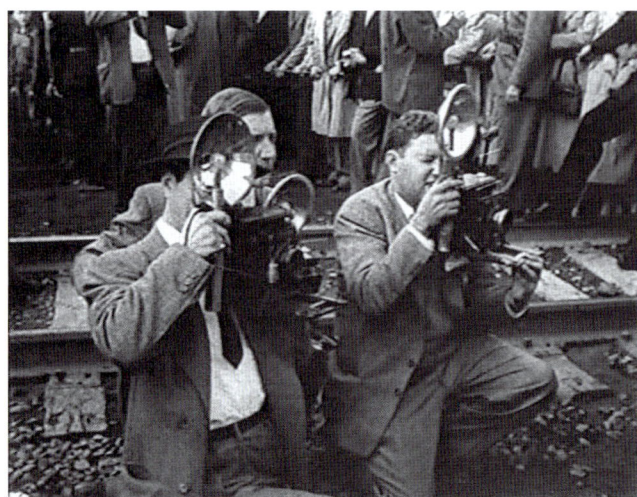

camps and even discovers a wide shot of a crafts class at Manzanar Camp that shows her own grandmother painting a carved bird that her mother had saved in her jewelry box for decades (Figure 20.5).

Metaphorical Imagery

Sometimes the relationship of archival imagery to your story is completely metaphorical. In Alan Berliner's film *Nobody's Business* (1996), about his father Oscar Berliner, we hear Oscar telling Alan, "I'm nobody. I'm just a regular person." This argument over whether Oscar's story is worth telling is one of the central themes of the hour-long documentary, and the images reflect this tension. We see black-and-white archival footage of a press conference, where photographers are taking pictures of people who presumably matter more than a "regular guy" like Oscar Berliner. In another scene, Alan and Oscar are heard sparring over whether Alan should make a film at all. We hear the starting bell for a boxing match, and see an old black-and-white film of a fight (Figure 20.6). These images are not of Alan and his father. Rather, they are metaphorical images that ask the audience to open up an active space for reflection about not only the relationships in the film, but documentary truth itself.

ORGANIZING YOUR MATERIAL

The advent of digital archives, where material can be searched online and even downloaded straight to your edit suite, has big advantages for filmmakers. It has presented a couple of big problems as well, however.

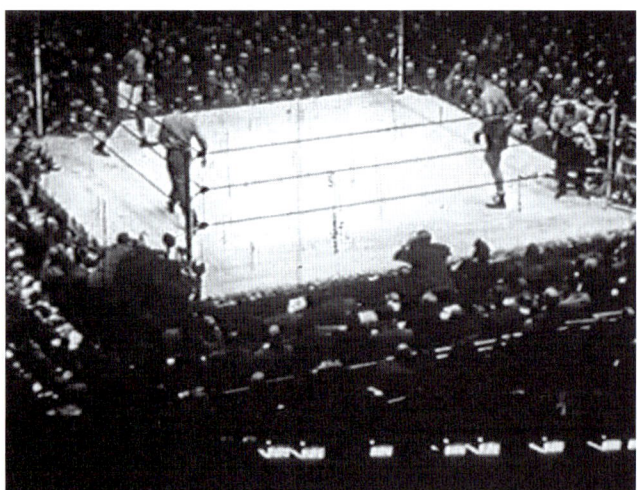

■ Figure 20.6
Archival images act as visual metaphor in *Nobody's Business*.

One of them is that it is incredibly tempting to pull images off the web and put them in your cut without knowing or worrying too much about where they originated. This separation of content from context is of concern for anyone who is interested in reality-based storytelling. To start with, an image may not be what it purports to be. A photograph identified as being from one battle may be from another, or even a complete fake. The other problem is that you can have a great image, but no idea whether you have rights to use it (p. 331). The best solution is to keep careful track of where you obtain images, and what their **provenance** is.

An additional problem is that you may end up with several versions of an image. Typically, archives and stock houses will have "screener" versions of material, either in low resolution or sporting a **watermark** (like the company's logo). It's common for the editor to use this temporary material until picture lock. At that point, though, you will need to know where to go for the high-quality versions of the images you've been using. In addition, you will need to develop a clear sense of which images you must pay for. Sometimes it takes a fair bit of research just to locate the rights holder, and it always takes time to negotiate licensing. If you are on a tight deadline for a festival or broadcast, be sure to start this process very early. You also need to keep careful paperwork, image by image, so that when you go to a broadcaster or distributor, you can prove that you own the rights to all the images in your film.

A good practice is to create a database of some kind for your images. This can be very basic, like a spreadsheet with columns for source, description, provenance, file type, image quality, etc., or you can use database software, such as Filemaker Pro or OpenOffice.

Using Metadata

One organizational tool you should be familiar with, especially for still images and audio files, is **metadata**. Metadata can include copyright info, what website you got the image or sound from, and more. Typical software such as Photoshop for images and Audacity for sound files make it easy to add such information. Having the data in the file gives you an easy way to keep track of an image's source. At present, it is more difficult to embed metadata in moving image files, but that is likely to change in the near future. Moving image files will always have some basic information imbedded in them, such as the format and the creation date. In Premiere Pro, you can add metadata in the Extensible Metadata Platform (XMP) format on a Metadata Panel (Figure 20.7).

For still images, it's a good idea to assign each image a number that is unique. In other words, NEVER give two images the same identification number or file name! Depending on how many images you are working with, you may decide to give each category of images a certain numerical range. For example, everything from one geographical area could have a number between 1000 and 1999, while material from somewhere else could start at 2000. When you import the images into your NLE, you can create keywords and categories in the project window that can help you find things easily.

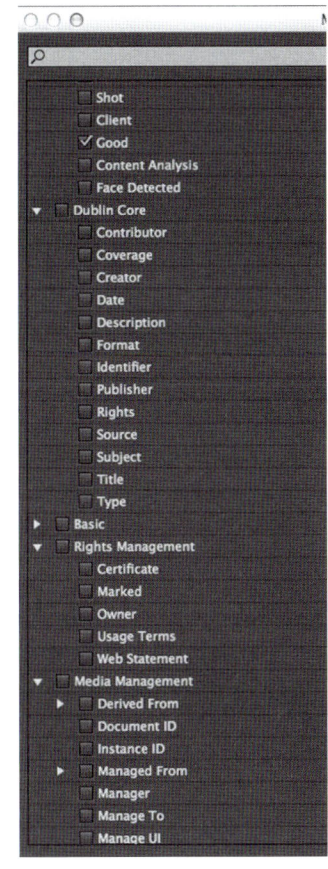

■ **Figure 20.7** The metadata logging panel from Premiere Pro.

WHO OWNS AN IMAGE? COPYRIGHT AND FAIR USE

While the topic of ownership of creative work and intellectual property is a complex one, here are some helpful guidelines that will help you negotiate this difficult terrain. The key is that intellectual property is protected by **copyright**. Copyright laws vary from country to country, but in all cases they ensure that the owner of the copyright has rights to determine where the image can be seen and especially into which works it can be incorporated. If you want to use a copyrighted image in your film, you will likely need their permission. You obtain these rights by **licensing** the image or footage in question. Music rights are another story and will be dealt with separately in Chapter 21. If you don't secure the rights, you risk at the very least a "cease and desist" letter from a lawyer, not to mention a lawsuit. In either case, you will end up going back to the editing room to change a film you thought was done.

As discussed in Chapter 5, though, our society is also based on the idea that culture is a shared field, a common patrimony that artists can draw on. This balance is achieved legally through **fair use doctrine**, which limits copyright in certain contexts. The complete ins and outs of fair use are outside the scope of this book, but the basic idea is that even copyrighted material can be used in a documentary under certain circumstances. These conditions are far from a blanket permission, and need to be examined carefully.

The Center for Media and Social Impact (CMSI) at American University has for many years been a key institution in developing a clear understanding of what fair use means in the context of documentary filmmaking.

CMSI's *Documentary Filmmakers' Statement of Best Practices in Fair Use* lists four main categories that could qualify your use as fair use[5]:

Category 1: Employing Copyrighted Material as the Object of Social, Political, or Cultural Critique

This class of uses involves situations in which documentarians engage in media critique, whether of text, image, or sound works. In these cases, documentarians hold the specific copyrighted work up for analysis.

Category 2: Quoting Copyrighted Works of Popular Culture to Illustrate an Argument of Point

Here the concern is with material (again, of whatever kind) that is quoted not because it is, in itself, the object of critique but because it aptly illustrates some argument or point that a filmmaker is developing—as clips from fiction films might be used (for example) to demonstrate changing American attitudes toward race.

Category 3: Capturing Copyrighted Media Content in the Process of Filming Something Else

Documentarians often record copyrighted sounds and images when they are filming in real-life settings. Common examples are a poster on a wall, music playing on a radio, and television programming heard (and perhaps seen) in the background. In the context of documentary, the incidentally captured material is an integral part of the ordinary reality being documented. Filmmakers argue that only by altering and thus falsifying the reality they film—for example by telling subjects to turn off the radio, take down a poster, or turn off the TV—could they avoid using this protected material.

Category 4: Using Copyrighted Material in a Historical Sequence

In many cases the best (or even only) effective way to tell a particular historical story or make a historical point is to make selective use of words that were spoken during the events in question, music that was associated with the events, or photographs and films that were taken at that time.

These categories offer legal protection but, like all laws, are subject to interpretation. In general the first two categories are stronger, meaning that if taken to court you are more likely to win than if you are relying on the last two categories. If you have a popular song playing in the background of a scene, you may have a hard time convincing a court that you have rights to leave it in if you could have asked the subjects to turn off the radio. Clips from movies, news footage, and music are most likely to present problems for a fair use argument.

Even if you meet one or more of these categories of use, the courts will still consider the *nature* of the use. This refers to how much your use will impact the value of the original. If you are taking "the heart," or most important part of the work, this will weigh against fair use. Finally, it's important that you use *as little of the copyrighted work as is absolutely necessary* to make your point. If using 5 seconds of an image or sound will suffice, don't use 7 or 10.

Because fair use is so integral to so many documentaries, it is essential that documentary filmmakers become familiar with **best practices** in this area. As attorney and producer Andrew Lund says,

> *Legal issues aren't separate from filmmaking. Just as it's important to understand cameras and lenses, documentary producers should have a strong grasp of the legal aspects of copyright and fair use so they can incorporate this knowledge into every stage of production and make smart, informed choices.*[6]

Lund makes the point that every filmmaker should be familiar with CMSI's *Documentary Filmmakers' Statement of Best Practices in Fair Use*. Why? If you are well-versed in these common practices, you will make more informed choices throughout preproduction and production instead of just confronting rights issues in postproduction. Also, if you do consult with an entertainment attorney when you are in postproduction and trying to resolve your rights issues, you will make a good impression and save yourself some money by having done much of the preparation for the legal work. Finally, fair use is based on legal precedent, and in making decisions the courts consider standard industry practice. So by being informed of the best practices and following them yourself, you are actually contributing to shaping the law so that it is more responsive to the needs of documentary filmmakers!

There is an extremely limited analogue to fair use in the United Kingdom and many Commonwealth countries called "fair dealing." Its application is narrower in scope and it varies from country to country, but generally it allows for some use of copyrighted material for review, research, or news reporting as well as parody and satire. The EU has, in the form of the European Copyright Directive, similar protections. In the United Kingdom, one useful source of information and discussion can be found at www.own-it.org, which offers "intellectual property advice for the creative sector."[7]

Public Domain Materials

Fortunately, many images are in the **public domain**, which means they can be used without clearance. The public domain includes images and footage that are out of copyright either because of their age or because they were created before copyright existed. In addition, images that were created by public institutions are in the public domain. Thus material produced by the government is considered to be free for use (although specific institutions may impose their own restrictions). For instance, in *History and Memory*, Tajiri uses archival material produced by the US government for wartime propaganda purposes (Figure 20.8). Since it was made by the government with taxpayers' money, anyone can access it and put it in a film. This area is obviously of great interest to filmmakers, and it includes material located in some of the nation's biggest collections, such as the US National Archives and the Library of Congress.

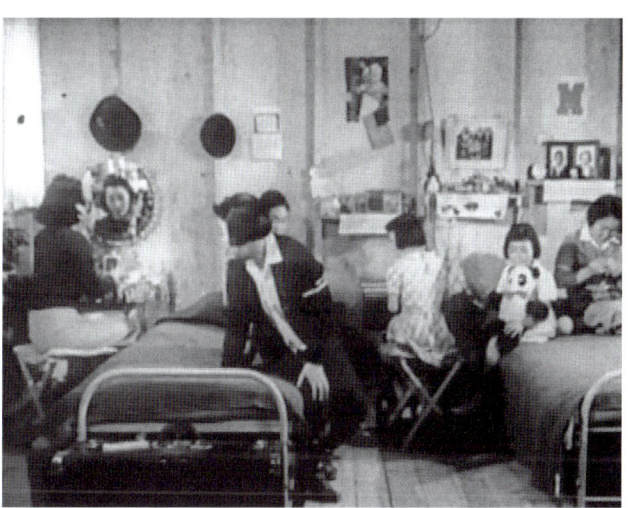

■ **Figure 20.8** This image of interned Japanese Americans taken from a 1944 propaganda film produced by the Office of War Information is in the public domain, and used in *History and Memory: For Akiko and Takashige*.

Clearing Rights

If you are planning to use material that may be covered by copyright, then you will need to license it. There are different approaches, including **royalty-free**, which means that you pay a flat one-time fee. Certain clip art or stock shot libraries may also fall into this category, as well as needle-drop music libraries (Chapter 21). A **rights-managed** approach means that you pay for rights that may be restricted by time (a certain number of years) or platform (broadcast, theatrical) or market (national, international).

It's important not to leave clearance to the last minute. Often, beginning filmmakers will throw anything and everything into their film, with the assumption that they will clear the rights when they need to. This is a dangerous practice, because once your film is finished and mastered, it will be expensive and time-consuming to go back into postproduction just because you got a broadcast or other distribution deal. Also, it's much easier to clear rights before your film has become a success and you have been offered a distribution deal. At that point, your negotiating power with the right holders is much weaker than it would have been at an earlier stage.

CREATIVE COMMONS: AN ALTERNATIVE TO COPYRIGHT

For filmmakers who see the creative space as a shared one, there are several alternatives to copyright with its "all-or-nothing" approach to intellectual property protection. The most popular of these is **Creative Commons** (Figure 20.9). Creative Commons is a licensing system that offers a variety of options for creators. Licensing your work is easy. As a maker, you decide first whether you will allow for commercial or noncommercial use. Next, you will decide if you allow **derivative work**, which means uses where someone incorporates your work into their new one.

If the alternative licensing movement has a guru, it is Larry Lessig, who as a founder of Creative Commons is a strong believer in a culture where creativity and innovation flourish in an environment where there is a healthy interchange of ideas and creative potential.[9] One of the outcomes of this movement is an acknowledgment of a need for a "commons," a space where media of all sorts can be seen and shared freely. Sites like Flickr Commons (www.flickr.com/commons) contain user-uploaded images with Creative Commons licenses, as well as images in the public domain (Figure 20.10). The ease of use and large size of the collection makes this a good first stop if you are looking for pictures of something you can't shoot yourself.

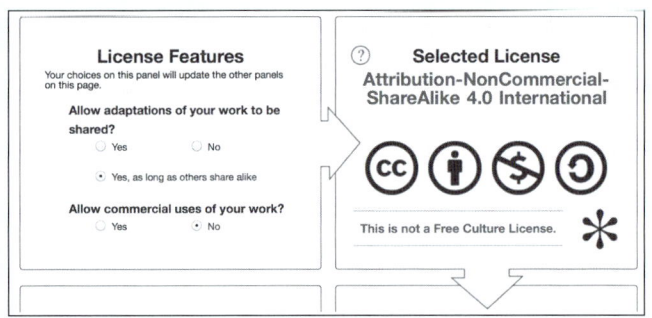

■ **Figure 20.9** The license-generating feature of creativecommons.org walks the maker through a series of simple choices to generate an appropriate license for your work.

Other sites like www.europeana.eu and Wikimedia Commons (www.commons.wikimedia.org) offer searchable databases of large numbers of images as well, along with clear indications of how you can use them. While these won't solve every need, they offer a good starting place for any documentary maker who needs to offer viewers representations of other times and places.

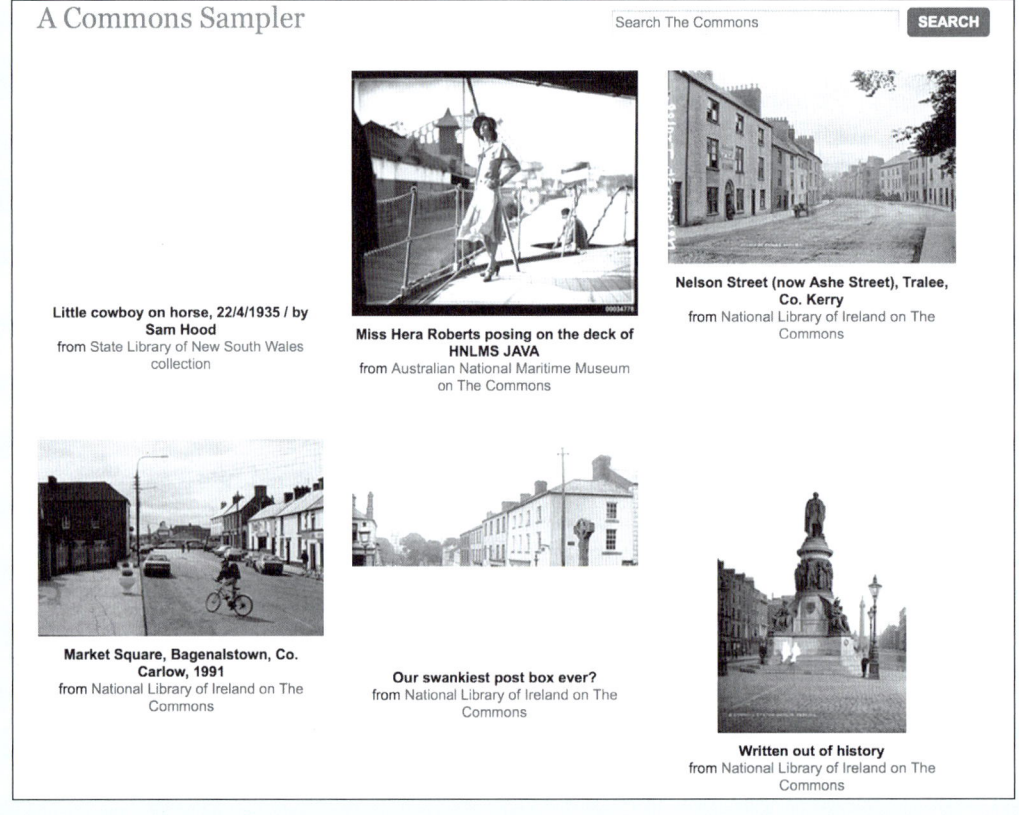

■ **Figure 20.10** Flickr Commons has over time become a repository for a wide variety of photos from around the world. Here we see historical images from Australian and Irish collections.

A good general guide to the complexities of this area can be found in Sheila Curran Bernard and Kenn Rabin's *Archival Storytelling: A Filmmaker's Guide to Finding, Using, and Licensing Third Party Visuals and Music*.[8]

As with all legal situations, we suggest consulting an attorney who specializes in rights clearances for media.

THE ETHICS OF USING ARCHIVAL MATERIAL

The ethics of using archival material is a complex question, and some of the issues are dealt with separately in Chapter 5. When you use an image from the past, you are creating an entirely new context for someone with whom you can't consult. As such, you bear some responsibility for their historical legacy. One film that deals with this issue directly is Elizabeth Barret's *Stranger with a Camera* (2000). Images of poor coal miners in the Appalachians were used by everyone from CBS to the BBC to President Johnson to illustrate poverty. The film discusses the complexity of using real people as evidence for political arguments. As Barret says, "The media companies mined the images the way the coal companies mined the coal." Does this mean we should never use archival imagery? Obviously not, but each filmmaker has to make a moral choice based on being fair to the subjects, and to the truth as they see it.

Another issue is accuracy. When you are talking about New York in the 1920s and you show archival material, it should really be New York, and not Philadelphia, and it should really be the 1920s, and not the '30s or '40s.

Another issue is whether or not you are obligated to identify archival material for viewers. As in other aspects of filmmaking ethics, people have a variety of approaches. In television news, it is standard procedure to identify the source of archival material. The WGBH public affairs program *Frontline*, on the other hand, suggests that it is not necessary to identify "non-original" material on screen unless doing so helps a viewer better understand the communication.[10]

Some documentary filmmakers take a completely different approach to using archival material. When Alan Berliner cut to a shot of a 1950s boxing ring in *Nobody's Business*, the ring is metaphorical, representing father–son conflict, and has no reference to a real match. On the other hand, when he cuts to a photo of a guy clowning in front of a microphone from the same era, it turns out to be a real photo of his father and we understand it as such. But anyone watching Berliner's film has a clear idea from the outset that they will be getting this more open, less literal, approach to archival materials.

TECHNICAL ISSUES

Another issue with using archival material has to do with the technical side. The gold standard for image quality is to have access to the original image, but this isn't always possible. If you can access an original photograph, you can scan it at a high resolution. How high is enough? The standard image resolution for anything on screen is 72 dpi or 72 pixels per inch. If you scan at double that, say 150 dpi, you will be able to digitally "zoom in" on the image digitally up to 50 percent of its original size without degradation. Another way to think of this is that a standard HD image is 1920 pixels across. If you want your image to fill the screen, then you need to scan it so that it has similar pixel width. For example, let's say you have a small passport photo of someone that you'd like in the film. The photograph may only be 2 inches high. You need to think how big you'd like this to appear on screen. If you want it to fill the frame, which is 1080 pixels high, you will need to scan the image at 500 dpi (2 inches x 500 pixels = 1000 pixels, or approximately the height of the screen).

You should be particularly wary of images or footage downloaded from the Internet. It is very easy to find material there that will not stand up in the context of a film. The overly pixilated look of low-resolution digital imagery will give your documentary an amateurish appearance you should strive to avoid. This, along with the difficulty of sourcing images online, means you should try to stick to known archival sources, or do as Ann Bennett and Thomas Allan Harris did and find your own!

Another issue that arises with archival materials is that of **aspect ratio** (Chapter 7). The difference between standard 4:3 aspect ratio, which is typical of archival film and SD NTSC video, and modern 16 x 9 screens presents another problem because the 4:3 image isn't wide enough to fill the sides of the 16 x 9 frame. One solution is to blow up the 4:3 image, cutting off the top and bottom, but sacrificing information and image resolution. Another is to **letterbox** your image, filling the empty edges of the frame with black (Figure 20.11). Doing this signals to viewers that they are seeing historical footage, and maintains image resolution that can be lost in a "blow up."

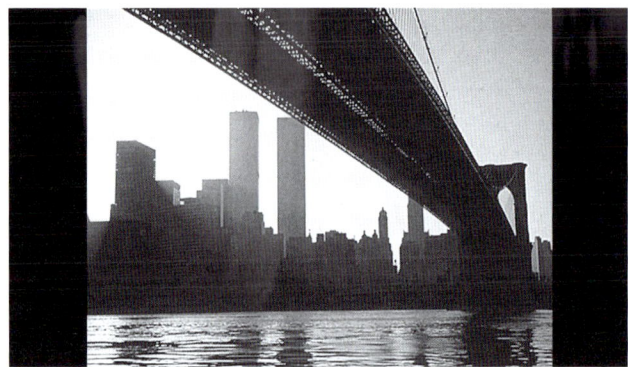

■ **Figure 20.11** Using letterboxing to integrate 4:3 archival material into a 16 x 9 frame.

DOCUMENTS

Archival material isn't just still and moving images and audio. It can consist of a variety of types of documents and **ephemera. Ephemera** is material that was originally thought of as something disposable, whether a greeting card, an advertisement, or a fruit box label.

When Ken Burns, whose documentary storytelling is based extensively on the use of archival materials, made his PBS historical documentary *The Civil War* (1990), one of the things that gave it a unique flavor was his use of original documents of all kinds (Figure 20.12). A good example is a letter home from a Union soldier, Sullivan Ballou:

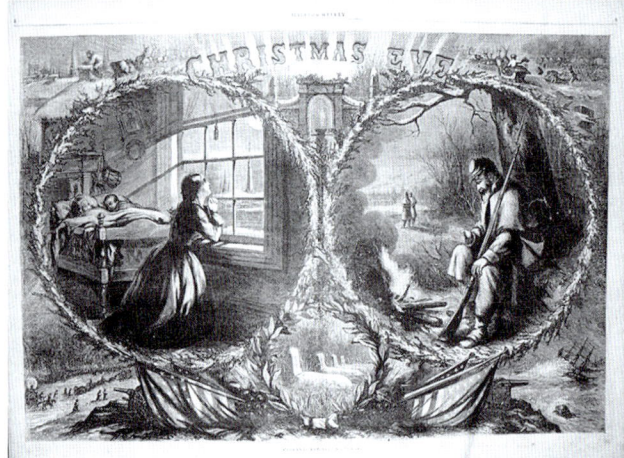

■ **Figure 20.12** Ken Burns used letters, photos, and illustrations from popular magazines like this Thomas Nast illustration from *Harper's Magazine* to give a rich sense of how the Civil War impacted daily life.

July 14, 1861
Camp Clark, Washington

My very dear Sarah:

The indications are very strong that we shall move in a few days—perhaps tomorrow. Lest I should not be able to write again, I feel impelled to write a few lines that may fall under your eye when I shall be no more . . .

I have no misgivings about, or lack of confidence in the cause in which I am engaged, and my courage does not halt or falter. I know how strongly American Civilization now leans on the triumph of the Government and how great a debt we owe to those who went before us through the blood and sufferings of the Revolution. And I am willing—perfectly willing—to lay down all my joys in this life, to help maintain this Government, and to pay that debt . . .

At the time of the Civil War, photography was in its infancy, and sound recording nonexistent. But Burns made a virtue of necessity by emphasizing the voices of the otherwise voiceless: ordinary citizens who fought and died.

Other types of documents such as maps, deeds, licenses, and reports can also play a role in your documentary. In Errol Morris's *The Thin Blue Line* (1989), a broad variety of documents appear in microscopic focus. While no single one of them is remarkable, the overall deluge of minutia gives the film an unmistakable visual style and serves the director's goals of raising questions about the veracity of evidence itself (Figure 20.13).

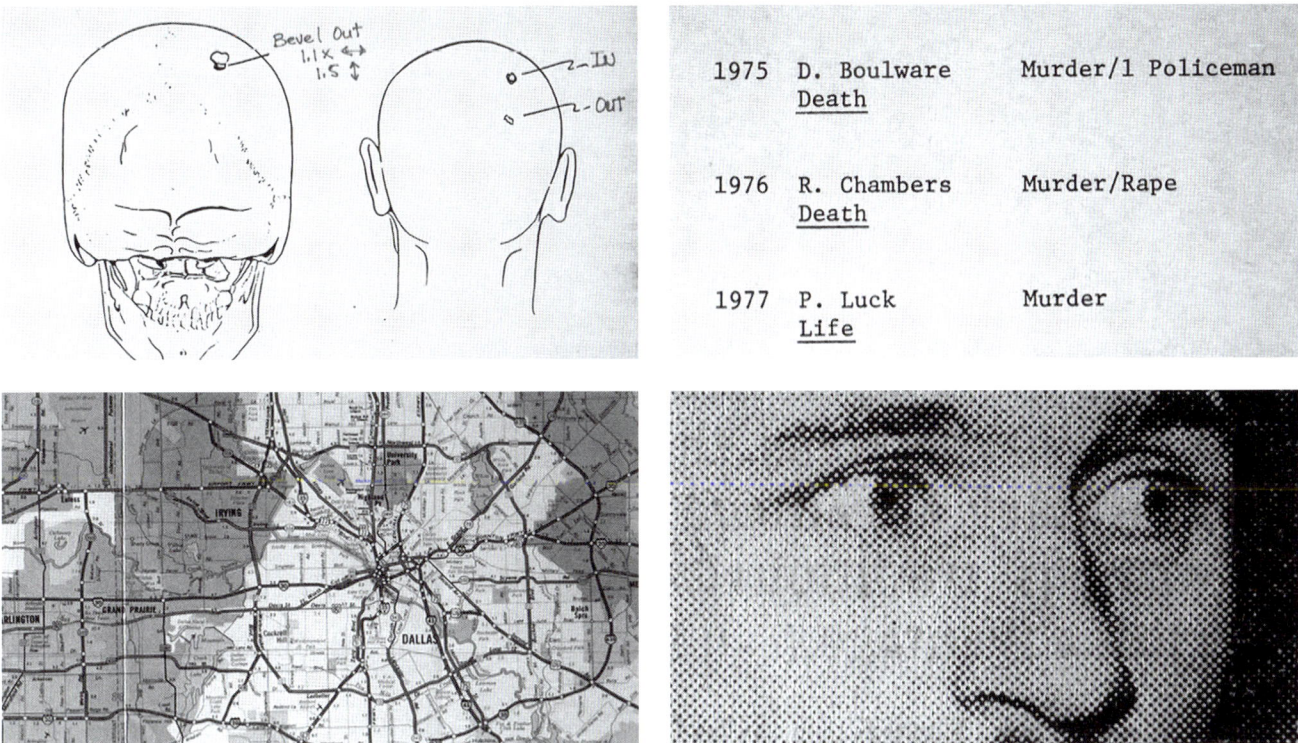

■ **Figure 20.13** In *The Thin Blue Line*, Errol Morris mixes court documents with extreme close-ups of newspaper clippings, and even an ordinary road map, to give the search for the facts about the murder of a Dallas police officer a haunting flavor that challenges the audience's assumptions about the nature of evidence.

CONCLUSION

This chapter can only offer a short overview of the vital subject of archival materials for documentary filmmaking. Just remember that thoughtful research and deft storytelling can enrich your own sense of your subject, and add a lot to the viewer's experience of your film without necessarily being a major drag on your budget. Also keep in mind that, while the number of online sources grows daily, going out and doing your own image research always pays off in unexpected ways.

CHAPTER 21

Sound Design and Finishing

Before the 1930s, documentaries—like all films—were a fundamentally *visual* art form, with images providing the entire narrative experience. Films like Robert Flaherty's *Nanook of the North* (1922) and Dziga Vertov's *Man with a Movie Camera* (1929) were silent, and sound was incorporated almost exclusively in the form of live musical accompaniment played during the screenings. The films made under John Grierson at the Empire Marketing Board were among the first documentaries to include sound in the form of **narration**, **music**, and **ambience**, often to creative effect. *Song of Ceylon* (1935, Dir. Basil Wright), about the Ceylonese tea trade, begins with images of people and places in Ceylon (now Sri Lanka) (Figure 21.1). Over them, the viewer hears Sri Lankan folk music, commentary from a 1680 travel book written by Robert Knox, and ambient sounds (children's voices, women pounding rice, and so on). Even in this early film, the directors used sounds to add additional meaning.

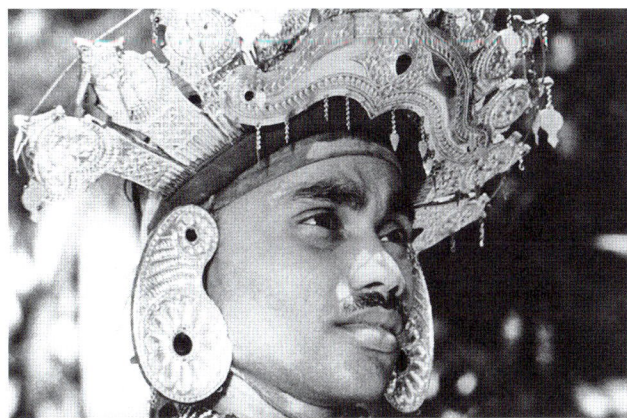

■ **Figure 21.1** The soundtrack of *Song of Ceylon* makes extensive use of multiple sound sources recorded on location, combined with a studio score and an evocative voice-over to help create a lyrical and impressionistic sense of Sri Lankan culture and society.

Towards the end of the film, we begin to hear market quotations of tea prices, telephone orders, invoices, and mail inquiries. As Erik Barnouw wrote, "The overriding impression is of commerce intruding on a lovely, age-old environment."[1] That same year, *Housing Problems* (1935, Dirs. Edgar Anstey and Arthur Elton) gave audiences a first taste of sync sound as slum-dwellers spoke for themselves about their decrepit living conditions. The four sound elements found in these early films—*music*, *narration*, *sound effects*, and *dialogue*—still form the basis of much sound design today.

Sound design refers to the final form of a film's total aural impression. Whether you are cutting to only a single music track, or layering 16 or 32 tracks of audio, there is virtually no end to the contributions a well-crafted sound design can bring to a documentary. Sound can establish a tone or mood with unmatchable nuance, and it can vividly signal the legitimacy and emotional impression of a location. Sound is able to bring dramatic emphasis to actions or details inside or outside of the frame. Sound can, in fact, create entire worlds off-screen. Sound can contribute to establishing a character's point of view, even to the point of reflecting their particular psychology. In short, sound is an essential storytelling component that deserves considerable attention throughout all phases of the documentary filmmaking process.

The creative manipulation, placement, layering, enhancing, composing, juxtaposing, and mixing of the various sound elements that comprise the sound design is done in the postproduction stage. As you gather and lay down your sound elements, you should place them on different audio tracks, keeping each type separate and distinct from the others. For example, you might have three or four audio tracks for your sync sound, a fifth and sixth track for the music (which is typically stereo), another track or two for sound effects, and another for **ambient sound** (also called **backgrounds**). Taken as a whole, all of these audio tracks and the way they are mixed together comprise the sound design.

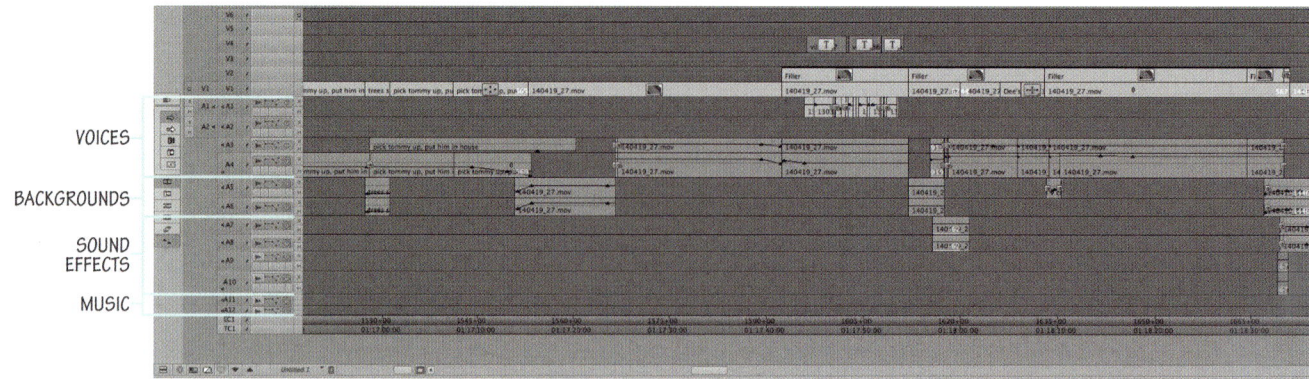

■ **Figure 21.2** The timeline from a scene in *Care*, showing the layering of audio tracks to build the sound design. Tracks 1–4 contain voices (dialogue, interviews, narration); Tracks 5 and 6 contain backgrounds; Tracks 7–10 contain sound effects; Tracks 11 and 12 contain music.

Figure 21.2 shows the NLE timeline from a scene in Deirdre Fishel's documentary *Care* (2016), about the elder care crisis in the United States. It is edited by Annukka Lilja, and you can see the way she has organized her audio tracks by the types of sounds.

Some of these tracks (like dialogue and certain effects) are synced with picture, while others (like music, backgrounds, and narration) are nonsync. The volume of each track can be adjusted independently to create an optimum blend of the various sounds.

TYPES OF SOUNDS: SPEECH, SOUND EFFECTS, AND MUSIC

The sound components of a film can be organized into three broad categories: speech, sound effects, and music. These sounds constitute the way a film can aurally communicate to an audience, but not every scene within a film will have all three types of sound. For example, many scenes are edited to music without any dialogue or sound effects at all, while other scenes may have dialogue and no music.

Speech

With very few exceptions, documentaries rely on human speech as a major element. A film like Tia Lessin and Carl Deal's *Trouble the Water* (2008), analyzed in detail in Chapter 18, has a fairly typical amount of speech for an **expository** documentary. In the first 10 minutes, there is more than 9 minutes of talking delivered by the film's characters, news broadcasters, and public officials (Figure 21.3). There are, of course, exceptions to this trend. One striking example is Ilisa Barbash and Lucien Castaing-Taylor's **observational** documentary *Sweetgrass* (2009), which follows sheep herders driving their flocks up into Montana's mountains for summer pasture. The film's first human speech is heard 19 minutes into the film, and the first dialogue between two characters occurs at 51 minutes!

Speech in documentaries comes in two basic forms: **dialogue** and **narration**. Dialogue is speech that emanates from characters within the film, whether they are on- or off-screen. **Synchronous (sync) dialogue** is recorded with the picture during the production phase, the picture and sound from the shot are both used **on-screen,** and frame-accurate sync is maintained during editing. Dialogue can also be **nonsynchronous**, meaning that it has no corresponding image and therefore no visible source. This occurs, for example, when we hear **off-screen** dialogue, where the voice of a person who is part of a scene is speaking but they are not in the view of the camera. An example from *Trouble the Water* would be Kimberly Roberts' voice, which we hear coming from behind the camera as she records scenes of her neighborhood before Hurricane Katrina.

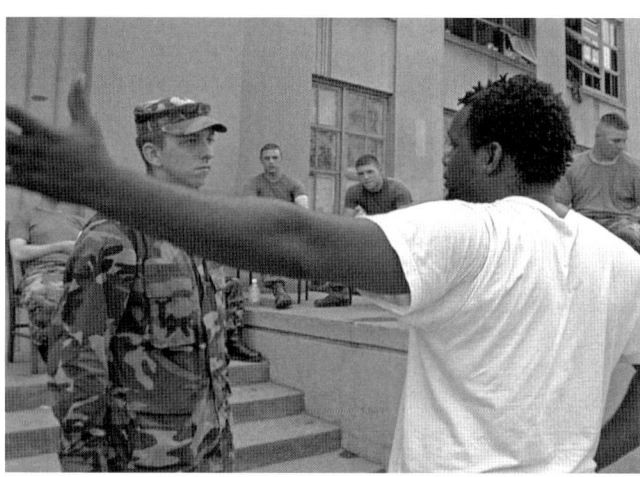 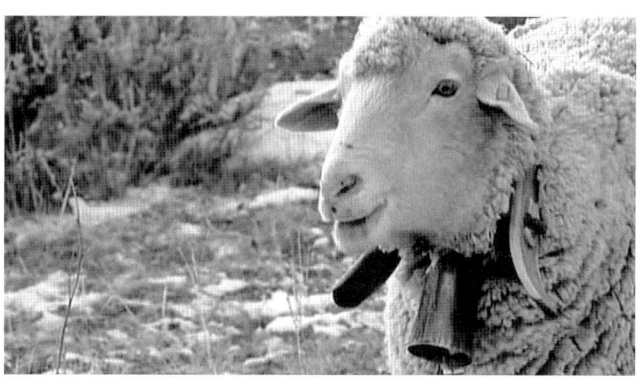

■ **Figure 21.3** Some documentaries, like *Trouble the Water* (left), rely heavily on speech. In this scene Scott Roberts is pleading with US army officials to let residents take shelter in an empty army base. Others, like *Sweetgrass* (right), focus instead on the sounds of the natural world and feature very little human dialogue.

It is common, in expository documentaries, to have a person being interviewed in sync, then cut to other visuals while the viewer continues to hear the person speaking. This is considered **voice-over dialogue** and is not to be confused with narration.

Narration is also nonsync sound and has no corresponding visual in the frame. It differs from voice-over and dialogue, however, in that it is understood by viewers that the voice cannot be heard by the people in the scene. This means that the voice is not in the time and space of the film world, and is instead an element that comes from outside the world of the characters in the film.

A key concept here, derived from film theory, is that of diegetic vs non-diegetic sound. The world of the film—the characters, actions, objects, locations, time, and story—is called the film's **diegesis**. A soundtrack can have sounds that seem to come from within the conceptual reality of the movie, called **diegetic sound**, as well as **non-diegetic sounds**, which don't come from any source in the world of the film. Examples of **diegetic sound** are the dialogue spoken by a character, music playing on a radio that is visible in the scene, and the sound of a siren that our characters respond to, whether it is on-screen or not. Examples of non-diegetic sounds are narration or music put into the film by the filmmaker to add emotion, context, or exposition. Observational films that adhere to the strict parameters of the **direct cinema** and **cinéma vérité** movements decline, as a matter of principle, to add non-diegetic sounds because it goes against the idea of capturing the truth in an immediate "fly on the wall" way (Chapter 2). The absence of non-diegetic elements strengthens the feeling of immediacy and realism in these films.

When considering the presence of speech in a film, keep in mind that sometimes the visual information we are getting from a scene is enough. Recently a student of ours had cut a documentary scene involving a young Pacific Islander who enlisted in the US Army. The new recruit found himself wandering through a typical American convenience store assessing all the products he could buy in the United States that weren't available in his home country. In the rough cut, the scene included voice-over dialogue of the character saying, "Here in Georgia, there are many things we cannot buy back home." During a rough cut screening, it became clear that the dialogue wasn't needed, as all the information was expressed powerfully through the scene's visuals. Audiences come to your film with a desire to decode the images before them. If the picture can tell the story, don't burden it with redundant voice-over or narration.

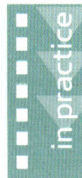

■ CUTTING DIALOGUE

Almost everybody speaks in a less direct and economical way than is ideal for documentary film purposes, so it is common to cut dialogue, and sometimes even rearrange it, to make it smoother and more efficient. Most students are amazed at the amount of cutting that goes into a simple statement by a character in a documentary. It is common to edit out utterances like "um," "ah," and "you know," and to streamline dialogue by cutting out tangents and backtracking. Consider this example from coauthor Kelly Anderson's film *Never Enough* (2010), about hoarding, collecting, cluttering, and people's relationships with their things. The text below comes from the transcript of an interview with Ron Alford, a central character in the film. The crossed out words were removed during the process of dialogue editing. Note that in addition to condensing dialogue, Anderson also used sections of three very different parts of the interview. One is labeled Ron 1 and comes from the beginning of the interview, whereas the others are Ron 9.2 and Ron 10 and come from much later.

Ron 1: ~~It's not from here out, it's from here out.~~ Clutter begins in the brain, and ends up on the floor. Look around. Everything that's in here, I brought in, and I have here for one of ~~two reasons. Either I like~~ — three reasons. I like it, I want it, or I may need it one day. ~~Those are the three classic reasons for this to occur.~~ And then the other thing is that, stuff that I'm not sure about, like this stuff over here, if you look through here, there's a whole pile of stuff here, and this is no different than them. Who are they? They are my clients. How do I know what they are? Because I, too, am one of them. The only difference is I know the difference and I'm able to act on it. ~~But if you look at this stuff, this pile, this pile is always, almost always about that tall. And what it is,~~ these are decisions that I have yet to make. ~~So the decision was, they're all decisions. We make decisions good, bad or indifferent.~~ So the good decision is to throw this in the trash, or to put it someplace or to deal with it. ~~The uh,~~ the bad decision is not to do anything with it but to let it sit there and pile up. ~~These are a lot of decision over here.~~

Ron 9.2: Here is Disaster Masters Website, ~~which is there~~. "The right people to know before things go wrong." Or the other tagline is, "The right people to call after things have gone wrong." ~~Done?~~ And here is the piece de resistance: disposophobia.com. This is the fear of getting rid of stuff. ~~This is what we provide for the internet.~~ If you type in the word "clutter" you are

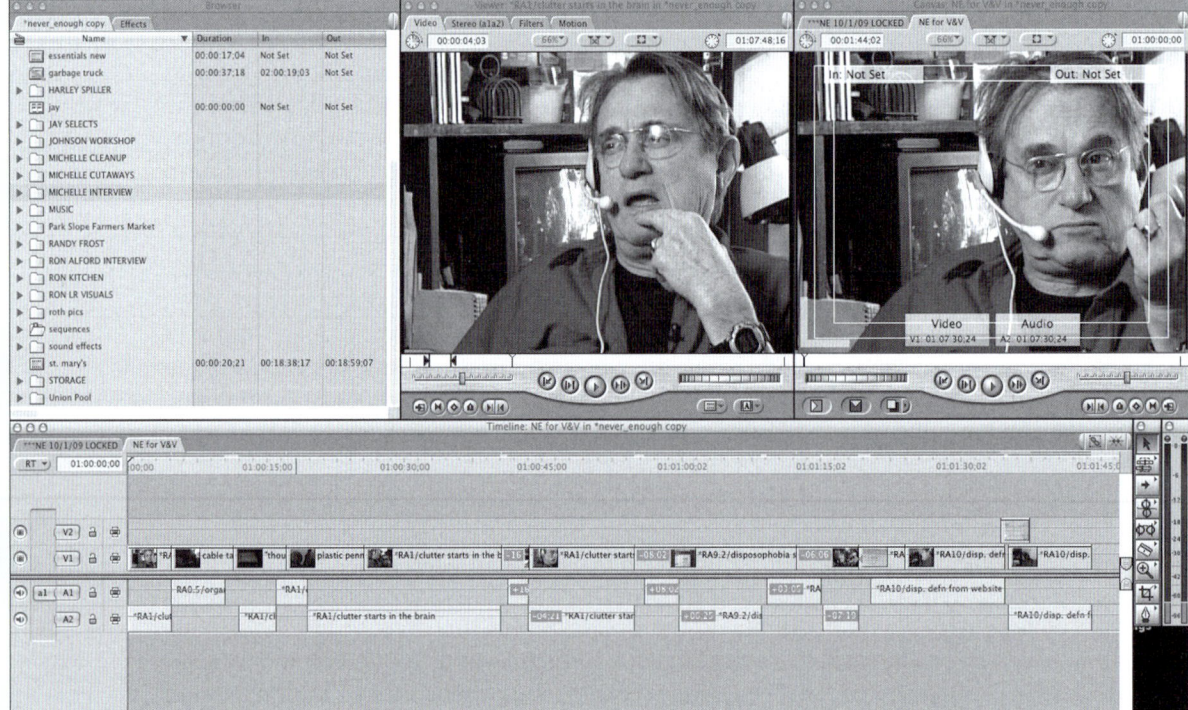

■ **Figure 21.4** Dialogue editing in *Never Enough* (2010). The transcript shows how many words are edited out in the progress of condensing the dialogue. This corresponding timeline shows how the dialogue (on audio channels 1 and 2) was cut up.

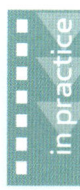

more than likely going to show up here. ~~If you type in the words "Collyer Brothers," let's try it. C-O-L-L-Y-E-R~~

Ron 10: ~~Disposophobics are generally very smart people who basically can't, don't or won't make fast value judgments about their stuff. Their solution for their dilemma is they keep everything. Here's about disposophobia: the fear of getting rid of stuff. The problem is that~~ Disposophobics are generally very smart people who basically can't, don't or won't make fast value judgments about their stuff. Their solution for their dilemma is they keep everything. ~~Example: Put $5, a magazine, a diamond ring and 2 dozen plastic chinese food containers and ask the disposophobic to trash two of them. Their response? I want them all. Their solution for this problem and it's available, so this is what we do at disposophobia.com.~~ We help these people make those decisions in an easy and non-threatening and non-judgmental way.

Figure 21.4 shows the Final Cut Pro timeline for the section of the film that corresponds with the marked up transcript. Note the number of dialogue edits in the timeline (they correspond with the cuts in the transcript). You can see the original clips and the edited sequence on our companion website (www.routledge.com/cw/Anderson).

What are the ethical implications of editing someone's dialogue? Most documentary filmmakers feel that, as long as you aren't changing the essence of what is being said, it's not a problem. Most film subjects are pleased that they sound more coherent and concise than they did when they made the statement the first time around! On the other hand, it would indeed be problematic to rework a person's interview in a way that changes their intentions or alters their statements in a significant way.

Of course, there is no rule that says you must edit out people's um's or ah's, stumbles, or redundancies. Sometimes leaving those in can reveal character, or help show how uncomfortable a particular interviewee was. If that's the goal, it can work well for the film to leave them in.

Sound Effects

Sound effects are perhaps best defined by what they are not: any sound that is not speech or music. **Hard effects** are sound effects that are gathered as nonsync sound and then inserted into the sound design either as **postsynchronous** sound (synced up to a corresponding image in editing) or as a nonsync sound effect. Hard effects are sounds like shattering glass, dog barks, gunshots, explosions, creaking stairs, doorbells, telephones, bird calls, or a helicopter fly-by. A hard sound effect can come from the production **wild** sound (e.g., a clean, nonsync recording of an actual car starting or birds chirping), or can be found as a prerecorded sound effect from a commercial **sound effects library**. There are many sound libraries online. Some are free while others will require that you purchase the rights to use the sound.

It's extremely important to record, create, or find the sound effect that will have the exact impact you need, and this is a task that requires great attention to detail. You don't just say, "I need a dog barking." You need to have a specific sense for the size and kind of dog (the "yap" of a Yorkie or the lazy "woof-woof" of a hound dog?), the kind of bark (playful, serious, or rabid?), and the dramatic context for the bark (is the barking realistic or expressionistic?).

Foley effects, named after Universal Pictures sound department head Jack Foley, differ from hard effects in that they are created and recorded in sync with the edited film. A foley session involves watching a scene in a soundproof room, with whatever objects or surfaces you need to create the right noise, and having a professional **foley artist** create and record the sounds as they watch each scene. The sounds are recorded digitally and put into the NLE system, where they are built into an effects track aligned with the picture.

A foley session can be an extremely elaborate and expensive event, requiring professional foley artists and a special foley room equipped with, among other things, different floor surfaces (gravel, concrete, wood, carpet, etc.) that are used to create just the right sounds

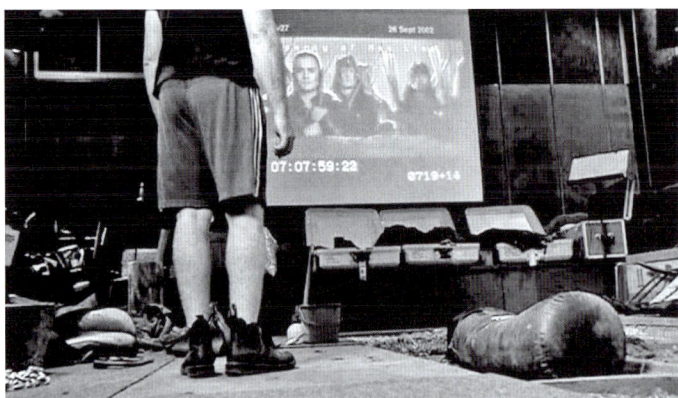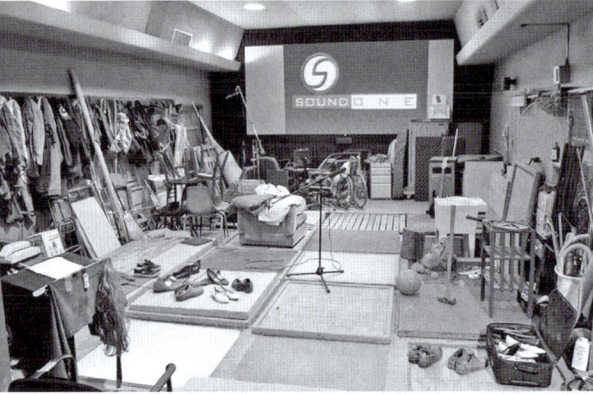

■ **Figure 21.5** Professional foley rooms are sound studios designed to record post-synchronous sound effects while the foley artist watches the scene on a screen. As you can see here, foley rooms are outfitted with a wide array of objects that can make a variety of noises.

(Figure 21.5). But for shorts and independent films, a foley session can simply mean watching your footage on a laptop computer in a soundproof room and re-creating a sound effect or two, recording it, and putting it back into the NLE where you can hopefully slide it into sync. Foley effects are relatively rare in documentary, but for those seeking an especially rich sound design, they can be useful. For example, in *The Immortalists* (2014), David Alvarado and Jason Sussberg foleyed every single effect. The intention, according to Alvarado, was "to make the visuals as real as possible, and the sound design as surreal as possible."[2]

In documentary, you will often find yourself working with footage, such as historical material, that comes to you with no soundtrack. This means you need to define your own approach to the sound design of the scenes that use the silent material. One approach is fairly literal: a shot of a fairground gets matched with the sound of a happy crowd and rides. The image of a World War II airplane gets matched with the sound of an engine from the period. But you might also choose to run the footage without effects to emphasize its historical nature, or use effects that are more impressionistic to create a more subjective feel.

Ambient Sounds

Ambient sounds, also called **backgrounds**, provide the background noises specific to a location. Ambient sound can come from the field recordings made at the actual locations, or it can be pulled from commercial sound effects libraries. These libraries offer thousands of different ambient environments ("rainforest with birds," "city streets/rush hour," "small restaurant," "children's playground," and so on) (Figure 21.6). Ambient sound in a final sound design can be a combination of the ambience that is already part of the sync field recordings and added sounds. It is not uncommon to use multiple ambient tracks in a single scene to get the atmosphere just right.

It's important to note that "silence" in film, as well as in real life, does not mean there is no sound at all. During "silent" passages, we should be able to hear the naturally occurring background noises. What this means is that there is never a time when a soundtrack has no audio. At the very least, it will contain very quiet **room tone** (Chapter 14) or ambiences like the ones in Figure 21.6.

As with everything else in film, ambient sound has both a practical use and a creative application. Practically speaking, ambience tracks are used to smooth out any shifts that would be apparent when cutting from one shot to another in the same scene. For example, in a scene where you cut between two people sitting at a sidewalk cafe, and one person is facing the traffic and the other is facing away, there will likely be a noticeable discrepancy between the traffic noise in their respective sound recordings. Often, this ambience shift

☐	💲	▶ MP3	Backgrounds - Interior Presence - Kitchen Roomtone - Int - 6:15am, Heater On Steady Throughout, Occasional Faint Clock Ticks.	59	$4.43
☐	💲	▶ MP3	Backgrounds - Interior Presence - Kitchen Roomtone - Int - 6:15am, Heater Turns On & Steady Throughout, Occasional Faint Clock Ticks.	54	$4.32
☐	💲	▶ MP3	Backgrounds - Interior Presence - Kitchen Roomtone - Int - 6:15am, Very Quiet, Still Air Atmosphere W/ Faint Clock Ticks.	54	$4.32
☐	💲	▶ MP3	Backgrounds - Interior Presence - Kitchen Roomtone - Int - 6:15am, Very Quiet, Still Air Atmosphere W/ Faint Clock Ticks.	55	$4.35
☐	💲	▶ MP3	Backgrounds - White House Control Room Ambiance - Some Beeping Tones, Occasional Soft BG Voices, Typing, Someone Coughs, Some BG Radio Calls After 2:30.	227	$6.52
☐	💲	▶ MP3	Backgrounds - White House Control Room Ambiance - Int - Busy With More Action, Phone Beeps, Hi-Tech Teletype, Occasional Light BG Voice & Typing, Printer Printing.	225	$6.50
☐	💲	▶ MP3	Backgrounds - White House Control Room Ambiance - Int - Medium Busy With Phone Beeps, Hi-Tech Teletype, Occasional Light BG Voice & Typing.	226	$6.51
☐	💲	▶ MP3	Backgrounds - Neighborhood Ambiance - Int - Quiet, Distant Traffic Rush, Occasional Bird, Distant Dogs Bark, Plane By, Little Medium Distant Activity, Mic'd Int House.	266	$6.82
☐	💲	▶ MP3	Backgrounds - Main Cable House - Interior - Industrial Hum, Slight Rubber Squeaking	69	$4.64
☐	💲	▶ MP3	Backgrounds - Urban House Ambience - Interior - Quiet Interior Sound With Very Light Off Stage Traffic, Background Prop Plane Overhead at 00:53, Background Birds, Inner City Neighborhood Feel	198	$6.27
☐	💲	▶ MP3	Backgrounds - Urban House Ambience - Interior - Distant Traffic, Distant Background Birds, Fly Buzzes Around Towards End, Inner City Neighborhood Feel	60	$4.46

■ **Figure 21.6** A search for "house backgrounds" on the website sounddogs.com shows the wide variety of available backgrounds. Note the level of detail in the descriptions, such as "Kitchen Roomtone, Int. 6:15am, Heater on Steady Throughout, Occasional Faint Clock Ticks."

can be too abrupt for continuity's sake when cutting from one shot to the other. Although you can't get rid of the traffic noise from one subject's audio, you could add a little traffic ambience on another track, under the character who has less, in order to even them out. You might find some traffic noise to layer under the entire scene. This can help unify the scene by subliminally affirming that the characters are in the same place.

The creative dimension of ambient sound is not to be underestimated. Finding just the right ambient sound for a scene can establish an environment that adds additional narrative information or an emotional tone. Ambience is also often used to create a subjective sound space, meaning that the sound environment the audience hears is a reflection of what a specific character is feeling. In Danfung Dennis' *Hell and Back Again* (2012), sound is used as a bridge between times and locations, and as a reflection of the main character's psychological state of mind. The film follows Sergeant Nathan Harris, who is struggling with physical injuries and post-traumatic stress disorder after being shot by the Taliban in Afghanistan. The film cuts back and forth between Harris at home in North Carolina and on duty a year earlier in Afghanistan. In one scene, Harris is in a North Carolina department store looking at the combat video game Call of Duty (Figure 21.7). The ambient sound of the department store fades, and we begin to hear the natural sounds of birds chirping and wind blowing. The change in backgrounds puts us in the subjective space of Harris' mind, as he becomes lost in thought and the outside world fades from his consciousness. It also creates a feeling of disconnection and tension, and signals that we are about to begin a flashback, picking up Harris' story before his injury, while he was still in the military.

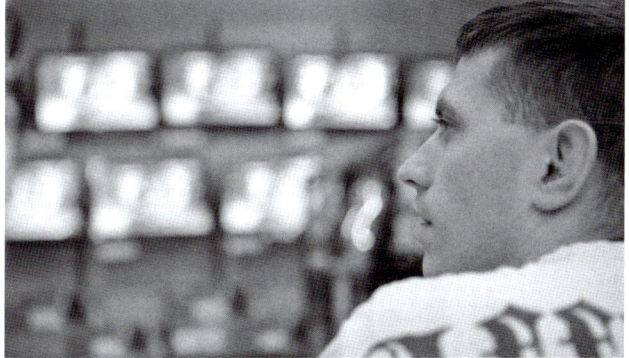
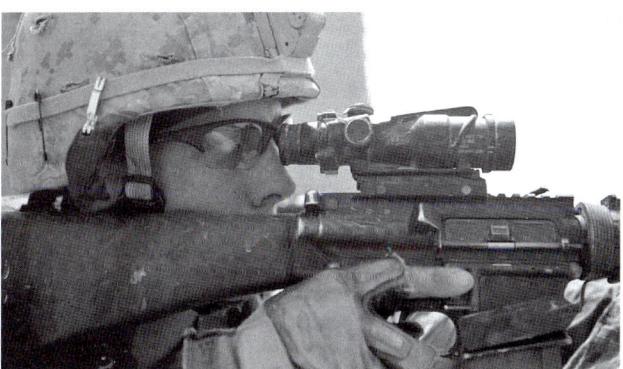

■ **Figure 21.7** In Danfung Dennis' documentary *Hell and Back Again*, sound from combat in Afghanistan is used over footage of Sergeant Nathan Harris as he watches video game screens in a store in the United States (top). The shift in sound signals a change in Harris' consciousness, and the beginning of a flashback to his time in combat (bottom), which follows.

Music: Source and Score

Source music is the name for any music that has a visible source in the scene. This could include a song playing on the car radio while your subject is driving, the guitar that a character is playing, or the song your characters are singing (think "Happy Birthday" at a party). Source music presents particular problems for documentary filmmakers. Although it would seem that a sound playing on the radio would be fair game to include in a scene, the copyright holders can, and have, claimed rights to be compensated for this use. A best practice is to have subjects turn off the radio, television, or any other device likely to transmit copyrighted material, before you begin filming, and then add material that you do have rights to in postproduction *as if* it were playing on the radio in the scene. Another good reason to do this is that having music recorded under dialogue will make it virtually impossible to edit.

There are times, however, when the content of the song or broadcast is essential to the meaning of your scene ("Happy Birthday" being sung at a birthday party, for example). As documentarians, we capture the world of our subjects, and that world includes the media they consume and perform. In these cases, there may be exceptions to copyright law. When in doubt, consult an entertainment attorney. Another good source of information is the Center for Media and Social Impact (CMSI), which, as we have mentioned in Chapter 5 and Chapter 20, has conducted extensive research around best practices for fair use and copyright clearance.

According to CMSI,

> *Fair use should protect documentary filmmakers from being forced to falsify reality. Where a sound or image has been captured incidentally and without prevision, as part of an unstaged scene, it should be permissible to use it, to a reasonable extent, as part of the final version of the film.*[3]

Documentarians should take care, however that:
- the music playing in the scene was not requested by the filmmaker
- the music is integral to the scene or action
- the scene has not been included primarily to exploit the incidentally captured music, or if the music functions as a substitute for non-source music in its own right (i.e., you show your character driving and then use the music on the radio under a montage of other images), and the captured content does not constitute the scene's primary focus of interest

There are times when you have no choice but to clear your music. If you are making a film about the Rolling Stones, as David and Albert Maysles did with *Gimme Shelter* (1970), you will have to clear the rights pertaining to both the composers (Jagger and Richards, and a few others), the record company whose recording you are using, and the performers.

The **musical score** (or background music) is nonsync and non-diegetic music that underscores the events of a scene with a tone, a mood, or musical commentary. Most people understand how a drawn-out note from a string instrument can add tension to a moment, how a song can unify a montage, or how a plaintive piano solo can infuse a scene with pathos. These uses are so common that audiences may barely notice them, but they will feel them deeply.

Score music can be existing music for which you've cleared the rights, or it can be original music composed specifically for the film. Given the hassles and costs associated with clearing music rights, many documentary filmmakers commission original score for most if not all of their film. The music can be performed by live musicians or created in a computer program. At times, computer-generated music is enhanced through the inclusion of one or more live instruments. Sometimes, the edited film is given to a composer who, in close consultation with the director, composes music timed to the actions, rhythms, and durations of specific scenes. This often occurs after **picture lock**, so the editor will cut to **temp music** that is later replaced by the composer's score.

Sometimes the composer will record a number of musical sketches or motifs (small musical phrases) that the editor can work with. Once picture is locked, the composer will finalize the cues based on what was used.

Sometimes a combination of acquired and commissioned music works best. Coauthor Kelly Anderson and Allison Lirish Dean commissioned composers Benjamin Fries and Simon Beins to create the score for their film *My Brooklyn* (2012), about the redevelopment of Downtown Brooklyn's Fulton Mall area. Since part of the film was about the importance of that commercial district to the emergence of hip-hop music, the filmmakers decided to clear the song "Brooklyn-Queens" by 3rd Bass because its music video was shot at Fulton Mall and they wanted to use the music video in the film. Even though 3rd Bass agreed to allow the filmmakers to use the song and the music video, the record company still insisted that they be paid for the **master use license** (p. 348).

Another option for filmmakers is to use prerecorded music from music libraries (also called **needle-drop music**). In these cases, you pay a flat fee per cue. This is generally much less expensive than clearing existing music. There are a wide variety of music libraries, and even some sites that offer free music for non-commercial projects.

For students and other low-budget filmmakers, we recommend finding low-cost music libraries, or working with a music student or aspiring composer who is looking for experience scoring film or material to include in their sample reel. Often you can find great music at low or no cost this way, and avoid the hassles of trying to clear music.

Common Music Pitfalls

Music, when used correctly, can be a profoundly expressive option in the filmmaker's toolbox of storytelling elements. The use of music to enhance a documentary's impact can seem so easy, and yet there are a number of pitfalls to be wary of. Most problems with poorly used music come from "too much." Music is like a strong cooking spice—just because a little bit is good does not mean that more is better. A few guidelines:

1. Use music only where it is necessary. Wall-to-wall music is the phenomenon of excessive and indiscriminate use of music from the beginning to the end of a film. Music that relentlessly cues emotions from the audience can be exhausting and counterproductive because it ultimately impedes authentic audience involvement.
2. Don't try to evoke an emotion that is not in the film. It doesn't help to throw music under a scene simply because the scene isn't working. If a scene is not suspenseful or poignant, adding music will not help. It will simply become an unsuccessful scene with mismatched music.
3. Too loud! Often in student films, the music is mixed in so loudly that it dominates anything else in the scene. In especially bad cases, loud music makes dialogue unintelligible.
4. Watch out for mismatched tempo. Rhythm and tempo come from many places: the cutting pace, the actions in the frame, the camerawork, and the dialogue. Be careful that your music fits well with the tempo you've established in the picture editing. This doesn't necessarily mean to duplicate the rhythms beat-for-beat—because music can often serve as a rhythmic counterpoint—but the energy of the image and the music should be complimentary.
5. Lyrics can be difficult to manage, especially in dialogue scenes. Lyrics tend to fight with dialogue for attention, even if you're using low-level source music, like a radio softly playing in the background.

6. Emotional associations are not fixed. While music is especially useful for conjuring emotions, the relationship between the particular music and the individual listener can be highly subjective. This is especially a problem when using popular music. You may decide to use a song in a love scene because it was on the radio two summers ago when you fell madly in love, so that piece of music resonates, for you, with all of those feelings. But this may not be a universal feeling about that song.

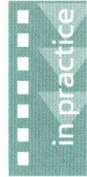

CLEARING MUSIC RIGHTS

If you want to use a piece of preexisting music in your documentary, here are some guidelines for clearing the rights. It is best to start this process as soon as you know what music you might want to use. It takes time, patience, and money to clear music. And you must clear it before you can exhibit your film! (The section below is adapted from "All Clear: A Music Clearance Primer" published by *The Music Bridge*.[4])

1. First you must ascertain and contact the person (or entity) who holds the rights to the song. The best places to start your investigation are ASCAP, BMI, and SESAC. These are performance rights societies, to which most professional songwriters and publishers belong. Each society has a website for easy online research of publisher/copyright owner contact information for songs, plus phone support. The rights you will obtain from the publisher are called **synchronization** (or **"sync"**) **rights**, and are basically permission to use the composition in your film for a fee.

2. The second type of license you must get is a **master use license**, controlled by the record label, that grants the right to include a specific recording of the composition in your film. A song will have one publisher you need to clear the sync rights with, but there may be multiple recordings of that song that you could clear through the corresponding record label.

You can also research rights information for commercially released recordings on sites such as amazon.com, as well as CD jackets and booklet credits. Usually, independently released artists, whom you can approach directly, will be self-published and will control both sync and master use rights.

3. Once you have contacted the rights holder, you need to state specifically (a) what you want, (b) how much of it you want, (c) in what context it will be used, and (d) how the music will be credited. As you can understand, people who create or control artistic works can be very particular about how the works are used.

4. If the rights holders are in agreement with your use of the music, then you negotiate a price. What's important to the rights holder is how much money you stand to make from your film. You need to be honest about what sort of distribution you expect. If it is a short movie made for a class and you hope to show it at only a few film festivals, then what you're asking for is called "festival rights." The cost of festival rights is often manageable. Occasionally, students are given permission to use commercial music in their films for nothing. A word of advice: the more rights you can clear up front, the better. Some low-budget, independent films can become surprise festival hits and attract the interest of a distributor or a broadcaster. One of the first questions they will ask you is, "Do you have the rights to all of the music?" If you don't, then they may well back away. Why? A music rights holder is more likely to give a filmmaker a cheap price for rights before it has a distribution company attached. If you attempt to buy music rights after your festival success, the earning potential of the movie has increased and the cost of clearing the music might be prohibitive.

SOUND PERSPECTIVE

What is the source of a sound? Film theorist Michel Chion makes the astute observation, in his book *Audio-Vision*, that in film, images are always contained within the confines of the frame. But sound has no such "container," no such strictly delineated limits.[5] Not only are you free to layer as many sounds as you want on top of other sounds, but you can also have various rationales for where those sounds are ostensibly coming from.

Sound perspective refers to the apparent distance of a sound. Clues to the distance of the source include the volume of the sound, the balance between the sound from the source and other sounds, and the amount of reverberation. Imagine you have filmed an observational scene of a character walking and talking in an exterior location. You have used a wireless lavalier microphone to record the dialogue, and also have a sound recordist using a shotgun microphone on a boom pole. During editing, you cut from a shot of the character in close-up to one of the same character in a long shot. For the close-up, the sound from the wireless microphone will likely work well, but when you cut to the long shot the close perspective of the lavalier will seem unnatural. At the cut point, you would likely want to mix in more of the sound from the boom microphone to create a more realistic **perspective**.

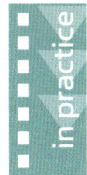

EXPERIMENTING WITH SOUND PERSPECTIVE

In *Sweetgrass* (2009), Ilisa Barbash and Lucien Castaing-Taylor follow sheep herders driving their flocks up into Montana's mountains for summer pasture. The film has a rich sound design, the foundations of which were established during preproduction. In addition to recording audio from a microphone mounted on the camera, the filmmakers put wireless lavalier microphones on the herders, and even occasionally on sheep and dogs. Because there was little radio interference up in the mountains, the mics could record sounds occurring far from the camera. "It meant that people could be three miles apart from each other, in different directions from me, and I would be getting this incredible signal of this super intimate, subjective . . . really embodied sound," Castaing-Taylor says (Figure 21.8).[6]

The filmmakers worked with experimental musician and sound artist Ernst Karel at Harvard's Sensory Ethnography Lab (where Castaing-Taylor is currently the director). Together they created a rich surround-sound mix that featured very little coherent human dialogue. Castaing-Taylor explains:

> When you think of documentary, spoken word is often just reduced to the content, the meaning, the propositional logic of what people are saying. But I was really interested in embodied sound, and what people are doing when they're hacking, or coughing, or they're crying or they're just mumbling under their breath to themselves, those fragments of noise that are half-language and half not. In many ways, that's a much more profound kind of noise than the words we issue when we're trying to make sense.[7]

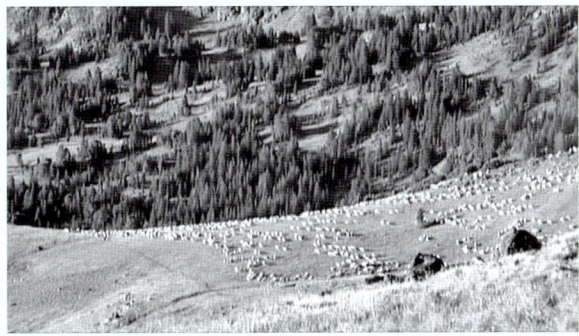

■ **Figure 21.8** Sound perspective in *Sweetgrass*. In this scene, we hear the close-up sounds of a sheep rancher saying "Good Morning" to the sheep, but the shot is such an extreme long shot that we can barely make him out amidst the herd.

Karel's soundscape also plays with the existing conventions around perspective in documentary sound. Castaing-Taylor explains:

> With documentary in general there's this set of conventions that's congealed that has you suppose that acoustic perspective has to coincide precisely with optical perspective. We really wanted to create some sort of aesthetic tension, so at times you'd have this very subjective, guttural, intimate proximate sound that would be playing over an image shot with a long lens that would really be a distant landscape or mountain shot.[8]

SOUND DESIGN STRATEGIES

The sound design for a particular documentary can generally be placed on a continuum with **realism** on one end and **expressionistic** or **stylized** sound design on the other. Realism obviously can be achieved through **direct sound**, which is the use of sounds recorded at the actual location. But depending on microphone placement, these sounds will be more or less convincing, and may require the careful and judicious addition

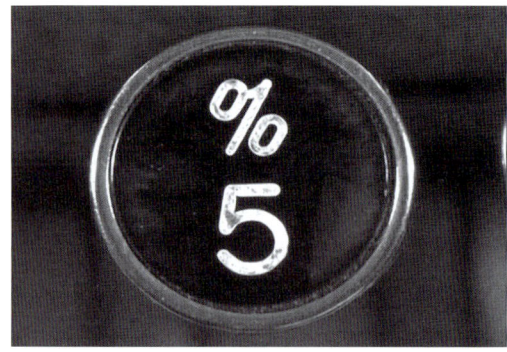

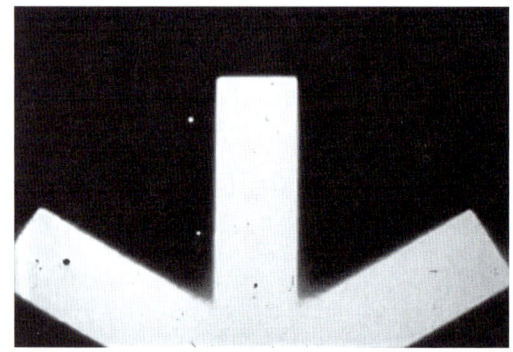

Figure 21.9 In Alan Berliner's *Intimate Stranger* (1991), sound effects like typewriter keys being hit and carriage returns bells are combined with iconic imagery to signal various types of footage are about to appear.

of other sounds. For example, a scene of a child on a playground may require the addition of ambient sounds of other children playing if the audio was recorded with a shotgun microphone that captured only the primary child and the sounds emanating from sources close to her.

One example of a documentary with a highly layered but realistic sound design is Florian Borchmeyer's *Habana: arte nuevo de hacer ruinas* (*Havana: The New Art of Making Ruins,* 2006). The film is a portrait of the inhabited ruins of Havana and their strange blend of magic and demolition, and captures the final moments of these buildings before they are either renovated or collapse. In addition to recording interviews, Borchmeyer recorded wild **surround sound** of the environment, and then layered multiple tracks of sound under and around the interviews. Blogger David Tamés wrote about the experience of viewing the film, "I felt as if I was enveloped by the landscape in a manner I have rarely experienced in a documentary."[9]

A more stylized use of sound is seen in the essay films of Alan Berliner. In several of Berliner's films, the aural motif of a typewriter reoccurs as part of a richly layered, highly expressive sound design (Figure 21.9). Berliner says,

Back in 1981, my film Myth in the Electric Age *made use of the sounds of a manual typewriter—the rat-tat-tat of the keys, the carriage return, and the small bell that always goes off when you reach the end of a line—to structure several rapid sequences of abstract imagery. Ten years later I brought back those same typewriter sounds as motifs in* Intimate Stranger, *this time to orchestrate and organize the voluminous documentary paper trail of my grandfather's life—all the letters, documents, stamps, envelopes, and photographs that he was so obsessed with. It felt like an appropriate metaphor. After all, the typewriter was the tool of my grandfather's autobiography and the primary tool of business during his lifetime. I wanted to transform it into a kind of musical instrument that would also function as a unifying editorial strategy, a way of allowing my unseen hand to "type" images on and off the screen with a kind of visceral immediacy. The sounds of the typewriter allowed me to "sculpt in time"—if I can borrow that phrase from Tarkovsky—and invigorate the film with rhythm.*

The typewriter sounds also allowed me to create a set of visual "codes" that appear throughout the film. For instance, before you see any passage of home-movie imagery in the film, a typewriter bell rings over a short fragment of film stock identification circles. Before historical documents come on-screen, a typewriter bell rings over a short image fragment of arrows that shake and tremble. Before any archival footage comes on screen, a typewriter bell rings over a short swish-pan. Still photographs are always preceded by a quick, abstract scissor-like animation, accompanied by the sound of a camera click. These sound-image identification markers are used consistently throughout the film. Eventually the viewer learns to associate each of them with a particular kind of visual and stylistic representation.[10]

While not all filmmakers will need to create the complex soundscapes of an Alan Berliner, you can see that thoughtful sound design is critical to the tone and meaning of every documentary. A creative strategy for your soundscape is just as important for the ultimate success of your film as the overall look or structure of your story. Achieving good sound design should start in the field, but ultimately, most of the work will happen when you do your sound editing.

SOUND EDITING

On a low-budget or student documentary, you will probably do your own **sound edit** and **sound mix** in your NLE program. On more professional productions, you will likely "prep" your sound elements in your NLE system and then deliver your project to a specialized **Sound Editor** and **Rerecording Mixer** (or **Dubbing Mixer** in Europe). For either scenario, you will begin in your NLE by building your audio tracks.

Building Your Audio Tracks

Even though NLE systems allow you to create as many as 100 or more audio tracks, most films use only a fraction of this capacity. The construction of your sound design occurs in various stages, from the most important sounds (those that are essential to understanding the story) to the supplementary sounds (those that add tone, mood, or other sonic dimensions to the film).

You begin to build your tracks from the moment you start to put shots together in the first rough cut. If your film is mostly dialogue based, then picture and dialogue editing will happen simultaneously. As you edit your early rough cuts, you will find it necessary to start adding other sound layers, like music or narration, that also play a vital role in the progress of the story and are therefore necessary for picture editing. As in editing your rough cut, build the basic structure first and fine-tune it later on. Don't spend a lot of time at the beginning of your process creating something that sounds beautiful but may have to be undone later because the whole concept doesn't work.

A typical progression for the gradual buildup of audio tracks for a documentary goes something like this:
1. Dialogue and/or narration. The first rough cuts include rough picture, scratch narration, and production dialogue. These only take up a few tracks of audio.
2. Music. Additional tracks are added for sequences where music is the primary sound element. Often this music will be scratch track—uncleared music that will be replaced later on with original score or cleared music.
3. Sound effects. Subsequent rough cuts add sound effects tracks for important hard sound effects, especially those that are central to the story. Many documentaries wait until the picture is locked to add effects, but if you have them in your production audio you can add them in during your fine cut stage. You can also add ambiences at this stage.

Refining Your Sound Design

Once you have arrived at picture lock, with the image and essential audio tracks in their fixed places, you then turn your attention to the supplementary sounds that provide extra layers of mood, tone, and information. This is where much of the creative sound design work begins. The first step in this process is called **spotting**. Spotting is the process of sitting down and closely watching the picture-locked film to identify, scene by scene, the placement and character of any additional sound effects, ambience tracks, or music. Notes are taken on a **spotting sheet** detailing the time code reference of each sound effect, along with a description and your thoughts on the contribution the sound is supposed to make to the scene. If someone else is creating the sound design, then this process is done by the director, the editor, and the sound designer (or sound editor).

Additional tracks are then added for room tone and backgrounds, especially where they are needed to smooth over dialogue edits and fill in sound gaps. If you are working with a composer, you will go through a similar process of watching the film together and creating a **music cue sheet**.

Splitting Tracks and Checkerboarding Your Audio

Often, it is easier to begin editing with most of the dialogue on two to four tracks. This way, you don't have to keep expanding the timeline vertically to see all your audio elements at the same time. As you progress towards picture lock, though, you will want to spread your audio out onto more tracks. The goal is to keep all the clips from one character on a single track (or set of two tracks if you have two sync tracks that go with the picture). This consolidation makes it easier to control volume and apply **equalization (EQ)** and effects to "sweeten" your audio (pp. 353–356) across a range of clips. It may not be feasible to give each character their own dedicated set of tracks, but the principle is to make it simpler to isolate each person for a given section of the film.

Even within each character, though, you will ultimately want to **checkerboard** the audio. This means alternating the clips of their audio over two (or four) tracks. So, for example, if you have chosen tracks 1–2 for Character A's dialogue, you would place the first audio clip on track 1, the second on track 2, and the third on track 1. If you are using stereo or linked tracks, you would use 1&2, then 3&4, then 1&2 again. This is called "checker-boarding" because it results in the alternating pattern found on a checkerboard (see Figure 21.4 for an example of what this looks like). The reason for checkerboarding is that it allows you to make more complex edits between clips, which may need to be faded up or down at different rates under the clips that immediately precede or follow them. The same principle applies for backgrounds and music.

Finessing Your Audio

If you are doing your own audio work, you should go through your cut carefully, making sure you have chosen the best audio tracks for each sound source. Make sure, for example, that if an interview was recorded with two microphones, you have chosen the best one. Make sure all intended sound effects are in the sequence and that they are high-quality

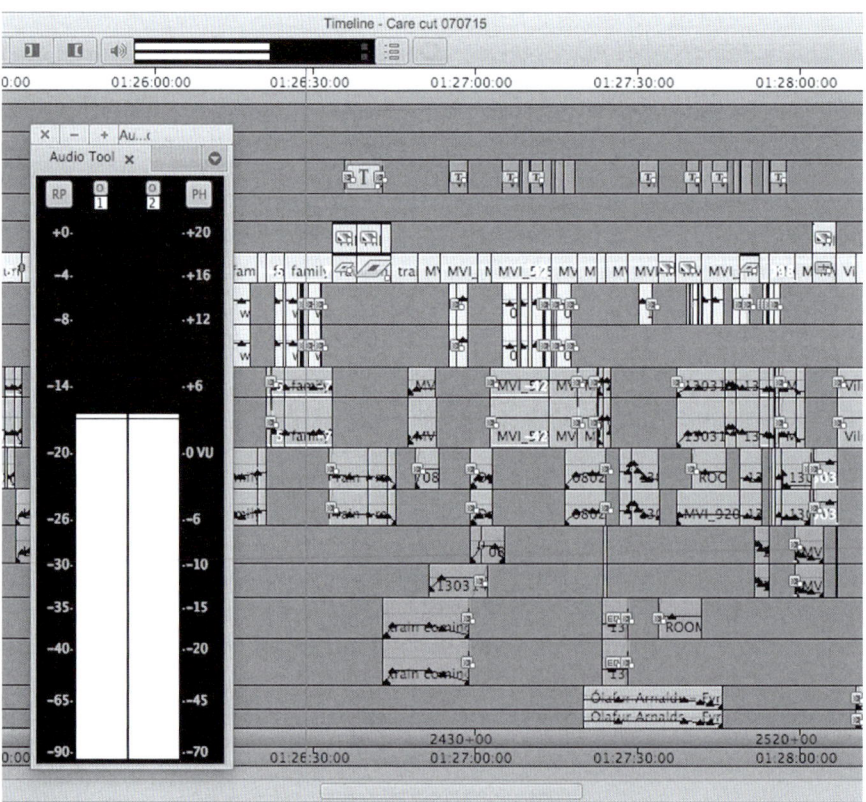

■ **Figure 21.10** Audio level adjustments are done right on the timeline and can be monitored on the sound tool's level meter window. Pictured here is Avid's Audio tool.

files. Replace scratch dialogue and music with their final versions. If you are working with a sound editor, you will want to deliver them your audio with as many choices as possible. If you have two channels of sync audio recorded, give them both so they can choose which to use or how to combine them. A sound editor will also add effects and backgrounds, but you should add any sync sources before you deliver the cut to them. An editor will be searching through libraries to find backgrounds and effects, and if you can provide them with production sound their process will be faster and your film may sound more authentic.

During the editing stage, you will need to adjust the audio levels of all your tracks to some extent, just to be able to hear everything and to get a sense of how the various sound elements are working to tell your story. All NLE systems offer some sort of easily accessible level control right in the timeline (Figure 21.10). You can adjust tracks globally, by selecting the entire track, or adjust individual clips. Adjusting clip levels in the timeline does not alter the master clip or the original media in any way. You can also add simple transitions like sound fades and cross-fades into your sequence to smooth out audio edits. This is especially useful for test screenings where viewers may be distracted by audio that's still too rough.

The editing stage is not the place to get the sound absolutely perfect. Finessing the track levels, creating transition effects, and enhancing the sound through equalization and audio filters are done in the next and final stage of the sound design process: **sound mixing**.

THE SOUND MIX

The **sound mix** is the process of polishing and finalizing the various audio tracks in your sound design and creating a single **mixtrack**. This is the **mono**, **stereo**, or even **surround sound** track that is then married to your images and accompanies your film into distribution and exhibition. On professional productions, your sound editor will set everything in place and leave it to the **rerecording mixer** to adjust levels and **sweeten** the sound. At the mix, the sound editor will be present, along with the director and perhaps the producer.

As a rule, everything is in its place before you arrive at the mix. In some cases, especially with low or medium budgets, one person may do the sound editing and mixing. For most student and independent films that are edited and finished on an NLE system, it's hard to strictly delineate the sound editing stage from the sound mixing stage. As you work with your rough cuts and build your sound design, you will be doing some rough sound mixing along the way. But at some point, after picture lock and after you've placed all your sounds where they need to be, you need to turn all your attention to perfecting the way your film sounds. The ultimate goal of a sound mix is to create a harmonious sonic environment for your film, meaning that the completed sound design is both believable and appropriate for the conceptual and aesthetic aims of your documentary. In this respect, the sound mix should not be viewed as merely a polishing process—there are substantial creative decisions to be made here.

The sound mix process involves the following four steps, generally in this order: (1) audio sweetening, (2) creating audio transitions, (3) audio level balancing, and (4) the mix down.

Step 1: Audio Sweetening

Audio sweetening means making your audio sound better. This is accomplished by evaluating, and adjusting when necessary, every individual audio clip in the film. Sweetening includes a variety of audio signal processing tools that can be employed to accomplish three goals: to generally enhance the quality of the audio, to repair poor audio, and to create audio effects. The reason your prep involves putting all the sound from one interview together on a track is that it allows the mixer to apply the setting to the whole track instead of having to evaluate and sweeten every clip from the same subject and location individually.

Audio Filters

At the heart of audio sweetening is the application of **audio filters**. Audio filters are audio signal processors that digitally alter the audio data, and therefore the characteristics of your sound. Each audio filter manipulates the spectrum in a unique way. It is certainly not possible here to explore the capabilities of every processing tool found in most NLE systems, but a few basics should get you started. The effect and function of a specific audio filter generally falls into one of three categories: (1) equalization, (2) reverb/echo, and (3) compression/expansion.

Filters for Frequency Equalization and Noise Reduction

Equalization, or EQ, means the manipulation of the various frequencies in your signal. Generally, we divide the frequency spectrum of an audio signal into three **frequency bands**: low frequencies, which are the deep, bass quality (around 25_Hz to 250 Hz); midrange frequencies, which are the most perceptible range for the human ear and include the human voice (250_Hz to 4 _kHz); and high frequencies, which include the bright, treble quality of the sound (4 _kHz to 20 _kHz). Most NLE systems offer a filter called a **three-band equalizer**, which allows you to manipulate these three broad areas of the sound spectrum independently (Figure 21.11).

When might you use an EQ filter? Let's say you shot a scene with a microphone that accentuated the high, treble end of the audio and, to your ear, it sounds too "crispy." You can use the EQ filter to bring down the high frequencies. Often a microphone will pick up the hum of a nearby refrigerator, for example, or the buzz of fluorescent lights overhead. Some of these unwanted noises can be reduced by isolating their frequencies and removing them from your track, or lessening them. Be aware, though, that if you need to EQ out a frequency that is found in other areas of the recorded sound, the filter will remove that frequency throughout the recording and will alter sounds you don't want changed in addition to the ones you are targeting. Completely removing high frequencies and low frequencies from a voice, for example, will make it sound like it's coming through the telephone or over a PA system. Also keep in mind, as a general rule, that you may be able

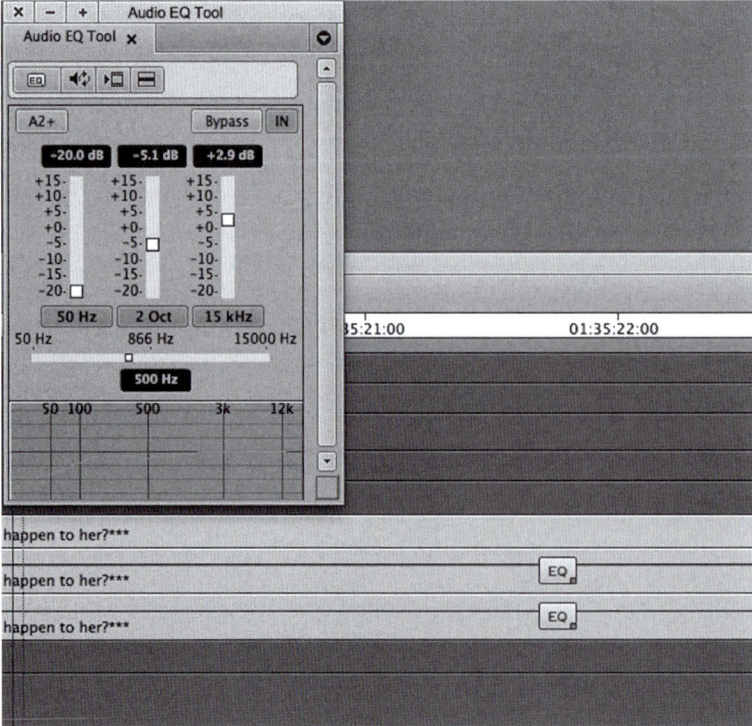

■ **Figure 21.11** The Audio EQ Tool in Avid's Media Composer.

to successfully remove (or accentuate) frequencies that are in the recording, but you cannot add frequencies that are not there in the first place. The removal of high- and low-frequency noise is so common in sound sweetening that you'll find numerous **filter presets** for high-end and low-end **roll-off filters** designed exactly for these problems.

Filters for Reverb and Echo

Echo and **reverb** are similar in that they both involve the reflection and return of sound after a slight delay. The return delay for reverb is fast, creating an effect like putting your source in a small tiled bathroom or concrete stairwell. The return delay for an echo is much longer, like you might hear in a Gothic cathedral or the Grand Canyon. Reverb and echo effects change the audio signal to make it sound as if it were recorded in an acoustically live space, where sound reverberates off hard surfaces. They are commonly used to add richness and depth to material recorded in an entirely dead space (Chapter 14).

In all popular NLEs, there are several preset filters (Figure 21.12). Reverb and echo can sound great, but be careful not to use too much or to use them without justification. Too much can make otherwise clear sound, especially dialogue, murky and unintelligible. Also remember that reverb filters do not remove reverberation—they can only add it!

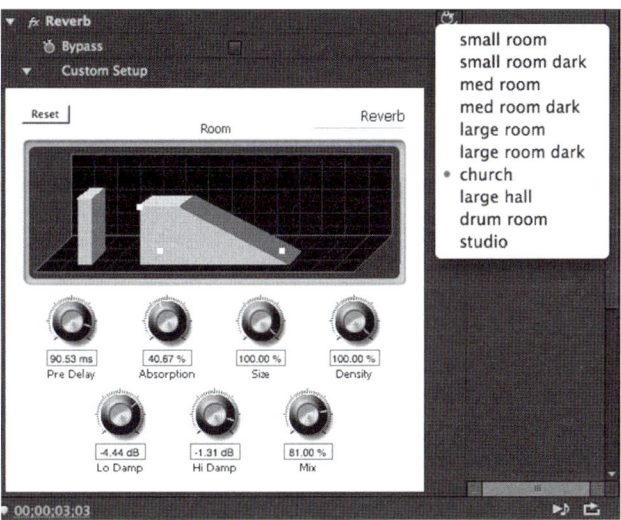

Figure 21.12 Do you want your audio to sound like it's reverberating in a church? A large hall? In Premiere Pro, you can choose from a range of acoustic effects when you apply the reverb filter.

Filters for Amplitude Compression or Expansion

Compression and **expansion** filters work on the amplitude of a sound signal or, more accurately, on the dynamic range (Chapter 13) of a given recording. As we know already, the result of audio that peaks above 0 dB on a peak meter is distortion. In digital audio, this means the loss of data and noticeable crackling in the sound. A compression filter detects when a sound will peak above or near 0 dB and it will suppress the sound to keep it within range without affecting the average audio levels of the track.

This is very different than lowering the overall audio level of a clip to keep loud sounds from peaking above 0 dB, which would also lower everything on that track. Let's say you have a scene in which a married couple is talking while the husband washes the dishes. The sound recordist did his job well and kept the sound from peaking above 0 dB in the field recordings, but now that you're mixing your sound, you want to be able to hear the dialogue clearly, and so you've set the audio levels for the dialogue track fairly high. But now you discover that every time the husband bumps a plate in the sink, the audio spikes above 0 dB and crackles. If you were to lower the track level overall, you'll be lowering the dialogue as well. The solution here is a compression filter, which will suppress only the audio that threatens to peak above 0 dB, leaving the rest at the level established in the timeline.

While compression filters lower loud, peaking sounds, **expansion filters** lower the amplitude of extremely quiet sounds in order to drop them below the level of audibility. Let's say you go into your sound mix, where you'll be listening on super high-quality speakers, and suddenly notice that during the shooting of a tight, close-up interview, the microphone picked up the ticking of the boom operator's watch. It's faint, but definitely distracting. An expansion filter will drop this very quiet noise even lower, hopefully out of the range of hearing, without affecting the rest of the audio on the track. Expansion filters can also be used to minimize the room tone in a dialogue recording, allowing you to more successfully replace it with another background if you so desire.

Filters for Sibilance Suppression or "P" Popping

Another useful set of filters relate to dialogue specifically. A **sibilance suppressor** decreases the hiss of an "S" sound, a common problem in voice recording. A **pop filter** is used to diminish the strength of a plosive "P," which is what happens when a person speaks into a microphone too vehemently.

Step 2: Creating Audio Transitions

Most of the creative audio editing choices, like split edits for dialogue, sound bridges, and ambient track layering, are accomplished during the picture and sound editing stages. During the sound mixing phase, the concern is the smoothness of the transitions from sound clip to sound clip across an entire track. This includes the use of room tone to fill in gaps of silence on the soundtrack, and to even out the qualities of two neighboring pieces of audio so they sound continuous. In the mix, almost every audio clip will get a little extra attention. A straight cut between two audio clips not only magnifies small ambient shifts, but the inconsistent waveforms of the two directly abutted audio clips will also result in an audible "pop" or "click" right at the edit point. To correct this, sound editors and/or mixers routinely add a very quick, four- to six-frame **cross-fade** (or **audio dissolve**) right at the edit point between two connected sound clips, and two- to four-frame **fades** (in and out) at the beginning and end of sound clips that are not directly joined to another audio clip (Figure 21.13). Obviously, like an image dissolve, you can create long cross-fades of many seconds to, for example, slowly introduce some background music. This is particularly important when you are transitioning between scenes with very different sound qualities, as from an interior to an exterior, where it is common to introduce the sound of the new scene as much as several seconds before the picture transition.

When you cross-fade between two clips, the dissolve can either be centered on the cut, or you can control how much of each clip is included. For example, if you decide that you need a 30-frame centered cross-fade to smooth out an ambience discrepancy, then the first shot will end 15 frames after the cut point before it completely fades out, and the second clip will begin 15 frames before the edit point to accommodate the fade-in. These extra frames are called **handles**, and you must be sure that there are no unwanted sounds, like the tail end of some dialogue that you wanted to cut out, within those extra frames (Figure 21.13).

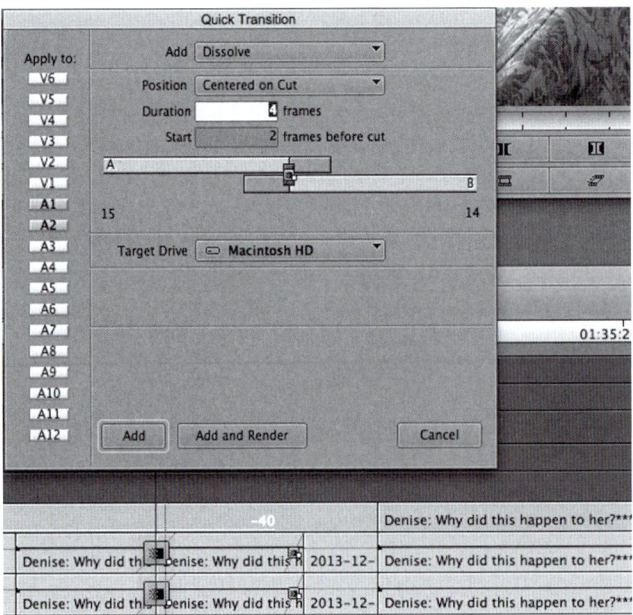

■ **Figure 21.13** An audio dissolve in Avid's Media Composer. Pictured here is four-frame cross-fade used to create an invisible dialogue edit. The dissolve is centered on the cut, with two-frame handles on each side.

Keep in mind that if you checkerboard your audio, you will not be using cross-fades. Because the audio clips are on alternating tracks, you will fade each up and out independently of its neighboring clips. The effect can be the same, but with checkerboarding you will have more control over the length of your sound transitions.

Step 3: Audio Level Balancing

Once all of the tracks sound good on their own, and all of the edit points are clean and smooth, it's time to think about adjusting the volume of the clips in each track and of the various tracks in relation to one another. This stage is critical not only for the intelligibility of your sound (important dialogue shouldn't be drowned out by music, for example). It also is critical for the general believability of the world of your film. An ambience track that is too loud can make a scene ring false; dialogue levels that are all over the map can make the editing painfully obvious; music that is too low will cause the audience to turn around and scream "louder!" at the poor projectionist. Track levels helps you to create emphasis and direct the ear and the eye to what is most important at a particular moment.

The Reference Track and Establishing Average Level Range

When establishing audio levels, you should start with the most important tracks first and then adjust all other tracks relative to this central reference. For example, if a film is primarily music driven with an occasional special effect tossed in here and there, then you'll set levels for the music track first. For dialogue-driven projects, start with dialogue tracks and then later adjust the effects, music, and ambience tracks relative to the dialogue. In either case, the first and most important track you mix is called your **reference track**.

Just as with field recording, you use a peak meter as your primary reference tool as you adjust levels. You monitor with headphones as well, but the peak meter helps maintain consistency across time, meaning from clip to clip, from start to finish, across your timeline. The first track that you adjust, your reference track, establishes your **average audio level range**. Your **headroom** is a safety area just above the place your audio peaks (Figure 21.14).

Let's say you are adjusting dialogue first. The area between –20 and –12 dB becomes your average audio range, with peaks going up to -6 dB. Now you can adjust the levels of each and every clip, across the dialogue tracks, relative to this reference. A whisper should obviously dip below –20 dB, loud voices will register around –16 dB, and a scream will clearly be even louder, but should not peak above –6 dB. As you adjust your clip levels for the reference track across time, you should use the peak meter to maintain consistency from clip to clip to clip. For example, if your narrator's average voice in the first scene held around –20 dB, then in the last scene it should also be at the same level. By comparing the levels of the two clips, you can easily see if your mix levels have drifted over time.

Adjusting the Other Tracks

Once you have established the levels of your reference track, you can then adjust the other tracks (sound effects, ambience, music) relative to this one. Keep in mind that "reference track" does not mean that this is always the loudest track in the movie. There are many times, for example, when music levels will be set well under dialogue levels and then later fade up to become the most prominent track in the sound design. Also, some sound effects, like explosions, should clearly be mixed louder than average dialogue.

NLE Systems and Audio Levels

As with most other functions in NLE systems, there are a number of ways to adjust the audio levels of clips and tracks. Most NLE systems make it extremely easy to adjust audio levels right in the timeline. To do this, you must select the track setting that shows the **audio waveforms**. The line that you see drawn through each clip is the system's default

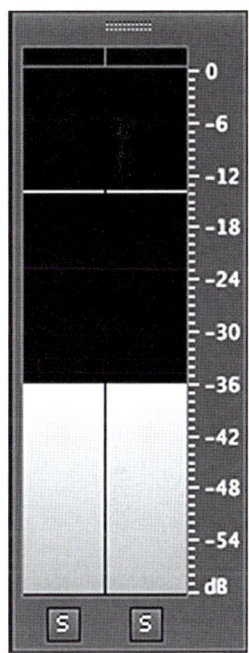

■ Figure 21.14
Your NLE's audio mixing tool allows you to monitor your audio levels as you work. The thin line towards the top shows that a sound has just peaked at –14dB, well within range, while the thicker bars show an average low of –36dB. Audio should never exceed –6 dB.

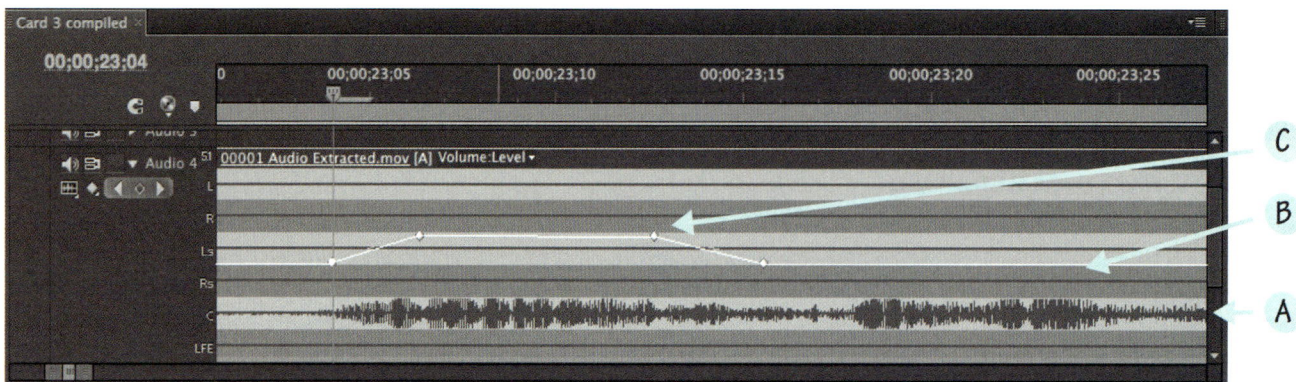

■ **Figure 21.15** Audio waveforms (A) in Premiere Pro. You can adjust audio levels in the timeline by clicking and dragging clip overlays (B). Here, key frames (C) are used to increase and then decrease the level of the audio.

level. Using your mouse or keypad, you can simply grab the audio overlay and manually raise or lower it to raise or lower the entire clip level (Figure 21.15). If you have a clip that has multiple dynamic level adjustments (for example, music in which the volume dips and then rises again), you can use **keyframes** to control the audio levels with precision. You can create as many keyframes as you need, allowing for enormous flexibility for level adjustment (Figure 21.15).

Step 4: The Mix Down

Finally, with all of the tracks sounding their best and their levels set to create a perfect balance of sounds, you are ready to mix down and output your multiple tracks to create a **master mix track**. Your NLE program's mix tool is used for this purpose (Figure 21.16). When you open the mix tool, you will see one audio gain slider for every audio track in

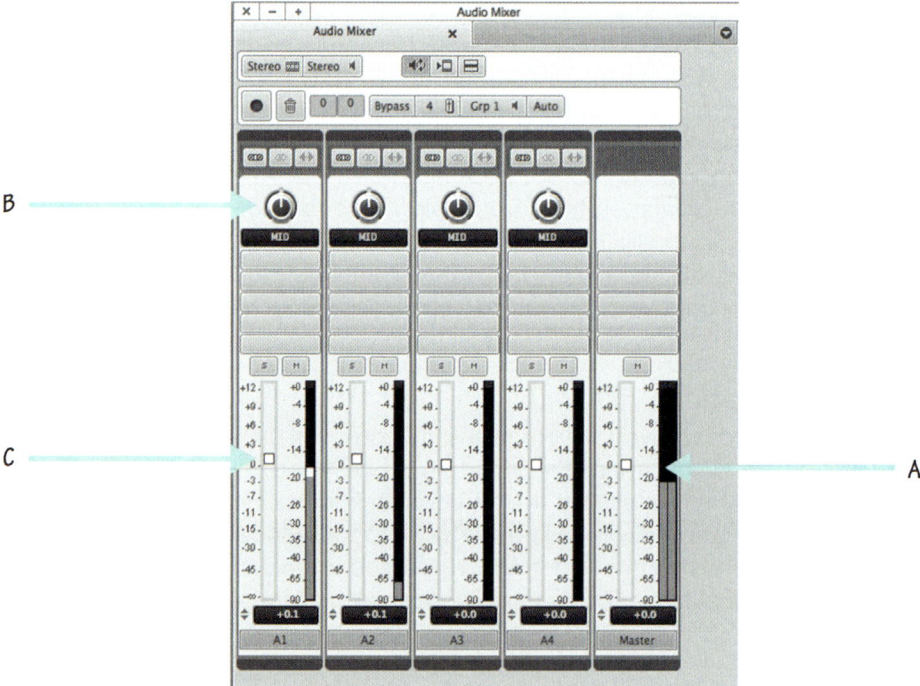

■ **Figure 21.16** Avid's audio mixer mixes all your audio tracks down to two master output stereo channels (A). With the panning slider (B), you can send each track to either one or both stereo channels. Each track also has its own fader (C) for independent level adjustment.

the program, and as you play through your sound design, the gain sliders will move, corresponding to the level adjustments you made in each clip. At the top of each level slider is a **pan slider**. Generally, you will be outputting your audio as a **two-channel stereo** master. The pan sliders allow you to select which channel on the mix track each audio track should be directed to. If you want both channels of audio to be the same (called a **mono mix**), then all of the pan sliders remain in their central position.

Surround sound is an increasingly common alternative to mono or stereo mixing, especially considering the popularity of sophisticated home viewing setups. Surround sound is also required for Digital Cinema Packages (Chapter 22) and may be required for other delivery situations. Essentially, surround sound uses five or more speakers behind and to the sides of the audience to create a more three-dimensional soundscape.

If you are going to be creating a surround sound mix track, you will likely work with a sound editor and/or rerecording mixer who specialize in creating surround sound mixes.

SOUND MIXING TIPS

The Mix Environment
Sound mixing should be done in an environment with audio playback equipment that accurately represents a high-quality exhibition space. In a professional mixing facility, the rerecording mixer handles the hardware and the mixing tasks while the director and the picture and sound editors watch the film projected on a fairly large screen, listening to the sound mix on high-quality speakers. The whole mixing suite is sound baffled to minimize reverberation. Most students in introductory or intermediate production courses, however, mix right on their NLE system. This is fine, but it is recommended to mix in a space that is quiet. It is essential that you use good speakers. Be aware that any traffic noise, reverberant surfaces, HVAC, and other noises in the environment will blend with what's coming out of your speakers. Mixing with headphones is also a viable alternative, but again, make sure the headphones are of very high quality and are isolation-type headphones, meaning that they have foam that surrounds your ears to keep external noises from leaking in. Poor-quality headphones, especially those that do not press firmly against your ear, can give you a less than accurate impression of your sound track. If you do mix with headphones, be sure to check your sound on a good set of speakers from time to time to get a more accurate impression of how the audience will hear it. One of the biggest weaknesses of most computer speakers and headphones is an inability to give you a clear sense of the bass sounds in your track.

Audio Monitor Reference
When setting audio levels during the sound mix, it is essential that you keep the output level of your speakers and headphones absolutely consistent. Audio levels are relative, so if your headphone level is low one day, you might raise the levels of your clips higher than you need, and if the headphone levels are higher another day, then you may be tempted to set clip levels lower than on the previous day. So set the output volume to a comfortable level and leave it alone for the duration of the sound mix.

ADVANCED SOUND EDITING AND MIXING PROGRAMS
The audio sweetening and sound mixing capabilities found in most NLE systems are truly remarkable, but to a professional sound mixer they offer only basic functions. As your films get more complex and your soundtrack needs become more demanding, you may find yourself wanting to use more advanced, stand-alone, sound mixing programs. Remember, Avid and Premiere Pro are picture editing programs, and professional sound mixers would never use them to mix sound. Instead, they use a **digital audio workstation (DAW)**. The most common DAW for documentary sound editing and mixing is **Avid Pro Tools** (Figure 21.17). Pro Tools offers much more powerful audio filters for special effects

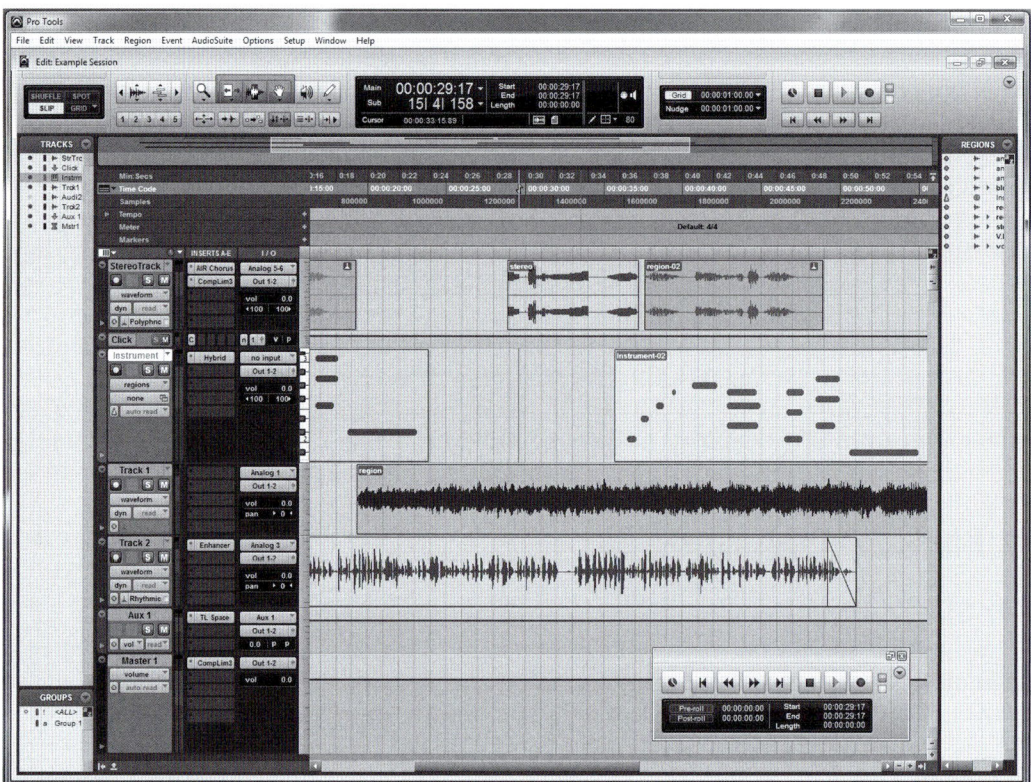

■ **Figure 21.17** DAWs are substantially more precise and powerful for audio work than NLEs. Pictured is the Pro Tools 9.0 desktop.

and audio sweetening than any NLE. It has more precise equalizers and many more transition effects. Its ability to make subframe edits and stretch audio without changing pitch allows for highly precise sound edits. Pro Tools is also designed to import both your edited video (for visual reference) as well as all of the sound tracks and adjustments you've made along the way. Pro Tools requires that all sound files be converted into the **open media framework (OMF)** file format. It is relatively easy to export audio from either AVID or Premiere Pro in OMF format. You can even set the conversion to export each clip with handles (p. 356).

Why Go Pro?

Certainly, as you are starting out, the benefits of mixing the soundtracks on your films on your own are enormous. Mixing your own sound gives you an intimate and nuanced understanding of the power of layered audio tracks. Placing a sound effect with perfect timing, adjusting the audio balance between clips to create dramatic emphasis, changing the mood by inserting a different ambience track, and literally seeing the way a music track can weave its way throughout a film are all invaluable experiences that will have an impact on the way you will use sound in future projects. Doing your own sound edit and mix may even convince you that you'd like to be a sound designer. If you find, though, that your ideas and requirements have become more complex than your abilities, it's time to turn to those people who absolutely adore postproduction sound, those who have dedicated their careers to it and have a talent for it, those people who know exactly what every one of those audio filters and third-party plug-ins in a Pro Tools system does.

Pros will have high-end mixing programs with audio processors, scopes, and equalizers, but more importantly, they have experience and a sensibility for the world of sound. A good sound editor or rerecording mixer can not only make everything sound much better, they can hear problems in the tracks you might not have noticed. They can make creative suggestions, especially for sound bridges between scenes that will improve your film. And that's why you go to a professional in any area of filmmaking: experience, talent, and technical expertise will enhance the expressive impact of your film.

When you decide to start using professional sound mixers, it is a good idea to consult with them before you start shooting your film. They will tell you the details of the mixing system they use and how it interfaces with your particular editing system. They will tell you what resources they have, what they need, and in what format they prefer the audio data and video delivered. It is especially important to consult with them ahead of time if you have sound that will need significant fixing in the mix. Some things can be fixed; others, like too much reverb in a recording, are nearly impossible to correct.

Keep in mind that the options are not limited to DIY or going with a professional sound mixer charging $200 an hour or more. Just as with cinematography, writing, or any other filmmaking task, there are people who have a talent for sound design and mixing who are good, but not yet professionals. This person might be your classmate or it might be you! These people need to establish themselves in the field and gain experience, and the only way to do that is to practice and show what they've got. You might just find the perfect match.

CHAPTER 22

Finishing Picture and Mastering

Once you have a picture-locked film and a mixed soundtrack, it may seem like the big creative choices are over. Yet there are still important aesthetic decisions to be made before exporting your film onto a format that will allow you to send it out into the world. This chapter looks at the picture finishing process for a variety of workflows. The determining factors in choosing your workflow will include 1) your budget, and 2) where your film is going to be seen. Student films that may show in a couple of festivals, and perhaps on YouTube or another online platform, will have a very different workflow than a film destined for more recognized festivals, for broadcast, or for theatrical presentation.

COLOR CORRECTION VS COLOR GRADING

Whereas historically, video color correction was done in an expensive **online session** in a postproduction facility that specialized in this work, the move to NLE editing meant that much color correction could be done using your NLE software tools. But in the last few years, the growing ability of digital cameras to handle a broad range of exposures has been accompanied by a similar growth in separate software specifically designed to give a whole new level of control over color at a low cost. Many of these new tools fall under the rubric of **color grading**. Adobe's Creative Suite, for example, now includes Adobe Speed Grade, and many other programs have come on the market. **Color grading** refers to the use of color to create mood, meaning, and a specialized look for your documentary. As such, it goes beyond the scope of **color correction**, which includes the more basic goals of getting appropriate and consistent color throughout your documentary. In this chapter, we will mostly focus on color correction adjustments you might expect to do on your own in your NLE system. If you are planning to work with **extended dynamic range** (Chapter 12) and do color grading, you will probably want to work with a colorist who specializes in this area. Like all workflow choices, it pays to consult with these specialists *before* you start shooting your project!

COLOR CORRECTION IN YOUR NLE SYSTEM

If you are working on a project that does not include funds for professional color grading, you will probably be using some standard tools that are incorporated into most NLE systems. These are, in fact, quite powerful correction features that take some time and patience to learn. Once you master them, though, you can correct many problems in your picture and put out a visually polished documentary.

Color correction is used primarily to accomplish four things:
1. Adjust **brightness** and **contrast** values for your shots.
2. Correct **color balance** so that skin tones in particular are correct, and the level of color saturation is appropriate for your desired look.
3. Create **consistent color and brightness values** across shots within a scene, and throughout the film.
4. Tweak subtle tonalities for a specific look or mood.

Adjusting Brightness and Contrast

Brightness refers to the overall lightness or darkness of your shot. **Contrast** refers to the range of dark and light values within the shot. If brights are too low, and darks too light, your image will look gray. Consider these two archival images of Coney Island's Dreamland in 1905, as they are displayed in Premiere Pro's Program Panel (Figure 22.1).

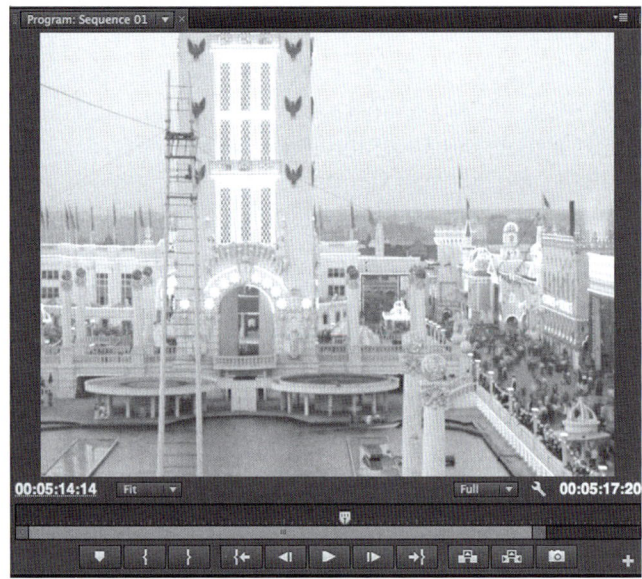 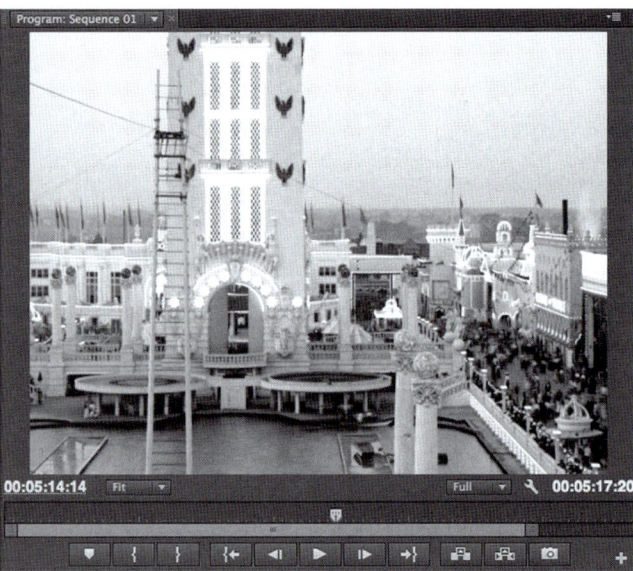

■ **Figure 22.1** Brightness and Contrast. The image on the left, the camera original, does not make use of the full range of white and black levels available. The image on the right has had its white and black levels adjusted using the Fast Color Corrector in Premiere Pro, resulting in higher contrast and a more dynamic image.

We measure white and black levels using the **waveform scope**, which gives us a graphical representation of the brightness levels across the image. Brightness is measured in IREs, with 100 representing pure white and 0 representing black, and is represented on the scope's y-axis (Figure 22.2).

Although there is some type of Brightness and Contrast filter in every NLE program, you will have better control using a more sophisticated filter. For our purposes, let's take a quick look at the **fast color corrector** filter in Premiere Pro (Figure 22.3).

If you are delivering a program for broadcast, you will need to pay close attention to your brightness levels as there are technical standards set by engineers that need to be closely adhered to. Black levels for broadcast, for example, need to be set at 0 IREs, and your whites at 100. Requirements for various platforms vary, so be sure to check the specifications for your particular exhibitor before you begin postproduction.

Adjusting Hue and Saturation

Hue refers to the color *values* of your image—in other words, the balance of red, blue, or green in your image. **Saturation** refers to the *intensity* of the colors. An image with rich, deep color would be considered highly saturated, while a washed-out image is less saturated. An image that has no saturation is black and white. Generally speaking, the most important hue and saturation adjustments are those that affect the way people's skin tones look. Hue and saturation can also be manipulated to create a look or mood for your film.

CHAPTER 22 365
Finishing Picture and Mastering

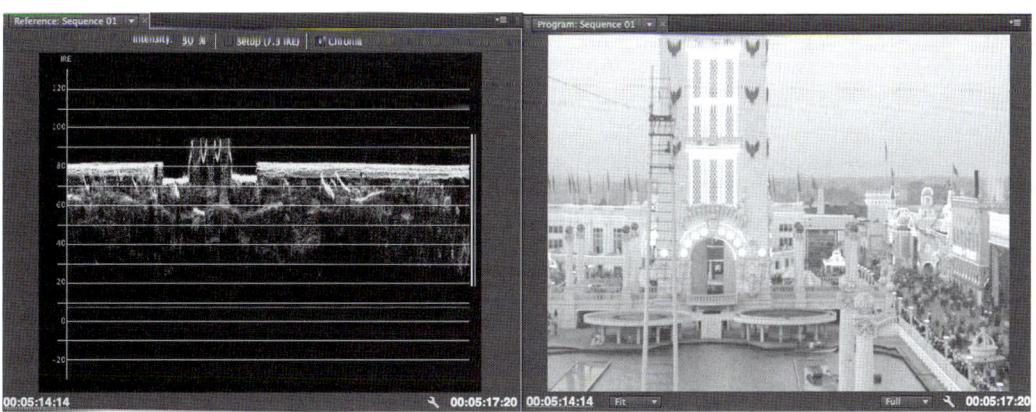

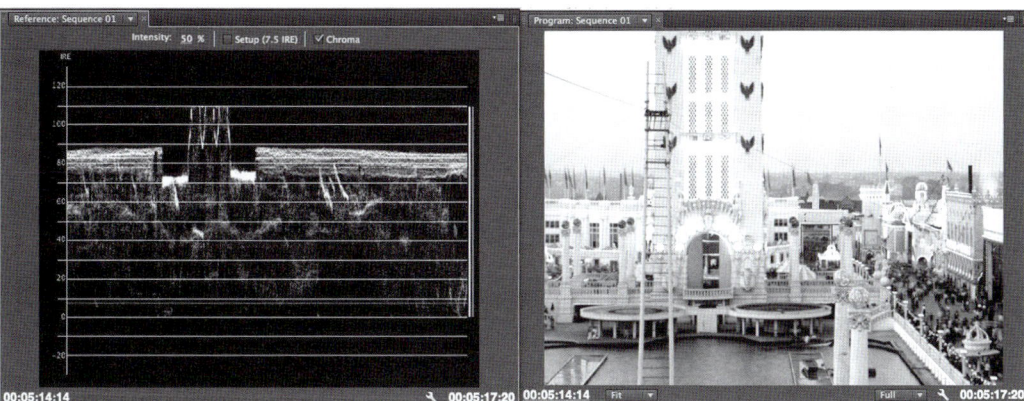

■ **Figure 22.2** The waveform scope shows the white and black levels of the image. The top photograph, which looks more "washed out," has a smaller range of white and black values than the one on the bottom. The range is indicated by a bar on the right-hand side of the scope.

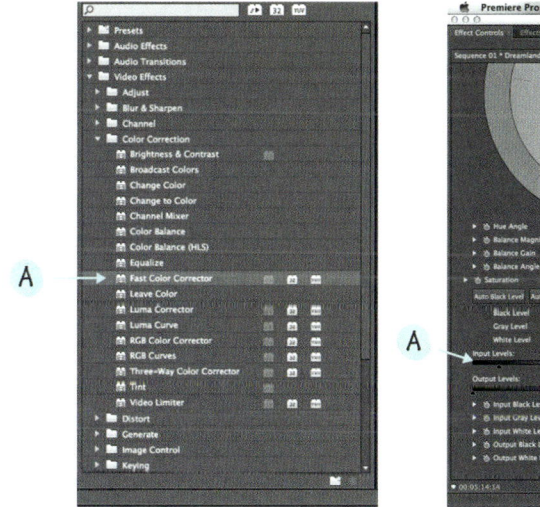
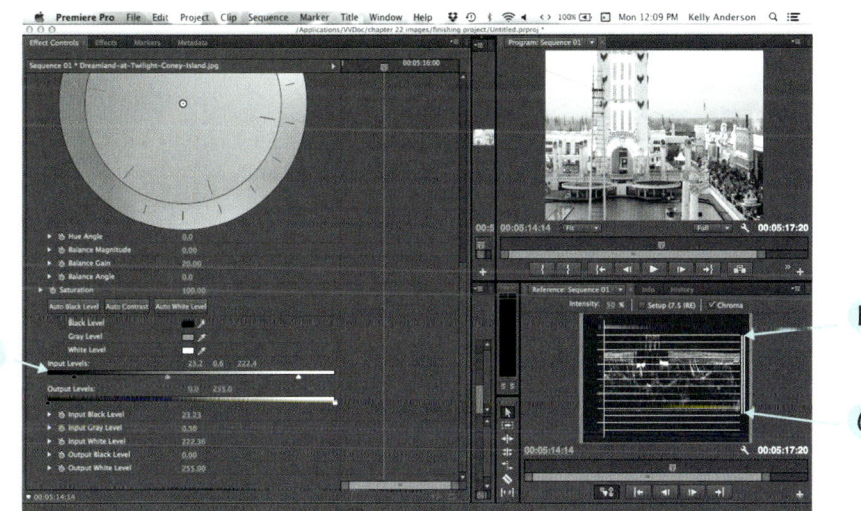

■ **Figure 22.3** The Fast Color Corrector filter in Premiere Pro (left, A) is a good choice for basic adjustments to Brightness and Contrast. Use the Input Level slider under "saturation" (right, A) to bring the white levels in the brightest part of the picture (the tower) to 100 IREs (B), and the darkest parts of the image (the bottom right corner) to 0 (C). The middle slider will adjust the range of gray values (you can do this by eye).

While there are many filters in your NLE toolbox for adjusting the hue and saturation of your image, here we will stick with the Fast Color Corrector filter. Consider the image in Figure 22.4, which was shot in **mixed light** (Chapter 12) and as a result has a blue tinge.

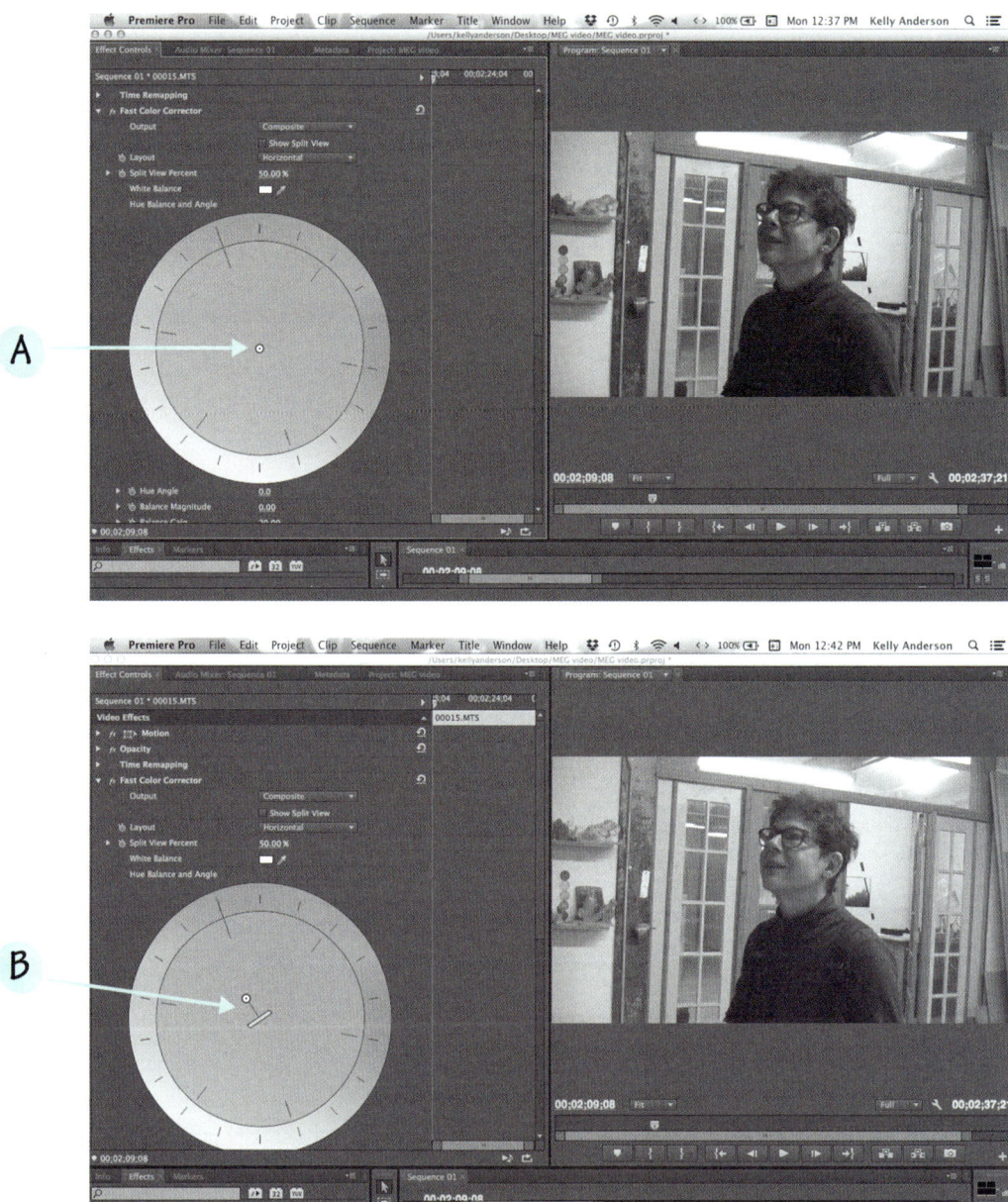

■ **Figure 22.4** Adjusting hue and saturation using the Fast Color Corrector in Premiere Pro. The dot in the middle of the color wheel (A) is in the center before the image is adjusted. In order to reduce the blue tint, and add orange, you drag the dot slowly away from the blue side of the color wheel and towards its opposite, orange (B). As you can see, the result is a warmer image. (See plate section for color.)

The Fast Color Corrector's color wheel has its roots in a **color wheel** that has been used for more than 300 years to help people understand the relationships between colors (Figure 22.5).

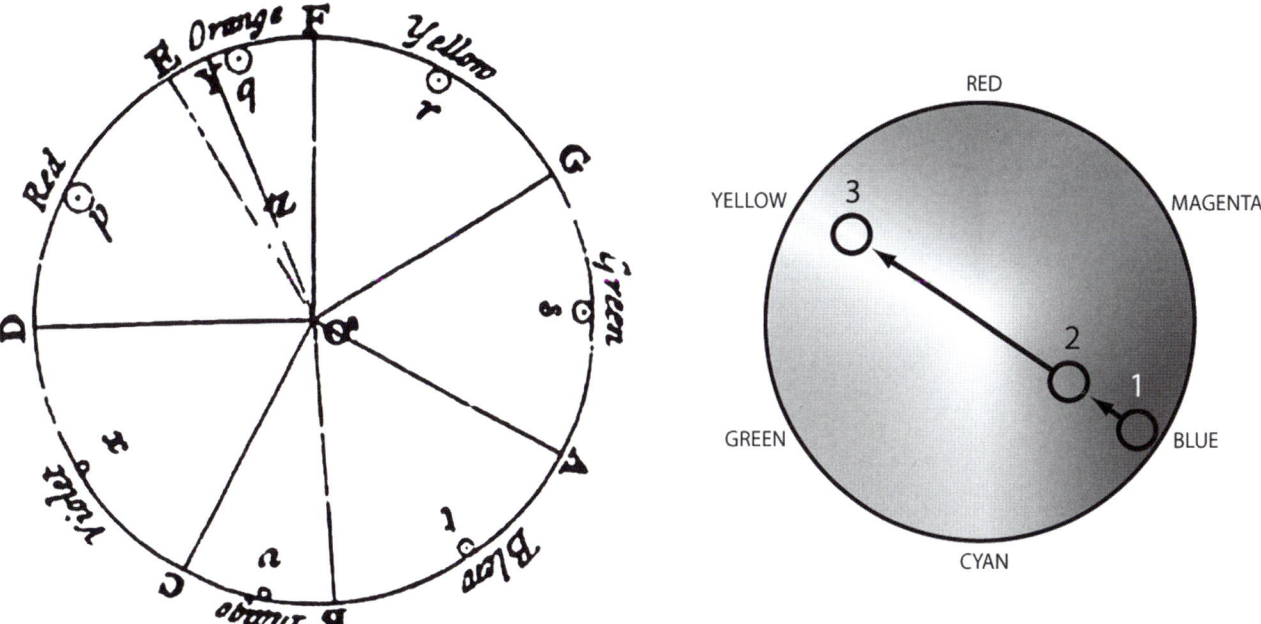

■ **Figure 22.5** The first color wheel is attributed to Isaac Newton, who in 1706 arranged red, orange, yellow, green, blue, indigo, and violet into a natural progression on a rotating disk (left). As the disk spins, the colors blur together so rapidly that the human eye sees white. The color wheel in many color correction programs follows the same principle (right). As you reduce the amount of blue, for example, you increase the amount of its complementary color, yellow. (See plate section for color.)

Another useful tool for adjusting color is the **Vectorscope** (Figure 22.6). The vectorscope represents the saturation of each color in the image.

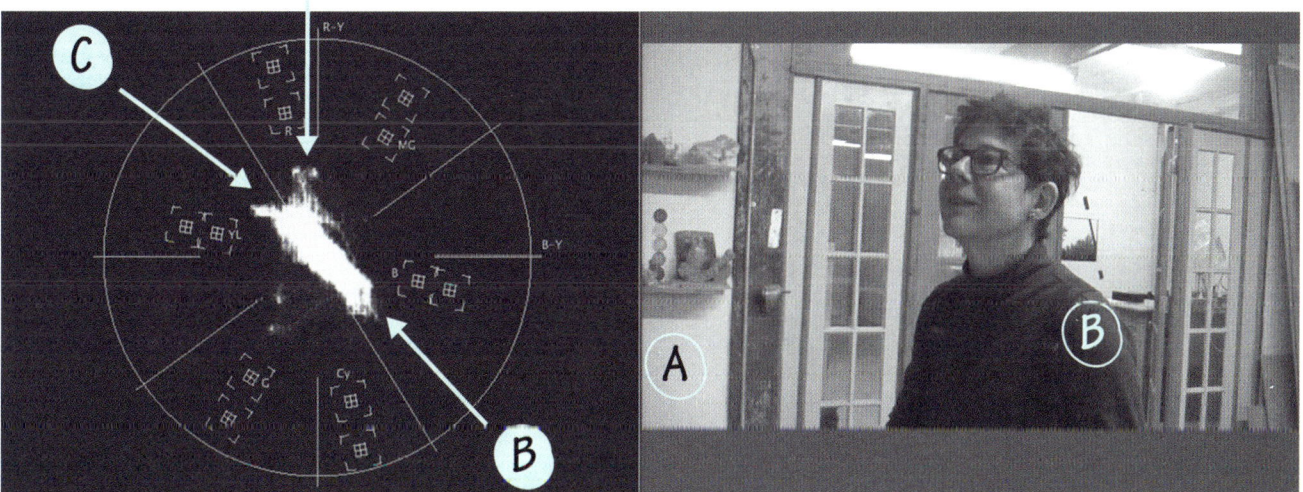

■ **Figure 22.6** The vectorscope represents the saturation level of the various colors in the image. The red object on the shelf (A) creates a spike on the "red" area of the vectorscope (A). Similarly, the blue shirt (B) registers strongly in the "blue" area of the vectorscope (B). The (C) line represents skin tones, and is a valuable reference point when correcting people's faces. Because what registers is the color of the blood, not the pigment of the skin, all skin tones should register along this exact line. (See plate section for color.)

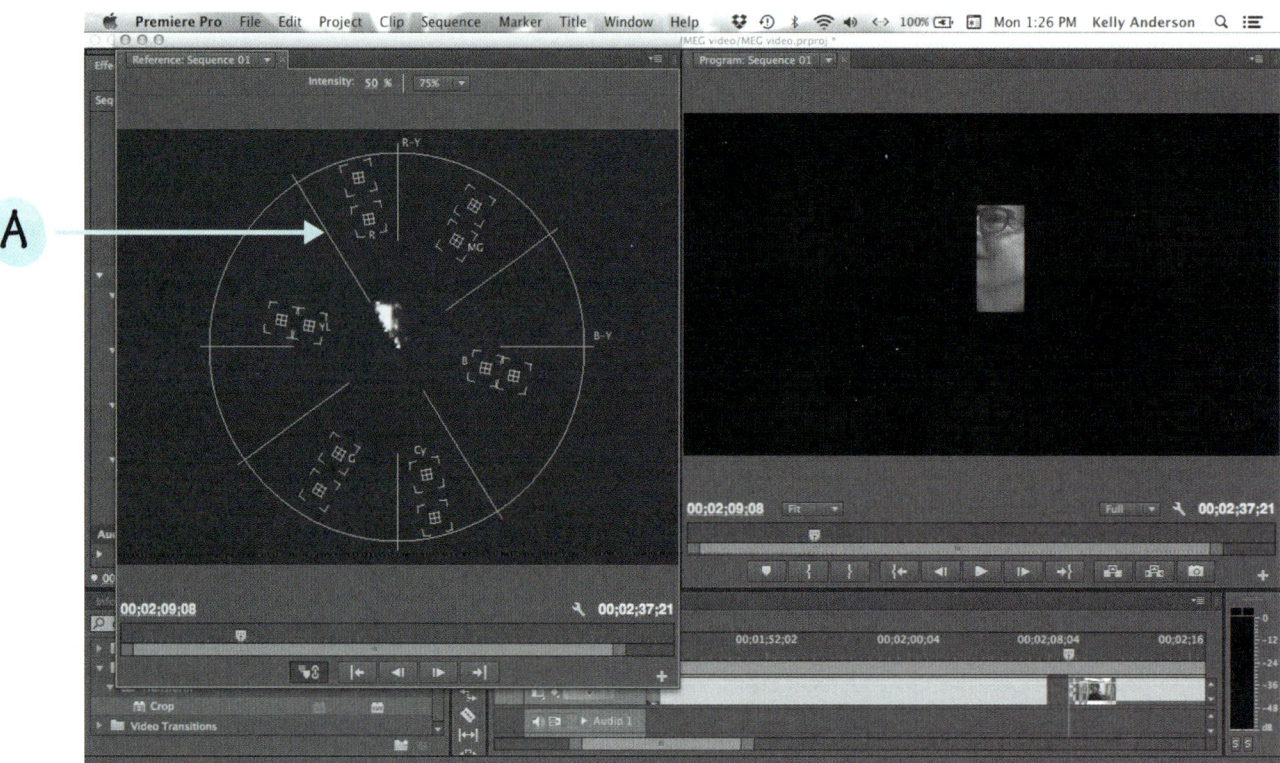

■ **Figure 22.7** The vectorscope's flesh tone line. Cropping the program panel image to reveal just the face of the subject illustrates how skin tones, when they are corrected properly, fall along the vectorscope's flesh tone line. (See plate section for color.)

When color correcting, keep in mind that your computer monitor is not necessarily calibrated to give you accurate colors. Whenever color correcting with your NLE, you should plan to screen the final results on a television **monitor** that has been calibrated to give the most accurate color possible (Chapter 8). It is also a good idea to work in a dark room, as the natural light coming from the outside will change over the course of the day, impacting what you see on your screen. Another tip is to look away from your computer quite frequently as you color correct. Your eyes and your brain are incredibly adept at adjusting to input. Before you know it, a green skin tone may begin to look normal if you don't take a break now and then.

And, finally, a word of caution: color correction tools are something that should be researched thoroughly before you go grabbing sliders and pushing them around. Color correction is not just about the buttons you need to push: there is considerable technique and aesthetic judgment involved.

■ TITLES AND CREDITS

The final step, before you master your film, is to put titles and credits on it. Most NLE systems contain a **title tool** with more typographical options than you could (or should!) use in a lifetime. You can choose from dozens of fonts, sizes, and colors. You can adjust the opacity of the text, create drop shadows or fuzzy edges, make the text scroll up or down, or crawl sideways, or fly in from the four corners of the screen. You can create titles against simple color backgrounds, like any color text on black or any color on white. Or, by adding an additional video track to your timeline, you can superimpose your opening or closing credits over scenes from your film (Figure 22.9).

If you are working with a colorist in a program like DaVinci Resolve, the film will generally be imported back into your NLE for titling. Some filmmakers prefer to create their titles in

CHAPTER 22
Finishing Picture and Mastering

■ WORKING WITH A PROFESSIONAL COLORIST

What can a professional **colorist** add to your documentary? If your documentary is going to be broadcast, you will be required to do a professional color correction or grading session to make sure you meet the technical specifications of the broadcaster to whom you are delivering. But there are also other reasons to draw on the expertise of someone who spends their days doing color correction.

Brian Boyd has worked doing color correction and creating cohesive looks for numerous television shows, as well as feature documentaries and dramas for theatrical and festival release. His documentary credits include *A Will for the Woods* (2014, Dirs. Amy Browne, Jeremy Kaplan, Tony Hale, and Brian Wilson) and *Next Year in Jerusalem* (2013, Dir. David Gaynes). He often collaborates with documentary director Morgan Spurlock. Asked what a professional colorist brings to a production, Brian says:

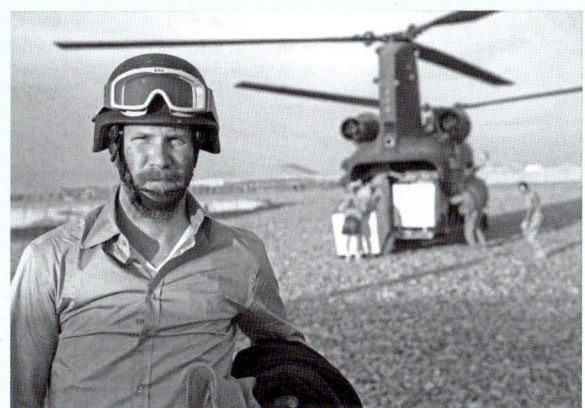

■ **Figure 22.8** In this scene from Morgan Spurlock's *Where in the World is Osama Bin Laden?* (2008), color grading brings out the subtle colors and textures of the Afghani landscape. (See plate section for color.)

> *Being a colorist can be an invisible art at times. Most documentarians just want the footage to look the best it can. Documentaries can't always shoot under ideal conditions, and from shot to shot drastic light and hue shifts can occur. A professional colorist has the ability to see these problems and make the best decisions as to how to balance the shots out so that nothing feels out of place or distracting.*
>
> *But a colorist can also help filmmakers enhance the power of their story. I've gotten to work on a lot of films and every single one has moments where we accomplish this. In A Will for the Woods (2014), a man goes through the process of preparing his own green burial. I received the footage after the subject had passed away, and I felt personally responsible for showing him in the best way possible during his final days. I've worked with Morgan Spurlock, creating slick commercial looks for his documentary Greatest Movie Ever Sold (2011), or showing how beautiful and harsh Afghanistan is in Where in the World is Osama Bin Laden? (2008) (Figure 22.8). I did a faux documentary The Bay (2012), directed by Barry Levinson. It's an eco disaster film set in a small town. Barry shot the film with a few cameras and it was my job to make it look like it was filmed with about 75 different cameras. I got to really degrade and "hurt" the footage for the look of the film. I took HD footage down to VHS and then back up. I messed with the timing of shots to create stuttered security cam footage. It was very experimental and fun.*[1]

The industry standard color correction tool at the moment, according to Boyd, is DaVinci Resolve, from Blackmagic Design.

> *Resolve did something that was unheard of in the post production world. They basically released their product for free. It works seamlessly with Final Cut Pro, and works extremely well with Premiere Pro and Avid. There is a paid version of the software that adds some needed tools for professional finishing, but a documentary could easily be finished on the free version of Resolve.*
>
> *What Blackmagic Design did by releasing DaVinci Resolve for free changed the industry. Suddenly everyone had access to professional color tools. There are positives and negatives to this. The industry was flooded with colorists who had no experience and didn't get the chance to learn the proper way to do color. You need to apprentice under a senior colorist for years before you understand the nuances of color for film and TV.*
>
> *On the more positive side, larger color systems like Assimilate's Scratch and FilmLight's Baselight are stuck playing catch-up, and have had to get creative with their products.*[2]

Brian's advice for students and emerging filmmakers? If you want to take full advantage of these new tools, you will want to investigate shooting with **log gamma** (Chapter 12) or another flat **camera profile**. The extended dynamic range will give the colorist much more to work with in terms of highlights and shadow detail, as well as color.

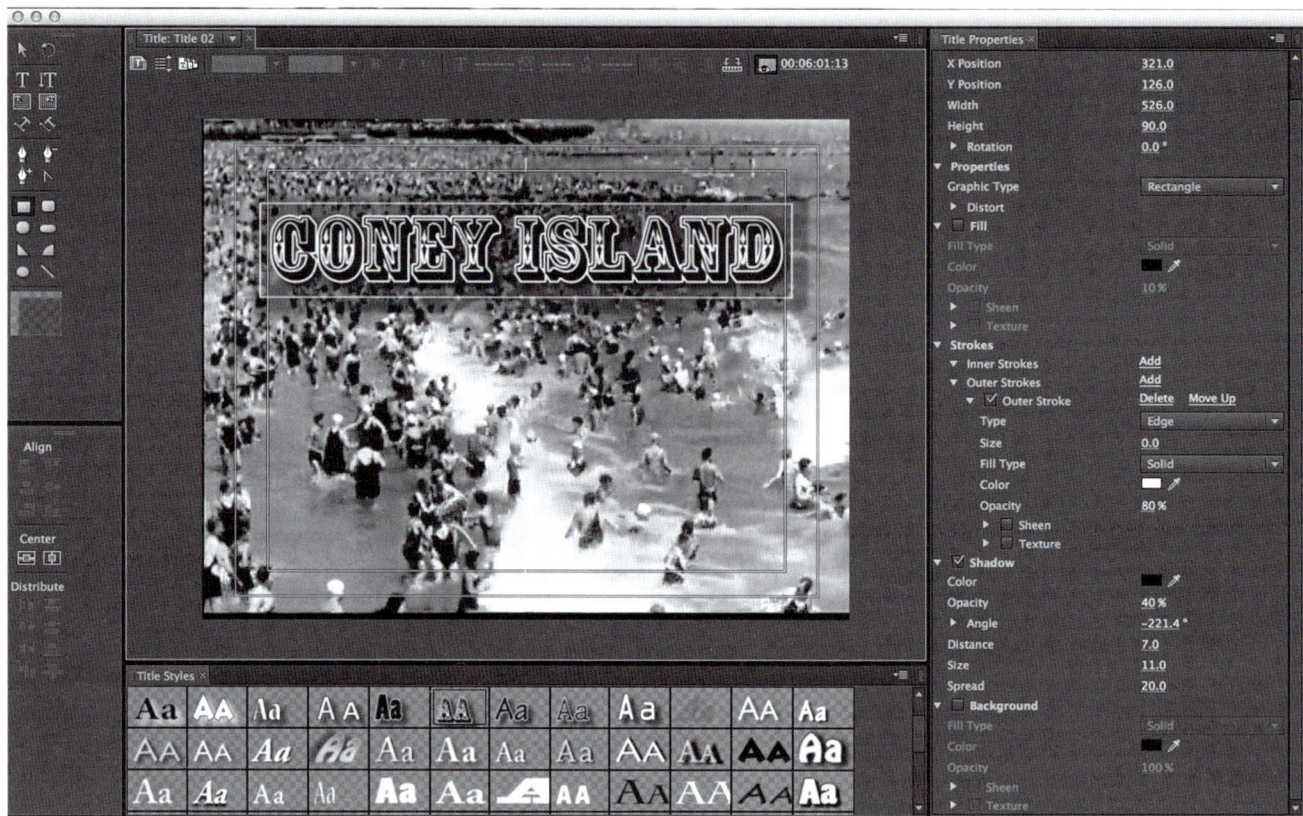

■ **Figure 22.9** The title tool in Premiere Pro allows you to select from a wide variety of fonts and effects, including "drop shadow" to make text superimposed over image pop out. In this case, a light gray rectangle has been placed behind the title to make it more legible.

a program like Adobe Illustrator or Photoshop, and then import them back into the NLE system. For complex layered or animated titles that require more sophistication than your NLE has, many designers use Adobe After Effects.

Think of your credits as an aspect of your film that is as important as any other visual element. Take time to design them. Do you want them to appear over moving images? Be combined with still images in some way? Just be simple but beautifully designed type on a black background? Do you want them to move (**scroll**) or to fade up and out one page at a time (**cards**)? It is easy, in the tired euphoria of locking picture and finishing sound, to short-change your titles. Think of them as adding a very important graphic touch that defines the overall tone of your film, and can be a simple way of adding style and production value (Figures 22.10 and 22.11).

A word of advice: the people who worked on your movie deserve proper credit. Especially for people initiating their careers in film, credits can be as important as pay. It is not unusual for talented people to work only for the credit, especially if they believe the film will be good. If you slap your credits together at the last minute, you run the risk of forgetting people, giving them improper credit, or misspelling their names. All of these are serious faux pas and can alienate the people you've worked with, who are among your most important resources as a filmmaker. Also, do not forget to acknowledge those people who helped make your film a reality, though they may not have directly worked on it, by including them in a "thanks to . . ." credit.

Lower Thirds

In addition to opening and end credits, documentaries often include titles that identify the people and locations in the film. As with opening and closing titles, these can easily be created within your NLE program, or imported from Photoshop or Illustrator.

CHAPTER 22 | 371
Finishing Picture and Mastering

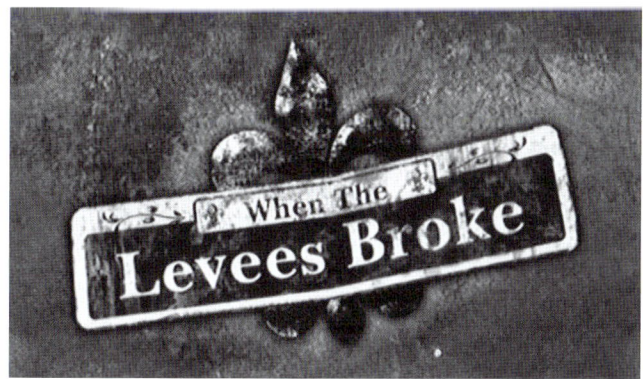

■ **Figure 22.10** The opening sequence of Spike Lee's *When The Levees Broke: A Requiem in Four Acts* (2006), about Hurricane Katrina, uses an appropriately simple style for the somber message of the opening card (left). The main title card (right) takes its graphic inspiration from the wrought iron street signs typical of New Orleans.

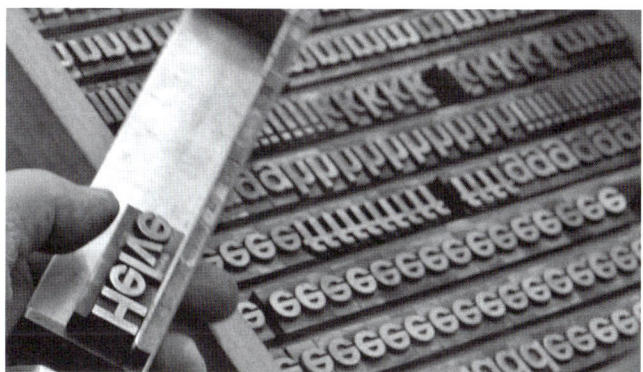 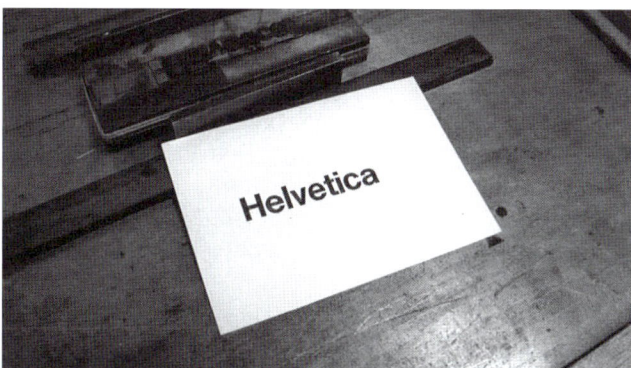

■ **Figure 22.11** *Helvetica* (Dir. Gary Hustwit, 2007) takes a live action approach that is appropriate for its subject matter (the Helvetica font). We see a typesetter arranging letters and applying ink to them. We see the results of his labor when he prints out a card with the film's title on it.

These titles are called **lower thirds** because traditionally they always appeared in the bottom third of the screen. In practice today, they can be anywhere in the frame, as long as they are placed within **title safety** (the inner portion of the frame that will be visible in a variety of exhibition venues, including older TV sets) (Figure 22.12). Titles that identify people generally include the person's name, as well as a professional association or some sense of who they are beyond just their name. For experts, this is often their professional title, like a university affiliation or other job-related information that will add credibility to their testimony. For other people, it can be trickier to figure out the right way to describe them. In a film about a murder trial, for example, you might interview a jury member who also happens to be a school teacher. In this case, it would probably make sense to identify them as "jury member" rather than as "science teacher," as the latter is irrelevant to the film. On the other hand, if it's a police misconduct trial and your jury member is also a retired police officer, it might be important to give your viewer both pieces of information. Use your own judgment, keeping your story in mind, and a sense of what information will best allow your viewer to put the speaker's comments and actions into perspective.

■ **Figure 22.12** Title and picture safety overlays. Because different monitors may clip some of your frame, it's important to keep your text within title safety (the inner green box) and any critical action within picture safety (the outer green box).

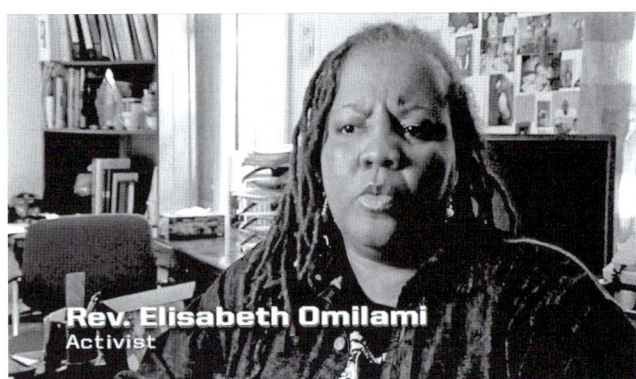 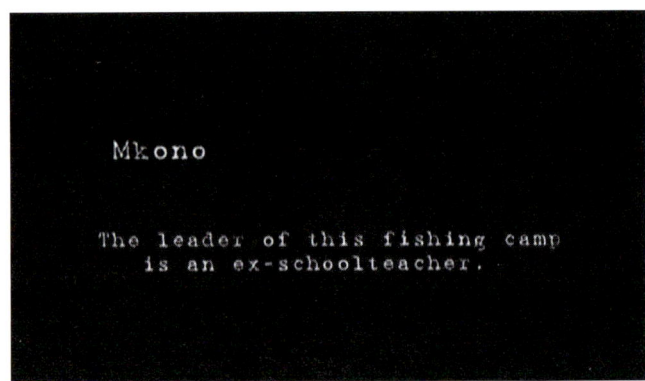

■ **Figure 22.13** A simple approach to lower thirds is used in *Banished* (Dir. Marco Williams, 2006) (left). A more stylized approach is used in Hubert Sauper's *Darwin's Nightmare* (2004): a black card with a degraded "typewriter" font is cut in over the interview to emphasize the investigative nature of the documentary (right).

Location identifiers, or **Location IDs**, present information that tells the audience where the events they are seeing are unfolding. Often they appear when the film moves to a new geographical place, or when the building we are looking at, for example, is significant to the story but not identifiable at first glance ("FBI headquarters," for example, or "Smith family home").

As with opening and closing credits, lower thirds should be designed carefully. Sometimes a very simple design is best, while at other times you can add production value through more stylized design choices (Figure 22.13). Just keep in mind that the titles should complement the film, not distract or shout out "look at me!"

MASTERING YOUR PROJECT

Picture locked, sound mixed, color corrected and titled, your film is now ready to be exported out of the computer and put into distribution. The first step in this process is to create full-resolution **program masters**. **Mastering** simply means outputting your film as a high-resolution digital file or onto a high-quality HD tape format (with a backup high-resolution digital file). The program masters serve dual purposes: they archive your film, and you use them to make distribution copies.

When creating your program masters, it's a good practice to create two versions. One is a **textless master**, without any titles or lower thirds. The textless master will be used to make copies for countries where the language differs from the one your film titles are in. Not having your titles married to the picture will allow a Brazilian broadcaster, for example, to add Portuguese versions of your titles with ease. The version of your film that includes your titles is called the **texted master**.

From your program master, you will output a range of files for different exhibition purposes. NLE systems offer a huge range of output options that employ various codecs, resolutions, frame sizes, and so on (Figure 22.14).

Different codecs are compatible with different uses. For example, the MPEG 2 codec is used for making DVDs, and MPEG 4 and H.264 are commonly used for distribution over the web. You can also export a QuickTime movie of your project at different levels of compression depending on your distribution outlet. Outputting to tape is done via a cable connected to your computer (such as Firewire or Thunderbolt), but many of these other output options, like QuickTime movies or MPEG 2, simply create media files that can be exported into third-party programs for multimedia playback, for further compression, for uploading to the web, or for authoring DVDs or Blu-rays.

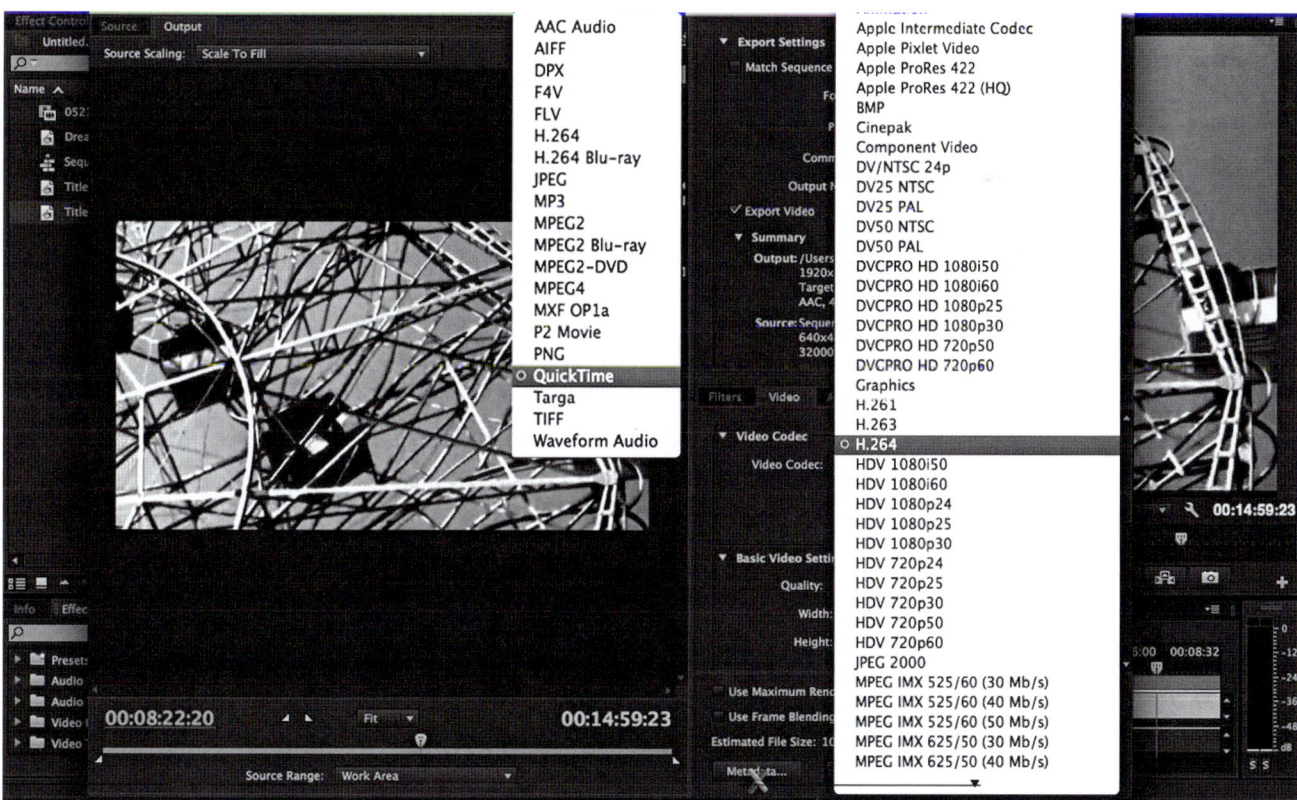

■ **Figure 22.14** The Export Settings window in Premiere Pro. Notice the wide variety of formats (left) and codecs (right) you can choose from.

Output Formats

These days, it can be very confusing to know what formats your exhibitors will be requesting from you. "Many broadcasters who request files ask for Apple ProRes HQ, but that's not standard by any means. Every broadcaster is different," says Keith Shapiro, the General Manager of Frame:Runner, Inc., a New York postproduction house. "And, many still ask for HD tapes."[3]

Common formats used for projection at film festivals include HDCAM, DigiBeta, Blu-ray disc, a hi-resolution file, or a Digital Cinema Package (see below).

Digital Cinema Package (DCP)

Increasingly filmmakers find themselves having to use the **Digital Cinema Package (DCP)** format for delivery. DCP, which is defined by the industry consortium Digital Cinema Initiatives, involves creating a collection of digital files used to store and convey digital cinema audio, image, and data streams. Finishing, mastering, and distributing on DCP is always expensive, primarily because it involves surround sound and other extensive postproduction services. This means that these processes are undertaken when a filmmaker knows that they have the budget to go this route, or after they have secured a theatrical release or have been accepted into a festival that requires a DCP. Increasingly, broadcasters also require a DCP.

If you anticipate that you'll be finishing on DCP, plan for this workflow before you start editing because all postproduction houses have their own requirements in terms of formats, processes, and elements. Though there is software you can use to create a DCP on your own, there are potential pitfalls and you should proceed with caution.

PROGRAM LEADER

Whether you are exporting to a high-resolution file or to tape, you should add a **program leader** to the head of your program master. Leaders include **color bars** and **tone**, a **slate**, and a **countdown** (Figures 22.15 and 22.16).

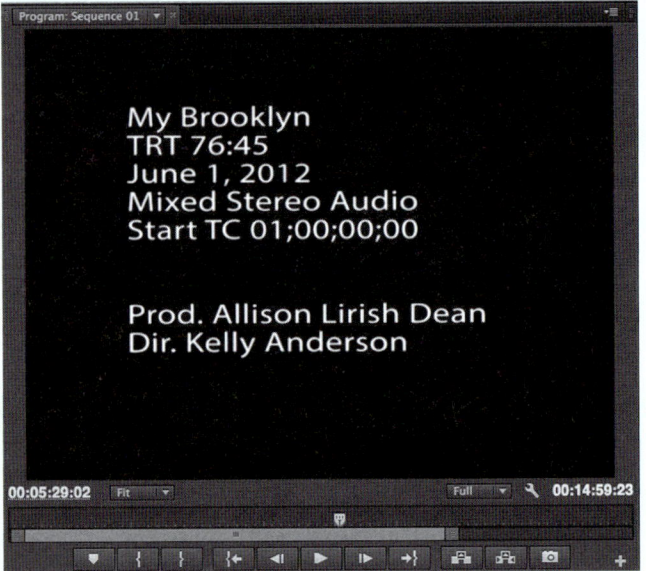

■ **Figure 22.16** A program slate, which is inserted for 10 seconds after the color bars and tone, and before the countdown. The slate generally includes the program title, the total running time (TRT), the creation date, technical information about the audio, the start time code, and the production company or creators of the film.

Bars and Tone

If you plan to broadcast your movie over television or cable, or submit it to film festivals, it's important to give the recipient of your film some way to accurately calibrate their equipment so that your film will look and sound as you intend. The standard calibration tools, which you lay down at the head of your tape, are **color bars** and **tone**. We have already mentioned color bars with respect to calibrating field monitors (Chapter 8). The leader elements discussed here are the Society of Motion Picture and Television Engineers (SMPTE) standard color bars, which allow the projectionist or broadcast engineer to accurately calibrate the chrominance and luminance of their playback equipment. The 1 kHz reference tone, which is recorded on the soundtrack under the color bars, allows them to calibrate the audio so that your program is played back neither too soft nor too loud.

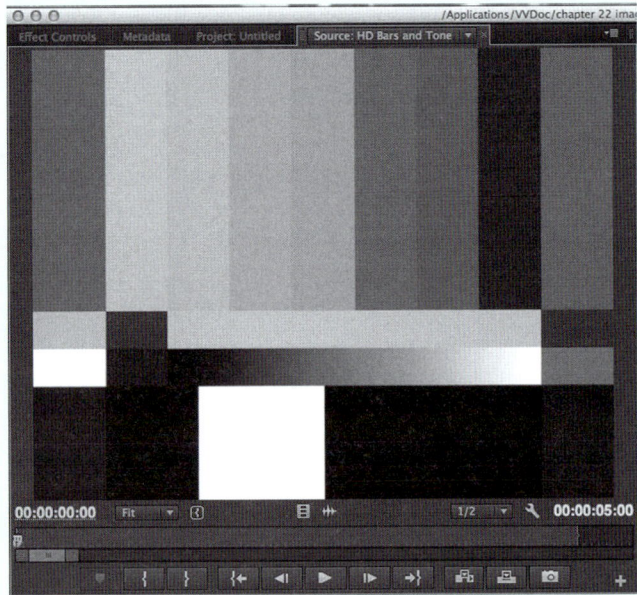

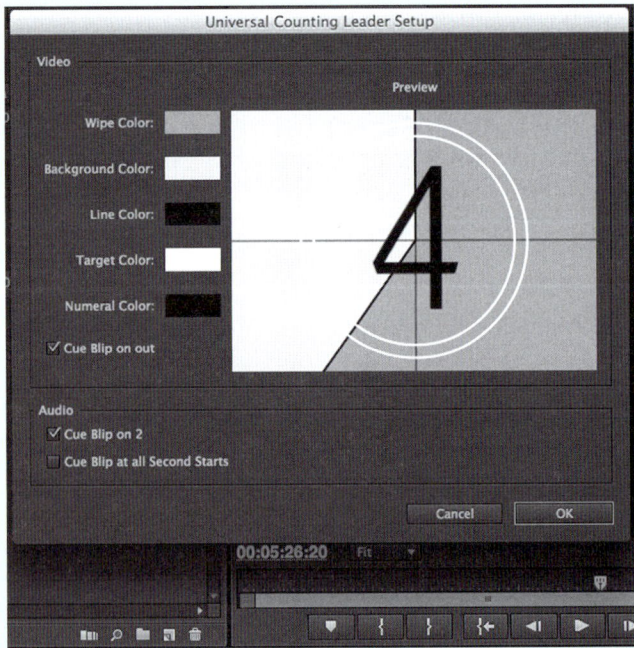

■ **Figure 22.15** The HD color bars and countdown in Premiere Pro. You insert these, as well as a 1 KHz tone, at the head of your program master as a reference for future duplication and exhibition.

The Program Slate

In addition, a standard professional program leader includes a **program slate**, which is a simple list of all of the information that would be important to a broadcaster or programmer, including (a) the film title, (b) total running time (TRT), (c) starting time code, (d) audio configuration (i.e., mixed or stereo unmixed), (e) production date, and

(f) producer or creators (Figure 22.16). Standard start time code is 01;00;00;00, which means that the actual start time code of the tape or file will have to be backtimed to give you room for these other elements before the program starts. The normal default for sequence starting time code is 01;00;00;00, so if you are exporting from your NLE you will have to change your sequence settings for this particular sequence to something like 00;59;00;00 and make sure your program starts at exactly 01;00;00;00.

SMPTE Countdown

SMPTE countdown is a numeric countdown in seconds, from 10 to 2, which cuts to black for the last 2 seconds of the countdown (Figure 22.15). Your project then begins precisely after the end of the 2 seconds of black. Countdown allows the broadcast engineer or projectionist to easily cue your tape for screening. By simply pausing in the black, after the #2 frame, they can be sure to begin your program with a little buffer of black before the first images appear on screen.

Exhibiting on Disc

Although Internet streaming and DCPs have gained huge ground in exhibition, **DVD** and **Blu-ray** discs are still common ways of distributing your documentary, particularly in the home video and educational markets. Discs are still used for exhibition at some festivals, though these are increasingly asking for high-resolution digital files or DCPs. A few years ago, DVDs were the standard for **festival screeners** or **demo reels**. Nowadays these functions are almost exclusively served by online (sometimes password-protected) screeners on websites like vimeo.com, imdb.com, or youtube.com.

DVDs play back at standard resolution, whereas Blu-ray discs are high definition. While DVDs play on practically all players (DVD, Blu-ray, and computers), Blu-ray discs will not play on standard DVD players. Both Blu-ray discs and DVDs are optical discs that store the binary data for your sounds and images as microscopic bumps and indentations, called **pits**, in the surface of the disc. These pits are written as one long, ultrafine spiral called the **data track** and are read with a laser beam as the disc spins in the drive bay. The primary difference between these two formats is the precision of the laser and the size and number of the data pits. The red laser found in the DVD system is capable of reading data tracks that are 0.74 microns wide, while the much sharper blue laser (hence the name) with its shorter wavelength can read data off tracks that are 0.32 microns wide. This allows for much more data to be packed on a disc, and the blue laser also provides for faster data rates.

A single-layer DVD holds 4.7 GB of data, and a dual-layer DVD can hold 8.5 GB. A single-layer Blu-ray disc, however, can hold 25 GB, and a dual-layer one holds 50 GB. The audio/video data transfer rates are similarly different with DVDs clocking in at 10.08 Mbps, and Blu-rays at a much faster 54.0 Mbps. What this all adds up to is resolution potential, and this is why DVDs can only support standard-definition video resolutions whereas Blu-ray is capable of high definition.

DVDs encode the image and sound data using the MPEG 2 compression codec. Blu-ray can use either MPEG-2 or the newer H.264/MPEG-4 AVC codec. For projects shot at 24p and edited at 24p or 23.976 fps, you can output, encode, and author either type of disc at these frame rates as well. Keeping your frame rate at 24p or 23.976 fps allows you to put more footage, less compressed, onto the disc, because you have fewer frames and less data per minute.

Pressed or Burned?

Not all DVD and Blu-ray discs are created equal. **Pressed discs** are created through a process called **replication**, which physically mold the pits of the data track into the surface of the polycarbonate plastic, which is then coated in aluminum. This is the kind of disc you find when you buy a commercial movie. **Burned discs**, created through **duplication**, use recordable media and are created using a laser to burn a color dye layer in the media surface, which turns various colors and densities that mimic the depth and shadows of the physical pits in a pressed disc.

Pressed discs offer much better compatibility and physical longevity but must be created by a professional disc mastering service. The cost for having discs professionally mastered is quite low, but they are only available in bulk quantities, which means 500 or more discs. If you plan to go this route, the disc mastering service you choose will instruct you as to the specific file format they prefer to work with. What if you need fewer discs? Then you're likely to burn your own using **recordable discs**. Recordable DVDs come in four flavors: **DVD+R** and **DVD–R** are record-once-only formats, and **DVD+RW** and **DVD–RW** can have their data erased and rewritten. Recordable Blu-ray discs are **BD–R** (record once only) and **BD-RE** (rewritable). In both cases, rewritable discs are not a good choice for distribution.

Encoding, authoring, and burning your own DVDs or Blu-rays requires a computer with a DVD burner or Blu-ray burner and a DVD authoring program like Adobe Encore or Pinnacle Studio for the PC (Figure 22.17). Make sure you thoroughly research the capabilities and options these programs offer before you encode, author, and burn your discs.

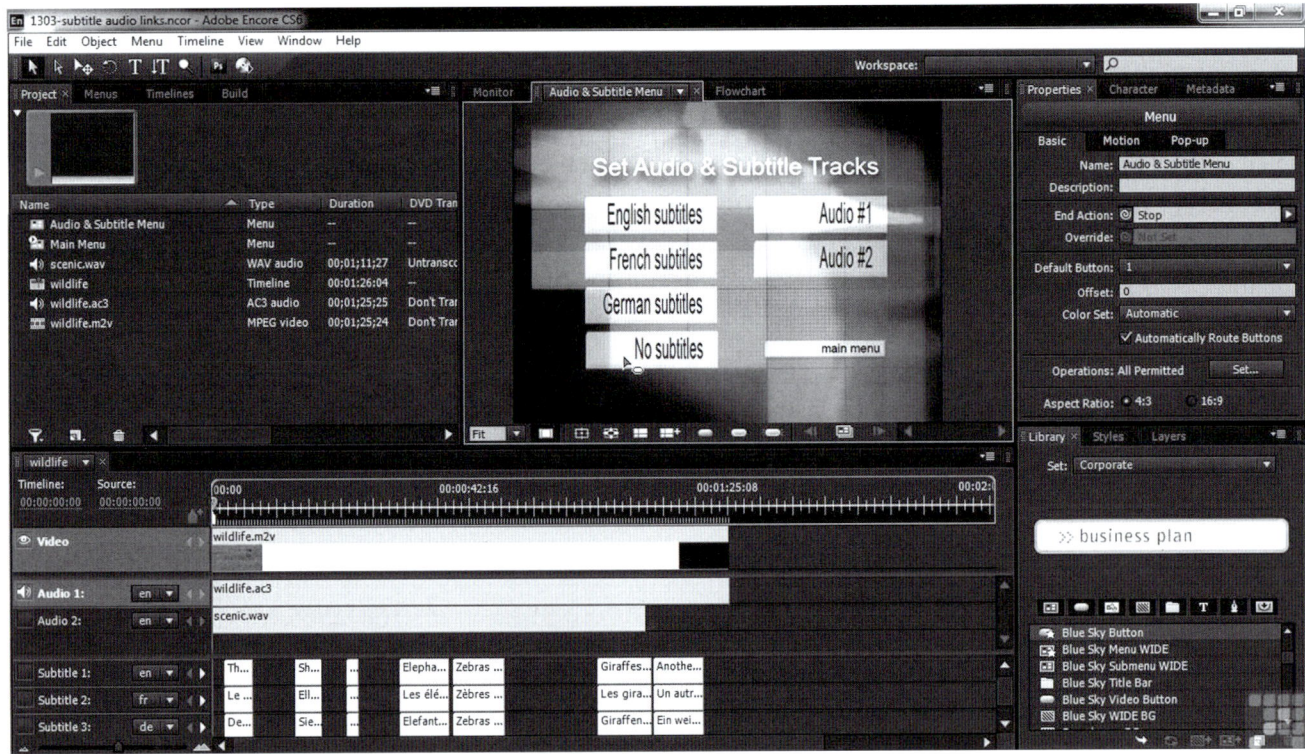

■ **Figure 22.17** The interface for Adobe Encore, a powerful disc authoring program.

CHAPTER 23

Distributing Your Documentary

Distribution refers to the process of getting your documentary out into the world and seen by audiences. Some documentary audiences may be very large and broad, while others may be highly targeted and specific. There are many ways of doing distribution, and the topic is complex enough to warrant its own book. In addition, **platforms** are changing very quickly. The changing nature of distribution requires filmmakers to educate themselves about the shifts and emerging opportunities of the moment. That said, there is one thing that will not change: distribution is hard and essential work. Filmmakers who take it seriously often say that making the film is only half the labor. Getting it out there is the other half and can take years. Distribution may be less glamorous than production, but the rewards here can be vast. During this phase you get to watch your film with audiences, hear their feedback, engage in discussion, and at times be reminded of the powerful tool for personal and political transformation that documentary film has the potential to be.

Often distribution is described in terms of **markets**. These can be loosely thought of as the various ways your film will reach audiences. These are the markets as currently understood in the documentary film world:
1. Festival
2. Theatrical
3. Semi-Theatrical/Special Events
4. Broadcast and Cable
5. Educational
6. Home Video (DVD/Blu-Ray)
7. Video on Demand

The **rights** to distribute in each market are generally handled separately. Some rights you will likely retain, while others you may delegate to a **distributor**. A distributor is a third-party entity (individual or organization) that specializes in the work of getting your film seen. In exchange for this work, they keep a percentage of the income generated. Sometimes a distributor will approach you, while at others times you will reach out to them to find out if they are interested in working with your documentary. A word of advice: don't sign the first distribution contract you are offered. Take time to research the distributor. Do they have other films like yours? What are their specific plans for your film? Are the people who made those films happy with how things have gone? Will they produce printed or online materials to promote your film?

When you sign a contract with a distributor, you will be granting them either **exclusive** or **nonexclusive** rights to sell your film in a particular market, for a specific **territory** (geographical area) and for an agreed upon **term** (amount of time). If the rights granted are exclusive for a particular market, you will not be able to assign those same rights to anybody else, or perhaps even to market in that area yourself. In exchange for these rights, the distributor will grant you **royalties** and possibly an **advance** against future royalties. The percentage of sales that you get back as royalties varies depending on the distributor, the market, and the other terms of the agreement.

One thing you should be aware of when evaluating a distribution contract is the difference between **"net"** and **"gross" revenue**. Gross refers to the total amount of sales revenue, without subtracting any expenses. Net refers to the total income minus any expenses the distributor has incurred marketing your film. These expenses could include the cost of creating print mailings, advertising, purchasing mailing lists, DVD duplication, and more. As a result, royalties based on 50 percent of gross sales would be a much larger amount than royalties based on 50 percent of net sales.

The order you release your work in these markets is also important, although the **windows** (or "holdback periods") between release times are shrinking. For example, several years ago, it was common to release a film in the educational market up to 3 years before making it available for home video, in order to reap the benefits of the higher educational pricing. Today, even a year holdback is rare. Sometimes films are released in theaters and via video on demand together. As we mentioned earlier, distribution avenues and opportunities are always in a state of flux.

One thing you should do, even before finishing your film, is begin to establish a relationship with potential audiences. If you do a **crowdsourced** funding campaign, like Kickstarter or Indiegogo, you will already have started to do this. Make sure you have a website, Facebook page, Twitter account, and other social media presence for your film. If you can keep people engaged through the production and editing phase, you will have begun to build your audience before you even lock picture.

FILM FESTIVALS

Before engaging a distributor, there is usually a period of self-distribution where you start to market your film yourself. The first area you will likely tackle is **film festivals**. Festivals are an important place to generate press, build "buzz," and even find a distributor. There are literally thousands of festivals globally, and the number is growing all the time. Just visit a website like withoutabox.com or filmfreeway.com and you'll get a sense of how overwhelming (not to mention expensive) it can be to submit your film to festivals. It is important to create a festival strategy before submitting blindly to hundreds of festivals you may know nothing about.

If you plan to submit to the most prestigious festivals, do it before submitting to smaller or more regional festivals. Examples of high-end festivals for documentary in North America are Sundance, South by Southwest (SXSW), the Tribeca Film Festival, and the Toronto International Film Festival. There are also documentary-specific festivals that have very good reputations, including Full Frame Documentary Film Festival, DOC NYC, and Hot Docs Canadian International Documentary Festival. This is by no means an exhaustive or even moderately inclusive list. The point here is that these festivals will not take your film unless it is a North American premiere, so if your strategy calls for a premiere at one of these festivals, don't show it anywhere else first! The same is true for international festivals. Some, like the Berlin Film Festival, the International Documentary Film Festival Amsterdam (IDFA), or the Rotterdam International Film Festival (The Netherlands), will likely require a world premiere. Others may be comfortable with a European premiere. In the United Kingdom, the most respected documentary-specific festival is Sheffield Doc/Fest, which generally requires at least a UK premiere.

Most films, however, are not going to premiere at one of these A-list festivals. There are many smaller festivals that are excellent at drawing audiences, and getting press to write about the films they program. Talk to other filmmakers to find out what festivals they think are worth submitting to. Research where other films similar to yours have played.

Many festivals are organized around themes. For example, there are many documentary film festivals you should consider. There are human rights festivals, Jewish film festivals,

CHAPTER 23
Distributing Your Documentary

in practice

■ MAXIMIZING FESTIVAL IMPACT

Iva Radivojevic was a graduate student in the Integrated Media Arts (IMA) MFA program at Hunter College when she completed her documentary *Evaporating Borders* (2014) (Figure 23.1). The film, a meditation on the experience of asylum seekers in Cyprus, had a festival run worthy of any top documentary filmmaker. It premiered at the Rotterdam International Film Festival, had its US premiere at South by Southwest (SXSW), and showed at more than 45 other festivals including Hot Docs and the Human Rights Watch Film Festival in New York. Here is how Iva explains her success[1]:

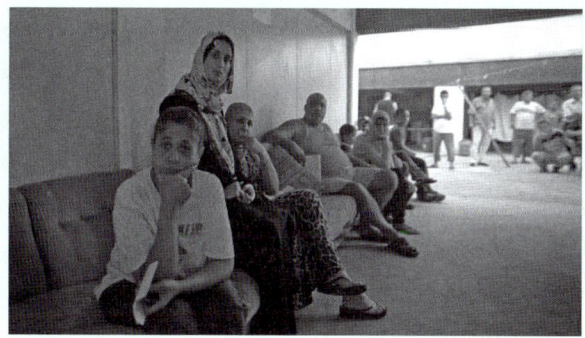

■ Figure 23.1 *Evaporating Borders*, which focuses on the migrant crisis in the Mediterranean island of Cyprus, owes much of its success to its director's determined efforts to get the film shown and talked about.

> *Independent Film Week [organized every year by the Independent Film Project (IFP)] was huge. I applied with a work-in-progress and got in, and they arranged meetings with distributors, producers, funders, and festival programmers. That's where I made my first contact with programmers from Berlin, Rotterdam, Sundance and so on. And from there you create a relationship. They give you a fee waiver, they know about your film, they are expecting it when you submit it. And some festivals even have specific sections that your film might fit into. Rotterdam, for example, had a special section that year they called "The State of Europe." So* Evaporating Borders *was perfect for that.*
>
> *Once I was accepted at Rotterdam, I had to worry about the US premiere. Because the film had such European subject matter, I was terrified nobody would want to show it here. I submitted to SXSW on a whim, the night before the deadline. Then when I got into Rotterdam I called SXSW and asked them "I just got into Rotterdam, do you guys need a world premiere?" I guess that put it on their radar, and they accepted me. From there, because I had two festivals with a lot of credibility, people started contacting me instead of me reaching out to them.*

Are festivals important to distribution? For Iva, the answer is an unequivocal "Yes!"

> *Festivals were critical for the visibility of* Evaporating Borders. *I didn't have money for a publicist, but SXSW sends you a list of press people who are going to be at the festival, including all the industry press. So I wrote them all, really emphasizing that I had been in* Filmmaker Magazine's *"25 filmmakers to watch," that (filmmaker) Laura Poitras was the Executive Producer, anything I could say to get their attention. I would wait for them to respond, and then I would send them a link to preview the film. A few of them did respond, and that's how I got into a few "Top Five" lists for the festival.* Hollywood Reporter *wrote about it,* Film Threat, Hammer to Nail—*all of them wrote about it just because of the festival circuit. The* Washington Post *wrote about it based on festivals, and also it got into the educational sphere too, because educators would come to see it at a festival, and they would contact me about screening it, and maybe coming to speak.*

Iva's advice for students and emerging filmmakers?

> *If at all possible, attach somebody with credibility to the film. I met Laura Poitras at a workshop in the Hunter College MFA program in Integrated Media Arts, and she consulted on my first short film. When I was making* Evaporating Borders, *I asked her to be a consultant again, and she offered to be the Executive Producer. That gave me a lot of credibility, and she also connected with me Jason Springarn-Koff, the editor of the* New York Times' OpDocs. *If you have a social issue film, that is a great way to get the word out about it. I knew Jay Rabinowitz, who is Jim Jarmusch's editor, because I used to have a job scheduling workshops for editors. I got to know him, and asked if he would be a Consulting Editor on* Evaporating Borders. *He said*

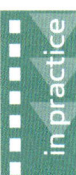

yes. These people are accessible. Even if you don't meet them directly, they are accessible in some way. I'm a big fan of workshops—any kind of workshop. I take them in editing or directing, even acting. And whenever I do these workshops, I make sure to connect with people and stay in touch (I use Facebook a lot for this). Not because I'm trying to get something out of them, but because I'm really interested in these relationships and connections, and I think we can make great things together. My point is that you stay in touch with all these people, and they become your supporters, and your community. But you have to love to do it. I really feel at this point like I have an incredible, supportive community of beautiful people around me.

This idea of support is critical. People who ask me to consult on their films, or edit their films, even if I don't have time, I will take some time to at least look at it, don't take any money at all, just to keep that relationship going, or to have somebody feel supported. And it's come back to me so many times. Somebody recommends me for a job, or nominates me for an award, or suggests me for a festival. I really feel that things come back around in a circle, and so the more you give and support, the more that support comes back to you.

As a filmmaker you not only create your audience. You also actively cultivate a community of other filmmakers and people who care about the issues in your film. Even if you are not in a major metropolitan area, you can find people and organizations who will connect you with audiences and help catalyze a conversation around your film and the issues it raises. And while the Internet hasn't made us a global village quite yet, it can be useful in connecting people of like minds and interests throughout the world.

women's film festivals, LGBT film festivals, environmental film festivals, festivals for films by and about specific ethnic identity groups, and many more. Research festivals whose mission fits your film, and submit!

If you are a student, take advantage of the "student" categories in the major festivals. The competition will be lighter, often the entry fees are less expensive, and you might end up getting up into a great festival! Also, be aware of what each festival can do for you. Some are good for getting industry press, while others are known for attracting distributors. Still others will help connect you with the grassroots educators, activists, and others who may give your film a long life in community and educational settings. All of these objectives, or only some, may be important to you. Design your festival strategy with your own priorities for your documentary in mind.

Finally, while most smaller festivals won't have resources to bring in and house filmmakers, many will pay a screening fee if asked. Don't be shy.

THEATRICAL

Theatrical distribution can be tough for documentaries, though over the past two decades, beginning with Michael Moore's *Roger and Me* (1989), they have had a consistent but small presence in the theatrical world. In general, you need a distributor to undertake a theatrical campaign.

The value of a theatrical release goes beyond prestige and getting films to local audiences. A review in *The New York Times*, for example, is almost impossible to secure unless you have a national television broadcast or a theatrical release.

Because of the value of reviews in major newspapers, some filmmakers pay for their own theatrical releases by renting a theater to promote the film themselves. This is known as **four-walling** and can cost upwards of $10,000 for a week in New York or Los Angeles. A theatrical run also makes a film eligible for the Academy Awards®, and many documentarians do it for that reason as well.

CHAPTER 23
Distributing Your Documentary

■ CASE STUDY: DIY SEMI-THEATRICAL DISTRIBUTION THROUGH TUGG.COM

In the semi-theatrical market, Tugg.com and Gathr.us are examples of the ways the Internet and crowdsourcing are converging to meet the needs of both filmmakers and audiences (Figure 23.2).

With Tugg, the first step is to submit your film. If it is accepted, you reach out to individuals and organizations in various communities and ask them to push for a screening in their area. Tugg has an exhibitor network that covers many screens in the United States, including nationwide chains such as AMC, Cinemark, and Carmike as well as hundreds of regional and independent cinemas around the country. They handle the operations, logistics, and customer service. You receive 35 percent of ticket sales, and your primary community supporter receives 5 percent for getting it going and turning people out.

Gregorio Smith's *Truth Be Told* (2012) is a documentary about growing up as a Jehovah's Witness. Smith four-walled the film four times in three cities (New York, Denver, and Boston) but felt the process was inefficient. "The screenings were well-received and well-attended," he says, "but scouting theaters, inspecting facilities, determining deliverable requirements, delivering content, performing picture tests/soundchecks, securing contracts, setting-up ticketing, waiting for reports/payments ... doing this for each location became an interminable and uncertain process."[2] Within the first four months of joining Tugg, *Truth be Told* had 10 well-attended screenings in 10 different cities. According to Tugg's website, the film grossed $12,645 at 13 events, and drew 1,077 people.

While this is still a very new strategy, and not all filmmakers are making a healthy return on these sites, the convergence of crowdsourcing and non-theatrical distribution seems like it will be around for a while.

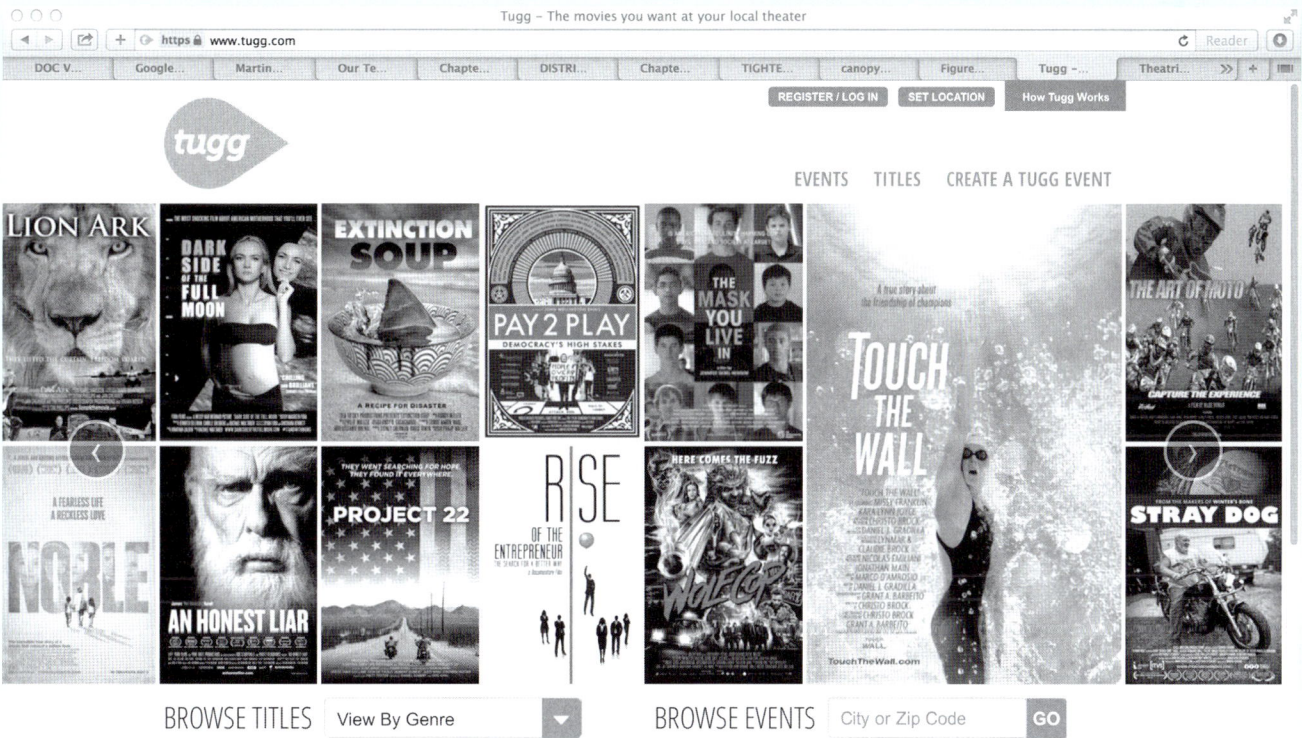

■ Figure 23.2 Tugg.com is one example of a site that allows filmmakers to crowdsource audiences for theatrical screenings.

SEMI-THEATRICAL

A semi-theatrical release refers to single screenings in a theater, museum, school, community center, religious institution, or even a community garden or bar (see *My Brooklyn* case study on p. 385).

Special "one-off" screenings have always been popular for documentaries, largely because these films often take up issues that people in institutions or at the community level want to learn about and discuss. They can also be an important revenue stream for filmmakers, depending on the size and budget of the organization sponsoring your screening. You should be up front and feel free to negotiate screening fees and honoraria for yourself (or any other speakers) if you are appearing with the film. Most filmmakers balance the desire to have their film seen with the need to recoup expenses or generate income. Many of us allow our films to be screened for free when a sponsoring organization is underfunded. Sometimes a group can "pass the hat" and collect contributions for the filmmaker. A museum or university may be able to pay $500 to $1,000. Screenings can also be a good place to sell home DVD copies and spread the word about the film in general.

At special events, be sure to pass around an e-mail sign-up list so you can develop a database of contacts. Many filmmakers send out newsletters about future events, updates to the stories in the film, awards won, future projects, and so on. Also, encourage people to connect with your project's social media pages (Facebook is popular, but there are other ways films maintain a presence on the Internet).

BROADCAST AND CABLE

Broadcast and cable TV are lucrative possibilities for documentary, but they can be difficult to secure. We recommend that you work with a **sales agent** who knows American and European programmers, as well as those in other parts of the world, and understands what kind of documentaries each is looking for. A sales agent differs from a distributor in that they represent the filmmakers' interest, often when selling to distributors. The sales agent will negotiate the contract and conditions of the sale of the film. A sales agent generally takes about 25 percent of the acquisition fee, which can range from a few thousand to tens of thousands of dollars.

In the United States, the Public Broadcasting Service (PBS) has served as an exhibition platform for many documentaries. On the national level there are two major independent documentary PBS **strands**: *POV* and *Independent Lens*. In addition, there are programs like *American Masters*, *Frontline*, and *The American Experience* that work with producers on shows for broadcast on their series. Individual PBS stations also program documentary content. In Europe, major buyers of documentary include the BBC and Channel 4 in Britain, Arte and Canal+ in France, and ZDF and Canal+ in Germany.

Broadcast also includes Cable TV. Channels like National Geographic, the History Channel, A&E, HBO, Al Jazeera, and others acquire documentaries. The competition for all broadcast is stiff, however, so proceed with reasonable expectations.

EDUCATIONAL

The educational market—colleges, universities, K-12 schools, and public libraries—has since the 1970s been a major source of revenue for many documentary filmmakers. Because educational institutions pay more for films than individuals in the home video market, it is not unusual for a documentary to gross upwards of $20,000 or $30,000 over a lifetime. There are many distributors that address niche educational markets, including Women Make Movies, Third World Newsreel, California Newsreel (African-American subject matter), Bullfrog Films (environmental subjects), and others. Some educational distributors have a broad selection that touches on many subject areas, like Icarus or Cinema Guild. These distributors take a commission of anywhere from 50 to 75 percent of net or gross income for creating a catalogue, maintaining a website, creating promotional materials, marketing your film, and fulfilling orders.

With the Internet, self-distribution has become more popular with documentary filmmakers. Some filmmakers purchase mailing lists of pertinent educational departments and programs, librarians, and professors. They also harness the power of social media and the Internet to sell directly to the educational market. An alternative that bridges the two models is New Day Films, a collective of more than 100 filmmakers who market their films individually but participate in collective curation and volunteer to perform most of the duties related to being a distributor—from finance to collection-wide promotion to website development.

HOME VIDEO (DVD)

DVD and Blu-ray are still viable ways of selling your films, especially in the home video market. The traditional video rental store may be a thing of the past, but people still buy DVDs on the Internet and at retailers. To make a healthy profit in this market, you will likely require the upfront expenditures and relationships that a home video distributor can offer.

STREAMING/VIDEO ON DEMAND

Internet streaming and **video on demand (VOD)** are areas that are changing fast. Every day new platforms emerge and others disappear. Some get revenue through advertising, like Snagfilms or YouTube, others through viewer subscriptions (Netflix, Hulu, Amazon Prime). Still others charge per transaction, like iTunes or Vimeo on Demand. This area is undoubtedly the future of film distribution and promises huge audiences, but it will also require crafty marketing and promotion to direct viewers to your specific film.

Historically, filmmakers have had to find a distributor to get their films onto VOD Platforms. The range of DIY options is expanding, however, and currently include such sites as Vimeo on Demand, CreateSpace (for Amazon only), VHX, and Distrify. Services like Quiver and Distribber can help you get on to the major VOD platforms like iTunes, Hulu and Netflix.

IMPACT: ENGAGEMENT CAMPAIGNS

Since its inception, documentary has been concerned with questions of audience engagement and social change. While not all documentaries make an explicit case for a particular kind of change, the genre's relationship to the real world makes it necessarily bound up with intentions of changing people's thinking about a pressing social issue or problem. Recent documentaries have fueled public debate and action on global and local issues, from the wars in the Middle East to global democracy movements, from droughts to healthy eating, from government surveillance to school bullying.

Over the past decade, there has been an explosion of interest in the kinds of social impact documentaries can have. This is partly spurred by funders, who want evidence that their investments in documentary are paying off in terms of measurable social change. The emergence of the BritDoc Impact Award, which gives five filmmakers $15,000 for their outreach campaigns, is evidence of this increased interest. In 2014, Hot Docs, a major annual documentary festival, market, and conference based in Toronto, released the report *Documentary Impact: Social Change through Storytelling*. In the introduction, they ask the question:

If documentary films generate empathy in audiences, illuminating new perspectives and activating powerful emotions, then what happens next? Audiences often walk out of documentaries saying, "I want to do something about the way I feel and what I just saw!" Empathy created by great storytelling can be great fuel for action. Coordinated, organized and strategic actions can facilitate major changes in a society's viewpoint, lexicons, values and practices. Coherent actions can shift this post-viewing inspiration into action, which can drive societal and legislative change, truly altering societal practice.[3]

These are compelling ideas, but how do we translate these audience reactions into concrete change? And how do we measure that change? Is a change of attitudes or way of thinking the goal? Is change reflected in participation in political action, like a letter-writing campaign or appearance at a demonstration? Or is specific policy change the goal? All of these are related, of course, and different filmmakers will answer these questions differently. The Fledgling Fund's 2009 report *Assessing Creative Media's Social Impact*[4] presents a diagram that maps out a possible relationship between compelling storytelling and social change (Figure 23.3).

There are at least two organizations that specialize in crafting **engagement plans** for films. Working Films, based in North Carolina, builds partnerships among non-fiction media makers, nonprofit organizations, educators, and advocates to advance social justice and environmental sustainability, and support community-based change. The staff trains and consults with filmmakers and works with NGOs (non-governmental organizations) to use documentaries to enhance their programs, extend their reach, and move their missions forward.

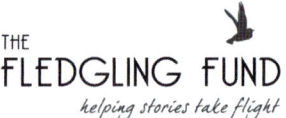

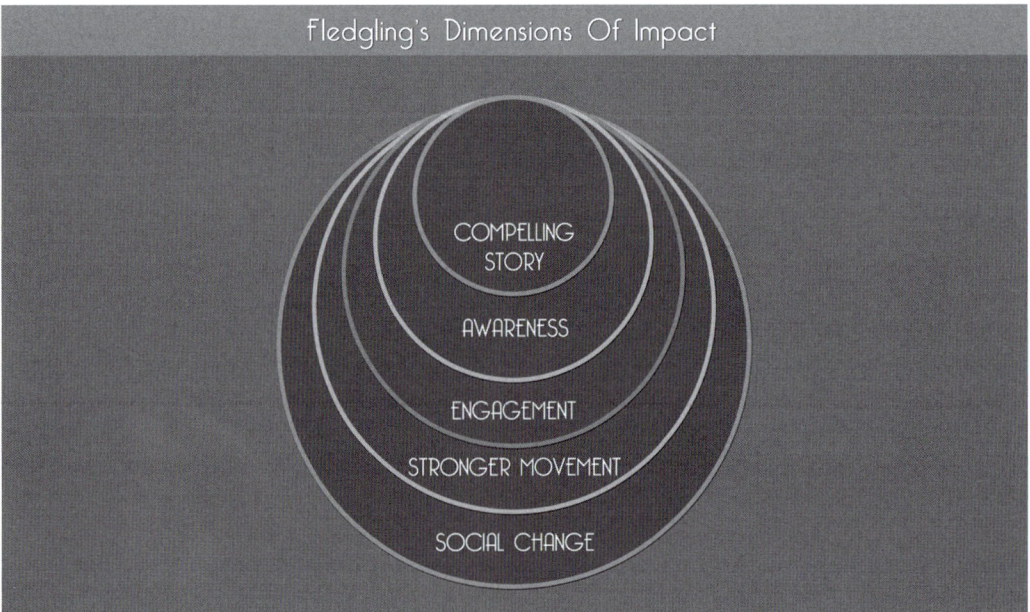

■ **Figure 23.3** The Fledgling Fund has created this diagram to illustrate their understanding of the "dimensions of impact" creative media can have. The model shows that there are many steps between a compelling story and social change.

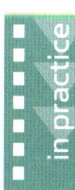

DIY AUDIENCE ENGAGEMENT

My Brooklyn (2012), coauthor Kelly Anderson and Allison Lirish Dean's documentary about the redevelopment of Downtown Brooklyn, shows how an engagement campaign can be done on a shoestring budget. The film reframes the gentrification debate to expose the policies and players behind seemingly natural neighborhood change. Anderson says,

> Audiences flocked to the film when it had a three-week theatrical run (organized by the Independent Filmmaker Project, or IFP) at a small theater in Brooklyn. After the film's premiere, many people and organizations reached out to us to ask if we could screen it for their constituents, so we knew there was a public out there that was hungry for the information in the film. This was 2012, and New York City was about to hold a historic mayoral election that would determine whether the city would continue with the real estate development policies of the previous 8 years, or embark on a new path with a more progressive mayor, Bill de Blasio. It was a political moment that provided an opportunity for the film to reach many people, and contribute valuable education about how cities change and why, but we weren't sure how to best translate the interest in the film into social change.
>
> The first step we undertook was to pull together some of the organizations we had come to know through the making of the film. There were activist organizations, not-for-profit affordable housing developers, and community planning experts. We held several meetings, during which we came up with the idea of My Brooklyn, Our City. The campaign essentially offered the film free of charge to any individual or organization who could commit to getting six people or more together to watch it, and to have a discussion using a resource guide we created to help guide them towards whatever action they felt would be most useful in their neighborhood context. We publicized the campaign through a list of local blogs we had compiled, through Facebook, and through an email list we had generated by asking people to sign in at the screenings we had held to date.
>
> The campaign was a huge success. During the summer of 2013 more than 50 screenings were held, without us organizing a single one of them. They ranged from a small showing in someone's apartment, to a 200-person screening in a café in Bedford-Stuyvesant, to screenings in parks and community gardens (Figure 23.4). Our expenses, beyond our time, were the cost of a few DVDs and some postage.

Focusing on impact doesn't necessarily mean you are sacrificing monetary gains. While *My Brooklyn, Our City* had the immediate political and social impact the filmmakers were seeking, the engagement campaign also raised the film's visibility and undoubtedly led to future sales in the educational and VOD realm.

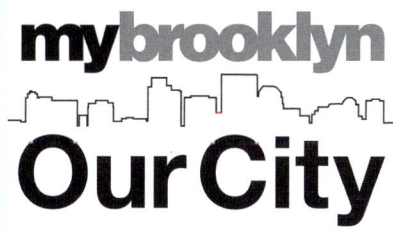 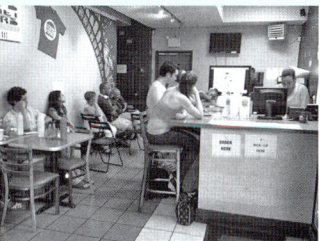 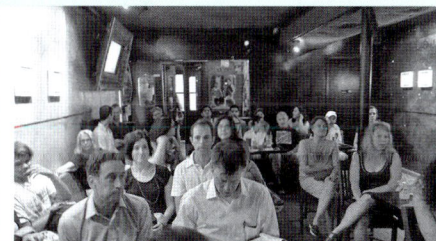

■ Figure 23.4 *My Brooklyn*'s DIY engagement campaign. Screenings were organized by community members all over New York City, including Mark's Burgers (Clinton Hill, Brooklyn) and Freddy's Bar (Prospect Heights, Brooklyn).

Active Voice is another organization that develops strategies for audience engagement. The organization recently launched a new website to help filmmakers, funders, and social change agents measure the impact of their strategies. The site, howdoweknow.net, presents a set of horticultural metaphors to help categorize the various ways films contribute to change. The categories include[5]:

- Rakes, which scratch the surface of an issue to engage people with different perspectives around common values
- Trowels, which dig in deeply and deliberately to plant a seed of advocacy
- Wheelbarrows, which transport audiences through a strong narrative structure, but refrain from offering simple solutions
- Trellises, which help movements grow by telling a story that affirms, directs, and heightens the visibility of existing efforts
- Shovels, usually investigative in nature, dig for the truth and expose alarming information

Which type of impact can your documentary have? Not all films have to act in all of the ways outlined above. If you are doing an investigative exposé, you might not have to also include all the solutions to the problem you are unearthing. Audiences can find their own way to appropriate actions by going to your website, perhaps, or connecting with an organization working on the same issue.

There are also individual consultants that filmmakers work with to craft engagement campaigns for their films. These campaigns cost money, as they require research and staff to implement. Even if you don't have a budget for engagement, however, you can still extend the impact of your film with some smart thinking and the involvement of community partners.

■ SKYLIGHT—THREE DECADES OF DOCUMENTARY IMPACT

Skylight is a New York-based company committed to producing artistic, challenging, and socially relevant media to strengthen human rights and the quest for justice. Their films include *When the Mountains Tremble* (1983), about the genocide of the Guatemalan Maya during the 1980s, *Granito: How to Nail a Dictator* (2011), which shows how *When the Mountains Tremble* was used as evidence in a Spanish trial to convict General Efraím Ríos Montt, and *Dictator in the Dock* (2013), about the 2012 Ríos Montt genocide trial in Guatemala. This last film is unique because it was released as short webisodes during the trial before being released as a full film. Skylight is known for the impact its films have had, and for its use of innovative technologies and strategies to get its films out to a broad range of audiences, from indigenous people in Guatemala to politicians and educators worldwide.

We spoke with Paco de Onís about how he and his partners Pamela Yates and Peter Kinoy think about impact, and about the models they are using.

Documentary Voice and Vision (DVV): *How do you think about audience?*

Paco de Onís (PdO): There are different audiences. For example, there's the indigenous Guatemalan audience, and then there's the whole Guatemalan audience, and then there's beyond that. One thing we do is make indigenous language versions of many of our films. In Guatemala, there are 22 languages. The biggest group are the Quiché, so we made a Quiché version. The group that was the most affected by the violence of the state were the Maya Ixil, so we made a version for them too. That process of making the indigenous

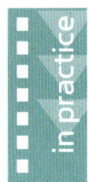

■ Figure 23.5 The process of recording indigenous language versions of *Granito: How to Nail a Dictator* (2011). Photo by Pamela Yates / http://skylight.is.

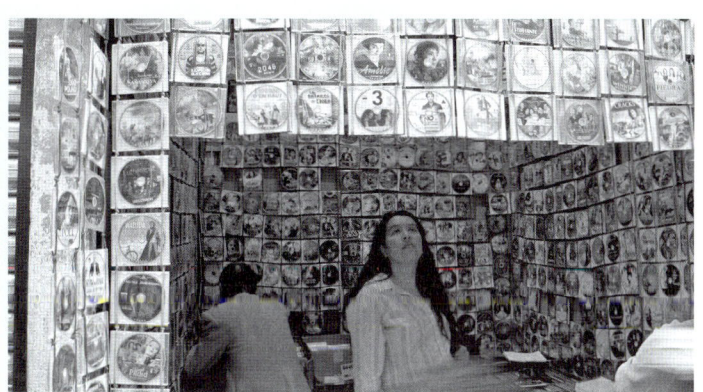
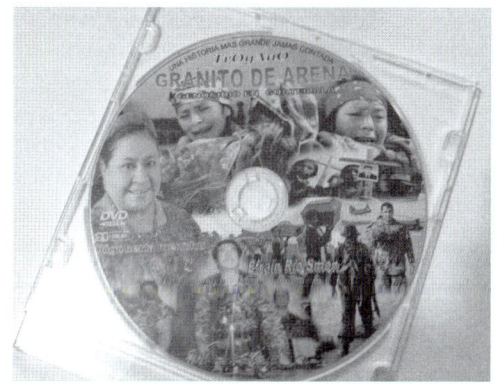

Figure 23.6 Skylight gives masters to bootleggers in Guatemala to reproduce and sell their films on DVD in marketplaces throughout the country in order to increase dissemination. The bootleggers create their own unique artwork for the DVDs. Photos by Pamela Yates / http://skylight.is

language version actually became a big outreach initiative, because first we had to work with somebody who is from that region and has the language, then we had to cast the voices (because it's not subtitled), and we went through a process of recording the voice-over translations (Figure 23.5). We discovered that the process of recording can become very emotional, because the people who are doing the recording actually lived through the events in the film. They become very invested in having people see it when it's done. The community radio stations also announced that anybody who came with a blank DVD could get a free copy of the film. That way we distributed a lot of copies of the film. Distribute is not really the right word—it's more disseminating, making it available.

DVV: *That goes against the idea many filmmakers have that you should never give your film away for free.*

PdO: We give our films away for free all the time. We would never sell the film in Guatemala, because it's their story, and it would feel wrong. In fact, we even identified the biggest bootlegger, he goes by the nickname "El Buki," and he really gets the film out there. In the Guatemalan markets, they have what look like curtains of DVDs in soft plastic cases—they clip them together. And they each have an image—the bootleggers actually create their own artwork for the DVDs. And it's culturally appropriate, it's artwork that speaks to their customers (Figure 23.6).

And then we sell to educators through New Day Films, we sell DVDs from our website, and we use Vimeo on Demand. And that's very steady.

DVV: *What is the social impact of screening the film in Guatemala?*

PdO: On a very basic level, it's the recovery of their historical memory. This history is not taught in the

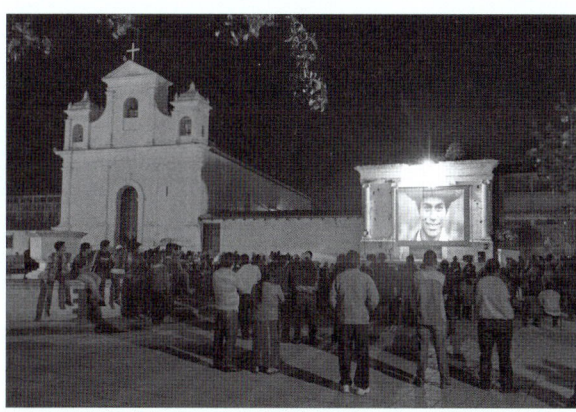

Figure 23.7 A screening of *Granito: How to Nail a Dictator* in Nebaj, Guatemala. Photo by James Rodríguez / mimundo.org / http://skylight.is.

Guatemalan school system. Also, what the screen does is it puts the Maya activist on the same platform as a dictator or powerful people. That has a very strong effect because they become powerful too. We often do public screenings in the plazas, and you can just see it on people's faces. It's very powerful (Figure 23.7).

The younger generation over the last few years has really become more and more empowered, and they tell us all the time that these films are very important for meetings they have, workshops, getting other people to understand what's happened, why the problems of today are related to the problems of before. It opens up a safe space to talk about what happened in the past.

DVV: *What about the companion website?*

PdO: That's called Granito: Every Memory Matters (www.granitomem.com). It is a space to share memories about the armed conflict in Guatemala, so that through our collective memory we can open a

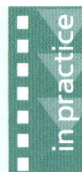

dialogue about the past. We built it, and we really tried to work it within the Guatemalan diaspora here in the US. It's a website, but people can access it from a smartphone. We thought of using some apps that are out there for phones that are just text-based. It was a big learning experience, and this is a lesson for every site: you should really have the users involved in the design. Not all the users, but people who represent that sector. After about three years, we're now migrating that site to a Guatemalan organization that was formed over the last couple of years to seek reconciliation among the parties: the Right, the Left, businessmen, politicians, the victims. It was always our goal to have somebody else take the site over—we don't want to run these sites forever because we don't think that's our role, and we don't really have the capacity to do it.

DVV: *How did you come up with the idea of releasing Dictator in the Dock as webisodes?*

PdO: We did that as a reaction to what was happening in the courtroom. The trial began 4 or 5 months before it was supposed to begin. The judge got a death threat, and she said "I'm just going to start the trial now." So we all had to scramble to get down there. And nobody knew if the trial was going to proceed because the defense lawyers for General Ríos Montt had succeeded for 15 years in stopping every attempt at a trial. But this one kept going, and it became very dramatic. Also, the mainstream media, controlled by the elite, was really making it look like the trial was a farce, there were hugely misogynistic comments about the judge, and the Attorney General, and (Mayan activist) Rigoberta Menchu, who was also in the courtroom a lot of the time. We decided to start putting up short episodes to kind of open up the doors of the courtroom to the world. We felt a responsibility to show a straighter version of what was happening. It got embedded all over the place, on alternative news sites, and episodes were embedded on many blogs.

DVV: *And then you made a film by putting the episodes together?*

PdO: Once we finished, we had 24 episodes in English and in Spanish. For the English version, we put 7 up for free viewing and the rest behind a paywall. And then we created a whole resource page around it, and it has sold well. We give away the Spanish version. Even in the US, you don't have to pay for that.

CONCLUSION

Whether you are distributing for financial return, for impact, or both, you are in a world where more and more documentaries are being made every day. In a changing distribution landscape that is being transformed by technological developments faster than anyone can keep pace with, you can't rely on any one avenue of distribution for all your success. You might find success in a place you never imagined. All markets have their value, and their importance. Stay nimble, keep on top of new developments, talk with other filmmakers, and keep in touch with the people who care about your issue. All of these, together, will ensure your film has a long life. After all, that's why you made it.

Notes

CHAPTER 1

1 "The Documentary Producer." *Cinema Quarterly*, 1933, 8.

2 Yates, Pam, and Paco de Onís. "Reflections on Getting Real: Debunking Five Myths That Divide Us." *Documentary Magazine*, International Documentary Association, February 23, 2015. Web. July 4, 2015.

3 Fitch, Nathan. "Mikrós Soldier," (MFA thesis, Integrated Media Arts, Hunter College (CUNY), 2014) 11–12.

4 Tharp, Twyla. *The Creative Habit: Learn It and Use It for Life* (New York, NY: Simon and Schuster, 2003) 6–8.

5 Sullivan, Graeme. "Artefacts as Evidence within Changing Contexts." *Working Papers in Art and Design 4* (2006), 1.

6 Buñuel, Luis. *My Last Breath* (London: Fontana Paperbacks, 1985) 42.

7 Vélez, Edin. Personal interview. March 9, 2014.

8 Rosenstein, Jay. Personal interview. May 27, 2014.

9 Cunningham, Megan. *The Art of the Documentary* (Berkeley, CA: New Riders, 2005) 52.

10 Rabiger, Michael. *Directing the Documentary* (Burlington, MA: Focal Press, 2009) 31–32.

11 Lucas, Martin. Personal interview. January 15, 2014.

12 Some of the points in this section are culled from "9 Filmmakers Tell Us What Makes the Perfect Documentary Character." Tribeca Film Institute Blog, Tribeca Film Institute, November 20, 2014. Web. July 4, 2015.

13 "If I Can't Do It (Film Description)." *POV*. PBS, n.d. Web. July 13, 2015.

14 Albert, Mitch. "A Family Affair: The Films of Alan Berliner." *The Independent Film and Video Monthly*. May 1997, 2.

15 Gold, Tami. Personal interview. May 12, 2014.

16 Ibid.

17 de Onís, Paco. Personal interview. March 27, 2015.

CHAPTER 2

1 Sachs, Lynne. Personal interview. February 14, 2014.

2 Sadoul, Georges, as quoted in Dai Vaughn, *For Documentary* (Berkeley, CA: University of California Press, 1999) 4–5.

3 Vaughn, Dai. *For Documentary* (Berkeley, CA: University of California Press, 1999) 5.

4 Balázs, Béla. "Filming Death." *Imagining Reality: The Faber Book of Documentary*. Ed. Mark Cousins and Kevin Macdonald (London: Faber and Faber, 1996) 29–36. Print.

5 Barnouw, Erik. *Documentary: A History of the Non-Fiction Film* (New York, NY: Oxford University Press, 1993) 77–80.

6 Grierson, John. "First Principles of Documentary." *Non-Fiction Film Theory and Criticism*. Ed. Richard M. Barsam (New York, NY: Dutton, 1976) 19–30. Print.

7 Rosenstein, Jay. Personal interview. May 27, 2014.

8 Ibid.

9 Maysles, Albert. "Sheffield Doc/Fest 2011: Albert Maysles Masterclass." YouTube. Sheffield Film Festival, April 17, 2012. Web. July 6, 2015.

10 Levin, G. Roy. *Documentary Explorations: 15 Interviews with Film-Makers* (New York, NY: Anchor Press, 1971) 316–331.

11 Barnouw, Erik. *Documentary: A History of the Non-Fiction Film* (New York, NY: Oxford University Press, 1993) 254–255.

12 Gustafson, Julie. Personal interview. 1991.

13 Ibid.

14 Winston, Brian. "Tsunami Hits Cannibal Tours: Documentary in the Twenty-first Century." Remarks delivered at Codes & Modes Conference, Hunter College, NY, November 7, 2014.

15 Turse, Nick. "What Sebastian Junger and Restrepo Won't Tell You about War." *The Huffington Post*. TheHuffingtonPost.com, July 13, 2010. Web. July 6, 2015.

16 Stoney, George. Interview. *Everyone's Channel*. Dir. David Shulman. 1990. VHS tape.

17 Morris, Errol. "Play It Again, Sam (Re-enactments, Part One)." New York Times Blog. *New York Times*, April 3, 2008. Web. July 9, 2015.

CHAPTER 3

1 Schank, Roger C. *Tell Me a Story: Narrative and Intelligence* (Boston, MA: Northwestern University Press, 1995).

2 Curran Bernard, Sheila. *Documentary Storytelling: Creative Nonfiction on Screen*, (Burlington, MA: Focal Press, 2011) 15.

3 Rosenstein, Jay. Personal interview. May 27, 2014.

4 Interview with Jennifer Baichwal. ETV Productions. myETVmedia, January 2014. Web. July 4, 2015.

5 Glassman, Marc. Interview with Jennifer Baichwal and Nick de Pencier. *Point of View* 91 (Fall 2013). Web. July 4, 2015.

6 Ibid.

7 Wilson, Keith. Personal interview. April 9, 2015.

CHAPTER 4

1 Chiang, S. Leo. A Village Called Versailles ITVS Proposal. n.d.TS. Personal collection of the author.

2 Ibid.

3 Ibid.

4 Alvarado, David, and Jason Sussman. *The Immortalists Press Kit*. 2014. TS.

5 Ibid.

6 Chiang, S. Leo. A Village Called Versailles ITVS Proposal. n.d.TS. Personal collection of the author.

7 Ibid.

8 Interview with S. Leo Chiang. *Independent Lens*. PBS.org, n.d. Web. July 4, 2015.

CHAPTER 5

1 See, for example: Gefter, Philip. "The Theater of the Street, the Subject of the Photograph." *The New York Times*, March 16, 2006. Web. July 4, 2015.

2 Gold, Tami. Personal interview. May 12, 2014.

3 Gentleman, Amelia. "Defeat for Teacher who Sued over Film Profits." *The Guardian*, September 29, 2004, US Edition. Web. July 5, 2015.

4 Chayet, Delphine. "Etre et avoir—un succés au goût amer." *Le Figaro*, October 14, 2003, 10. Print.

5 Lund, Andrew. Personal interview. July 13, 2015.

6 Ibid.

7 Swami, Praveen. "A Missionary Enterprise." *Frontline*, March 12, 2005. Web. July 5, 2015.

8 Ibid.

9 "Finalists for 2011 PUMA. Creative Impact Award Announced at Durban International Film Festival." News.puma.com. *Puma*. July 25, 2011. Web. July 5, 2015.

10 Rabiger, Michael. *Directing the Documentary* (Burlington, MA: Focal Press, 2009) 351–354.

11 "RTDNA Code of Ethics." RTDNA. Radio Television Digital News Association, n.d. Web. July 6, 2015.

12 "PBS National Program Funding Standards and Practices." PBS.org. *PBS*. February 3, 2014. Web. July 5, 2015.

13 Hampe, Barry. *Making Documentary Films and Videos* (New York, NY: Henry Holt and Company, 2007) 141.

14 Boykoff, Jules, and Maxwell Boykoff. "Journalistic Balance as Global Warming Bias." *Fairness and Accuracy in Reporting*. November 1, 2004. Web. July 5, 2015.

15 Bullert, B. J. *Public Television: Politics and the Battle over Documentary Film* (New Brunswick, NJ: Rutgers University Press, 1997) 156.

CHAPTER 6

1 Alvarado, David. Personal interview. May 10, 2014.

2 "Get Permission." *Film London—Get Permission*. Film London, n.d. Web. July 25, 2015.

3 www.bbc.co.uk/filmnetwork/filmmaking/guide/production/insurance. Web. Feb 4, 2016.

4 Bahar, Robert. "Don't Fudge on Your Budget: Toeing the Line Items." *Documentary Magazine*, International Documentary Association, February 2006. Web. July 5, 2015.

5 Ibid.

CHAPTER 7

1. Mackendrick, Alexander. *On Film-Making: An Introduction to the Craft of the Director* (New York, NY: Faber and Faber, 2005) xxxv.

2. Chiang, S. Leo. Personal interview. May 15, 2014.

3. Hampe, Barry. *Making Documentary Films and Videos* (New York, NY: Henry Holt and Company, 2007) 112.

4. Heinzerling, Zachary. "Documentary Shooting and Directing." (panel presentation, Documentary Fundamentals 2014, UnionDocs Center for Documentary Art. Brooklyn, NY, May 16, 2014).

5. Chiang, S. Leo. Personal interview. May 14, 2014.

6. Ibid.

CHAPTER 8

1. Anderson, Joseph, and Barbara Anderson. "The Myth of Persistence of Vision Revisited." *Journal of Film and Video* 45 (1993), 3–12.

2. Barnouw, Erik. *Documentary: A History of the Non-Fiction Film* (New York, NY: Oxford University Press, 1993) 236–242.

3. Chiang, S. Leo. "Re: Format Question." Message to Kelly Anderson. June 25, 2014. E-mail.

4. Alvarado, David. "Re: Format Question." Message to Kelly Anderson. June 29, 2014. E-mail.

5. Laforet, Vincent. "The Hobbit: An Unexpected Masterclass in Why HFR fails, and a Reaffirmation of what makes Cinema Magical." vincentlaforet.com. December 19, 2012. Web. July 5, 2015.

6. Grossman, Todd. *Shooting Action Sports: The Ultimate Guide to Extreme Filmmaking* (Burlington, MA: Focal Press, 2008) 26.

7. "POV's 2013 Documentary Filmmaking Equipment Survey." *POV*. PBS, n.d. Web. July 5, 2015.

8. Cook, Adam. "Heavy Metal: An Interview with Liviathon Co-Director Véréna Paravel." *Notebook*, August 28, 2012. Web. July 5, 2015.

9. Cain, Bennett. "HD Monitor Calibration—White Balance and Color Bars." *RSS*. Bennett Cain, n.d. Web. July 06, 2015.

CHAPTER 9

1. Chiang, S. Leo. Personal interview. May 14, 2014.

2. Herzog, Werner. "On the Absolute, the Sublime, and Ecstatic Truth." Arion, Boston University College of Arts and Sciences, n.d. Web. July 5, 2015.

3. Alvarado, David. Personal Interview. July 8, 2013.

CHAPTER 10

1. "POV's 2013 Documentary Filmmaking Equipment Survey." *POV*. PBS, n.d. Web. July 5, 2015.

2. Alvarado, David. Personal Interview. May 10, 2014.

CHAPTER 11

1 Ray, Man. *La Photographie N'est Pas L'Art* (Paris: GLM, 1937).

CHAPTER 12

1 Brown, Blain. *Cinematography: Theory and Practice: Image Making for Cinematographers and Directors* (Burlington, MA: Focal Press, 2002).

2 Chiang, S. Leo. Personal interview. May 14, 2014.

3 Gustafson, Julie. Personal interview by Tami Gold and Kelly Anderson. 1991.

4 Azoury, Philippe. "Caméras Libres", *Libération*, Paris, August 11, 2004.

CHAPTER 13

1 Barbash, Ilisa, and Lucien Taylor. *Cross-Cultural Filmmaking: A Handbook for Making Documentary and Ethnographic Films and Videos* (Berkeley: University of California Press, 1997) 172.

2 Brooks, Daniel. Personal Interview. September 10, 2014.

3 Takagi, JT. Personal Interview. September 11, 2014.

4 Brooks, Daniel. Personal Interview. September 10, 2014.

CHAPTER 14

1 Alvarado, David. Personal interview. May 10, 2014.

2 Takagi, JT. Personal Interview. September 11, 2014.

3 Ibid.

4 Brooks, Daniel. Personal Interview. September 10, 2014.

5 Brooks, Daniel. Personal Interview. July 11, 2015.

CHAPTER 15

1 Heinzerling, Zachary. "Documentary Shooting and Directing." (panel presentation, Documentary Fundamentals 2014, UnionDocs Center for Documentary Art. Brooklyn, NY, May 16, 2014).

2 Spence, Louise, and Vinicius Navarro. *Crafting Truth: Documentary Form and Meaning* (Piscataway, NJ: Rutgers University Press, 2011) 51–53.

3 Gold, Tami. Personal Interview. May 12, 2014.

4 Rabiger, Michael. *Directing the Documentary* (Burlington, MA: Focal Press, 2009) 463.

5 Gold, Tami. Personal Interview. May 12, 2014.

6 Fan, Lixin. Interview by Adnaan Wasey. Rooftop Films Blog. *Rooftop Films*, August 12, 2010. Web. July 5, 2015.

CHAPTER 16

1 Brooks, Daniel. Personal Interview. September 10, 2014.

2 Many thanks to educator, author, and DP Harry Box for his valuable input on this section.

CHAPTER 17

No notes

CHAPTER 18

1 Oldham, Gabriella. *First Cut: Conversations with Film Editors* (Berkeley, CA: University of California Press, 1992) 45.

2 "Documentary Film and Nonfiction Programming." wga.org. Writer's Guild of America, n.d. Web. July 4, 2015.

3 Alter, Nora. *Chris Marker* (Champaign-Urbana, IL: University of Illinois Press, 2006).

CHAPTER 19

1 Eisenstein, Sergei. *Film Form: Essays in Film Theory* (New York, NY: Harcourt, Brace and World, 1949) 72.

2 Morris, Errol. Interview by Homi Bhabha. errolmorris.com. n.d. Web. July 5, 2015.

3 Vélez, Edin. Personal interview. March 9, 2014.

CHAPTER 20

1 Bennett, Ann. Personal Interview. February 8, 2015.

2 Ibid.

3 Ibid.

4 Ibid.

5 "Documentary Filmmakers' Statement of Best Practices in Fair Use." Center for Media & Social Impact. American University School of Communications, November 2005. Web. July 10, 2015.

6 Lund, Andrew. Personal interview. July 10, 2015.

7 "Own-it | Intellectual Property Advice for Creative Businesses." Own-it. University of the Arts London, n.d. Web. July 22, 2015.

8 Bernard, Sheila Curran, and Kenn Rabin. *Archival Storytelling: A Filmmaker's Guide to Finding, Using, and Licensing Third Party Visuals and Music* (Burlington, MA: Focal Press, 2009).

9 www.free-culture.cc

10 "Journalistic Guidelines." *Frontline*. n.d. PBS. Web. July 5, 2015.

CHAPTER 21

1 Barnouw, Erik. *Documentary: A History of the Non-Fiction Film* (New York, NY: Oxford University Press, 1993) 93.

2 Alvarado, David. Personal Interview. May 10, 2014.

3 "Documentary Filmmakers' Statement of Best Practices in Fair Use." Center for Media & Social Impact. American University School of Communications, November 2005. Web. July 10, 2015.

4 "All Clear—Music Clearance Primer." *The Music Bridge*. The Music Bridge, 2005. Web. July 23, 2015.

5. Chion, Michel. *Audio-Vision: Sound on Screen* (New York, NY: Columbia University Press, 1994).

6. Castaing-Taylor, Lucien. Audio Commentary. *Sweetgrass*. Dir. Lucien Castaing-Taylor and Ilisa Barbash. PBS. 2009. DVD.

7. "Sweetgrass Documents a Dying Tradition through Quiet Observation." Art Beat. *PBS Newshour*. March 25, 2010. Web. July 5, 2015.

8. Castaing-Taylor, Lucien. Audio Commentary. *Sweetgrass*. Dir. Lucien Castaing-Taylor and Ilisa Barbash. PBS. 2009. DVD.

9. Tamés, David. "Sound for Documentary, Part 2: What Is It and Why Is It so Important?" KinoEye.com. March 16, 2013. Web. July 11, 2015.

10. Berliner, Alan. Interviewed by Scott MacDonald in *A Critical Cinema 5: Interviews with Independent Filmmakers* (Berkeley, CA: University of California Press, 2006) 169.

CHAPTER 22

1. Boyd, Brian. "Re: Interview for our Book." Message to Kelly Anderson. February 21, 2015. E-mail.

2. Ibid.

3. Shapiro, Keith. "Re: Quick Question for our Book." Message to Kelly Anderson. January 5, 2015. E-mail.

CHAPTER 23

1. Radivojevic, Iva. Personal Interview. February 21, 2015.

2. Interview with Gregorio Smith. Tugg School. Tugg. com. n.d. Web. July 5, 2015.

3. Finneran, Patricia, "Documentary Impact: Social Change through Storytelling." Hot Docs, Inspirit Foundation and Panicaro Foundation. 2014. pdf via web. July 13, 2015.

4. "Assessing Creative Media's Social Impact." *The Fledgling Fund RSS*. The Fledgling Fund, January 2009. Web. July 13, 2015.

5. "Horticulture Tools." Howdoweknow.net. Active Voice Lab, n.d. Web. July 13, 2015.

Glossary

.AIFF (audio interchange file format)—An uncompressed audio format created by Apple

.WAV—An uncompressed audio file format developed by Microsoft and IBM

.WMV—A Windows audiovisual media container format

1/3–2/3 Rule—A rule for depth of field, which tells us that two-thirds of the depth range that will be in focus along the z-axis is behind the focal point, and one-third is in front

180° Lighting—A lighting setup with lights pointing toward the subject at two ends or sides of a space

180° Principle/180° Line/Line of Action—An imaginary line drawn through a scene used to maintain consistent sightlines and screen direction; all shots used in a sequence must be filmed from one side of the line

3:2 Pulldown—A method of recording video at 24 frames per second in a 30 fps timespace, or a method for converting from 24 fps (23.976) to 30 fps (29.97) in postproduction

3-Point Edit—Editing method that uses either 2 in-points and 1 out-point, or 1 in-point and 2 out-points, to define the length of a source clip and it's placement in a sequence

3-to-2 Adapter—Connector used for plugging 3-pronged, grounded AC plugs into 2-pronged outlets

4K Image Format/4K Video—A video format that has approximately four times the image area of HD video, with a horizontal resolution of approximately 4,000 pixels. See **UHD** and **DCP**

Acquisition Format—A video format used for recording with a camera

Advance—An amount of money loaned to a person before their work is due or completed

Advanced Television Systems Committee (ATSC)—A consortium of engineers, telecommunications companies, and government policy makers responsible for setting broadcast video standards in North America and certain other regions

Ambient Sound/Backgrounds—The aural environment in which a scene takes place

Amp—A unit of electrical current equal to a flow of one coulomb per second, short for "ampere"

Amplitude—The measure of the loudness of a sound

Analog—A recording medium in which the light and color of the image correspond to the strength and frequency of its analogous electronic signal

Analog-to-Digital Converter (ADC)—A digital signal processor that samples analog audio or video information and translates it into binary code

Angle of Acceptance—The area from which a microphone will gather acceptable sound

Angle of View—The maximum angle a camera is capable of capturing through a lens of a specific focal length

Aperture—An opening that all light gathered by a lens must pass through before it is registered on the sensor

Aperture Ring/F-Stop Ring—The adjustable ring on a lens that controls the iris

APS-C—An image sensor size used in DSLRs, approximately equivalent in size to the Advanced Photo System film negative size of 25.1 x 16.7 mm

Archival Footage—Footage retrieved from a public or private archive that can be used in films

Archival Material—Historical footage or stills not created for the film it is included in

Artificial Light—Any light source that generates light through electricity

Artistic Identity—The creative voice within an individual shaped by their experiences and worldviews

Aspect Ratio—The relationship between the width and the height of the frame expressed as a ratio of width:height

Associate Producer/Production Coordinator—Crew member who handles a variety of tasks including confirming locations and meeting times, coordinating transportation, helping things stay on schedule, making sure release forms are signed, and generally providing backup for the director and other crew

Associative Editing—An editing technique characterized by comparing or contrasting the content of the shots to create an association that is not contained in the individual shots

Audio Continuity—A seamless sound transition between cuts or scenes

Audio Filter—Audio signal processing that alters the audio data, and therefore the characteristics of the sound

Audio Outputs—The jacks on a camera or sound recording device where cables can be connected to send audio signals to another device

Audio Record Level—Setting on an audio recording device that will give maximum audio quality with sufficient dynamic range and minimum noise or distortion

Audio Sample Rate—Determines how many times a sound is measured or "sampled" per second by a digital recorder. See **sample rate**

Audio Sweetening—Process of enhancing the quality of the audio, including repairing poor audio and creating audio effects

Audio Waveform—Audio levels shown in the timeline or viewer of an NLE

Authenticity—The apparent sincerity or truthfulness of a film's intentions

Authority—The position and knowledge of a filmmaker or subject in relation to the subject matter of the film, and how their position, background, education, and upbringing gives their stance believability in the documentary

Auto Exposure/Auto Iris—A camera function that will take the average meter reading for a scene and automatically set the camera's aperture

Auto Functions—Modes of automatic function that allow a camera to determine exposure, aperture, focusing, light metering, and white balance

Autofocus—A camera setting that focuses automatically

Auto-knee/Auto Highlight Control—An automatic setting that is designed to give a maximum level of detail depending on the highlight values of the particular image in the frame

Automatic Gain Control (AGC)—A sound recording option that automatically adjusts audio levels to a predetermined average

Autosync (Avid)—A command used to create a single synced clip

Available Light—The light available in a particular shooting situation without adding lights

Average Audio Level Range—The consistent audio level across time, from clip to clip, from start to finish, across a timeline

Avid Pro Tools—A common DAW/software for sound editing and mixing

B-Roll—Images and footage that will accompany a voice-over or narration

BD-R—Recordable Blu-ray disc only able to record once

BD-RE—Recordable Blu-ray disc that is rewritable

Baby Legs—A set of short tripod legs that have a height range from 1 foot to about 3 feet

Backlight—A light positioned at a high angle from behind the subject to help separate the subject from the background

Back Plate—The fixed plate in a capacitor

Back Up—The process of creating a copy of digital material and saving it, usually on a separate drive

Balance—In journalism, the idea that if one side of a story is told, the opposing side should be represented as well

Balanced Audio—An audio signal that runs through a 3-wire cable: two wires for the signal and a hum-resistant shielding cable that is usually grounded

Balanced Output—A signal free from interference caused by AC or fluorescent hum and radio frequencies

Bandwidth—In broadcasting, the bit-rate of available or consumed information capacity in a system, expressed typically in multiples of bits per second

Barn Doors—Attachment with several metal leaves placed in front of a light to keep light off of areas of the set where light is not needed

Bars and Tone—The color bars and reference tone at the head of recorded media used to calibrate sound levels and color and luminance settings for broadcast and post-production

Bass—Sound frequencies at the low end of audibility

Bass Roll-Off—A filter used to suppress unwanted low frequency sound from sources such as wind, traffic, and low machinery hum

Bayer Pattern Filter—On an image sensor, an array of color filters that allocate pixels to the three colors: green, red, and blue

Best Practices—Refers to industry standard approaches to using copyrighted material, dealing with subjects, and so on

Bias—A systematic judgment in favor of or against a person, group, or thing. In documentary, it can be linked to questions about funding or sponsorship

Binary Code—A base-2 numerical system using ones and zeros, so that 1=1, 10=2, 11=3, etc. The basic numerical system used in computers

Bins—Second-level folders that are used to organize all audio and video clips and graphic files in an NLE

Bit Depth—The number of bits of information in each sample of a digital video or audio file

Bit Depth Setting—The sample size for an individual digital sample. In video the RAW sample size could be 14 bits, while the recorded size could be as low as 8 or 10 bits. In audio, 16-bit or 24-bit sample sizes are common

Bit Rate—The number of bits conveyed or processed per unit of time. Also called the data rate; in video it is measured in Mbps, and is a crude measure of overall image quality

Bits—Digital information expressed as binary digits

Black Diffusion—Special effects filter that softens the image by delicately flaring the dark, shadow areas

Black Stretch—A setting that can extend a digital camera's sensor sensitivity range in the darkest parts of the image

Blacks—The darkest parts of the image, such as dark objects, dark clothing, and shadows

Blown Out/Clipped Whites—Complete overexposure

Blu-ray—A digital optical disc data storage format

BNC—A locking connector used to carry composite video [SDI] and uncompressed HD [HD-SDI] signals

Boom Pole—A long, lightweight pole that telescopes out to various lengths, designed to hold a microphone for film recording

Booming—Lifting a camera up and down. Alternatively, recording sound with a boom pole

Bounce Card/Show Card—A card with a reflective surface used to bounce light. See **reflector**

Breakaway Cable—A cable that sends two channels of audio to the camera and then brings the output of the camera back to the sound person so they can monitor the recorded signal through headphones

Breaker Box/Fuse Box—A box containing circuit breakers (or fuses), safety devices that will disconnect when the circuit overheats or short-circuits. It is located where raw power comes into a building and is divided into separate circuits

Breaker Switch—A switch that is automatically operated to protect an electrical circuit from damage caused by overload or short circuit

Brightness—The overall lightness or darkness of a shot

Broads—Open-faced lights with no spotting capability used to deliver a hard, efficient bright light

Bubble Leveler—A level found on some tripods that is designed to assist in leveling the head

Burned Discs—Disc created through a process called duplication

C-stand/Century Stand—All-purpose grip stand, used for hanging, holding, or positioning flags, scrims, or other rigging on a film location

Call Sheet—A document that is circulated before a shoot to everyone involved in a production that includes crucial information including location, key personnel, contact information, necessary equipment, and transportation information

Camcorder—An electronic device that is a combination of a video recorder and a video camera

Camera Adjustment—A small alteration of a framed shot to maintain composition or focus on a person or object that is moving slightly

Camera Filter—Glass or hard plastic elements mounted on the camera, in front of the lens, to change the quality of the light from all sources entering the camera

Camera Microphone—The typically low quality microphone built into a camera. See also **onboard microphone**

Camera Mounting Plate—A removable piece of the tripod head where the camera is attached

Camera Profile—A specific exposure curve and color response used by a digital camera. These are available as presets on many cameras, and can be user-generated as well

Camera Take—The footage generated from the moment the camera is on to the moment it is turned off

Canted Angle/Dutch Angle—Tilting the camera to the side so that the horizon of the composition is oblique

Capacitor—A device capable of storing a small amount of electricity made of two plates oriented parallel to each other, with a very narrow space between them. Also called a condenser, as in a condenser microphone

Capture Drive (Avid)—Determines where the NLE will put any files it creates while importing or during editing

Cardioid—A somewhat directional microphone with a heart-shaped pickup pattern

Cards—Titles or credits that appear one page at a time

CCD / Charge Coupled Device—A type of image sensor (an array of light sensitive pixels on a silicon chip) that captures the entire image at once, and then sends the result to the camera's signal processor one line of video at a time

Center-Averaging—Basing exposure on light values at the center of the image

Center On Cross-Fade—The process of cross-fading between two clips; the audio of the first clip is extended beyond the cut point by half the duration of the cross-fade in order to accommodate the full fade-out, and the incoming shot is extended at the head by half the cross-fade duration to accommodate the fade-in

Character—The personality, aspirations, and internal conflicts of the people in a film

Character-Based—The type of film where characters' actions and interactions are the main action

Characteristic Exposure Curve—A curve that represents how the camera sensor responds to the light hitting it

Checkerboard—To alternate audio clips over 2 (or more) tracks

Chinese Lanterns—A paper lantern that throws a soft even glow in all directions

Chroma Subsampling—A compression system that eliminates color data from a video signal to save space. Chroma subsampling is expressed as a ratio of color samples (red and blue) to luminance (identified with the green signal). Typical subsample ratios are 4:1:1 and 4:2:2

Chrominance (chroma)—The color component of a video signal

CineGamma/Log Gamma—A camera profile setting that flattens the straight-line portion of the video signal's characteristic curve and introduces a shoulder to the highlight areas, resulting in highlight detail and added dynamic range in terms of f-stops

Cinéma Vérité/Direct Cinema—A style characterized by the use of small crews, lightweight handheld equipment, and filming unscripted action with a highly observational "fly-on-the-wall" approach

Cinematographer—Chief operator of the camera, in charge of lighting crew and the general look and shooting style of the film

Climax—The moment of highest emotional impact, where the conflicts that have been put into motion come to a head

Clipping—Overexposure of bright areas of the image. It results in a uniform white area

Clipping (Audio)—When the limiter suppresses the loudness by cutting the sound before it can peak

Clips—In an NLE, the icon that points to an underlying media file. Or, the media file itself

Close-Up (CU)—A shot that places the primary emphasis on the face or other part of the body

Closed Frame—When all of the essential information in the shot is neatly contained within the parameters of a frame

CMOS/Complementary Metal–Oxide–Semiconductor—A type of image sensor (an array of light sensitive pixels on a silicon chip) that creates an image one row of pixels at a time

Codec—A specific compression scheme used to reduce digital file size while maintaining image quality. Short for "compression/decompression."

Color Balance—The adjustment of the intensities of colors in a frame

Color Bars—A screen display of specific colors used to calibrate the projector or recording device to match that of a camera's viewing system

Color Correction/Grading—Part of the postproduction process where image color and light values are evaluated and altered to create a consistent look

Color Grading—The adjustment of color and brightness to achieve a specific mood or look

Color Sampling—The number of times brightness and color information are measured and translated into data by the DSP

Color Space—A model that indicates the reproducible color possibilities in a specific system. Common color spaces are CMYK (print) and RGB (video)

Color Subsampling—See **chroma subsampling**

Color Temperature—The color hue of light, measured using the Kelvin scale.

Color Wheel—A wheel that arranges red, orange, yellow, green, blue, indigo, and violet into a natural progression on a rotating disk

Colorist—A member of the postproduction team who alters and enhances the color of a film using specialized software

Combing—A visual artifact generated when an interlaced image is viewed on a computer screen (with progressive scan)

Compact Flash (CF) Card—A flash memory mass storage device that is used in portable devices such as digital cameras and audio recording devices

Composite Video—An analog video signal that carries both chrominance (color) and luminance (brightness) information

Compositing—The combining of visual elements from separate sources in a single frame

Compositional Frame—A two-dimensional space defined by its horizontal and vertical dimensions

Compound Lens—A lens made up of multiple glass elements

Compound Move—A type of shot created by combining two or more different camera moves, such as a dolly and a pan

Compression—A method of reducing file size or the amount of data by discarding visual detail in the case of an image file, or through analogous methods for audio data

Compression Filter—A filter that detects when a sound will peak above or near 0 dB, used to suppress the sound to keep it within range without affecting the average audio levels of the track

Condenser Microphones—A microphone that uses a capacitor with two charged plates, one fixed and the other forming a diaphragm that is moved by sound waves

Consistency (Sound)—Ensuring there are no noticeable differences in overall sound quality and character as a scene unfolds

Consistent Color and Brightness Values—Color and brightness continuity created through the process of color correction, e.g., no abrupt shifts in luminance or color temperature

Constant Bit Rate (CBR)—A compression type which compresses the image the same amount regardless of the content. Used particularly in NLEs

Constants—Recurring portions of a budget such as monthly charges or days of shooting

Container Format—A metafile format such as Quicktime or MXF that packages image, audio, and other data into a format that a computer can recognize. See **file wrapper**

Content—The actual information in a film, usually used to delineate aspects of a film that do not relate to **form**

Continuity (Continuity Style Editing)—An approach to film editing that assures that individual shots, when cut together, will give the illusion of smooth and continuous time, movement, and space

Contrast—The difference in dark and light values within a shot

Contrast Range/Luminance Range—The difference between the brightest and the darkest areas of the scene being shot

Cookie (Cucoloris)—A metal or foam core gobo with shapes cut into it, used to create patterns on a wall, floor, or other surface

Copyright—Law used to ensure that the creator of a work of art has rights to determine where an image, for example, can be seen, and especially into which works it can be incorporated

Countdown—A numeric on-screen title counting backwards in seconds, from 10 to 2, placed at the head of recorded media intended for exhibition

Coverage—A strategy for filming in a way that will tell the needed story as completely as possible. Includes what will be shot, where the camera is positioned, and how the frame is arranged

Crane Shot—A shot in which the camera is raised very high in the air, above a subject's head, using either a crane or a jib

Creative Commons—A licensing system that offers a variety of options for creators to license their work

Crop Factor—The ratio of a camera's imaging area, typically to that of a 35mm frame, used to calculate relationship between sensor size, focal length and angle of view

Cross Lighting—A lighting setup, often used for two-person interviews, where lights act as both key and fill

Cross-Fade/Audio Dissolve—An audio transition where one sound slowly diminishes while another rises into audibility

Crowdfunding /Crowdsourced—A method of funding a film by raising money from a large number of people, usually via the Internet

Crushed Blacks—Underexposure in video, such that black levels are at or below 0 IRE units

CTB—Color temperature blue, a color conversion gel used to convert a tungsten light source to daylight color temperature

CTO—Color temperature orange, a color conversion gel used to convert daylight into tungsten

Cut—The joining of two shots

Cutaway—A shot used to help "smooth out" discontinuity in the main action, or a jump cut. It is usually followed by a return to the shot before it

Cycles Per Second—The measure of frequency in a wave, whether of sound or electricity

Data Card—A small removable device for data storage

Data Rate—Bit rate in Megabits per second (Mbps) used to determine the amount of storage space needed for a project, type of recording and storage media, and connector types

Data Track—A long, ultrafine spiral track of data, as on disc media such as Blu-ray or DVD

DCI (Digital Cinema Initiatives)—A working group that has developed the digital image and sound standards for exhibition of digital media

Dead—An acoustic environment with poor reflective surfaces that absorbs sound after it leaves the source

Deal Memo—A contract between the filmmakers, cast, and crew, defining the specifics of the production

Decibels (dB)—A logarithmic measurement of audio volume or loudness

Deep Depth of Field—When objects along the z-axis, from foreground to background, are in crisp detail. Also called "deep focus."

Deep Frame—A frame that accentuates the compositional element of depth through use of foreground and background elements

Deliverables—This refers to what a filmmaker actually delivers to a broadcaster (or to a festival, etc.). Deliverables can include the actual film, a list of music used, credits, subject releases, a script for closed captioning, and more

Demo Reels—A video or audio presentation of a person's specific expertise

Depth of Field (DOF)—The range of distances along the z-axis where objects appear to be in sharp focus

Derivative Work—Refers to creative work based on an existing work, such as a film based on a novel

Detail Budget—A line item budget that specifies all expenditures

Dialogue—Speech that emanates from characters within the film, whether they are on- or off-screen

Diaphragm—The thin vibrating membrane that is the sound sensitive portion of a microphone

Diegesis—The world of the film, consisting of the characters, actions, objects, locations, time, and story

Diegetic—Sounds that naturally occur in the world of a film

Dielectric—In a condenser microphone, the space between the two plates that holds the electrical charge

Diffused/Soft Light—Lighting typically coming from a unit that does not illuminate directly from the bulb, but instead bounces the light off a reflective surface, or light from an overcast sky

Diffusion Media—Gel or lighting filter used to soften the output of a hard light source

Digital Audio Recorder—Device for recording sound where an input audio waveform is sampled and recorded digitally

Digital Audio Workstation (DAW)—Editing hardware/software combination designed specifically for professional sound editing

Digital Cinema—The use of digital technology to distribute or use digital theatrical projection

Digital Cinema Package (DCP)—A set of specifications for digital exhibition defined by the industry consortium Digital Cinema Initiatives

Digital Loader/Digital Imaging Technician (DIT)—A crew member specifically devoted to media management, preparing media for editing, transcoding, syncing picture, and downloading media from cards into a computer or onto hard drives

Digital Signal Processor (DSP)—A DSP combines the three sets of color information from the sensor(s) and determines the brightness and color value of every pixel in every frame of video to create the full-color image, and encodes it, along with the audio signal, to create the final digital signal

Digital Sound Recorder—See **Digital Audio Recorder**

Digital Zoom—An in-camera digital special effect in which the circuitry in the camera magnifies the captured video signal by selecting specific pixels and blowing them up

Digital-to-Analog Converter (DAC)—A converter that changes digital audio information into analog electronic waveforms and outputs a line level signal

Diopter—A magnifying lens, part of the camera's viewfinder, that can be set for the camera operator's eye

Direct Address—When a subject speaks directly to an audience, or straight to the camera

Direct Cinema—A documentary genre that focused on directly capturing reality, using flexible camera movement and a highly observational "fly-on-the-wall" approach

Direct Sound—Sounds recorded at the actual location

Directionality—Where light is coming from, or appears to be coming from

Directionality/Pickup Pattern—In sound recording, the tendency of a microphone to be more sensitive to sound from a particular direction

Display Format—A set of specifications for how video is broadcast, received, and displayed

Dissolve—A transition in which the outgoing shot gradually disappears as the incoming shot gradually appears

Distribution—The process of getting a film seen by audiences or viewers

Distributor—A third party entity that specializes in the work of getting a film seen, and getting financial return in the process

Ditty Bag—A filmmaker's general utility tool kit

Documentary Director—The person responsible for the vision of a documentary film

Documentary Producer—A person whose duties vary but typically include raising the funds for a documentary, budgeting, and making sure a film is delivered on budget and on schedule

Dolly—A camera support on wheels that is used when the shot requires a smooth, controlled, and dynamic move

Dolly Shots—Moving shots in which the camera moves closer or farther away from a subject. May or may not involve an actual dolly

Dolly-In—To move the camera closer to a subject

Dolly-Out—To move the camera farther away from a subject

Double-System—A version of sync sound where sound is recorded on a separate audio recorder and combined with the picture in postproduction

Drag—On a tripod head, the amount of resistance to a pan or tilt

Drama—The entire tradition of narrative storytelling

Dramatic Arc—The introduction and resolution of conflict over the course of a film

Dramatic Structure—The shape of the story arc of a film, over time

Dressing Cables—An on-set term for taping down and safetying cables

Drone—A flying device that can mount tiny cameras

Drop-Frame Time Code (DF TC)—A time code that does not drop any video frames, but skips over some time code numbers from time to time in order to adjust the frame count to accurately reflect the true 29.97 fps of SD video

DSLR (Digital Single Lens Reflex) Camera—A digital camera that combines a single-lens reflex camera's optics and mechanisms with a digital imaging sensor

DTMB (Digital Terrestrial Multimedia Broadcast)—Digital television standards used in China and Hong Kong

Duplication—In DVD burning for distribution, the process of creating a disc by using a laser to burn a color dye layer in the media surface, which turns various colors and densities that mimic the depth and shadows of the physical pits in a pressed disc

DVB-T (Digital Video Broadcasting-Terrestrial)—Digital television standards used throughout Western and Eastern Europe, Russia, Australia, and many nations throughout Asia and Africa

DVD—Optical discs that store the binary data for sound and images as microscopic bumps and indentations and play back at standard resolution

DVD+R—Record-once only DVD format

DVD-R—Record-once only DVD format

DVD+RW—DVDs that can be erased and rewritten

DVD-RW—DVDs that can be erased and rewritten

Dynamic Camera Moves—A shot where the camera moves along any of the axes of motion

Dynamic Microphone/Moving Coil Microphone—A microphone that generates a signal through an electromagnetic moving coil attached to the diaphragm

Dynamic Range—The range of signal levels a system can handle. In audio, the range between the loudest and quietest sounds recorded and/or played back, usually expressed in dB

Echo—A long delay return of sound caused by the reflection of sound waves from a surface

Edit Decision List (EDL)—A list of all of the editing decisions made to create a sequence or film—length of shots, order of shots, layering of audio—in a standard format

Electret Condenser—A type of condenser microphone that uses a permanently charged material (the electret) to create the electrical signal, eliminating the need for a polarizing power supply

Elements—The components that create a film, which includes interviews, observational footage, archival materials, etc.

Encoding System—In the world of digital media, a system for turning picture or sound information into digital information that can be stored and manipulated in a computer environment

End Credits—The credits shown after a film that acknowledge subjects, cast, and crew, and other people/organizations that helped with the production of the film

Engagement Plan—A strategy for developing audience engagement and action in relationship to a documentary

Equalization—The manipulation of the frequencies in an audio signal to improve audibility and clarity

Errors and Omissions—Insurance that protects a filmmaker from claims involving violation of certain personal rights or copyright infringement

Essay Documentary—A type of documentary film that typically foregrounds the process of thought and the processes of representation, while employing a poetic or personal voice-over

Establishing Shot—A shot that gives the viewer a sense of the location of a particular sequence

European Broadcast Union (EBU)—Organization of European Broadcasters. They develop shared broadcast and transmission standards

Exclusive—The rights detailed in a contract a filmmaker signs with a distributor ensuring that they will not be able to assign those same rights to a distributor in or outside of the designated market

Exclusivity—A deal that a documentary subject makes with a filmmaker guaranteeing exclusive access to their story in return for specified compensation

Expansion Filters—A filter used to lower the amplitude of extremely low-level sounds in order to drop them below the level of audibility

Exposition—Information a viewer needs to know in order to understand what is happening on the screen

Expository—An informative style of documentary that typically proceeds by argument, employs narration, graphics, etc. and has educational goals

Exposure—Amount of light per unit area that reaches an electronic image (or film) sensor in relation to shutter speed, lens aperture, and scene luminance

Exposure Control—Controlling the amount of light coming through the camera lens by balancing the various factors such as scene lighting, filtering, and camera factors such as f-stop and gain

Exposure Range/Dynamic Range—The range of luminance values a specific imaging device can render with detail before falling off into complete overexposure or underexposure

External Hard Drive—A data storage device that is separate from a computer

External Microphone Input—The connection for audio coming from sources other than the camera's internal microphone

Extract—A type of edit performed by placing in- and out-points and taking selected material out of a timeline, closing the gap, or rippling

Extreme Close-Up (ECU)—A stylistically potent shot that isolates a very small detail or feature of the subject

Extreme Long Shot/Wide Shot (ELS)—A shot that shows a large view of the location, setting, or landscape

Eye Light—A very small spot light carefully set to put a bit of sparkle into the eyes of a subject

Eye-Level—A shot where the lens of the camera is positioned at eye level with a subject regardless if they are sitting, standing, or lying down

Eyeline—The direction a subject on screen appears to be looking in

F-stop Scale—A measure of the amount of light entering a lens, based on a particular aperture or iris opening. It is a ratio of the lens's focal length and its diameter, and proceeds in steps such that each f-stop represents a doubling or halving of the light from the next one

Faceplate (Front of Image Sensor)—Place directly behind the camera lens where the light information strikes the sensor or prism

Fade-In—A slow appearing of an image

Fade-Out—A slow disappearing of an image into a color, usually black

Fair Use Doctrine—A doctrine, written into law in some countries, including the United States, that allows creators to use copyrighted material in certain specific contexts

Fast Color Corrector—A filter in Premiere Pro used to adjust brightness, contrast and color

Fast Lens—A lens with a small f-stop that can open up for low lighting

Festival Screener—A copy of a film designed for use by film festival judges

Field (video)—In interlaced video, a half frame, containing half of the picture information, and displayed for half of the time of the full frame

Field Monitor—A flat-screen LCD display that can mount on the camera or the shoulder mount of a DSLR or stand alone, used during a shoot to display live footage of the camera for framing, critical focus, lighting, or continuity

File-Based Media—Said of digital sound or picture to differentiate from analog media stored on film or videotape

File Format—A scheme for storing information in a computer. For video, this usually includes a compression codec, and a file wrapper, often proprietary, and the possibility of including different types of data (sound and image) and metadata (time code, etc.)

File Wrapper—A metafile format whose specification describes how different elements of data and metadata coexist in a computer file. It does not describe how the media is encoded. It does tell the computer that the file may contain video, audio, time code, and more. See **container format**

Fill Light—A soft light that is positioned to fill in the shadows created by a key light

Film Festival—An organized event for presenting and premiering films

Film Permit—A permit to film in public spaces, typically issued by a city government

Filter—In cinematography, a piece of glass placed in front of the lens to alter the light entering. Typically affects color, the amount of light, or distorts the image

Filter Preset—In audio recording and postproduction, a filter that offers a specific effect (for example on defined frequencies)

Filtering—A method of controlling light by putting it through something that will alter the amount or quality of light. See **audio filter** for sound

Fine Cut—The last stage of editing before sound editing/mix and color correction

Firewire/IEEE 1394—A high-speed interface developed by Apple, used to send digital data from a camera to a computer at speeds of 400/800 Mbps

Fiscal Sponsorship—A service that allows individual filmmakers to receive money from funders that only give to non-profit organizations

Fisheye Lens—An extreme wide-angle lens, with an angle of view greater than 180°

Fixer—The person who knows the lay of the land, speaks the local language, or otherwise has specialized knowledge that will help filming in a foreign environment

Flags—Free-standing frames covered with black cloth, used to sharply define where light falls and where it doesn't

Flaring—Visual effect created when light enters the lens and reflects off the elements

Flat Frame—A frame that emphasizes the two-dimensionality of an image

Flat Response—An equal response throughout all frequencies of the sound spectrum resulting in a flat line graph of frequency response

Flicker Effect—The unsteady strobe-like visual effect that happens when film is projected or filmed at a low frame rate

Flood/Spot Control—A control used to alter the quality of light and intensity along a soft (flood) to hard (spot) spectrum

Fluid Head—A type of resistance mechanism in a tripod head that uses pressurized hydraulic fluid to provide the adjustable drag necessary for smooth camera moves

Fluorescent—A light that generates illumination by passing an electric charge through mercury gas trapped within a hollow tube coated with phosphors, causing it to glow

Focal Length—The distance between the optical center of the lens and the focal plane determining the degree of magnification or demagnification of the subject being filmed

Focal Plane/The Recording Surface—The plane inside the camera where the image is in focus. Generally coincides with the recording surface

Focus—In optics, the point where light rays originating from a point on the object converge, hence where the clearest and most exact reproduction of the image will be found

Focus Assist—A focusing aid which magnifies a portion of the image allowing critical focus with the viewfinder or LCD viewscreen

Focus Point—The subject or area that is in sharpest focus

Focus Ring—A device on a lens that brings a subject into focus by very precisely moving the front elements of the lens forward and backward in relation to the focal plane

Foley Artist—A person who creates and records foley effects as they watch each scene in a film

Foley Effects—A system for recording sound effects in postproduction, where a **foley artist** watches scenes and produces sounds with whatever objects or surfaces needed to create the right sound

Follow Focus—A situation where the camera operator or assistant retains focus on a subject while they are moving along the z-axis either closer to or farther away from the camera

Foot-Candles—Unit of measurement for the intensity of light. Foot-candles is a measurement, used in the United States, based on the light intensity of one lux per square foot. Equal to approximately 10 3/4 **lux**

Foreshortening/Diminishing Perspective—The perceptual understanding that objects will appear to be smaller the farther they are from the viewer, and conversely, that objects will appear larger the closer they are to the viewer

Form—A film's stylistic approach, usually used to differentiate from the content

Format—See **file format**

Four-Walling—A situation where filmmakers pay for the theatrical release of their own film by renting a theater to promote the film themselves

Frame—Each individual still image captured on film or on video

Frame Rate—Refers to the number of still frames that are captured by a camera, or played back on a viewing system, expressed in frames per second (fps)

Frequency—The number of waves that pass a fixed point over a period of time, expressed in terms of number of waves per second and measured in Hertz (Hz)

Frequency Bands—In audio, the different ranges of sound frequencies, typically divided into low, midrange, and high frequencies

Frequency Filters—Filters used to automatically remove unwanted portions of the frequency range

Frequency Range—The range of detectable pitches for a given apparatus

Frequency Response—The frequency range that a microphone or a sound recorder can duplicate in a useful way, measured in a frequency response chart

Fresnel—A type of closed face spotlight that uses a lens with series of concentric focusing rings to achieve a long throw with a soft edged spot

Friction Head—A type of tripod head that uses a resistance mechanism employing surface friction between internal plates to create movement resistance

Frontal Light—Illumination that comes from the angle of the camera

Frontal Shot—A shot taken from directly in front of a subject

Full Blue—A color conversion gel that converts 3,200K light into 5,600K

Full CTO—A color conversion gel that converts 5,600K light directly into 3,200K

Fundamental Tone—The central and dominant shape of a sound wave

Fuse—A safety device inserted into an electrical circuit that will "blow" or melt when the circuit overheats or is short-circuited

Gaffer—Crewmember who is the head electrician

Gaffer's Tape—Special tape used on set, rips easily into any width and length strip you need, holds well, and leaves no adhesive residue behind

Gain—A measure of electronic amplification, said of the boosting of the video signal coming from the image sensor or the record level of a sound signal, expressed in dB

Gamma—The way that an imaging device differentiates between the various luminance tonalities in a scene. It is represented by the deviation from the straight-line portion of the **characteristic exposure curve**. Gamma defines the relationship between a pixel's numerical value and its actual luminance

Gator Clamp—Heavy-duty spring clamp with rubber teeth that ensure a very tight grip

Gel—Sheet of material used in front of a lighting unit (or over a window) to alter the color or quality of that particular light source before it falls on the scene

Genre—A way to categorize film according to its narrative and stylistic elements

Gimbal Mount—A camera stabilizer rig that uses gyroscopes to allow the camera to remain suspended on a horizontal plane regardless of how it is moved

Global Shutter—A method of electronic image capture where all the pixels on a sensor are exposed to light at the same moment and register a complete image

Gloves—Protective garment worn on the hands, important to wear when handling lights

Goals—What a character would ideally like to accomplish

Gobo—The general name given to anything placed between a light source and the scene that throws a shadow pattern

Gobo Head/Gobo Arm—The adjustable parts that attach to a C-stand to hold gobos, flags, and scrims, etc.

Graduated Filter—A filter that incrementally introduces a filter effect into only a portion of the frame, leaving the rest of the frame unaffected

Graphic Match—When shots are connected for their compositional similarities

Graphics—Visual material that can be created using your NLE's title tool or other software such as Photoshop or Aftereffects

Grid Cloth—A waterproof textile or fabric diffusion that is reinforced to allow it to be sewn or grommeted

Grip—The crewmember who sets up, rigs, and supports camera equipment

Gross Revenue—The total amount of sales revenue without subtracting any expenses

Group Shot—A shot that includes more than three people

Gyroscope—A camera stabilizer rig that functions on a spinning wheel or disc so the axis of rotation can assume any orientation and correct for tilt, roll, and pan movements

Half Blue—CTB gel that converts 3,200K to 4,100K

Handles—The extra frames at either side of a cross-fade. Alternatively, any extra media added when exporting media files

Hard Effects—The sound effects that are gathered as nonsync sound and then inserted into the sound design either as postsynchronous sound or as a nonsync sound effect

Hard Light/Directional Light—Light that travels directly from a lamp to the subject

Harmonic—An audio frequency or tone that accompanies the main tone at another fixed frequency

HDMI (High-Definition Multimedia Interface)—An audio/video interface for transferring uncompressed video data and compressed or uncompressed digital audio data from a source device, such as a digital camera, to a compatible field monitor or projector, etc.

Head—The part of the tripod where the camera is mounted. If it is a pan head, it swivels left and right for panning, and up and down for tilting

Head (Editing)—Beginning of a frame

Headphone Jack—A connector used for standard headphones, typically a 1/4″ miniplug

Headroom—In digital audio recording, the range between the maximum record volume and 0dB, which allows a buffer for any unforeseen and sudden audio spikes

Height/Vertical Angle—The vertical position of a lighting unit

Hertz (Hz)— A unit of frequency equal to one cycle per second

High Angle (Lighting)—When the lighting unit is positioned high above the subject

High-Angle (Camera)—A shot composed when raising the camera above eye level

High-Definition—Higher resolution and quality than SD or standard resolution video. Measured in lines of horizontal image resolution, as in 720P with 720 lines, or 1080i, with 1080

High-Key Lighting—Lighting with bright and even illumination, minimizing shadows, texture, and dimensionality

Histogram—A graph shown on cameras and monitors displaying the light value of every pixel registered by the sensor on an axis from black to white

HMI (Hydrargyrum Medium-arc Iodide)—Large mercury vapor lights developed as an alternative to tungsten lighting, they are daylight balanced (5,600K)

Hue—The color values of an image

Hybrid Large Sensor Camera—A camera that attempts to bridge the gap between the ease of use of video cameras and the large sensors and interchangeable lenses of DSLRs

Hypercardioid/Supercardioid—A microphone with a pickup pattern that has a narrow range of acceptance and increased sensitivity

Hypothesis—A basic claim about the world or society that your film expresses, subject to change over the course of the production process

I/O Connector—**Input/Output** connector used for outputting digital video and audio

Icon—A symbol used in computer software to indicate a specific function; in editing an icon corresponds to a specific item, task, or tool

Ideation—The process of conceptualizing a project

Image Plane—The place where the image coming from the camera lens resolves or focuses. In digital video the image plane is the sensor surface. See **focal plane**

Image Resolution—The reproduction of visual detail, sharpness of line, subtlety and degrees of luminance, and accuracy of color, usually expressed as lines of resolution or number of pixels

Impressionistic—A stylistic approach, whether to storytelling, camerawork, lighting, or sound, with a focus on emotion and subjectivity, associations, and patterns often contrasted with realism

In Sync—When sound and picture correspond with frame accuracy

In-Kind—Donated financial support, can include the directors and producers' time, airfare, office rent, or equipment rental

In-Point—The point indicated in editing where a shot will begin

Incident Meter—A light meter that can read the intensity of light falling directly on a subject. Readings are taken from the position of the subject

Infinity—The situation where an infinitely distant object would be in focus, represented on the focus ring scale with the symbol ∞

Infographic—An image used to represent information or data, such as a chart or other visualization

Informed Consent—The principle that subjects should know what a film is about and what their role will be, and what the possible consequences of participation might be, before giving consent to be filmed

Ingest—The process of bringing material into a NLE environment

Input Connectors—On a camera these are how external signals, audio, and time code, are brought in for recording

Inputs/Channels—The signal route for a device that processes or reproduces signals, typically audio

Insert—An edit which works by opening up a space in the timeline for the new clip and pushing any existing material further down the timeline

Intellectual Montage—Conceptual editing that juxtaposes shots with the goal of creating new meaning, or illustrating a concept

Intensity—The strength of an emitted source, whether sound or light

Interlaced Scanning—A method of scanning in which the camera's imaging device first outputs the odd-numbered horizontal pixel lines, one at a time, from the top to the bottom, creating a half-resolution image that is called a field of video. Then, the imaging device returns to the top of the frame to output the even-numbered rows, from the top to the bottom, to fill in the rest of the information with a second field. These two fields of video are interlaced to make up one full frame

International Driver's Permit—A permit issued by most national drivers' associations that allows a person with a driver's license to drive in a foreign country

International Telecommunications Union (ITU)—A specialized agency of the United Nations that is responsible for issues that concern information and communication technologies; they are also involved in defining video standards globally, as for 4K UHD

Interview—A face-to-face meeting where a person poses questions to a subject

Introduction/Synopsis—A concise, one-paragraph description of a project: what the film is about, how long it will be, and what the general significance of the story is

Inverse Square Law—A law that states the intensity of a given sound or image decreases by the square of its distance from the source

Iris—A diaphragm inside the camera lens made up of flat metal blades that controls the amount of light striking the sensor

ISDB-T (Integrated Services Digital Broadcasting-Terrestrial)—Digital television standards used in Japan, Brazil, and most of South America

Isolated Tracks—Unmixed single recorded audio tracks

Isolation Pads—Found on over-the-ear headphones to ensure that what is being heard is only the audio being picked up by the microphone

J-Cut—An edit where the sound comes in before the picture

Jamming—Refers to matching the time code of two devices such as a camera and a sound recorder, or two cameras, usually by briefly connecting with a cable

Jello Artifact/Skew—An effect caused by a rolling shutter where the image wobbles unnaturally

Jib—A boom device that holds the camera on one end and a counterweight on the other, with a balance point close to the counterweight, used to create acrane or boom shot

Jump Cut—When two shots of the same subject are cut together and the frames are very similar, causing the image to "jump"

Juxtaposition—The placing of two shots one after the other to create filmic meaning

Kelvin Scale—Unit of measurement for color temperature. In the Kelvin scale 0 is absolute zero, and the units are the equivalent of centigrade degrees. The color is based on what is known as black body radiation where a piece of iron, for example, will glow first red, then orange, up the spectrum as it is heated

Key Light—A light that provides main illumination of a scene

Keyframe—In computer graphics, a frame used to indicate the beginning or end of a change made to the signal. Used in NLE systems for image transitions, audio level alterations, etc.

Key-to-Fill Ratio—The ratio between the key and the fill lights as they hit a subject. The formula is **Key + fill: fill**

Kicker—A small low-powered hard light source that shines from a side or back angle to provide definition in the subject's body, face, or hair

L-Cut—An edit with new picture coming in before the new sound

LCD Monitor—A liquid crystal display flat screen video monitor, typically backlit

LCD Viewscreen—A small LCD monitor that flips open, found in most digital cameras

Lead Room—Extra vertical space in front of a moving figure in the frame. Also called "walking room."

LED (Light Emitter Diode)—A technology that uses sets of tiny individual cells for both monitor and lighting applications. As light sources they are highly efficient, and use DC power, which means that LED lights can be powered with batteries

LED Monitor—A display that uses tiny LED lights

Legs/Sticks—The part that holds the tripod up, the legs adjust to define the tripod's height and therefore the camera angle

Lens—A set of one or more elements, typically glass, taking light reflecting off of a scene to create an image in conjunction with a camera body or other sensing device

Lens Element—An optical lens that is part of a series that go to make up a compound lens

Lens Filter—A filter used to adjust the quality, color, or intensity of the light entering the camera

Lens Flare—When light scatters in a lens system creating visible artifact across an image. See **flaring**

Lens Housing/Barrel—A light-tight housing where lens elements are held parallel to each other

Lens Speed—The largest possible aperture opening of a particular lens, hence a definition of its maximum light gathering capability

Letter of Inquiry—A short version of a proposal, often the first approach to a funder

Level Control/Gain Control/Pot (Potentiometer)—On an audio mixer or recording device, the control that increases or diminishes the strength of the incoming audio signal

Levels—The strength of your audio as it enters the recorder, as in, "Your levels are too high"

Licensing Agreement—A legal contract that grants the rights to use a still image, a piece of music, a sound effect, or a film clip in a person's work

Lift—An edit that is performed by placing in- and out-points and removing selected material from a timeline, leaving a gap in the timeline where the deleted material used to be

Light Stand—A stand for mounting lights

Lighting Ratio—The ratio that reflects the relative intensities of light sources illuminating a subject or scene. See **key-to-fill ratio**

Limiter—An automatic volume control that brings down peaking sounds that are unacceptably high

Line Level Signal—The audio signal used between audio devices such as cameras, mixers, and amplifiers. Distinguished from the mic level signal, which is much weaker

Line Producer—A producer who focuses specifically on the daily logistics of the shoot

Link—An editing command that is used to marry two files, such as a video file with its corresponding sync audio

Live—An acoustic environment with hard surfaces that reverberate easily

Location or ID Shot—A shot that tells an audience where the events they are seeing are unfolding

Location Permit—A permit allowing one to film in an institutional or restricted locale, whether privately owned or public

Location Scout—In documentary this is typically someone on the production crew, whether the director, producer, or cinematographer who will be involved in location choices and assessing a location

Location Survey—A visit to a location before shooting to develop a shooting plan, and to assess resources and issues that may arise in terms of sound or picture recording

Log Gamma/Extended Dynamic Range—A camera setting that stretches the dynamic range of the exposure to the maximum the sensor is capable of, typically expressed in the added number of f-stops between the darkest and brightest parts of the image

Logging—The process of naming and describing clips at the beginning of the editing process

Long Shot (LS)—Generally a shot that contains the whole human figure

Long Throw—The capability for hard light to travel a long distance

Looking Room—Extra vertical space, to one side or the other of a frame in the direction a subject is looking. Also "look room."

Lot—A box of archival material

Loudness—The magnitude of sound

Low Angle (Lighting)—When the lighting unit is positioned low, below the subject

Low-Angle (Camera)—A shot composed when lowering the camera below eye level

Low-End Roll-Off—A microphone switch that makes the microphone less sensitive to low frequencies

Low-Frequency Attenuation Filters—A filter used to automatically suppress low frequencies

Low-Key Lighting—A lighting setup with a high key-to-fill ratio

Low-Pass Filter—A filter used to pass signals with a frequency lower than a certain cutoff frequency and attenuate signals with frequencies higher than the cutoff frequency

Lower Third—Title used to identify the people in a film, as well as locations

LPCM Audio (Linear Pulse Code Modulation)—A system used for converting an analog sound signal to digital data via sampling

Lumen—An SI (metric) measurement of light intensity, about a tenth of a foot-candle

Luminance—The part of a video signal that carries information about different light levels, or shades of black and white

Macro Lens—A special type of lens that allows for very close focusing on an object

Mafer Clamp—Heavy-duty clamp designed to lock onto pipes, doors, etc., featuring a stud for holding a light, or other grip gear

Magic Hour—The period just before sunset when there is still enough light to film, but the strong shadows of normal daylight are missing

Manual Aperture Override—A function used to turn the auto iris on briefly to get an average exposure and then return to manual iris function for fine tuning

Manual Mode—A camera setting that forces the user to manually adjust aperture, shutter speed, gain/ISO, or other functions

Manual Override—When the user is given control over an otherwise automatic system, as on a camera or sound recording device

Marker—A reference tab that can be put on audio and visual files while editing

Market—As in film market, one of the various ways a film will reach audiences, such as theatrical, broadcast, or video-on-demand

Master List—In editing, a list of all the elements of footage shot, and sound recorded, with the date created and a short description of the material

Master Mix Track—In audio postproduction, the final mix track used to create versions for distribution

Master Shot—A shot used to establish a space and where characters are relative to one another and their environment

Master Use License—Grants the right to include a specific recording of the composition in a film, controlled by the record label

Mastering—The process of outputting the final film to a sturdy, archivally sound digital form from which distribution copies can be made

Material Exchange Format (.mxf)—A container or wrapper format used extensively for media files in both acquisition and editing contexts

Matte Box—Equipment that is attached to the front of the camera and allows for the use of external filters in front of the lens

Media Bay—The place on a digital camera where media is inserted for recording

Media File Indicator—In an NLE system, the time code and clip name used to "point" to or identify the original media file

Media Files—In digital production, the data form of visual or audio footage

Media Format—The physical medium on which video or audio data is recorded

Media Transfer Device—A camera or card reader used to download footage into an NLE system

Medium Close-Up (MCU)—A shot that generally frames a subject from the chest or shoulders up

Medium Shot (MS)—A shot that frames a subject from approximately the waist up

Merge Clips (Premiere Pro)—A command used to create a single synced clip out of components including, for example, separate sound and picture files

Metadata—In digital files, information included along with the media. It can include data from creation date, and iris settings, to copyright info, and other user-defined information

Metric Montage—Editing where cuts are based on regularities in the duration of the shots

Microphone Attenuation—A switch that cuts the overall volume of incoming audio by 10 or 20 dB

Microphone Level Signal—The fluctuating voltage created by a microphone sent as electronic signal to a preamp or amplifier

Mids—The central range of luminances in an image, between the shadow area and the highlights

Milky Blacks—Blacks that are not rich in all portions of an image and that have low luminance levels. Typically a side effect of adding shadow detail

Mini-Jack—Electrical connector used to carry line audio and microphone audio with an adaptor

Miniplug Connector—A 1/8" connector for external microphone input

Mirrorless Shutter Camera—A digital camera, typically with a still photography form factor and lacking an optical viewfinder

Mise-en-Scène—Everything that the audience sees on the screen, including props, costume design, staging

Mix Track—A master track, either stereo, mono, or surround sound, that is mixed down from the output of multiple tracks to accompany the image for exhibition and distribution

Mixed Lighting—A situation where available light sources and film lighting units are combined

Modeling—In cinematography, creating depth by casting shadows

Moleskin—Soft, heavy cotton fabric, using to wrap lavalier microphones and prevent rustling noises

Monitor/Receiver—A screen capable of playing back a video (and audio) signal from a camera or other playback device, as in field monitor and studio monitor

Monitor Hood—A cover for a monitor that protects from sun glare in location situations

Mono Mix—An audio mix designed for single channel playback where both channels of audio are the same

Mono Recording—An audio setup where each microphone or sound source has its own recorded channel

Monopod—A type of camera support with a single pole or leg that can be used to reduce camera shake in the vertical plane

Motivated Light Source—A light that appears to come from a natural source such as the sun, or an overhead light in a room

Music Cue Sheet—A schedule of the music contained in a film or television program. It is the essential document for a licensing company to distribute royalties for musical performances in audiovisual media

Musical Score—Nonsync and non-diegetic music that generally accompanies action or dialogue to underscore the events of a scene with a tone, a mood, or musical commentary

Narration—Spoken commentary in a film from a source that is non-diegetic or outside the story

Narrative Promise—A point early in a documentary where you give your audience a taste of what is to come

National Television System Committee (NTSC) A committee in the United States that creates broadcast standards for television

Natively—Said of a situation where digital files can be ingested as they are, without transcoding

Natural Light—The light coming from a natural source or another source that is not electric

Naturalistic/Realistic—A filmmaking approach that strives to appear as plausible and harmonious with the real environment as possible

Needle-Drop Music—Prerecorded music from music libraries

Net Revenue—The total income of a film minus any expenses a distributor has incurred marketing the film

Nets—Netting material stretched across a frame used purely to cut the intensity of light, by one, two, or three stops, mounted on a C-stand

Neutral Density Filter (ND Filter)—Gray-tinted filters that cut down the amount of light entering the lens in measured steps

Neutral Density Gels—A gel used to cut down the intensity of a light source without affecting the color or light quality

Noise—Residual low-level sound generated by a sound recording system that is always present, as in signal-to-noise ratio

Non-Diegetic Sound—Sound that has no source in the world of film. Examples are film music and narration

Non-Drop-Frame Time Code (NDF TC)—A time code that counts frames according to the original black-and-white video frame rate, assigning a new number to each video frame at a consistent rate of 30 frames per second

Nonexclusive—Rights granted to a party with the understanding that the licensor can grant those same rights to another third party

Nonlinear Editing System—Video or audio software that uses nondestructive editing

Nonsynchronous—In sound recording, audio that has no corresponding image

Nonvolatile—Said of computer memory that can be stored and retrieved after the device has been powered down

Normal Lens/Medium Lens—A lens that creates a field of view close to what to the human eye would experience

Object Overlapping—When one object overlaps with another to achieve a feeling of deep receding space

Objectivity—Judgment ostensibly not formed by personal opinion or emotion, but by fact

Observational Filmmaking—Style of filmmaking characterized by unscripted action with a highly observational "fly-on-the-wall" approach

Observational Material—Material within the raw footage that passively observes a subject or situation

Obstacle—In dramatic terms, an opposition or a conflict that needs to be overcome

Off-Line Editing—Using low-resolution proxies for editing

Off-Screen—The real world environment that is cropped, and not shown in the frame

Off-Screen Dialogue—When the voice of a person who is part of a scene is speaking but they are not in the view of the camera

On-Axis—Correct placement of the mic in relation to the audio source so that it is directly in line with the microphone's optimal sensitivity range

Onboard Microphone—An external microphone mounted on a camera or camera rig

Online Editing/Conforming—Re-creating a cut on a high-end edit system using high-resolution footage or original source material; can include color correction or insertion of final graphics

Online Session—A picture finishing session in a postproduction facility

On-Screen Dialog—When the voice of a person who is part of a scene is speaking while being in view of the camera

Open Frame—When the composition leads the audience to be aware of the area beyond the edges of the visible shot

Open Media Framework (OMF)—A file format for moving sound files as well as edit information, and even effect information, between applications

Open-Faced Spot—A common lighting unit producing hard light that has a movable lamp, allowing one to focus its throw from a broad to a more narrowly defined area

Opening—The beginning of a dramatic arc; is meant to draw the audience into a story, give them a basic sense of what the topic is, introduce the audience to at least one of the main characters, establish the style of a film, including major elements, and give the viewer a sense of the scope of the discussion

Opening Montage—Associative editing montage located at the beginning of a film

Optical Center—The point inside a lens where the image reverses itself

Optical Refraction—A process of gathering the light reflecting off a scene and bending it to form an image on the **focal plane**

Optical Zoom—A type of lens that allows for the alteration of the focal length, for instance, from wide to telephoto by adjusting the front lens elements

Out-Point—The point indicated in editing where a shot will end

Output Connectors—A connector used for monitoring sound or picture, or transferring files

Outtake—The shots within the raw footage a filmmaker does not use

Overexposed—What happens to an image when too much light goes through the lens, creating a washed out image with no definition in the highlights

Overlay Edit—A type of edit that will cover over the excess portion of the outgoing shot starting at the edit insertion point

Overmodulated/Overloaded—In sound recording when a signal is too strong to be sampled accurately and the result is distorted sound, or "clipping"

Overtonal/Associational Montage—A montage that is the combination of metric, rhythmic, and tonal montage properties

Overtones—Any frequency that is higher than the fundamental frequency of a sound. See **harmonic**

Overwrite—An edit that covers up whatever was in the timeline before the source material came in

P2—Short for "Professional Plug-In," a professional digital recording solid-state memory storage media format created by Panasonic

Pacing—The rate of speed that a scene, or sequence of scenes, plays out

PAL (Phase Alternate Line)—Analog SD video standard based on 50 fps and 625 lines of resolution. Since replaced with Digital Video Broadcasting (DVB) standards in countries using PAL

Pan—A dynamic camera move that scans space horizontally by pivoting the camera left or right

Pan Handle—A handle used to control the movements of the tripod head

Pan Head—A type of tripod head that gives the camera independent rotation horizontally and vertically

Pan Slider—In NLEs and audio software, a tool used to select which channel on a mix track each audio track should be directed to, or the real world equivalent on a hardware audio mix board

Pan With/Follow Pan—A pan that follows a subject as they move through space

Panning From/To—A pan that moves from one subject to another

Paper Edit—A preliminary edit written on paper, and based on an initial evaluation of the raw material before actual editing

Participatory—Style of filmmaking where the filmmaker catalyzes events within the film

Payroll Service—A service that can be used to pay the salaries of staff, such as a film crew, and deal with workman's compensation, social security, and other tax-related issues

Peak Reading Meter—A hardware or software device that measures and indicates the momentary highest levels of sound entering the recorder

Perspective—Relationship between objects in a scene based on the focal length and field of view of the lens

Phantom Power—A method for powering condenser microphones where electrical current flows through the output to the microphone from the recorder or camera

Phase Error—An error that occurs when sound waves arrive at different times from the same source, canceling each other out. The result is a noticeable muffling of the audio

Photosphere—The light sensitive half-globe light diffuser on an incident light meter that gathers the light falling on a subject from the front and sides and averages out these light intensities to arrive at an overall incident light intensity reading

Picture Lock—The point in postproduction when the placement of all the picture elements is perfect, and all of the creative editing decisions are complete

Pillarboxing—A system for inserting an image with a 4:3 aspect ratio into a wider aspect ratio frame, where the sides of the frame are filled with black

Pistol Grip—A small handle attached to a shock mount to allow the handholding of a microphone

Pitch—The property of sound caused by the frequency of the sound waves that determine how high (treble) or low (bass) the sound is

Pits—The microscopic bumps and indentations found on DVDs, CDs, and Blu-rays

Pivot Camera Move—A shot where the camera pivots, horizontally or vertically, from a stationary spot

Pixel—Light-sensitive photodiode, mounted in an array on a CCD or CMOS image sensor

Plane of Critical Focus—The precise region in front of the camera that will be in sharp focus

Plasma Display—A flat display screen or monitor in which pixels are colored fluorescent cells

Platforms—A hardware/software context for seeing media. Used particularly for video on demand and other net-based distribution situations, but also applicable to broadcast television or cable

Playhead—On an NLE timeline, a horizontally scrolling vertical line running through all edited tracks indicating where the media will play back from the timeline

Plot—What happens during a film, what the characters do, and what happens to them, including how and why those things happen, and the results

Pluraleyes—A software program by Singular Software that synchronizes audio and video clips automatically without the need for time code or slates

Point of View—A type of shot that reflects the perspective of someone in the film

Point Source—In lighting, a light that is generated from something approximating a single point, for example a filament in a light bulb, or a candle

Polarizing Filter—A filter used to reduce or eliminate the obstructing glare and reflections coming off transparent surfaces like glass and water, works by eliminating all light waves except for those with one orientation

Pop Filter—A filter used to diminish the strength of a plosive "P"

Portable Field Mixer/Microphone Mixers—Small audio consoles that allow for independent level control of multiple microphone inputs, and then output this audio as either a microphone or a line signal to your camcorder through two channels

Postproduction—The creative and technical processes that go on after the shooting stops

Postproduction Binder—A binder that holds important information such as the master list of footage, logs, and transcripts, used while editing

Postproduction Supervisor—Someone who oversees the postproduction process, organizing the workflow, and taking care of aspects other than editing such as obtaining archival material, clearing rights, maintaining schedule between different personnel

Postsynchronous—Sound such as effects that is synced up to a corresponding image in the editing

Practical—Lights that are part of your location, such as household lamps or overhead fixtures

Preamplifier/Preamps—Part of electronic sound reproduction equipment that boosts the incoming signal

Presence—The overall sound of a location

Presetting Focus—Finding focus on a subject by zooming in and focusing on a detail and then zooming back out to one's frame

Pressed Discs—A way of making DVDs or Blu-ray discs in large quantities, also called replication

Pressure Zone Microphones (PZMs)/Boundary Mics—Specialized mics mounted on a plate that eliminates reverb in situations where many people are speaking from different parts of a room

Preview Monitor (Avid)—Window used to view an entire clip and then set in-points and out-points to delineate the exact piece of footage from a longer shot. A source monitor

Primary Sources—People in a documentary who have experienced an event such as eyewitnesses or participants

Prime Lens—A lens with one fixed focal length

Prism Block—A solid geometrical grouping of optical glass where light gathered from the lens is split into the three primary colors of light

Pro-Filmic Reality—The real world that encompasses the world of the film

Production Assistants—Crewmembers who help with various logistical aspects of production

Production Insurance—An insurance package that will cover liability, as well as loss or damage to production equipment

Production Management—The practical dimension of producing a film, including the organizing of scheduling and personnel and managing expenses

Production Sound—Audio gathered on location, also called field recordings

Production Value—The overall quality and aesthetic impact of a film's technical aspects like lighting, sound, and cinematography

Profile Shot—A shot of the subject taken from the side

Program Leader—Footage placed at the head of your program master, including color bars and tone, a slate, and a countdown

Program Master—The definitive version of a film, used for creating exhibition and distribution copies

Program Panel (Premiere Pro)—The window used to watch the sequence as you build it, displays wherever the timeline playhead rests

Program Slate—A simple title at the beginning of a film intended for a broadcaster or programmer that typically includes title, running time, audio information, production date, and maker's name

Progressive Scanning—A method of scanning in which the sensor scans a full frame of video from top to bottom in a continuous line

Project File—The main file created by a NLE; it includes EDLs for various sequences, source media information, user preferences, and settings

Project Panel (Premiere Pro)—The main window for storing, organizing, and accessing all of the visual and audio elements for a project

Project Window (Avid)—The main window for storing, organizing, and accessing all of the visual and audio elements for a project

Proposal—Initial plan for filmmaking used to communicate the vision for a film clearly and powerfully, and used for fundraising efforts

Provenance—The history of origin and ownership of an image or an object

Proxies—Lower-resolution versions of high-resolution media files used for off-line editing

Public Domain—Material that has either aged out of copyright, was produced before a copyright existed, or material produced by a government agency

Pulldown Menus—A type of software interface. In NLE software, these menus are a place where any given command can be found

Pulling Focus—The act of changing the camera's focus distance so the subject can remain in focus while changing position

Quality (of Light)—The texture of a light: how hard or soft its beam is

Quantizing—The process of transforming analog information into digital data

Quantizing Error—The round-off error introduced by quantization, noticeable in lower bitrate digital sound or image

Quick Release—A small easily detachable plate used to pop the camera on and off the head of a tripod quickly

Radio Mic/Wireless Mic—A small pocket-size transmitter/receiver system (typically transmitting in the UHF band) to which a microphone is attached

Random Access—The ability of a computer to access any piece of media instantly

Rarefaction—Low pressure in a sound wave

Rationale—The portion of a proposal that informs readers why the film needs to be made

RAW File Format—A digital image file that has not been compressed

Raw Footage—Everything shot during production

Raw Media—Uncompressed media

RCA Plug—Electrical connector used to carry line audio and composite analog video signals

Reenactment—The recreation of prior events for film

Re-Link—Reestablishing the relationship between the media file indicator (the clip) and the underlying media files if it has broken for some reason

Remix Culture—The generational idea that creators can easily borrow and adapt images and sounds created by others

Rerecord Mixer/Dubbing Mixer—A postproduction audio engineer who mixes recorded dialog, sound effects, and music for a film

Reaction Shot—A shot that breaks away from the action of the film in order to show a character's reaction to that action, particularly other people speaking

Realism—An approach to documentary filmmaking that creates the effect of reality, of being a "slice of life," without any manipulation of events

Recordable Disc—A media storage disc such as a DVD, Blu-ray, or CD that can be used to record and play back using lasers

Recording Level—The levels that are monitored while recording audio during production, also known as record level

Recording Media Format—Includes both the type of media the data is stored on and the file type, sample rate, etc.

Recording Surface—In a camera, the faceplate of the sensor, or the face of the prism block. This is where the image is registered

Reference Audio—In double-system shooting, audio recorded with the camera's built-in microphone, used as a reference while syncing sound in post

Reference Tone—A 1-kHz pure tone used to calibrate a chain of audio devices in the field

Reference Track—The most important track in a mix, used as the base for creating sound levels

Reflecting/Bouncing—A method of moving light where it is needed using a specular or light-colored surface

Reflective Light Meter—A light meter that measures the light bouncing off of a surface

Reflector—Any device that can be used to bounce light, either cloth, metallized cloth, or a show card

Reflexive—Style of filmmaking that draws attention to the film's construction, often through the presence of the filmmaker on- or off-screen

Reflexivity—When the filmmaking process is revealed in the film

Refutative Argument—Presenting the opinions of people who counteract the essential claim of the documentary

Release Form—A legally binding contract between the filmmaker and the subject being filmed, stipulating that the subject consents to being filmed and included in the final work

Render Files—Process of creating temporary video and audio render files for segments of a sequence that are altered digitally in editing, such as transitions, or sound level alterations

Replication—Process of physically molding the pits of the data track into the surface of the polycarbonate plastic, which is then coated in aluminum to create a disc

Resistance Mechanism—The mechanism that creates the resistance or drag of the tripod head against the weight of the camera and the speed of a pan or tilt

Resolution—In story structure, the final outcome of rising action and climax. For cinematographic definition, see **image resolution**

Reveal—A single shot that starts with one frame, and then gives new information, often through a camera move

Reverberation (Reverb)—A very short delay in the return of a sound

RGB—The three primary colors of light: red, green, and blue as used in a computer color space

Rhetoric—Effective use of language or speech and the impact of a message on an audience

Rhetorical Approaches—A filmmaking approach that explores real-life situations and conflict, crafting arguments through the presentation of events, evidence, information, and analysis

Rhythm—The duration of shots relative to each other, and the patterns of emphasis, or pulses, these durations create

Rhythmic Montage—Montage where changes in rhythm create new meaning

Riding the Gain/Riding Levels—Raising or lowering the record level as needed

Rights-Managed—A way to license copyrighted work where a person pays for rights that may be restricted by time (a certain number of years) or platform (broadcast, theatrical) or market (national, international)

Rim Light—A lighting unit that is positioned 180° away from the camera and pointing near or toward it, illuminating the subject's back

Rising Action—The bulk of a film, includes the development of voices, events, and the nuances that contextualize the basic conflict to create a larger and more complex picture

Rocker Switch—A pressure sensitive switch that controls the servo zoom control on a camera lens

Roll-Off Filter—In audio recording, a roll-off filter cuts the sensitivity to unwanted frequencies, typically very low or high sounds. They can be found on microphones, mixers, and recorders

Rolling Shutter—A method of image capture that exposes and reads out one line of pixels at a time (as opposed to the whole frame)

Room Tone—The ambient sound of a location when no one is talking

Rough Cut—Preliminary cuts of a film that follow a paper edit, and precede the fine cut; where the scenes and structure of the documentary are worked out

Rough Cut Screenings—A screening of an unfinished film for sample audiences

Royalties—Money paid to a filmmaker for the sale or use of their film

Royalty-Free—Category of material that is owned, but that can be used freely under some circumstances without licensing

Rule of Thirds—A guide to composing an aesthetically pleasing frame where it is divided into thirds with imaginary lines along the horizontal and vertical axes (making four points of particular interest), where significant objects, focus points, and elements of interest are positioned along these lines

Sales Agent—A person who represents the filmmakers' interest, often when selling to distributors, and negotiates the contract and conditions of the sale of a film

Sample—In digital recording, a single measurement of a waveform whether sound or light

Sample Rate—In digital media, the number of samples per second. For an HD video luminance signal, the sample rate is 75.25 MHz. For audio, a sample rate of 48 kHz is standard for film work

Sample Size—A measure of the accuracy and detail of each audio sample, determined by the number of binary digits assigned to each sample. See **bit depth**

Sandbags—A bag or sack made from sturdy material filled with sand, placed over the legs of light or grip stands as a safety measure to prevent their toppling over

Saturation—The intensity of a particular color, expressed as the degree to which it differs from white

Scanning—In video, the process that analyzes an image line by line and outputs it as a continuous signal for recording

Scanning Type—There are two types of scanning used in digital recording, interlaced (i) and progressive (p)

Scene—A dramatic unit in which action ostensibly happens in continuous time and within a single location

Scratch—A placeholder to indicate any footage or elements that remain to be acquired, typically said of preliminary music or narration

Scratch Disk (Premiere Pro)—The destination storage drive for any files created by an NLE, such as render files

Scratch Mix—A preliminary mix where audio levels are at a comfortable range without spending too much time developing a full mix

Scratch Narration—Temporary narration, a placeholder for final narration

Scratch Track—A placeholder audio track used to sync audio and visual footage, usually deleted after the syncing process is complete

Screen Direction—The movement of a character through the frame in an edited shot must maintain the same direction, left to right or right to left, in order to sustain continuity

Scrim—Wire mesh screens that fit directly in front of the lighting unit and reduce the light's intensity

Script—A written description of what the audience sees and hears

Scroll—The movement of titles or credits from bottom to top or top to bottom of the screen

SDI/HD-SDI (Serial Digital Interface)—The US broadcast standard for digital video signals (set by the Society of Motion Picture and Television Engineers, or SMPTE)

SECAM (Séquential Couleur Avec Mémoire)—Former European analog standard

Secondary Sources—Experts, academics, or policy makers used in interviews

Secure Digital (SD)—A type of small nonvolatile memory card commonly used in cameras and sound recording devices

Selective Focus—Focusing on an aspect of the frame to isolate and highlight a particular part of the image

Selects—In editing, shots chosen by the editor from the raw footage that a filmmaker deems most usable

Sensor (Image Sensor)—In a camera, the light sensitive device that converts an image from the lens into a digital file. See **CMOS** and **CCD**

Sequence—In story structure, a part of a film, usually longer than a shot or a scene, that is unified by a theme or a larger idea. In NLE editing, the actual series of shots in one timeline

Sequence Monitor (Avid)—The window used to watch the sequence as you build it, displays wherever the timeline playhead rests

Sequence Settings—The settings for frame rate and size and codec, used to determine the format of any new sequence created

Servo Zoom Mechanism/Servo Zoom Motor—A motorized system that enables a user to glide through the zoom range, from wide-angle to telephoto and back smoothly at different speeds

Set Lights—Lights used to light the space of a set, as opposed to the main action

Setting Levels—Adjusting the strength of the recorded audio signal

Setting Tone—A process that uses a standard tone to calibrate the gain levels of linked recording devices, such as a mixer and camera or digital audio recorder in order to maintain audio level consistency

Shallow Depth of Field—In cinematography, when a narrow vertical plane is sharply defined and objects in front of or behind that plane are blurry

Shock Mount—A device that holds the microphone securely in place using rubber or other mounting that absorbs vibrations or handling noise

Shooting Flat—A shooting approach where the image has extended dynamic range in highlights and shadow detail, but looks flat and unnatural to the eye until it is corrected or graded in postproduction

Shooting from Behind—When the camera is directly behind the subject

Shooting Ratio—The ratio of total footage shot to footage being used in the final film

Short Lens—See **wide-angle lens**

Short-Range Apparent Motion—A phenomenon that happens when shown a rapidly changing series of sequential still images in which there is only slight difference from image to image; humans process this visual stimulus with the same perceptual mechanism used in the visual processing of real motion transforming the still images into motion through the psychological and physiological interpolation of information between the still frames

Short Throw—Light that spreads rapidly and does not travel far, said of soft light

Shortcut—In editing, a quick alternative way to perform a function, usually a designated keystroke

Shot—A continuous run of images, unbroken by an edit. Technically speaking, a shot is the footage generated from the moment the camera rolls to the moment it is turned off

Shot/Reverse Shot—A shooting technique used when two characters are speaking to each other. One character is shown looking at the other from his point of view, then the second character is shown looking back at the first character, from the first character's point of view

Shotgun Mic/Unidirectional—A microphone with a narrow pickup pattern and hence excellent response in one direction

Shoulder—In cinematography, the brighter end of a characteristic curve where you will find the highlights

Shoulder Mount—A device that allows the support of camera equipment on the shoulder

Show and Tell Sequence—A sequence where a subject explains something to an off-screen director

Shutter Speed—The amount of time for which each frame of film or video is exposed

Sibilance Suppressor—A filter used to decrease the hiss of an "S" sound in dialog or narration

Sidelight—A lighting unit that is positioned at 90° from the camera

Sightline—The direction a character is looking

Signal—In communications, refers to the part of image or sound that contains information, as opposed to noise

Signal-to-Noise (S/N)—The ratio between the part of the signal, typically audio, that we want to record and unwanted interference that contaminates that signal

Significant Detail—A shot that provides important information

Silk—Said of any material that is stretched on a frame to diffuse light

Single-System—A sync sound recording system where audio and video are gathered at the same time and recorded to one apparatus as linked files on the same media

Sit-Down Interview—A formal interview, one where the subject or subjects are seated and focusing their attention on the interviewer or camera

Sizzle Reel—A collection of a filmmaker's best material, used to give viewers a sense of the documentary's style and the range of material that has been shot

Slate—When shooting **double-system**, a device that creates a one-frame, easily identifiable reference "moment" of an image and sound event with which to line up the picture and sound, which is recorded by the camera and the audio recorder at the beginning of every take

Slider—A small lateral dolly capable of a few feet of motion

Slow Lens—A lens with a larger f-stop and hence a reduced ability to let in light

Snap—In NLE software, an editing tool that connects two clips together as if they were magnetic, allowing quick placement of shots end-to-end

Solid State Drive (SSD)—A data storage device with no moving parts that uses integrated circuit assemblies as memory to store data persistently

Solid-State Memory—A nonvolatile method of storing data that does not use magnetism, found on solid state drives

Sound Design—The formal approach to a film's total aural impression

Sound Design Element—The layers of sound that add to the overall feel of a film

Sound Designer—A member of the postproduction team who is responsible for the overall aural impression of a film

Sound Edit—The part of the postproduction process that focuses on preparing the sound tracks for the **sound mix**

Sound Editor—The person who performs the sound editing, and prepares the sound tracks for the sound mix

Sound Effect/SFX—A sound in a film that is not speech or music, typically of short duration

Sound Effects Library—A resource that houses pre-recorded sound effects to use in films, either off- or online

Sound Mix—The process of setting levels, polishing and finalizing the various audio tracks in your sound design, and creating a mixtrack

Sound Perspective—Refers to the apparent distance of a sound. Clues include the volume of the sound and the balance with other sounds, and the amount of echo and reverberation

Sound Recordist—In media production, the crew member who decides on a sound recording strategy for a given scene, places microphones, and makes sound recordings

Sound Scout—Refers to a stage of preproduction where the sound recordist examines a location for sound issues

Sound Wave—A pressure wave, consisting of an alternating pattern of high pressure and low pressure traveling through the air or other medium

Source—In production, the origin point of a sound, or alternatively, of a particular light hitting the scene

Source Music—The name given to any music that has a visible origin in a scene

Source Panel (Premiere Pro)—A window used to view an entire clip and then set in-points and out-points to delineate the exact piece of footage used from a longer shot

Special—Low-wattage, unobtrusive light whose function is to illuminate a specific object or a small area of the frame for emphasis

Special Effect—Category of camera filter that alters or distorts the quality of the light. Also an illusion created for movies and television by props, camerawork, or generated using computer software

Specular—A mirror-like reflector, as behind the bulb of an open-faced light

Speed of Sound—How fast sound travels, at sea level in dry air, can be about 340.2 meters/sec or 1,126 feet per second

Spill Light—In cinematography, light that falls where it should not on the set

Split Edits—Edits in which the transition from one image to the other happens at a different time than the transition in the audio track

Splitters—Extension cord used for plugging multiple devices into one outlet

Spotting—In sound editing, the process of watching the picture-locked film to identify, scene by scene, the placement and character of any additional sound effects, ambience tracks, or music that are needed

Spotting Sheet—A sheet detailing the location of each sound effect, along with thoughts on the tone, mood, or other contribution that each sound is supposed to make

Spreader—A piece of the tripod attached to the legs, which keeps them from sliding out from under the camera

Staging Area—On set, an area for equipment that is safe and secure, where the subjects and crew can store their personal belongings while they are on set

Stakes—The investment the characters in a film, or the audience have in the outcome of the story or argument

Standard Legs—A type of tripod leg that has two or three stages of extension and can position the camera between about 3 feet and 6 feet high

Standard Sample Rate—In sound recording, the number of samples of audio recorded per second. For media production, this is 48 kHz

Standard-Definition/SD—The standard image resolution for broadcast television before the advent of HD recording. 525 lines in the US NTSC system, and 625 in the European PAL system

Stereo Recording—An audio setup where two microphones are used for each sound source to give a sense of sound dimensionality and perspective

Still Photo—A non-moving photograph

Stinger—The on-set name for an extension cord

Stock Footage—Footage that can be used in other films

Stock Houses—Large private collections that are in the business of collecting and licensing still and moving images

Stop—In cinematography, signifies each number on the f-stop scale

Straight Cut—An edit where picture and sound are both cut together at the same point

Strands—A television term referring to a particular program or series that acquires media of a particular type

Stream—A file structure found in cameras that shoot in the AVCHD format where the media typically is accompanied by external metadata and must be "wrapped" in a container file format for editing

Structure—How the film is organized and arranged

Stylistic Approach—A filmmaker's aesthetic strategy for telling a filmic story

Stylized/Expressionistic—A filmmaking approach used to draw attention to the aesthetic dimensions of representation, or to the emotional import of the situation by being overt or exaggerated in ways that make a specific narrative or thematic point

Subcarrier Frequency—A digital or analog signal riding on a main radio transmission carrying extra information like voice, color, or data

Subclips—In NLE editing, excerpted sections of an original long take that can act as independent clips

Submaster—A copy of the master film used for a specific purpose, such as duplication

Superimposition—When two images are layered one on top of the other

Surround Sound—A technique for playing back sound that provides sound from a 360° radius around the listener, typically on six or more channels

SxS—A flash memory standard used by Sony for camera recording

Synchronization Rights—An aspect of music licensing that refers to the rights to use a particular composition (as opposed to a particular recording of that music)

Synchronous (sync) Dialogue—Dialogue recorded with the picture during the production phase, and the picture and sound from the shot are both used on-screen, and frame-accurate sync is maintained during editing

Synchronous Sound—Audio that is recorded with the image, so sound and picture correspond to each other with frame accuracy

System Noise—The electronic junk that contaminates the audio signal being recorded

Tail—The end of a shot

Talking Heads—Interview footage that prominently features people talking

Target Audiences—A group of people a film is aimed toward, an intended audience

Telephoto Lens/Long Lens—A lens with a long focal length that magnifies the subject and gives a narrow field of view

Temp Music—In editing, music from any source used to get a feel for the style and tone that will work for a scene

Term—The amount of time noted in a distribution contract

Territory—The geographical area noted in a distribution contract

Texted Master—The version of a master that includes titles

Textless Master—A master without any titles or lower thirds

Theme—The deep central ideas in a film, that may not be referenced directly but are at the core of its meaning

Three Shot—A shot that includes three subjects

Three-Band Equalizer—A filter used to manipulate three broad areas of the sound spectrum more or less independently

Three-Point Lighting—A three light unit set up with a key light, fill light, and backlight

Three-Quarter Back—The camera shoots the subject facing away from the camera at a three-quarter angle

Three-Quarter Backlight—A lighting unit that is positioned at 45° from the camera, behind the subject

Three-Quarter Frontal (Camera)—When the camera is positioned at a 45° from where the subject is facing

Three-Quarter Frontal Light—A lighting unit that is positioned at 45° from the camera, in front of the camera

Three-Way Color Corrector—A filter used to make brightness, contrast, hue, and saturation adjustments to three regions of exposure of an image, shadow, midrange, and highlights

Threshold Level—The amplitude level above which or below which a sound must be in order to be affected by a filter

Threshold of Hearing—The minimum a human ear can hear when there are no other sounds present (0 dB)

Threshold of Pain—Where the threshold of pain and hearing meet (120 dB)

Through the Lens (TTL) Metering—A reflective light meter used to measure light levels from a scene after it has entered the lens

Throw—The ability for light from a lighting unit to reach a subject

Tilt—A dynamic camera move that employs a shift in the camera's perspective vertically, as in "tilt up" or "tilt down"

Tilt From/To—A tilt that moves from one subject to another

Tilt Lock—A device on the tripod head that locks the head mechanism, preventing tilt

Tilt With/Follow Tilt—A tilt that follows a subject as they move

Timbre—The unique tonal composition and characteristics of a sound

Time Code—A coded signal in video that marks each frame with a unique number in hours, minutes, seconds, and frames

Time Lapse—A type of filming where a long time period is condensed to a short one by shooting frames at a very slow rate

Timeline—In an NLE display, the window where an editor inserts, deletes, arranges, rearranges, and fine-tunes clips

Timing—The specific placement of a shot within a sequence

Title Safety—The inner portion of a frame that will be visible in a variety of exhibition venues

Title Tool—Tool that creates titles and credits

Toe—The dark end of a characteristic curve

Tonal Montage—Montage that uses the emotional meaning or "mood" of the shots to determine their placement relative to one another

Tool Palette—A window used to access timeline tools

Toolbar Window—On an NLE display, a small window used to access timeline tools

Topsheet—A one-page summary of a film budget

Tough—In lighting, indicates any gel that is heat resistant and can be used on lights

Tough Frost—A heat-resistant diffusion that attaches to barn doors to create a softer light

Tough Opal—A heat-resistant diffusion that attaches to barn doors to create a slightly softer light

Tough Spun—Diffusion made of spun glass

Tracking Shot—A dynamic camera move where the camera follows a subject, typically from side to side

Trailer—A short preview of a film

Transcode—The act of converting media to a new codec, for instance, one that a NLE is optimized to work with

Transcribing—The process of a creating a word-for-word transcript of interviews and dialog from a documentary

Transcript—Word-for-word written account of an interview or other dialog

Transfer—The act of moving sound and visual components as digital data to a computer, especially one running specialized editing software

Transition Shot—A shot used to start or end a scene or sequence

Treatment—Part of a film proposal, describes what viewers will see and hear as they watch the film

Trimming—In lighting, the process of blocking light to keep it from falling where it is not needed

Tripod—A three-legged device designed to both hold the camera steady for precise subject framing and allow for fluid pans, tilts, and compound moves

Tungsten-Halogen Light/Quartz Light—A common artificial lighting source for documentary production, with a color temperature of 3,200K. Employs a tungsten filament in a halogen gas such as iodine or bromine

Two Shot—A shot that includes two subjects

Two-Channel Stereo—See **stereo recording**

UHD (Ultra High Definition)—The broadcast standard for 4K digital video developed by the NHK and supported by the International Telecommunications Union. Typically an option on 4K cameras. UHD-1 supports 3840 x 2160 pixels

Unbalanced—A two wire system for audio, prone to interference and hum

Underexposed—What happens to an image when there is not enough light in a scene or part of one to get an exposure, creating an image that is too dark

USB—Universal Serial Bus, one of several connectors used to carry digital audio, video, and auxiliary data

User Preferences—In an NLE, the settings created at the start of editing that define personal preferences such as layout and display

Variable Bit Rate (VBR)—Codecs that compress less when there is more movement or color shifting from frame to frame than when the image is more static

Vectorscope—A vectorscope shows a waveform representing the amount of saturation of each color in an image, used for color correction and grading

Venue—The place where an audience encounters a film

Veracity—The truthfulness of a film

Video and Audio Tracks—The parts of the timeline where video and/or audio clips are assembled

Video Diary—A method in documentary filmmaking where subjects speak to the camera directly, often in a confessional mode, with the assumption that there is no interviewer present

Video Knee—A signal compression adjustment that, confusingly enough, affects the representation of highlights in what is also known as the "shoulder" in a characteristic exposure curve

Video Noise—Unwanted electronic aberrations and artifacts noticeable at higher gain

Video on Demand (VOD)—A service that allows users to view a selection of video or audio online whenever they choose

Video Only Icon—A button used in Premiere Pro to edit video without accompanying audio

Video Standards—In broadcasting the specifics including frame rate, image size, resolution, and more, as defined by a governing body such as the ATSC

Viewfinder—The viewing system built into a video camera that is designed for the eye

Visual Evidence—Images that convey the story or confirm a point being made with little or no explanation

Voice Coil—A wire coil with a permanent magnetic charge found in a dynamic microphone

Voice-Over Dialogue—When the film cuts to other visuals while the interviewee or subject continues speaking

VU Meter (Volume Unit Meter)—A meter used to monitor the incoming audio signal by indicating an average sound level

Walk-and-Talk—A scenario where the main subject walks around a neighborhood, or some other location, and speaks, for instance to an off-camera director

Watermark—A mark holding a company logo or icon used to mark footage

Wattage—A unit of electrical power used to rate lighting and other film equipment

Watts = Volts x Amps—Formula used to determine how many watts of lighting can be plugged into any single circuit

Wave Cycle—Refers to the frequency of a wave, for example a sound wave. Measured in cycles per second, or Hertz

Waveform Scope / Waveform Monitor—A tool, based on an oscilloscope, used to measure luminance levels in a video image by displaying a graphical representation of the brightness levels across the image

Wavelength—The length of one cycle of a sound wave plotted from one highest pressure point to the next highest pressure point

White Balance—The act of adjusting a video camera's color circuitry to compensate for the color temperature of a light source

White Diffusion—Special effect filter that creates a soft haze, from the subtle refracting of white highlights

Whites—Brightest parts of an image

Wide-Angle Lens/Short Lens—A lens with a short focal length that broadens the angle of view

Wild Sound/Nonsync Sound—Audio that is recorded on location, but not simultaneously with the picture

Wild Sound Effects—Sounds recorded from the environment that can be added in to help build a richer, more complex soundtrack

Wind Noise—Audio disturbance caused by wind

Windows—In distribution, holdback periods between release times

Windscreens—A microphone attachment used to dampen the effects of wind on the diaphragm without altering the incoming sound waves

Witness Mark—A line etched into a nonmovable part of the lens barrel used while setting the focus

Work Sample—A sample of previous or current work to show potential funders the filmmaker is capable of completing a high-quality project

Workers' Compensation—A form of insurance providing wage replacement and medical benefits to employees injured in the course of employment. In the United States, it is paid as part of a worker's salary by the employer

Workflow—The technical path a project will take from acquisition to exhibition

Wrapping—Involves putting media into a container file format that the NLE can understand and work with, without necessarily changing the original shooting format encoding

X-Axis—The horizontal dimensions on a screen

XLR Connectors—The professional standard three-pin connector for microphones and mic cables used to send balanced, distortion-free audio between microphones and recorders

XLR-to-Mini Adaptor/Pigtail—An audio input that connects an XLR cable to a mini adapter to connect balanced audio to an unbalanced input on a camera or recorder

Y-Axis—The vertical dimensions on a screen

Z-Axis—The dimension of depth and distance to and from screen

Zebra Function—A setting that uses a striped overlay to indicate areas of the image that are over a specified luminance level

Zone Lighting—A naturalistic lighting strategy where certain areas of a location will be lit and others not

Zoom Lens/Variable Focal Length—A lens that offers a range of focal lengths usually expressed in a ratio between long and short focal lengths, as 10:1 or 20:1

Zoom Ring—A device on the camera that allows you to manually set the desired focal length of a variable focal length lens

Zooming In—Making the image size larger by manipulating the focal length of the image while keeping the camera stationary

Zooming Out—Making the image size smaller by manipulating the focal length of the image while keeping the camera stationary

Filmography

CHAPTER 1

An Inconvenient Truth (Dir. Davis Guggenheim, 2006)
    Stream on Amazon

Dance of Darkness (Dir. Edin Velez, 1989)
    Educational Distribution: Electronix Arts Intermix

Every Mother's Son (Dir. Tami Gold and Kelly Anderson, 2004)
    Stream at New Day Films
    Educational Distribution: New Day Films

If I Can't Do It (Dir. Walter Brock, 1998)

In Whose Honor? (Dir. Jay Rosenstein, 1997)
    Stream at New Day Films
    Educational Distribution: New Day Films

Inside Job (Dir. Charles Ferguson, 2010)
    Stream on Amazon

Island Soldier (Dir. Nathan Fitch)
    Not yet completed. Visit www.islandsoldiermovie.com for information.

Man with a Movie Camera (Dir. Dziga Vertov, 1929)
    Stream on Amazon
    Educational Distribution: Academic Video Store (Alexander Street Press)

The Meaning of the Interval (Dir. Edin Velez, 1987)
    Educational Distribution: Electronix Arts Intermix

The Missing Picture (Dir. Rithy Panh, 2013)
    Stream on iTunes or Vimeo on Demand

My Brooklyn (Dir. Kelly Anderson and Allison Lirish Dean, 2012)
    Stream on Vimeo on Demand
    Educational Distribution: New Day Films

Nanook of the North (Dir. Robert Flaherty, 1922)
    Stream on Archive.org
    Educational Distribution: contact mulvaney@criterion.com

No Room to Move! (Dir. Martin Lucas, 1993)
    Educational Distribution: United Nations Population Fund

State of Fear (Dir. Pamela Yates, 2005)
    Stream on Vimeo on Demand
    Educational Distribution: New Day Films

The Thin Blue Line (Dir. Errol Morris, 1988)
    Stream on Amazon

Waltz with Bashir (Dir. Ari Folman, 2008)
    Stream on Google Play and iTunes

The Wolfpack (Dir. Crystal Moselle, 2015)
  Stream on Amazon

CHAPTER 2

All My Babies: A Midwife's Own Story (Dir. George Stoney, 1952)
  Stream on Amazon
  Educational Distribution: Documentary Educational Resources

An American Family (Prod. Craig Gilbert, 1972)
  DVD reissued 2011

Chronicle of a Summer (Dir. Jean Rouch, 1961)
  Stream on Hulu Plus
  Educational Distribution: Academic Video Store (Alexander Street Press)

Citizenfour (Dir. Laura Poitras, 2014)
  Stream on iTunes or HBO GO

Crush (Dir. Bianca Giaever and Rachel Antonoff, 2014)
  Stream on Short of the Week

Drifters (Dir. John Grierson, 1929)
  Stream on University of East Anglia Film Archive website
  Educational Distribution: Academic Video Store (Alexander Street Press)

Grey Gardens (Dir. Albert and David Maysles, Muffie Meyer, Ellen Hovde, 1975)
  Stream on Amazon
  Educational Distribution: Academic Video Store (Alexander Street Press)

Handsworth Songs (Dir. John Akomfrah and the Black Audio Collective, 1986)
  Stream at the Birmingham Black Oral History Project:
  www.bbohp.org.uk/node/20

History and Memory: For Akiko and Takashige (Dir. Rea Tajiri, 1991)
  Stream at www.reatajiri.com/videos.html
  Educational Distribution: Women Make Movies

The House I Live In (Dir. Eugene Jarecki, 2012)
  Stream on Google Play or iTunes

Housing Problems (Dir. Edgar Anstey and Arthur Elton, 1935)
  Stream on BFI screenonline

Manufactured Landscapes (Dir. Jennifer Baichwal, 2006)
  Stream on Amazon
  Educational Distribution: Zeitgeist Films

Outfoxed: Rupert Murdoch's War on Journalism (Dir. Robert Greenwald, 2004)
  Stream on Amazon
  Educational Distribution (free) at www.bravenewfilms.org/educators

Paint It Again (Dir. Sasha Wortzel, 2011)
  Stream on Vimeo

The Polymath (Dir. Fred Barney Taylor, 2008)
  Educational Distribution: email polymath@maestromedia.net

Regen (Dir. Joris Ivens, 1929)
  Stream on Vimeo

Restrepo (Dir. Tim Hetherington and Sebastian Junger, 2010)
  Stream on iTunes

Titicut Follies (Dir. Frederick Wiseman, 1967)
    Educational Distribution: Zipporah Films

Tongues Untied (Dir. Marlon Riggs, 1989)
    Educational Distribution: California Newsreel

Workers Leaving the Factory (Dir. Louis Lumière, 1898)
    Stream on archive.org

CHAPTER 3

A Conversation with My Black Son (Dir. Geeta Gandbhir and Blair Foster, 2015)
    Stream on the New York Times Op-Doc Channel

Every Third Bite (Meerkat Media, 2008)
    Stream at http://meerkatmedia.org/2008/06/every-third-bite/

Hotel 22 (Dir. Elizabeth Lo, 2014)
    Stream on the New York Times Op-Doc Channel

Last Minutes with ODEN (Dir. Eliot Rausch, 2009)
    Stream on Vimeo

Marie's Dictionary (Dir. Emmanuel Vaughan-Lee, 2014)
    Stream on Vimeo

The Shrimp (Dir. Keith Wilson, 2009)
    Educational Distribution: New Day Films

Waiting for Superman (Dir. Davis Guggenheim, 2010)
    Stream on Google Play

Watermark (Dir. Jennifer Baichwal and Edward Burtynsky, 2013)
    Stream on Amazon

CHAPTER 4

A Village Called Versailles (Dir. S. Leo Chiang, 2009)
    Stream on Amazon
    Educational Distribution: New Day Films

The Immortalists (Dir. David Alvarado and Jason Sussberg, 2014)
    Stream on Amazon
    Educational Distribution: http://theimmortalists.com/education/

CHAPTER 5

Born Into Brothels (Dir. Zana Briski, 2004)
    See: www.zanabriski.com/born-into-brothels-1

Burma VJ: Reporting From a Closed Country (Dir. Anders Ostergaard, 2008)
    Stream on Amazon

Etre et Avoir (Dir. Nicolas Philibert, 2002)
    Stream at Sundance Doc Club

Mr. Cao Goes to Washington (Dir. S. Leo Chiang, 2012)
    Stream on Vimeo on Demand
    Educational Distribution: New Day Films

Never Enough (Dir. Kelly Anderson, 2010)
　Stream at New Day Films
　Educational Distribution: New Day Films

Roger and Me (Dir. Michael Moore, 1989)
　Stream on VUDU or Google Play

Snakeheads (Dir. Ying Chang, Jon Alpert, and Peter Kwong, 1994)
　Stream on Amazon
　Educational Distribution: Downtown Community Television Center

VTR St. Jacques (Dir. Bonnie Sherr Klein, 1969)
　Streaming and Educational Distribution: National Film Board of Canada

You Are on Indian Land (Dir. Mort Ransen, 1969)
　Streaming and Educational Distribution: National Film Board of Canada

CHAPTER 7

Chile, Obstinate Memory (Dir. Patricio Guzman, 1997)
　Educational Distribution: Icarus Films

Crumb (Dir. Terry Zwigoff, 1994)
　Stream on Amazon

Cutie and the Boxer (Dir. Zachary Heinzerling, 2013)
　Stream on Amazon

Fog of War (Dir. Errol Morris, 2003)
　Stream on Amazon

Night and Fog (Dir. Alain Resnais, 1955)
　Stream on Amazon
　Educational Distribution: Academic Video Store (Alexander Street Press)

Nostalgia for the Light (Dir. Patricio Guzman, 2010)
　Stream on Amazon
　Educational Distribution: Icarus Films

Our Daily Bread (Dir. Nikolaus Geyrhalter, 2005)
　Stream on Amazon
　Educational Distribution: Icarus Films

Primary (Dir. Robert Drew, 1960)
　Educational Distribution: Academic Video Store (Alexander Street Press)

CHAPTER 8

Bully (Dir. Lee Hirsch, 2011)
　Stream on Google Play
　Educational Distribution: http://shop.thebullyproject.com/products/educators-dvd-and-toolkit

Cave of Forgotten Dreams (Dir. Werner Herzog, 2010)
　Stream on iTunes and Amazon

Leviathan (Dir. Lucien Castaing-Taylor and Véréna Paravel, 2012)
　Stream on Google Play
　Educational Distribution: The Cinema Guild

Pina (Dir. Wim Wenders, 2011)
　Stream on Google Play
　Educational Distribution: contact mulvaney@criterion.com

The Police Tapes (dir. Susan and Alan Raymond, 1977)
    Stream at SundanceNow Doc Club

CHAPTER 9

Description of a Memory (Dir. Dan Geva, 2006)
    Educational Distribution: Icarus Films

Lessons of Darkness (Dir. Werner Herzog, 1992)
    Stream on Amazon

CHAPTER 10

A Lion in the House (Dir. Julia Reichert and Steven Bognar, 2006)
    DVD available on Amazon

CHAPTER 11

Split (Dir. Ellen Bruno, 2013)
    Educational Distribution: New Day Films

War Photographer (Dir. Christian Frei, 2001)
    Educational Distribution: First Run Features

CHAPTER 12

Border (Dir. Laura Waddington, 2004)
    See: www.laurawaddington.com/film.php?film=1

Casting the First Stone (Dir. Julie Gustafson, 1991)
    Educational Distribution: Icarus Films

Don't Look Back (Dir. D.A. Pennebaker, 1967)
    See: www.criterion.com/films/28655-dont-look-back

Frantz Fanon: Black Skin, White Mask (Dir. Isaac Julien, 1996)
    Educational Distribution: Educational Distribution: Academic Video Store (Alexander Street Press)

Resisting Paradise (Dir. Barbara Hammer, 2003)
    Educational Distribution: email barbarahammer@gmail.com

The War (Dir. Ken Burns and Lynn Novick, 2007)
    Stream on Netflix and Amazon

CHAPTER 13

Good People Go to Hell, Saved People Go to Heaven (Dir. Holly Hardman, 2013)
    Stream on Amazon
    Educational Distribution: http://goodpeoplegotohell.com

My Little Friends (Dir. Megan Mylan, 2013)
    Stream at Living with Alzheimer's Website

CHAPTER 15

Last Train Home (Dir. Lixin Fan, 2009)
    Educational Distribution: Zeitgeist Films

Looking for Love: Teenage Mothers (Dir. Tami Gold, 1982)
    Educational Distribution: AndersonGold Films

Mr. Death: The Rise and Fall of Fred A. Leuchter, Jr. (Dir. Errol Morris, 1999)
    Stream at Sundance Doc Club
    Purchase DVD on amazon

Out at Work (Dir. Kelly Anderson and Tami Gold, 1999)
    Stream at New Day Films
    Educational Distribution: New Day Films

Particle Fever (Dir. Mark Levinson, 2013)
    Stream at http://particlefever.com/
    Educational Distribution: Roco Films

Sherman's March: A Meditation on the Possibility of Romantic Love in the South during an Era of Nuclear Weapons Proliferation (Dir. Ross McElwee, 1985)
    Stream on Amazon

CHAPTER 17

Care (Dir. Deirdre Fishel)
    Not yet available

Visitors (Dir. Godfrey Reggio, 2013)
    Stream on Amazon
    Educational Distribution: New Video

CHAPTER 18

High School (Dir. Frederick Wiseman, 1968)
    Educational Distribution: Zipporah Films

The Last Bolshevik (Dir. Chris Marker, 1992)
    Stream on Amazon
    Educational Distribution: Icarus Films

Night Mail (Dir. Harry Watt and Basil Wright, 1936)
    British Film Institute: www.screenonline.org.uk/film/id/530415 (UK only)

State of Rest and Motion (Dir. Edin Velez, 2015)
    Not yet in distribution

Trouble the Water (Dir. Tia Lessin and Carl Deal, 2008)
    Stream on iTunes and Amazon
    Educational Distribution: www.troublethewaterfilm.com

CHAPTER 19

Barque sortant du port (Dir. Louis Lumière, 1895)
    Stream on archive.org

Darwin's Nightmare (Dir. Hubert Sauper, 2004)
    See: http://archive.org/details/Darwins.Nightmare.2004

Le Repas de Bébé (Dir. Louis Lumière, 1895)
    Stream on YouTube

The Most Dangerous Man in America (Dir. Judith Ehrlich and Rick Goldsmith, 2009)
    Educational Distribution: New Day Films

Nobody's Business (Dir. Alan Berliner, 1996)
    Stream on Amazon
    Educational Distribution: Kino Lorber Edu

The Plough That Broke the Plains (Dir. Pare Lorentz, 1936)
    Stream on archive.org

The River (Dir. Pare Lorentz, 1938)
　　Stream on archive.org

CHAPTER 20

Atomic Cafe (Dir. Kevin and Pierce Rafferty, Jayne Loader, 1982)
　　Stream at Sundance Doc Club
　　Educational Distribution: New Video

The Civil War (Dir. Ken Burns, 1990)
　　Stream on Amazon
　　Educational Distribution: PBS

Hiroshima Bound (Dir. Martin Lucas, 2015)
　　Educational Distribution: Martin Lucas Media, email info@www.hiroshimabound.com

Sidney Poitier, an Outsider in Hollywood (Dir. Catherine Arnaud, 2008)
　　Not available for distribution

Stranger with a Camera (Dir. Elizabeth Barret, 1999)
　　Stream on Vimeo
　　Educational Distribution: Appalshop

Through a Lens Darkly: Black Photographers and the Emergence of a People
(Dir. Thomas Allen Harris, 2014)
　　Stream on iTunes
　　Educational Distribution: First Run Features

CHAPTER 21

Gimme Shelter (Dir. David and Albert Maysles, Charlotte Zwerin, 1970)
　　Stream on Hulu
　　Educational Distribution: contact mulvaney@criterion.com

Habana: arte nuevo de hacer ruinas (Havana: The New Art of Making Ruins)
(Dir. Florian Borchmeyer, 2006)
　　Educational Distribution: The Cinema Guild

Hell and Back Again (Dir. Danfung Dennis, 2011)
　　Stream on Amazon
　　Educational Distribution: New Video

Intimate Stranger (Dir. Alan Berliner, 1991)
　　Stream on Amazon
　　Educational Distribution: Kino Lorber Edu

Song of Ceylon (Dir. Basil Wright, 1934)
　　Stream on archive.org

Sweetgrass (Dir. Ilisa Barbash and Lucien Castaing-Taylor, 2009)
　　Educational Distribution: Cinema Guild

CHAPTER 22

Banished: How Whites Drove Blacks Out of Town in America (Dir. Marco Williams, 2006)
　　Educational Distribution: California Newsreel

Helvetica (Dir. Gary Hustwit, 2007)
　　Stream on Amazon

When the Levees Broke: A Requiem in Four Acts (Dir. Spike Lee, 2006)
    Stream on Amazon

Where in the World is Osama Bin Laden? (Dir. Morgan Spurlock, 2008)
    Stream on Amazon

CHAPTER 23

Evaporating Borders (Dir. Iva Radivojevic, 2014)

Granito: How to Nail a Dictator (Dir. Pamela Yates, 2011)
    Stream at Vimeo on Demand
    Educational Distribution: New Day Films

Truth Be Told (Dir. Gregorio Smith, 2012)
    Stream at http://buy.hereliesthetruth.com/

Photograph and Illustration Credits

PHOTOGRAPHS BY NATALIE CONN

ADDITIONAL PHOTOGRAPHS BY Gustavo Mercado, Peter Jackson, Martin Lucas, and Mick Hurbis-Cherrier

COVER PHOTOS BY Robin Canfield/Actuality Media and G. Betancourt (CGIAR Research Program on Climate Change, Agriculture, and Food Security—CCFAS)

Figure 1.1 from *The Missing Picture*; **Figure 1.2** from *Waltz with Bashir*; **Figure 1.3** courtesy of Nathan Fitch; **Figure 1.4** courtesy of Edin Velez; **Figure 1.5** from *In Whose Honor?*; **Figure 1.6** courtesy of Jamel Shabazz; **Figure 1.7** from *If I Can't Do It*, courtesy of Noel Salzmann; **Figure 1.8** from *Nobody's Business*; **Figure 1.9** courtesy of Anderson Gold Films, Inc.; **Figure 2.3** from *Workers Leaving the Factory*; **Figure 2.4** from *Regen*; **Figure 2.5** from *The Polymath*; **Figure 2.6** from *Housing Problems*; **Figure 2.7** from *In Whose Honor?*; **Figure 2.8** from *Titicut Follies*; **Figure 2.9** from *Chronique d'un Été*; **Figure 2.10** from *Tongues Untied*; **Figure 2.11** from *All My Babies*; **Figure 2.12** from *The Thin Blue Line*; **Figure 3.2** from *Every Mother's Son*; **Figure 3.4** from *Inside Job*; **Figure 3.5** from *Watermark*; **Figure 3.6** from *A Conversation with My Black Son*; **Figure 3.7** from *Marie's Dictionary*; **Figure 3.8** from *Hotel 22*; **Figure 3.9** from *Last Minutes with ODEN*; **Figure 3.10** from *The Shrimp*; **Figure 4.1** from *A Village Called Versailles*; **Figure 4.2** from *The Immortalists*; **Figure 5.1** from *Etre et Avoir*; **Figure 5.2** courtesy of Zana Briski; **Figure 5.3** from *Darwin's Nightmare*; **Figure 5.4** from *Snakeheads*; **Figure 5.5** from *Outfoxed: Rupert Murdoch's War on Journalism*; **Figure 6.4** courtesy of Renato Tonelli; **Figure 6.5** from *Mr. Cao Goes to Washington*; **Figure 6.6** from *Never Enough*; **Figure 6.7** from *The Immortalists*; **Figure 6.9** courtesy of Robert Bahar; **Figure 6.11** courtesy of Robert Bahar; **Figure 7.1** from *Sweetgrass*; **Figure 7.4** from *Nostalgia for the Light*; **Figure 7.5** from *Nostalgia for the Light*; **Figure 7.6** from *Manufactured Landscapes*; **Figure 7.7** from *The Thin Blue Line*; **Figure 7.8** from *Nostalgia for the Light*; **Figure 7.10** from *Chile: Obstinate Memory*; **Figure 7.12** from *Fog of War*; **Figure 7.13** from *Sweetgrass*; **Figure 7.17** from *Crumb*; **Figure 7.21** from *Manufactured Landscapes*; **Figure 7.23** from *Primary*; **Figure 7.24** from *Night and Fog*; **Figure 7.25** courtesy of Jai Mansson; **Figure 7.28** from *Crumb*; **Figure 7.29** from *Roger and Me*; **Figure 7.30** from *Cutie and the Boxer*; **Figure 7.32** from *Mr. Cao Goes to Washington*; **Figure 7.33** from *Mr. Cao Goes to Washington*; **Figure 7.34** from *Mr. Death: The Rise and Fall of Fred A. Leuchter, Jr.*; **Figure 7.35** from *Our Daily Bread*; **Figure 7.36** from *Mr. Death: The Rise and Fall of Fred A. Leuchter, Jr.*; **Figure 8.1** from *Butterfly Dance*; **Figure 8.3** courtesy of Edin Velez, Philip Johnston, and Prudence Hill; **Figure 8.4** from *The Police Tapes*; **Figure 8.9** courtesy of Gustavo Mercado; **Figure 8.10** courtesy of Gustavo Mercado; **Figure 8.12** from *Bully*; **Figure 8.14** from *Leviathan*; **Figure 8.15** courtesy of Sony Corporation and Anna Ozbek; **Figure 8.17** courtesy of Sony Corporation; **Figure 8.33** courtesy of AJA Video Systems, Inc.; **Figure 8.34** courtesy of Arjen Van de Merwe; **Figure 8.38** courtesy of Bennett Cain; **Figure 8.39** from *Pina*; **Figure 9.13** from *Description of a Memory*; **Figure 9.17** courtesy of Kitmondo Marketplace; **Figure 9.20** from

Lessons of Darkness; **Figure 9.25** from *Nobody's Business*; **Figure 9.26** from *Helvetica*; **Figure 10.1** courtesy of Gary Griffin and Andre Baranowski; **Figure 10.3** courtesy of Vocal-NY; **Figure 10.4** from *Nostalgia for the Light*; **Figure 10.5** from *Man with a Movie Camera*; **Figure 10.14** from *The Immortalists*; **Figure 10.15** courtesy of Erika Kapin; **Figure 10.16** courtesy of Edelkrone; **Figure 10.17** courtesy of Philip Johnston; **Figure 10.18** courtesy of Shari Sperling; **Figure 10.19** courtesy of DJI; **Figure 11.1** from *Split*; **Figure 11.6** courtesy of Mole-Richardson; **Figure 11.8** courtesy of Gustavo Mercado; **Figure 11.11** courtesy of Renato Tonelli; **Figure 11.13** courtesy of De Sisti; **Figure 11.15** courtesy of Chimera Lighting; **Figure 11.19** courtesy of Curt Pair; **Figure 11.27** from *War Photographer*; **Figure 12.5** from *The War* and *Sherman's March*; **Figure 12.6** courtesy of Sekonic; **Figure 12.8** from *Don't Look Back*; **Figure 12.10** from *Casting the First Stone*; **Figure 12.11** from Franz Fanon: *Black Skin, White Mask*; **Figure 12.12** from *Resisting Paradise*; **Figure 12.14** from *Border*; **Figure 12.15** courtesy of Eastman Kodak Company; **Figure 12.19** courtesy of Canon USA, Inc.; **Figure 13.3** courtesy of Principe Productions; **Figure 13.8** courtesy of Holly Hardman; **Figure 13.12** courtesy of Beachtek; **Figure 13.16** courtesy of Sound Devices LLC and Zaxcom, Inc.; **Figure 13.28** courtesy of Lectrosonics; **Figure 14.1** courtesy of Principe Productions; **Figure 14.2** courtesy of Professional Sound Services; **Figure 15.1** from *Out at Work*; **Figure 15.2** from *Sherman's March*; **Figure 15.3** from *My Brooklyn*; **Figure 15.4** from *Inside Job*; **Figure 15.5** from *Hiroshima Bound*; **Figure 15.6** from *Every Mother's Son*; **Figure 15.7** from *Mr. Death: The Rise and Fall of Fred Leuchter, Jr.*; **Figure 15.8** from *Particle Fever*; **Figure 15.9** courtesy of Tami Gold; **Figure 16.2** from *Man with a Movie Camera*; **Figure 17.8** courtesy of Adobe Systems Inc.; **Figure 17.20** from *Visitors*; **Figure 18.1** from *Trouble the Water*; **Figure 18.2** from *Trouble the Water*; **Figure 18.3** from *Trouble the Water*; **Figure 18.4** from *Last Train Home*; **Figure 18.5** from *Last Train Home*; **Figure 18.6** from *Trouble the Water*; **Figure 18.8** from *In Whose Honor?*; **Figure 18.9** from *Night Mail*; **Figure 18.10** from *The Last Bolshevik*; **Figure 19.1** from *Barque Sortant du Port*; **Figure 19.2** from *The Plough that Broke the Plains*; **Figure 19.3** from *Banished: How Whites Drove Blacks Out of Town in America*; **Figure 19.4** from *Banished*; **Figure 19.5** from *Banished*; **Figure 19.6** from *Banished*; **Figure 19.7** from *Regen*; **Figure 19.8** from *Nostalgia for the Light*; **Figure 19.9** from *The Most Dangerous Man in America*; **Figure 19.11** from *Cutie and the Boxer*; **Figure 19.14** from *Darwin's Nightmare*; **Figure 19.15** from *Darwin's Nightmare*; **Figure 19.16** from *Mr. Cao Goes to Washington*; **Figure 19.17** from *Fog of War*; **Figure 19.18** from *Nobody's Business*; **Figure 19.19** from *Etre et Avoir*; **Figure 19.20** from *Nostalgia for the Light*; **Figure 19.21** from *Darwin's Nightmare*; **Figure 19.22** from *Manufactured Landscapes*; **Figure 19.23** from *The Thin Blue Line*; **Figure 19.24** from *State of Rest and Motion*; **Figure 20.1** from *Hiroshima Bound*; **Figure 20.2** courtesy of The Digital Diaspora Family Reunion; **Figure 20.3** from *Sidney Poitier: An Outsider in Hollywood*; **Figure 20.4** from *Atomic Cafe*; **Figure 20.5** from *History and Memory: For Akiko and Takashige*; **Figure 20.6** from *Nobody's Business*; **Figure 20.8** from *History and Memory: For Akiko and Takashige*; **Figure 20.11** from *My Brooklyn*; **Figure 20.12** from *The Civil War*; **Figure 20.13** from *The Thin Blue Line*; **Figure 21.1** from *Song of Ceylon*; **Figure 21.3** from *Trouble the Water* and *Sweetgrass*; **Figure 21.5** courtesy of Sound One/Ascent Media; **Figure 21.7** from *Hell and Back Again*; **Figure 21.8** from *Sweetgrass*; **Figure 21.9** from *Intimate Stranger*; **Figure 21.17** courtesy of Avid; **Figure 22.8** from *Where in the World is Osama Bin Laden?*; **Figure 22.10** from *When the Levees Broke: A Requiem in Four Acts*; **Figure 22.11** from *Helvetica*; **Figure 22.13** from *Banished* and *Darwin's Nightmare*; **Figure 22.17** courtesy of Adobe Systems, Inc.; **Figure 23.1** from *Evaporating Borders*; **Figure 23.3** courtesy of The Fledgling Fund; **Figure 23.5** courtesy of Skylight Pictures; **Figure 23.6** courtesy of Skylight Pictures; **Figure 23.7** courtesy of Skylight Pictures.

Index

Page numbers in *italics* refer to figures

1/3-2/3 rule 152, *152*
3D documentaries 135
3-point edit 286–288, *287*
4K image format 119–120
-12 audio levels 235
-20 audio levels 235
24p 115
60i 115
180° principle 100, *101*, *103*, 193, 315

A

acquisition video formats 110
actions continuity 314–315, *315*
active characters 12–13
Active Voice 386
ADCs *see* analog-to-digital converters
Advanced Television Systems Committee (ATSC) 110, *111*
advances 377
aesthetics, locations 68–69
AGC (automatic gain control) 216
air risks 262
All My Babies documentary 27, *27*
Alter, Nora 305
Alvarado, David 44, 63–64, 69, 115, 151, 161, *161*, 227–228, 344
ambient sound 205, 212, 241, 339, 344–345, *345*
amplitude *206*, *207*; compression 355
analog-to-digital converters (ADCs) 129, 213, *215*
analog video 110
angle of view 142, *143*
angles, camera 91–93, *91–93*
aperture of lens 148–150, *149*, 167
APS-C 118
archival footage 8, 44
archival storytelling 325–337
art of editing 307–324
artificial light 168–169
artistic identity 7–10
artists, documentary filmmakers as 4
aspect ratio 85, *85*, 113, 336
associate producers 64, *65*

associative editing 311–313, *312*
Atomic Café documentary 329, *329*
ATSC (Advanced Television Systems Committee) 110
audience 46, 57–58, 385
audio 351–359; clips 294; connectors, camcorders 125–126, *125*; filters 354–356; ingestion 277; monitor reference 359; outputs, digital recorders 218, *221*; recording 237–242; sweetening 353–356; tracks 278, 351–353; transitions 356–357; *see also* sound
audio levels 100, 193, 315, 357–358, *357*
audio/video codecs 111
authenticity 154
authority 27
autofocus 139, *139*
auto functions 123–124, 139–140, 149, 202
autoiris (autoexposure) 149
auto-knee 202
automatic gain control (AGC) 216
available light 165, 169

B

baby legs, tripods 159, *159*
back camera angles 92, *92*
background information 42–43
background sound *see* ambient sound
backing up media 276, 294
backlight 186, 187, *187*, 188, *188*
Bahar, Robert 73–81
Baichwal, Jennifer 36–37, 93, 153, 160, 322
balance 57–58; audio signals 214; frames 88; *see also* white balance
Balázs, Béla 19
bandwidth, scanning types 114
Banished documentary 308–310, *309–310*, 372
barn doors 172, 173, 181–182, *181–182*
barrel of lens 137, *138*

Barret, Elizabeth 26–27, 335
bars: color 374; and tone 237
bass-roll off 238
Bayer pattern filter 127
being-on-axis 239–241, *239*
"being present" 19
Bennett, Ann 328–329
Berliner, Alan 12–13
bias 57
binary code 110
bins 278, 280, *280*, 284–285, 294
bit depth 120, 129–130, *130*, 214–215
black diffusion 177
black stretch 201–202
blocking light 172
booming 94, 162, *162*, 239–241, *241*
boom poles 239–240, *239–240*
Border documentary 198, *198*
Born Into Brothels documentary 54, *54*, 56
bouncing light 172, 197, *197*
Boyd, Brian 369
breakaway cables 209, 211, *211*
breakers, electrical 263, *264*
brightness 364, *364*
Briski, Zana 54, *54*, 56
British Film Movement 22–23
broadcasting 382
broadcast standards 110, 111–112, 135
broads 172, *172*
Brock, Walter 12, *12*
B-Roll 99
Brooks, Daniel 211, *211*, 213, *213*, 228, 231–232, 234–235, *235*, 256
budgets 47–48, 73–82
burned discs 375–376

C

cables, coiling 240–241, *240*
cable TV 49, 382
calibrating monitors 133–134
call sheets 71, *72*
camcorders *109*, 120–133, 216

INDEX

camera 18–19, 91–98, 116–126, 196–198; adjustment 97–98; angles 91–93, *91–93*; filters 175–183, *176–178*; function menus/switches 123–124; mounting plate 158; moves 93–98, *94*; positions, lighting 196–197; profile 369; support 153–164; takes, camcorders 123; types 18–19, 116–126
camera crew 64
camera-mounted lighting 198
canted angle 92, *92*
capacitors, microphones 221
cardioid microphones 223, *223*
cash support 48
Castaing-Taylor, Lucien 118, 349
casting documentaries 11–13
Casting the First Stone documentary 25, 195, *195*
cathode ray tube 108, *108*
CBR (constant bit rate) 131
CCD (charge coupled device) 126–127
center-averaging 190
Center for Media and Social Impact (CMSI) 346
CF (compact flash) card 122
character-based films 29, 33
characteristic curves/gamma 200–201, *200–201*
characters 296–298; identification 90–91; main characters 44; see also casting documentaries
charge coupled device (CCD) 126–127
checkerboarding 352
chemical media 107–108
Chiang, S. Leo 42–43, 44, 46, 68, 84, 102–103, 105, 115, 145, 193
Chinese lanterns 174, *174*
chrominance 131
Chronique d'un Eté documentary 25, *25*
chronology 301–302
CineGamma 202
cinematic time/space 83–106
cinematographer *64*, 65
cinéma vérité 23–25, *25*, 154, 192, 252, 341
The Civil War documentary 336–337
clamps 182
clean sound 239–241
clearing rights 333, 335, 348
clipping 202, 237
clips 278, 284, 294
closed frames 86, *86*
CMOS see complementary metal oxide semiconductor sensor
CMSI (Center for Media and Social Impact) 346
codecs 111, 130–131, *131*
color 131–134; bars 133–134, *133–134*, 374; conversion gels 178–180;

correction 363–368; encoding 131–132; grading 363; sampling 131–132; settings 203; temperature 171, *171*, 180, *180*
colorists 369, *369*
communication: crews 70–71; tools for 71–72
community involvement 47, 54–55
complementary metal oxide semiconductor (CMOS) sensor 117, 126–127, *126–127*
compositing 324, *324*
composition 85–93
compositional frame 85, *85*
compound lenses 142, *142*
compression 130–131
compression filters 355
condenser microphones 220–222, *221*
condensing space 147, *147*
conflict 11, 29–30, 32
consent 53
consistency, sound 239
constant bit rate (CBR) 131
continuity 24, 99–100, 307, 313–318, 315
contrast 198–199, *199*, 364, *364*
A Conversation With my Black Son documentary 38, *38*
copyright 59, 331–334
cost reports 79, 82, *82*
countdown 375
counterpoint narration 304
coverage 99–105
crane shots 94, 162
Creative Commons 334, *334*
creativity 4–7, *4–5*, 328–329
credits 368–372
crews 63–65, 227–228, *227*, 255; communication 70–71; responsibilities 65; size 63–64, *63*
crop factor 144–145
cross-fade 356, *356*
cross lighting 193
crowdsourcing 49, 378, *381*
Crumb documentary 91, *91*, 98, *98*
C-stands 181, *181*
culture 59
cutaway shot 90, 315, 317–318, *317*
Cutie and the Boxer documentary 100–101, *100*, 243–244, 314–315, 315
cuts 322, 342–343, *342*

D

DACs (digital-to-analog converters) 214, 215
Darwin's Nightmare documentary 55, *55*, 317, *317*, 322, *322*, 372, *372*

data rate: camcorders 132, *132*; video images 111
DAWs (digital audio workstations) 359, *360*
DC power 123
dead recording space 212
deal memos 71
deep depth of field/focus 87, *87*, 150–151, *150–151*
deep frames 86, *86*
Delany, Samuel 20–21, *21*
deliverables 228
de Onís, Paco 14–15, 386–388
depth of field (DOF) 87, *87*, 150–152; deep vs shallow 150, *150–151*; factors impacting 151
derivative work 334
detail budgets *75–78*, 79
DF TC (drop-frame time code) 116, *116*
diagonal lines 86–87
dialogue 340–341, 342–343, *342*
diaphragm, microphones 220
diegetic sound 341
diffused light see soft light
diffusion filters 177, *177*
diffusion media 170–171, 171, 180–181, *181*
digital audio quality 214–215, *215*
digital audio recorders 69, 218
digital audio workstations (DAWs) 359, *360*
Digital Cinema 111, 373
digital editing 269, 272–277
digital imaging technician/loader 64
digital signal processor (DSP) 129–130
digital single-lens reflex (DSLR) camera 117, *117*
digital sound recording 213–217, *215*
digital-to-analog converters (DACs) 214, 215
digital video cameras 116–126
digital video systems 107–136
digital zoom 122
diopter viewer 121
direct cinema 23–25, *25*, 108, 154, 192, 341
directing/director *64*, 65, 252–253
directionality 185, 222
directional light see hard light
direct sound 349
disc exhibiting 375–376
dissolve 323, 356, *356*
distribution 46–47, 377–388
ditty bags 183
documentary: art and *4*, 307–324; brief/selective history 18–28; ideas 3–16; impact of 383–388; origins 3; process value 14; styles 17–28, 44–45
documents 336–337

INDEX

DOF *see* depth of field
dollies 160–162, *160*
dolly shots 94, *95*
double-system sound 69, 117, 209–211, *209*, 227
drag 157
drama 29, 30–34, *31*, 44
drones 163, *163*
drop-frame time code (DF TC) 116, *116*
DSLR (digital single-lens reflex) camera 117
DSP (digital signal processor) 129–130
dusk-for-night light 197
Dutch angle *see* canted angle
DVD format 375–376, 383, *387*
dynamic microphones 220–222
dynamic range 191, 199–201, 203, 207, 237, 363

E

echo 355
Edison, Thomas 18, 107
editing 269; art of 307–324; making simple edits 283, 285–289; overview of stages 293–294; patterns 321–322; process 272–277, *273*; shooting and 98–99; sound 351–353, 359–361; stages 289–292
educational markets 47, 382–383
Eisenstein, Sergei 311
electret condenser microphones 220–222, *221*
electricity 261, 263–265, *264*
electronic media 108–116
employment rules 260
engagement campaigns 383–388, *385*
entering frame 104
ephemera 336
equalization (EQ) 352, 354–355, *354*
equipment 69–70; respect for 257–258; setting up 233–237; sound recording 205–226
errors/omissions insurance 70
essay documentary style 26–27, 304–305
ethics 52–59, 335
etiquette 255–258
Etre et Avoir documentary 53, *53*, 319–320, *320*
European Broadcast Union 111
Evaporating Borders documentary 379, *379*
Every Mother's Son documentary *13*, 31–34, *32–33*, 58, *249*
exclusivity 56
exhibiting work 375–376
exiting frame 104
expansion filters 355
exposition 31, 34, 296–298
expository films 22–23, *23*, 307–310, 340
exposure: beyond basics 185, 198–203; control 190–192; elements 167–168, *167*
expressionistic techniques 194–196, *196*, 349
expressive sequences 105
exterior lighting 196–198
external microphone inputs 125
extract edits 288
eye-level shot 91
eye light 194
eyeline 248–250, *249*

F

fades 323, 356, *356*
fairness 57–58
fair use 59, *59*, 331–333
Fan, Lixin 253, 299
fast color corrector filter 364–367, *365–366*
feasibility 14
festivals 378–380
field of video 113
file-based media 123
fill light 187–188, *187–188*
film festivals 46, 378–380
filmmaking types 3; *see also* documentary
film medium 107–108, *107*, 199
film research 8
filters 167, 172–183, *176–178*, 354–356, 364–367, *365*
fine cut 292
finishing: film 292–293; picture 363–376; sound design 339–361
first-person narration 302–303
fiscal sponsorship 49
fisheye lenses 142–143, *143*
Fitch, Nathan 3–4
fixers 260
flags 181
flash memory recorders 217, 218, 219
flat frames 86
flat response, microphones 222
flicker effect 107
flood/spot control 170
fluid heads, tripods 157
fluorescent lights 174, *174*
focal lengths: lenses 137, *137*, 141–148, *142–145*; and sensor size 144, *144*; video camcorders 122, *122*; *see also* crop factor
focal plane, lens 137
focus 87, 138–141
focus assist *139*
Fog of War documentary 88, *88*, 300, 318, *318*
foley effects 343–344, *344*
follow focus 140–141
footage organization 284–285
fore-shortening 86
formats: common sources 275, *275*; NLE projects 274; video 110–111
four-walling 380
frame 85–93; balanced/unbalanced 88; dimensions of 85; entering/exiting 104; graphic qualities 85–86; moving frame 95–97
frame rate 114–115; broadcast standards 112; exposure 167; film 107; postproduction 275–276; scanning types 114
framing: compositing and 324; lenses 137; *Manufactured Landscapes* 93, *93*
frequency 222; filters 238, 354–355; response, microphones 222, *222*
Fresnels 173, *173*
friction heads, tripods 157
frontal light 185–186
front shot 92, *92*
f-stop scale 148, *148*
funding sources 48–49, 56
fuses 263

G

gaffer 64, 69
gaffer's tape 182, *182*, 257
gain 128–129, 167, 218
gamma 200–201, *200–203*
gels 172, 175, 178–181, *178*, *180*
gobo 182
Gold, Tami 52, 243, 244, 248, 252, *252*
government funding 48
graduated filters 178, *178*
Granito: How to Nail a Dictator documentary 386–388, *386–387*
graphic frame qualities 85–86
graphic match 313
graphics files 294
gray scale 191–192
Grierson, John 3, 22, 108, 303, 339
grips 64, 181–183
Gustafson, Julie 25, 195

H

Hampe, Barry 57–58, 99
handheld devices 153–154, *153*, 223–224
handles 356
"Handsworth Songs" documentary 21
hard drive recorders 219
hard light 170–171, *170*
hard sound effects 343
hardware 273–274
HD (high-definition) broadcast 85, *85*

INDEX

HD (high-definition) cameras 107
HDMI *see* high-definition multimedia interface
headphones 225, 238–239, *238*
headroom 234, 357
heads, tripods 156, 157–159, *158*
Hell & Back Again documentary 345, *345*
Helvetica documentary 151, *151*, 371, *371*
Herzog, Werner 135, 147
high angles 91, *91*
high-definition multimedia interface (HDMI) 125, 126
high-end finishing workflows 292–293
high-key lighting 189–190
Hiroshima Bound documentary 247, *247*
histograms 168, *168*
historical approach 18–28, 329–330
History and Memory documentary 21–22, 329–330, *330*, 333
HMI (Hydrargyrum Medium-arc Iodide) lights 175
home video 383
horizontal lines 86–87, 92
Hotel 22 documentary 38–39, *39*
The House I Live In documentary 301–302, 303, *303*
hue 131, 364–368, *366*
hybrid cameras 118, *118*
Hydrargyrum Medium-arc Iodide (HMI) lights *see* HMI (Hydrargyrum Medium-arc Iodide) lights
hypercardioid microphones 223, *223*
hypotheses 10–11, 296

I

ideation 63
identity 7–10
If I Can't Do It documentary 12, *12*
illegal actions 57
image combination 324
image ownership 331–333
image sensor, camcorders 126–127, *126*
image transitions 322–323
imaging devices 167
The Immortalists documentary 45, *45*, 68–69, *68*, 161, *161*
impressionistic films 20–21, 29, 36, 310–313
incident meter 190, 191
infographics 105
informed consent 53
ingesting: audio 277; video 274–276
in-kind support 48
inquiry letter 41
insert edits 288

Inside Job documentary 34–35, *35*, 56, *247*
insurance 70, 260
intellectual property rights 58–59
intensity of light 167, 169–170
interlaced scanning 113–115, *113–114*
International Telecommunications Union 111, 133
international travel 260–261
Internet 47
interviews 14, 43, 243–253; conducting 250–252; jump cutting *317–318*, 318; lighting 186–188, 246; locations 245–248; preparing 244–245; structuring 298–301; tips for 251
Intimate Stranger documentary 350, *350*
introduction *see* synopsis
inverse square law 169–170, *170*, 208
In Whose Honor? documentary 6, *6*, 12, 22–23, *23*, 35, 304, *304*
iris, lenses 148
isolated tracks 229, 233
isolation pads, headphones 238
ISO settings 167
issue-based films 37–38, *38*
Ivens, Joris 20–21, 310–311

J

J-cut edits 289
jello artifact 127
jib arms 162, *162*
jump cutting interviews *317–318*, 318
juxtaposition 307

K

keyframes 358
key light 187, *187–188*
key-to-fill ratios *see* lighting ratios
knee, exposure 201–202

L

The Last Bolshevik documentary 305, *305*
Last Minutes with ODEN documentary 39, *39*
Last Train Home documentary 299–300, *299–300*
lavalier microphones 224, *224*, 234–235, *235*, 241
LCD equipment 114, 121, *121*
lead room 89, *89*
LEDs *see* light emitter diodes
legal issues 52–59
legs, tripods 156, 159, *159*
lens 137–152; aperture 148, *148*; and camcorders 121–122; defined 137–152; exposure 167; focal length 141–143, *142–145*; focus 138; functions *138*; optics of 137–141; prime 145; speed 149; video camcorders 121–122; zoom 145–146, *145–146*
lens housing *see* barrel of lens
Lessons of Darkness documentary 147, *147*
letter of inquiry 41
level controls, sound 216, 217–218, *217*
Leviathan documentary 118–119, *119*
licensing agreements 58, 331
lift edits 288
light emitter diodes (LEDs) 114, 174–175, *175*
lighting 69, 246; basics 165–183; beyond basics 185–203; properties of light 169–171; ratios 189–190; safety tips 265–266, *265*; sources of light 167–169, *167*; styles 188–190; units 172–175
light stands 181
limiters 237–238, *238*
line of action 100
linear pulse code modulation (LPCM) 215
line level signal 214
line producer 65
live environments 212–213
location 65–69; agreements/contracts 66–68; evaluation 231; IDs 372; interviews 245–248; permits 53; respect/protect 257; risk and 262; scouts/scouting 65–66, 196; sound techniques 227–242
log gamma 191, 201, 203, *203*, 369
long takes 104–105, *104*
Looking for Love: Teenage Mothers documentary 252, *252*
looking room 88–89, *89*
loudness 207
low angles 91, *91*
low-budget documentaries 79
lower thirds 370–372, *372*
low-key light 166, *166*, 190
LPCM (linear pulse code modulation) 215
Lucas, Martin 9
Lumière, Auguste and Louis 18–20, 24, 107, 307–308
Lumière camera 18–19, *19*
luminance 131
Lund, Andrew 53, 332–333

M

macro lenses 138
mafer clamps 182
magic hour 197

manual exposure control 190–191
manual override: aperture 149; camcorders 149
Manufactured Landscapes documentary 86, 93, *93*, 322
Man With a Movie Camera documentary 3, 21, 156, *156*, 259, *259*, 339
Marey, Etienne-Jules 18, *18*
Marie's Dictionary documentary 38, *38*
Marker, Chris 305
markets for distribution 377–383
master clips 294
mastering 284, 293, 363–376
master mix track 358
master shot 100
master use license 347, 348
materials: organization 330–331; resources 255–258
matte boxes 175–176, *176*
Maysles, Albert 24, 64, *64*, 313, 346
mechanical media 107–108
media backups 276, 294
media bay, camcorders 122–123
media file indicators 272, *272*
media formats 110, 275, *275*
media transfer device 273
memory 28
memory cards 122
metadata 331, *331*
metaphorical imagery 330
metering light 190–192, *191*
microphone 125, 220–225; attenuation 237–238, *238*; inputs, digital recorders 216–217, *217*; level signal 213; location techniques 234–235, *235*, 239–241, *239*, *241*, *242*; support for 225, *225*
minicams 118–119
mirrorless shutter cameras 118
mise-en-scène 18, 313–314
mixed-lighting situations 179, *180*
mixing 353, 358–361, *358*
monitor hoods 121, *121*
monitoring 132–134, *134*; audio 359; exposure 168; headphones 238–239
mono mix 359
monopods 159–160, *160*
mono recording 242
montage categories 311–312, *311*
Morris, Errol 6–7
The Most Dangerous Man in America documentary 312, *312*
Motion Picture Experts Group (MPEG) 111
motivated lighting 169, 187, 192
motivation 97
movement 93–98, *94*
MPEG (Motion Picture Experts Group) *see* Motion Picture Experts Group (MPEG)

Mr. Cao Goes to Washington documentary 68, *68*, 102–103, *102–103*, 317, *317*
Mr. Death documentary 103–104, 105, *105*, 249, *249*
music 339, 340; common pitfalls 347–348; cue sheets 351; source and score 346–347
My Brooklyn documentary 8, *8*, 9, 212, 245, 246, *246*, 284, 347, 385, *385*

N

narration 339–341; B-Roll 99; reflexivity and 21–22; scratch narration 291; structure 44; styles 303–305; writing 302–305
narrative promise 31
National Television System Committee (NTSC) 111
natively working 275
natural light 168, 188–189, *189*, 192, *193*
ND *see* neutral density
NDF TC (non-drop-frame time code) 116
needle-drop music 347
nets 182
neutral density (ND) filter 129, *129*, 150, 176–177, *176*
neutral density (ND) gels 179–180
Never Enough documentary 68, *68*, 342–343, *342*
Night Mail documentary 303–304, 305
night shooting 197–198, *198*
NLE system *see* nonlinear editing system
Nobody's Business documentary 12–13, *13*, 151, *151*, 319–320, *320*, 330, *330*, 335
noise 206, 217, 354–355
non-diegetic sound 341
non-drop-frame time code (NDF TC) 116
nonlinear editing (NLE) system 210, 270–274, *271*, *273*; audio levels 357–358, *357*; color correction 363–368; interface 278–283
nonsynchronous dialogue 340
nonsync sound *see* wild sound
No Room To Move! documentary 9
Nostalgia for the Light documentary 86, 86–87, 87, 155–156, *156*, 311, *311*, 313, 321, *321*
NTSC (National Television System Committee) 111

O

objectivity 7, 57–58
observational work 23–27, 29, 44, 307, *310*, 313–318, 340; covering 99–105;

directing participants 252–253; editing 289; lighting 192–195, *193*, *195*; structuring 298–301
off-line work 276–277, 284
off-screen images/action 85
omnidirectional microphones 222, *222–223*
onboard microphones 225
one-chip cameras 127
online editing 276–277
open-faced lights 172
open frames 86, *86*
opening montages 312
optical center 137, *137*
optical zoom 122
organizational elements 294, 330–331
Our Daily Bread documentary 104–105, *104*, 153
Outfoxed documentary 59, *59*
output formats 373
outtakes 327
overexposed images 148, 199, 202
overlapping objects 86
overmodulation 234
overwrite edits 288

P

pacing 318–322, *320*
pan 94, *94*, *96*; dampers 157; handle 157; heads 155; locks 157; slider 359
paper edit 289–290
Paravel, Véréna 118–119
participatory observation 25
passive characters 12–13
pattern editing 321–322
peak meters 218, *218*, 234, *236*
permits 66, 68
personal profiles 38
perspective: and focal length 146–148; moving frame 95–97; *see also* sound perspective
phase error 242
photosphere 191
picture look 292, 347
picture syncing with sound 277–278
pillarboxed images 336
Pina documentary 135, *135*
pistol grip 241, *241*
pitch *206*, 207
pivot camera moves 93–94, *94*
pixels 126
place portraits 38–39
plane of critical focus 138, 150
plasma display 113–114
platforms 46, 377
playhead 281
plots 296–298
Pluraleyes 278

point of view 102
polarizing filters 177–178, *177–178*
The Polymath documentary 20–21, *21*
pop filter 356
portable field mixers 219–220, *219–220*
postproduction process 24, 269–294
postproduction supervisor 269
postsynchronous sound 343
pots 218
practicals 194
preamp 213, 217, *217*, 221
presence 232
presetting focus 139
pressed discs 375–376
pressure zone microphones (PZMs) 225, *225*
primary sources 245
prime lenses 145–146
process films 39–40
producer roles 65
production: insurance 70, 260; management 63; procedures 255–266; proposal and 41; scheduling 71–72; sound 208–211, 216–225
production assistants 64, 65
production coordinators 64, 65
profile shot 92, *96*
pro-filmic reality 99
program leader 374–375
program masters 372
program slate 374–375, *374*
progressive scanning 114–115, *114*
projects: description 43–46; files 272; organization 294; timeline 49; window/panel 278, 294
proposals 41–49
Pro Tools system 359–361
provenance, archives 330
proxies 276–277
public domain 59, 326, 333–335
pulldown process 115, 276, 282
pulling focus 140
PZMs (pressure zone microphones) 225, *225*

Q

quality of light 170–171
quality of sound 208
quantizing 129, 215
quartz lights *see* tungsten-halogen lights
quick release tripods 158

R

radio mics *see* wireless microphones
Radivojevic, Iva 379–380
ratios, lighting 189–190
raw footage 289

raw media 120, 132
reaction shots 101
realist approach 22, 34, 154, 169, 192, 349
Rec 709 133, *133*
receding planes 86
recordable discs 376
reenactment 27–28, *27*
reference: audio 232, 357; tone 236–237
reflective light meters 190
reflectors 175, *175*, 197
reflexivity 21–22, 26–27, 44
Regen (Rain) documentary 20–21, *21*, 310, *310*
relationships *see* subject relations
release forms 14, 52–57
remix culture 59
render files 273
rerecording mixer 353
research 8–10, 15–16, 325–327, 328–329
resistance mechanisms 157
resolution 112–113, *112*, 120
respect 166, 257–258
responsibilities: to audiences 57–58; to other creators 58–59; to subjects 52
Restrepo documentary 26
reveals 97
reverberation 212, 355, *355*
rhetoric 29, 34–35, 44
rhythm 318–322
riding the gain 237
rights: clearance 333, 335, 348; distribution 377; *see also* copyright
rim light 186
rising action 32–33
risk 57, 262
rocker switch 122
Roger and Me documentary 58, 99, *99*, 302, 380
rolling shutters 127
roll-off setting, microphones 222, *222*
room acoustics 212–213
room tone 212, 241, 344
Rosenstein, Jay 22–23, 35
rough cuts 290–291
royalties 377
royalty-free approach 333
rule of thirds 88–89, *89*

S

Sachs, Lynne 17–18
Sadoul, Georges 19
safety 258–266
sample rates: digital audio quality 214–215, *215*; ND filters 129
sample reels 49
saturation 131, 364–368, *366*
scanning type 112, 113–115, *113–114*

scenes 83–84; observational 99–105, 289, 298–301; paper edit 289–290
scheduling 71–73
score music 346–347
scouting 65–66, 69, 196, 228–234, *230*
scratch folders 294
scratch narration 291, 303
scratch tracks 277–278
screen direction 100, 104
scrims 182, 266
SDI (serial digital interface) 125
SD (secure digital) card 122, *123*
SD (standard-definition) video 85, 110
secondary sources 245
secure digital (SD) card 122, *123*
security 258, 262–263
selective focus 141, *141*
selects 289
semi-theatrical distribution 381–382
sensors 126–127, *126*, 144–145, *144*
sequences 83–84; digital editing 272, 274; editing elements 294; monitor/program panel, NLE 282; NLE system 278, 281; reflexivity 21
serial digital interface (SDI) 125
servo zoom mechanism 122, *122*, 145
set etiquette 255–258
set lights 194
setting levels, locations 234, 236
setting tone, locations 236–237, *236*
setting up 233–237, 248, 274
shade 197
shadows 88, *88*
shallow depth of field/focus 87, 150–151, *150–151*
shared shot content *see* mise-en-scène
Sherman's March documentary 188–189, *189*, 246, *246*
shock mounts 239, *240*
shooting: from behind 92; with editing in mind 98–99; flat 203; planning 63–82; prepping/scouting 228–234; *see also* shots
short documentaries 37–40, *80–81*
short-range apparent motion 107
shotgun microphones 223, 224
shot/reverse shot technique 100, *100*
shots 83–84; adjusting 97–98; camera angles 91–92, *91–92*; composition 85–86; dynamic moves 94; size 90–91, *90*; too-similar-shots 316–317, *316*; *see also* shooting
shoulder, exposure 201
shoulder mounts 154–155, *155*
show and tell sequence 103–104, *103*
The Shrimp documentary 39–40, *39*
shutter speed 129, 167
sibilance suppression 356
sidelight 186

Sidney Poitier: An Outsider in Hollywood documentary 328–329, *328*
sightline 100
signal 206
signal compression 130–131
signal-to-noise (S/N) ratio 217
single event stories 39
single frame 324
single-system sound 69, 209, *209*, 211, 227, 277–278
sizzle reels 49
Skylight company 386–388, *387*
slate 21, *209–210*, 210, 277, 374–375, *374*
sliders 94, 162, *162*
SMPTE countdown 375
Snakeheads documentary 57, *57*
S/N (signal-to-noise) ratio 217
soft light 170–171, *170*, 173–174, *174*, *181*
software 276, *276*, 278–283
solid state drives (SSDs) 124
solid-state memory cards 122–123, *123*
Song of Ceylon documentary 108, 339, *339*
sound 22; editing 351–353, 359–361; film 108; importance 205; location techniques 227–242; postproduction 269–271, 274, 277–278; recording 69–70, 205–226, 231–233, *232*; syncing picture and 277–278; types 340–348; understanding 206–208; *see also* audio
sound design 105, 339–361
sound effects 340, *340*, 343–345, *350*
sound mix 351, 353–359
sound perspective 348–349, *349*
sound recordist 63, *64*, 65, 117, 227
soundtrack building 291
source music 346
speakers 274
specials, lighting 194
specific filmmaking 14–15
speech 340–341
speed: lenses 149–150; of sound 208
spill light 181
Split documentary 166, *166*
split edits 288–289
splitting electrical loads 265
splitting tracks 352
sponsorship 49
spotting 351
spreaders 159
SSDs (solid state drives) 124
stabilizing arm systems 162–163, *163*
standard-definition (SD) video 85, 110
stands, lighting 181
State of Fear documentary 14–15
stereo recording 242, *242*

stock footage 8
stock houses 326
Stoney, George 26, 27, 54
stops 148
storage media 124, *124*
storytelling 29–35, *33*, 296–298, 325–337
straight cuts 288
Stranger With a Camera documentary 26–27, 335
streaming 383
structuring documentaries 29–40, 44–45, 295–306
stylistic approach 7, 17–28, 44–45, 349
stylized expressive sequences 105
stylized images 188, *189*, 194–196
subcarrier frequency 115
subclips 294
subject positions 196–197, 248–250, *249*
subject relations 52, 243–253
subsampling 131–132
sunlight 197
superimposition 323
surround sound 350
sweetening audio 353–356
Sweetgrass documentary 85, *85*, 89, *89*, 224, 340–341, *341*, 349, *349*
sync rights 348
sync sound 22, 108, 205, 208–211, *210*, 277–278, 340
synopsis 42
system noise 217

T

Tajri, Rea 21–22
Takagi, J. T. 212, 227, 229, 231
talking heads 244
target audiences 46
TC *see* time code
team structure 256
telephoto lenses 142, 147, *147*
television 23, 46, 49, 382
text cards 31–32
texted/textless master 372
theatrical releases 46–47, 380–382, *381*
The Thin Blue Line documentary 6–7, 27–28, *27*, 87, *87*, 166, 323, *323*, 337, *337*
third-person narration 302
three-chip cameras 127
three-point lighting 186–187, *187*, 246
three-quarter back position 92
Through a Lens Darkly documentary 327–329, *327*
through the lens (TTL) metering 190
tilt 94, *94*; dampers 157; locks 157
timbre 208
time code (TC) 116, *116*, 210, 272, 278
time lapse photography 156

timeline window, NLE 278, 281
timing 318–322; electrical load limits 264–265; light and 196; organization 83–106; structure 301–302
titles 368–372, *371*
toe, exposure *200*, 201
tone 236–237, *236*, 374
Tongues Untied documentary 26, *26*
too-similar-shots 316–317, *316*
topics 10, 15
topsheets 74, *74*
track adjustment 357
tracking shot 94, *95*
trailers 49
transcoding 275
transcripts 285
transitions: audio 356–357; shots 321–323
travel 260–261
trimming light 181
tripod heads 156–159, *158*
tripod-mounted slider 94
tripods 155–159, *155–157*
Trouble the Water documentary 296–297, *296–298*, 300–301, *301*, 326, *341*
Truth Be Told documentary 381
TTL (through the lens) metering 190
Tugg.com 381, *381*
tungsten-halogen lights 171
TV documentary *see* television

U

ultra high-definition (UHD) 111, 119
ultra high end cameras 119–120
U-matic 109, *109*
unbalanced audio signals 214
unbalanced frames 88
underexposed images 148, 199
underwater photography 164
universal filmmaking 14–15

V

value 14
variable bit rate (VBR) 131
vectorscope 367–368, *367–368*
Vélez, Edin 5, 109, *109*, 324
velocity 208
veracity 17
Vertov, Dziga 21–22
video 108–116; camcorders *109*, 120–133, 216; camera lenses 137–138; connectors, camcorders 125–126, *125*; diaries 249; images today 110–116; knee 202; standards 111, *111*; tracks 278
video on demand (VOD) 383
viewfinders 121

A Village Called Versailles documentary 42–43, *42*, 44, 45
visual evidence 23, 99, 298–301, *301*, 308
visual language 83
visual perspective *see* perspective
VOD (video on demand) 383
voice coil 220, *220*
voice-over 99, 341
volume unit (VU) meters 236, *236*

W

walking (lead) room 88–89
walk and talk sequence 103–104, 233, 246, *246*
Watermark documentary 36–37, *37*
watermarks, archives 330
water risks 262
waveform scope 364–365, *365*
wavelength *206*, 207, *208*
weather checks 196, 262
white balance 127–128, *128*, 171
white diffusion 177
wide-angle lenses 142
wild sound 205, 208, 212, 343
Wilson, Keith 37, 39–40
wind noise 241–242, *241*
windows 194, *194*
wireless microphones 224, *224*
Wiseman, Frederick 24–25, 252, 301, 313
witness mark 138
worker's compensation 70, 260
workflow 270–272, *271*, 292–293
work samples 49
wrapping 274
writing documentaries 295–306

X

XLR connectors 214, 216, *216*, 222

Y

Yates, Pamela 14–15

Z

zebra function 168, *168*, 202
zone systems *192*
zoom lenses 145–146, *145–146*; defined 145–146; lens speed 150; optical vs digital 122; using for critical focus 139; zooming in and out 94